THE PHILOSOPHY OF RELIGION
Selected Readings

Yeager Hudson
Colby College

Mayfield Publishing Company
Mountain View, California
London • Toronto

Library of Congress Cataloging-in-Publication Data
The Philosophy of religion: selected readings / [compiled by]
    Yeager Hudson.
        p.   cm.
    Includes bibliographical references and index.
    ISBN 0-87484-959-4
    1. Religion—Philosophy.   I. Hudson, Yeager, 1931– .
BL51.P545   1991
200'.1—dc20   90-45173
                                                   CIP

Manufactured in the United States of America

10 9 8 7 6 5 4 3 2 1

Mayfield Publishing Company
1240 Villa Street
Mountain View, California 94041

Sponsoring editor, James Bull; managing editor, Linda
Toy; production editor, Carol Zafiropoulos; manuscript
editor, Victoria Nelson; cover design, Anna George. This
text was set in 9½/11 Meridien Light by Harrison
Typesetting, Inc., and printed on 50# Finch Opaque by
Edwards Brothers.

Contents

iii

Author/Title Index   633

Preface

The present era has been characterized by some as an age of doubt, skepticism, cynicism, and a time in which religion, if it has not been definitely refuted or undermined by the progress of human thought, has in any case been abandoned, laid aside as irrelevant to modern human concerns. Today we look to science for answers to the questions that only religion used to address—questions about the origin of the world and about how human beings came to occupy their place in the scheme of things. We look to medicine for the healing that once was sought from priests and religious medicine men, and to psychiatry for the peace of mind once thought to come only from God. We try not to think about death. When we are forced to face it, we mostly assume that it is an unfathomable mystery to which religious teachings have nothing to contribute and probably the final end of our individual human existence. Even some Christian theologians during the past several decades have talked about the "death of God," and some of the most popular literary and philosophical movements of our century have been not merely atheistic but explicitly antireligious.

For centuries small numbers of commentators have prophesied the eventual demise of religion, arguing that humankind would eventually reach a level of maturity that would enable them to see through the superstitious explanations and to outgrow their need for myths of hope and encouragement. But these prognostications have never been widely accepted. Anthropologists have nearly always declared with scientific indifference, and theists with optimistic confidence, that religion is a universal and permanent aspect of human life. It was with cynical scorn that Sigmund Freud, the founder of psychoanalysis, argued that human beings are altogether too infantile and dependent upon their imaginary divine father-image to be able to outgrow religion.

A close examination of the human situation, even in our so-called "age of doubt," gives every indication that the forecasters of the demise of religion will be found to be false prophets. Even in the agnostic West, indeed, even in the skeptical United States, interest in religion persists. Church attendance and participation has declined in some of the so-called mainline churches, but growth in some other denominations more than makes up for it, and even when week-by-week religious activity seems on the wane, the strength of religion in influencing legislation, court judgments, and political rhetoric appears to grow. Seemingly indifferent persons turn to religion at major transitions in their lives such as births, marriages, grave illnesses, and deaths.

Whenever the large issues of moral concern impinge on our consciousness, it is nearly always in terms of the teachings of the religious traditions that the arguments are carried out. Politics and concerns about the economy may dominate casual conversation in election years or when the stock market is not doing well, but religion is the topic that is always in the background and often in the foreground of thought and discussion whatever the political or economic climate.

This book is designed to present significant writings on the philosophy of religion by some of the most thoughtful and best-informed minds in the history of our civilization. The book is arranged into nine parts, each addressing one of the most important issues in the philosophy of religion. In each part, readings have been provided that present several points of view so that students may become acquainted with the various principal positions and so be in a better position to reflect for themselves on the central questions. An effort has been made to provide a balance also between classical and contemporary writings and to give some sense of the progress that has been made and of the direction in which thought is moving at the present time. The philosophy of religion is one of the most active and creative branches of philosophy in our day, so a number of selections have been included from very recent sources. In the interest of inclusiveness, a very large number of readings is provided—more that any other leading book of readings in the philosophy of religion in print today. The book is designed to supply a complete set of readings for an entire course in the philosophy of religion. The topics are arranged in a logical and carefully thought out order so that the sequencing provides an appropriate pathway through the field of philosophy of religion. It would be appropriate to assign the entire collection of readings and to follow the order given here; such an assignment should not be more than most college students could handle. But it is also possible, of course, for instructors to be selective, putting together their courses in their own way, and finding here abundant resources. If it is thought desirable to supplement readings from primary sources with the kind of guidance provided by a textbook, a companion volume by the editor of this book, titled *The Philosophy of Religion* (Mayfield, 1990), is available. The textbook is organized into nine chapters paralleling the nine parts of this book of readings, so that the two books nicely supplement one another.

This book begins with an attempt to understand just what philosophers and ordinary persons mean by such terms as religion, philosophy, theology, and the philosophy of religion. Selections are included in which the authors attempt to define religion and to explain how theology differs from the philosophy of religion. Part I devotes considerable attention to the question of the rationality of religious belief, offering readings that attack reason, readings that raise questions about the meaningfulness of religious language, and readings that make a case for the claim that religious beliefs, carefully formulated and thought out, can appropriately be called rational.

Because theism has been such a dominant position in Western religious thought since ancient times, and continues to be so today, four parts of the book are devoted to theism, exploring the attributes or perfections usually attributed to the theistic God, the major arguments put forward to support theism, the principal arguments offered against theism, and a few world views that have been offered as alternatives to theism by persons who find theism not a plausible position.

Part II treats the major divine attributes of omnipotence, omniscience, and omni-benevolence or divine goodness, and also explores several other features of theism including some of the so-called metaphysical attributes, the question whether personality is a characteristic of God, the idea that God might not be infinite but might be limited in some way(s), and the question whether the divine attributes are mutually compatible.

Part III, after a brief look at the place of rational proofs in supporting religious belief, examines the major arguments for the existence of God, namely the ontological, the cosmological, and the teleological. Selections are also included that deal with two less prominent arguments, the moral and the pragmatic arguments.

Part IV takes a look at the major objections that have been raised to theism and the ways in which these objections have been used as arguments designed to undermine theism. The problem of evil, widely recognized as the most serious threat to theism, is addressed through selections from four important thinkers. Selections are provided that raise and press the psychological objections to religion generally and to theism in particular, including Sigmund Freud's characterization of religion as illusion and mass delusion, and Karl Marx's claim that religion is the opiate of the people. Selections dealing with the relationship of religion to science and with miracles explore the widespread belief that religion has either been disproved or rendered irrelevant by the progress of modern science.

In every age there have been at least a few serious thinkers who have found theism unacceptable and who have generated philosophical theories designed to answer many of the questions addressed by theists without embracing a belief in God. Books on the philosophy of religion have tended simply to ignore these thinkers. One of the special features of the present volume is its inclusion of material dealing with non-theistic positions, examining two such world views, naturalism and humanism. Part V also includes a selection that addresses the question, "Is theism the most plausible world view?"

Many of the most religious of persons, the founders and the most devoted practitioners of religion, would be inclined to say that rational argument is not the surest path to religious understanding; some would say that it is quite beside the point. Such persons point to the direct experiences of the divine dimensions of reality that saints, avatars, and mystics allegedly have through religious and mystical experience. Part VI provides a selection of readings dealing with both the phenomenology of religious and mystical experience, i.e., the actual nature of the experiences themselves, and with philosophical questions concerning the value of these experiences as a source of trustworthy knowledge about religious claims.

Theists in the West, and most ordinary people as well, frequently assume an intimate, perhaps even a necessary, connection between religion and morality. Part VII examines this allegedly inextricable relationship. Judaism is the source of the ten commandments, and Christianity sets forth many ethical teachings both in its scriptures and in its Church doctrines. The divine command theory of ethics, which claims that morality is derived from God's will, seems to many people who are steeped in the Western religious milieu to be the natural and obvious account of the relationship between religion and ethics. But problems with this theory began to be noticed at least as early as the sixth century B. C. E., as is evidenced in a selection from Plato. The great nineteenth-century Danish philosopher Søren Kierkegaard also found the divine command theory disturbing; his discussion of Abraham and Isaac is included in this section, along with selections from the Bible. Part VI ends with an essay by the editor of this book that argues for the independence of Ethics and Religion.

The great religions of humankind, Hinduism, Buddhism, Islam, Judaism, Christianity, Taoism, etc., arose and evolved in a world of isolated cultures where the peoples of one country had little occasion to know about the beliefs and practices of others. In the last several centuries, and especially in the twentieth century, the isolation has disappeared and peoples of every race, nationality, ethnic group, and religion interact with one another on a regular basis. The confrontation of religion with religion has become a dilemma and a serious source of tensions in our age. Books on the philosophy of religion have not usually paid any attention to this issue. A distinctive feature of this book is its examination of questions concerning how we should think about the relationship among the great religions. Ethnocentrism seems to be the natural response of humans, and thus we assume that our own religion, whatever it may be, is the true one and that others are false, or at least inferior. Some writers on comparative religions take an exclusivistic position, maintaining that only one of the religions can be right and thus that the rest must be wrong. But others are more inclusive in their vision, suggesting that the several religions might be different paths to the same destination, or different interpretations, colored by cultural differences, of the same divine dimension of reality. These issues are addressed by the readings in Part VII.

The book concludes with readings about the question of the meaning or significance of human life, and about how religious beliefs relate to those questions. Death has often been regarded as the phenomenon that raises the most serious problems about life's meaning, so a reading on death and what might happen after death is included. Existentialism is the philosophy that, during the twentieth century, has preoccupied itself most directly with questions about the meaningfulness of human life. Besides a reading from what we might call an "existentialist from antiquity," the author of the biblical book of Ecclesiastes, readings from two of the most prominent of the twentieth-century existentialists represent this viewpoint. Part IX concludes with an essay by William James that argues that how we live our lives determines whether or not they have meaning.

The philosopher of religion, unlike the theologian of some particular religion, makes no attempt either to support or to undermine religious belief. It is the role of the philosopher of religion to look, with as much objectivity and as little bias as is humanly possible, at the claims made by the advocates of religious belief and to subject to rational scrutiny the problems these claims raise for reasonable persons. Thus philosophers go about their work in as disinterested a way as they can, seeking insights that any reasonable person, religious, indifferent, or anti-religious, could recognize as plausible and for arguments that stand up at the bar of reason without regard to whether they agree with or oppose the received religious orthodoxy.

At the same time, the philosopher's deliberately disinterested approach does not in any sense suggest that he or she is *un*interested in the issues the philosophy of religion treats. These issues are inevitably of keen interest to every thoughtful person whatever his or her religious persuasion. Religious beliefs dominate moral discussions, influence lawmaking and court decisions, govern the behavior of countless individuals in nearly every society, and drive the international policies of nations up to the brink of war—and beyond. The concerns of the philosopher of religion are of paramount importance for nearly everyone. But quite apart from these serious and sometimes dangerous implications, and perhaps more significantly for the student, these issues are matters of great intellectual and personal interest. The student who begins genuinely to engage with these questions is likely to find a lure to a fascinating process of thought and discovery. The topics are important and interesting for their own sakes, but they also have direct relevance to our lives. The study of the philosophy of religion involves not just the study of abstract philosophical puzzles and of what learned thinkers have said about them; it also involves the study of oneself, one's beliefs, one's values, and one's vision of what kind of life is worth living and what kind of person one will choose to be. This book is not intended to provide a set of ready-made answers to be accepted without question; rather, it offers a set of stimulating questions and some suggestions concerning how these questions might be approached. And it offers an invitation to an enchanting journey of discovery, a challenge to think these questions through and to find answers that are individually satisfying and rationally persuasive. The study of philosophy is a path toward the examined life, a life that is not only worth living, but that many persons find to be the most gratifying life open to humans. If this book awakens or enlivens the sense of wonder that is philosophy in the minds of some of its readers, my efforts will have been abundantly rewarded.

ACKNOWLEDGMENTS

A book of readings designed for use in a college course is shaped importantly by the experience of teaching that course and especially by the students with whom the teacher interacts in the process of teaching. My students have taught me a great deal—I only hope that I have taught them as much. I have also learned of the contents and been infected by the fascination of the philosophy of religion from my own teachers, particularly Peter A. Bertocci, who died earlier this year, and from many colleagues with whom I have worked, such as Francis A. Parker. I have received valuable assistance on matters of detail from Colin E. McKay and Thomas R. W. Longstaff, and encouragement, in his own way, from Frederick A. Geib. My student research assistants, William Priestly and Gina Rogers, themselves committed students of the philosophy of religion, undertook in a good-natured spirit such detailed chores as searching out sources and tracking down bibliographical details. My secretary, Pauline Wing, cheerfully and patiently worked far above and beyond any reasonable demands of duty. I am grateful also to my colleagues who reviewed the manuscript: Robert Miller, Eastern Kentucky University; R. Duane Thompson, Indiana Wesleyan University; Robert A. Goff, University of California, Santa Cruz. And my wife, Louise, provided unflagging encouragement, tireless proofreading, and valuable stylistic suggestions.

My two sons to whom this volume is affectionately dedicated, although grown up and pursuing their own careers, provided distractions that sometimes seemed to threaten its completion, but that actually helped to save me from the undivided immersion in work that makes Jack, or anyone else, a dull person.

For Paul and Gary

Part I

The Philosophical Study of Religion

Religious beliefs and practices seem to be a permanent feature of human life. Just as archaeologists find signs of religious behavior among the earliest human remains, religion is also present and widespread in every contemporary society, even those that have made an effort to discourage or eliminate it. It appears in a great variety of forms, as diverse as the cultures that foster it, yet scholars also find many common features and similarities. The attempt to define religion is the effort to discover these common features, to articulate the essence of religion amid its multitude of variations.

The philosophical study of religion endeavors to apply the methods of philosophy—analysis and critique—to religious teachings so that we may understand the claims of religious doctrines and how these claims are supported by their advocates. The philosophy of religion also seeks to judge the plausibility of the claims and the validity of the arguments. Philosophy of religion differs from theology in this way: Whereas theology speaks from within a specific religious tradition, philosophy of religion takes a position outside religious doctrine and attempts to speak about religion as a universal human phenomenon.

Another major difference between theology and the philosophy of religion is that theology usually presupposes that the basic teachings of religion are true. Theology is a process of explaining and clarifying doctrines presumed to be true, systematizing these doctrines and making them coherent, and

1

providing arguments designed to support the teachings and convince nonbelievers. The philosophy of religion, on the other hand, attempts an open-minded examination of religious teachings, setting aside—insofar as this is possible—all preconceived assumptions. It makes an effort to uncover all presuppositions and to analyze and criticize them. Rather than assuming the truth of some one tradition, it raises questions about the teachings of religion in general, attempts to discover criteria for evaluating all sorts of religious claims, and tries to judge as objectively as possible the plausibility of these claims, scrutinizing the arguments offered to support them and bringing to bear on them relevant knowledge from other areas of human cognitive endeavor such as science, history, sociology, politics, and psychology.

Part I consists of selections that examine the problem of defining religion or deciding what counts as a religion; the distinction between theology and the philosophy of religion; and the large and important philosophical question of whether or not any religious beliefs can be regarded as rational. The opposing points presented convey some sense of the range of positions on these issues. Instead of simply adopting some proffered position, readers will, it is hoped, think through each issue and make up their own minds, based on what they take to be the weightiest evidence and the soundest arguments.

ANNOTATED GUIDE TO FURTHER READINGS

Abernethy, George L., and Langford, Thomas A., eds. *Philosophy of Religion*. New York: Macmillan, 1962.
A collection of short essays offering a wide variety of viewpoints; authors include Kant, James, Aquinas, and Tillich. Chapter 1 discusses the nature of religion; chapter 2, the relationship between the philosophy of religion and theology; chapter 5, religious language.

Clifford, William K. "The Ethics of Belief." In *Philosophy of Religion: Selected Readings*, 2nd ed., edited by William L. Rowe and William J. Wainwright. New York: Harcourt Brace Jovanovich, 1989.
Clifford argues that we are morally obligated to believe only what is supported by the evidence. A belief not backed up in such a manner should, according to morality, be rejected. Other readings in this section, "Faith and the Need for Evidence," are by Aquinas, James, Plantinga, and Wykstra.

Delaney, C.F., ed. *Rationality and Religious Belief.* Notre Dame: University of Notre Dame Press, 1979.
Eight essays dealing with the link between rationality and religious belief. There are two central themes: (1) the concept of rationality must be scrutinized and not blindly accepted, and (2) religion is more than a mere assortment of beliefs, it plays an inseparable role in how we define ourselves.

Flew, Antony, Hare, R.M., and Mitchell, Basil. "Theology and Falsification." In *New Essays in Philosophical Theology*, edited by Antony Flew and Alasdair MacIntyre. London: SCM Press, 1955.
To what extent are theological utterances assertions or explanations? Flew, Hare, and Mitchell address this question, along with that of maintaining faith when faced with evidence that may make this faith seem irrational. Each thinker uses a parable to clarify his position, a format that makes the argument highly readable.

Hick, John H. *Philosophy of Religion.* Englewood Cliffs, N.J.: Prentice-Hall, 1983.
Hick's introduction attempts a definition of the philosophy of religion. Chapters 6 and 7 deal with religious language. Presenting various viewpoints, Hick examines the question of whether or not religious statements should be seen as assertions of truth. The idea that religious language should be regarded as symbolic rather than literal is presented by an analysis of the theories of Paul Tillich and J.H. Randall, Jr.

Plantinga, Alvin, and Nicholas Wolterstorff, eds. *Faith and Rationality: Reason and Belief in God.* Notre Dame: University of Notre Dame Press, 1983.
Eight essays dealing with the question of whether faith can be rational, by such notable thinkers as Alvin Plantinga, George I. Mavrodes, William P. Alston, and Nicholas Wolterstorff.

I.A. Religion

I.A.1. Religion and Solitariness

A. N. WHITEHEAD

*Alfred North Whitehead (1861–1947) was a British mathematician and philosopher. *Religion in the Making* treats religion as a process rather than a finished product delivered by revelation; in this brief excerpt Whitehead defines religion not so much in terms of its truth claims as its effects on human character, not as a social phenomenon but as a product and expression of individual solitariness.*

It is my purpose. . . to consider the type of justification which is available for belief in doctrines of religion. This is a question which in some new form challenges each generation. It is the peculiarity of religion that humanity is always shifting its attitude towards it.

The contrast between religion and the elementary truths of arithmetic makes my meaning clear. Ages ago the simple arithmetical doctrines dawned on the human mind, and throughout history the unquestioned dogma that two and three make five reigned whenever it has been relevant. We all know what this doctrine means, and its history is of no importance for its elucidation.

But we have the gravest doubt as to what religion means so far as doctrine in concerned. There is no agreement as to the definition of religion in its most general sense, including true and false religion; nor is there any agreement as to the valid religious beliefs, nor even as to what we mean by the truth of religion. It is for this reason that some consideration of religion as an unquestioned factor through the long stretch of human history is necessary to secure the relevance of any discussion of its general principles.

There is yet another contrast. What is generally disputed is doubtful, and what is doubtful is relatively unimportant—other things being equal. I am speaking of general truths. We avoid guiding our actions by general principles which are entirely unsettled. If we do not know what number is the product of 69 and 67, we defer an action pre-supposing the answer, till we have found out. This little arithmetical puzzle can be put aside till it is settled, and it is capable of definite settlement with adequate trouble.

But as between religion and arithmetic, other things are not equal. You *use* arithmetic, but you *are* religious. Arithmetic of course enters into your nature,

From *Religion in the Making* (New York: Macmillan, 1927), pp. 13–18.

so far as that nature involves a multiplicity of things. But it is there as a necessary condition, and not as a transforming agency. No one is invariably "justified" by his faith in the multiplication table. But in some sense or other, justification is a basis of all religion. Your character is developed according to your faith. This is the primary religious truth from which no one can escape. Religion is force of belief cleansing the inward parts. For this reason the primary religious virtue is sincerity, a penetrating sincerity.

A religion, on its doctrinal side, can thus be defined as a system of general truths which have the effect of transforming character when they are sincerely held and vividly apprehended.

In the long run your character and your conduct of life depend upon your intimate convictions. Life is an internal fact for its own sake, before it is an external fact relating itself to others. The conduct of external life is conditioned by environment, but it receives its final quality, on which its worth depends, from the internal life which is the self-realization of existence. Religion is the art and the theory of the internal life of man, so far as it depends on the man himself and on what is permanent in the nature of things.

The doctrine is the direct negation of the theory that religion is primarily a social fact. Social facts are of great importance to religion, because there is no such thing as absolutely independent existence. You cannot abstract society from man; most psychology is herd-psychology. But all collective emotions leave untouched the awful ultimate fact, which is the human being, consciously alone with itself, for its own sake.

Religion is what the individual does with his solitariness. It runs through three stages, if it evolves to its final satisfaction. It is the transition from God the void to God the enemy, and from God the enemy to God the companion.

Thus religion is solitariness; and if you are never solitary, you are never religious. Collective enthusiasms, revivals, institutions, churches, rituals, bibles, codes of behavior are the trappings of religion, its passing forms. They may be useful or harmful; they may be authoritatively ordained, or merely temporary expedients. But the end of religion is beyond all this.

Accordingly, what should emerge from religion is individual worth of character. But worth is positive or negative, good or bad. Religion is by no means necessarily good. It may be very evil. The fact of evil, interwoven with the texture of the world, shows that in the nature of things there remains effectiveness for degradation. In your religious experience the God with whom you have made terms may be the God of destruction, the God who leaves in his wake the loss of the greater reality.

In considering religion, we should not be obsessed by the idea of its necessary goodness. This is a dangerous delusion. The point to notice is its transcendent importance; and the fact of this importance is abundantly made evident by the appeal to history.

I.A.2.   What Religion Is

W. T. STACE

Walter T. Stace (1886–1967) was born in England, spent twenty-two years in the British civil service in Ceylon (Sri Lanka) and then taught philosophy for twenty-three years at Princeton University. An empiricist in the tradition of David Hume, Stace had a keen interest in the philosophy of religion and mysticism. His definition of religion is the definition of a mystic who expresses himself through metaphor: Religion is a hunger nothing earthly can fully satisfy. Contradiction and paradox Stace sees as the essence of religion; the attempt to render a rational account of religion produces a rendition that no longer belongs to religion. Religion aspires after that bliss of which the material or the temporal knows not even an approximation, a qualitatively different bliss that belongs to the dimension of eternity.

"Religion," says Whitehead, "is the vision of something which stands beyond, behind, and within, the passing flux of immediate things; something which is real, and yet waiting to be realized; something which is a remote possibility, and yet the greatest of present facts; something which gives meaning to all that passes, and yet eludes apprehension; something whose possession is the final good, and yet is beyond all reach; something which is the ultimate ideal, and the hopeless quest."[1]

These words evidently express a direct intuition of the writer. They well up from his own personal religious experience and therefore stir the depths in us who read. What he says is not a faded copy of what someone else has felt or thought or seen, as the majority of pious utterances are—hackneyed and worn-out clichés, debased by parrot-like repetition, although they too, poor dead things, once issued fresh-minted from a living human soul. Here and there amid the arid hills of human experience are well-springs and fountain-heads of religious intuition. They are the original sources of all religion. They need not always be of great grandeur. They may be humble rivulets of feeling. Or they may give rise to great rivers of refreshment flowing through the centuries. But always, great or small, they bear upon themselves the stamp of their own authenticity. They need no external proof or justification. Indeed they are incapable of any. We know them because the God in us cries out, hearing the voice of the God in the other, answering back. The deep calls to the deep.

---

[1] A. N. Whitehead, *Science and the Modern World*, chapter 12.

Whitehead's words are of this kind.

Note first their paradoxical character. To the "something" of which they speak are attributed opposite characters which barely avoid, if they do avoid, the clash of flat contradiction. Each clause is a balance of such contradicting predicates. The meaning cannot be less than that paradox and contradiction are of the very essence of that "something" itself.

Note, too, the final words. That something which man seeks as his ultimate ideal is the "hopeless quest." This is not a careless expression, an exaggeration, a loose use of words. It is not rhetoric. If this phrase had come at the beginning of the passage, it might have been toned down in the succeeding sentences. But it strikes the final note. It is the last word.

And one can see why. For religion is the hunger of the soul for the impossible, the unattainable, the inconceivable. This is not something which it merely happens to be, an unfortunate accident or disaster which befalls it in the world. This is its essence, and this is its glory. This is what religion *means*. The religious impulse in men *is* the hunger for the impossible, the unattainable, the inconceivable—or at least for that which is these things in the world of time. And anything which is less than this is not religion—though it may be some very admirable thing such as morality. Let it not be said that this makes religion a foolish thing, fit only for madmen—although indeed from the world's point of view the religious man *is* a madman. For, mad or not, this impulse lies deep down in every human heart. It is of the essence of man, quite as much as is his reason.

Religion seeks the infinite. And the infinite by definition is impossible, unattainable. It is by definition that which can never be reached.

Religion seeks the light. But it is not a light which can be found at any place or time. It is not somewhere. It is the light which is nowhere. It is "the light which never was on sea or land." Never was. Never will be, even in the infinite stretches of future time. The light is non-existent, as the poet himself says. Yet it is the great light which lightens the world. And this, too, the poet implies.

Religion is the desire to break away from being and existence altogether, to get beyond existence into that nothingness where the great light is. It is the desire to be utterly free from the fetters of being. For every being is a fetter. Existence is a fetter. To be is to be tied to what you are. Religion is the hunger for the non-being which yet is.

In music sometimes a man will feel that he comes to the edge of breaking out from the prison bars of existence, breaking out from the universe altogether. There is a sense that the goal is at hand, that the boundary wall of the universe is crumbling and will be breached at the next moment, when the soul will pass out free into the infinite. But the goal is not reached. For it is the unspeakable, the impossible, the inconceivable, the unattainable. There is only the sense of falling backward into time. The goal is only glimpsed, sensed, and then lost.

One thing is better than another thing. Gold is perhaps better than clay, poetry than push-pin. One place is pleasanter than another place. One time is happier than another time. In all being there is a scale of better and worse. But just because of this relativity, no being, no time, no place, satisfies the ultimate hunger. For all beings are infected by the same disease, the disease of existence. If owning a marble leaves your metaphysical and religious thirst unquenched, so will owning all the planets. If living on the earth for three-score years and ten leaves it unsatisfied, neither will living in a fabled Heaven for endless ages satisfy it. For how do you attain your end by making things bigger, or longer, or wider, or thicker, or more this or more that? For they will still be *this* or *that*. And it is being this or that which is the disease of things.

So long as there is light in your life, the light has not yet dawned. There is in your life much darkness—that much you will admit. But you think that though this thing, this place, this time, this experience is dark, yet that thing, that place, that time, that experience is, or will be, bright. But this is the great illusion. You must see that all things, all places, all times, all experiences are equally dark. You must see that all stars are black. Only out of the *total* darkness will the light dawn.

Religion is that hunger which no existence, past, present, or future, no actual existence and no possible existence, in this world or in any other world, on the earth or above the clouds and stars, material or mental or spiritual, can ever satisfy. For whatever is or could be will have the curse on it of thisness or thatness.

This is no new thought. It is only what religious men have always said. To the saint Narada the Supreme Being offered whatsoever boon his heart could imagine—abundance of life, riches, health, pleasure, heroic sons. "That," said Narada "and precisely that is what I desire to be rid of and pass beyond." It is true that things here spoken of—health, riches, even heroic sons—are what we call worldly, even material, things. But they are symbolic only. They stand for all things of any kind, whether material or non-material—for all things, at least, which could have an existence in the order of time, whether in the time before death or in the time after.

It is true that simple-minded religious men have conceived their goal as a state of continued existence beyond the grave filled with all happy things and experiences. But plainly such happy things and experiences were no more than symbolic, and the happy heavens containing such things have the character of myth. To the human mind, fast fettered by the limits of its poor imagination, they stand for and represent the goal. One cannot conceive the inconceivable. So in place of it one puts whatever one can imagine of delight; wine and houris if one's imagination is limited to these; love, kindness, sweetness of spiritual living if one is of a less materialistic temper. But were these existences and delights, material or spiritual, to be actually found and enjoyed as present, they would be condemned by the saint along with all earthly joys. For they would have upon them the curse, the darkness, the disease, of all existent things, of all that is this or that. This is why we cannot conceive of any particular pleasure, happiness, joy, which would not *cloy*, which—to be quite frank—would not in the end be boring.

"In the Infinite only is bliss. In the finite there is no bliss" says the ancient Upanishad.[2] And we are apt to imagine that this is a piece of rhetoric, or at least an exaggeration. For surely it is not strictly speaking true that in the finite there is no happiness at all. No doubt the saint or the moralist is right to speak disparagingly of the mere pleasures of sense. But is there, then, no joy of

---

[2] Chandogva Upanishad.

living? What of the love of man and woman, of parent and child? What of the sweetness of flowers, the blue of the sky, the sunlight? Is it not quite false that there is no bliss in these? And yet they are finite. So we say. But we fail to see that the author of the verse is speaking of something quite different from what we have in mind, namely of that ultimate bliss in God which is the final satisfaction of the religious hunger. And we think that this ultimate blessedness differs only *in degree* from the happy and joyful experiences of our lives. Whereas the truth is that it differs *in kind*. The joys, not only of the earth, but of any conceivable heaven—which we can conceive only as some fortunate and happy prolongation of our lives in time—are not of the same order as that ultimate blessedness. We imagine any joyful, even ecstatic, experience we please. We suppose that the blessedness of salvation is something like this, only more joyful. Perhaps if it were multiplied a million times. . . . But all this is of no avail. Though we pile mountain of earthly joy upon mountain of earthly joy, we reach no nearer to the bliss which is the end. For these things belong to different orders; the one, however great, to the order of time; the other to the order of eternity. Therefore all the temporal joys which we pile upon one another to help our imaginations, are no more than symbolic, and the accounts of possible heavens mere myths.

Hence the religious soul must leave behind all things and beings, including itself. From being it must pass into Nothing. But in this nothing it must still be. Therefore also what it seeks is the being which is non-being. And God, who is the only food which will appease its hunger, is this Being which is Non-Being. Is this a contradiction? Yes. But men have always found that, in their search for the Ultimate, contradiction and paradox lie all around them. Did we not see that the words of Whitehead, with which we opened this chapter, must mean at least that contradiction and paradox lie at the heart of things? And is there any more contradiction here than we find—to give the most obvious example from traditional theology—in the doctrine of the Trinity? That, too, proclaims in unmistakable terms that there is contradiction in the Ultimate. The rationalizing intellect, of course, will not have it so. It will attempt to explain away the final Mystery, to logicize it, to reduce it to the categories of "this" and "that." At least it will attempt to water it down till it looks something like "common sense," and can be swallowed without too much discomfort! But the great theologians knew better. In the self-contradictory doctrine of the Trinity they threw the Mystery of God uncompromisingly in men's faces. And we shall see that all attempts to make religion a purely rational, logical thing are not only shallow but would, if they could succeed, destroy religion. Either God is a Mystery or He is nothing at all.

I.B. Philosophy of Religion Versus Theology

I.B.1. Philosophy and Theology

WILLIAM L. ROWE

William Rowe (1931–), professor of philosophy at Purdue University, specializes in the philosophy of religion. Here he distinguishes philosophy of religion from theology and several other disciplines, pointing out that theology functions from within a single religious tradition whereas philosophy of religion, operating from a vantage point beyond any particular tradition, engages in the critical examination of basic religious beliefs and concepts.

Philosophy of religion is one of the branches of philosophy, as are philosophy of science, philosophy of law, and philosophy of art. We may best understand what philosophy of religion is by beginning with what it is not. First, philosophy of religion must not be confused with the study of the history of the major religions by which human beings have lived. In studying the history of a particular religion, Christianity, for example, one would read something about its origin in Judaism, the life of Jesus, the emergence of the Christian church within the Roman Empire, and the development of the doctrines distinctive of the Christian faith. Similar studies might be carried out with respect to the other major religions: Judaism, Islam, Buddhism, and Hinduism. While such studies are important to the philosophy of religion, and at times may overlap with it, they should not be confused with it.

Second, philosophy of religion is not to be confused with theology. Theology is a discipline largely *within* religion. As such, it develops the doctrines of some particular religious faith and seeks to ground them either within the reason common to humankind (natural theology) or within the revealed word of God (revealed theology). Although philosophy of religion is fundamentally concerned with the study of the ways in which religious beliefs are justified by those who hold them, its primary concern is not to justify or refute some particular set of religious beliefs but to assess the sorts of reasons that thoughtful people have advanced for and against religious beliefs. Philosophy of religion, unlike theology, is not primarily a discipline *within* religion, but a

From *Philosophy of Religion* (Enrico, Calif.: Dickenson, 1978), pp. 1–3. Reprinted by permission of the author.

discipline which studies religion from a vantage point beyond. Like philosophy of science and philosophy of art, philosophy of religion is not a part of the subject matter it studies. It is important to recognize, however, that there is considerable overlap between theology, particularly *natural* theology, and philosophy of religion. When Aquinas discusses the various arguments for God's existence or tries to analyze what is meant by the idea that God is omnipotent, or when Anselm examines certain important notions like eternity and self-existence, it is difficult to classify their work as belonging solely to theology. It clearly can also be viewed as philosophizing about certain issues in religion. Despite these overlaps, however, the philosophy of religion, as a discipline, should not be identified with theology.

We may best characterize philosophy of religion as *the critical examination of basic religious beliefs and concepts*. Philosophy of religion critically examines basic religious concepts like the concept of God, the concept of faith, the notion of a miracle, the idea of omnipotence. To critically examine a complex concept like the concept of God is to do two things: to distinguish the basic conceptions of God that have emerged in religion, and to analyze each conception into its basic components. The notion of God, as we shall see, stands for several distinct conceptions of the divine. There is, for example, the *pantheistic* idea of God as well as the *theistic* idea of God. What the philosophy of religion seeks to do is to distinguish these different ideas of God and to elaborate each of them. A comprehensive philosophy of religion would analyze each of these distinct ideas of God. . . .

Philosophy of religion critically examines basic religious beliefs: the belief that God exists, that there is life after death, that God knows before we are born whatever we will do, that the existence of evil is somehow consistent with God's love for his creatures. To critically examine a religious belief involves explicating the belief, and examining the reasons that have been given for and against the belief, with a view to determining whether there is any rational justification for holding that belief to be true or holding it to be false. Our purpose in carrying out this examination is not to persuade or convince but to *acquaint* the reader with the sorts of reasons that have been advanced for and against certain basic religious beliefs.

I.B.2.   The Truth of Faith and Philosophical Truth

PAUL TILLICH

Paul Tillich (1886–1965), one of the leading theologians of the twentieth century, taught theology and philosophy in his native Germany until Hitler's rise to power obliged his immigration to the United States. Tillich taught theology and philosophy of religion at Union Theological Seminary from 1933 to 1956 and at Harvard and the University of Chicago from 1956 to 1965. In Dynamics of Faith, *he interprets religious doctrines as symbolic expressions of faith and defines faith as ultimate concern about whatever one takes to be ultimate. There can be no conflict between science and faith or between history and faith, he argues, because science and history seek to express empirical truth by means of literal concepts, whereas the claims of faith are attempts to express spiritual truth through the medium of symbols and myths. In this selection, Tillich contrasts the disinterested philosophical effort to describe ultimate reality in rational concepts with the involved attempt of the religious person or community to express in appropriate symbols the ultimate as the object of faith—that is, the ultimate concern.*

Neither scientific nor historical truth can affirm or negate the truth of faith. The truth of faith can neither affirm nor negate scientific or historical truth. Then the question arises whether philosophical truth has the same relation to the truth of faith or whether the relation is more complex. This, indeed, is the case. What is more, the complexity of the relation between philosophical truth and the truth of faith makes the relation of scientific and historical truth more complex than it appeared in the preceding analysis. This is the reason for the innumerable discussions about the relationship of faith and philosophy and for the popular opinion that philosophy is the enemy and destroyer of faith. Even theologians who have used a philosophical concept in order to express the faith of a religious community have been accused of betraying the faith.

The difficulty of every discussion concerning philosophy as such is the fact that every definition of philosophy is an expression of the point of view of the philosopher who gives the definition. Nevertheless, there is a kind of pre-philosophical agreement about the meaning of philosophy, and the only thing one can do in a discussion like the present one is to use this prephilosophical notion of what philosophy is. In this sense philosophy is the attempt to answer the most general questions about the nature of reality and human existence. Most general are those questions which do not ask about the nature of a specific sphere of reality (as the physical or the historical realms) but about the nature of reality, which is effective in all realms. Philosophy tries to find the universal categories in which being is experienced.

If such a notion of philosophy is presupposed, the relation of philosophical truth to the truth of faith can be determined. Philosophical truth is truth about the structure of being; the truth of faith is truth about one's ultimate concern. Up to this point the relation seems to be very similar to that between the truth of faith and scientific truth. But the difference is that there is a point of identity between the ultimate of the philosophical question and the ultimate of the religious concern. In both cases ultimate reality is sought and expressed—conceptually in philosophy, symbolically in religion. Philosophical truth consists in true concepts concerning the ultimate; the truth of faith consists in true symbols concerning the ultimate. The relation between these two is the problem with which we have to deal.

The question will certainly be raised: Why does philosophy use concepts and why does faith use symbols if both try to express the same ultimate? The answer, of course, is that the relation to the ultimate is not the same in each case. The philosophical relation is in principle a detached description of the basic structure in which the ultimate manifests itself. The relation of faith is in principle an involved expression of concern about the meaning of the ultimate for the faithful. The difference is obvious and fundamental. But it is, as the phrase "in principle" indicates, a difference which is not maintained in the actual life of philosophy and of faith. It cannot be maintained, because the philosopher is a human being with an ultimate concern, hidden or open. And the faithful one is a human being with the power of thought and the need for conceptual understanding. This is not only a biographical fact. It has consequences for the life of philosophy in the philosopher and for the life of faith in the faithful.

An analysis of philosophical systems, essays or fragments of all kinds shows that the direction in which the philosopher asks the question and the preference he gives to special types of answers is determined by cognitive consideration and by a state of ultimate concern. The historically most significant philosophies show not only the greatest power of thought but the most passionate concern about the meaning of the ultimate whose manifestations they describe. One needs only to be reminded of the Indian and Greek philosophers from Leibnitz and Spinoza to Kant and Hegel. If it seems that the positivistic line of philosophers from Locke and Hume to present-day logical positivism is an exception to this rule, one must consider that the task to which these philosophers restricted themselves were special problems of the doctrine of knowledge and, in our time especially, analyses of the linguistic tools of scientific knowledge. This certainly is a justified and very important endeavor, but is not philosophy in the traditional sense.

Philosophy, in its genuine meaning, is carried on by people in whom the passion of an ultimate concern is united with a clear and detached observation of the way ultimate reality manifests itself in the process of the universe. It is this element of ultimate concern behind philosophical ideas which supplies the truth of faith in them. Their vision of the universe and of man's predicament within it unites faith and conceptual work. Philosophy is not only the mother's womb out of which science and history have come, it is also an ever-present element in actual scientific and historical work. The frame of reference within which the great physicists have seen and are seeing the universe of their inquiries is philosophical, even if their actual inquiries verify it. In no case is it a result of their discoveries. It is always a vision of the totality of being which consciously or unconsciously determines the frame of their thought. Because this is so one is justified in saying that even in the scientific view of reality an element of faith is effective. Scientists rightly try to prevent these elements of faith and philosophical truth from interfering with their actual research. This is possible to a great extent; but even the most protected experiment is not absolutely "pure"—pure in the sense of the exclusion of interfering factors such as the observer, and as the interest which determines the kind of question asked of nature in an experiment. What we said about the philosopher must also be said about the scientist. Even in his scientific work he is a human being, grasped by an ultimate concern, and he asks the question of the universe as such, the philosophical question.

In the same way the historian is consciously or unconsciously a philosopher. It is quite obvious that every task of the historian beyond the finding of facts is dependent on evaluations of historical factors, especially the nature of man, his freedom, his determination, his development out of nature, etc. It is less obvious but also true that even in the act of finding historical facts philosophical presuppositions are involved. This is especially true in deciding, out of the infinite number of happenings in every infinitely small moment of time, which facts shall be called historically relevant facts. The historian is further forced to give his evaluation of sources and their reliability, a task which is not independent of his interpretation of human nature. Finally, in the moment in which a historical work gives implicit or explicit assertions about the meaning of historical events for human existence, the philosophical presuppositions of history are evident. Where there is philosophy there is expression of an ultimate concern; there is an element of faith, however hidden it may be by the passion of the historian for pure facts.

All these considerations show that, in spite of their essential difference, there is an actual union of philosophical truth and the truth of faith in every philosophy and that this union is significant for the work of the scientist and the historian. This union has been called "philosophical faith."[1] The term is misleading, because it seems to confuse the two elements, philosophical truth and the truth of faith. Further, the term seems to indicate that there is *one* philosophical faith, a "philosophia perennis," as it has been termed. But only the philosophical question is perennial, not the answers. There is a continuous process of interpretation of philosophical elements and elements of faith, not *one* philosophical faith.

---

[1] In the book of this name by Jaspers.

There is truth of faith in philosophical truth. And there is philosophical truth in the truth of faith. In order to see the latter point we must confront the conceptual expression of philosophical truth with the symbolical expression of the truth of faith. Now, one can say that most philosophical concepts have mythological ancestors and that most mythological symbols have conceptual elements which can and must be developed as soon as the philosophical consciousness has appeared. In the idea of God the concepts of being, life, spirit, unity and diversity are implied. In the symbol of the creation concepts of finitude, anxiety, freedom and time are implied. The symbol of the "fall of Adam" implies a concept of man's essential nature, of his conflict with himself, of his estrangement from himself. Only because every religious symbol has conceptual potentialities is "theo-logy" possible. There is a philosophy implied in every symbol of faith. But faith does not determine the movement of the philosophical thought, just as philosophy does not determine the character of one's ultimate concern. Symbols of faith can open the eyes of the philosopher to qualities of the universe which otherwise would not have been recognized by him. But faith does not command a definite philosophy, although churches and theological movements have claimed and used Platonic, Aristotelian, Kantian or Humean philosophies. The philosophical implications of the symbols of faith can be developed in many ways, but the truth of faith and the truth of philosophy have no authority over each other.

I.C.   Rationality and Religious Belief

I.C.1.   Philosophy the Instigator of Heresies

ST. TERTULLIAN

St. Tertullian (c 160–220), an African church father who wrote his polemical works on Christian theology in Latin, was convinced that human reason is tainted because of our sinful nature inherited from Adam, and thus that religious truths must be received without question through revelation: The more they seem contrary to what our "bastard reason" dictates, the more confident we can be that they are true. In De Carne Christi Tertullian says that the incarnation of God in Christ is certain because it is impossible. In the following selection he draws a sharp contrast between philosophy and religion (Athens and Jerusalem), accusing philosophy of being an instigator of heresies.

These are, "the doctrines" of men and "of demons" produced for itching ears of the spirit of this world's wisdom: this the Lord called "foolishness," and "chose the foolish things of the world" to confound even philosophy itself. For [philosophy] it is which is the material of the world's wisdom, the rash interpreter of the nature and the dispensation of God. Indeed heresies are themselves instigated by philosophy. From this source came the Ænos, and I known not what infinite forms, and the trinity of man in the system of Valentinus, who was of Plato's school. From the same source came Marcion's better god, with all his tranquillity; he came of the Stoics. Then, again, the opinion that the soul dies is held by the Epicureans; while the denial of the restoration of the body is taken from the aggregate school of all the philosophers; also, when matter is made equal to God, then you have the teaching of Zeno; and when any doctrine is alleged touching a god of fire, then Heraclitus comes in. The same subject-matter is discussed over and over again by the heretics and the philosophers; the same arguments are involved. Whence comes evil? Why is it permitted? What is the origin of man? and in what way does he come? Besides the question which Valentinus has very lately proposed—Whence comes God?... Unhappy Aristotle! who invented for these men dialectics, the art of building up and pulling down; an art

From *The Prescription against Heretics*, in Alexander Roberts and James Donaldson, eds., *The Ante-Nicene Fathers* (Buffalo: Christian Literature Publishing Company, 1885), vol. 3, p. 246.

so evasive in its propositions, so far-fetched in its conjectures, so harsh, in its arguments, so productive of contentions—embarrassing even to itself, retracting everything, and really treating of nothing! Whence spring those "fables and endless genealogies," and "unprofitable questions," and "words which spread like a cancer?" From all these, when the apostle would restrain us, he expressly names *philosophy* as that which he would have us be on our guard against. Writing to the Colossians, he says, "See that no one beguile you through philosophy and vain deceit, after the tradition of men, and contrary to the wisdom of the Holy Ghost." He had been at Athens, and had in his interviews [with its philosophers] become acquainted with that human wisdom which pretends to know the truth, whilst it only corrupts it, and is itself divided into its own manifold heresies, by the variety of its mutually repugnant sects. What indeed has Athens to do with Jerusalem? What concord is there between the Academy and the Church? what between heretics and Christians? Our instruction comes from "the porch of Solomon," who had himself taught that "the Lord should be sought in simplicity of heart." Away with all attempts to produce a mottled Christianity of Stoic, Platonic, and dialectic composition! We want no curious disputation after possessing Christ Jesus, no inquisition after enjoying the gospel! With our faith, we desire no further belief. For this is our palmary faith, that there is nothing which we ought to believe besides.

I.C.2.   Verification and the Meaning of Religious Language

A. J. AYER AND FATHER COPLESTON

Alfred Jules Ayer (1910–1989), a British philosopher teaching at Oxford and University College London, was an aggressive advocate of logical positivism who attempted to narrow the scope of philosophy in order to exclude metaphysics, the philosophy of religion, ethics, and aesthetics. Frederick C. Copleston (1907–) a British priest, taught philosophy in Oxford, London, and Rome. In 1949, the British Broadcasting Corporation sponsored a discussion between Ayer and Copleston about the nature and function of philosophy. The following selection consists of excerpts from that broadcast. Ayer states the now-discredited verifiability criterion, which Copleston argues was designed not for a disinterested purpose but as a means of ruling out metaphysics and the philosophy of religion. Copleston points out further that the criterion is arbitrary because it is put forth without a rational justification, and also "self-stultifying," because it not only rules out metaphysical propositions as meaningless but also convicts itself of meaninglessness, since it cannot itself pass the test it imposes on all meaningful propositions.

AYER: Well, Father Copleston, you've asked me to summarize logical positivism for you, and it's not very easy. For one thing, as I understand it, logical positivism isn't a system of philosophy; it consists, rather, in a certain technique, a certain kind of attitude towards philosophical problems. Perhaps one thing which those of us who are called logical positivists tend to have in common is that we deny the possibility of philosophy as a speculative discipline. We should say that if philosophy was to be a branch of knowledge as distinct from the sciences it would have to consist in logic or in some form of analysis; and our reason for this would be somewhat as follows:

We maintain that you can divide propositions into two classes—formal and empirical. Formal propositions, like those of logic and mathematics, depend for their validity on the conventions of a symbol system. Empirical propositions, on the other hand, are statements of observation—actual or

From a BBC broadcast, 1949, reprinted in David Stuart, *Exploring the Philosophy of Religion* (Englewood Cliffs, N.J.: Prentice-Hall, 1980), pp. 186ff.

possible—or hypotheses from which such statements can be logically derived; and it is they that constitute science insofar as science isn't purely mathematical. Now our contention is that this exhausts the field of what we may call speculative knowledge. Consequently we reject metaphysics, if this be understood—and I think it commonly has been—as an attempt to gain knowledge about the world by non-scientific means. Inasmuch as metaphysical statements are not testable by observation, we hold they're not descriptive of anything; and from this we should conclude that if philosophy is to be a cognitive activity, it must be purely critical. It would take the form of trying to elucidate the concepts that were used in science or mathematics or in everyday language.

COPLESTON: Well, Professor Ayer, I can quite understand, of course, philosophers confining themselves to logical analysis if they wish to do so, and I shouldn't dream of denying or of belittling in any way its utility; I think it's obviously an extremely useful thing to do, to analyze and clarify the concepts used in science. In everyday life, too, there are many terms used that practically have taken on an emotional connotation—"progressive,"or "reactionary," or "freedom," or "the modern mind." To make clear to people what's meant—or what *they* mean—by those terms, or the various possible meanings, is a very useful thing. But if the logical positivist means that logical analysis is the *only* function of philosophy, that's the point at which I should disagree with him; and so would many other philosophers disagree, especially, I think, on the Continent.

Don't you think that by saying what philosophy is one presupposes a philosophy or takes up a position as a philosopher? For example, if one divides significant propositions into two classes—namely, purely formal propositions and statements of observation—one is adopting a philosophical position, one is claiming that there are no necessary propositions which are not purely formal. Moreover, to claim that metaphysical propositions to be significant should be verifiable as scientific hypotheses are verifiable is to claim that metaphysics—to be significant—should not be metaphysics.

AYER: Oh, I agree that my position is philosophical, though not that it's metaphysical, as I hope to show later. To say what philosophy is is certainly a philosophical act, but this I mean is itself a question of philosophical analysis. We have to decide, among other things, what it is we're going to call philosophy—and I've given you my answer. It is not, perhaps, an obvious answer, but it at least has the merit that it rescues philosophical statements from becoming either meaningless or trivial. . . .

COPLESTON: . . . Well, perhaps we'd better attend to your principle of verifiability. You mentioned the principle of verification earlier. I thought possibly you'd state it. Professor, would you?

AYER: Yes, I'll state it in a very loose form; namely, that to be significant a statement must be either on the one hand a formal statement—one that I should call analytic—or on the other hand empirically testable. I should try to derive this principle by an analysis of understanding. I should say that understanding a statement meant knowing what would be the case if it were true. Knowing what would be the case if it were true means knowing what observations would verify it. And this in turn means being disposed to accept some situations as warranting the acceptance or rejection of the statement in question. From which there are two corollaries. One—which we've been talking about to some extent—: The statements to which no situations are relevant one way or the other are ruled out as non-factual. And, secondly, the contents of the statement, the cash value, to use James's term, consists of a range of situations, experiences, that would substantiate or refute it.

COPLESTON: Thank you. Now I don't want to misinterpret your position, but it does seem to me that we're supposing a certain philosophical position. What I mean is this. If you say that any factual statement, in order to be meaningful, must be verifiable, and if you mean, by verifiable, verifiable by sense experience, then surely you are presupposing that all reality is given in sense experience. If you are presupposing this, you are presupposing that there can be no such thing as a metaphysical reality, and if you presuppose this you are presupposing a philosophical position which cannot be demonstrated by the principle of verification. It seems to me that logical positivism claims to be what I might call a neutral technique, whereas in reality it presupposes the truth of positivism. And please pardon my saying so, but it looks to me as though the principle of verifiability was cogitated partly in order to exclude metaphysical propositions from the range of meaningful propositions.

AYER: Even if that were so it doesn't prove anything, really. But to go back. I certainly shouldn't make any statement about all reality. That's precisely the kind of statement I use my principle in order not to make. Nor do I wish to restrict experience to sense experience. I shouldn't at all mind counting what might be called introspectable experiences or feelings; mystical experiences, if you like.

It would be true then that people who haven't had certain experiences won't understand propositions which refer to them, but that I don't mind either. I can quite well believe that your experience is different from mine. Let's assume, which is after all an empirical assumption, that you even have a sense difference from mine. I should then be in the position of a blind man, and I should admit that statements that are unintelligible to me might be meaningful to you. But I should then go on to say that the factual content of your statement was determined by your experiences—which contents are verifiers or falsifiers.

COPLESTON: Yes, you include introspection, and just assumed it, but my point is that you assumed that a factually informative statement is significant only if it is verifiable—at least in principle—by direct observation. Now obviously the existence of a metaphysical reality is not verifiable by direct observation. I'm not very keen on appealing to intuition, though I see no compelling reason to rule it out from the beginning. However, if you mean, by verifiable, verifiable by direct sense observation, and/or by introspection, you seem to me to be ruling out metaphysics from the start. In other words, I suggest that acceptance of the principle of verification, as you appear to understand it, implies the acceptance of philosophical positivism. I think I should probably be prepared to accept the principle if it were understood in a very wide sense—that is, if verifiable by experience is understood as including intellectual intuition, and also as meaning simply that some experience, actual or conceivable, is relevant to the truth or falsity of the proposition concerned. But what I object to is any statement of the principle which tacitly assumes the validity of the definite philosophical position. Now you've made a distinction, I think, between the analytic statements, on the one hand, and the empirical statements, and the metaphysical and ethical statements on the other. Or at any rate the metaphysical statements—let's leave ethical out of it. You call the first group cognitive statements and the second emotive. Is that so?

AYER: I think the word "emotive" isn't very happy, though I've used it in the past, and I suggest I make it "emotion," which isn't necessarily the case. But I accept what you say if you mean by emotive simply not cognitive.

COPLESTON: Very well, I accept, of course, your substitution of non-cognitive for emotive, but my objection still remains that by cognitive statements I presume that you mean statements which satisfy the criterion of meaning—that is to say, the principle of verifiability; and by non-cognitive statements I presume you mean statements which do not satisfy that criterion. If this is so, it seems to me that when you say that metaphysical statements are non-cognitive you are not saying much more than that statements which do not satisfy the principle of verification do not satisfy the principle of verification In this case, however, no conclusion follows as to the significance or non-significance of metaphysical propositions, unless, indeed, one has previously accepted your philosophical position—that is to say, unless one has assumed that they are non significant.

AYER: It's not so simple as that. My procedure is this. I shall claim that the account I have given you of what understanding a statement is. . . does apply to ordinary common-sense statements and scientific statements. So I'd give a different account of how a mathematical statement functions, and a different account again of value judgment.

COPLESTON: Yes.

AYER: I then say that statements which don't satisfy these conditions are not significant, not to be understood; and I think you can quite correctly object that by putting my definitions together all I come down to saying is that statements that are not scientific or common-sense statements are not scientific or common-sense statements. But then I want to go further and say that I totally fail to understand—and, again, I'm afraid I'm using my own sense of understanding; what else can I do?—I fail to understand what these other non-scientific statements and non-common-sense statements, which don't satisfy these criteria, propose to be. Someone may say he does understand them, in some sense of understanding other than the one I've defined. I reply: It's not clear to me what that sense of understanding is, nor, a fortiori, what it is he understands, nor how these statements function. But of course you may still say that in making it a question of how these statements function I'm presupposing my own criterion.

COPLESTON: Well, then, in your treatment of metaphysical propositions you are either applying the criterion of verifiability or you are not. If you are, then the significance of metaphysical propositions would seem to be ruled out of court a priori, since the truth of the principle, as it is seems to be understood by you, inevitably involves the non-significance of metaphysical propositions. In this case the application of the criterion to concrete metaphysical propositions constitutes a proof neither of the non-significance of metaphysical propositions nor of the truth of the principle. All that is shown, it seems to me, is that metaphysical propositions do not satisfy a definite assumed criterion of meaning. But it does not follow that one has to accept that criterion of meaning. You may legitimately say, if you like, "I will accept as significant factual statements only those statements which satisfy these particular demands or conditions." But it doesn't follow, does it, that I or anybody else has to make those particular demands before we are prepared to accept a statement as meaningful?

AYER: What I do is to give a definition of certain related terms: "understanding," "meaningful," and so on. I can't possibly accept them, either. But I can perhaps make you unhappy about the consequences of not accepting them. What I should do is this. I should take any given proposition, and show how it functions. In the case of a scientific hypothesis, I would show that it had a certain function—namely, that, with other premises, you could deduce certain observational consequences from it. I should then say this is how this proposition works. This is what it does, this is what it amounts to. I then take mathematical propositions and play a slightly different game with them, and show that they function in a certain way, in a calculus, in a symbolic system. You then present me with these other statements, and I say: On the one hand, they have no observational consequences. On the other hand, they aren't statements of logic. All right. So you understand them. I have given a definition of understanding according to which they are not, in my usage of the term, capable of being understood. Nevertheless, you reject my definition; you are perfectly entitled to, because you can give understanding a different meaning if you like. I can't stop you. But now I say: Tell me more about them. In what sense are they understood? They are not understood in my sense. They aren't parts of a symbolic system. You can't do anything with them in the sense of deriving any observational consequences from them. What do you want to say about them? Well, you may just want to say they're facts or something of that sort. Then again I press you on your use of the word "facts."

COPLESTON: You seem to me to be demanding that in order for a factual statement to be significant, one must be able to deduce observational consequences from it. But I don't see why that should be so. If you mean directly observable consequences, you appear to me to be demanding too much. In any case, are there some propositions which are not verifiable, even in principle, but which would yet be considered by most people to have meaning and to be either true or false. Let me give an example. I don't want to assume the mantle of a prophet, and I hope the statement is quite false. But it is this. "Atomic warfare will take place and it will blot out the entire human race." Now, most people would think that this statement has meaning. It means what it says. But how could it possibly be verified empirically? Supposing it were fulfilled; the last man could not say with his last breath, "Copleston's prediction has been verified," because he would not be entitled to say this until he was dead—that is, until he was no longer in a position to verify the statement.

AYER: It is certainly practically unverifiable. You can't be a man surviving all men. On the other hand, there's no doubt it describes a possible situation. Putting the observer outside the story, one knows quite well what it would be like to observe devastation and fail to observe any men. Now it wouldn't necessarily be the case that, in order to do that, one had to observe oneself. Just as, to take the case of the past, there were dinosaurs before there were men. Clearly, no man saw that, and clearly I, if I am speaker, I can't myself verify it, but one knows what it would be like to have observed animals and not to have observed men.

COPLESTON: The two cases are different. In regard to the past, we have empirical evidence. For example, we have fossils of dinosaurs. But in the case of the prediction I mentioned, there would be nobody to observe the evidence and so to verify the proposition.

AYER: In terms of the evidence, of course, it becomes very much easier for me. That would be too easy a way of getting out of our difficulty, because there is also evidence for the atomic thing.

COPLESTON: Yes, but there would be no evidence for the prediction that it will blot out the human race, even if one can imagine the state of affairs that would verify it. Thus by imagining it, one's imagining oneself into the. . .

AYER: No, no.

COPLESTON: Yes, yes. One can imagine the evidence and one can imagine oneself verifying it; but in point of fact, if the prediction were fulfilled, there would be no one there to verify it. By importing yourself imaginatively into the picture, you are canceling out the condition of the fulfillment of the prediction. But let us drop the prediction. You have mentioned imagination. Now, what I should prefer to regard as the criterion of the truth or falsity of an existential proposition is simply the presence or absence of the asserted fact or facts, quite irrespective of whether I can know whether there are corresponding facts or not. If I can at least imagine or conceive the facts, the existence of which would verify the proposition, the proposition has significance for me. Whether I can or cannot know that the facts correspond is another matter.

AYER: I don't at all object to your use of the word "facts" so long as you allow it to be observable facts. But take the contrary case. Suppose I say, "There's a drogulus over there." And you say, "What?" and I say, "Drogulus," and you say, "What's a drogulus?" "Well," I say, "I can't describe what a drogulus is because it's not the sort of thing you can see or touch; it has no physical effects of any kind; it's a disembodied being." And you say: "Well, how am I to tell if it's there or not?" And I say: "There's no way of telling. Everything's just the same if it's there or it's not there. But the fact is it's there. There's a drogulus there standing just behind you, spiritually behind you." Does that make sense?

COPLESTON: It seems to me to do so. I should say that a drogulus in the room or not is true or false, provided that you can—that you at any rate, I have some idea of what is meant by a drogulus, and if you can say to me it's a disembodied spirit, then I should say that the proposition is either true or false whether one can verify it or not. If you said to me: "By 'drogulus' I merely mean the word 'drogulus' and I attach no other significance to it whatsoever," then I should say that it isn't a proposition any more than if I said "piffle" was in the room.

AYER: That's right. But what is "having some idea" of something? I want to say that having an idea of something is a matter of knowing how to recognize it. And you want to say that you can have ideas of things even though there's no possible situation in which you could recognize it because nothing would count as finding it. I would say that I understand the words "angel," "table," "clock," "drogulus" if I'm disposed to accept certain situations as verifying the presence or absence of what the word is supposed to stand for. But you want to admit these words without any reference to experience, whether the thing they are supposed to stand for exists, and everything is to go on just the same.

COPLESTON: No, I should say that you can have an idea of something if there's some experience that's relevant to the formation of the idea, not so much to its verification. I should say that I can form the idea of a drogulus or a disembodied spirit from the idea of body and the idea of mind. You may say that there's no mind and there's no spirit, but, at any rate, there is, as you'll admit, certain internal experience of thinking and so on which at any rate accounts for the formation of the idea. Therefore I can say I have an idea of a drogulus or whatever it is, even though I'm quite unable to know whether such a thing actually exists or not.

AYER: You would certainly not have to know that it exists, but you would have to know what would count as its existing.

COPLESTON: Yes, well, if you mean by count as its existing that there must be some experience relevant to the formation of the idea, then I should agree.

AYER: Not to the formation of the idea, but to the truth or falsity of the propositions in which it is contained.

COPLESTON: The word "metaphysics" and the phrase "metaphysical reality" can have more than one meaning, but when I refer to a "metaphysical reality" in our present discussion I mean a being which in principle (and not merely in fact) transcends the sphere of what can be sensibly experienced. Thus God is a metaphysical reality. Since God is, *ex hypothesi*, immaterial, he cannot, in principle, be apprehended by the senses.

May I add two remarks? My first remark is that I do not mean to imply that no sense experience is in any way relevant to establishing or discovering. I certainly do believe that metaphysics must be based on experience of some sort, but metaphysics involves intellectual reflection on experience. No amount of immediate sense experience will disclose the existence of a metaphysical reality. In other words, I should say, there is a halfway house between admitting only the immediate data of experience and, on the other hand, leaping to the affirmation of a metaphysical reality without any reference to experience at all. You yourself reflect on the data of experience. The metaphysician carries that reflection a stage further.

My second remark is this. Because one cannot have sense experience of a metaphysical reality it doesn't follow that one couldn't have another type of experience of it, and if anybody had such experience it does not seem to me that the metaphysical reality is deprived, as it were, of its metaphysical character and become non-metaphysical. I think that's an important point.

AYER: Yes, but asking are there metaphysical realities isn't like asking are there still wolves in Asia, is it? It looks as if you've got a clear usage for metaphysical reality and then ask does it occur or not, does it exist or not, as if I'm arbitrarily denying that it exists. My difficulty is not in answering the question—are there not metaphysical realities?—but in understanding what usage is being given to the expression "metaphysical reality." When am I to count a metaphysical reality? What would it be like to come upon a metaphysical reality? That's my problem. It isn't that I arbitrarily say there can't be such things, already admitting the use of the term, but that I'm puzzled about the use of the term. I don't know what people who say there are metaphysical realities mean by it.

COPLESTON: Well, that brings us back to the beginning—the function of philosophy, I think. I should say that one can't simply raise in the abstract the question: Are there metaphysical realities? Rather, one asks: Is the character of observable reality of such a kind that it leads one to postulate a metaphysical reality, a reality beyond the physical sphere? If one grants that it is, even then one can only speak about that metaphysical reality within the framework of human language. And language is, after all, primarily developed to express our immediate experience of surrounding things, and therefore there's bound, I fully admit, to be inadequacy in any statements about a metaphysical reality.

AYER: But you're trying to have it both ways, you see. If it's something that you say doesn't have a meaning in my language, then I don't understand it. It's no good saying: "Oh, well, of course, it really has a meaning," because what meaning could it have except in the language in which it is used?

COPLESTON: Well, let's take a concrete example. If I say, for example, God is intelligent—well, you may very well say to me, "What meaning can you give to the word 'intelligent'?—because the only intelligence you have experienced is the human intelligence, and are you attributing that to God?" and I should have to say no, because I'm not. Therefore, if we agree to use the word "intelligent" simply to mean human intelligence, I should have to say God is not intelligent. But when I say that a stone is not intelligent I mean that a stone is less than intelligent; when I say God is intelligent I mean that God is more than intelligent, even though I can't give an adequate account of what that intelligence is in itself.

AYER: Do you mean simply that he knows more than any given man knows? But to what are you ascribing this property? You haven't begun to make that clear.

COPLESTON: It's a point, of course. But what you are inviting me to do is to describe God in terms which will be as clear to you as the terms in which one might describe a familiar object of experience or an unfamiliar object which is yet so like familiar objects that it can be adequately described in terms of things which are really familiar to you. But God is *ex hypothesi* unique; and it's quite impossible to describe him adequately by using concepts which normally apply to all ordinary objects of experience. If it were possible, then God wouldn't be God. So I think you're really asking me to describe God in a manner possible only if he weren't God.

I freely admit that all human ideas on God are inadequate. I also affirm that this must be so, owing to the finitude of the human intellect and to the fact that we can come to a philosophical knowledge of God only through reflection on the things we experience. But it doesn't follow that we can have no knowledge of God. It does follow, though, that our philosophical knowledge of God cannot be more than analogical.

AYER: Yes, but in the case of an ordinary analogy when you say that something is like something else you understand what both things are. But in this case, if you do say something is analogical I say: Analogical of what? And you don't tell me of what. You merely repeat the first term of analogy. Well, I get no analogy. It's like saying that something is "taller than," and I say, "Taller than?" and you repeat the first thing you say. Then I understand it's taller than itself, which is nonsense.

COPLESTON: I think that one must distinguish physical analogy and metaphysical analogy. If I say that God is intelligent, I don't say so simply because I want to call God intelligent, but either because I think that the world is such that it must be ascribed, in certain aspects at least, to a Being which can be described in human terms only as intelligent or because I am satisfied by some argument that there exists an absolute Being and then deduce that that Being must be described as intelligent. I am perfectly well aware that I have no adequate idea of what that intelligence is in itself. I am ascribing to God an attribute which, translated into human terms, must be called intelligence. After all, if you speak of your dog as intelligent, you are using the word in an analogous sense, and it has some meaning for you, even though you don't observe the dog's physical operations. Mathematicians who speak of multidimensional space have never observed, I suppose, such a space, but presumably they attach some meaning to the term. Or when we speak of "extrasensory perception" we are using the word "perception" analogously.

AYER: Yes, but mathematical physicists do test their statements by observation, and I know what would count as a case of extrasensory perception. In the case of your statement I don't know what counts. Of course, you might give it an empirical meaning: you might say that by "God is 'intelligent' " you mean that the word had certain features. Then we'd inspect it to see if it had the features or not.

COPLESTON: Well, of course I do argue from the world to God. I must start from the world to God. I wouldn't wish to argue from God to the features of the world. But to keep within your terms of reference of empiricism, I should say that if God is personal then he's capable, for example, of entering into relationship with human beings. Then it's possible to find human beings who claim at any rate they have a personal intercourse with God.

AYER: Then you've given your statement a perfectly good empirical meaning. But it would then be like a scientific theory, and you would be using it in exactly the same way as you might use a concept like "electron"—to account for, explain, predict a certain range of human experience—namely, that certain people did have these experiences which they described as "entering into communion with God." Then one would try to analyze it scientifically, find out in what conditions these things happened. Then you might put it up as a theory. What you'd done would be psychology.

COPLESTON: Well, as I said, I was entering into your terms of reference. I wouldn't admit that when I was saying God is personal I merely meant that God could enter into intercourse with human beings. But I should be prepared to say that he was personal even if I had no reason for supposing that he entered into intercourse with human beings.

AYER: No, but it's only in that case one has anything one can control. The facts are that these human beings have these experiences. They describe these experiences in a way which implies more than that they're merely having them. But if one asks what more, then what answer does one get? Only, I'm afraid, repetition of the statement that was questioned in the first place.

COPLESTON: Well, let's come back to this religious experience. However you subsequently interpret the religious experience, you'd admit, then, that it was relevant to the truth or falsity of the proposition that God existed.

AYER: Relevant only insofar as the proposition that God existed is taken as a prediction or description of the occurrence of their experience. But not, of course, that one has any inference you might want to draw, such as that the world was created, or anything of that kind.

COPLESTON: No. We'll leave that out. What I'm trying to get at is that you'd admit the proposition "God exists" could be a meaningful form of metaphysical proposition.

AYER: No, it wouldn't then be a meaningful metaphysical proposition. It'd be a perfectly good empirical proposition, like the proposition that the unconscious mind exists.

COPLESTON: The proposition that people have religious experience would be an empirical proposition, I quite agree. And the proposition that God exists would also be an empirical proposition, provided that all I meant by saying that God exists was that some people have a certain type of experience. But actually that's not all I mean by it. All I originally said was that if God is personal then one of the consequences would be that he could enter into communication with human beings. If he does so that doesn't make God an empirical reality in the sense of not being a metaphysical reality, but God can perfectly well be a metaphysical reality—that is, independent of physics or nature even if intelligent creatures have a non-sensible experience of him. However, if you wish to call metaphysical propositions empirical propositions, by all means do so. It then becomes a question of terminology, I think.

AYER: Oh, no. I suggest that you're again trying to have it both ways. You see, you allow me to give these words, these shapes, or noises an empirical meaning. You allow me to say that the test. . . [of whether] what you call God exists or not is to be that certain people have certain experiences, just as the test whether the table exists or not is that certain people have experiences. Only the experiences are a different sort. Having got that admission, you then shift the meaning of the words "God exists"; you no longer make them refer simply to the possibility of having these experiences, and so argue that I have admitted a metaphysical proposition, but of course I haven't. All I've admitted is an empirical proposition, which you've chosen to express in the same words as you also want to use to express your metaphysical proposition.

COPLESTON: Pardon me. I didn't say that the test. . . [of whether] what I call God exists or not is that certain people have certain experiences. I said that if God exists one consequence would be that people could have certain experiences. However, even if I accept your requirements, it follows that in one case at least you are prepared to recognize the word "God" as meaningful.

AYER: Of course I recognize it as meaningful if you give it an empirical meaning, but it doesn't follow there's any empirical evidence for the truth of your metaphysical proposition.

COPLESTON: But then I don't claim that metaphysical propositions are not in some way founded on reflection on experience. In a certain sense I should call myself an empiricist, but I think that your empiricism is too narrow.

AYER: My quarrel with you is not that you take a wider view of experience than I do, but that you fail to supply any rules for the use of your expressions. Let me try to summarize. I'm not asking you for explicit definitions: All that I require is that some indication be given of the way in which the expression relates to some possible experience. It's only when a statement can't be interpreted as referring even indirectly to anything observable that I wish to dismiss it as metaphysical. It's not necessary that the observation should actually be made; there are cases, as you've pointed out, where for practical, or even for theoretical, reasons, the observation couldn't, in fact, be made, but one knows what it would be like to make it. The statements which refer to it would be said to be verifiable in principle, if not in fact. To put the point more simply, I understand a statement of fact, I know what to look for on the supposition that it's true. My knowing what to look for is itself a matter of my being able to interpret the statement as referring, at least, to some possible experience.

Now you may say—indeed, you have said—that this is all entirely arbitrary. The principle of verifiability is not itself a descriptive statement; its status is that of a persuasive definition. I am persuaded by it, but why should you be? Can I prove it? Yes—on the basis of other definitions. I have in fact tried to show you how it can be derived from an analysis of understanding. But if you're really obstinate you'll reject these other definitions, too, so it looks as if we reach a deadlock. . . . I claim for my method that it does yield valuable results in the way of analysis, and with this you seem disposed to agree. You don't deny the importance of the analytic method in philosophy, nor do you reject all the uses to which I put it; therefore you accept in the main the account that I gave of empirical propositions. You have indeed objected to my treatment of the propositions of logic, but there I think that I'm in the right. At least I'm able to account for their validity, whereas on your view it is utterly mysterious.

The main difference between us is that *you* want to leave room for metaphysics. But now look at the result that you get. You put forward your metaphysical statements as ultimate explanations of fact, yet you admit that they're not explanations in any accepted sense of the term, and you can't say in what sense they *are* explanations. You can't show me how they're to be tested, and you seem to have no criterion for deciding whether they are true or false. This being so, I say they're unintelligible. You say no, you understand them; but for all the good they do you—I mean cognitively, not emotionally— you might just as well abandon them.

This is my case against your metaphysical statements. You may decline to be persuaded by it, but what sort of case can you make *for* them? I leave the last word to you.

COPLESTON: Well, I've enjoyed our discussion very much. I've contended that a metaphysical idea has meaning if some experience is relevant to the formation of the idea, and that a rational metaphysic is possible if there are—as I still think there are—principles which can express an intellectual apprehension and a nature of being. I think that one *can* have an intellectual experience—or intuition, if you like—of being. A metaphysical proposition is testable by rational discussion, but not by purely empirical means. When you say that metaphysical propositions are meaningless because they are unverifiable in your sense, I don't really think that this amounts to more than saying that metaphysics are not the same thing as empirical science.

In short, I consider that logical positivism, apart from its theory of analytic propositions, really embodies the notion of nineteenth-century positivism; that the terms "rational" and "scientific" have the same extension. This notion certainly corresponds to a popularly held prejudice, but I don't see any adequate reason for accepting it. I still find it difficult to understand the status of the principle of verification. It must be, I should have thought, either a proposition or not a proposition. If it is a proposition it must be, on your premises, either a tautology or an empirical hypothesis. If it's a tautology, then no conclusion follows as to metaphysics; if it's an empirical hypothesis, then the principle itself would require verification. But the principle of verification cannot itself be verified. If, however, the principle is not a proposition, it should be, on your premises, meaningless. In any case, if the meaning of an existential proposition consists, according to the principle, in its verifiability, it is impossible, I think, to escape an infinite regress, since the verification will itself need verification, and so on indefinitely; and if that is so, then all propositions, including scientific propositions, are meaningless.

I.C.3. The Meaning of Rationality and the Rationality of Religious Belief

YEAGER HUDSON

Yeager Hudson (1931–), the editor of this volume, is pro fessor of philosophy at Colby College and author of a companion text, The Philosophy of Religion, *from which the following selection is taken. Hudson analyzes the claim that all religious beliefs are irrational via a scrutiny of rationality. The category of irrational beliefs, he argues, consists of all of those beliefs that are forbidden by reason, but the category of rational beliefs includes not only those beliefs required by reason but also those permitted by reason—that is, those concerning which, because the evidence is not conclusive, there is reasonable room for disagreement. Many of the teachings of science fall into this latter class of beliefs, as do many religious beliefs. Such religious beliefs are thus permitted by reason. It follows that they are also rational, although the question whether any of them are true must be answered on other grounds.*

When we look a bit more closely at what it means to say that a belief is rational or irrational, we discover that the distinction is not

From *The Philosophy of Religion* (Mountain View, Calif.: Mayfield, 1990), pp. 25–29.

as simple as it may appear at first. Rationality is not a concept created arbitrarily by the mathematician or logician to serve some narrow purpose. Rather, it represents the pattern or the structure according to which the normal, mature mind operates, and we find it natural to believe that rationality also represents the pattern of the world as well. There is an objectivity and necessity about rationality that the informed and unclouded mind cannot avoid.

It is this necessity that coerces us when we think logically and mathematically. When we understand what the expressions *2*, *plus*, *equals*, and *4* mean, it is impossible (that is, irrational) for us to think that $2 + 2 = 4$ is false. The mind is built in such a way that we cannot avoid believing the conclusion of a mathematical sum or of a logical argument. It is not merely difficult, it is literally impossible to understand "All men are mortal" and "Socrates is a man" without believing "Socrates is mortal." In cases such as these, where the requirements of reason are so luminous and obvious, the mind finds itself definitely unable to believe in an irrational conclusion. In order to accept irrational beliefs, it is necessary for us not to see the irrationality. We do sometimes hold mutually contradictory beliefs, but only if we do not notice that they are contradictory. As soon as their inconsistency is pointed out, we undergo the curious experience of finding that we simply cannot any longer accept both beliefs. Among the large number of beliefs that we accept, there are bound to be inconsistencies that go unnoticed; we do not always bring to bear on a belief the evidence we may have that, if juxtaposed with the belief, would force us to abandon it.

When religious leaders urge the faithful to accept beliefs that are irrational in the sense of being contradictory or inconsistent with other things we know to be true, they often make use of devices to obscure the fact that the beliefs are irrational. Political leaders follow a similar strategy. This is undoubtedly the reason that religious authorities have often discouraged laypersons from attempting to understand or reason about the articles of faith. Doctrines are called mysterious and above reason, and sometimes teachings that seem distinctly contradictory—such as the claim that God can be three and at the same time one—are called *paradoxes*, a word intended to designate teachings that appear to be contradictory but that allegedly, at a deeper or more sacred level, are not.

Thus, to say of a belief that it is irrational is to denounce it in the strongest possible way. It is a very serious matter to say that religious beliefs are not or cannot be rational. This means that if the people who hold such beliefs really understood them and the evidence related to them, they would not be able to accept them. It means, in other words, that persons could be religious only if they were ignorant or very dishonest—willing to hide from themselves the truths that undermine their beliefs.

Is religion actually rendered untenable by reason when it is clearly examined and fully understood? It is quite likely that some of the teachings of the various religions are indeed irrational. Many of the tenets put forward by religious teachers incorporate the current scientific or commonsense beliefs of the era in which the teacher lived. The progress of human knowledge reveals that these opinions are false, but because they have become part of sacred writings, the defenders of the religion often feel that they must continue to present these opinions as revealed truth. This is the most serious epistemological fault of fundamentalism, whether Christian, Moslem, Buddhist, or Hindu.

One of the important tasks that many modern theologians assign themselves is that of separating such unessential, time-bound, empirical or commonsense teachings that do not pertain to the spiritual core of the religious revelation from the essential religious teachings that pertain to every era. The fact that religious scriptures or doctrines have in them such time-bound beliefs means that some religious teachings are indeed irrational. But the charge that all religious belief is irrational is based on a mistaken and too simple-minded understanding of the meaning of rationality and irrationality, an understanding that assumes that every belief is either required by reason or forbidden by reason. But the two classes "forbidden by reason" and "required by reason" do not exhaust all of the possibilities. Some beliefs—indeed, the great majority are neither forbidden nor required by reason.

Reason requires us to believe that bachelors are unmarried men, that a whole is greater than any one of its parts, that two plus seven is nine. It also requires us to believe, apart from distorting or deceiving circumstances, that what we see before us is approximately as it appears to be; it even requires us to believe with a considerable degree of confidence various scientific and commonsense claims for which there is very strong appropriate evidence: that smoking causes lung cancer, that the material things in the world are all made of various combinations of approximately 100 basic elements, that the sun produces energy by fusing hydrogen atoms into helium, that racial and ethnic prejudice are fairly widespread in the world in the twentieth century, and so on. Reason forbids us to believe that there are any five-sided triangles, that by the year 2000 the world will have existed for a shorter period of time than it had existed in 1900, that three times three is eleven, or that a man could be his grandfather's sister. Reason also forbids us to believe with any substantial degree of conviction that there is no connection between serum cholesterol and heart disease, that the moon is made of a substance totally different from what constitutes the earth, or that it is safe to expose humans to very high levels of radioactivity.

When we talk about beliefs that reason requires and the beliefs that reason forbids, we speak of the areas of well- or of relatively well-established human knowledge. But there is much we do not yet know. There is some justification for believing that a vaccine effective in preventing AIDS will be discovered before the year 2015, but there are also substantial reasons for believing that this will not happen. Evidence suggests that the mean temperature of the earth is rising very gradually; but this evidence is far from conclusive. Reason neither requires nor forbids us to believe these and a very large number of similar claims. About such beliefs we say that there is room for reasonable doubt and reasonable disagreement. It is not irrational to believe; neither is it irrational to disbelieve. Indeed, we actually find numbers of very reasonable persons on both sides of many of these issues.

We must conclude, therefore, that the question of rationality involves not just two but three categories: (1) "required by reason" (2) "forbidden by reason," and a third that is neither required nor forbidden but is rather (3) "permitted by reason." Now it is clear that persons would be irrational if they adopted beliefs forbidden by reason and rational if they adopted beliefs required by reason. But what about the very large category of beliefs about which the sum of our evidence is insufficient to enable us to say that they are either required or forbidden? Certainly it would not be irrational to believe them, since the evidence is inconclusive and thus they might be true. Likewise, it would not be irrational to disbelieve them for a similar reason. We must say of those beliefs that are "permitted by reason" that it is rational to believe them *and* that it is rational not to believe them.

We may summarize our findings, therefore, by saying that when we call a belief irrational, we mean that it is forbidden by reason. That means that the belief is known to be false or that the evidence against it is strong enough that no reasonable person could be justified in accepting the belief. But when we say that a belief is rational, we mean not necessarily that it is required by reason, but perhaps that it is permitted by reason. In other words, the class of rational beliefs includes those that are required and also those that are permitted by reason. Perhaps a diagram will help:

Irrational Beliefs	Rational Beliefs	
Beliefs forbidden by reason	Beliefs permitted by reason	Beliefs required by reason

But where, in this framework, do religious beliefs fall? Clearly the positivists believed that religious beliefs were excluded from the whole scheme of classification because they are not true assertions and thus do not count as beliefs at all. But we have already seen that the positivists were not justified in that position. We must find the proper place, then, for religious assertions that make genuine claims.

It is clear that some religious beliefs are required by reason, particularly those whose truth is determined exclusively by the meaning of their terms: for example, "God is the creator of the world according to Christian doctrine," or "The Buddha is the enlightened one." And any parallel claims that are false by virtue of the meaning of their constituent terms are forbidden by reason: for example, "God is a created being according to Christian doctrine" or "An avatar is not an incarnate deity." The overwhelming majority of religious claims, however, are neither forbidden nor required by reason. "God exists" is supported by certain plausible arguments, but there are also substantial counterarguments. "God is omnipotent" is maintained by Christians on fairly convincing grounds, but opponents have brought forward strong objections. "Mystical experiences are merely abnormal psychological states with no religious significance" has been argued with a certain plausibility, but there are good reasons on the other side. Thus, these claims may not be either required nor forbidden by reason. This means that such beliefs are permitted by reason: It is reasonable to believe them; it is also reasonable to disbelieve them. But we must be very careful not to become lax in weighing the evidence. Only those beliefs concerning which the available evidence is quite evenly balanced can be considered in this sense rational to believe. Those for which there is even a small balance of negative over affirmative evidence cannot be affirmed rationally.

Beliefs that are permitted by reason are not irrational. They are, in fact, one of the categories of rational beliefs. It follows, therefore, that it is not irrational to hold some religious beliefs or, stated another way, that some religious beliefs can be rational. But we must remember that this is not a very strong claim about religious beliefs. It does not amount to saying that any religious beliefs are true; that is an entirely separate question. Many beliefs that it is rational to hold may turn out to be false. Of course, once we discover that they are false, it is no longer rational to hold them. Indeed, as soon as there is a preponderance of evidence against a belief, it ceases to be rational to hold it.

Many religious beliefs, however, have strong arguments in their favor that many honest and careful thinkers find convincing. The business of the philosophy of religion is to examine the claims made in the name of religion. In so doing, we must keep in mind at all times William James's injunction to think without arbitrariness or dogmatism. Thus we will give rank or privilege to no belief, whether favorable to or critical of religion, but will attempt to place all on an equal footing, demanding of every one satisfactory epistemological credentials and standing ready to reject any that do not pass muster. We will make use of all the tools of evidence and reasoning and will hope for illuminating results. But whether our conclusions are meager or substantial, we will learn in the process a great deal about religion, philosophy, and perhaps also ourselves.

I.C.4. Can Religious Belief Be Rational?

LOUIS POJMAN

Louis Pojman (1935–), professor of philosophy at the University of Mississippi, takes an entirely rationalistic position on faith, reflecting W. K. Clifford's (1845–1879) attitude of moral disapproval toward anyone who embraces doctrines blindly or without the rational warrant of evidence. Pojman rejects the notion of groundless or "properly basic" beliefs as the foundation of our belief systems, which are themselves unsupported, and argues for a coherence theory in which our beliefs form a mutually supporting network. Religious beliefs find their place and rational standing in a coherent web within which all our beliefs are analyzed, clarified, and justified by the extent to which they cohere with, are supported by, and reciprocally support all that we have reason to believe.

INTRODUCTION

In this essay I argue for a thoroughly rationalistic faith. I argue that religious faith has a moral dimension underlying it, so that any faith that is not rational for a person to hold may also be immoral. I outline a notion of an ethics of belief that makes rational believing a *prima facie* moral duty and casts moral censure at leaps of faith beyond the evidence. Then I outline a coherentist strategy for justifying religious belief within the bounds of reason.

Nearly every Christian theologian has demurred from the idea of a wholly rational faith. The Catholic tradition, stemming from Thomas Aquinas, avers that the subset of doctrines, the preambles, are in accordance with reason but that such doctrines as the incarnation and the trinity are beyond its pale. On the other side of the spectrum we have the antirationalists, who believe that the key to religious belief is a miracle of faith "which subverts all the principles of understanding," as Hume skeptically but Hamann and Kierkegaard approvingly put it. (It's a fascinating intellectual anecdote in the history of philosophy that Hamann discovered Hume's dictum and set it forth in his writings as the essence of faith, where it was read by Kierkegaard, who thought Hamann had originated it and applauded him for his brilliant insight.) For Tertullian, Hamann, Kierkegaard, and Shestov the very irrationality of Christianity is reason for embracing it. If God is wholly other, we should expect his truth to seem contradictory to sinful human minds. Modern fideists, following some remarks by Wittgenstein, claim that religious belief is groundless and not subject to rational scrutiny. Somewhere in between these opposing positions is the reformed view (that of Calvin, Warfield, and Bavinck) of natural theology as somehow an irreverent activity. As Barth puts it, to reason about faith is to assume the standpoint of unbelief; it "makes reason a judge over Christ." Most recently, a well-argued version of this position has been developed by Alvin Plantinga, which claims that belief in God may be properly basic to the foundations in one's noetic structure, as justified as our belief that there are other minds or as any of our immediate empirical or memory beliefs (e.g., the memory belief that I had breakfast this morning).[1]

Although I have learned much from Plantinga and have sympathy for a great deal in his position, especially since he has modified it lately to include the notion that reason could infirm faith's stance, I find two problems with his position, which I have tried to remedy:

(1) The criteria of proper basicality for Plantinga seem so open-ended that virtually any world view, no matter how implausible to thoughtful people, could be justified. Although honest people will certainly differ about what is properly basic, one should suspect or even not fully accept one's own beliefs as basic if they fail to win support from the consensus of rationally informed people or epistemologists as basic or evidential. There are limits to what can count as properly basic, and although exact criteria are hard to come by, not everything can properly be part of the foundations of a noetic structure. As far as I understand the logic of Plantinga's position, there are no epistemically neutral criteria that would eliminate anyone's favorite insane belief. Here his position reminds one of Hare's famous paranoid student who had a *blik* (read "properly basic belief") that all dons were out to harm him.

(2) Secondly, I doubt that theoretical beliefs such as the existence of a divine creator of the universe fit as well into a foundationalist view of epistemology as they do into a coherentist framework. Would we believe in God if the concept had no support at all from our beliefs about the world's having a cause, a design or order, if we didn't have testimony of various encounters with the divine, if there were no claims to miraculous events confirming divine authority? Theistic belief does not stand unsupported, alone and in isolation, but as part and parcel of many other considerations that together helps us make sense of the world. Although a great many of our core beliefs cannot easily be traced back to their origins or justificatory basis, we can still offer considerations for them, showing that they are supported by other beliefs in an all-encompassing network of beliefs. Our noetic structure may well be more in the metaphorical shape of a web than in the shape of a house with a foundation. It is the very foundational metaphor that makes Plantinga's view so implausible to some of us.

THE ETHICS OF BELIEF

First let me state why there are ethical duties to believe according to the best evidence available. Often the beliefs that we have affect the well-being of others. Suppose that you are a physician who is consulted about certain symptoms. You prescribe a drug that you have a hunch will help the patient, but your diagnosis is wrong and the patient dies. When examiners inquire into the situation, they discover that you hadn't kept up on your medicine and that your mistake would have been easily prevented had you been aware of side effects of the drug in question (and had you not misdiagnosed the symptoms). Since you could have had correct beliefs about these matters had you read the latest literature in the area, which was abundantly available, you are rightly judged to be culpably ignorant. You had an obligation to keep up with the literature. At bottom, an ethic of belief may reduce to an ethic of investigation and openness to criticism, but the point is that we are responsible for many of the beliefs that we have and that, as guides to actions, eventually result in action that may harm or help our fellow humans.

Of course, the duty to believe according to the best evidence is not our only moral duty, and perhaps there are times when another duty overrides it, but it is a duty that ought to be taken with the utmost seriousness, more than most thinkers have afforded it. Besides, how confident can we be of our beliefs if we know deep down that they are not backed up by good evidence?

If we apply this to religious belief, we can see that it is also important that we follow the best reasons in forming our belief states. Since the best justified beliefs have the best chance of being true and hence reliable, we should seek to justify even our most personal religious beliefs or doubt them. It would seem that a morally good God who created us as rational would honor doxastic honesty even if it led to unbelief.[2]

RATIONALITY AND CONCEPTUAL FRAMEWORKS

Sometimes it is claimed that we use a clear-cut decision-making process, similar to the one used in mathematics and empirical science, when we arrive at justified belief or truth. A person has a duty to believe exactly according to the available evidence. Hence there is no excuse for anyone to believe anything on insufficient evidence. Such is the case of Descartes and logical positivism, which is echoed in Clifford's classical formula, "it is wrong always, everywhere, and for anyone to believe anything on insufficient evidence." Laying aside the criticism that the statement itself is self-referentially incoherent (it doesn't give us sufficient evidence for believing itself), the problem is that different data will count as evidence to different degrees according to the background beliefs a person has. The contribution of Polanyi, Popper, and Wittgenstein has been to demonstrate the power of perspectivism, the thesis that the way we evaluate or even pick out evidence is determined by our prior picture of the world, which itself is made up of a loosely connected and mutually supporting network of propositions. Do the farmer, the real estate dealer, and the landscape artist on looking at a field see the same field?

The nonperspectivist position, seen in Plato, Aquinas, Descartes, Locke, Clifford, and Chisholm, seems damaged beyond repair. However, the reaction has been to claim that since what is basic is the conceptual (fiduciary) framework, no interchange between world views is possible. As Karl Barth says,

"Belief can only preach to unbelief." No argument is possible. We may call this reaction to the postcritical critique of rationalism "hard-perspectivism."

The nonperspectivist writes as though arriving at the truth were a matter of impartial evaluation of the evidence, and the hard-perspectivist writes as though no meaningful communication were possible. The world views (*Weltanschauungen*) are discontinuous. As fideists often say, "The believer and unbeliever live in different worlds."[3] There is an infinite qualitative distinction existing between various forms of life that no amount of argument or discussion can bridge. For hard-perspectivists, including Wittgensteinian fideists, reason can only have intramural significance. There are no bridges between world views.

However, hard-perspectivism is not the only possible reaction to the postcritical revolution. One may accept the insight that our manner of evaluating evidence is strongly affected by our conceptual frameworks without opting for a view that precludes communication across world views. One may recognize the depth of a conceptual framework and still maintain that communication between frameworks is possible and that reason may have an intermural as well as intramural significance in the process. Such a view has been called soft-perspectivist. The soft-perspectivist is under no illusion regarding the difficulty of effecting a massive shift in the total evaluation of an immense range of data, of producing new patterns of feeling and acting in persons, but he or she is confident that the program is viable. One of the reasons given in support of this is that there is something like a core rationality common to every human culture, especially with regard to practical life. Certain rules of inference (deductive and inductive) have virtually universal application. Certain assumptions (basic beliefs) seem common to every culture (e g , that there are other minds, that there is time, that things move, that perceptions are generally to be trusted, and so on). Through sympathetic imagination one can attain understanding of another's conceptual system; through disappointment one can begin to suspect weakness in one's own world view and thus seek for a more adequate explanation. It is not my purpose here to produce a full defense of a soft-perspective position, but only to indicate its plausibility. The assumption on which this essay is written is that the case for soft-perspectivism can be made. And if it is true, then it is possible for reason to play a significant role in the examination, revision, and rejection of one's current beliefs and in the acquisition of new beliefs.

DOES RATIONALITY IMPLY A NEUTRALITY THAT IS INCOMPATIBLE WITH RELIGIOUS FAITH?

We may say that postcritical rationalists of the soft-perspectivist variety are individuals who seek to support all their beliefs (especially their convictions)[4] with good reasons. They attempt to evaluate the evidence as impartially as possible, to accept the challenge of answering criticisms, and to remain open to the possibility that they might be wrong and may need to revise, reexamine, or reject any one of their beliefs (at least those not involving broadly logical necessity). This character description of the rationalist is often interpreted to mean that rationalists must be neutral and detached with regard to their beliefs.[5] This is a mistake. It is a confusion between *impartiality* and *neutrality*. Both concepts imply conflict situations (e.g., war, a competitive sport, a legal trial, an argument), but to be neutral signifies not taking sides, doing nothing to influence the outcome, remaining passive in the fray; whereas impartiality *involves* one in the conflict in that it calls for a judgment in favor of the party that is right. To the extent that one party is right or wrong (measured by objective criteria) neutrality and impartiality are incompatible concepts. To be neutral is to detach oneself from the struggle; to be impartial (rational) is to commit oneself to a position—though not partially (i.e., unfairly or arbitrarily) but in accordance with an objective standard. The model of the neutral person is an atheist who is indifferent about football watching a game between Notre Dame and Southern Methodist. The model of the partial or prejudiced person is the coach who, on any given dispute, predictably judges his team to be in the right and the other to be in the wrong and for whom it is an axiom that any judgment by a referee against his team is, at best, of dubious merit. The model of the impartial person is the referee in the game, who, knowing that his wife has just bet their life savings on the underdog, Southern Methodist, still manages to call what any reasonable spectator would judge to be a fair game. He does not let his wants or self-interest enter into the judgment he makes.

To be rational does not lessen the passion involved in religious beliefs. Rational believers, who believe that they have good grounds for believing that a perfect being exists, are not less likely to trust that being absolutely than believers who do not think that they have reasons. Likewise, persons who live in the hope of God's existence may be as passionate about their commitment as persons who entertain no doubts. In fact the rational hoper or believer will probably judge it to be irrational not to be absolutely committed to such a being. Hence the charge leveled against the rationalist by Kierkegaard and others that rational inquiry cools the passions seems unfounded.

However, nonrationalists have a slightly different but related argument at hand. They may argue that if there were sufficient evidence available, it might be the case that one might be both religious and rational. But there is not sufficient evidence; hence the very search for evidence simply detracts believers from worship and passionate service, leading them on a wild-goose chase for evidence that does not exist. The believer is involved in cool calculation instead of passionate commitment, questioning instead of obeying.

There are at least two responses to this charge. First of all, how does the nonrationalist know that there is not sufficient evidence for a religious claim? How does the nonrationalist know that not merely a demonstrative proof but even a cumulative case with some force is impossible? It would seem reasonable to expect that a good God would not leave his creatures wholly in the dark about so important a matter. The nonrationalist's answer (that of Calvin and Kierkegaard, and suggested by Plantinga) that sin has destroyed the use of reason or our ability to see God seems unduly ad hoc and inadequate. It would seem that little children in nontheistic cultures should manifest some theistic tendencies on this view, for which there is no evidence. Second, why cannot the search for truth itself be a way of worshipping God? A passionate act of service? Again one would expect the possession of well-founded beliefs to be God's will for us. Is the person who in doubt prays, "God, if you exist, please show me better evidence," any less passionate a worshipper than the person who worships without doubts?

A word is in order about the relation of the emotions and passions to religious belief. The claims of a religion cannot but move a person. Anyone who does not see the importance of its claims either does not have a sense of selfhood or does not understand what is being said, for a religion claims to explain who and why one is and what one can expect to become. It claims to make sense out of the world. For example, to entertain the proposition that a personal, loving Creator exists is to entertain a proposition whose implications affect every part of a person's understanding of self and world. If the proposition is true, the world is personal rather than mechanistic, friendly rather than strange, purposeful rather than simply a vortex of chance and necessity. If it is not true, a different set of entailments follow that are likely to lead to different patterns of feeling and action. If Judeo-Christian theism is accepted, the believer has an additional reason for being a moral person, for treating fellow humans with equal respect. It is because God has created all persons in his image, as infinitely precious, destined to enjoy his fellowship forever. Theism can provide a more adequate metaphysical basis for morality. Hence it can be both descriptively and prescriptively significant.

TOWARDS A THEORY OF RATIONALITY

It is often said that rational persons tailor the strength of their beliefs to the strength of the evidence. The trouble with this remark is that it is notoriously difficult to give sense to any discussion of discovering objective criteria for what is to count as evidence and to what extent it is to count. One of my criticisms of Swinburne's usually perceptive work is that he tries to apply the concept of probabilities to world views, as though we somehow could identify evidential wholes without comparing them to other outcomes.

Deciding *what* is to count as evidence for something else in part depends on a whole network of other considerations, and deciding to *what extent* something is to count as evidence involves weighing procedures that are subjective. Two judges may have the same evidence before them and come to different verdicts. Two equally rational persons may have the same evidence about the claims of a religion and still arrive at different conclusions in the matter. It would seem that the prescription to tailor one's beliefs according to the evidence is either empty or a shorthand for something more complex. I think that it is the latter. Let me illustrate what I think it signifies.

Consider any situation in which our self-interest may conflict with the truth. Take the case of three German wives who are suddenly confronted with evidence that their husbands have been unfaithful. Their surnames are Uberglaubig, Misstrauisch, and Wahrnehmen. Each is disturbed about the evidence and makes further inquiries. Mrs. Uberglaubig is soon finished and finds herself rejecting all the evidence, maintaining resolutely her husband's fidelity. Others, even relatives of Mr. Uberglaubig, are surprised by her credulity, for the evidence against Mr. Uberglaubig is the sort that would lead most people to conclude that he was unfaithful. No matter how much evidence is adduced, Mrs. Uberglaubig is unchanged in her judgment. She seems to have a fixation about her husband's fidelity. Mrs. Misstrauisch seems to suffer from an opposite weakness. If Mrs. Uberglaubig overbelieves, she seems to underbelieve. She suspects the worst and even though others who know Mr. Misstrauisch deem the evidence against him weak (especially in comparison to the evidence presented against Mr. Uberglaubig), she is convinced that her husband is unfaithful. No evidence seems to be sufficient to reassure her. It is as though the very suggestion of infidelity were enough to stir up doubts and disbelief. Mrs. Wahrnehmen also considers the evidence, which is considerable, and comes to a judgment, though with some reservations. Suppose she finds herself believing that her husband is faithful. Others may differ in their assessment of the situation, but Mrs. Wahrnehmen is willing and able to discuss the matter, gives her grounds, and considers the objections of others. Perhaps we can say that she is more self-aware, more self-controlled, and more self-secure than the other women. She seems to have the capacity to separate her judgment from her hopes, wants, and fears in a way that the other two women do not.

This should provide some clue to what it means to be rational. It does not necessarily mean having true beliefs (though we would say that rationality tends toward truth), for it might just turn out that by luck Mr. Wahrnehmen is indeed an adulterer and Mr. Uberglaubig innocent. Still, we would want to say that Mrs. Wahrnehmen was justified in her beliefs but Mrs. Uberglaubig was not.

What does characterize rational judgment are two properties, one being *intentional* and the other being *capacity-behavioral*. First, rationality involves an intention to seek the truth or the possession of a high regard for the truth, especially when there may be a conflict between it and one's wishes. It involves a healthy abhorrence of being deceived combined with a parallel desire to have knowledge in matters vital to one's life. Mrs. Wahrnehmen and Mrs. Misstrauisch care about the truth in a way that Mrs. Uberglaubig does not. But secondly, it involves a skill or behavioral capacity to judge impartially, to examine the evidence objectively, to know what sort of things count in coming to a considered judgment. It is as though Mrs. Wahrnehmen alone were able to see clearly through the fog of emotion and self-interest, focusing on some ideal standard of evidence. Of course, there is no such simple standard of evidence, any more than there is for the art critic in making a judgment on the authenticity of a work of art. Still, the metaphor of the ideal standard may be useful. It draws attention to the objective feature in rational judgment, a feature that is internalized in the person of the expert. Like learning to discriminate between works of art or with regard to criminal evidence, rationality is a learned trait that calls for a long apprenticeship (a lifetime?) under the cooperative tutelage of other rational persons. Some people with little formal education seem to learn this better than some "well-educated" people, but despite this uncomfortable observation, I would like to believe that it is the job of education to train people to judge impartially over a broad range of human experience.

As a skill combined with an intention, rationality may seem to be in a shaky situation. How do we decide who has the skill or who has the right combination of traits? There is no certain way, but judge we must in this life, and the basis of our judgment will be manifestations of behavior that we classify as truth directed, noticing that persons with this skill seek out evidence and pay attention to criticism and counterclaims, that they usually support their judgment with recognizable good reasons, that they revise and reject their beliefs in the light of new information. These criteria are not foolproof, and it seems impossible to give an exact account of the process involved in rational decision or belief, but this seems to be the case with any skill. In the end rationality seems more like a set of trained intuitions than anything else.

Let us carry our story a little further. Suppose now Mrs. Wahrnehmen receives some new information to the effect that her husband has been un-faithful. Suppose it becomes known to others who were previously convinced by her arguments acquitting her husband, and suppose that the new evidence infirms many of those arguments, so that the third parties now come to believe that Mr. Wahrnehmen is an adulterer. Should Mrs. Wahrnehmen give up her belief? Perhaps not. At least, it may not be a good thing to give it up at once. If she has worked out a theory to account for a great many of her husband's actions, she might better cling to her theory and work out some ad hoc hypotheses to account for this evidence. This principle of clinging to one's theory in spite of adverse evidence is what Peirce debunkingly and Lakatos approvingly call the principle of tenacity.[6] It receives special attention in Lakatos's treatment of a progressive research program. In science, theoretical change often comes as a result of persevering with a rather vaguely formulated hypothesis (a core hypothesis), which the researcher will hold on to in spite of a good many setbacks. Scientists must be ready to persevere (at least for a time) even in the face of their own doubts and their recognition of the validity of their opponents' objections. If maximum fruitfulness of the experiment is to be attained, it must endure through many modifications as new evidence comes in. As Basil Mitchell has pointed out, a scientific thesis is like a growing infant, which "could be killed by premature antisepsis." The biographies of eminent scientists and scholars, are replete with instances of going it alone in the face of massive intellectual opposition and finally overturning a general verdict. Hence researchers cushion the core hypothesis against the blows and shocks that might otherwise force them to give it up. They invent ad hoc explanations in the hope of saving the core hypothesis. They surround the core hypothesis with a battery of such hypotheses, and as the ad hoc hypotheses fall, they invent new ones. Mitchell compares this process to a criminal network, in which the mastermind (core hypothesis) always manages to escape detection and punishment "by sacrificing some of his less essential underlings, unless or until the final day of reckoning comes and his entire empire collapses."[7]

Admittedly, each ad hoc hypothesis weakens the system, but the core hypothesis may nevertheless turn out to approximate a true or adequate theory. But the more ad hoc hypotheses it becomes necessary to invent, the less plausibility attaches to the core hypothesis, until the time comes when the researcher is forced to give up the core hypothesis and conclude that the whole project has outlived its usefulness. In Lakatos's words, it has become a "degen-erative research project."[8] No one can say exactly when that time comes in a particular project, but every experimental scientist fears it and, meanwhile, lives in hope that the current project will bear fruit.

Let us apply this paradigm to rational religious believers. Once they find themselves with a deep conviction, they have a precedent or model in science for clinging to it tenaciously, experimenting with it, drawing out all its implications, and surrounding it with tentative ad hoc or auxiliary explanations in order to cushion it from premature antisepsis. Nevertheless, if the analogy with the scientist holds, they must recognize that the time may come when they are forced to abandon their conviction because of the enormous accumulation of counterevidence. Such rational persons probably cannot say exactly when and how this might happen, and they do not expect it to happen, but they acknowledge the possibility of its happening. There is no clear decision procedure that tells us when we have crossed over the fine line between plausibility and implausibility, but suddenly the realization hits us that we now disbelieve theory A and believe theory B, whereas up to this point the reverse was true. Conversions or paradigm switches occur every day in the minds of both the highly rational and the less rational. There is also a middle zone where a person considering two seemingly incompatible explanatory theories can find something plausible in each of them, so that the person cannot be said to believe either one. Still, such individuals may place their hope in one theory and live by it in an experimental faith, keeping themselves open to new evidence and maintaining the dialogue with those who differ so as not to slip into a state of self-deception. The whole matter of double vision and experimental faith is quite complicated, but often we can see the world in more than one way and yet find our moral bearings. What I want to emphasize is the Kierkegaardian point (used in an unKierkegaardian manner) that more important than *what* one believes is the manner in which one believes, the *how* of believing, the openness of mind, the willingness to discuss the reasons for one's belief, the carefulness of one's examination of new and conflicting evidence, one's commitment to follow the argument and not simply one's emotions, one's training as a rational person that enables one to recognize what is to count as a good argument.

This leads me to say a few things about the role and mode of argument in rationality. One of the problems that has plagued discussion in philosophy of religion through the ages is that the way philosophers have written has implied that unless one had a deductive proof for a religious thesis, one had no justification for it. The result of this narrow view of argument in religious matters has pushed those who believe in religion to the point of conceding too much, that is, that religion is not rational. This is one of the main reasons for the incommensurabilist position. I think that this is a mistake. Our concept of argument must be broadened from mere deductive and strict inductive argument to include non–rule-governed judgments. What I have in mind is the sort of intuitive judgment illustrated by the art critic in assessing an authentic work of art, the chicken sexer in identifying the sex of the baby chicks without knowing or being able to tell us how he knows the chick's sexual identity, or the water diviner in discovering underground springs without knowing how he does so. Another example of non–rule-governed reasoning is a child's invention of new sentences. The child follows rules, which seem to be programed into her, but she does not do it consciously and cannot tell us what the rules are. Later, however, she may be able to do so.

Perhaps even more typical of everyday non–rule-governed reasoning is the process whereby judges or juries make judgments when the evidence is ambiguous or there is considerable evidence on both sides of an issue. In weighing pros and cons and assessing conflicting evidence, the judge or jury does not normally go through standard logical procedures to arrive at a verdict. They rely on intangible and intuitive weighing procedures. It is hard to see how the deductive and strict inductive schemes of argument can account for our judgments when we have good reasons for and against a conclusion. Nor is it easy to see how deductive and strict inductive reasoning account for the decisions experts make in distinguishing the valuable from the mediocre. They cannot formalize their judgment, and we may not be able to offer an account of it, but we would still recognize it as valid and importantly rational. Perhaps we ought generally to aim at formalizing our judgments as carefully as possible, using the traditional forms of reasoning, but it is not always necessary or possible to do this. We can be said to be rational because we typically arrive at decisions and judgments that other rational creatures would regard as a fair estimation of the evidence (this excuses the occasional idiosyncratic judgment); because we attempt to face the challenge of our opponent with the grounds of our beliefs, and because we are honest about the deficiencies of our positions. It is a whole family of considerations that leads us to an overall conclusion about whether another person is rational and not simply whether or not the person is able to provide sound deductive or inductive arguments. Of course, induction plays a strong role in our relying on another's judgments. It is because we have generally found that people of this sort usually make reliable judgments in cases of such-and-such a type that we are ready to take their intuitions as credible.

A great deal more needs to be said about non-rule-governed judgments, but this discussion at least shows that something broader than the standard moves is needed in an account of rational argument. There is a need to recognize the important role that intuition plays in reasoning itself or, at least, in the reasoning of the trained person. This is what the Greeks called *phronesis* ("wise insight") and *ortho logos* ("correct thinking"), and it should be given greater emphasis in modern philosophy.

IS A RATIONAL ACCOUNT OF RELIGION COMPATIBLE WITH THE BIBLICAL PICTURE OF FAITH?

Let me turn finally to the important objection that the position that I have outlined distorts the biblical notion of faith. Biblical faith is, the critic affirms, believing against or without sufficient evidence. As Hick points out, there is little deductive reasoning in the Scriptures, but the Holy of Holies is taken as the starting point of all thinking.[9]

But the claim that this is the sole meaning of faith in the Bible seems an unwarranted generalization. Actually, several different but related concepts of faith are found in the Bible, including loyalty, trust, fear, and obedience, as well as propositional belief. What we have called rational faith seems duly accounted for in the miracles and prophecy of the Bible, especially the Old Testament, which in part serve as evidence for the Hebrew faith. When Elijah, in 1 Kings 18, competes with the priests of Baal on Mt. Carmel to determine which god is more powerful, we are given a concrete scientific testing of competing hypotheses. When John the Baptist's disciples come to ask Jesus if he is the Messiah, Jesus does not rebuke them for seeking grounds for their beliefs but immediately "cures many diseases and plagues and evil spirits" and opens the eyes of the blind; only after this does he answer them. "Go and tell John what you have seen and heard: the blind receive their sight, the lame walk, lepers are cleansed, and the deaf hear, the dead are raised up, the poor have the good news preached to them" (Luke 7:20–22). When Jesus does chide his disciples for unbelief it seems to be for good reasons. "Don't you remember what the Scriptures demand? Don't you trust me in spite of my being with you so long and having proved my reliability over and over?" What the Scriptures deny is *sight*. We cannot see God directly and live, for there is another dimension of his reality, but we can see him *indirectly* through his works (Rom. 1:20f). When Thomas doubts good evidence (viz., the witness of his fellow disciples and the words of Jesus' prophecy), he is given evidence, the point being not that evidence is contrary to faith but that dependence on too much outward evidence may get in the way of inward discernment. There is just enough evidence to satisfy a person passionately concerned but not enough to produce a comfortable proof.

Usually, nonrationalists make their point about the antipathy between faith and reason in the Bible by pointing to Abraham's reliance on God even to the point of being willing to kill his son, Isaac. Abraham, the father of faith, is put forth as the paradigm of believing against all evidence. As Kierkegaard puts it, "Abraham believed by virtue of the absurd," despite the impossibility of the promise to give him a son when he was old or to bring him back after he was sacrificed. He believed God would somehow bring it about that Isaac would live in spite of the fact that he was going to kill him. The reader will recall the story. God tells Abraham to go to Mt. Moriah and sacrifice Isaac in order to prove his love for God. Abraham proceeds to carry out the command, but at the last moment an angel stops him, showing him a lamb in the thicket to be used for the offering. The story of Abraham and Isaac has usually been taken as the height of religious faith: believing God when it really affects one's deepest earthly commitments. It is taken to prove that faith is irrational, that faith involves believing against all standards of rationality.

Of course, many Old Testament scholars dismiss the literalness of the story and interpret it within the context of Middle Eastern child sacrifice. The story, according to these scholars, provides the pictorial grounds for breaking with the custom. But even leaving aside this plausible explanation, we might contend that Abraham's action can be seen as rational given his noetic framework. One can imagine him replying to a friendly skeptic years after the incident in the following manner:

> I heard a voice. It was the same voice (or so I believed) that
> commanded me years before to leave my country, my kindred, and my
> father's house to venture forth into the unknown. It was the same voice
> that promised me that I would prosper. I hearkened, and though the
> evidence seemed weak, the promise was fulfilled. It was the same voice
> that promised me a son in my old age and Sarah's old age, when
> childbearing was thought to be impossible. Yet it happened. My trust
> was vindicated. My whole existence has been predicated on the reality

of that voice. I already became an exception by hearkening unto it the first time. I have never regretted it. This last call was in a tone similar to the other calls. The voice was unmistakable. To deny its authenticity would be to deny the authenticity of the others. In doing so, I should be admitting that my whole life has been founded on an illusion. But I don't believe that it has, and I prefer to take the risk of obeying what I take to be the voice of God and disobey certain norms than to obey the norms and miss the possibility of any absolute relation to the Absolute. And what's more, I'm ready to recommend that all people who feel so called by a higher power do exactly as I have done.

It seems to me that even if we accept the story of Abraham's offering his son as a sacrifice at face value, we can give it an interpretation not inconsistent with the commensurabilist's position. Abraham has had inductive evidence that following the voice is the best way to live. We can generalize the principle on which Abraham acted to be as follows:

If one acts on a type of intuition I in an area of experience E, over a period of time t and with remarkable success, and no other information is relevant or overriding, one can be said to have good reason for following that intuition (I_n, an instance of type I) the next time it presents itself in an E-type situation.

Given the cultural context of Abraham's life, his actions seem amenable to a rationalist account. Of course, what this shows is that given enough background data, almost any proposition could be considered *rational* for an individual believer. Irrationality would occur if Abraham neglected counterevidence at his disposal.

My point in all this has not been to prove that the Bible contains a fully developed philosophy of faith and reason but simply to indicate that it seems far closer to the commensurabilist's position than the fideist might imagine. My impression is that the Scriptures pay a great deal of attention to evidence, acts of deliverance, and the testimony of the saints and prophets who hear God's voice and sometimes even get a vision of his splendor.

Let me end this article on a conciliatory note. I can appreciate the criticism of someone who feels that my approach overemphasizes the rational and intellectual aspects of believing at the expense of the emotional and volitional aspects, the feelings of divine presence and inner certainty and devotion. I do not want to deny the importance of these feelings. My point has been simply that they are compatible with a rationalist perspective. Further thought on the matter may reveal that my approach to religion as an experimental faith in a viable hypothesis fails to get at the heart of religious commitment. But even so, the general quest for justification may not be inappropriate. Complex as religious phenomena are, profound as the feelings are, at some point religious experience needs to be scrutinized honestly and carefully by the believer him- or herself. When Barth and Bultmann protest that God does not need to justify himself before man, the proper response is to echo Karl Jasper's reply to Bultmann: "I do not say that God has to justify himself, but that everything that appears in the world and claims to be God's word, God's act, God's revelation, has to justify itself."[10] This outline of a commensurabilist position with regard to religious belief is intended as a small step in doing just that.

NOTES

1. The most complete version of Plantinga's views is his essay "Reason and Belief in God," in *Faith and Rationality*, edited by Alvin Plantinga and Nicholas Wolterstorff (Notre Dame: Univ. of Notre Dame Press, 1983).

2. See my book, *Religious Belief and the Will* (London: Routledge & Kegan Paul, forthcoming), part 2, chap. 2.

3. Alvin Plantinga suggests that the believer and the unbeliever have different conceptions of reason. Op. cit., 91.

4. I follow McClendon and Smith's definition of *conviction* here as "a persistent belief such that if *X* has a conviction, it will not be easily relinquished without making *X* a significantly different person than before." James McClendon and James Smith, *Understanding Religious Convictions* (Notre Dame: Univ. of Notre Dame Press, 1975), 7.

5. Even McClendon and Smith make this mistake in their usually reliable work. Ibid., 108.

6. Basil Mitchell, "Faith and Reason: A False Antithesis?" *Religious Studies* 16 (June 1980); I. Lakatos, "Falsification and Methodology of Scientific Research Programs," in *Criticism and the Growth of Knowledge*, edited by I. Lakatos and A. Musgrave (Cambridge: Cambridge Univ. Press, 1970) 91–196.

7. Mitchell, op. cit.

8. Lakatos, op. cit., 118.

9. John Hick, *Arguments for the Existence of God* (New York: Macmillan, 1971), chap. 7.

10. Quoted in John Macquarrie, *Twentieth Century Religious Thought* (New York: Harper & Row, 1966), 334.

Part II

Theism: The Attributes or Perfections of God

Theism, the belief that there exists a divine being or God who is the creator and controller of the universe, has been the shared core ingredient of developed religions in the West. Although polytheism, the belief in more than one god, is to be found in the early writings of both cultural traditions (Hebrew and Greek) from which the Western civilization largely derives, the mature religions of the West and the Middle East—Judaism, Christianity, and Islam—are all (mono)theistic. Theism is also to be found in the East, but there it is a minority position. Popular Hinduism is clearly polytheistic (although many of its theologians claim that Hinduism at a more profound level is theistic); some schools of Hinduism are pantheistic or monistic, teaching that everything that exists is identical with God (Brahman); and other schools are explicitly theistic. Buddhism is generally regarded as atheistic or nontheistic, denying the existence of God or gods, although in a number of its popular forms it also becomes polytheistic. Sikhism is explicitly theistic, teaching the oneness of God, and Confucianism is nontheistic.

The central philosophical issues that arise in connection with theism, besides questions about the existence of God that will be addressed in later parts, concern the characteristics or perfections usually attributed to God. Philosophers analyze the attributes of omnipotence, omniscience, and omnibenevolence or divine goodness, as well as the so-called metaphysical attributes, such as immutability, impassibility, eternity or timelessness, and simplicity, in order to discover whether or not these concepts are intelligible, mutually compatible, and compatible with the kind of world of which we find ourselves a part.

The selections in Part II explore the three major attributes—omnipotence, omniscience, and divine goodness—and several of the metaphysical attributes. We also take a brief look at the claim that personality is an attribute of God; consider John Stuart Mill's notion of a limited noninfinite God; and reflect briefly on the question of whether or not the attributes are mutually compatible. Selections in the next three parts explore arguments for the existence of God, examine the major kinds of objections to theism, and present several alternatives to theism.

The attribute of omnipotence is often interpreted to mean "all powerful," and that in turn is sometimes taken to mean "able to do anything." But such a broad interpretation of the claim that God is omnipotent raises a number of problems. Can an all-powerful God do logically contradictory things, such as creating a four-sided triangle or making $2 + 2 = 7$? Some philosophers, such as Descartes, maintained that God's omnipotence means that God creates the laws of logic and mathematics and thus could have made them differently. Many others, however, have taught that omnipotence does not mean able to do literally anything at all, but rather able to do any possible thing—that is to say, anything that does not involve contradiction.

A number of other problems arise from the interpretation of omnipotence as all powerful. Some have to do with time-related matters, such as changing the past and control over future contingent events. It would appear that although God might have determined a past event *before* it happened, he could not change it once it happened. But if we say that all events are subject to God's control before they occur, then the concept of a future contingent event disappears and all things become predetermined. What about the free actions of human agents? If God controls everything, then it seems to make no sense to call our actions free or designate us as agents.

These have been topics of considerable controversy in the philosophy of religion. One group of philosophers has claimed that human free will and responsibility are compatible with God's full omnipotence, arguing that God determines our future actions based on his foreknowledge of our choices. Another group argues that humans are free inasmuch as we do as we choose, but that God determines our choices. Many, however, insist that neither alternative is compatible with real human freedom. Thus certain philosophers suggest that there are a number of things that even an omnipotent being cannot do—and that this does not compromise God's omnipotence. God cannot do logically contradictory things, cannot change the past, determine future contingent events, or control the actions of free agents; cannot break promises; and cannot sin or commit acts incompatible with divine goodness. Such incapacities, however, do not diminish God's omnipotence, because omnipotence does not imply the ability to do impossible things. P. T. Geach analyzes four major ways in which the concept of omnipotence has been interpreted, and C. Wade Savage treats the so-called paradox of omnipotence by the examination of a specific instance: the question of whether God can create a stone so heavy that he cannot lift it.

Omniscience has traditionally been understood to mean "all knowing." But when the concept is interpreted to mean that God knows literally everything, time-related problems arise that are somewhat similar to those raised by the broad interpretation of omnipotence. If God infallibly knows what will happen in the future, it would seem that no future events can be contingent; and if God infallibly knows ahead of time every action every person will perform, it would seem that no action can be free and no person a free agent. Some have attempted to answer this problem by the doctrine that God is a timeless being who sees and knows all events occurring in time, not sequentially as finite beings do, but simultaneously in a great eternal Now. Thomas Aquinas takes this view, arguing that God surveys the whole sweep of history in a single glance from the perspective of eternity. What is future from the point of view of a particular human at a specific time is not future to a being that exists outside the flow of time. Thus God's knowledge of what, from our point of view, is future does not imply that future events cannot be contingent or that human actions cannot be free. It is not clear, however, that placing God outside time clears the way for God to know all things. Can a timeless God know what the passing of time is like, what it is to remember, anticipate, or wonder about the future—things that humans clearly can know?

The notion of timelessness raises other problems as well. How can such a being be involved in human affairs, as religions such as Judaism, Christianity, and Islam teach that God is? The concept of omniscience understood to mean "knowing all things" thus seems at least as problematic as a similar understanding of omnipotence, leading some contemporary philosophers to suggest giving it up or interpreting it in a very different way. A prominent contemporary philosopher of religion who favors the more traditional approach is Alvin Plantinga, who argues that God's omniscience is not incompatible with the real contingency of future events or with human free will. Plantinga attempts to show that the supposition of inconsistency is based on a confusion.

Divine goodness or omnibenevolence is perhaps the most fundamental attribute of God, according to the major theistic religions. Theologians who, pressed by the threats of such enigmas as the problem of evil (how can an all-powerful, all-knowing, all-loving God allow evil to exist in the world?), allow themselves to be persuaded that God's power might not be infinite or that there might be things that God does not know, never waver in their insistence that God is good. The goodness of God is said to be expressed in the creation of the world and the creation of humans in the divine image. Some thinkers argue that God's goodness is so far above and beyond that of humans, or of anything they can conceive, that our standards quite fail to measure or to reflect divine goodness. Others maintain that although God's goodness exceeds the best of which we are capable, it remains true that God's goodness is not different in kind from human goodness. Thomas Aquinas argues that God is essentially good and that goodness, human or divine, is related to the being of whatever is good, since evil is privation of being. Thomas V. Morris discusses the relationship between the idea of duty and divine goodness.

Although philosophers of religion have not always included personality among the list of divine attributes, clearly the major theistic traditions have understood God to be personal or a person. Richard Swinburne is a prominent contemporary defender of the claim that God is a person. Adrian Thatcher discusses Swinburne's position, arguing that God is properly conceived as personal, but that it is a mistake to hold that God is a person.

Philosophers of religion have also explored a variety of characteristics of God, called the metaphysical attributes: eternity, simplicity, immutability, impassibility, impeccability, and the like. These attributes, often discussed within the context of Aristotle's scheme of metaphysics, concern various features thought to be involved in calling God absolute or infinite. God is supposed to be immutable, exempt from change, because any change of a perfect being would be a move away from perfection. Impassibility refers to God's alleged imperturbability, grounded in the belief that the divine being is sufficient in every way and could not be disturbed or stirred from complete calmness. Simplicity refers to God's complete oneness and unity, which means that there is no complexity that might fail to be in complete harmony and no parts. Readings are provided touching on several of these metaphysical attributes. Swinburne attempts to offer an analysis of the concepts of eternity and immutability to show that such attributes are coherent with the divine nature. Charles Hartshorne, a contemporary process philosopher, raises serious objections concerning several of these attributes, insisting that such characteristics imply that God is uninvolved with the world and uncaring about humans.

Only rarely in the history of the West has a philosopher put forward a version of theism that explicitly recognizes limitations on the divine attributes. This has usually been done in an effort to deal with the problem of evil, which might seem otherwise fatal to theism. The nineteenth-century utilitarian philosopher John Stuart Mill attempts, by an examination of evidences found in nature and the human world, to infer what kind of deity these evidences support and finds that God must be regarded as very powerful, wise, and good, but by no means infinite in these and other characteristics.

An objection sometimes raised against theism generally is that the characteristics attributed to God are not mutually compatible: that is, that these qualities could not consistently coexist harmoniously in a being. George Schlesinger argues that we can infer from the very concept of God as absolutely perfect that all the divine attributes are compatible.

ANNOTATED GUIDE TO
FURTHER READINGS

Creel, Richard E. *Divine Impassibility*. Cambridge: Cambridge University Press, 1986.
A thorough discussion of the metaphysical attribute of impassibility. Creel closely examines the meaning of this attribute and concludes that it has four facets. He also treats some of the other divine attributes as they relate to impassibility.

Crombie, I.M. "Eternity and Omnitemporality." In *The Rationality of Religious Belief*, edited by William J. Abraham and Steven W. Holtzer. Oxford: The Clarendon Press, 1987.
Deals with the debate over God's relationship with time. Some say that God resides outside of time; others maintain that God exists forever within time. Crombie points out that the finite human being's comprehension of time may differ from God's understanding of the nature of time.

Kenny, Anthony. *The God of the Philosophers*. Oxford: Clarendon Press, 1979.
Omniscience and omnipotence are the subjects of this book. Kenny examines in considerable depth the problems and ramifications that arise when these attributes are assigned to God. Special attention is given to the topic of divine foreknowledge.

Kvanivig, Jonathan L. *The Possibility of an All-Knowing God*. New York: St. Martin's Press, 1986.
A defense of the traditional conception of omniscience. It is not only possible, but even necessary, Kvanivig argues, for an omniscient being to know the future. Kvanivig attempts to resolve the dilemma raised by his stance: If God has knowledge of the future, how then can there be free human action?

Langston, Douglas C. *God's Willing Knowledge*. University Park: The Pennsylvania State University Press, 1986.
The attribute of omniscience analyzed in the writings of John Duns Scotus, along with the conflict between humankind's free will and God's omniscience. Writings of Molina, Leibniz, Pike, and Plantinga on omniscience are also examined.

Rowe, William L., and Wainwright, William J., eds. *Philosophy of Religion: Selected Readings*, 2nd ed. New York: Harcourt Brace Jovanovich, 1989.
A useful general examination of the various characteristics attributed to God: omniscience, omnipotence, the metaphysical characteristics, along with their accompanying problems and inconsistencies, as attributes of God. An article by Charles Hartshorne addresses the conflict between a personal God who loves people and an impassive, immutable God.

Swinburne, Richard. *The Coherence of Theism*. Oxford: Clarendon Press, 1977.
An excellent source that not only discusses several of the characteristics commonly attributed to God, but also explains how these characteristics can coexist together in God. Also deals with the question of whether or not

God is perfectly good and, if so, whether this is compatible with the other attributes.

Wierenga, Edward R. *The Nature of God: An Inquiry into Divine Attributes.* Ithaca: Cornell University Press, 1989
A good contemporary discussion of the whole range of divine attributes.

II.A. Omnipotence

II.A.1. Omnipotence

P. T. GEACH

P. T. Geach (1916–) is professor of logic at the University of Leeds. Distinguishing between almighty (God's power over all things) and omnipotence (the ability to do everything), Geach argues that any reasonable understanding of deity involves the recognition that there are many things that no being, no matter how powerful, can do and thus that we appropriately regard God as almighty but not as omnipotent.

It is fortunate for my purposes that English has the two words 'almighty' and 'omnipotent', and that apart from any stipulation by me the words have rather different associations and suggestions. 'Almighty' is the familiar word that comes in the creeds of the Church; 'omnipotent' is at home rather in formal theological discussions and controversies, e.g. about miracles and about the problem of evil. 'Almighty' derives by way of Latin 'omnipotens' from the Greek word *'pantokratōr'*; and both this Greek word, like the more classical *'pankratēs'*, and 'almighty' itself suggest God's having power *over* all things. On the other hand the English word 'omnipotent' would ordinarily be taken to imply ability to *do* everything; the Latin word 'omnipotens' also predominantly has this meaning in Scholastic writers, even though in origin it is a Latinization of *'pantocratōr'*. So there already is a tendency to distinguish the two words; and in this paper I shall make the distinction a strict one. I shall use the word 'almighty' to express God's power over all things, and I shall take 'omnipotence' to mean ability to do everything.

I think we can in a measure understand what God's almightiness implies, and I shall argue that almightiness so understood must be ascribed to God if we are to retain anything like traditional Christian belief in God. The position as regards omnipotence, or as regards the statement 'God can do everything', seems to me to be very different. Of course even 'God can do everything' may be understood simply as a way of magnifying God by contrast with the impotence of man. McTaggart described it as 'a piece of theological etiquette' to call God omnipotent: Thomas Hobbes, out of reverence for his Maker, would rather say that 'omnipotent' is an attribute of honour. But McTaggart and Hobbes would agree that 'God is omnipotent' or 'God can do everything' is not to be treated as a proposition that can figure as premise or conclusion in a serious theological argument. And I too wish to say this. I have no objection to

P. T. Geach, "Omnipotence," *Philosophy*, vol. 48 (April, 1973): pp. 7–20. Reprinted with the permission of Cambridge University Press.

such ways of speaking if they merely express a desire to give the best honour we can to God our Maker, whose Name only is excellent and whose praise is above heaven and earth. But theologians have tried *to prove* that God can do everything, or to derive conclusions from this thesis as a premise. I think such attempts have been wholly unsuccessful. When people have tried to read into 'God can do everything' a signification not of Pious Intention but of Philosophical Truth, they have only landed themselves in intractable problems and hopeless confusions; no graspable sense has ever been given to this sentence that did not lead to self-contradiction or at least to conclusions manifestly untenable from a Christian point of view.

I shall return to this; but I must first develop what I have to say about God's almightiness, or power over all things. God is not just more powerful than any creature; no creature can compete with God in power, even unsuccessfully. For God is also the source of all power; any power a creature has comes from God and is maintained only for such time as God wills. Nebuchadnezzar submitted to praise and adore the God of heaven because he was forced by experience to realize that only by God's favour did his wits hold together from one end of a blasphemous sentence to the other end. Nobody can deceive God or circumvent him or frustrate him; and there is no question of God's trying to do anything and failing. In Heaven and on Earth, God does whatever he will. We shall see that some propositions of the form 'God cannot do so-and-so' have to be accepted as true; but what God cannot be said to be able to do he likewise cannot will to do; we cannot drive a logical wedge between his power and his will, which are, as the Scholastics said, really identical, and there is no application to God of the concept of trying but failing.

I shall not spend time on citations of Scripture and tradition to show that this doctrine of God's almightiness is authentically Christian; nor shall I here develop rational grounds for believing it is a true doctrine. But it is quite easy to show that this doctrine is indispensable for Christianity, not a bit of old metaphysical luggage that can be abandoned with relief. For Christianity requires an absolute faith in the promises of God: specifically, faith in the promise that some day the whole human race will be delivered and blessed by the establishment of the Kingdom of God. If God were not almighty, he might will and not do; sincerely promise, but find fulfillment beyond his power. Men might prove untamable and incorrigible, and might kill themselves through war or pollution before God's salvific plan for them could come into force. It is useless to say that after the end of this earthly life men would live again; for as I have argued elsewhere, only the promise of God can give us any confidence that there will be an after-life for men, and if God were not almighty, this promise too might fail. If God is true and just and unchangeable and almighty, we can have absolute confidence in his promises: otherwise we cannot—and there would be an end of Christianity.

A Christian must therefore believe that God is almighty; but he need not believe that God can do everything. Indeed, the very argument I have just used shows that a Christian must not believe that God can do everything: for he may not believe that God could possibly break his own word. Nor can a Christian even believe that God can do everything that is logically possible; for breaking one's word is certainly a logically possible feat.

It seems to me, therefore, that the tangles in which people have enmeshed themselves when trying to give the expression 'God can do everything' an intelligible and acceptable content are tangles that a Christian believer has no need to enmesh himself in; the spectacle of others enmeshed may sadden him, but need not cause him to stumble in the way of faith. The denial that God is omnipotent, or able to do everything, may seem dishonouring to God; but when we see where the contrary affirmation, in its various forms, has led, we may well cry out with Hobbes: 'Can any man think God is served with such absurdities? . . . As if it were an acknowledgment of the Divine Power, to say, that which is, is not; or that which has been, has not been.'

I shall consider four main theories of omnipotence. The first holds that God can do everything absolutely; everything that can be expressed in a string of words that makes sense; even if the sense can be shown to be self-contradictory, God is not bound in action, as we are in thought, by the laws of logic. I shall speak of this as the doctrine that God is *absolutely* omnipotent.

The second doctrine is that a proposition 'God can do so-and-so' is true when and only when 'so-and-so' represents a logically consistent description.

The third doctrine is that 'God *can* do so-and-so' is true just if 'God does so-and-so' is logically consistent. This is a weaker doctrine than the second; for 'God is doing so-and-so' is logically consistent only when 'so-and-so' represents a logically consistent description, but on the other hand there may be consistently describable feats which it would involve contradiction to suppose done *by God*.

The last and weakest view is that the realm of what can be done or brought about includes all future possibilities, and that whenever 'God *will* bring so-and-so about' is logically possible, 'God *can* bring so-and-so about' is true.

The first sense of 'omnipotent' in which people have believed God to be omnipotent implies precisely: ability to do absolutely everything, everything describable. You mention it, and God can do it. McTaggart insisted on using 'omnipotent' in this sense only; from an historical point of view we may of course say that he imposed on the word a sense which it, and the corresponding Latin word, have not always borne. But Broad seems to me clearly unjust to McTaggart when he implies that in demolishing this doctrine of omnipotence McTaggart was just knocking down a man of straw. As Broad must surely have known, at least one great philosopher, Descartes, deliberately adopted and defended this doctrine of omnipotence: what I shall call the doctrine of absolute omnipotence.

As Descartes himself remarked, nothing is too absurd for some philosopher to have said it some time; I once read an article about an Indian school of philosophers who were alleged to maintain that it is only a delusion, which the wise can overcome, that anything exists at all—so perhaps it would not matter all that much that a philosopher is found to defend absolute omnipotence. Perhaps it would not matter all that much that the philosopher in question was a very great one; for very great philosophers have maintained the most preposterous theses. What does make the denial of absolute omnipotence important is not that we are thereby denying what a philosopher, a very great philosopher, thought he must assert, but that this doctrine has a live influence on people's religious thought—I should of course say, a pernicious influence. Some naive Christians would explicitly assert the doctrine; and moreover, I think McTaggart was right in believing that in popular religious thought a covert appeal to the doctrine is sometimes made even by people who would deny it if it were explicitly stated to them and its manifest consequences pointed out.

McTaggart may well have come into contact with naive Protestant defenders of absolute omnipotence when he was defending his atheist faith at his public school. The opinion is certainly not dead, as I can testify from personal experience. For many years I used to teach the philosophy of Descartes in a special course for undergraduates reading French; year by year, there were always two or three of them who embraced Descartes' defence of absolute omnipotence *con amore* and protested indignantly when I described the doctrine as incoherent. It would of course have been no good to say I was following Doctors of the Church in rejecting the doctrine; I did in the end find a way of producing silence, though not, I fear, conviction, and going on to other topics of discussion; I cited the passages of the Epistle to the Hebrews which say explicitly that God cannot swear by anything greater than himself (vi. 13) or break his word (vi. 18). Fortunately none of them ever thought of resorting to the ultimate weapon which, as I believe George Mavrodes remarked, is available to the defender of absolute omnipotence; namely, he can always say: 'Well, you've stated a difficulty, but of course being omnipotent God can overcome that difficulty, though I don't see how.' But what I may call, borrowing from C. S. Lewis's story, victory by the Deplorable Word is a barren one; as barren as a victory by an incessant demand that your adversary should prove his premises or define his terms.

Let us leave these naive defenders in their entrenched position and return for a moment to Descartes. Descartes held that the truths of logic and arithmetic are freely made to be true by God's will. To be sure we clearly and distinctly see that these truths are necessary; they are necessary in our world, and in giving us our mental endowments God gave us the right sort of clear and distinct ideas to see the necessity. But though they are necessary, they are not necessarily necessary; God could have freely chosen to make a different sort of world, in which other things would have been necessary truths. The possibility of such another world is something we cannot *comprehend*, but only dimly *apprehend*; Descartes used the simile that we may girdle a tree-trunk with our arms but not a mountain—but we can *touch* the mountain. Proper understanding of the possibility would be possessed by God, or, no doubt, by creatures in the alternative world, who would be endowed by God with clear and distinct ideas corresponding to the necessities of their world.

In recent years, unsound philosophies have been defended by what I may call shyster logicians: some of the more dubious recent developments of modal logic could certainly be used to defend Descartes. A system in which 'possibly p' were a theorem—in which everything is possible—has indeed never been taken seriously; but modal logicians have taken seriously systems in which 'possibly possibly p', or again 'it is not necessary that necessarily p', would be a theorem for arbitrary interpretation of 'p'. What is more, some modern modal logicians notoriously take possible worlds very seriously indeed; some of them even go to the length of saying that what you and I vulgarly call the actual world is simply the world we happen to live in. People who take *both* things seriously—the axiom 'possibly possibly p' and the ontology of possible worlds—would say: You mention any impossibility, and there's a possible world in which that isn't impossible but possible. And this is even further away out than Descartes would wish to go; for he would certainly not wish to say that 'It is possible that God should not exist' is even *possibly* true. So *a fortiori* a shyster logician could fadge up a case for Descartes. But to my mind all that this shows is that modal logic is currently a rather disreputable discipline: not that I think modal notions are inadmissible—on the contrary, I think they are indispensable—but that current professional standards in the discipline are low, and technical ingenuity is mistaken for rigour. On that showing, astrology would be rigorous.

Descartes' motive for believing in absolute omnipotence was not contemptible: it seemed to him that otherwise God would be *subject* to the inexorable laws of logic as Jove was to the decrees of the Fates. The nature of logical truth is a very difficult problem, which I cannot discuss here. The easy conventionalist line, that it is our arbitrary way of using words that makes logical truth, seems to me untenable, for reasons that Quine among others has clearly spelled out. If I could follow Quine further in regarding logical laws as natural laws of very great generality—revisable in principle, though most unlikely to be revised, in a major theoretical reconstruction—then perhaps after all some rehabilitation of Descartes on this topic might be possible. But in the end I have to say that as we cannot say how a non-logical world would look, we cannot say how a supra-logical God would act or how he could communicate anything to us by way of revelation. So I end as I began: a Christian need not and cannot believe in absolute omnipotence.

It is important that Christians should clearly realize this, because otherwise a half-belief in absolute omnipotence may work in their minds subterraneously. As I said, I think McTaggart was absolutely right in drawing attention to this danger. One and the same man may deny the doctrine of absolute omnipotence when the doctrine is clearly put to him, and yet reassure himself that God can certainly do so-and-so by using *merely* the premise of God's omnipotence. And McTaggart is saying this is indefensible. At the very least this 'so-and-so' must represent a logically consistent description of a feat; and proofs of logical consistency are notoriously not always easy. Nor, as we shall see, are our troubles at an end if we assume that God *can* do anything whose description is logically consistent.

Logical consistency in the description of the feat is certainly a *necessary* condition for the truth of 'God can do so-and-so': if 'so-and-so' represents an inconsistent description of a feat, then 'God can do so-and-so' is certainly a false and impossible proposition, since it entails 'It could be the case that so-and-so came about'; so, by contraposition, if 'God can do so-and-so' is to be true, or even logically possible, then 'so-and-so' must represent a logically consistent description of a feat. And whereas only a minority of Christians have explicitly believed in absolute omnipotence, many have believed that a proposition of the form 'God can do so-and-so' is true whenever 'so-and-so' represents a description of a logically possible feat. This is our second doctrine of omnipotence. One classic statement of this comes in the *Summa Theologica* Ia q. xxv art. 3. Aquinas rightly says that we cannot explain 'God can do everything' in terms of what is within the power of some agent; for 'God can do everything any created agent can do', though true, is not a comprehensive enough account of God's power, which exceeds that of any created agent; and

'God can do everything God can do' runs uselessly in a circle. So he puts forward the view that if the description 'so-and-so' is in itself possible through the relation of the terms involved—if it does not involve contradictories' being true together—then 'God can do so-and-so' is true. Many Christian writers have followed Aquinas in saying this; but it is not a position consistently maintainable. As we shall see, Aquinas did not manage to stick to the position himself.

Before I raise the difficulties against this thesis, I wish to expose a common confusion that often leads people to accept it: the confusion between self-contradiction and gibberish. C. S. Lewis in *The Problem of Pain* says that meaningless combinations of words do not suddenly acquire meaning simply because we prefix to them the two other words 'God can', and Antony Flew has quoted this with just approval. But if we take Lewis's words strictly, his point is utterly trivial, and nothing to our purpose. For gibberish, syntactically incoherent combination of words, is quite different from self-contradictory sentences or descriptions; the latter certainly have an intelligible place in our language.

It is a common move in logic to argue that a set of premises A, B, C together yield a contradiction, and that therefore A and B as premises yield as conclusion the contradictory of C; some logicians have puritanical objections to this manoeuvre, but I cannot stop to consider them; I am confident, too, that neither Aquinas nor Lewis would share these objections to *reductio ad absurdum*. If, however, a contradictory formula were gibberish, *reductio ad absurdum* certainly would be an illegitimate procedure—indeed it would be a nonsensical one. So we have to say that when 'so-and-so' represents a self-contradictory description of a feat, 'God can do so-and-so' is likewise self-contradictory, but that being self-contradictory it is *not* gibberish, but merely false.

I am afraid the view of omnipotence presently under consideration owes part of its attractiveness to the idea that then 'God can do so-and-so' would never turn out *false* so that there would be no genuine counterexamples to 'God can do everything'. Aquinas says, in the passage I just now cited: 'What implies contradiction cannot be a word, for no understanding can conceive it.' Aquinas, writing seven centuries ago, is excusable for not being clear about the difference between self-contradiction and gibberish; we are not excusable if we are not. It is not gibberish to say 'a God can bring it about that in Alcalá there lives a barber who shaves all those and only those living in Alcalá who do not shave themselves'; this is a perfectly well-formed sentence, and not on the face of it self-contradictory; all the same, the supposed feat notoriously is self-contradictory, so this statement of what God can do is not nonsense but false.

One instance of a description of a feat that is really but not overtly self-contradictory has some slight importance in the history of conceptions of omnipotence. It appeared obvious to Spinoza that *God can bring about everything that God can bring about*, and that to deny this would be flatly incompatible with God's omnipotence (*Ethics* I.17, scholium). Well, the italicized sentence is syntactically ambiguous. 'Everything that God can bring about God can bring about' is one possible reading of the sentence, and this is an obvious, indeed trivial predication about God, which must be true if there is a God at all. But the other way of taking the sentence relates to a supposed feat of *bringing about everything that God can bring about—all* of these bringable-about things *together—* and it says that God is capable of *this* feat. This is clearly the way Spinoza wishes us to take the sentence. But taken this way, it is not obvious at all; quite the contrary, it's obviously false. For among the things that are severally possible for God to bring about, there are going to be some pairs that are not *com*possible, pairs which it is logically impossible should both come about; and then it is beyond God's power to bring about such a pair together—let alone, to bring about all the things together which he can bring about severally.

This does not give us a description of a *logically possible* feat which God cannot accomplish. However, there is nothing easier than to mention feats which are logically possible but which God cannot do, if Christianity is true. Lying and promise-breaking are logically possible feats: but Christian faith, as I have said, collapses unless we are assured that God cannot lie and cannot break his promises.

This argument is an *ad hominem* argument addressed to Christians; but there are well-known logical arguments to show that on any view there must be some logically possible feats that are beyond God's power. One good example suffices: making a thing which its maker cannot afterwards destroy. This is certainly a possible feat, a feat that some human beings have performed. Can God perform the feat or not? If he cannot there is already some logically possible feat which God cannot perform. If God can perform the feat, then let us suppose that he does: *ponatur in esse*, as medieval logicians say. Then we are supposing God to have brought about a situation in which he *has* made something he cannot destroy; and in that situation destroying this thing is a *logically* possible feat that God cannot accomplish, for we surely cannot admit the idea of a creature whose destruction is logically *im*possible.

There have been various attempts to meet this argument. The most interesting is that the proposition 'God cannot make a thing that he cannot destroy' can be turned round to 'Any thing that God can make he can destroy'—which does not even look like an objection to God's being able to do everything logically possible. But this reply involves the very same bracketing fallacy that I exposed a moment ago in Spinoza. There, you will remember, we had to distinguish two ways of taking 'God can bring about everything that God can bring about':

A. Everything that God can bring about, God can bring about.

B. God can bring about the following feat: to bring about everything that God can bring about.

And we saw that A is trivially true, given that there *is* a God, and B certainly false. Here, similarly, we have to distinguish two senses of 'God cannot make a thing that its maker cannot destroy':

A. Anything that its maker cannot destroy, God cannot make.

B. God cannot bring about the following feat: to make something that its maker cannot destroy.

And here A does contrapose, as the objectors would have it, to 'Anything that God can make, its maker can destroy', which on the face of it says nothing against God's power to do anything logically possible. But just as in the Spinoza example, the B reading purports to describe a single feat, *bringing about everything that God can bring about* (this feat, I argued, is impossible for God, because logically impossible): so in our present case, the B reading purports to describe a single feat, *making something that its maker cannot destroy*. This, as I said, is a logically possible feat, a feat that men sometimes do perform; so we may press the question whether this is a feat God can accomplish or not; and either way there will be some *logically possible* feat God cannot accomplish. So this notion of omnipotence, like the Cartesian idea of absolute omnipotence, turns out to be obviously incompatible with Christian faith, and moreover logically untenable.

Let us see, then, if we fare any better with the third theory: the theory that the only condition for the truth of 'God can do so-and-so' is that 'God does so-and-so' or 'God is doing so-and-so' must be logically possible. As I said, this imposes a more restrictive condition than the second theory: for there are many feats that we can consistently suppose to be performed but cannot consistently suppose to be performed by God. This theory might thus get us out of the logical trouble that arose with the second theory about the feat: *making a thing that its maker cannot destroy*. For though this is a logically possible feat, a feat some creatures do perform, it might well be argued that '*God* has made a thing that its maker cannot destroy' is a proposition with a buried inconsistency in it; and if so, then on the present account of omnipotence we need not say 'God *can* make a thing that its maker cannot destroy'.

This suggestion also, however, can easily be refuted by an example of great philosophical importance that I borrow from Aquinas. 'It comes about that Miss X never loses her virginity' is plainly a logically possible proposition: and so also is 'God brings it about that Miss X never loses her virginity'. All the same, if it so happens that Miss X already has lost her virginity, 'God *can* bring it about that Miss X never loses her virginity' is false (Ia q. xxv art. 4 ad 3 um). Before Miss X had lost her virginity, it would have been true to say this very thing; so what we can truly say about what God can do will be different at different times. This appears to imply a change in God, but Aquinas would certainly say, and I think rightly, that it doesn't really do so. It is just like the case of Socrates coming to be shorter than Theaetetus because Theaetetus grows up; here, the change is on the side of Theaetetus not of Socrates. So in our case, the change is really in Miss X not in God; something about her passes from the realm of possibility to the realm of *fait accompli*, and thus *no longer* comes under the concept of the accomplishable—*deficit a ratione possibilium* (Aquinas, *loc. cit.*, ad 2 um). I think Aquinas's position here is strongly defensible; but if he does defend it, he has abandoned the position that God can do everything that it is not *a priori* impossible *for God to do*, let alone the position that God can bring about everything describable in a logically consistent way.

Is it *a priori* impossible for God to do something wicked? And if not, *could* God do something wicked? There have been expressed serious doubts about this: I came across them in that favourite of modern moral philosophers, Richard Price. We must distinguish, he argues, between God's natural and his moral attributes: if God is a free moral being, even as we are, it must not be absolutely impossible for God to do something wicked. There must be just a chance that God should do something wicked: no doubt it will be a really infinitesimal chance—after all, God has persevered in ways of virtue on a vast scale for inconceivably long—but the chance must be there, or God isn't free and isn't therefore laudable for his goodness. The way this reverend gentleman commends his Maker's morals is so startling that you may suspect me of misrepresentation; I can only ask any sceptic to check in Daiches Raphael's edition of Price's work! Further comment on my part is I hope needless.

A much more restrained version of the same sort of thing is to be found in the Scholastic distinction between God's *potentia absoluta* and *potentia ordinata*. The former is God's power considered in abstraction from his wisdom and goodness, the latter is God's power considered as controlled in its exercise by his wisdom and goodness. Well, as regards a man it makes good sense to say: 'He has the bodily and mental power to do so-and-so, but he certainly will not, it would be pointlessly silly and wicked.' But does anything remotely like this make sense to say about Almighty God? If not, the Scholastic distinction I have cited is wholly frivolous.

Let us then consider our fourth try. Could it be said that the 'everything' in 'God can do everything' refers precisely to things that are not in the realm of *fait accompli* but of futurity? This will not do either. If God can promulgate promises to men, then as regards any promises that are not yet fulfilled we know that they certainly will be fulfilled: and in that case God clearly has not a *potentia ad utrumque*—a two-way power of either actualizing the event that will fulfill the promise or not actualizing it. God can then only do what will fulfill his promise. And if we try to evade this by denying that God can make promises known to men, then we have once more denied something essential to Christian faith, and we are still left with something that God cannot do.

I must here remove the appearance of a fallacy. God cannot but fulfill his promises, I argued; so he has not a two-way power, *potentia ad utrumque*, as regards these particular future events. This argument may have seemed to involve the fallacy made notorious in medieval logic treatises, of confusing the necessity by which something follows—*necessitas consequentiae*—with the necessity of that very thing which follows—*necessitas consequentis*. If it is impossible for God to promise and not perform, then if we know God has promised something we may infer with certainty that he will perform it. Surely, it may be urged, this is enough for Christian faith and hope; we need not go on to say that God *cannot not* bring about the future event in question. If we do that, are we not precisely committing the hoary modular fallacy I have just described?

I answer that there are various senses of 'necessary'. The future occurrence of such-and-such, when God has promised that such-and-such shall be, is of course not logically necessary; but it may be necessary in the sense of being, as Arthur Prior puts it, now unpreventable. If God *has* promised that Israel shall be saved, then there is nothing that anybody, even God, can do about that; this past state of affairs is now unpreventable. But it is also necessary in the same way that if God has promised then he will perform; God cannot do anything about that either—cannot make himself liable to break his word. So we have as premises 'Necessarily p' and 'Necessarily if p then q', in the same sense of 'necessarily'; and from these premises it not merely necessarily follows that q—the conclusion in the necessitated form, 'Necessarily q' with the same sense of 'necessarily', follows from the premises. So if God has promised that Israel shall be saved, the future salvation of Israel is not only certain but inevitable; God must save Israel, because he cannot not save Israel without breaking his word given in the past and he can neither alter the past nor break his word.

Again, in regard to this and other arguments, some people may have felt discomfort at my not drawing in relation to God the sort of distinction between various applications of 'can' that are made in human affairs: the 'can' of knowing how to, the 'can' of physical power to, the 'can' of opportunity, the 'can' of what fits in with one's plans. But of course the way we make these distinct applications of 'he can' to a human agent will not be open if we are talking about God. There is no question of God's knowing how but lacking the strength, or being physically able to but not knowing how; moreover (to make a distinction that comes in a logical example of Aristotle's) though there is a right time when God may bring something about, it is inept to speak of his then having the opportunity to do it. (To develop this distinction: if 'x' stands for a finite agent and 'so-and-so' for an act directly in x's power, there is little difference between 'At time t it is suitable for x to bring so-and-so about' and 'It is suitable for x to bring so-and-so about at time t': but if 'x' means God, the temporal qualification 'at time t' can attach only to what is brought about; God does not live through successive times and find one more suitable than another.)

These distinct applications of 'can' are distinct only for finite and change-able agents, not for a God whose action is universal and whose mind and character and design are unchangeable. There is thus no ground for fear that in talking about God we may illicitly slip from one sort of 'can' to another. What we say God can do is always in respect of his changeless supreme power.

All the same, we have to assert different propositions at different times in order to say truly what God can do. What is past, as I said, ceases to be alterable even by God; and thus the truth-value of a proposition like 'God can bring it about that Miss X never loses her virginity' alters once she has lost it. Similarly, God's promise makes a difference to what we can thereafter truly say God can do; it is less obvious in this case that the real change involved is a change in creatures, not in God, than it was as regards Miss X's virginity, but a little thought should show that the promulgation or making known of God's intention, which is involved in a promise, is precisely a change in the creatures to whom the promise is made.

Thus all the four theories of omnipotence that I have considered break down. Only the first overtly flouts logic; but the other three all involve logical contradictions, or so it seems; and moreover, all these theories have consequences fatal to the truth of Christian faith. The last point really ought not to surprise us; for the absolute confidence a Christian must have in God's revelation and promises involves, as I said at the outset, both a belief that God is almighty, in the sense I explained, and a belief that there are certain describable things that God cannot do and therefore will not do.

If I were to end the discussion at this point, I should leave an impression of Aquinas's thought that would be seriously unfair to him; for although in the passage I cited Aquinas appears verbally committed to our second theory of omnipotence, it seems clear that this does not adequately represent his mind. Indeed, it was from Aquinas himself and from the *Summa Theologica* that I borrowed an example which refutes even the weaker third theory, let alone the second one. Moreover, in the other Summa (Book II, c. xxv) there is an instructive list of things that *Deus omnipotens* is rightly said not to be able to do. But the mere occurrence of this list makes me doubt whether Aquinas can be said to believe, in any reasonable interpretation, the thesis that God can do everything. That God is almighty in my sense Aquinas obviously did believe; I am suggesting that here his 'omnipotens' means 'almighty' rather than 'omnipotent'. Aquinas does not say or even imply that he has given an *exhaustive* list of kinds of case in which 'God can do so-and-so' or 'God can make so-and-so' turns out false; so what he says here does not commit him to 'God can do everything' even in the highly unnatural sense 'God can do everything that is not excluded under one or the other of the following heads'.

I shall not explore Aquinas's list item by item, because I have made open or tacit use of his considerations at several points in the foregoing and do not wish to repeat myself. But one batch of items raises a specially serious problem. My attention was drawn to the problem by a contribution that the late Mr. Michael Foster made orally during a discussion at the Socratic Club in Oxford. Aquinas tells us that if 'doing so-and-so' implies what he calls passive potentiality, then 'God can do so-and-so' is false. On this ground he excluded all of the following:

God can be a body or something of the sort.

God can be tired or oblivious.

God can be angry or sorrowful.

God can suffer violence or be overcome.

God can undergo corruption.

Foster pointed out that as a Christian Aquinas was committed to asserting the contradictory of all these theses. *Contra factum non valet ratio*; it's no good arguing that God cannot do what God has done, and in the Incarnation God did do all these things Aquinas said God cannot do. The Word that was God *was* made flesh (and the literal meaning of the Polish for this is: The Word became a body!); God the Son *was* tired and did sink into the oblivion of sleep; he *was* angry and sorrowful; he was bound like a thief, beaten, and crucified; and though we believe his Body did not decay, it suffered corruption in the sense of becoming a corpse instead of a living body—Christ in the Apocalypse uses of himself the startling words 'I became a corpse', *'egenomēn nekros'*, and the Church has always held that the dead Body of Christ during the *triduum mortis* was adorable with Divine worship for its union to the Divine Nature.

Foster's objection to Aquinas is the opposite kind of objection to the ones I have been raising against the various theories of omnipotence I have discussed. I have been saying that these theories say by implication that God *can* do certain things which Christian belief requires one to say God *cannot* do; Foster is objecting that Aquinas's account says God *cannot* do some things which according to Christian faith God *can* do and has in fact done.

It would take me too far to consider how Aquinas might have answered this objection. It would not of course be outside his intellectual milieu; it is the very sort of objection that a Jew or a Moor might have used, accepting Aquinas's account of what God cannot do, in order to argue against the Incarnation. I shall simply mention one feature that Aquinas's reply would have had; it would have to make essential use of the particle 'as', or in Latin 'secundum quod'. God did become a man, so God can become man and have a human body; but God as God cannot be man or have a body.

The logic of these propositions with 'as' in them, reduplicative propositions as they are traditionally called, is a still unsolved problem, although as a matter of history it was a problem raised by Aristotle in the *Prior Analytics*. We must not forget that such propositions occur frequently in ordinary discourse; we use them there with an ill-founded confidence that we know our way around. Jones, we say, is Director of the Gnome Works and Mayor of Middletown; he gets a salary *as* Director and an expense allowance *as* Mayor; he signs one letter *as* Director, another *as* Mayor. We say all this, but how far do we understand the logical relations of what we say? Very little, I fear. One might have expected some light and leading from medieval logicians; the theological importance of reduplicative propositions did in fact lead to their figuring as a topic in medieval logical treatises. But I have not found much that is helpful in such treatments as I have read.

I hope to return to this topic later. Meanwhile, even though it has nothing directly to do with almightiness or omnipotence, I shall mention one important logical point that is already to be found in Aristotle. A superficial grammatical illusion may make us think that 'A as P is Q' attaches the predicate 'Q' to a complex subject 'A as P'. But Aristotle insists, to my mind rightly, on the analysis: 'A' subject, 'is, as P, Q' predicate—so that we have not a complex subject-term, but a complex predicate-term; clearly, this predicate entails the simple conjunctive predicate 'is both P and Q' but not conversely. This niggling point of logic has in fact some theological importance. When theologians are talking about Christ as God and Christ as Man, they may take the two phrases to be two logical subjects of predication, if they have failed to see the Aristotelian point; and then they are likely to think or half think that Christ as God is one entity or *Gegenstand* and Christ as Man is another. I am sure some theologians have yielded to this temptation, which puts them on a straight road to the Nestorian heresy.

What Aquinas would have done, I repeat, to meet Foster's objection in the mouth of a Jew or Moor is to distinguish between what we say God can do, *simpliciter*, and what we say God *as* God can do, using the reduplicative form of proposition. Now if we do make such a distinction, we are faced with considerable logical complications, particularly if we accept the Aristotelian point about the reduplicative construction. Let us go back to our friend Jones: there is a logical difference between:

1. Jones as Mayor can attend this committee meeting.

2. Jones can as Mayor attend this committee meeting.

as we may see if we spell the two out a little:

1. Jones as Mayor has the opportunity of attending this committee meeting.

2. Jones has the opportunity of (attending this committee meeting as Mayor).

We can easily see now that 1 and 2 are logically distinct: for one thing, if Jones is not yet Mayor but has an opportunity of becoming Mayor and *then* attending the committee meeting, 2 would be true and 1 false. And if we want to talk about what Jones as Mayor *cannot* do, the complexities pile up; for then we have to consider how the negation can be inserted at one or other position in a proposition of one of these forms, and how all the results are logically related.

All this is logical work to be done if we are to be clear about the implications of saying that God can or cannot do so-and-so, or again that God *as God* can or cannot do so-and-so. It is obvious, without my developing the matter further, that the logic of all this will not be simple. It's a far cry from the simple method of bringing our question 'Can God do so-and-so?' under a reassuring principle 'God can do *everything*'. But I hope I have made it clear that any reassurance we get that way is entirely spurious.

II.A.2. The Paradox of the Stone

C. WADE SAVAGE

C. Wade Savage (1932–), professor of philosophy at the University of Minnesota, examines here the paradox of the stone, the problem of whether an omnipotent being can create a stone so heavy that he cannot lift it. Traditionally the paradox has been construed as demonstrating that God could not be omnipotent because God either cannot create such a stone or cannot lift it. Savage argues that this interpretation reflects confusion: An omnipotent being can create a stone of any weight. An omnipotent being can also lift a stone of any weight. There is, then, no threat to God's omnipotence in this paradox.

A. **(1)** Either God can create a stone which He cannot lift, or He cannot create a stone which He cannot lift.

  (2) If God can create a stone which He cannot lift, then He is not omnipotent (since He cannot lift the stone in question).

  (3) If God cannot create a stone which He cannot lift, then He is not omnipotent (since He cannot create the stone in question).

  (4) Therefore, God is not omnipotent.

Reprinted from *The Philosophical Review* 76 (1967) 74–79 by permission of the publisher and author.

Mr. Mavrodes has offered a solution to the familiar paradox above;[1] but it is erroneous. Mavrodes states that he assumes the existence of God,[2] and then reasons (in pseudo-dilemma fashion) as follows. God is either omnipotent or He is not. If we assume that He is omnipotent, the task of creating a stone which He cannot lift is not self-contradictory. And we can conclude that God is not omnipotent on the grounds that both His ability and His inability to perform this task imply that He is not omnipotent. But to prove his non-omnipotence in this way is trivial. "To be significant [the paradoxical argument] must derive this same conclusion *from the assumption that God is omnipotent*; that is, it must show that the assumption of the omnipotence of God leads to a *reductio*." However, on the assumption that God is omnipotent, the task of creating a stone which God cannot lift is self-contradictory. Since inability to perform a self-contradictory task does not imply a limitation on the agent, one of the premises of the paradoxical argument—premise A(3)—is false. The argument is, in consequence, either insignificant or unsound.

There are many objections to this solution. First, the paradoxical argument need not be represented as a *reductio*; in A it is a dilemma. Mavrodes' reasoning implies that the paradoxical argument must either assume that God is omnipotent or assume that He is not omnipotent. This is simply false: neither assumption need be made, and neither is made in A. Second, "a stone which God cannot lift" is self-contradictory—on the assumption that God is omnipotent—only if "God is omnipotent" is necessarily true. "Russell can lift any stone" is a contingent statement. Consequently, if we assume that Russell can lift any stone we are thereby committed only to saying that creating a stone which Russell cannot lift is a task which *in fact* cannot be performed by Russell or anyone else. Third, if "God is omnipotent" is necessarily true—as Mavrodes must claim for his solution to work—then his assumption that God exists begs the question of the paradoxical argument. For what the argument really tries to establish is that the existence of an omnipotent being is logically impossible. Fourth, the claim that inability to perform a self-contradictory task is no limitation on the agent is not entirely uncontroversial. Descartes suggested that an omnipotent God must be able to perform such self-contradictory tasks as making a mountain without a valley and arranging that the sum of one and two is not three.[3] No doubt Mavrodes and Descartes have

---

[1] George I. Mavrodes, "Some Puzzles Concerning Omnipotence," *Philosophical Review*, LXXII (1963), 221–223. The heart of this solution is contained in pars. 6, 7, and 11.

[2] See n. 1, p. 221.

[3] Harry G. Frankfurt, "The Logic of Omnipotence," *Philosophical Review*, LXXIII (1964), 262–263. The relevant passage from Descartes is quoted by Frankfurt in a long footnote.

Mavrodes assumes (on his "significant" interpretation of the paradox) that creating a stone which God cannot lift is a self-contradictory task, and contends that God therefore cannot perform it. This forces him onto the second horn of dilemma A, which he tries to break by arguing that inability to perform a self-contradictory task does not imply a limitation on the agent. Frankfurt also assumes that creating a stone which God cannot lift is a self-contradictory task, but he contends with Descartes (for the sake of argument) that God can

different theories about the nature of contradictions; but that is part of the controversy.

Mavrodes has been led astray by version A of the paradox, which apparently seeks to prove that *God is not omnipotent*. Concentration on this version, together with the inclination to say that God is by definition omnipotent, leads straight to the conclusion that the paradox is specious. For if God is by definition omnipotent, then, obviously, creating a stone which God (an omnipotent being who can lift any stone) cannot lift is a task whose description is self-contradictory. What the paradox of the stone really seeks to prove is that the notion of an omnipotent being is logically inconsistent—that is, that *the existence of an omnipotent being, God or any other, is logically impossible*. It tries to do this by focusing on the perfectly consistent task of creating a stone which the creator cannot lift. The essence of the argument is that an omnipotent being must be able to perform this task and yet cannot perform the task.

Stated in its clearest form, the paradoxical argument of the stone is as follows. Where x is any being:

B. (1) Either x can create a stone which x cannot lift, or x cannot create a stone which x cannot lift.

(2) If x can create a stone which x cannot lift, then, necessarily, there is at least one task which x cannot perform (namely, lift the stone in question).

(3) If x cannot create a stone which x cannot lift, then, necessarily, there is at least one task which x cannot perform (namely, create the stone in question).

(4) Hence, there is at least one task which x cannot perform.

(5) If x is an omnipotent being then x can perform any task.

(6) Therefore, x is not omnipotent.

Since x is any being, this argument proves that the existence of an omnipotent being, God or other, is logically impossible.

It is immediately clear that Mavrodes' solution will not apply to this version of the paradox. B is obviously a significant, nontrivial argument. But since it does not contain the word "God," no critic can maintain that B assumes that God is omnipotent. For the same reason, the point that "a stone which God cannot lift" is self-contradictory is simply irrelevant. Notice also that B is neutral on the question of whether inability to perform a self-contradictory task is a limitation on the agent's power. We can, however, replace every occurrence of "task" with "task whose description is not self-contradictory" without damaging the argument in any way.

---

nevertheless perform it. This forces him onto the first horn of the dilemma, which he tries to break with the following argument. If God can perform the self-contradictory task of creating a stone which He cannot lift, then He can just as easily perform the additional self-contradictory task of lifting the stone which He (creates and) cannot lift. Frankfurt's fundamental error is the same as Mavrodes': both suppose that on any significant interpretation the paradox sets for God the self-contradictory task of creating a stone which God (an omnipotent being who can lift any stone) cannot lift.

The paradox does have a correct solution, though a different one from that offered by Mavrodes. The two solutions are similar in that both consist in arguing that an agent's inability to create a stone which he cannot lift does not entail a limitation on his power. But here the similarity ends. For, as we shall see presently, the basis of the correct solution is not that creating a stone which the creator cannot lift is a self-contradictory task (which it is not). Conse quently, the correct solution side-steps the question of whether an agent's inability to perform a self-contradictory task is a limitation on his power.

The fallacy in the paradox of the stone lies in the falsity of the second horn—B(3)—of its dilemma: "x can create a stone which x cannot lift" does indeed entail that there is a task which x cannot perform and, consequently, does entail that x is not omnipotent. However, "x cannot create a stone which x cannot lift" does not entail that there is a task which x cannot perform and, consequently, does not entail that x is not omnipotent. That the entailment seems to hold is explained by the misleading character of the statement "x cannot create a stone which x cannot lift." The phrase "cannot create a stone" seems to imply that x is limited in power. But this illusion vanishes on analysis: "x cannot create a stone which x cannot lift" can only mean "If x can create a stone, then x can lift it." It is obvious that the latter statement does not entail that x is limited in power.

A schematic representation of B(1)–B(3) will bring our point into sharper focus. Let S = stone, C = can create, and L = can lift; let x be any being; and let the universe of discourse be conceivable entities. Then we obtain:

C. (1) $(\exists y)(Sy \cdot Cxy \cdot - Lxy) \lor - (\exists y)(Sy \cdot Cxy \cdot - Lxy)$.

   (2) $(\exists y)(Sy \cdot Cxy \cdot - Lxy) \supset (\exists y)(Sy \cdot - Lxy)$.

   (3) $- (\exists y)(Sy \cdot Cxy \cdot - Lxy) \supset (\exists y)(Sy \cdot - Cxy)$.[4]

That the second alternative in C(1) is equivalent to "$(y)[(Sy \cdot Cxy) \supset Lxy]$"[5] schematically explains our interpretation of "x can create a stone which x cannot lift" as meaning "If x can create a stone, then x can lift it." It is now quite clear where the fallacy in the paradoxical argument lies. Although C(2) is logically true, C(3) is not. "$(\exists y)(Sy \cdot Cxy \cdot - Lxy)$"[6] logically implies "$(\exists y)(Sy \cdot - Lxy)$."[7] But "$- (\exists y)(Sy \cdot Cxy \cdot - Lxy)$"[8] does not logically imply "$(\exists y)(Sy \cdot -$

---

[4] [(**1**) *Either*: there exists something called "y" such that y is a stone and any being "x" can create y, and x cannot lift y, *or* there does not exist a y such that x can create y and x cannot lift y.

(**2**) *If* there exists a y such that y is a stone and x can create y and x cannot lift y, *then* there exists a y such that y is a stone and x cannot lift y.

(**3**) *If* there does not exist a y such that y is a stone and x can create y and x cannot lift y, *then* there exists a y such that y is a stone and x cannot create y.]

[5] [For any y, *if* y is a stone and x can create y, *then* x can lift y.]

[6] [There exists a y such that y is a stone and x can create y and x cannot lift y.]

[7] [There exists a y such that y is a stone and x cannot lift y.]

[8] [There does not exist a y such that y is a stone and x can create y and x cannot lift y.]

Cxy)";[9] nor does it logically imply "(∃y)(Sy · – Lxy)."[10] In general, "x cannot create a stone which x cannot lift" does not logically imply "There is a task which x cannot perform."

For some reason the above analysis does not completely remove the inclination to think that an agent's inability to create a stone which he himself cannot lift does not entail his inability to perform some task, does not entail a limitation on his power. The reason becomes clear when we consider the task of creating a stone which someone *other than* the creator cannot lift. Now if x cannot create a stone which Y cannot lift, then x cannot create a stone heavier than seventy pounds, and is indeed limited in power. But suppose that y is omnipotent and can lift stones of any poundage. Then x's inability to create a stone which y cannot lift does not necessarily constitute a limitation on x's power. For x may be able to create stones of any poundage, although y can lift any stone x creates. If y can lift stones of any poundage, and x cannot create a stone heavier than seventy pounds, then x cannot create a stone which y cannot lift, and x is limited in power. But if x can create stones of any poundage, and y can lift stones of any poundage, then x cannot create a stone which y cannot lift, and yet x is not thereby limited in power. Now it is easy to see that precisely parallel considerations obtain where x is both stone-creator and stone lifter.

The logical facts above may be summarized as follows. Whether x = y or x ≠ y, x's inability to create a stone which y cannot lift constitutes a limitation on x's power only if (i) x is unable to create any stones of any poundage, or (ii) y is unable to lift stones of any poundage. And, since either (i) or (ii) may be false, "x cannot create a stone which y cannot lift" does not entail "x is limited in power." This logical point is obscured, however, by the normal context of our discussions of abilities and inabilities. Since such discussions are normally restricted to beings who are limited in their stone-creating, stone-lifting, and other abilities, the inability of a being to create a stone which he himself or some other being cannot lift *normally* constitutes a limitation on his power. And this produces the illusion that a being's inability to create a stone which he himself or some other being cannot lift *necessarily* constitutes a limitation on his power, the illusion that "x cannot create a stone which y cannot lift" (where either x = y or x ≠ y) entails "x is limited in power."

Since our discussions normally concern beings of limited power, the erroneous belief that "x cannot create a stone which x cannot lift" entails "x is limited in power" will normally cause no difficulty. But we must beware when the discussion turns to God—a being who is presumably unlimited in power. God's inability to create a stone which He cannot lift is a limitation on His power only if (i) He is unable to create stones of any poundage, or (ii) He is unable to lift stones of any poundage—that is, only if He is limited in His power of stone-creating or His power of stone-lifting. But until it has been proved otherwise—and it is difficult to see how this could be done—we are free to suppose that God suffers neither of these limitations. On this supposition God's inability to create a stone which He cannot lift is nothing more nor less than a

---

[9] [There exists a y such that y is a stone and x cannot create y.]

[10] [There exists a y such that y is a stone and x cannot lift y.]

necessary consequence of two facets of His omnipotence.[11] For if God is omnipotent, then He can create stones of any poundage and lift stones of any poundage. And "God can create stones of any poundage, and God can lift stones of any poundage" entails "God cannot create a stone which He cannot lift."

---

[11] Mavrodes apparently sees this point in the last three paragraphs of his article. But his insight is vitiated by his earlier mistaken attempt to solve the paradox.

II.B. Omniscience

II.B.1. On God's Knowledge

THOMAS AQUINAS

*Thomas Aquinas (1224–1274), one of the greatest of Western
theologians, produced a massive and comprehensive system of
thought treating the whole range of theological subjects.
Thomas was strongly influenced by Aristotle ("The Philosopher," as Thomas refers to him), whose metaphysical system
in* De Anima *he virtually takes over and retrofits with
Christian concepts ("The Apostle" is St. Paul). Readers unaccustomed to his rather cumbersome argumentation style
sometimes find Thomas a bit difficult to follow at first. He
begins each article by stating the objections that might be
raised against the position he is going to defend. Then he offers
his own teachings, usually prefaced by "I answer that . . ."
Finally he offers answers to the objections he raised before.*

*Thomas argues here for a strong sense of divine omni-
science that is nonetheless compatible with the contingency of
future events and therefore of the future free actions of other
agents. Thomas believes he escapes the problem of alleged
incompatibility of divine foreknowledge with future contingency and future free agency by placing God outside the
flow of time. What is future from the point of view of any
human individual is not future from God's perspective, because God surveys the entire sweep of time in a simultaneous,
eternal Now.*

QUESTION XIV: ON GOD'S KNOWLEDGE

First Article: Whether There is Knowledge in God?

We proceed thus to the First Article:—

Objection 1. It seems that in God there is not knowledge [*scientia*]. For
knowledge is a habit; and habit does not belong to God, since it is the mean
between potentiality and act. Therefore knowledge is not in God.

From *Summa Theologica,* question XIV, articles 1, 5, 8, 9, and 13, in Anton C. Pegis, *An
Introduction to St. Thomas Aquinas* (New York: Random House, 1945), pp. 127–128; 134–136;
141–144; 151–155. Reprinted by permission.

Objection 2. Further, since science is about conclusions, it is a kind of knowledge caused by something else, namely, the knowledge of principles. But nothing caused is in God; therefore science is not in God.

Objection 3. Further, all knowledge is universal, or particular. But in God there is no universal or particular. Therefore there is no knowledge in God.

On the contrary, The Apostle says, *O the depth of the riches of the wisdom and of the knowledge of God (Rom.* xi. 33).

I answer that, In God there exists the most perfect knowledge. To prove this, we must note that knowing beings are distinguished from non-knowing beings in that the latter possess only their own form; whereas the knowing being is naturally adapted to have also the form of some other thing, for the species of the thing known is in the knower. Hence it is manifest that the nature of a non knowing being is more contracted and limited; whereas the nature of knowing beings has a greater amplitude and extension. That is why the Philosopher says that *the soul is in a sense all things.* Now the contraction of a form comes through the matter. Hence, as we have said above, according as they are the more immaterial, forms approach more nearly to a kind of infinity. Therefore it is clear that the immateriality of a thing is the reason why it is cognitive, and that according to the mode of immateriality is the mode of cognition. Hence, it is said in *De Anima* ii. that plants do not know, because of their materiality. But sense is cognitive because it can receive species free from matter; and the intellect is still further cognitive, because it is more *separated from matter and unmixed,* as is said in *De Anima* iii. Since therefore God is in the highest degree of immateriality, as was stated above, it follows that He occupies the highest place in knowledge.

Reply Objection 1. Because perfections flowing from God to creatures exist in a higher state in God Himself, whenever a name taken from any created perfection is attributed to God, there must be separated from its signification anything that belongs to the imperfect mode proper to creatures. Hence knowledge is not a quality in God, nor a habit; but substance and pure act.

Reply Objection 2. Whatever is divided and multiplied in creatures exists in God simply and unitedly as was said above. Now man has different kinds of knowledge, according to the different objects of his knowledge. He has *understanding* as regards the knowledge of principles; he has *science* as regards knowledge of conclusions; he has *wisdom,* according as he knows the highest cause; he has *counsel* or *prudence,* according as he knows what is to be done. But God knows all these by one simple act of knowledge, as will be shown. Hence the simple knowledge of God can be named by all these names; in such a way, however, that there must be removed from each of them, so far as they are predicated of God, everything that savors of imperfection; and everything that expresses perfection is to be retained in them. Hence it is said, *With Him is wisdom and strength, He hath counsel and understanding. (Job* xii. 13).

Reply Objection 3. Knowledge is according to the mode of the one who knows, for the thing known is in the knower according to the mode of the knower. Now since the mode of the divine essence is higher than that of creatures, divine knowledge does not exist in God after the mode of created knowledge, so as to be universal or particular, or habitual, or potential, or existing according to any such mode.

Fifth Article: Whether God Knows Things Other Than Himself?

We proceed thus to the Fifth Article:—

Objection 1. It seems that God does not know other things besides Himself. For all other things but God are outside of God. But Augustine says that *God does not behold anything out of Himself.* Therefore He does not know things other than Himself.

Objection 2. Further, the object understood is the perfection of the one who understands. If therefore God understands other things besides Himself, something else will be the perfection of God, and will be nobler than He; which is impossible.

Objection 3. Further, the act of understanding is specified by the intelligible object, as is every other act from its own object. Hence the intellectual act is so much the nobler, the nobler the object understood. But God is His own intellectual act, as is clear from what has been said. If therefore God understands anything other than Himself, then God Himself is specified by something other than Himself; which cannot be. Therefore He does not understand things other than Himself.

On the contrary, It is written: *All things are naked and open to His eyes* (Heb. iv. 13).

I answer that, God necessarily knows things other than Himself. For it is manifest that He perfectly understands Himself; otherwise His being would not be perfect, since His being is His act of understanding. Now if anything is perfectly known, it follows of necessity that its power is perfectly known. But the power of anything can be perfectly known only by knowing to what that power extends. Since, therefore, the divine power extends to other things by the very fact that it is the first effective cause of all things, as is clear from the aforesaid, God must necessarily know things other than Himself. And this appears still more plainly if we add that the very being of the first efficient cause—viz., God—is His own act of understanding. Hence whatever effects pre-exist in God, as in the first cause, must be in His act of understanding, and they must be there in an intelligible way: for everything which is in another is in it according to the mode of that in which it is.

Now in order to know how God knows things other than Himself, we must consider that a thing is known in two ways: in itself, and in another. A thing is known *in itself* when it is known by the proper species adequate to the knowable object itself; as when the eye sees a man through the species of a man. A thing is seen *in another* through the species of that which contains it; as when the part is seen in the whole through the species of the whole, or when a man is seen in a mirror through the species of the mirror, or by any other way by which one thing is seen in another.

So we say that God sees Himself in Himself, because He sees Himself through His essence; and He sees other things, not in themselves, but in Himself, inasmuch as His essence contains the likeness of things other than Himself.

Reply Objection 1. The passage of Augustine in which it is said that God *sees nothing outside Himself* is not to be taken in such a way, as if God saw nothing that was outside Himself, but in the sense that what is outside Himself He does not see except in Himself, as was explained above.

Reply Objection 2. The object understood is a perfection of the one understanding, not by its substance, but by its species, according to which it is in the intellect as its form and perfection. For, as is said in *De Anima* iii, *a stone is not in the soul, but its species*. Now those things which are other than God are understood by God inasmuch as the essence of God contains their species, as was explained above; and hence it does not follow that anything is the perfection of the divine intellect other than the divine essence.

Reply Objection 3. The intellectual act is not specified by what is understood in another, but by the principal object understood in which other things are understood. For the intellectual act is specified by its object inasmuch as the intelligible form is the principle of the intellectual operation, since every operation is specified by the form which is its principle of operation, as heating by heat. Hence the intellectual operation is specified by that intelligible form which makes the intellect to be in act. And this is the species of the principal thing understood, which in God is nothing but His own essence in which all the species of things are comprehended. Hence it does not follow that the divine intellectual act, or rather God Himself, is specified by anything other than the divine essence itself.

Eighth Article: Whether the Knowledge of God is the Cause of Things?

We proceed thus to the Eighth Article:—

Objection 1. It seems that the knowledge of God is not the cause of things. For Origen says (on *Rom.* viii. 30): *A thing will not happen, because God knows it as future, but because it is future, it is on that account known by God before it exists.*

Objection 2. Further, given the cause, the effect follows. But the knowledge of God is eternal. Therefore if the knowledge of God is the cause of created things, it seems that creatures are eternal.

Objection 3. Further, *The knowable thing is prior to knowledge, and is its measure*, as the Philosopher says. But what is posterior and measured cannot be a cause. Therefore the knowledge of God is not the cause of things.

On the contrary, Augustine says, *Not because they are, does God know all creatures spiritual and temporal, but because He knows them, therefore they are.*

I answer that, The knowledge of God is the cause of things. For the knowledge of God is to all creatures what the knowledge of the artificer is to things made by his art. Now the knowledge of the artificer is the cause of the things made by his art from the fact that the artificer works through his intellect. Hence the form in the intellect must be the principle of action; as heat is the principle of heating. Nevertheless, we must observe that a natural form, being a form that remains in that to which it gives being, denotes a principle of action according only as it has an inclination to an effect; and likewise, the intelligible form does not denote a principle of action in so far as it resides in the one who understands unless there is added to it the inclination to an effect, which inclination is through the will. For since the intelligible form has a relation to contraries (inasmuch as the same knowledge relates to contraries), it would not produce a determinate effect unless it were determined to one thing by the appetite, as the Philosopher says. Now it is manifest that God causes things by His intellect, since His being is His act of understanding; and hence His knowledge must be the cause of things, in so far as His will is joined to it. Hence the knowledge of God as the cause of things is usually called the *knowledge of approbation.*

Reply Objection 1. Origen spoke in reference to that aspect of knowledge to which the idea of causality does not belong unless the will is joined to it, as is said above.

But when he says that the reason why God foreknows some things is because they are future, this must be understood according to the cause of consequence, and not according to the cause of being. For if things are in the future, it follows that God foreknows them; but the futurity of things is not the cause why God knows them.

Reply Objection 2. The knowledge of God is the cause of things according as things are in His knowledge. But that things should be eternal was not in the knowledge of God; hence, although the knowledge of God is eternal, it does not follow that creatures are eternal.

Reply Objection 3. Natural things are midway between the knowledge of God and our knowledge: for we receive knowledge from natural things, of which God is the cause by His knowledge. Hence, just as the natural things that can be known by us are prior to our knowledge, and are its measure, so the knowledge of God is prior to them, and is their measure; as, for instance, a house is midway between the knowledge of the builder who made it, and the knowledge of the one who gathers his knowledge of the house from the house already built.

Ninth Article: Whether God Has Knowledge of Things That Are Not?

We proceed thus to the Ninth Article:—

Objection 1. It seems that God has not knowledge of things that are not. For the knowledge of God is of true things. But *truth* and *being* are convertible terms. Therefore the knowledge of God is not of things that are not.

Objection 2. Further, knowledge requires likeness between the knower and the thing known. But those things that are not cannot have any likeness to God, Who is very being. Therefore what is not, cannot be known by God.

Objection 3. Further, the knowledge of God is the cause of what is known by Him. But it is not the cause of things that are not, because a thing that is not has no cause. Therefore God has no knowledge of things that are not.

On the contrary, The Apostle says: *Who. . . calleth those things that are not as those that are (Rom.* iv. 17).

I answer that, God knows all things whatsoever that in any way are. Now it is possible that things that are not absolutely should be in a certain sense. For, absolutely speaking, those things are which are actual; whereas things, which are not actual, are in the power either of God Himself or of a creature, whether in active power, or passive; whether in the power of thought or of imagination, or of any other kind whatsoever. Whatever therefore can be made, or thought, or said by the creature, as also whatever He Himself can do, all are known to

God, although they are not actual. And to this extent it can be said that He has knowledge even of things that are not.

Now, among the things that are not actual, a certain difference is to be noted. For though some of them may not be in act now, still they have been, or they will be; and God is said to know all these with the *knowledge of vision*: for since God's act of understanding, which is His being, is measured by eternity, and since eternity is without succession, comprehending all time, the present glance of God extends over all time, and to all things which exist in any time, as to objects present to Him. But there are other things in God's power, or the creature's, which nevertheless are not, nor will be, nor have been; and as regards these He is said to have the knowledge, not of vision, but of *simple intelligence*. This is so called because the things we see around us have distinct being outside the seer.

Reply Objection 1. Those things that are not actual are true in so far as they are in potentiality, for it is true that they are in potentiality; and as such they are known by God.

Reply Objection 2. Since God is very being, everything is in so far as it participates in the likeness of God; as everything is hot in so far as it participates in heat. So, things in potentiality are known by God, even though they are not in act.

Reply Objection 3. The knowledge of God is the cause of things when the will is joined to it. Hence it is not necessary that whatever God knows should be, or have been or is to be; but this is necessary only as regards what He wills to be, or permits to be. Further, it is not in the knowledge of God that these things be, but that they be possible.

Thirteenth Article: Whether the Knowledge of God is of Future Contingent Things?

We proceed thus to the Thirteenth Article:—

Objection 1. It seems that the knowledge of God is not of future contingent things. For from a necessary cause proceeds a necessary effect. But the knowledge of God is the cause of things known, as was said above. Since therefore that knowledge is necessary, what He knows must also be necessary. Therefore the knowledge of God is not of contingent things.

Objection 2. Further, every conditional proposition, of which the antecedent is absolutely necessary, must have an absolutely necessary consequent. For the antecedent is to the consequent as principles are to the conclusion: and from necessary principles only a necessary conclusion can follow, as is proved in *Poster*. i. But this is a true conditional proposition, *If God knew that this thing will be, it will be*, for the knowledge of God is only of true things. Now, the antecedent of this conditional proposition is absolutely necessary, because it is eternal, and because it is signified as past. Therefore the consequent is also absolutely necessary. Therefore whatever God knows is necessary; and so the knowledge of God is not of contingent things.

Objection 3. Further, everything known by God must necessarily be, because even what we ourselves know must necessarily be; and, of course, the knowledge of God is much more certain than ours. But no future contingent thing must necessarily be. Therefore no contingent future thing is known by God.

On the contrary, It is written (*Ps.* xxxii. 15), *He Who hath made the hearts of every one of them, Who understandeth all their works,* that is, of men. Now the works of men are contingent, being subject to free choice. Therefore God knows future contingent things.

I answer that, Since, as was shown above, God knows all things, not only things actual but also things possible to Him and to the creature, and since some of these are future contingent to us, it follows that God knows future contingent things.

In evidence of this, we must observe that a contingent thing can be considered in two ways. First, in itself, in so far as it is already in act, and in this sense it is not considered as future, but as present; neither is it considered as contingent to one of two terms, but as determined to one; and because of this it can be infallibly the object of certain knowledge, for instance to the sense of sight, as when I see that Socrates is sitting down. In another way, a contingent thing can be considered as it is in its cause, and in this way it is considered as future, and as a contingent thing not yet determined to one; for a contingent cause has relation to opposite things: and in this sense a contingent thing is not subject to any certain knowledge. Hence, whoever knows a contingent effect in its cause only, has merely a conjectural knowledge of it. Now God knows all contingent things not only as they are in their causes, but also as each one of them is actually in itself. And although contingent things become actual successively, nevertheless God knows contingent things not successively, as they are in their own being, as we do, but simultaneously. The reason is because His knowledge is measured by eternity, as is also His being; and eternity, being simultaneously whole, comprises all time, as was said above. Hence, all things that are in time are present to God from eternity, not only because He has the essences of things present within Him, as some say, but because His glance is carried from eternity over all things as they are in their presentiality. Hence it is manifest that contingent things are infallibly known by God, inasmuch as they are subject to the divine sight in their presentiality; and yet they are future contingent things in relation to their own causes.

Reply Objection 1. Although the supreme cause is necessary, the effect may be contingent by reason of the proximate contingent cause; just as the germination of a plant is contingent by reason of the proximate contingent cause, although the movement of the sun, which is the first cause, is necessary. So, likewise, things known by God are contingent because of their proximate causes, while the knowledge of God, which is the first cause, is necessary.

Reply Objection 2. Some say that this antecedent, *God knew this contingent to be future,* is not necessary, but contingent; because, although it is past, still it imports a relation to the future. This, however, does not remove necessity from it, for whatever has had relation to the future, must have had it, even though the future sometimes is not realized. On the other hand, some say that this antecedent is contingent because it is a compound of the necessary and the contingent; as this saying is contingent, *Socrates is a white man.* But this also is to no purpose; for when we say, *God knew this contingent to be future,* contingent is used here only as the matter of the proposition, and not as its principal part. Hence its contingency or necessity has no reference to the necessity or contingency of the proposition, or to its being true or false. For it may be just as true that I said a man is an ass, as that I said Socrates runs, or God is: and the same applies to necessary and contingent.

Hence it must be said that this antecedent is absolutely necessary. Nor does it follow, as some say, that the consequent is absolutely necessary because the antecedent is the remote cause of the consequent, which is contingent by reason of the proximate cause. But this is to no purpose. For the conditional would be false were its antecedent the remote necessary cause, and the consequent a contingent effect; as, for example, if I said, *if the sun moves, the grass will grow.*

Therefore we must reply otherwise: when the antecedent contains anything belonging to an act of the soul, the consequent must be taken, not as it is in itself, but as it is in the soul; for the being of a thing in itself is other than the being of a thing in the soul. For example, when I say, *What the soul understands is immaterial*, the meaning is that it is immaterial as it is in the intellect, not as it is in itself. Likewise if I say, *If God knew anything, it will be*, the consequent must be understood as it is subject to the divine knowledge, that is, as it is in its presentiality. And thus it is necessary, as is also the antecedent; *for everything that is, while it is, must necessarily be*, as the Philosopher says in *Periherm*. i.

Reply Objection 3. Things reduced to actuality in time are known by us successively in time, but by God they are known in eternity, which is above time. Whence to us they cannot be certain, since we know future contingent things only as contingent futures; but they are certain to God alone, Whose understanding is in eternity above time. Just as he who goes along the road does not see those who come after him; whereas he who sees the whole road from a height sees at once all those traveling on it. Hence, what is known by us must be necessary, even as it is in itself; for what is in itself a future contingent cannot be known by us. But what is known by God must be necessary according to the mode in which it is subject to the divine knowledge, as we have already stated, but not absolutely as considered in its proper causes. Hence also this proposition, *Everything known by God must necessarily be*, is usually distinguished, for it may refer to the thing or to the saying. If it refers to the thing, it is divided and false; for the sense is, *Everything which God knows is necessary*. If understood of the saying, it is composite and true, for the sense is, *This proposition, 'that which is known by God is' is necessary.*

Now some urge an objection and say that this distinction holds good with regard to forms that are separable from a subject. Thus if I said, *It is possible for a white thing to be black*, it is false as applied to the saying, and true as applied to the thing: for a thing which is white can become black; whereas this saying, *a white thing is black*, can never be true. But in forms that are inseparable from a subject, this distinction does not hold: for instance, if I said, *A black crow can be white*; for in both senses it is false. Now to be known by God is inseparable from a thing; for what is known by God cannot be not known. This objection, however, would hold if these words *that which is known* implied any disposition inherent in the subject; but since they import an act of the knower, something can be attributed to the known thing in itself (even if it always be known) which is not attributed to it in so far as it falls under an act of knowledge. Thus, material being is attributed to a stone in itself, which is not attributed to it inasmuch as it is intelligible.

II.B.2.   God's Omniscience and Human Freedom

ALVIN PLANTINGA

Alvin Plantinga's (1932–) concern here is to answer the claim that God's omniscience is incompatible with human freedom. Plantinga summarizes an argument in which Nelson Pike attempts to show that God's foreknowledge of future human actions implies that those actions must occur and thus that the actions are not free. Plantinga makes use of the language of possible worlds to argue that Pike's claim is based on confusion. The claim that God is essentially omniscient implies that God is omniscient in every possible world. The confused position takes this to mean that God holds in every possible world exactly the beliefs he holds in the actual world (which Plantinga calls Kronos). What it actually implies is that God holds no false beliefs in any possible world. This means that in any possible world where some individual performs a certain act, God knows that she will perform it, but in any possible world where the same individual refrains from the act, God's knowledge is different—that is, God knows that the person refrains. Thus, says Plantinga, God's essential omniscience does not rule out human freedom.

The last argument I wish to discuss is perhaps only mildly atheological. This is the claim that God's omniscience is incompatible with *human freedom*. Many people are inclined to think that if God is omniscient, then human beings are never free. Why? Because the idea that God is omniscient implies that at any given time God knows not only what *has* taken place and what *is* taking place, but also what *will* take place. He knows the future as well as the past. But now suppose He knows that Paul will perform some trivial action tomorrow—having an orange for lunch, let's say. If God knows in advance that Paul will have an orange for lunch tomorrow, then it must be the case that he'll have an orange tomorrow; and if it *must* be the case that Paul will have an orange tomorrow, then it isn't possible that Paul will *refrain* from so doing—in which case he won't be free to refrain, and hence won't be free with respect to the action of taking the orange. So if God knows in advance that a person will perform a certain action *A*, then that person isn't free with respect to that action. But if God is omniscient, then for any person and any action he performs, God knew in advance that he'd perform that action. So if God is omniscient, no one ever performs any free actions.

From Alvin Plantinga, *God, Freedom, and Evil* (Grand Rapids: William B. Eerdmans, 1974), pp. 66–72.

This argument may initially sound plausible, but the fact is it is based upon confusion. The central portion can be stated as follows:

(49) If God knows in advance that X will do A, then it must be the case that X will do A

and

(50) If it must be the case that X will do A, then X is not free to refrain from A.

From (49) and (50) it follows that if God knows in advance that someone will take a certain action, then that person isn't free with respect to that action. But (49) bears further inspection. Why should we think it's *true*? Because, we shall be told, if God *knows* that X will do A, it *logically follows* that X will do A: it's necessary that if God knows that p, then p is true. But this defense of (49) suggests that the latter is *ambiguous*, it may mean either

(49a) Necessarily, if God knows in advance that X will do A, then indeed X will do A

or

(49b) If God knows in advance that X will do A, then it is necessary that X will do A.

The atheological argument requires the truth of (49b); but the above defense of (49) supports only (49a), not (49b). It is indeed necessarily true that if God (or anyone else) knows that a proposition P is true, then P is true; but it simply doesn't follow that if God knows P, then P is *necessarily* true. *If I know that Henry is a bachelor, then Henry is a bachelor* is a necessary truth; it does not follow that if I know that Henry is bachelor, then it is necessarily true that he is. I know that Henry is a bachelor: what follows is only that *Henry is married* is false; it doesn't follow that it is necessarily false.

So the claim that divine omniscience is incompatible with human freedom seems to be based upon confusion. Nelson Pike has suggested[1] an interesting revision of this old claim: he holds, not that human freedom is incompatible with God's being omniscient, but with God's being *essentially* omniscient. Recall that an object X has a property P *essentially* if X has P in every world in which X exists—if, that is, it is impossible that X should have existed but *lacked* P. Now many theologians and philosophers have held that at least some of God's important properties are essential to him in this sense. It is plausible to hold, for example, that God is essentially omnipotent. Things could have gone differently in various ways; but if there had been no omnipotent being, then God would not have existed. *He* couldn't have been powerless or limited in power. But the same may be said for God's *omniscience*. If God is omniscient, then He is unlimited in knowledge; He knows every true proposition and believes none that are false. If He is *essentially* omniscient, furthermore, then He not only *is not* limited in knowledge; He *couldn't* have been.

---

[1] Nelson Pike, "Divine Omniscience and Voluntary Action," *Philosophical Review* 74 (January 1965), 27.

There is no possible world in which He exists but fails to know some truth or believes some falsehood. And Pike's claim is that this belief—the belief that God is essentially omnipotent—is inconsistent with human freedom.

To argue his case Pike considers the case of Jones, who mowed his lawn at T_2—last Saturday, let's say. Now suppose that God is essentially omniscient. Then at any earlier time T_1—80 years ago, for example—God believed that Jones would mow his lawn at T_2. Since He is *essentially* omniscient, furthermore, it isn't possible that God falsely believes something; hence His having believed at T_1 that Jones would mow his lawn at T_2 entails that Jones does indeed mow his lawn at T_2. Pike's argument (in his own words) then goes as follows:

1. "God existed at T_1" entails "If Jones did X at T_2, God believed at T_1 that Jones would do X at T_2."

2. "God believes X" entails "X is true."

3. It is not within one's power at a given time to do something having a description that is logically contradictory.

4. It is not within one's power at a given time to do something that would bring it about that someone who held a certain belief at a time prior to the time in question did not hold that belief at the time prior to the time in question.

5. It is not within one's power at a given time to do something that would bring it about that a person who existed at an earlier time did not exist at that earlier time.

6. If God existed at T_1 and if God believed at T_1 that Jones would do X at T_2, then if it was within Jones' power at T_2 to refrain from doing X, then (1) it was within Jones' power at T_2 to do something that would have brought it about that God held a false belief at T_1, or (2) it was within Jones' power at T_2 to do something which would have brought it about that God did not hold the belief He held at T_1, or (3) it was within Jones' power at T_2 to do something that would have brought it about that any person who believed at T_1 that Jones would do X at T_2 (one of whom was, by hypothesis, God) held a false belief and thus was not God—that is, that God (who by hypothesis existed at T_1) did not exist at T_1.

7. Alternative 1 in the consequent of item 6 is false (from 2 and 3).

8. Alternative 2 in the consequent of item 6 is false (from 4).

9. Alternative 3 in the consequent of item 6 is false (from 5).

10. Therefore, if God existed at T_1 and if God believed at T_1 that Jones would do X at T_2, then it was not within Jones' power at T_2 to refrain from doing X (from 1 and 10).[2]

What about this argument? The first two premises simply make explicit part of what is involved in the idea that God is essentially omniscient; so there

---

[2] Ibid., pp. 33–34.

is no quarreling with them. Premises 3–5 also seem correct. But that complicated premise (6) warrants a closer look. What exactly does it say? I think we can understand Pike here as follows. Consider

(51) God existed at T_1, and God believed at T_1 that Jones would do X at T_2, and it was within Jones' power to refrain from doing X at T_2.

What Pike means to say, I believe, is that either (51) entails

(52) It was within Jones' power at T_2 to do something that would have brought it about that God held a false belief at T_1

or (51) entails

(53) It was within Jones' power at T_2 to do something that would have brought it about that God did not hold the belief He did hold at T_1

or it entails

(54) It was within Jones' power at T_2 to do something that would have brought it about that anyone who believed at T_1 that Jones would do X at T_2 (one of whom was by hypothesis God) held a false belief and thus was not God—that is, that God (who by hypothesis existed at T_1) did not exist at T_1.

[The remainder of Pike's reasoning consists in arguing that each of (52), (53), and (54) is necessarily false, if God is essentially omniscient, which means that God's being essentially omniscient is incompatible with human freedom.] Now suppose we look at these one at a time. Does (51) entail (52)? No. (52) says that it was within Jones' power to do something—namely, refrain from doing X—such that if he had done that thing, then God *would have* held a false belief at T_1. But this does not follow from (51). If Jones had refrained from X, then a proposition that God *did in fact* believe would have been false; but if Jones had refrained from X at T_2, then God (since He is omniscient) *would not have believed at T_1 that Jones will do X at T_2*—indeed, He would have held the true belief that Jones will *refrain* from doing X at T_2. What follows from (51) is not (52) but only (52'):

(52') It was within Jones' power to do something such that if he had done it, then a belief that God *did hold* at T_1 *would have been false*.

But (52') is not at all paradoxical and in particular does not imply that it was within Jones' power to do something that would have brought it about that God held a false belief.

Perhaps we can see this more clearly if we look at it from the vantage point of possible worlds. We are told by (51) both that in the actual world God believes that Jones does X at T_2 and also that it is within Jones' power to *refrain* from doing X at T_2. Now consider any world W in which Jones *does* refrain from doing X. In *that* world, a belief that God holds in the actual world—in Kronos—is false. That is, if W had been actual, then a belief that God does *in fact* hold would have been false. But it does not follow that in W God holds a false belief. For it doesn't follow that if W had been actual, God would have believed that Jones would do X at T_2. Indeed, if God is essentially omniscient

(omniscient in every world in which He exists) what follows is that in *W* God did *not* believe at T_1 that Jones will do *X* at T_2. He believed instead that Jones will *refrain* from *X*. So (51) by no means implies that it was within Jones' power to bring it about that God held a false belief at T_1.

What about

(53) It was within Jones' power at T_2 to do something that would have brought it about that God did not hold the belief He did hold at T_1?

Here the first problem is one of understanding. How are we to take this proposition? One way is this. What (53) says is that it was within Jones' power, at T_2, to do something such that if he had done it, then at T_1 God would have held a certain belief and also *not* held that belief. That is, (53) so understood attributes to Jones the power to bring about a contradictory state of affairs [call this interpretation (53a)]. (53a) is obviously and resoundingly false; but there is no reason whatever to think that (51) entails it. What (51) entails is rather

(53b) It was within Jones' power at T_2 to do something such that if he had done it, then God would not have held a belief that in fact he did hold.

This follows from (51) but is perfectly innocent. For suppose again that (51) is true, and consider a world *W* in which Jones refrains from doing *X*. If God is essentially omniscient, then in this world *W* He is omniscient and hence does not believe at T_1 that Jones will do *X* at T_2. So what follows from (51) is the harmless assertion that it was within Jones' power to do something such that if he had done it, then God would not have held a belief that in fact (in the actual world) He did hold. But by no stretch of the imagination does it follow that if Jones had done it, then it would have been true that God *did* hold a belief He didn't hold. Taken one way (53) is obviously false but not a consequence of (51); taken the other it is a consequence of (51) but by no means obviously false.

(54) fares no better. What it says is that it was within Jones' power at T_2 to do something such that if he had done it, then God would not have been omniscient and thus would not have been God. But this simply doesn't follow from (51). The latter does, of course, entail

(54′) It was within Jones' power to do something such that if he'd done it, then anyone who believed at T_1 that Jones would do *X* at T_2 would have held a false belief.

For suppose again that (51) is in fact true, and now consider one of those worlds *W* in which Jones refrains from doing *X*. In that world

(55) Anyone who believed at T_1 that Jones will do *X* at T_2 held a false belief

is true. That is, if *W* had been actual, (55) would have been true. But again in *W* God does not believe that Jones will do *X* at T_2; (55) is *true* in *W* but isn't relevant to God there. If Jones had refrained from *X*, then (55) would have been true. It does not follow that God would not have been omniscient; for in those worlds in which Jones does not do *X* at T_2, God does not believe at T_1 that He does.

Perhaps the following is a possible source of confusion here. If God is *essentially* omniscient, then He is omniscient in every possible world in which He exists. Accordingly there is no possible world in which He holds a false belief. Now consider any belief that God does in fact hold. It might be tempting to suppose that if He is essentially omniscient, then He holds that belief in every world in which He exists. But of course this doesn't follow. It is not essential to Him to hold the beliefs He does hold; what is essential to Him is the quite different property of holding only true beliefs. So if a belief is true in Kronos but false in some world *W*, then in Kronos God holds that belief and in *W* He does not.

II.C.   Divine Goodness

II.C.1.   The Goodness of God

THOMAS AQUINAS

Thomas Aquinas (1224–1274), the great systematizer of Catholic theology, offers interpretations in his writings of all of the traditional attributes of God. Here he argues that God and God alone is essentially good, and that the goodness of other things is measured by its resemblance to the goodness of God. God's goodness is identical with his being. Indeed, everything is good to the extent that it has being, because evil is precisely the lack of being in a way similar to the way in which darkness is an absence of light. Aquinas is reflecting Aristotle's philosophy of degrees of being or actuality: God is pure actuality with no admixture of potentiality; thus God is supremely good.

QUESTION VI: THE GOODNESS OF GOD (In Four Articles)

We next consider the goodness of God, under which head there are four points of inquiry: (1) Whether to be good belongs to God? (2) Whether God is the

---

From *Summa Theologica*, in Anton C. Pegis, *An Introduction to St. Thomas Aquinas* (New York: Random House, 1945), pp. 46–52. Reprinted by permission.

highest good? (3) Whether He alone is essentially good? (4) Whether all things are good by the divine goodness?

First Article: Whether to be Good Belongs to God?

We proceed thus to the First Article:—

Objection 1. It seems that to be good does not belong to God. For goodness consists in limit, species and order. But these do not seem to belong to God, since God is immense, and is not ordered to anything. Therefore to be good does not belong to God.

Objection 2. Further, the good is what all things desire. But all things do not desire God, because all things do not know Him; and nothing is desired unless it is known. Therefore to be good does not belong to God.

On the contrary, It is written (*Lam.* iii. 25): *The Lord is good to them that hope in Him, to the soul that seeketh Him.*

I answer that, To be good belongs pre-eminently to God. For a thing is good according to its desirableness. Now everything seeks after its own perfection, and the perfection and form of an effect consist in a certain likeness to the agent, since every agent makes its like; and hence the agent itself is desirable and has the nature of good. For the very thing which is desirable in it is the participation of its likeness. Therefore, since God is the first producing cause of all things, it is manifest that the aspect of good and of desirableness belong to Him; and hence Dionysius attributes good to God as to the first efficient cause, saying that *God is called good as by Whom all things subsist.*

Reply Objection 1. To have limit, species and order belongs to the essence of caused good; but good is in God as in its cause, and hence it belongs to Him to impose limit, species and order on others; wherefore these three things are in God as in their cause.

Reply Objection 2. All things, by desiring their own perfection, desire God Himself, inasmuch as the perfections of all things are so many similitudes of the divine being, as appears from what is said above. And so of those beings which desire God, some know Him as He is in Himself, and this is proper to a rational creature; others know some participation of His goodness, and this belongs also to sensible knowledge; and others have a natural desire without knowledge, as being directed to their ends by a higher knower.

Second Article: Whether God is the Highest Good?

We proceed thus to the Second Article:—

Objection 1. It seems that God is not the *highest* good. For the *highest* good adds something to good, or otherwise it would belong to every good. But everything which is an addition to anything else is a composite thing: therefore the highest good is composite. But God is supremely simple, as was shown above. Therefore God is not the highest good.

Objection 2. Further, *Good is what all desire*, as the Philosopher says. Now what all desire is nothing but God, Who is the end of all things: therefore there is no other good but God. This appears also from what is said (*Luke* xviii. 19): *None is good but God alone.* But we use the word highest in comparison with others, as, *e.g.*, the highest hot thing is used in comparison with all other hot things. Therefore God cannot be called the highest good.

Objection 3. Further, highest implies comparison. But things not in the same genus are not comparable; as sweetness is not properly called greater or less than a line. Therefore, since God is not in the same genus as other good things, as appears above, it seems that God cannot be called the highest good in relation to them.

On the contrary, Augustine says that the Trinity of the divine persons *is the highest good, discerned by purified minds.*

I answer that, God is the highest good absolutely, and not only in any genus or order of things. For good is attributed to God, as was said, inasmuch as all desired perfections flow from Him as from the first cause. They do not, however, flow from Him as from a univocal agent, as was shown above, but as from an agent that does not agree with its effects either in species or genus. Now the likeness of an effect in the univocal cause is found uniformly; but in the equivocal cause it is found more excellently, as heat is in the sun more excellently than it is in fire. Therefore as good is in God as in the first, but not the univocal, cause of all things, it must be in Him in a most excellent way; and therefore He is called the highest good.

Reply Objection 1. The highest good does not add to good any absolute thing, but only a relation. Now a relation, by which something is said of God relatively to creatures, is not really in God, but in the creature, for it is in God in our idea only. In the same way, what is knowable is so called with relation to knowledge, not that it depends on knowledge, but because knowledge depends on it. Thus it is not necessary that there should be composition in the highest good, but only that other things be deficient in comparison with it.

Reply Objection 2. When we say that *good is what all desire,* it is not to be understood that every kind of good thing is desired by all, but that whatever is desired has the nature of good. And when it is said, *None is good but God alone,* this is to be understood of the essentially good, as will be explained.

Reply Objection 3. Things not of the same genus are in no way comparable to each other if they are in diverse genera. Now we say that God is not in the same genus with other good things. This does not mean that He is in any other genus, but that He is outside genus, and is the principle of every genus. Thus He is compared to others by excess, and it is this kind of comparison that the highest good implies.

Third Article: Whether to be Essentially Good Belongs to God Alone?

We proceed thus to the Third Article:—

Objection 1. It seems that to be essentially good does not belong to God alone. For as *one* is convertible with *being,* so is *good,* as we said above. But every being is one essentially, as appears from the Philosopher. Therefore every being is good essentially.

Objection 2. Further, if good is what all things desire, since being itself is desired by all, then the being of each thing is its good. But everything is a being essentially: therefore every being is good essentially.

Objection 3. Further, everything is good by its own goodness. Therefore if there is anything which is not good essentially, it is necessary to say that its goodness is not its own essence. Therefore its goodness, since it is a being, must be good; and if it is good by some other goodness, the same question applies to that goodness also. Therefore we must either proceed to infinity, or come to some goodness which is not good by any other goodness. Therefore the first supposition holds good. Therefore everything is good essentially.

On the contrary, Boethius says that *all things but God are good by participation*. Therefore they are not good essentially.

I answer that, God alone is good essentially. For everything is called good according to its perfection. Now perfection in a thing is threefold: first, according to the constitution of its own being; secondly, in respect of any accidents being added as necessary for its perfect operation; thirdly, perfection consists in the attaining to something else as the end. Thus, for instance, the first perfection of fire consists in its being, which it has through its own substantial form; its secondary perfection consists in heat, lightness and dryness, and the like; its third perfection is to rest in its own place. This triple perfection belongs to no creature by its own essence; it belongs to God only, Whose essence alone is His being, in Whom there are no accidents, since whatever belongs to others accidentally belongs to Him essentially: *e.g.*, to be powerful, wise, and the like, as appears from what is stated above. Furthermore, He is not directed to anything else as to an end, but is Himself the last end of all things. Hence it is manifest that God alone has every kind of perfection by His own essence, and therefore He alone is good essentially.

Reply Objection 1. *One* does not include the idea of perfection, but only of indivision, which belongs to everything according to its own essence. Now the essences of simple things are undivided both actually and potentially, but the essences of composite things are undivided only actually; and therefore everything must be one essentially, but not good essentially, as was shown above.

Reply Objection 2. Although everything is good in that it has being, yet the essence of a creature is not being itself, and therefore it does not follow that a creature is good essentially.

Reply Objection 3. The goodness of a creature is not its very essence, but something superadded; it is either its being, or some added perfection, or the order to its end. Still, the goodness itself thus added is called good, just as it is called being. But it is called being because by it something has being, not because it itself has being through something else. Hence it is called good because by it something is good, and not because it itself has some other goodness whereby it is good.

Fourth Article: Whether All Things Are Good by the Divine Goodness?

We proceed thus to the Fourth Article:—

Objection 1. It seems that all things are good by the divine goodness. For Augustine says: *This and that are good. Take away this and that, and see good itself if thou canst; and so thou shalt see God, good not by any other good, but the good of every good*. But everything is good by its own good: therefore everything is good by that very good which is God.

Objection 2. Further, as Boethius says, all things are called good according as they are directed to God, and this is by reason of the divine goodness: therefore all things are good by the divine goodness.

On the contrary, All things are good inasmuch as they have being. But they are not called beings through the divine being, but through their own being: therefore all things are not good by divine goodness, but by their own goodness.

I answer that, As regards relative things, we may admit extrinsic denomination. Thus, a thing is denominated *placed* from *place*, and *measured* from *measure*. But as regards what is said absolutely, opinions differ. Plato held the separate existence of the essences of all things, and that individuals were denominated by them as participating in the separate essences; for instance, that Socrates is called man according to the separate Form of man. Now just as he laid down separate Forms of man and horse which he called absolute man and absolute horse, so likewise he laid down separate Forms of *being* and of *one*, and these he called absolute being and absolute oneness, and by participation in these everything was called *being* or *one*. What was thus absolute being and absolute one, he said was the highest good. And because good is convertible with being, as is also one, he called the absolute good God, from whom all things are called good by way of participation.

Although this opinion appears to be unreasonable in affirming that there are separate forms of natural things subsisting of themselves—as Aristotle argues in many ways—still, it is absolutely true that there is something first which is essentially being and essentially good, which we call God, as appears from what is shown above. Aristotle agrees with this. Hence from the first being, essentially being and good, everything can be called good and a being inasmuch as it participates in the first being by way of a certain assimilation, although distantly and defectively, as appears from the above.

Everything is therefore called good from the divine goodness, as from the first exemplary, effective and final principle of all goodness. Nevertheless, everything is called good by reason of the likeness of the divine goodness belonging to it, which is formally its own goodness, whereby it is denominated good. And so of all things there is one goodness, and yet many goodnesses.

This is a sufficient Reply to the Objections.

II.C.2. Duty and Divine Goodness

THOMAS V. MORRIS

Thomas V. Morris (1952–) is assistant professor of philosophy at the University of Notre Dame. In this article he discusses the duty model of divine goodness according to which God always acts in accordance with universal moral principles and also performs acts of supererogation. But to do one's duty is to act freely. If God necessarily does what morality requires, he seems to lack freedom, which implies that he has no duties and that his acts have no moral worth. Morris offers an analogical version of the duty model, arguing that a being who always acts according to the requirements of morality and performs the works of supererogation is good in the highest sense.

Throughout the history of western theology, divine goodness has been explicated in a number of different ways. Central among these is the important religious claim that God is morally good. This form of divine goodness usually is thought to consist in God's acting always in accordance with universal moral principles, satisfying without fail moral duties and engaging in acts of gracious supererogation. Divine moral goodness is understood basically on the model of human moral goodness. Let us refer to the part of this conception having to do with duty as "the duty model" of divine goodness. According to the common employment of this model, God like us has moral duties, but unlike us satisfies those duties perfectly.

Now of course God is not thought on any reasonable construal of the duty model to have all and only those moral duties also had by human beings. We, for example, have a duty to worship God and be thankful for his benefits. Presumably, he has no such duty. Conversely, in virtue of his exalted role *vis à vis* the entire universe, God may well have duties shared by no one else, and even of which we have no conception. So divine and human duties presumably diverge. But it is a widespread and fundamental religious belief that they must also overlap. If God deigns to communicate with us, he will speak the truth, in accordance with a universal duty. Likewise, if he makes a promise, he will keep it, consistent with another general duty. This area of overlap between human and divine obligation is vital to religious faith. In our ability to know moral principles which bind human conduct we have the ability to anticipate features of divine activity. The belief that such duties as truthtelling and promise-keeping govern divine conduct grounds the trust the religious believer has in God.

Yet two other common, and also quite important, traditional theistic

---

From Thomas V. Morris, "Duty and Divine Goodness." *American Philosophical Quarterly* 21, no. 3 (July 1984): 261–263, 265–268.

commitments create a serious logical problem for the duty model of divine goodness. I shall indicate what this problem is, comment on some unsatisfactory attempts to avoid it, and then propose an adequate solution which involves a new account of the way in which the notion of a moral duty can be used to characterize divine action.

I

A great many theists favor a libertarian (agent-causation) analysis of free action. Nearly all are committed to a libertarian account of divine action. At the same time, it is a standard theistic belief that God is necessarily good, that goodness is an essential property of the individual who in fact, and of necessity, is God. If God is necessarily good, and part of what that goodness involves is given by the duty model, then it follows that God necessarily acts in accordance with moral principles. But if this is so, a quite modest libertarian principle will entail that God does not exemplify the kind of freedom requisite for being a moral agent with any duties at all. On this principle it will be logically impossible for any individual to have moral duties he necessarily satisfies. In short, there can be no necessarily good moral agent. It is this entailment which will generate our problem. The logical problem then is one of compatibility among three common theistic commitments: (1) the duty model of divine goodness, (2) a libertarian account of moral freedom, and (3) the claim that God is necessarily good.

Most accounts of free action include a condition to the effect that an act is performed freely only if its agent in some sense *could have done otherwise*. The libertarian characteristically insists on a strong, categorical construal of this condition. It is exceeding difficult to stage an unproblematic formulation of this requirement, but it is clear that it must contain *at least* the relatively modest principle that an agent S performs an act A at a time t freely only if no conditions exist prior to t which render it necessary, or unavoidable, in a broadly logical sense, and by doing so in fact bring it about, that S performs A.[1] Let us refer to this condition as the Principle of Avoidance (PA). The libertarian will insist on conditions a good deal more stringent than PA as well, but at least all forms of the libertarian account of freedom will incorporate this requirement, and it is all that is needed to produce our problem. According to the libertarian, it is only acts satisfying this minimal condition which are free acts. And only free acts are morally characterizable as the satisfaction or violation of duties.

PA is to be understood as specifying that whenever there are *any* conditions prior to the time of an act (other than any immediately efficacious decision or intention of the agent to perform that act) which render it in a broadly logical sense unavoidable, it is not a morally characterizable act. Such an act will be judged not to exemplify the sort of freedom necessary for its being morally assessable. Likewise, any *feature* of an act which is such that it can not be avoided by the agent is not such that the agent is morally responsible for it. And this in particular is relevant to the case of God.

Suppose God promises to bless Abraham. If God necessarily acts in accordance with moral principles, it seems that once the promise is made he is logically bound, bound in such a way as to deprive him of the freedom the libertarian analysis requires of a morally characterizable act. Suppose the promise is made at t to bless Abraham at $t + n$. At that later time is God free to bless and free to refrain from blessing Abraham, all relevant prior conditions remaining the same? If he is free to refrain, he is free to break a promise. But God can be free to break a promise only if there is a possible world in which he does so. And if he is necessarily good, there is no such world. Jonathan Edwards once put this point strongly by saying:

> God's absolute promise of any things make the things promised
> necessary and their failing to take place impossible. . . . [2]

There is no possible world containing both a promise of God's and the everlasting lack of that promise's fulfillment. So when God blesses Abraham, his act of blessing fails to satisfy PA. Conditions prior to the time of his act render it necessary, or unavoidable, in a broadly logical sense that he perform that act. Thus, on the libertarian analysis, it is not morally characterizable, and so cannot count as the fulfillment of a duty. And surely this result of PA will be entirely general. From the necessity of God's acting in accordance with moral principles, it will follow, for example that no divine act can possibly constitute in a moral sense the keeping of a promise, and so it will follow that God cannot make any promises at all. Likewise, analogous reasoning will show that God cannot act in such a way as to *morally* satisfy *any* duty, and thus cannot be such as to have any moral duties at all. [3]

It should be pointed out at this stage that libertarian principles do not entail that God is not in any sense free. Nor do they entail that by making a promise he would deprive himself of all freedom with respect to the act promised. God always has a range of free choice, but the argument is that it is not such as to ground moral characterization with respect to duty. For example, if God were to promise to give Abraham a son, he could not then do otherwise. But suppose that in keeping his promise he gives Abraham Isaac. The exact way in which he keeps the promise is such that he could have done otherwise. He could have given Abraham another son. It was in no sense necessary or unavoidable that he give Abraham Isaac. There is always this sort of "open texture" to promises and promise-keeping. This sort of freedom God does have. And of course God is presumably free with regard to whether he will ever make such a promise in the first place. So God is free both to promise and not to promise. Likewise he is free in exactly how he keeps the promise. He lacks freedom only with respect to whatever feature of a state of affairs or event will render his actualization of it the keeping of his promise. He is not free to refrain from bringing it about that something have that particular feature. Given prior conditions, it is necessary or unavoidable in the broadly logical sense that he bring that about. So on the libertarian analysis he is not free in his bringing it about that that feature obtain.

The case of truth-telling may serve to highlight these distinctions. Suppose God chooses to reveal some proposition P at time t. If he is necessarily good, then anything he asserts must be true. He cannot lie. Now according to PA, why can't we count God's telling the truth in uttering P at t as the satisfaction of a moral duty not to lie? Is God free to assert P at t and free to refrain from asserting P at t? Surely circumstances are easily conceivable in which this is so, in which God's revealing *P* satisfies the Principle of Avoidance. He could have revealed some other true proposition *Q* instead, or just have chosen not to communicate anything at *t*. His act of revelation is thus in this sense a free act. But the libertarian principle generates the following argument: At *t* God freely tells a truth. But there is a sense in which he could not have done otherwise. He could not have asserted intentionally a falsehood at *t*. This is the morally significant alternative from which he is debarred by his character. And his having such a character is a condition which obtains, and obtains of necessity, prior to *t*. If he chooses to communicate, God cannot refrain from bringing about that feature of an assertion which alone would render its utterance the satisfaction of a duty not to lie. If he decides to speak his goodness logically necessitates his telling the truth. So on the libertarian analysis, since he is not free to utter a falsehood knowingly, he does not have the sort of freedom requisite for his uttering a true statement to count as morally characterizable, and thus as the satisfaction of any duty. . . .

I would like to suggest that there is a way of applying the duty model to God which avoids completely the logical problem which otherwise arises between the libertarian account of freedom, the claim that God is necessarily good, and the use of that model as at least a partial explication of what religious people mean to convey when they ascribe goodness to God. Should it be judged successful, there will be no need to give up any of the three commitments which have seemed to form an inconsistent triad. If what I have to suggest is right, employing the duty model as at least a partial explication of divine goodness need not commit one to holding that God actually has any duties at all. A fairly simple distinction will render intelligible this admittedly paradoxical claim.

For a number of years, philosophers have drawn a distinction between following a rule and merely acting in accordance with a rule. Behavior which results from obeying a rule can be distinguished logically from behavior which otherwise accords with that rule, even though the two may be empirically indistinguishable to an observer. Although we cannot appropriate this precise distinction to solve our problem, the application of this *sort* of distinction to our employment of the duty model of divine goodness is relatively simple and will give us exactly what we need. We can hold that those moral principles which function as either deontically prescriptive or proscriptive for human conduct stand in some other relation to divine conduct. We could even go so far as to claim that they are merely descriptive of the shape of divine activity. But the important difference is as follows. We human beings exist in a state of being *bound* by moral duty. In this state we act under obligation, either satisfying or contravening our duties. Because of his distinctive nature, God does not share our ontological status. Specifically, he does not share our relation to moral principles—that of being bound by some of these principles as duties. Nevertheless, God acts *in accordance with* those principles which would express duties for a moral agent in his relevant circumstances. And he does so necessarily. So although God does not literally have any duties on this construal of the duty model, we still can have well grounded expectations concerning divine conduct by knowing those moral principles which would govern the conduct of a perfect, duty bound moral agent who acted as God in fact does act. We understand and anticipate God's activity in analogy with the behavior of a completely good moral agent. And this is an application of analogy in our understanding of God which in no way impedes that understanding. On this application of the duty model, just as much as on its literal employment, we know that if God says that he will do A, then he will do A. We can depend on it. Likewise, if he communicates any proposition, we can be assured that it will be a true one. When we use the duty model in this way, we retain all that is religiously important about it while avoiding the problems a literal application would generate.

A couple of objections to this application of the duty model easily come to mind. First, it might be pointed out that on this interpretation, God can never actually make any promises, since promising generates literal duties. And this surely seems counter-intuitive. Don't traditional theists often talk of "the promises of God"?

There is no substance to this objection. R. L. Franklin has characterized the purpose of promising as "that of committing a man reliably to future acts."[4] God can certainly declare his intention to bless Abraham, thereby committing himself reliably to do so (where 'committing himself' amounts to intentionally generating justified expectations in his hearers). The libertarian can hold that in making this sort of declaration God is doing something for his creatures with an effect analogous to that of promising, or even that in an analogical sense he is making a promise. In holding that God cannot literally make promises, the libertarian would only be acknowledging in a particular type of case that the relation holding between God and moral principles is different from that holding between us and those moral principles. And so long as God necessarily acts in the way a perfectly good moral agent would act, nothing of religious importance is lost in this difference.

A more substantial objection would go as follows. If God does not actually have any moral duties he satisfies, we have no basis on which to praise him. Praise, according to this line of thought, is appropriate only for acts which satisfy moral duties, and only for agents in so far as they perform such acts. On this understanding of praise, a theology which claims that God can have no duties thereby debars God from ever being praiseworthy.

This objection is based on a very common mistaken assumption about moral praise. It is the position that fulfillment of duty, and that alone, merits praise. I would argue, on the contrary, that praise is never strictly appropriate for duty satisfactions. The proper response of one moral agent to another when the latter has done his duty, and when none other than moral considerations obtain, is something weaker than, and distinct from, praise. One who does his duty ought to be morally acknowledged, accepted, or commended by his fellows, not praised. Admittedly, in this world of ours, where duty fulfillment under difficult conditions is somewhat rare, there can be significant social utility in praising such accomplishment. But strictly speaking, praise is morally proper only for acts of supererogation.

God's lacking duties, then, will not amount to his being unworthy of praise. In so far as he actualizes great value he is not bound to bring about, he is worthy of praise. For example, when God "makes a promise," do we praise him for being so good as to keep it? I think not. When he speaks to his people, is he praised for restraining himself from lying? Clearly not. What we praise him for is for condescending to make us promises or communicate with us at all, for deigning to involve himself at all in our small lives. And these are acts of supererogation, not fulfillments of duty.

Are there any costs incurred by employing the duty model in this new analogical manner? It might seem that at least we lose any answer for such questions as "Why does God keep his promises?" or "Why does God do what is morally right?" We can no longer say "Because he ought to." But actually nothing is lost. It can be maintained that as a maximally perfect being, God necessarily acts in accordance with those principles which lesser beings ought to comply with. This is his nature. And as his activity and nature is, in a less than Cartesian sense, the ground of all possibility, it is impossible that he not so act. We would have a troubling unanswered question about his activity only if it were a contingent fact that his conduct accords perfectly with moral principles. But of course, the traditional theist denies that this is a contingent matter.

IV

One final question remains. In applying the duty model in an analogical manner, are we any longer giving an account of God's *goodness*? Can divine goodness even partially consist in God's acting in accordance with moral principles if none of those principles provides him with moral duties? The most obvious answer to this may seem to be—no. Human action in accord with moral principles can count as the moral satisfaction of duties, because of the nature of the human condition. Our ontological status and our freedom is such that we have duties we can morally fulfill and thereby count as good agents. With the analogical deployment of the duty model, the theist could say that it is not strictly true that God's goodness partly consists in his acting in accordance with moral principles. With this model, we are just explicating part of what religious people usually *mean to convey* when they say that God is good. Strictly speaking, God's non-metaphysical goodness consists only in his disposition to, and effectuation of, supererogatory activity.

But this answer is not forced on the theist. It seems at least possible to argue without absurdity that some conditions for goodness vary with the ontological status of the agent concerned. I have referred to both moral and metaphysical goodness in the case of God. It is possible to treat both these sorts of goodness as species of a broader category of what we might call "axiological goodness." To be an agent, such as a human being, who gladly engages in deeds of supererogation and freely acts in accordance with moral principles, satisfying moral duties, is to be in a state of axiological goodness. To be an agent such as God who freely engages in acts of grace, or supererogation, but necessarily acts in accordance with moral principles, is to be in the greatest possible state of axiological goodness. It may be held that for human beings, axiological goodness and moral goodness coincide. For God, however, one form of moral goodness (supererogation) is a component of his axiological goodness; whereas another aspect of his axiological goodness is his necessarily acting in accordance with moral principles—not literally a form of moral goodness at all on the libertarian analysis, but on this view a contributing element or aspect of divine axiological goodness.

On this possible view, God's intentionally acting in accordance with what for us are moral principles specifying duties would be sufficient, given his nature and ontological status, for that conduct counting as good, not morally but axiologically. Axiological agency need not be thought of as logically incompatible, on every ontological level, with all forms of necessitation. Brand Blanshard once argued that being determined by the moral law is, unlike being causally determined by prior states of the physical universe, a condition of the highest (i.e. most valuable) sort of freedom.[5] Of course, because of PA the libertarian cannot hold this to be true of moral freedom. But it could be reasonable for the libertarian theist to hold that a form of moral necessitation is compatible with, indeed a condition of, God's being a perfectly good axiological agent, a greater than which is not possible.

With these distinctions in hand, the theist could say that an analogical employment of the duty model is indeed a partial explication of divine goodness. Part of God's goodness does consist in his acting in perfect accord with those principles which would provide duties for a lesser being. This use of the model would be an explication not of God's moral goodness, but of his axiological goodness. When religious people claim that God is morally good, meaning that he acts in accord with moral principles, they are merely using that axiological conception with which they are most familiar, moral goodness, to describe or model an aspect of divinity functionally isomorphic with, though ontologically different from, human goodness. The point of importance here is that either answer to our question could be defended, whichever is preferred. And neither is obviously inimical to traditional theology.

It seems then that a traditional theist can hold to (1) a libertarian analysis of free action, (2) the position that God is necessarily good, and (3) the duty model of divine goodness without incurring any logical inconsistency among these commitments just by employing the duty model in a carefully controlled analogical manner. The resolution of the problem we have examined seems to be attended by no peculiar difficulties of its own, and seems to be perfectly consistent with any broadly orthodox theology in the Judeo-Christian tradition. And as the same problem of logical consistency may arise on any plausible analysis of free action, this new understanding of the duty model of divine goodness may be of importance to any traditional theist, whatever reasonable position he adopts concerning the conditions of moral freedom.

NOTES

1. The principle stated here circumvents well known counter-examples to the stronger Principle of Alternate Possibilities. See for example Harry Frankfurt's "Alternate Possibilities and Moral Responsibility," *The Journal of Philosophy*, vol. 66 (1969).

2. *Freedom of the Will*, ed. Paul Ramsey (New Haven, 1957), p. 283.

3. The argument here treats God as a temporal agent lacking power to change the past, but this is strictly unnecessary for the generation of our problem. Note also that the inference bears a superficial resemblance to, but on reflection can be seen not to commit, a famous modal fallacy.

4. *Free Will and Determinism* (New York, 1968), p. 41.

5. See "The Case For Determinism," in *Determinism and Freedom in the Age of Modern Science*, ed. by Sidney Hook (New York, 1958).

II.D. Personality

II.D.1. The Personal God and a God Who Is a Person

ADRIAN THATCHER

Adrian Thatcher teaches at the College of St. Mark and St. John, Plymouth. Here he examines Richard Swinburne's definition of God as a person without a body. Thatcher finds serious problems with such a conception, concluding that although most Christians and perhaps most theists have thought of God as personal, for a number of good reasons we do not properly think of God as a person.

If one believes in a personal God, must one also believe that God is a person? I hold that the former is essential to Christian faith, the latter an impediment to it. Several recent writers in the philosophy of religion have however assumed that to believe in God *is* to believe in a person. The most subtle and influential proponent of 'bodiless person theism' is Richard Swinburne. I hope to show that this philosophical presentation of theism is unwarrantable and misrepresents what the theological tradition says about God. In section (I) I describe how Swinburne justifies his view that God is a person. In section (II) I show that this view is defective. In section (III) I uncover a common, though mistaken, procedure among several other advocates of this type of theism. In section (IV) I suggest that the belief that God is a person is foreign to Christian theology, with the unfortunate consequence that a philosophical defense of it is not only mistaken: it is also pointless.

I

Swinburne's working definition of belief in God, presupposed throughout his recent trilogy of works in philosophical theology, occupies the opening lines of the first volume: 'By a theist I understand a man who believes that there is a God. By a "God" he understand (*sic*) something like a "person without a body (i.e. a spirit) who is eternal, free, able to do anything, knows everything, is perfectly good, is the proper object of human worship and obedience, the

From *Religious Studies*, vol. 21 (1985), pp. 61–67; 71–73. Reprinted with the permission of Cambridge University Press

creator and sustainer of the universe".'[1] The troublesome phrase 'person without a body' is incorporated into the root meaning of belief in God. 'That God is a person, yet one without a body, seems the most elementary claim of theism.'[2] The term 'person' is used in the modern English sense, not the classical sense of *persona* or *hypostasis*.[3] The tendency of 'some recent Protestant theologians' to affirm that God is personal but to deny God is a person on the grounds that the latter pictures God 'as too much like ordinary created persons', is rejected. This is because the differences between the divine person who is God and human persons can be sufficiently picked out by ascribing only to God certain characteristics, e.g. omnipotence, omniscience.[4] The key notion of 'person without a body', thought to be synonymous with 'spirit', is defended at length. I cannot summarize all Swinburne's arguments for the coherence of theism's 'most elementary claim', though I shall identify the main moves. These are (i) a transformation of the concept of person as originally defined by P. F. Strawson; (ii) a Cartesian account of the mind-body relationship; (iii) an attempt to show that the notion 'person without a body' is free from logical objection; and (iv) a non-bodily account of personal identity.

Swinburne uses Strawson's well-known concept of person as the basis for the answer to his own question 'What is a person?'[4],[5] Strawson, it will be recalled, tried to avoid the twin pitfalls of Cartesian dualism (which insists a person is a composite of two substances, mind and body) and outright materialism (which insists a person is a single substance, body only) by a middle position which assumes that a person is a single substance of which two fundamentally different sorts of predicates can be made. These refer either to its physical or its mental properties. A person is 'a type of entity such that *both* predicates ascribing states of consciousness *and* predicates ascribing corporeal characteristics, a physical situation, etc., are equally applicable to an individual entity of the type.'[6] Predicates ascribing states of consciousness are 'P-predicates'; predicates ascribing corporeal characteristics are 'M-predicates'. So 'is cold', 'weighs a ton' are M-predicates: 'is laughing', 'is thinking about his lunch' are P-predicates ascribable only to persons. A weakness of this distinction is that 'states of consciousness' can also be ascribed to some higher animals with the result that the range of application of P-predicates becomes too wide. Swinburne helpfully suggests the difficulty be set right by noting that persons have a capacity for language, private thought, 'second order wants', making moral judgments, and so on. P-predicates could be reserved for these.

This concept of a person lies at the root of the doctrine that God is a person without a body. Swinburne next asks 'whether it is coherent to suppose that there exists a person without a body who is present everywhere'. He thinks it *is* coherent. The argument rests on a transformation of Strawson's concept of

---

[1] Richard Swinburne, *The Coherence of Theism* (Oxford, 1977) p. 1.

[2] *Op. cit.* p. 99.

[3] *Op. cit.* p. 1, note 1; p. 99.

[4] *Op. cit.* pp. 99–100.

[5] *Op. cit.* pp. 99–102.

[6] P. F. Strawson, *Individuals* (London, 1957), p. 102.

person, which begins with the innocent-looking question 'whether the concept of "person" which we have derived from seeing it applied to individuals with bodies is such that it could also be applied to an individual lacking a body.' The question, he continues, is 'not so much about the word "person", but about whether there could be an individual to whom M-predicates did not apply, but to whom many P-predicates did apply . . . If there were such an individual, it would, I suggest, be natural to call him a "person".'

Of course we now have a different concept of a person, viz. one which cannot be the subject of M-predicates. The plausibility of this concept of a person, i.e. a spirit, is defended by asking 'what it is for a person to have a body'.[7] The experience of having a body can be accounted for in five ways. 'When I say that this body is my body' I mean first, 'that disturbances in it cause me pains, aches, tingles, etc.'; second, 'I feel the inside of this body'; third, 'I can move directly many parts of this body'; fourth, 'I look out on the world from where this body is'; and fifth, 'my thoughts and feelings are affected by goings-on in this body'. Clearly, says Swinburne, 'a person has a body if there is a material object to which he is related in any of the above ways'. In the special case of an 'Omnipresent Spirit' a very limited embodiment is allowable on the basis of the third and fourth ways. 'God is supposed to be able to move any part of the universe directly; he does not need to use one part of the universe to make another part move.' And while God does not look out on the world from where his body is, as we are said to do, none the less 'He knows without inference about any states of the world (whether he "sees" it or "feels" it we do not know).' To this limited extent God can be embodied. 'The claim that God has no body is the denial of more substantial embodiment.'

An attempt is made next to show that the idea of a bodiless person is free from logical objections. We are invited to 'imagine . . . that you cease to feel any pains, aches, and thrills, although you remain aware of what is going on in what has been called your body'. We are also to imagine seeing things from any point of view we choose, uttering words which can be heard anywhere, moving the hands of other people, etc. We are then invited to conclude 'Surely anyone can thus conceive of himself becoming an omnipresent spirit. So it seems logically possible that there be such a being. If an opponent still cannot make sense of this description, it should be clear to many a proponent how it could be spelt out more fully.'

More support for the idea of a bodiless person comes from standard philosophical discussions about the nature of personal identity.[8] The traditional means of affirming the continued identity of a person through time, either by bodily continuity, memory or character, are rejected as insufficient, and a theory of personal identity is proposed according to which 'personal identity is something ultimate—unanalysable into conjunctions or disjunctions of other observable properties'. So 'while evidence of continuity of body, memory, and character is evidence of personal identity, personal identity is not constituted by continuity of body, memory and character'. What is it con-

---

[7] Swinburne, *op. cit.* pp. 102–5. His source is Jonathan Harrison, 'The embodiment of mind, or what use is having a body?', *Proceedings of the Aristotelian Society*, LXXIV (1973–4), 33–55.

[8] *Op. cit.* pp. 111–25.

stituted by, then? Swinburne will not say, contenting himself with the view that relevant empirical states of a person cannot in principle provide sufficient evidence for the continued identity of a person, because what is involved in talking about the continued identity of a person rests on non-empirical factors. They are ultimate. And their transcendence over the merely empirical is thought to lend further credibility to the contention that whatever is essential about persons can be divorced from their bodies.

II

In this section I give my grounds for thinking that the case for the intelligibility of 'person without a body' fails.

First, Swinburne uses Strawson's concept of person in a manner of which Strawson could not possibly approve. Strawson's sophisticated purpose in defining a person as a single individual to whom M-predicates and P-predicates are both applicable was to rule out in advance any Cartesian separation of mental and physical states. Developed mental states and physical states there certainly are, but the only individuals having them are persons. The genius of Strawson's account of a person is that in ascribing a P-predicate to an individual, one is ascribing it to an entity to whom many M-predicates must also apply. Mental states are necessarily states of entities which are also physical bodies. A conceptual veto is successfully placed on attempts to identify a logical subject of consciousness while at the same time excluding that subject's essential materiality. According to Strawson 'a necessary condition of states of consciousness being ascribed at all is that they should be ascribed to the very same things as certain corporeal characteristics, a certain physical situation, etc.'. The temptation to think of a person 'as a sort of compound of two kinds of subject' must be firmly resisted. 'Many questions arise when we think in this way.'

When Swinburne asks whether there could be an individual to whom M-predicates did not apply, but to whom many P-predicates did apply, he has already broken the logical rules governing this concept of person, for the rules exclude the very possibility which Swinburne wants to import into the discussion about a God who is a person. If P-predicates were applied to an individual to whom no M-predicates applied, that individual could not possibly be a person. Swinburne uses Strawson's concept of a person as a vehicle for his own version of Cartesian dualism, while overlooking that this concept excludes such a dualism from the beginning. Of course Swinburne might reply that his use of Strawson's concept of person was just a preliminary move in getting his own discussion about a bodiless person off the ground. But then the obvious counter-reply is that Swinburne is advocating a full-blown Cartesian dualism, disguised in a more fashionable costume.

Cartesian dualism is also assumed by admitting into the discussion what it is for a person to have a body. There is an oddity about the phrase 'having a body'. I can have glandular fever, a son, a holiday in Brittany, etc., and I can speak about having these things not least because I can identify them by marking them off from other things that I have or do not have. But as I need to have a body as a precondition of having anything else at all, from a cold to a philosophical argument, I can't identify having a body by marking it off from something else, like not having a body. This is a small matter. What loom larger are the Cartesian assumptions built into the question. It has already been decided in advance that a person is separate from his or her body, that one can intelligibly discuss the having of a body, that one is 'related' to one's body and can speak literally of this relation as a relation to a 'material object'. Never is the alternative question 'What is it to *be* a body?' raised. If it were it might lead to the embarrassing conclusion that being a body is a necessary condition of an individual being a person in the first place as Strawson rightly holds. And this conclusion prevents Swinburne's enterprise getting started.

It is claimed that since we can imagine becoming an omnipresent spirit, there can be no logical objection to the possibility of there being such a being. But is this so? There does seem to be a connexion between being able to imagine a state of affairs and the purely logical possibility of there being this state of affairs, but can one ever coherently imagine being without a body? Suppose one tried to imagine one had the body of a fairy, like Puck in *A Midsummer Night's Dream*—could one imagine being a fairy, flying about, having supernatural powers, becoming invisible at will? A problem here is that one only has human experience to work on, and whereas one might imagine having great increases or decreases in human capability, being non-human is finally unimaginable to humans, and having no body is not being human. One would still need a physical brain to imagine becoming disembodied, and once one had imagined being without one's brain what could one imagine then?

Perhaps Wittgenstein's illustration of the talking pot can make the matter clearer. Of a fairy tale where a pot talks, Wittgenstein asks 'Is it false or nonsensical to say that a pot talks? Have we a clear picture of the circumstances in which we should say of a pot that it talked? (Even a nonsense-poem is not nonsense in the same way as the babbling of a child.)'[9] A lesson to be drawn from the illustration concerns the relation between what one can imagine and what one can understand. Fairy tales cannot be dismissed as nonsense. People enjoy them. But one does not inquire too closely into the sense a fairy tale has because one knows that in a fairy tale the normal rules for recognizing the sense of something are suspended. We do not have 'a clear picture of the circumstances' and we do not need to have. Now we can imagine a person without a body playing an exciting role in a fairy tale. Imagining such a person would not be nonsense, for fairy tales are not nonsense. But now the price to be paid for admitting 'person without a body' into sensible discourse is that any sense it has is the sense one gives to a fairy tale, and that unfortunately tells us nothing about logical or ontological possibilities, even though it may amuse us. In imagining a person without a body we cannot get very far; in understanding one we hardly set off. We do not have 'a clear picture of the circumstances'. It is a fairy tale. Yet a clear picture of the circumstances is what Swinburne must provide if we are to be convinced of its logical possibility.

Swinburne's admission that God has a limited embodiment is a curious modification of his picture of the Omnipresent Spirit. He is forced into conced-

---

[9] L. Wittgenstein, *Philosophical Investigations* (Oxford: Blackwell, 1972), section 282.

ing limited embodiment to the Christian God for this God is believed by Christians to be a God who acts, and in order to perform an action (not merely to intend to perform it) a person needs a body. Swinburne tries to resolve this antinomy by drawing on one of the ways in which he says a person is related to his body, viz. that a person can move many parts of his body directly. An argument from analogy is set up which runs: as a person is able to move many parts of his body, so is God able to move any part of the world. When God is said to move any part of the universe directly, or to know any state of the universe without inference, this talk is supposed to be rendered intelligible by comparison with a human individual who is said to move many parts of his body directly, and to know something of what is going on inside it. God's body is whatever God moves and knows.

There are two new problems about this account of God's actions. First the analogy. I can cause my arm to move, and I can cause my car to move. In one case I act on myself (we might say): in the other case I act on something else, outside me. Now when God moves a part of the world this part of the world is presumably outside God. So any analogy illustrating how God moves a part of the world, drawn from human beings moving things, will need to be taken from our moving things external to our bodies, not from our moving parts of our bodies. And this is why Swinburne's analogy unfortunately does not work. Swinburne holds that a person without a body (God) can move something not himself. So an analogy drawn from human agency would have to start from a human agent moving something not himself or herself. But, telekinesis apart, a human person needs his or her body to move anything outside that body. What has happened is that once corporeality has been removed from the God who is a person, it now has to be smuggled back in the attempt to make this God's actions and knowledge intelligible. And that is the second problem. Limited embodiment is reintroduced in an attempt to meet a logical requirement of talk about agency. But there is nothing corresponding to it among human agents. Human persons with bodies tell us little about a divine person without one, and still less about this person's partial re-embodiment. The term 'limited embodiment' functions as a logical substitute for genuine personal embodiment.[10]

The account of personal identity is also aimed at showing that 'person without a body' is coherent. As we have seen, personal identity is 'something ultimate—unanalysable into conjunctions or disjunctions of other observable properties.' One might wonder whether on this view personal identity can be positively characterized at all, or remark that it looks very like a Cartesian *res cogitans* or a Kantian transcendental self, in which case it runs into deep historical difficulties unexplored in this paper. But that is not the issue at present. Swinburne rightly denies that person can be exhaustively described in empirical terms—my worry is that when he subtracts body, memory and character from what he calls personal identity, there is nothing left over to be identical with anything. Body, memory and character provide evidence for continued personal identity but do not constitute it, because it cannot be

---

[10] W. D. Hudson, for similar reasons, ascribes to God a substitute body. See his *A Philosophic Approach to Religion* (London and Basingstoke: Macmillan, 1974), pp. 166–76.

constituted empirically. So while one or more of these conditions is a necessary condition of personal identity, it or they can never be a sufficient condition of it because it is something ultimate. But this 'something ultimate' is arrived at by stripping away all the empirical features of persons on which it depends, so whatever is left is more a residue of a person than a person. Everything bodily must be moved . .

IV

. . . Christians, reflecting on their belief in a personal God, can provide various accounts of it which do not require that God be a person. Obviously more is at stake here than the verbal similarity between adjectival and nominal forms of 'person'. This similarity is itself a source of much confusion, for it masks a crucial dissimilarity in meaning. Christians do need to hold that God is personal: they do not need to hold that God is a person. They might say that since Jesus is a (human) person who fully reveals God, then God must be fully personal too. But this does not make God a person. They might want to agree with Keith Ward that there is 'a personal depth of reality' which is called God.[11] They might want to say, with Hans Küng, that God is 'one who faces me as founding and embracing all interhuman personality'.[12] They might think that since God is love and the sharing of love goes on among persons, then a loving God is a personal God. On a different tack they might make the observation that in an act of worship one can feel addressed 'as a person', and that only a personal God could do this. More ambitiously they might say that through Jesus Christ God is enabling them to become new persons and so God is supremely personal. And so on. Philosophers of course are interested in the intelligibility of these and similar claims. The point to be stressed, though, is that there is no obvious theological connection, still less a logical or ontological one, between plausible theological accounts of belief in a personal God and the quite separate hypothesis that God is a person.

Perhaps the biggest difficulty for bodiless person theism is that the most respected theologians for the church, ancient and modern, have no use for the modern term 'person' in relation to God. Swinburne cannot evade this weight of testimony against his idea of God by a remark that theologians are over anxious about identifying God too closely with 'ordinary created persons'. Here the complicated history of the term 'person' is important. In its modern family of uses it refers to individual men and women, perhaps as intelligent agents (following Locke), moral beings worthy of respect (following Kant), or existents becoming what they choose (following the existentialists). God is not a person in these senses (especially the last two) and theologians avoid talking as if he is. More importantly God is not called a person in the bible, not even by Jesus. Of course the familiar words *persona*, *prosōpon* and *hypostasis* which came to dominate later Christological and Trinitarian discussion had not in biblical

---

[11] Keith Ward, *Holding Fast to God* (London: S.P.C.K., 1982), p. 6.

[12] Hans Küng, *Does God Exist?* (London: Collins, 1980) p. 633.

times acquired the senses they later came to have (though even then God is three Persons, not a divine superperson). But to draw attention to the fact that God is not called a person in the bible is to do more than begin an argument from silence. Nothing can be made out of the tautology that new testament writers did not use words that they did not use. What is overlooked though is that if they had wanted to convey the idea of God as a bodiless person, language was certainly available to them to do it. *Anthrōpos*, and perhaps even *anēr*, could have done the job. If we grant to St. Paul the license to do with *anthrōpos* what bodiless person theists do with 'person', i.e. dematerialize it, then God (not Jesus) might have been called a *theios anthrōpos*. Of course the suggestion sounds bizarre, not least because St. Paul had too deep a sense of human embodiment to be attracted by this kind of dualism and *anthrōpos* was too associated with human frailty to permit its application to God. But the suggestion is no more bizarre than the modern attempt to speak of God as a person without a body. The bible is a record of Judaeo-Christian belief in a personal God who is spoken of symbolically. There is no record in its pages of a God who is a person who is spoken of literally.

In the present century too theologians avoid the term. John Macquarrie has rightly identified the theism which asserts that God is a person 'but a strange metaphysical kind of person without a body' as pre-scientific, as a phase in the historical development of the idea of God.[13] None the less he insists we have excellent reasons for speaking of God as personal. Personal language about God is symbolic, and 'the test of a symbol is its *adequacy* in lighting up Being'. Personal language becomes the most appropriate language we have for speaking of God, for 'In man, a material body and an animal organism are united with his distinctively personal being. This is the widest range of being that we know, and therefore symbols and images drawn from personal life have the highest degree of adequacy accessible to us.[14] Similar considerations lead Hans Küng to say God is not 'an individual person among other persons, is not a superman or superego. . .God is not the supreme person among other persons. God transcends also the concept of person. God is more than person.' 'It will be better to call the most real reality not personal or nonpersonal—but—if we attach importance to the terminology—transpersonal or suprapersonal.'[15]

Philosophers and theologians have other alternatives open to them. One of them is that long and distinguished tradition in Christian thought which was developed by Augustine and the Franciscans, and later by Aquinas and the Dominicans according to which God is no person but is being, or being-itself.[16] A related alternative is panentheism, the view that in some respects the world is included within the divine reality. Panentheism allows a place for materiality in its approach to the being and actions of God, and this is surely a

---

[13] John Macquarrie, *Principles of Christian Theology* (London: S.C.M. Press, rev. edn. 1977), p. 116.

[14] *Op. cit.* p. 143.

[15] Küng, *op. cit.* p. 633.

[16] I defend this idea in ch. 8 of my *The Ontology of Paul Tillich* (Oxford, 1978).

key advantage given that the God of faith is One whose Word becomes flesh in Jesus Christ and who makes men and women (i.e. embodied beings) in his image. A more theological account of a personal God might be one which begins with Jesus Christ, and derives the affirmation that God is personal not from a philosophical agency model but from the theological conviction that Jesus Christ is the revelation of God in his being and actions. As a person, and in his personal life, Jesus is believed to show us what is meant by 'God'. So God is 'personal'. The materiality of the man who was God makes possible a theological doctrine of nature: the temporality of this man makes possible a theological doctrine of history. But this is not the time to develop any of these alternatives, only to say that they, and others, are available.

Modern Christian theism in its philosophical and theological forms profits from the diversity of approaches to be found within it. This diversity is usually to be welcomed, though in the case of bodiless person theism I am unconvinced that it can make a positive contribution. As well as its internal inconsistencies, the consequences of accepting it may be also unfortunate. In philosophy a God who is a person without a body looks like a return to a *deus ex machina*, to a remote deistic deity whose existence reason tries in vain to corroborate. In theology a crude supernaturalism which is an obstacle to intelligent faith is likely to be encouraged once a bodiless person becomes the direct referent of religious discourse. In academic philosophy of religion we can perhaps look forward to the ebb and flow of argument about whether 'person without a body' is coherent, and the unbelievers will have an easy task showing it won't work. And as for religious people themselves, a few literalists will be pleased to learn that God is a person after all (as they have all along believed). The rest will manage without it. Whichever way one looks at it, it is a doctrine we can do without.

II.E. The Metaphysical Attributes

II.E.1. Eternal and Immutable

RICHARD SWINBURNE

Richard Swinburne (1934–), Nolloth Professor of Religion at Oxford, examines the metaphysical attributes of eternity, timelessness, and immutability. Swinburne argues that the concepts of timelessness and immutability, when interpreted to mean "totally unchanging," are incoherent with the notion of God as a person, but he goes on to show that these attributes actually seem to be products of neo-Platonism and thus need not be regarded as essential features of theism. Offering an interpretation of all the major characteristics usually attributed to God, he undertakes to show that they are mutually coherent as well as coherent with the idea of God as personal, the creator of the world, and the ground of moral obligation.

The argument . . . so far has been that it is coherent to suppose that there exists now an omnipotent spirit, who is perfectly free, the creator of the universe, omnipotent, omniscient, perfectly good, and a source of moral obligation—so long as 'omnipotent' and 'omniscient' are understood in somewhat restricted senses. I shall consider in this chapter two further suppositions which the theist makes—that this being is an eternal being and is immutable.

ETERNAL

The property of being creator of the universe is different from the other properties which we have considered so far in the following respect. To say that there exists now a being with the other properties does not entail the existence of such a being at any other time. A being with all the other properties could come into existence yesterday and cease to exist today—though his ceasing to exist today could not have been something which was against his choice; otherwise he would not have been omnipotent before ceasing to exist. However, if a creator of the universe exists now, he must have existed at least as long as there have been other logically contingent existing things. For a creator of the universe is. . .one who brings about or makes or permits other beings to bring about the existence of all logically contingent things which exist, i.e. have existed, exist, or will exist. On the assumption that an agent can only bring about effects subsequent to his action, he must have existed at least as long as created things.

However, traditionally theists believe not merely that this spirit, God, exists now or has existed as long as created things, but that he is an eternal being. This seems to mean, firstly, that he has always existed—that there was no time at which he did not exist—and that he has always had the properties which we have been considering. Let us put this point by saying that they believe that he is backwardly eternal. The supposition that a spirit of the above kind is backwardly eternal seems to be a coherent one. If, as I have argued, it is coherent to suppose that such a spirit exists at the present time, then it would seem coherent to suppose that he exists at any other nameable time; and, if that is coherent, then surely it is coherent to suppose that there exists a being now such that however far back in time you count years you do not reach the beginning of its existence. The above spirit could surely be of that kind. Then he would be backwardly eternal. Various writers have suggested that endless life would be tedious, boring, and pointless. An omnipotent being could, however, if he so chose, ensure that his life was not tedious or boring. And given, as I have argued, that there are true moral judgments, there will often be a point in doing one thing rather than another.

The doctrine that God is eternal seems to involve, secondly, the doctrine that the above spirit will go on existing for ever, continuing for ever to possess the properties which I have discussed. I will put this point by saying that he is forwardly eternal. This too seems to be a coherent suggestion. We, perhaps, cease to exist at death. But we can surely conceive of a being now existent such that whatever future nameable time you choose, he has not by that time ceased to exist; and the spirit described above could be such a being. A being who is both backwardly and forwardly eternal we may term an eternal being.

The above seems the natural way of interpreting the doctrine that God is eternal, and it is, I have urged, a coherent one. However, there is in the Christian theistic tradition an alternative way of interpreting this doctrine, and I shall consider this alternative after considering the doctrine of God's immutability.

IMMUTABLE

Closely connected with the doctrine of God's eternity is the doctrine of his immutability. Theists traditionally claim that God is immutable, that he cannot change.

We can understand 'immutable' in a weaker or stronger way. In the weaker way to say of a person that he is immutable is simply to say that he cannot change in character. To say of a free and omniscient creator that he is immutable is simply to say that, while he continues to exist, necessarily he remains fixed in his character. We saw [earlier] that of logical necessity a person who is perfectly free and omniscient will be perfectly good. Hence a person cannot change in character while he remains perfectly free and omniscient. According to traditional theism God is eternally perfectly free and omniscient, and so it follows that he will not change in character. Given the doctrine which I shall discuss later that God necessarily possesses such properties as freedom and omniscience, it will follow that he cannot change in character, and so is immutable in the weaker sense. God's immutability in this sense is of course something which theism has always wished to affirm.

Theists have, however, sometimes understood immutability in a much stronger sense. On this understanding to say that God is immutable is to say that he cannot change *at all*. The doctrine of divine immutability in this sense is often combined with the doctrine of divine timelessness. But for the moment I shall consider it independently of the latter doctrine. To investigate the coherence of the suggestion that a person with the properties so far delineated be immutable in this strong sense, we must begin by asking what it is to change.

There is a famous but clearly unsatisfactory criterion of change, which Professor Geach has called the Cambridge criterion.[1] According to this a thing x changes if some predicate 'Φ' applies to it at one time, but not at another. Thus my tie has changed if it was clean yesterday, but is not clean today. But although everything which 'changes' in the ordinary sense does seem to 'change' by the Cambridge criterion, the converse is not true. Sometimes a predicate 'Φ' applies to an object x at one time, but not at another without that thing having 'changed' in the ordinary sense of the word. Socrates may at one time be thought about by Smith and at a later time not be thought about by Smith, without Socrates having changed. Or John may be at one time taller than James and at another time John may not be taller than James—without John having changed at all. It may be simply the case that James has grown.

Real change must be distinguished from mere Cambridge change. An attempt to bring out the difference has been made by T. P. Smith.[2] He claims that the Cambridge criterion is perfectly satisfactory for non-relational predicates. A relational predicate is one which expresses a relation to some individual. Thus 'moves,' 'talks,' 'is green,' 'is square' are non-relational predicates; whereas 'hits John,' 'thinks of the man in the moon,' 'opens the door,' etc. are relational predicates. Where we have a relational predicate of the form '$\ldots Ry$' (viz. '$\ldots$ has relation R to y'), all that follows from x being Ry at one time and not being Ry at another is that either x has changed or y has changed or both have changed—given that '$\ldots Ry$' is not a predicate of spatial relation, such as 'is to the left of Jones,' in which case we cannot conclude even that. So, given that '$\ldots Ry$' is not a predicate of spatial relation, x has changed if x is Ry at one time and not at another, and if y has not changed between these times. (If y has changed, x may have changed also, or it may not.) Thus if James has not changed, and John is at one time shorter than James, and at another and later time not shorter than James, then John has changed by getting taller. But something does not change merely because it is now thought about, and then not thought about by John. The criterion can only be applied to yield results in

---

[1] P. T. Geach, 'What Actually Exists,' *Proceedings of the Aristotelian Society*, Suppl. Vol., 1968, 42, 7–16. Reprinted in his *God and the Soul*, pp. 65–74; see pp. 71 f.

[2] T. P. Smith, 'On the Applicability of a Criterion of Change,' *Ratio*, 1973, 15, 325–33.

the case of relational predicates if we already have some understanding of what it is for something to change (for one can only conclude that *x* has changed if one knows that *y* has not). Nor, if we know that *y* has changed can we conclude whether or not *x* has changed merely from knowing that *x* has a certain relation to *y* at one time but not at another. But the criterion does bring out to some limited extent what is involved in real as opposed to mere Cambridge change.

Now given this understanding of change, what is it to say that God does not change at all? This would not rule out God at one time not being worshipped by Augustine, and at a later time being worshipped by Augustine. For in such case, intuitively, Augustine changes but God does not. It might seem that it rules out God acting—for acts take place at particular times; in acting God changes from not doing a certain action to doing that action. This difficulty could be avoided if one said that all that God brings about he has chosen 'from all eternity' to bring about. The effects (e.g. the fall of Jerusalem, the fall of Babylon) which God brings about occur at particular times (587 B.C. and 538 B.C. respectively). Yet God has always meant them to occur at those times—i.e. there was no time at which God did not intend Jerusalem to fall in 587 B.C. When 587 B.C. arrived there was no change in God—the arrival of the moment to put into effect the intention which God always had. This view would need to be made more sophisticated to deal with the suggestion that God's bringing out one state of affairs, say *A*, rather than another, say *B*, was due to his reaction to the behaviour of men (e.g. men may have behaved badly and so God gave them drought instead of rain). The view in question would have to claim that in such circumstances 'from all eternity' God had intended that *A*-occur-if-men did so-and-so, and that *B*-occur-if-men did such-and-such.

If God had thus fixed his intentions 'from all eternity' he would be a very lifeless thing; not a person who reacts to men with sympathy or anger, pardon or chastening because he chooses to there and then. Yet . . . the God of the Old Testament, in which Judaism, Islam, and Christianity have their roots, is a God in continual interaction with men, moved by men as they speak to him, his action being often in no way decided in advance. We should note, further, that if God did not change at all, he would not think now of this, now of that. His thoughts would be one thought which lasted for ever.

It seems to me that although the God of the Old Testament is not pictured as such a being, nevertheless a perfectly free person might act in fact only on intentions which he had had from all eternity, and so in a strong sense never change. However, a perfectly free person could not be immutable in the strong sense, that is *unable* to change. For an agent is perfectly free at a certain time if his action results from his own choice at that time and if his choice is not itself brought about by anything else. Yet a person immutable in the strong sense would be unable to perform any action at a certain time other than what he had previously intended to do. His course of action being fixed by his past choices, he would not be perfectly free. Being perfectly free is incompatible with being immutable in the strong sense. We could attempt to save the coherence of the supposition that God is both perfectly free and immutable (in the strong sense) by pleading that words are being used analogically, but there seems no need whatever for this manoeuvre here, because there is no need whatever for the theist to say that God is immutable in the strong sense.

Why should many theists have wished to suppose that God is immutable in the strong sense? The belief that God is immutable in this sense does not seem to me to be much in evidence in Christian tradition until the third or fourth century A.D. It came, I suspect, from neo-Platonism. For a Platonist things which change are inferior to things which do not change. Aquinas, claiming that God is altogether unchangeable, gives as one of his reasons that 'anything in change acquires something through its change, attaining something not previously attained. Now God . . . embracing within himself the whole fullness of perfection of all existence cannot acquire anything.'[3] Being perfect already he can lack nothing. However, an obvious answer to this point is to suggest that the perfection of a perfect being might consist not in his being in a certain static condition, but in his being in a certain process of change. Only neo-Platonic dogma would lead us to suppose otherwise. That God is completely changeless would seem to be for the theist an unnecessary dogma. It is not, I have suggested, one implicit in the Old or New Testaments. Nor, I would think, is it one to which very many modern theists are committed, unless they have absorbed Thomism fairly thoroughly.

TIMELESSNESS

Armed with the results of the last few pages, I now return to consider an alternative interpretation of the doctrine that God is eternal, alternative to the simple interpretation that God's eternity consists in his always having existed and his going to exist for ever. This simple interpretation, I urged earlier, was a coherent one.

The alternative interpretation of God's eternity is that to say that God is eternal is to say that he is timeless, that he exists outside the 'stream' of time. His actions are timeless, although they have their effects in time. His thoughts and reactions are timeless, although they may be thoughts about or reactions to things in time. His knowledge is timeless, although it includes knowledge of things in time. There is no temporal succession of states in God. Another way of putting these points is to say that God has his own time scale. There is only one instant of time on the scale; and everything which is ever true of God is true of him at that instant. In a sense, however, that instant of time lasts for ever. In this chapter I wish to consider whether it is a coherent claim that God is timeless and whether it is one which the theist needs to make.

Most of the great Christian theologians from Augustine to Aquinas taught that God is timeless. The best-known exposition of this doctrine occurs in the last section of the *Consolation of Philosophy* of the sixth-century Christian philosopher Boethius. Let us look at Boethius's exposition. God, Boethius says, is eternal, but not in the sense that he always has existed and always will exist. Plato and Aristotle thought that the world always had existed and always would exist. Christian revelation had shown that the world had a beginning and would have an end in time. But even if Plato and Aristotle had been right,

---

[3] *Summa Theologiae*, vol. ii, Ia.9.I.

that would not mean that the world was eternal in the sense in which God is eternal. 'Let us say that God is eternal, but that the world lasts for ever.' God, however, is eternal in being present at once to all times which from our view at any one time may be past or future. God is thus outside the stream of temporal becoming and passing away. Boethius's much-quoted definition of eternity is that it is 'the complete and perfect possession at once of an endless life'. 'For it is one thing to be carried through an endless life which Plato attributed to the world, another thing to embrace together the whole presence of an endless life, a thing which is the manifest property of the divine mind.'[4] The obvious analogy is to men travelling along a road; at each time they can see only the neighbourhood on the road where they are. But God is above the road and can see the whole road at once. Taking man's progress along the road as his progress through time, the analogy suggests that while man can enjoy only one time at once, God can enjoy all times at once. God is present to all times at once, just as he is present to all places at once. This doctrine of God's eternity provided Boethius with a neat solution of the problem of divine foreknowledge. Because all times are present to God, God can just as easily see our future acts as other men can see our present acts. But this does not affect their freedom. Just as the fact that we see a man acting now does not mean that he is not acting freely, so God's seeing a man acting in the future does not mean that the man will not act freely. For God does not ever see what are from our point of view future acts, *as* future. He always (on his time scale) sees them as present, and hence the difficulties discussed [earlier] concerning God's present knowledge of our future free actions do not arise.

This doctrine of divine timelessness is very little in evidence before Augustine. The Old Testament certainly shows no sign of it. For Old Testament writers, as has been noted, God does now this, now that; now destroys Jerusalem, now lets the exiles return home. The same applies in general for the New Testament writers, although there are occasional sentences in the New Testament which could be interpreted in terms of this doctrine. Thus in the Revelation of St. John the Divine God is described more than once as 'Alpha and Omega, the beginning and the end' and also as he 'which was and is and is to come.' But it seems to be reading far too much into such phrases to interpret them as implying the doctrine of divine timelessness. Like the doctrine of his total immutability, the doctrine of God's timelessness seems to have entered Christian theology from neo-Platonism, and there from Augustine to Aquinas it reigned. Duns Scotus seems to have rejected it and so did William of Ockham. It seems to have returned to Catholic theology from the sixteenth century onwards, but to have had comparatively little influence in Protestant theology. Post-Hegelian Protestant theology explicitly rejects it. For Hegel the Absolute or God was essentially something in process and Tillich acknowledged his debt here to Hegel, by claiming that Hegel's 'idea of a dialectical movement within the Absolute is in agreement with the genuine meaning of eternity. Eternity is not timelessness.'

Tillich claims that God is not outside the temporal process, for, if he were, he would be lifeless. Only a God who acts and chooses and loves and forgives is

---

[4] Boethius, *On the Consolation of Philosophy*, 5.6.

the God whom we wish to worship, and the pursuit of these activities, since they involve change of state, means being in time. "If we call God a living God, we affirm that he includes temporality and with this a relation to the modes of time.'[5] Exactly the same point is made by Barth,[6] though he argues not only from the the general fact God is a living God but also from the particular fact of the Incarnation. The Incarnation means, according to Barth, that God acts at a particular temporal moment. Only a temporal being can do this. 'Without God's complete temporality the content of the Christian message has no shape.'[7,8]

The reasons why theists would wish to adopt this doctrine are interior to theism. That is, it is felt by some theists to be better consonant with other things which they wish to say, to say that God is timeless than to say that he lives through time. However, it seems to me that the reasons which the scholastics had for putting forward the doctrine of timelessness were poor ones. A major consideration for them seems to have been that this doctrine would provide backing for and explanation of the doctrine of God's total immutability. For if God is timeless he is totally immutable—although it does not follow that if he is totally immutable he is timeless. Aquinas seems to have thought that the latter did follow: 'something lacking change and never varying its mode of existence will not display a before and after'.[9] God's eternity (in the sense of timelessness), he claimed, 'follows upon unchangeableness, and God alone . . . is altogether unchangeable'.[10] However, this seems mistaken. A totally immutable thing could just go on existing for ever without being timeless—especially if other things, such as the universe, changed, while the immutable thing continued changeless. The change of other things would measure the passage of time during which the immutable thing changed not. Still, the timelessness of God would explain God's total immutability, if he was totally immutable. But we have seen no reason why the theist should advocate God's total immutability.

A second reason why the scholastics adopted the doctrine of timelessness is, as we saw for Boethius, that it allowed them to maintain that God is omniscient in the very strong sense which was discussed [earlier]. God outside

---

[5] *Systematic Theology*, vol. i, p. 305.

[6] Also by O. Cullman in *Christ and Time* (London, 1951), Pt. I, Chs. 3 and 4. Cullman owes an obvious debt to Barth.

[7] K. Barth, *Church Dogmatics*, II (i) (Edinburgh, 1957), p. 620.

[8] For a fuller statement of the history of the doctrine in Christian theology, see Nelson Pike, *God and Timelessness* (London, 1970), esp. pp. 180-7, and the opening pages of an article of mine, 'The Timelessness of God,' *Church Quarterly Review*, 1965, 323-37 and 472-86. The later philosophical part of this article now seems to me mistaken both in its argumentation and in its conclusion. It mistakenly assumed that the only proper kind of explanation was scientific explanation, and reached the conclusion, which I now regard as mistaken, that the timelessness of God was a doctrine needed by Christian theism. Pike's book, in contrast, is a very careful systematic treatment of this issue which reaches the opposite conclusion, which now seems to me the correct one.

[9] *Summa Theologiae*, vol. ii, Ia.10.1.

[10] Ibid., Ia.10.3.

time can be said never not to know our free actions, even though they may sometimes be future from our point of view. Since they are never future for God, he sees them as present and this does not endanger their free character. In view of the general Christian tradition that God's omniscience includes knowledge of future free human actions, the doctrine of timelessness does seem to have the advantage of saving the former doctrine against obvious difficulties. I urged [earlier], however, that the view that God's omniscience includes knowledge of future free human actions is easily detachable from the theistic tradition.

A further reason why a theist might want to adopt the doctrine, although, as far as I know, it was not one put forward by the scholastics is the following. A man, especially a modern man, might feel that a temporal being was as such less than perfect in that his mere existence in time would mean that he was as it were continually losing parts of his existence all the while. As today ends and tomorrow begins, the being has lost today—his existence today is dead and gone, for ever unrecallable:

> Time, you old gypsy man, will you not stay,
> Put up your caravan just for one day?

But *why* does the continual passage of time mean loss for those who live in it? Obvious answers are—that they get older and so weaker, that new experiences are not so exciting as old ones, and that they draw nearer to death, which, they fear, is the end. All of these are indeed proper reasons for regretting the passage of time; and if the passage of time had these consequences for God, he would indeed have cause for regret. But these are mere factual consequences of the passage of time for mortal finite man; an omnipotent being need not suffer them. But still, it might be felt, there are some consequences of life in time which even an omnipotent being would have to suffer. These are that the moment certain states, experiences, and actions are past, they are for ever unrepeatable. If he performed a certain *A* on one day, he could not perform exactly that action on another day—he could only perform one qualitatively similar. This is true of logical necessity. States, experiences, actions, etc. are individuated by the time of their occurrence. An 'action' is a numerically different individual 'action' from a similar action tomorrow, because of the criteria which we have for distinguishing one 'action' from another. But what real loss does this fact mean? If I can tomorrow have states and do actions qualitatively as similar as I like to those of today, why should the passage of time cause me regret? And anyway, even if this limitation is a logically necessary one for all beings in time it is one which a being who lives and acts, chooses and reacts in anything like a literal sense will—of logical necessity— have to endure. Such a being may still be as close as it is logically possible for a being to be to being perfect.

So much for the reasons why a theist might wish to claim that God is timeless. I have urged that they are not very good reasons. Further, the claim that God is timeless, as I have expounded it, seems to contain an inner incoherence and also to be incompatible with most things which theists ever wish to say about God.

The inner incoherence can be seen as follows. God's timelessness is said to consist in his existing at all moments of human time—simultaneously. Thus he is said to be simultaneously present at (and a witness of) what I did yesterday, what I am doing today, and what I will do tomorrow. But if t_1 is simultaneous with t_2 and t_2 with t_3, then t_1 is simultaneous with t_3. So if the instant at which God knows these things were simultaneous with both yesterday, today, and tomorrow, then these days would be simultaneous with each other. So yesterday would be the same day as today and as tomorrow—which is clearly nonsense. To avoid this awkward consequence we would have to understand 'simultaneously' in a somewhat special stretched sense. The 'simultaneously' holding between God's presence at my actions and those actions would have to differ from normal simultaneity.

The second difficulty is that so many other things which the theist wishes to say about God—that he brings about this or that, forgives, punishes, or warns—are things which are true of a man at this or that time or at all times. If we say that P brings about x, we can always sensibly ask *when* does he bring it about? If we say that P punishes Q, we can always sensibly ask *when* does he punish Q? If P really does 'bring about' or 'forgive' in anything like the normal senses of the words, there must be answers to these questions even if nobody knows what they are. Further, many of these things which the theist wishes to say about God seem to be things the doing of which at one time carries entailments of things being true at later or earlier times. If P at t brings about x, then necessarily x comes into existence (simultaneously with or) subsequently to P's action. If P at t forgives Q for having done x, then Q did x prior to t. If P at t warns Q not to do x, in such a way that Q has an opportunity to heed his warning, then there must be a time subsequent to t at which Q has this opportunity. And so on. So, superficially, the supposition that God could bring things about, forgive, punish, warn, etc. etc. without his doing these things at times before or after other times (often, times on the human scale of time) seems incoherent. Once again, the theist will need to say that God only 'brings about', 'forgives', etc. in senses very different from the normal, if the sentence in which God is said to do these things are to express coherent suppositions.

Generally, the theist's only hope for maintaining the inner coherence of his claim that God is timeless and its coherence with others of his claims would be to maintain that many words are being used in highly analogical senses. When he says that God is a 'person' or 'brings about' states of affairs, or 'knows' what happened yesterday 'at the same time as' he 'knows' what happens tomorrow and that he 'knows' all these things at and only 'at the same time as' they happen, the theist could claim that the words involved here are being used in highly stretched senses, so that there is no incoherence in what is being said and no incompatibility with other things which the theist wishes to say. When discussing the analogical use of words. . . , I warned that although a theist would be justified on occasion in using words in an analogical sense, nevertheless too many appeals to analogical senses of words would make sentences in which the words were used empty of content. In this case it seems to me that the theist has no need to make such an appeal. For as I have been urging, the theist has no need to incorporate the doctrine of the timelessness of God into his theism. He can easily do without it and all the difficulties which it brings,[11] and rely instead on the simple and easy coherent understanding of God's eternity which I delineated earlier.

THE PERSONAL GROUND OF BEING

Apart from the property of necessity I have now considered all the main properties traditionally ascribed to God, properties which, in some sense which I shall be discussing shortly, are inalienable from him. Are there any logical relations between the predicates ascribing properties to God or are they just a string of predicates, such that it is coherent to suppose that there might be beings with different combinations of them? I argued [earlier] that—of logical necessity—an omniscient and perfectly free person would be perfectly good, and that a perfectly good creator of the universe would be a source of moral obligation. So, if my arguments are correct, any being which had the other properties would—of logical necessity—be perfectly good and a source of moral obligation.

I wish now to argue for two further entailments between the properties discussed. The first is that any person who is omnipotent and omniscient will be of logical necessity an omnipresent spirit. A person who is omnipotent is able to bring about effects everywhere by basic actions. One who is omniscient at a certain time has justified true beliefs about all things which are going on anywhere at that time. Now if he depended for his knowledge on the proper functioning of intermediaries such as eyes and ears, then if they were to behave in unusual ways, his beliefs would be false (as are ours when our eyes and ears malfunction). But if there were such intermediaries, as an omniscient being he would know if they were behaving unusually and so would correct his beliefs in the light of this knowledge. Malfunctioning of intermediaries could not lead an omniscient being astray. Hence an omniscient being does not depend for his knowledge on the correct functioning of intermediaries. Hence an omnipotent and omniscient person, in my senses of the terms, is of logical necessity an omnipresent spirit.

The other entailment for which I shall argue is that an eternally omnipotent person (who is also omniscient and perfectly free in our senses of these terms) is necessarily the creator of the universe. A person P who is omnipotent at a time t (in my sense [E]...) is able to bring about the existence of any logically contingent state of affairs after t (the description of the occurrence of which does not entail that P did not bring it about at t), given that he does not believe that he has overriding reason for refraining from bringing it about. Now consider for any time t all the logically contingent things which exist at that time. At a time t' immediately precedent to t, an omnipotent being P would have had it in his power to bring about the non-existence of all those

---

[11] The doctrine of the timelessness of God is connected in the Thomist system with various connected doctrines, expressed in Aristotelian terminology, that there is no potency in God, that God is pure act, and that God is one pure act. There seem to me similar reasons for adopting or rejecting these doctrines as for adopting or rejecting the doctrine of timelessness.

things—with the exception to which we will come shortly. In that case, if they exist, they only exist because he brought them about (or permitted them to exist) or made or permitted some other being to bring them about. For each time t there will be a precedent time t' of which this holds. Hence an eternally omnipotent being will at some time have brought about (or permitted to exist) or made or permitted other beings to bring about the existence of, all the things which exist.

The only kind of thing existent at t such that an omnipotent being P would not at t' have had the power to bring about its non-existence is anything such that P believes that he has overriding reason for refraining from bringing about its nonexistence, viz. anything for which he believes that he has overriding reason for bringing about its existence. But then, although P's being omnipotent does not entail that he brings about the existence of such things, it follows from his being omnipotent, omniscient, and perfectly free that he will do so. For being omnipotent he will have the power to do so.[12] Being omniscient and perfectly free, he is perfectly good, and hence will bring about those things.

The complex argument of the last two paragraphs may be summarized as follows. If there is an omnipotent being, whatever exists at some time must have existed because he did not stop it existing. The only things which he could not stop from existing are any things which he has overriding reason to bring about. If he is also perfectly free and omniscient, of logical necessity he will bring those things about. I conclude that an eternally omnipotent person who is omniscient and perfectly free is of logical necessity the creator of the universe. Note that God being creator of the universe in my sense does not entail the existence of our universe or any other material universe—only that if any universe does exist God created it or permitted some other being to do so. Theists have always held that God did not have to create the universe.

So then I have claimed that a person who is eternally perfectly free, omnipotent, and omniscient will have the other divine properties which I have considered. He will be an omnipresent spirit, creator of the universe, perfectly good, and a source of moral obligation. I now define such a person as a personal ground of being.[13] The theist's claim is that there exists a personal ground of being. The arguments [so far] have been arguments designed to show that the concept of a personal ground of being is a coherent one. I claim that those arguments do show that.

Although the properties associated together with the property of being a personal ground of being do not, I think, entail each other in any further way, they do belong very naturally together. A person who brings about effects clearly does so in virtue of his powers or capacities. An omnipotent person is a person to whose powers there are no limits but those of logic. If all power is really to be in the hands of some agent, it is natural to suppose that how that power is exercised lies also within his hands, and that involves him in being

---

[12] Unless the things are such as to entail that he does not bring them about. But a being can hardly have overriding reason for bringing about a state of affairs, the description of which entails that he does not bring it about; and an omniscient being will know this.

[13] The terminology is of course based on that of Tillich. See, e.g., his *Systematic Theology*, vol. i, Ch. 10.

perfectly free. Now an omnipotent being must be able to acquire knowledge of anything, but he need not actually possess knowledge of everything. Yet he clearly has to possess some knowledge. He must, for example, surely know of the basic actions which he is performing, that he is performing them. I can only move my hand, or open my mouth, as basic actions, things which I do meaning to do them, if I know that I am doing them. Further, it would seem very odd to suppose that an omnipotent being might try to do something and yet fail to do it. Yet unless he knew all the truths of logic, this would be possible. For he might try to do something which was (unknown to him) logically impossible. If this is to be ruled out, any omnipotent being would need to know all the truths of logic. However, omnipotence does not seem to entail omniscience. An omnipotent being might well not know how many pennies I have in my pocket—so long as he could acquire that knowledge when he wanted to do anything about them. But given that he must have much knowledge, the most natural assumption about the knowledge of an omnipotent person is that there are no limits to it except those of logic, viz. that he is omniscient. If such a being came into existence at any time, there would clearly in a wide sense be limits to his power. Hence it seems natural to suppose that he is backwardly eternal. Forward eternity seems to fit not unnaturally with backward eternity.

There can only be one personal ground of being. This is because there cannot be causation in a circle. It is incoherent, philosophers generally agree, to suppose that A brings about the existence of B and that B in turn brings about the existence of A. Let us suppose A to be one personal ground of being and B to be another. Let us further suppose, as I shall argue below, that the existence of a personal ground of being is a logically contingent matter; that is, although it may be necessary in some sense, it is not logically necessary. Then A as creator of the universe will have brought about the existence of B, since B is a logically contingent thing apart from A. Conversely, B will have brought about the existence of A. But that is absurd. Therefore there can only be one personal ground of being. Henceforward instead of talking of 'a personal ground of being' we can talk of 'the personal ground of being'. There can be at most one such.

'GOD' A PROPER NAME

In subsequent discussion it will be useful to have a name for the individual who is, on the theist's claim, the personal ground of being. Proper names are words such as 'Socrates,' 'Aristotle,' 'Disraeli,' 'Stalin,' 'Edward Heath,' used to denote unique individuals. (In the cases cited the individuals are people, but they need not be. 'Red Rum' is the proper name of a horse, and 'Italy' of a country.) Proper names apply to individuals, so long as they remain the same individuals, however they may change in other ways. Proper names are contrasted with definite descriptions. A definite description is a phrase such as 'the Queen of England,' 'the President of France,' 'the world chess champion.' Like proper names, definite descriptions pick out unique individuals. But a definite description applies to a certain individual only while he has the characteristics set out in the description. These are characteristics which he may lose while continuing to be the same individual. Some writers tend to treat the word 'God' as a definite description shorthand for 'the one and only one perfectly free omnipresent spirit, who is the creator of the universe, omnipotent, omniscient, perfectly good, and a source of moral obligation,' or something similar. In that case 'God' would apply to an individual only as long as he retained the stated characteristics. However, I propose henceforward[14] to use 'God' as the proper name of the individual, if there is one, who is the personal ground of being. I suspect that, in treating 'God' as a proper name, I am conforming to majority use.[15]

---

[14] It has been necessary to use the word 'God' earlier in this book, before it was convenient to introduce the distinction between proper names and definite descriptions. In general, however, throughout the book I have used 'God' only as a proper name, but one or two earlier statements will need to be read slightly differently in order to conform to this precise usage. Thus when [earlier] I talk of there being 'different definitions of "God"', this should be understood as claiming that there are different definitions, that is different descriptions, by which an individual who is then given the name 'God' is supposedly picked out.

[15] But not, however, to the use of Aquinas. He treats 'God' as a description roughly equivalent to 'a simple, perfectly good creator'. This is an indefinite description, in the sense that its applicability to a certain individual does not immediately entail that he is the only individual to whom it applies (in English indefinite descriptions are indicated by the occurrence of 'a' instead of 'the' in front of the description). Aquinas needs to produce an argument to show that there is only one God—this he does in *Summa Theologiae* I.ii.3; it does not follow immediately from the definition.

II.E.2. God As Supreme, Yet Indebted to All

CHARLES HARTSHORNE

Charles Hartshorne (1897–), professor emeritus of philosophy at the University of Texas, is one of the leading proponents of process theology. He maintains that most of the metaphysical attributes—indeed, the whole scheme of thought that conceives of God as absolute—contributes an image of God that is very unappealing. Hartshorne finds a much higher religious value in a view of God as social and personal, but he is convinced that such a conception implies relativity. Such terms as infinite, immutable, simple, *and* impassive *are attempts to express the human experience of God as supreme, but they clash with the God of love. A being so impassive as to be unmoved by any measure of human suffering is hardly a being to be worshipped or admired. To say that God is perfect does not mean that God is changeless, simple, impassive; it means that God is completely worthy of trust, admiration, and respect.*

Why is it religiously significant that God be supposed absolute? The reason is at least suggested by the consideration that absoluteness is requisite for complete reliability. What is relative to conditions may fail us if the conditions happen to be unfavorable. Hence if there is to be anything that *cannot* fail, it must be nonrelative, absolute, in those respects to which "reliability" and "failure" have reference. But it is often not noted that this need not be every respect or aspect from which God's nature can be regarded. For there may be qualities in God whose relativity or variability would be neutral to his reliability. To say of a man that (as human affairs go) his reliability is established refers not to every quality of the man, but only to certain principles exhibited in his otherwise highly variable behavior. We do not mean that if something comes close to his eye he will not blink, or that if he is given bad-tasting food he will enjoy it as much as better fare. We mean that his fixed intention to act according to the requirements of the general welfare will not waver, and that his wisdom and skill in carrying out this aim will be constant. But in all this there is not only no implication that conditions will not have effect upon the man, but the very plain implication that they will have plenty of effect. Skill in one set of circumstances means one form of behavior, in another set another form, and the same is true of the intention to serve the general good. Of course, one may argue that complete fixity of good intention and complete constancy of skill imply every other sort of fixity as well. But this has never yet been definitely shown by careful, explicit reasoning, and any-

From Charles Hartshorne, *The Divine Relativity* (New Haven: Yale University Press, 1948) pp 22–34. © Yale University Press

thing less is inappropriate in as difficult a subject as we are dealing with. General hunches will not do.

A typically invalid argument in this connection is that unless God surveys at once the whole of time and thus is independent of change, he cannot be relied upon to arrange all events with due regard to their relations to all that has gone before and all that is to come after. This argument either rests on an equivocation or it destroys all religious meaning for the divine reliability. For, if it is meant in any clear sense, it implies that every event has been selected by deity as an element in the best of all possible worlds, the ideal total pattern of all time and all existence. But this ideal pattern includes all acts of sin and the most hideous suffering and catastrophe, all the tragedies of life. And what then becomes of the ideas of human responsibility and choice, and of the notion that some deeds ought not to have taken place? These are only the beginning of the absurdities into which the view thrusts us. To mitigate these absurdities theologians introduce various more or less subtle equivocations. Would they not do better to take a fresh start (as indeed many have done) and admit that we have no good religious reason for positing the notion of providence as an absolute contriving of all events according to a completely detailed plan embracing all time? The religious value of such a notion is more negative than positive. It is the mother of no end of chicanery (see the book of Job for some examples), of much deep feeling of injustice (the poor unfortunate being assured that God has deliberately contrived everything as exactly the best way events could transpire), and of philosophical quagmires of paradox and unmeaning verbiage. The properly constituted man does not want to "rely" upon God to arrange all things, including our decisions, in accordance with a plan of all events which fixes every least detail with reference to every other that ever has happened or ever "is to" happen. How many atheists must have been needlessly produced by insistence upon this arbitrary notion, which after all is invariably softened by qualifications surreptitiously introduced *ad hoc* when certain problems are stressed! We shall see later that the really usable meaning of divine reliability is quite different and is entirely compatible with a profound relativity of God to conditions and to change. For the present, I suggest that all we can assert to have obvious religious value is the faith that God is to be relied upon to do for the world all that ought to be done for it, and with as much survey of the future as there ought to be or as is ideally desirable, leaving for the members of the world community to do for themselves and each other all that they ought to be left to do. We cannot assume that what ought to be done for the world by deity is everything that ought to be done at all, leaving the creatures with nothing to do for themselves and for each other. Nor can we assume that the ideal survey of what for us at least constitutes the future is one which fully defines it in every detail, leaving no open alternatives of possibility. So far from being self-evidently of religious value, these assumptions, viewed in the light of history, seem clearly of extreme disvalue. Yet they are often either asserted, or not unequivocally denied or avoided, in the intemperate insistence upon the total absoluteness of deity.

GOD AS SOCIAL

We have also to remember that if there is religious value in the absoluteness of God, as requisite for his reliability, there is equally manifest religious value in another trait which seems unequivocally to imply relativity rather than abso-luteness. This is the social or personal nature of God. What is a person if not a being qualified and conditioned by social relations, relations to other persons? And what is God if not the supreme case of personality? Those who deny this have yet to succeed in distinguishing their position from atheism, as Hume pointedly noted. Either God really does love all beings, that is, is related to them by a sympathetic union surpassing any human sympathy, or religion seems a vast fraud. The common query Can the Absolute or Perfect Being be personal or social? should really run In what sense, if any, can a social being be absolute or perfect? For God is conceived socially before he is conceived absolutely or as perfect God is the highest ruler, Judge, benefactor; he knows, loves, and assists man; he has made the world with the design of sharing his bliss with lesser beings. The world is a vast society governed by laws instituted by the divine monarch—the supreme personal power to whom all other persons are subject. These are all, more or less clearly, social conceptions— if you like, metaphors (though aimed, as we shall see, at a literal, intuited meaning) drawn from the social life of man. They constitute the universal, popular meaning of "God," in relation to which descriptions such as "abso-lute," "perfect," "immutable," "impassive," "simple," and the like, are tech-nical refinements aimed at logical precision. They seek to define the somewhat vague ideas of *highest* ruler, *supreme* power, or *author of all*, himself without author or origin. "Immutable," for example, is an attempted definition of the superiority of deity with respect to death and degeneration, and also with respect to vacillation of will due to fear, or other weakness. Earthly rulers are all brought low by death; and their promises and protection and execution of justice must always be discounted somewhat in anticipation of the effect upon them of changing circumstances and the development of their own motives, the growth of good and evil in their own hearts. God is not under sentence of death, cannot decay; and his covenant abides, nor is his wisdom ever clouded by storms of blind passion, the effects of strong drink or of disease.

The future of theology depends, I suggest, above all upon the answer to this question: can technically precise terms be found which express the su-premacy of God, among social beings, without contradicting his social char-acter? To say, on the one hand, that God is love, to continue to use popular religious terms like Lord, divine will, obedience to God, and on the other to speak of an absolute, infinite, immutable, simple, impassive deity, is either a gigantic hoax of priestcraft, or it is done with the belief that the social connota-tions of the popular language are ultimately in harmony with these descrip-tions. Merely to speak of the "mysteriousness" of God is not sufficient. If he escapes all the resources of our language and analysis, why be so insistent upon the obviously quite human concepts, absolute, infinite, perfect, immuta-ble? These too are our conceptions, our terms, fragments of the English or Latin languages. Perhaps after all it is not correct to say God is absolute. How shall we know, if the subject is utterly mysterious and beyond our powers?

THE SOCIAL NATURE OF EXISTENCE

The question Can a supreme being be social? is important not merely because men generally have meant by God a supreme social being. There are grounds for thinking that the popular religious emphasis is philosophically sound, that a supreme being must, for rational reasons, be conceived socially. Human nature is the supreme instance of nature in general, as known to us (apart from the "nature" of God himself), and moreover, it is the instance which in some respects at least is much more certainly and intimately known to us than any other. Human nature is social through and through. All our thought is some sort of conversation or dialogue or social transaction; when we have no one else to converse with, we converse, silently or even aloud, with ourselves. We love and hate and sympathize, not only in relation to others but in relation to our own past, future, or potential selves. Not only human beings stimulate such response, but animals, plants, mountains, ships, the moon, colors, sounds (think of groaning brakes, growling thunder, merry sunshine). One may say simply, all classes of concrete objects at least can be social objects for man. What would poetry be without personification, overt or implicit; what would art be without empathy, which is social response of a kind?

Now, further, not simply man, but all life whatsoever, has social structure. All organisms on the multicellular level are associations of cells. There is scarcely a line between societies and individuals formed by societies which reach a sufficient grade of integration. Cells themselves are associations of similar molecules and atoms. It becomes a question of how broadly one wishes to use terms where one says that the social begins, if indeed it ever begins, in the ascending scale of emergence. And the higher one goes in the scale the more obviously do the social aspects assume a primary role. Does this point to the conclusion that the supreme being is not social at all?

There are even more ultimate considerations. Logical analysis shows, according to such high authorities as Peirce and Whitehead, that the "social" in its most general sense is definable as the synthesis of all the universal categories. It is the union of absolute and relative, independent and dependent, freedom and order, individual and universal, quality and structure, and so on. A nonsocial conception is only arrived at by reducing some category to the zero case. Thus a mere "machine" is what society would become if the element of routine interdependence should completely suppress the aspect of individual initiative or originality, or if quality (feeling) should vanish, leaving mere structure. And a wholly absolute and hence nonsocial deity is one to which the category of relation—without reference to which even "absolute" has no meaning—is denied application. Thus mechanism, materialism, and absolutism can all be viewed as special cases of the same error, the arbitrary reduction of one or more aspects of sociality to zero. A category so completely ultimate for thought and life as relation (or as felt quality) can, it seems, be assigned null value only in the case of "nonentity." Those who spoke of the wholly absolute deity as the great void perhaps spoke a little more truly than they intended.

The purpose of the foregoing discussion—whose implications could be fully set forth only in a treatise on metaphysics—is not to prove that all things, and therefore even God, must or can be conceived as social in nature; but only to show that the common antithesis between the personal or social deity of religion, and the impersonal or nonsocial supreme being of philosophy, is to be viewed with suspicion. Some of the greatest philosophies, from Plato to Whitehead, have held, with varying degrees of explicitness and consistency, that the social structure is the ultimate structure of all existence; and never has this idea been so explicitly and competently defended as during the last hundred years. Whitehead's supreme conception, for example, is that of a society of actual occasions, related one to another by the sympathetic bond of "feeling of feeling." Peirce's doctrine of agapism was similar. So was Fechner's "daylight view." And Fechner and Whitehead—in some passages, also Peirce—and many other recent thinkers, have held that deity is the supreme case of the social principle, rather than an exception to it.

SOCIAL DEITY AND CREATION

It may be thought that a socially conceived God could not be the creator. Can a member of a society create that society? Here we must remember the theological principle of "eminence." God, if social, is eminently or supremely so. On the other hand, that which in the eminent form is called divine creation, in a milder or ordinary form must be exhibited by lesser beings such as man. Man certainly is social. If then ordinary sociality is ordinarily creative, eminent sociality will be eminently creative, divinely creative. And ordinary sociality is, in a humble sense, creative. A man contributes creatively to the concrete actuality of his friends and enemies, and they to his. We *make* each other what we are, in greater or less degree.

The more important members of a society contribute more largely and vitally to the actuality of other members. The supreme member of a society would contribute most vitally and largely to the actuality of all. However, we shall be told, all this is not really "creation," since it presupposes a matter and at most adds a new form. In the first place, no one has proved or can possibly prove (against Peirce, Whitehead, et al.) that there is any "matter," apart from social terms and relations. Electrons and protons are, for all that anyone knows, simply the lowest actual levels of social existence. It may well be that a human mind is not sufficiently important in the world to call an electron into being where none was before. However, we do, by our thoughts and feelings, influence the formation of nerve cells (in the first years of life), and even more, of molecules in the nerves. This is not creation in the eminent sense, but it differs from this only as we might expect the ordinary to differ from the eminent. And the influence of our thought and feeling upon nerve cells and molecules is either a blind mystery, or it is a social influence, as Peirce and Whitehead, and before them (less clearly) Leibnitz, have pointed out.

That the human creator always has a given concrete actuality to work with does not of itself establish a difference between him and God, unless it be admitted as made out that there was a first moment of creation. For if not, then God, too, creates each stage of the world as successor to a preceding phase. Only a dubious interpretation of an obscure parable, the book of Genesis, stands between us and this view. What does distinguish God is that the preceding phase was itself created by God, so that he, unlike us, is never confronted by a world whose coming to be antedates his own entire existence. There is no presupposed "stuff" alien to God's creative work; but rather everything that influences God has already been influenced by him, whereas we are influenced by events of the past with which we had nothing to do. This is one of the many ways in which eminence is to be preserved, without falling into the negations of classical theology.

ANALOGICAL CONCEPTS AND
METAPHYSICAL UNIQUENESS

It would be a misunderstanding of the social doctrine to accuse it of denying the radical difference between God and nondivine beings. Whitehead (and something similar might be said of Fechner) is so anxious that this difference should not be slurred over that he never, save once in conversation, has described God as a "society of occasions" (with "personal order") because, although that is what, in his system, God must be, it is equally clear that *this* society has a metaphysically unique status and character. By a metaphysically unique status and character I mean one whose distinctiveness can be defined through purely universal categories. It is impossible to define what is unique about my youngest brother in terms of categories alone. And if deity were conceived merely as very superior to man, this description might, for all we could know, apply to myriads of individuals somewhere in the universe. Besides, the description contains a nonmetaphysical term, man. But according to the view presented in this book, a purely metaphysical description applicable only to the one individual, God, is possible. Thus God is the *one individual conceivable a priori*. It is in this sense that concepts applied to him are analogical rather than simply univocal, in comparison to their other applications. For in all other cases, individual otherness is a mere specificity under more general characteristics—thus, my (not wholly definable) nuance of wisdom rather than yours. But in the case of deity, the most general conceptions, without anything more specific, suffice to "individuate" (though not, as we shall see, to particularize or concretize). The old dualities of creating and created, necessary and contingent, perfect and imperfect, expressed this metaphysical or a priori otherness of God. But, as generally stated, they did so in self-contradictory fashion. And it was not seen that, with respect to the category of relation, for example, a metaphysically unique status is definable in another way than through the simple denial of relativity. If the negative "nonrelatedness" is purely categorical, the positive "all-relatedness" is equally so. And we shall find that there is no logical reason why both may not apply to diverse aspects of deity. Then the metaphysical uniqueness would be a double one: no other being, in *any* aspect, could be either wholly relative or wholly nonrelative. Thus, while all beings have some measure of "absoluteness" or independence of relationships and some measure of "relativity," God, and only God, is in one aspect of his being strictly or maximally absolute, and in another aspect no less strictly or maximally relative. So both "relative" and "nonrelative" are analogical, not univocal, in application to deity. And since "social" is, in this reference, equivalent to the synthesis of independent and dependent, social also is analogical in its theological application. Accordingly, our doctrine does not "humanize" or anthropomorphize deity, but preserves a distinction that is completely metaphysical between deity and all else.

The distinction may be expressed under any category. For example, God is the only unconditionally "necessary" existent. What is unconditionally necessary in God, however, is not all of God, though it is unique to him. And in another aspect, God is not only possessed of accidents, but he is the sole being who possesses or could possibly possess all actual accidental being as his own actuality. Other beings are in no aspect strictly necessary, and in no aspect maximally accidental, but always and in all aspects something middling under both categories. In this middling character lies their "imperfection." The mediocre way in which they illustrate categories like possibility, necessity, relativity, independence, is their real otherness to the divine, not the mere fact that they do illustrate this or that category. Tradition put it otherwise, thus: "God is not subject to the category of relation, or of potentiality, or of passivity, etc."

To be sure, there are some apparent qualifications to be made of this historical account. There was said to be relation among the persons of the Trinity; and also God could be said to have "extrinsic potentiality," since his existence is the possibility of the world's existence. But these qualifications amount to little. "Relation" here is not the category of relativity in the basic or primary sense which is in question in this book. For that sense is the ability of a thing to express in its own nature those other things which, among alternatively possible or contingent things, happen to exist. (Persons of the Trinity, of course, are noncontingent.) This meaning of relation is, as we shall see, the fundamental one. Without it there could be no knowledge of what contingent things actually exist, and what possibilities of existence are unactualized. Moreover, necessity is a negative or at least an abstract conception. It may be defined as that whose nonexistence is not possible; or as that which, being common to all possibility (its least common denominator, or abstract identity), has no possible alternative. On the other hand, Peirce[1] has shown that the definition of the possible as the nonnecessary presupposes another and positive meaning, that of spontaneous variety, particularity. Extrinsic potentiality is also, like relation between exclusively necessary factors, a derivative or negative form of its category. Plato extrinsically "produced" Leibnitz, in that the actual coming to be of Leibnitz did not change or enrich the actuality of Plato. He who causes others to reach the promised land but himself remains outside—as the historical Plato remained outside the philosophy of Leibnitz (in the sense that he did not know or enjoy it)—exercises extrinsic potency, potency of producing but not of being. Alternative possible effects of such an agent cannot be regarded as deliberate deeds on his part. To decide this, when deciding that was possible, is to be in one state of decision when another was possible. In so far as Plato consciously chose the kind of successors he was to have, just so far his potency was intrinsic as well as extrinsic. And he was a human being, able to produce a human being's characteristic effects, only because he did exercise intrinsic potency. Conscious freedom is decision among alternative possibilities of intrinsic being. Plato chose the sort of influence he was to have by choosing what he was himself to be. This is all that can be meant by conscious choice. It may be that God has only to say, "Let there be light," and there is light. But God's saying "Let there be light" is a state of his

---

[1] See, in *Collected Papers*, especially Vols. I and VI, discussions of firstness, possibility, chance variety, spontaneity.

being, and a nonnecessary state, for otherwise either we have a vicious regress, the "Let there be light" becoming something outside himself, so that he must have said Let such a saying be; or else the saying is his very essence, and then he could not possibly have failed to say "Let there be light," and the saying can have been no decision, no free act at all.

II.F.   The Notion of a Limited God

II.F.1.   Attributes

JOHN STUART MILL

John Stuart Mill (1806–1873) was a leading advocate of utilitarianism, political liberalism, and rational religion. Although the implications of the work of Peter Bertocci and Charles Hartshorne seem to be that God may not be possessed of every infinite attribute that traditional theology has insisted on, Mill explicitly argues that the creator of the world we know could not be omnipotent. The evidence of design proves contrivance on the part of the creator, but a creator who could bring his objectives about merely by an act of volition would not use contrivance. Thus God must not be omnipotent. What we know about the world does not preclude God's omniscience, but neither does it prove it. Similarly, if God's omnipotence is conceded, there is no impediment (as there otherwise would be) to presuming God's supreme goodness, although again the evidence of nature does not suffice to prove it.

The question of the existence of a Deity, in its purely scientific aspect, standing as is shown [earlier], it is next to be considered, given the indications of a Deity, what *sort* of a Deity do they point to? What attributes are we warranted, by the evidence which nature affords of a creative mind, in assigning to that mind?

It needs no showing that the power, if not the intelligence, must be so far superior to that of man as to surpass all human estimate. But from this to

From *Three Essays on Religion* (New York: AMS Press, 1970), pp. 176–195.

omnipotence and omniscience there is a wide interval. And the distinction is of immense practical importance.

It is not too much to say that every indication of design in the cosmos is so much evidence against the omnipotence of the designer. For what is meant by design? Contrivance: the adaptation of means to an end. But the necessity for contrivance—the need of employing means—is a consequence of the limitation of power. Who would have recourse to means if to attain his end his mere word was sufficient? The very idea of means implies that the means have an efficacy which the direct action of the being who employs them has not. Otherwise they are not means but an encumbrance. A man does not use machinery to move his arms. If he did, it could only be when paralysis had deprived him of the power of moving them by volition. But if the employment of contrivance is in itself a sign of limited power, how much more so is the careful and skillful choice of contrivances? Can any wisdom be shown in the selection of means when the means have no efficacy but what is given them by the will of him who employs them, and when his will could have bestowed the same efficacy on any other means? Wisdom and contrivance are shown in overcoming difficulties, and there is no room for them in a being for whom no difficulties exist. The evidences, therefore, of natural theology distinctly imply that the author of the cosmos worked under limitations; that he was obliged to adapt himself to conditions independent of his will and to attain his ends by such arrangements as those conditions admitted of.

And this hypothesis agrees with what we have seen to be the tendency of the evidences in another respect. We found that the appearances in nature point indeed to an origin of the cosmos or order in nature, and indicate that origin to be design, but do not point to any commencement, still less creation, of the two great elements of the universe, the passive element and the active element, matter and force. There is in nature no reason whatever to suppose that either matter or force, or any of their properties, were made by the being who was the author of the collocations by which the world is adapted to what we consider as its purposes; or that he has power to alter any of those properties. It is only when we consent to entertain this negative supposition that there arises a need for wisdom and contrivance in the order of the universe. The Deity had on this hypothesis to work out his ends by combining materials of a given nature and properties. Out of these materials he had to construct a world in which his designs should be carried into effect through given properties of matter and force, working together and fitting into one another. This did require skill and contrivance, and the means by which it is effected are often such as justly excite our wonder and admiration; but exactly because it requires wisdom, it implies limitation of power, or rather the two phrases express different sides of the same fact.

If it be said that an Omnipotent Creator, though under no necessity of employing contrivances such as man must use, thought fit to do so in order to leave traces by which man might recognize his creative hand, the answer is that this equally supposes a limit to his omnipotence. For if it was his will that men should know that they themselves and the world are his work, he, being omnipotent, had only to will that they should be aware of it. Ingenious men have sought for reasons why God might choose to leave his existence so far a matter of doubt that men should not be under an absolute necessity of knowing it, as they are of knowing that three and two make five. These imagined reasons are very unfortunate specimens of casuistry; but even did we admit their validity, they are of no avail on the supposition of omnipotence, since if it did not please God to implant in man a complete conviction of his existence, nothing hindered him from making the conviction fall short of completeness by any margin he might choose to leave. It is usual to dispose of arguments of this description by the easy answer that we do not know what wise reasons the Omniscient may have had for leaving undone things which he had the power to do. It is not perceived that this plea itself implies a limit to omnipotence. When a thing is obviously good and obviously in accordance with what all the evidences of creation imply to have been the Creator's design, and we say we do not know what good reason he may have had for not doing it, we mean that we do not know to what other, still better object—to what object still more completely in the line of his purposes, he may have seen fit to postpone it. But the necessity of postponing one thing to another belongs only to limited power. Omnipotence could have made the objects compatible. Omnipotence does not need to weigh one consideration against another. If the Creator, like a human ruler, had to adapt himself to a set of conditions which he did not make, it is as unphilosophical as presumptuous in us to call him to account for any imperfections in his work, to complain that he left anything in it contrary to what, if the indications of design prove anything, he must have intended. He must at least know more than we know, and we cannot judge what greater good would have had to be sacrificed or what greater evil incurred if he had decided to remove this particular blot. Not so if he be omnipotent. If he be that, he must himself have willed that the two desirable objects should be incompatible; he must himself have willed that the obstacle to his supposed design should be insuperable. It cannot therefore *be* his design. It will not do to say that it was, but that he had other designs which interfered with it; for no one purpose imposes necessary limitations on another in the case of a Being not restricted by conditions of possibility.

Omnipotence, therefore, cannot be predicated of the Creator on grounds of natural theology. The fundamental principles of natural religion as deduced from the facts of the universe negative his omnipotence. They do not, in the same manner, exclude omniscience: if we suppose limitation of power, there is nothing to contradict the supposition of perfect knowledge and absolute wisdom. But neither is there anything to prove it. The knowledge of the powers and properties of things necessary for planning and executing the arrangements of the cosmos is no doubt as much in excess of human knowledge as the power implied in creation is in excess of human power. And the skill, the subtlety of contrivance, the ingenuity as it would be called in the case of a human work, is often marvelous. But nothing obliges us to suppose that either the knowledge or the skill is infinite. We are not even compelled to suppose that the contrivances were always the best possible. If we venture to judge them as we judge the works of human artificers, we find abundant defects. The human body, for example, is one of the most striking instances of artful and ingenious contrivance which nature offers, but we may well ask whether so complicated a machine could not have been made to last longer and not to get so easily and frequently out of order. We may ask why the human race should have been so constituted as to grovel in wretchedness and degradation for countless ages before a small portion of it was enabled to lift itself into the very imperfect state of intelligence, goodness, and happiness which we enjoy. The divine power may not have been equal to doing more; the obstacles to a better arrangement of things may have been insuperable. But it is also possible that they were not. The skill of the *demiourgos* was sufficient to produce what we see; but we cannot tell that this skill reached the extreme limit of perfection compatible with the material it employed and the forces it had to work with. I know not how we can even satisfy ourselves on grounds of natural theology that the Creator foresees all the future, that he foreknows all the effects that will issue from his own contrivances. There may be great wisdom without the power of foreseeing and calculating everything; and human workmanship teaches us the possibility that the workman's knowledge of the properties of the things he works on may enable him to make arrangements admirably fitted to produce a given result, while he may have very little power of foreseeing the agencies of another kind which may modify or counteract the operation of the machinery he has made. Perhaps a knowledge of the laws of nature on which organic life depends, not much more perfect than the knowledge which man even now possesses of some other natural laws, would enable man, if he had the same power over the materials and the forces concerned which he has over some of those of inanimate nature, to create organized beings not less wonderful nor less adapted to their conditions of existence than those in nature.

Assuming then that while we confine ourselves to natural religion we must rest content with a Creator less than almighty; the question presents itself, of what nature is the limitation of his power? Does the obstacle at which the power of the Creator stops, which says to it: "Thus far shalt thou go and no further," lie in the power of other intelligent beings, or in the insufficiency and refractoriness of the materials of the universe, or must we resign ourselves to admitting the hypothesis that the author of the cosmos, though wise and knowing, was not all-wise and all-knowing, and may not always have done the best that was possible under the conditions of the problem?

The first of these suppositions has until a very recent period been, and in many quarters still is, the prevalent theory even of Christianity. Though attributing, and in a certain sense sincerely, omnipotence to the Creator, the received religion represents him as for some inscrutable reason tolerating the perpetual counteraction of his purposes by the will of another being of opposite character and of great, though inferior, power, the Devil. The only difference on this matter between popular Christianity and the religion of Ormuzd and Ahriman[1] is that the former pays its good Creator the bad compliment of having been the maker of the Devil and of being at all times able to crush and annihilate him and his evil deeds and counsels, which nevertheless he does not do. But, as I have already remarked, all forms of polytheism, and this among the rest, are with difficulty reconcilable with a universe governed by general laws. Obedience to law is the note of a settled government

---

[1] [Mill here emphasizes the point that in Zoroastrianism, contrary to the Christian belief, the good spirit (Ormuzd) and the evil (Ahriman) are coeval. They are constantly at war against each other in their effort to influence the conduct of men.]

and not of a conflict always going on. When powers are at war with one another for the rule of the world, the boundary between them is not fixed but constantly fluctuating. This may seem to be the case on our planet as between the powers of good and evil when we look only at the results; but when we consider the inner springs we find that both the good and evil take place in the common course of nature, by virtue of the same general laws originally impressed—the same machinery turning out now good, now evil things, and oftener still, the two combined. The division of power is only apparently variable, but really so regular that, were we speaking of human potentates, we should declare without hesitation that the share of each must have been fixed by previous consent. Upon that supposition, indeed, the result of the combination of antagonistic forces might be much the same as on that of a single creator with divided purposes.

But when we come to consider, not what hypothesis may be conceived and possibly reconciled with known facts, but what supposition is pointed to by the evidences of natural religion, the case is different. The indications of design point strongly in one direction—the preservation of the creatures in whose structure the indications are found. Along with the preserving agencies there are destroying agencies which we might be tempted to ascribe to the will of a different creator; but there are rarely appearances of the recondite contrivance of means of destruction except when the destruction of one creature is the means of preservation to others. Nor can it be supposed that the preserving agencies are wielded by one being, the destroying agencies by another. The destroying agencies are a necessary part of the preserving agencies: the chemical compositions by which life is carried on could not take place without a parallel series of decompositions. The great agent of decay in both organic and inorganic substances is oxidation, and it is only by oxidation that life is continued for even the length of a minute. The imperfections in the attainment of the purposes which the appearances indicate have not the air of having been designed. They are like the unintended results of accidents insufficiently guarded against, or of a little excess or deficiency in the quantity of some of the agencies by which the good purpose is carried on, or else they are consequences of the wearing out of a machinery not made to last forever: they point either to shortcomings in the workmanship as regards its intended purpose, or to external forces not under the control of the workman, but which forces bear no mark of being wielded and aimed by any other and rival intelligence.

We may conclude, then, that there is no ground in natural theology for attributing intelligence or personality to the obstacles which partially thwart what seem the purposes of the Creator. The limitation of his power more probably results either from the qualities of the material—the substances and forces of which the universe is composed not admitting of any arrangements by which his purposes could be more completely fulfilled; or else, the purposes might have been more fully attained, but the Creator did not know how to do it; creative skill, wonderful as it is, was not sufficiently perfect to accomplish his purposes more thoroughly.

We now pass to the moral attributes of the Deity, so far as indicated in the creation; or (stating the problem in the broadest manner) to the question, what indications nature gives of the purpose of its author. This question bears a very different aspect to us from what it bears to those teachers of natural theology who are encumbered with the necessity of admitting the omnipotence of the Creator. We have not to attempt the impossible problem of reconciling infinite benevolence and justice with infinite power in the Creator of such a world as this. The attempt to do so not only involves absolute contradiction in an intellectual point of view but exhibits to excess the revolting spectacle of a jesuitical defense of moral enormities.

On this topic I need not add to the illustrations given of this portion of the subject in my Essay on Nature.[2] At the stage which our argument has reached there is none of this moral perplexity. Grant that creative power was limited by conditions the nature and extent of which are wholly unknown to us, and the goodness and justice of the Creator may be all that the most pious believe; and all in the work that conflicts with those moral attributes may be the fault of the conditions which left to the Creator only a choice of evils.

It is, however, one question whether any given conclusion is consistent with known facts, and another whether there is evidence to prove it; and if we have no means for judging of the design but from the work actually produced, it is a somewhat hazardous speculation to suppose that the work designed was of a different quality from the result realized. Still, though the ground is unsafe we may, with due caution, journey a certain distance on it. Some parts of the order of nature give much more indication of contrivance than others; many, it is not too much to say, give no sign of it at all. The signs of contrivance are most conspicuous in the structure and processes of vegetable and animal life. But for these, it is probable that the appearances in nature would never have seemed to the thinking part of mankind to afford any proofs of a God. But when a God had been inferred from the organization of living beings, other parts of nature, such as the structure of the solar system, seemed to afford evidence, more or less strong, in confirmation of the belief; granting then, a design in nature, we can best hope to be enlightened as to what that design was by examining it in the parts of nature in which its traces are the most conspicuous.

To what purpose, then, do the expedients in the construction of animals and vegetables, which excite the admiration of naturalists, appear to tend? There is no blinking the fact that they tend principally to no more exalted object than to make the structure remain in life and in working order for a certain time: the individual for a few years, the species or race for a longer but still limited period. And the similar, though less conspicuous, marks of creation which are recognized in inorganic nature are generally of the same character. The adaptations, for instance, which appear in the solar system consist in placing it under conditions which enable the mutual action of its parts to maintain, instead of destroying, its stability, and even that only for a time, vast indeed if measured against our short span of animated existence, but which can be perceived even by us to be limited; for even the feeble means which we possess of exploring the past are believed by those who have examined the subject by the most recent lights to yield evidence that the solar system was once a vast sphere of nebula or vapor and is going through a process which in the course of ages will reduce it to a single and not very large

---

[2] [Reference is to the first of the *Three Essays on Religion*, of which the present is the third, and "Utility of Religion" the second.]

mass of solid matter frozen up with more than arctic cold. If the machinery of the system is adapted to keep itself at work only for a time, still less perfect is the adaptation of it for the abode of living beings, since it is only adapted to them during the relatively short portion of its total duration which intervenes between the time when each planet was too hot and the time when it became or will become too cold to admit of life under the only conditions in which we have experience of its possibility. Or we should perhaps reverse the statement and say that organization and life are only adapted to the conditions of the solar system during a relatively short portion of the system's existence.

The greater part, therefore, of the design of which there is indication in nature, however wonderful its mechanism, is no evidence of any moral attributes, because the end to which it is directed, and its adaptation to which end is the evidence of its being directed to an end at all, is not a moral end: it is not the good of any sentient creature, it is but the qualified permanence, for a limited period, of the work itself, whether animate or inanimate. The only inference that can be drawn from most of it respecting the character of the Creator is that he does not wish his works to perish as soon as created; he wills them to have a certain duration. From this alone nothing can be justly inferred as to the manner in which he is affected toward his animate or rational creatures.

After deduction of the great number of adaptations which have no apparent object but to keep the machine going, there remain a certain number of provisions for giving pleasure to living beings, and a certain number of provisions for giving them pain. There is no positive certainty that the whole of these ought not to take their place among the contrivances for keeping the creature or its species in existence; for both the pleasures and the pains have a conservative tendency; the pleasures being generally so disposed as to attract to the things which maintain individual or collective existence, the pains so as to deter from such as would destroy it.

When all these things are considered it is evident that a vast deduction must be made from the evidences of a Creator before they can be counted as evidences of a benevolent purpose—so vast indeed that some may doubt whether after such a deduction there remains any balance. Yet endeavoring to look at the question without partiality or prejudice and without allowing wishes to have any influence over judgment, it does appear that granting the existence of design, there is a preponderance of evidence that the Creator desired the pleasure of his creatures. This is indicated by the fact that pleasure of one description or another is afforded by almost everything, the mere play of the faculties, physical and mental, being a never-ending source of pleasure, and even painful things giving pleasure by the satisfaction of curiosity and the agreeable sense of acquiring knowledge; and also that pleasure, when experienced, seems to result from the normal working of the machinery, while pain usually arises from some external interference with it and resembles in each particular case the result of an accident. Even in cases when pain results, like pleasure, from the machinery itself, the appearances do not indicate that contrivance was brought into play purposely to produce pain: what is indicated is rather a clumsiness in the contrivance employed for some other purpose. The author of the machinery is no doubt accountable for having made it susceptible to pain; but this may have been a necessary condition of its susceptibility to pleasure; a supposition which avails nothing on the theory of an omnipotent Creator but is an extremely probable one in the case of a contriver working under the limitation of inexorable laws and indestructible properties of matter. The susceptibility being conceded as a thing which did enter into design, the pain itself usually seems like a thing undesigned; a casual result of the collision of the organism with some outward force to which it was not intended to be exposed, and which, in many cases, provision is even made to hinder it from being exposed to. There is, therefore, much appearance that pleasure is agreeable to the Creator, while there is very little, if any, appearance that pain is so: and there is a certain amount of justification for inferring on the grounds of natural theology alone, that benevolence is one of the attributes of the Creator. But to jump from this to the inference that his sole or chief purposes are those of benevolence, and that the single end and aim of Creation was the happiness of his creatures, is not only not justified by any evidence but is a conclusion in opposition to such evidence as we have. If the motive of the Deity for creating sentient beings was the happiness of the beings he created, his purpose, in our corner of the universe at least, must be pronounced, taking past ages and all countries and races into account, to have been thus far an ignominious failure; and if God had no purpose but our happiness and that of other living creatures it is not credible that he would have called them into existence with the prospect of being so completely baffled. If man had not the power by the exercise of his own energies for the improvement both of himself and of his outward circumstances to do for himself and other creatures vastly more than God had in the first instance done, the Being who called him into existence would deserve something very different from thanks at his hands. Of course it may be said that this very capacity of improving himself and the world was given to him by God, and that the change which he will be thereby enabled ultimately to effect in human existence will be worth purchasing by the sufferings and wasted lives of entire geological periods. This may be so; but to suppose that God could not have given him these blessings at a less frightful cost is to make a very strange supposition concerning the Deity. It is to suppose that God could not, in the first instance, create anything better than a Bosjesman or an Andaman Islander,[3] or something still lower, and yet was able to endow the Bosjesman or the Andaman Islander with the power of raising himself into a Newton or a Fénelon.[4] We certainly do not know the nature of the barriers which limit the divine omnipotence; but it is a very odd notion of them that they enable the Deity to confer on an almost bestial creature the power of producing by a succession of efforts what God himself had no other means of creating.

Such are the indications of natural religion in respect to the divine benevolence. If we look for any other of the moral attributes which a certain class of philosophers are accustomed to distinguish from benevolence, as, for exam-

---

[3] [Both the Bosjesman and the Andaman Islanders are Indian tribes known for their backward state of civilization.]

[4] [François de Salignac de La Mothe Fénelon (1651–1715). French prelate and writer. Consecrated archbishop of Cambrai 1695. His major works are *Fables, Dialogues des mortes,* and *Télémaque.*]

ple, justice, we find a total blank. There is no evidence whatever in nature for divine justice, whatever standard of justice our ethical opinions may lead us to recognize. There is no shadow of justice in the general arrangements of nature; and what imperfect realization it obtains in any human society (a most imperfect realization as yet) is the work of man himself, struggling upward against immense natural difficulties into civilization, and making to himself a second nature, far better and more unselfish than he was created with. But on this point enough has been said in another Essay, already referred to: on Nature.

These, then, are the net results of natural theology on the question of the divine attributes. A being of great but limited power, how or by what limited we cannot even conjecture; of great, and perhaps unlimited, intelligence, but perhaps also more narrowly limited than his power; who desires and pays some regard to the happiness of his creatures, but who seems to have other motives of action which he cares more for, and who can hardly be supposed to have created the universe for that purpose alone. Such is the Deity whom natural religion points to; and any idea of God more captivating than this comes only from human wishes or from the teaching of either real or imaginary revelation.

II.G. Are the Divine Attributes Compatible?

II.G.1. On the Compatibility of the Divine Attributes

GEORGE N. SCHLESINGER

*George N. Schlesinger is professor of philosophy at the Univer-
sity of North Carolina. He argues in the short piece here that if
we begin our reflection on the divine attributes with the
central concept of God as absolutely perfect, there can be no
question of incompatibility. An absolutely perfect being is one
possessed of every attribute that contributes to perfection; and
that being possesses each attribute in exactly the measure that
contributes maximally.*

According to Anselm, all Divine qualities are tightly interrelated: they are implied by the unique central property of being absolutely perfect. In the second chapter of the *Proslogium*, Anselm claims that it is the essence of our concept of God that He is a being greater than which nothing can be conceived. From this, he argues, it is possible to infer that He is eternal, omnipotent, omniscient, omnibenevolent, and so on. In other words, given an absolutely perfect being we can derive all the attributes commonly ascribed to Him.

The remarkable predicate 'absolutely perfect' has the unique feature that it contains, and thus by itself implies, all the other predicates traditionally ascribed to God. In proclaiming the existence of an absolutely perfect, or the greatest possible being, the theist offers a complete description of the deity thus postulated. The theist's brief statement, that his object of worship exemplifies a maximally consistent set of great-making properties, enables us in principle to determine for any property P, whether his Deity does or does not possess P: if through having P one's excellence is enhanced, then P is a member of the set of attributes characteristic of an absolutely perfect being, otherwise it is not.

Now suppose there is a P such that it is advantageous to have it up to, but not beyond, a certain degree. Obviously then, a perfect being will have P but

From *Religious Studies* 23, no. 4 (December 1987): 539–542. Reprinted with the permission of
Cambridge University Press.

not to higher than the desired degree. It would surely be a mistake to regard a being as inadequately exemplifying P and thus treat it as inferior, simply because it possessed P less than to its full measure. For, on the contrary, it is a mark of perfection to have P just to the degree it is excellence-enhancing and no more. To give a simple example illustrating the point, suppose it has been stated that a certain person enjoys an absolutely perfect health. Surely that statement is not to be taken to imply that he has, for example, an infinitely fast heartbeat, nor again that he has an infinitely slow heartbeat, since neither a too fast nor a too slow heartbeat promotes the kind of blood circulation that ensure the best functioning of the body. The heart of an individual who is perfectly healthy will beat precisely at a rate that is not slower nor faster than is required for the optimum functioning of his various organs. It would clearly be absurd to maintain that since the heart of a person, who was in fact absolutely sound of mind and body, did not beat faster than it was good for him, he was after all handicapped by an inadequate pulse. It is thus very hard to follow Professor Pearl when he says:

> Schlesinger's attempt to protect God's perfection from challenge by lowering the standards for someone's deserving the title 'God' leaves the door open for idolatry.[1]

How can there be a lowering of standards in maintaining that God exemplifies every attribute to a degree that is neither more nor less than the exact degree it is desirable? And clearly an idolater is one who pays Divine honours to a deficient deity, one that is inferior and thus different from the superexcellent being of theism. By definition then, a person who worships a being greater than which nothing can be conceived, cannot be practicing idolatry.

Once we grasp this elementary point it will not be hard to see how any attempt to demonstrate an incompatibility among the Divine attributes cannot succeed. Consider, for example, one such attempt which consists in posing the supposedly damaging question: could God create a person S who knows a secret no one else knows? Each answer we might wish to offer could seem to lead to the defeat of theism. If the answer we give is yes, then we concede that He is not omniscient since we have admitted the possibility of something He would be ignorant of, namely, the secret known to S only. If the correct answer is no, He is not omnipotent as He is incapable of creating S.

There exist a number of wrong approaches to this problem which should be avoided. For example, one might be tempted to say that it is logically impossible that there be a secret not known to an omniscient being. Hence one might wish to argue, it is logically impossible to create a person like S. Thus God is unable to create S, since as is well known he cannot do, and is not required to do (and His inability to do does not diminish His power) that which is logically impossible.

This suggestion does not help to solve the problem since it offers no reason

---

[1] Leon Pearl "The Misuse of Anselm's Formula For God's Perfection,' *Religious Studies* xxii (1987), 385.

why we should not instead claim that on the contrary God is able to create S who would indeed have a secret not known to anyone, not even to Him. We might claim that God is simply not required to know S's secret and His inability to discover it does not diminish His omniscience, as it was logically impossible for Him to do so. The reason why it would be logically impossible for God to know S's secret is that it is logically impossible to know that which had been ensured by an omnipotent being to remain a secret.

Another unhelpful line, a line adopted by Pearl, is to say that it is irrational for God to create S. Such a suggestion will not work since it leaves open the question, given that an act is irrational and therefore God is certain not to perform it, still, would He have the power to perform it, that is to say, could He do so if He wanted to? Furthermore, this approach provides no clue as to what would happen if rationality did require the creation of S. This last question need not be interpreted as a counterfactual; the universe being so exceedingly complex and its management by far surpassing human understanding, Pearl could not insist on knowing for certain that some long-range Divine plan did not involve the need for having just the kind of person S is.

But the correct view, in my opinion is, that the question relevant in the present context is: which is more desirable, the property of having the power to create S, and thus lacking the knowledge of S's secret, or instead lacking the power to create S but being fully informed about everything? As I have stated in my original paper, we may never know the answer to this question, but can . . . rest assured that a perfect being will have whichever is the more desirable of these two properties. At this juncture, however, Pearl expresses his belief to have uncovered a difficulty serious enough to prevent a theist from knowing what deity to worship. He says:

> This approach (if interpreted as not requiring us to make principled choices) is not acceptable. For without either intuitive conviction in this matter or a rational procedure for choosing, we are in no position to identify God. A can lift every stone but not create every one; B, on the other hand, can create every stone but not lift every one. If we insist on remaining monotheists who ought we to worship, A or B. (p. 358)

It seems to me, that if Pearl's was a damaging objection then even without anything I have said, theism would be in a hopeless state. Most scientists, for example, agree that at the moment there is no sufficient evidence that intelligent life exists or does not exist outside our planet, and also that we have nothing to go by to determine whether or not our galaxy contains a planet having a mass exactly seven times as large as the earth. Also I take it that not many would claim to have a clear view as to which of the two otherwise equal, impeccable beings X and Y is superior: X, who is disposed to create a universe where intelligent creatures are confined to a single planet, or Y who will allow more than one planet to be inhabited by sentient beings? Similarly, there seems to be no way of deciding whether of U and V, who are no different from one another except that U places in our galaxy a planet sevenfold as massive as our own, whereas V does not do so, which one is to be preferred? Thus according to Pearl the theist finds himself in the unwieldy predicament, is he to adopt as his object of worship a deity like X, like Y, like U or like V?

Part III

The Arguments for Theism

The surest foundation for theism, it has often been assumed, is a set of solid arguments proving the existence of God. The attempt to provide such arguments or proofs has preoccupied the energies of a great many Western philosophers and theologians for more than two millennia. Although some have assumed, and others have attempted to demonstrate by argument, that the existence of God is not the sort of thing that human reason can prove, many have felt confident that proofs can be found. Theologians such as St. Tertullian (c. 160–220) condemn efforts to prove God's existence on grounds that human reason, tainted by the sin of Adam, is incapable of understanding such high things and that it is the folly of sinful pretension to try. Faith, according to Tertullian, is our path to knowledge of God; when the articles of faith received through revelation appear contradictory to reason, that is a clue to the feebleness and corrupted nature of reason and a sign that the revelation is profoundly true. Others such as David Hume (1711–1776), though not scornful of the power of reason, are nonetheless convinced by the use of reason that humans lack the kind of knowledge that would make proofs of God's existence valid. The efforts to provide proofs have been persistent, however, and many thinkers are convinced not only that proofs are needed and useful but also that valid proofs are possible.

In the strictest sense of the word, a *proof* is a valid argument whose premises are known to be true. Thus the evaluation of alleged proofs involves not only an assessment of their validity but especially a scrutiny of the premises. Some premises of some of the arguments, even if they are true, may not be of the sort that human reason can *know* to be true. This is the problem that Thomas Aquinas (1224–1274) finds with the ontological argument. Thomas says that the argument is valid from God's perspective but that since *knowing* the truth of the premises would require comprehending the divine nature, something not possible for humans, the argument is not, from the human point of view, a legitimate proof. But there are other arguments that, according to Thomas, do not require knowledge beyond the reach of human reason, and therefore God's existence can be proved. Thomas provides five such arguments, his famous "five ways."

Many supporters of rational proofs interpret arguments for the existence of God not as demonstrations but as ways of arranging evidence to offer strong support for belief in God. A. E. Taylor (1869–1945) sees theistic arguments not as knock-down proofs that coerce reason by showing that the denial of their conclusions involves a contradiction, but as analogous to scientific arguments, which provide a plausible interpretation of human experience and the order of nature in terms that strongly suggest or provide credible evidence for a divine creator. Using the teleological and the moral arguments, Taylor not only provides support for the claim that God exists but also an interpretation of how arguments that do not attempt absolute demonstration may still offer valuable evidence.

The ontological argument attempts a logical demonstration of God's existence. It is the single argument that has perhaps raised the most controversy among philosophers and theologians. Commencing from the meaning of the term "God," it proceeds, allegedly without making use of any empirical premises (thus avoiding the uncertainty that accompanies every empirical claim) to demonstrate that a being so defined must exist because the denial would involve a contradiction. God, that being than which no greater can be conceived, must exist, else a greater could be conceived—one just like the first but also existing, which would be a contradiction. Put forward in its classic form by St. Anselm (1033–1109) and elaborated among others by René Descartes (1596–1650), this argument was declared impossible by Immanuel Kant (1724–1804) and widely neglected until the twentieth century when it has enjoyed a considerable renaissance.

The cosmological argument begins with the empirical assumption of the existence of the observed world and usually involves what some philosophers regard as a logical assumption of the so-called principle of sufficient reason—that is, there is a sufficient reason or cause for the existence of whatever exists. The argument claims that the world is a contingent being, that is, something whose existence is not self-explanatory, but that depends on something else. It holds that the events in the world that we experience all turn out to depend on antecedent events that we understand as their causes. It then asserts that the chain of causation cannot be infinite; there must be a first cause. Thus God is suggested as the first cause. God, an eternal and infinite being, is said to contain within his own nature the sufficient reason for his existence and thus to require no further explanation.

This argument has been attacked at virtually every point. The principle of sufficient reason has been alleged to be suspect. How do we know, after all, that there is indeed a sufficient reason or a cause for everything? Defenders, though conceding that we cannot know for sure, have pointed out that the whole and rather successful enterprise of science is based on this assumption and that the denial of the principle implies what scarcely anyone is likely to concede—namely, that things might pop into and out of existence fortuitously and that events might happen for no reason at all.

The claim that an infinite regress of causes is impossible has also been questioned. Why, after all, must the chain have a beginning? If each link is supported by the one before it and we never reach a link that is not so supported, then no step is without support or explanation. The postulation of a divine being, moreover, is sometimes said to be an attempt to explain the obscure in terms of the more obscure. To say that God is the first cause and sufficient reason for the existence of the world is simply to name something whose nature we do not understand at all to explain a cosmic process whose nature we do understand in some measure. And if it is legitimate to say that God is eternal, self-existent, and in no need of explanation, why not simplify our theory by omitting God and making the same claim about the world? But the criticisms of the cosmological argument have failed to persuade everyone; many still find it a strong argument for the existence of God.

The teleological argument, like the cosmological argument, begins with empirical assumptions, but in this case not simply the contingent existence of the world is assumed but its orderliness, which is said to bespeak deliberate design. The argument often makes use of analogies between complex, humanly contrived objects and objects in nature that also seem to have been contrived to serve certain purposes. Then the comparison is extended to the entire universe, which is said to be machinelike, orderly, rational, and on such a grand scale as to require as its creator a divine mechanic or engineer with intelligence and purpose resembling, but vastly superior to, that of the smartest of humans.

This argument has also been subject to considerable criticism. David Hume, one of the most powerful critics, points out that arguments relying on analogy always fall short of proof; the wider the analogy, the weaker the argument. He also notes that the argument at best points to some sort of intelligence and purpose, not necessarily a single being or one like our conception of God. Supporters of the argument, however, reply that we should hardly scorn an argument that supports its conclusion in the same way, and with the same degree of evidence, that scientists use to support their conclusions. Further, if the argument justifies our believing that the world is the product of a great intelligence, we have come a long way toward showing that the world is created by God; the rest of the proving can come from supplementary arguments.

From the human experience of urgent moral obligation, the moral argument attempts to infer the existence of a God who is the source of the laws that define the nature of that obligation and who is the ground of the obligation itself. Immanuel Kant, a major proponent of this argument, concedes that it provides no proof and calls God's existence a postulate of pure practical (i.e., moral) reason. He insists, however, that the nature of morality, and the universality and inescapability of its demands, are unintelligible unless we postulate God as lawgiver and sustainer of a moral universe in which ultimately justice prevails. Thus in Kant's mind the nature of our experience of moral obligation justifies the postulation of three things, none of which can otherwise be justified: God, the freedom of the human will, and the immortality of the human soul. Serious objections have been raised against this argument, which in any case makes only modest claims, but some of its defenders believe that those claims are legitimate.

The pragmatic argument does not so much claim to prove or provide strong evidence for the existence of God as it claims to provide justification, in the absence of positive proofs or disproofs, for affirming a belief. The argument concedes—indeed, insists on the point—that the evidence for the existence of God is inconclusive. But it also maintains that the practical consequences of believing or not believing are of surpassing importance, both in the present life and, if there is one, in the life to come. Thus even in the face of those who denigrate the holding of beliefs for which there is not sufficient rational warrant, the supporters of this position insist that it is, after all, justifiable to affirm a belief in God.

ANNOTATED GUIDE TO FURTHER READINGS

General

Mackie, J. L. *The Miracle of Theism*. Oxford: Clarendon Press, 1982.
A comprehensive survey of the arguments for the existence of God. Hume, Descartes, Berkeley, and Swinburne among others are given special attention. Mackie's own position is skeptical.

Rowe, William L., and Wainwright, William J., eds. *Philosophy of Religion: Selected Readings*, 2nd ed. New York: Harcourt Brace Jovanovich, 1989.
Contains an excellent collection of readings dealing with the ontological, cosmological, teleological, and moral arguments. The section on the ontological argument provides a particularly good introduction; it contains Anselm's argument and Gaunilo's response, selections from Descartes and Plantinga, and Kant's attack upon the argument.

Swinburne, Richard, *The Existence of God*. Oxford: Clarendon Press, 1979.
A somewhat technical analysis of the topic. Swinburne thoroughly examines the evidence for the existence of God, including traditional proofs as well as arguments based on historical and religious experience.

The Ontological Argument

Hartshorne, Charles. *The Logic of Perfection*. La Salle, Ill.: Open Court, 1962.

Chapter 2 of this book extensively examines various forms of the ontological argument. Hartshorne's analysis, although somewhat technical at times, is excellent; he thoroughly discusses most of the arguments and counter-arguments.

Hick, John, and McGill, Arthur C., eds. *The Many-Faced Argument.* New York: Macmillan, 1967.
This comprehensive study of the traditional ontological argument focuses on the writings of St. Anselm but also deals with the more recent reformulations of the argument.

Plantinga, Alvin. *The Nature of Necessity.* Oxford: Clarendon Press, 1974.
Plantinga looks at the concept of necessity in this challenging book. Through such means as the notion of possible worlds, Plantinga creates a solid foundation for the understanding of the term necessity, *using this framework to examine the ontological argument.*

Plantinga, Alvin, ed. *The Ontological Argument.* Garden City, N.Y.: Doubleday, 1965.
A collection of essays tracing the ontological argument from its beginnings (Anselm, Aquinas, and Descartes) through contemporary times (Moore, Alston, Hartshorne, Malcolm). Especially intriguing is the piece by J. N. Findlay, in which he tries to disprove the existence of God by turning the ontological argument back on itself.

The Cosmological Argument

Craig, William Lane, *The Cosmological Argument from Plato to Leibniz.* New York: Barnes and Noble, 1980.
Craig gives a comprehensive history of the cosmological argument, then distinguishes arguments of three different types: those based on the principle of determination, those based on the principle of causality, and those based on the principle of sufficient reason.

Kenny, Anthony. *The Five Ways.* Notre Dame, Ind.: University of Notre Dame Press, 1969.
Kenny recounts and analyzes Aquina's five ways to prove the existence of God: The first four of these ways are forms of the cosmological argument and the fifth is the deductive form of the teleological argument. Aquinas's writings form a vital part of the basic historical foundation of the cosmological argument and are important to the study of the argument.

Rowe, William L. *The Cosmological Argument.* Princeton, N.J.: Princeton University Press, 1975.
An excellent source for analysis. Rowe first discusses the various forms of the argument and then examines some of its faults.

The Teleological Argument

Hume, David. *Dialogues Concerning Natural Religion,* edited by John Valdimir Price. Oxford: Clarendon Press, 1976.
This classic contribution to the philosophy of religion, from which two selections are included in this Part, deserves reading in its entirety by the serious student. Hume's wit provides amusing but devastating criticisms of several theistic arguments and of theism in general.

Paley, William. "The Watch and the Watchmaker." In *Philoso-phy of Religion: An Anthology*, edited by Louis P. Pojman. Belmont, Calif.: Wadsworth, 1987.
Paley's famous analogy. This section of Pojman's text also has a fine article by Swinburne and an excerpt from Hume.

The Moral Argument

Adams, Robert Merrihew. "Moral Arguments for Theistic Be-lief." In *Rationality and Religious Belief*, edited by C. F. De-laney. Notre Dame, Ind.: University of Notre Dame Press, 1979.
Through the framework of the divine command theory, Adams discusses the existence and nature of God. He talks about two types of moral arguments for the existence of God, the theoretical (which tries to prove that God exists) and the practical (which seeks to show that it is morally desirable to believe in God).

Mackie, J. L. *The Miracle of Theism*. Oxford: Claredon Press, 1982.
Mackie devotes a chapter to analyzing and criticizing several forms of the moral argument, including that of Newman, Kant, and Sedgwick.

The Pragmatic Argument

Cargile, James. "Pascal's Wager." In *Contemporary Philosophy of Religion*, edited by Steven M. Cahn and David Shatz. New York: Oxford University Press, 1982.
Cargile denigrates the importance of Pascal's pragmatic argument for religious belief by saying that realistically it probably will not sway anyone's opinion.

Mackie, J. L. *The Miracle of Theism*. Oxford: Claredon Press, 1982.
In a chapter titled "Belief Without Reason," Mackie offers a critique of Pascal's Wager, James's Pragmatic Argument, and Kierkegaard's notion of the Primacy of Commitment.

III.A. The Place of Rational Proofs

III.A.1. The Five Ways

THOMAS AQUINAS

Thomas Aquinas (1224–1274) was a Benedictine monk and one of the greatest systematic theologians in the history of the West. An enthusiastic supporter of rational theology, Thomas denied that there could be any inconsistency between what God reveals to humans through scripture and the Church and what the God-given human faculty of reason discovers. Thus he set out to reconcile faith or revelation with reason. Thomas argues that, although some mysteries are beyond the power of reason to understand, many of the most important religious truths lie within the competency of reason. Revelation is the means by which God vouchsafes to make known to us those essential things that we cannot discover by the right use of reason. But God gave us reason so that we could find out the truth by tracing the paths and patterns of God's work in the world.

One of the essential aspects of knowledge that reason is able to discern, says Thomas, is that God exists. To be sure, the existence of God is also made known to us through divine revelation. God intentionally revealed some things that reason could also discover so that these revelations might serve as a verifier and trainer of reason. In the following selection, one of the most frequently cited passages from Thomas's writings, he offers his famous five proofs of the existence of God. The first four are versions of the cosmological argument; the fifth is an example of the deductive form of the teleological argument.

QUESTION II: THE EXISTENCE OF GOD

Third Article: Whether God Exists?

We proceed thus to the Third Article:—
  Objection 1. It seems that God does not exist; because if one of two con-

From *Summa Theologica*, in Anton C. Pegis, *An Introduction to St. Thomas Aquinas* (New York: Random House, 1945), pp. 24–27.

traries be infinite, the other would be altogether destroyed. But the name *God* means that He is infinite goodness. If, therefore, God existed, there would be no evil discoverable; but there is evil in the world. Therefore God does not exist.

Objection 2. Further, it is superfluous to suppose that what can be accounted for by a few principles has been produced by many. But it seems that everything we see in the world can be accounted for by other principles, supposing God did not exist. For all natural things can be reduced to one principle, which is nature; and all voluntary things can be reduced to one principle, which is human reason, or will. Therefore there is no need to suppose God's existence.

On the contrary, It is said in the person of God: *I am Who am* (*Exod.* iii. 14).

I answer that, The existence of God can be proved in five ways.

The first and most manifest way is the argument from motion. It is certain, and evident to our senses, that in the world some things are in motion. Now whatever is moved is moved by another, for nothing can be moved except it is in potentiality to that towards which it is moved; whereas a thing moves inasmuch as it is in act. For motion is nothing else than the reduction of something from potentiality to actuality. But nothing can be reduced from potentiality to actuality, except by something in a state of actuality. Thus that which is actually hot, as fire, makes wood, which is potentially hot, to be actually hot, and thereby moves and changes it. Now it is not possible that the same thing should be at once in actuality and potentiality in the same respect, but only in different respects. For what is actually hot cannot simultaneously be potentially hot; but it is simultaneously potentially cold. It is therefore impossible that in the same respect and in the same way a thing should be both mover and moved, *i.e.*, that it should move itself. Therefore, whatever is moved must be moved by another. If that by which is moved be itself moved, then this also must needs be moved by another, and that by another again. But this cannot go on to infinity, because then there would be no first mover, and, consequently, no other mover, seeing that subsequent movers move only inasmuch as they are moved by the first mover; as the staff moves only because it is moved by the hand. Therefore it is necessary to arrive at a first mover, moved by no other; and this everyone understands to be God.

The second way is from the nature of efficient cause. In the world of sensible things we find there is an order of efficient causes. There is no case known (neither is it, indeed, possible) in which a thing is found to be the efficient cause of itself: for so it would be prior to itself, which is impossible. Now in efficient causes it is not possible to go on to infinity, because in all efficient causes following in order, the first is the cause of the intermediate cause, and the intermediate is the cause of the ultimate cause, whether the intermediate cause be several, or one only. Now to take away the cause is to take away the effect. Therefore, if there be no first cause among efficient causes, there will be no ultimate, nor any intermediate, cause. But if in efficient causes it is possible to go on to infinity, there will be no first efficient cause, neither will there be an ultimate effect, nor any intermediate efficient causes; all of which is plainly false. Therefore it is necessary to admit a first efficient cause, to which everyone gives the name of God.

The third way is taken from possibility and necessity, and runs thus. We find in nature things that are possible to be and not to be, since they are found to be generated, and to be corrupted, and consequently, it is possible for them to be and not to be. But it is impossible for these always to exist, for that which can not-be, at some time is not. Therefore if everything can not-be then at one time there was nothing in existence. Now if this were true, even now there would be nothing in existence, because that which does not exist begins to exist only through something already existing. Therefore, if at one time nothing was in existence, it would have been impossible for anything to have begun to exist; and thus even now nothing would be in existence—which is absurd. Therefore, not all beings are merely possible, but there must exist something the existence of which is necessary. But every necessary thing either has its necessity caused by another, or not. Now it is impossible to go on to infinity in necessary things which have their necessity caused by another, as has been already proved in regard to efficient causes. Therefore we cannot but admit the existence of some being having of itself its own necessity, and not receiving it from another, but rather causing in others their necessity. This all men speak of as God.

The fourth way is taken from the gradation to be found in things. Among beings there are some more and some less good, true, noble, and the like. But *more* and *less* are predicted of different things according as they resemble in their different ways something which is the maximum, as a thing is said to be hotter according as it more nearly resembles that which is hottest; so that there is something which is truest, something best, something noblest, and consequently, something which is most being, for those things that are greatest in truth are greatest in being, as it is written in *Metaph.* ii. Now the maximum in any genus is the cause of all in that genus, as fire, which is the maximum of heat, it the cause of all hot things, as is said in the same book. Therefore there must also be something which is to all beings the cause of their being, goodness, and every other perfection; and this we call God.

The fifth way is taken from the governance of the world. We see that things which lack knowledge, such as natural bodies, act for an end, and this is evident from their acting always, or nearly always, in the same way, so as to obtain the best result. Hence it is plain that they achieve their end, not fortuitously, but designedly. Now whatever lacks knowledge cannot move towards an end, unless it be directed by some being endowed with knowledge and intelligence; as the arrow is directed by the archer. Therefore some intelligent being exists by whom all natural things are directed to their end; and this being we call God.

Reply Objection 1. As Augustine says: *Since God is the highest good, He would not allow any evil to exist in His works, unless His omnipotence and goodness were such as to bring good even out of evil.* This is part of the infinite goodness of God, that He should allow evil to exist, and out of it produce good.

Reply Objection 2. Since nature works for a determinate end under the direction of a higher agent, whatever is done by nature must be traced back to God as to its first cause. So likewise whatever is done voluntarily must be traced back to some higher cause other than human reason and will, since these can change and fail; for all things that are changeable and capable of defect must be traced back to an immovable and self-necessary first principle, as has been shown.

III.A.2. From Nature and Man to God

A. E. TAYLOR

Alfred E. Taylor (1869–1945), a scholar of ancient Greek philosophy, offers here an exposition of two arguments for the existence of God: the teleological and the moral. But he also provides us with a discussion of the place of rational proofs, suggesting that even though some or perhaps all of the arguments may fall short of absolute demonstration, they are at least as strong as the arguments scientists provide for their conclusions and should therefore be accorded at least as much respect and credibility.

Speaking quite generally, I suppose we may say that no great and far-reaching scientific theory is ever adopted because it has been demonstrated. It is not believed because it can be shown by stringent logic that all other accounts of facts involve self-contradiction. The real reason for belief is that the theory provides a key for the interpretation of the facts on which it is said to be founded, that on further investigation it is found also to provide a key to the interpretation of numerous groups of often very dissimilar facts, which were either uninterpretable or actually unknown when the theory was first put forward, and that even where at first sight there are facts which seem refractory to the proposed interpretation, the general theory can be made to fit them by some modification which does not interfere with its continued use for the interpretation of the facts by which it was first suggested. In this respect the interpretation of the "book of Nature" is exactly similar to the process of deciphering a cryptogram or an inscription in a hitherto unknown language. The decipherer has first to be in possession of a "key" of promising make. Thus, the inscription may be bilingual and one language may be a known one; there may be good reasons for believing that the cipher message is in English, and this enables the reader to make a probable conjecture from the relative frequency of certain signs alone or in combination. The original identifications will usually be in part erroneous, but even where they are so, if enough of them are correct, the partial decipherment will make the words of the text sufficiently intelligible to lead to subsequent correction of initial mistakes; though, when all our ingenuity has been expended, it may still remain the case that some of the signs we are trying to decipher have to be left uninterpreted owning to the insufficiency of our data. If our inscription were interminable, we might readily have to acknowledge that, though successive scrutiny made each new reading more nearly correct than those which went before, a final and definitive transcription was beyond our reach, and that all we could do was to make the tentative and provisional element in our readings

From "The Veneration of Religion," in E. G. Selwyn, ed., *Essays Catholic and Critical* (London: Society for Promoting Christian Knowledge, 1927), pp. 34f, 38f, 46–64, 70.

steadily smaller. It is hardly necessary to mention the way in which this tentative process of decipherment of symbols, applied to the hieroglyphs of Egypt and the cuneiform of Babylon, has already enriched our historical knowledge of the early civilisations by making real to us the politics and social life of people who, a few generations ago, were little but names to us, or the still greater flood of light on the past of our race which may yet come from the successful reading of Cretan and Hittite records. . . .

If all this is so, we cannot be fairly asked to justify religion by producing a different kind of vindication, or a fuller degree of vindication, of the "religious view" of the world than the man of science would think adequate if he were called on to "vindicate" the "scientific view" of the world. In either case the most that can be demanded of us is to show that there are real and undeniable facts which call for explanations and must not be explained *away*; that the interpretation supplied brings coherence and "sense" into them, where they would, without it, be an unintelligible puzzle; that the more steadily and systematically the principles we fall back on are employed, the less puzzling does the reality we are trying to interpret become. In a word, we need to show that there is the same solid ground for holding that religion cannot be dismissed as a passing illusion incident to a particular stage in the mental growth of humanity as there is for holding the same view about science. If we cannot *demonstrate* that religion is not temporary illusion, neither can we *demonstrate* that science is in any better position. And it may be worth while to observe in express words that the real weight of the "evidence" which is accepted as sufficient ground for assurance can only be judged by a mind of the right kind and with the right training. This holds good without exception in all branches of "secular" learning. An experiment which the trained chemist or physicist sees to be "crucial" as deciding for or against a speculation will often seem of no particular significance to a layman; it requires another and a different type of mind and a different training to appreciate the sort of considerations which a trained palaeographer will regard as decisive for the authenticity of a document, the soundness of a reading, the worth of a speculation about the relations between the various extant manuscripts of an ancient author.[1]

---

[1] This is why even men of high intellectual power so often make themselves merely ridiculous when they venture into fields of knowledge where they are amateurs. Their training has not prepared them to be sound judges of the kind of considerations which are decisive in dealing with the unfamiliar matter. It is notorious that some of the very worst Biblical and Shakespearean "criticism" has been produced by lawyers who are very sound judges of evidence within their own sphere. The trouble is that their training disposes them to assume that what cannot be "proved" under the rules of the English or some other law of evidence cannot be adequately established in history or in literary criticism, or that what would be regarded as sufficient evidence for a British jury must always be sufficient evidence for the historian or the critic. Both assumptions are mistaken. Thus a "lawyer turned apologist" will argue that the critical analysis of the Pentateuch must be rejected because no one can "produce to the court" copies of the earlier documents into which it is analysed, or again that he has proved the correctness of the traditional ascription of a work like the Fourth Gospel to a particular author by merely showing that the tradition is ancient, as though some sort of law of "prescription" held good in questions of authorship.

I. FROM NATURE TO GOD

(1) The argument "from Nature up to Nature's God" can be presented in very different forms and with very different degrees of persuasiveness, corresponding with the more or less definite and accurate knowledge of different ages about the detailed facts of Nature and the greater or less degree of articulation attained by Logic. But the main thought underlying these very different variations is throughout the same, that the incomplete points to the complete, the dependent to the independent, the temporal to the eternal. Nature, in the sense of the complex of "objects presented to our notice," the bodies animate and inanimate around us, and our own bodies which interact with them and each other, is, in the first place, always something incomplete; it has no limits or bounds; the horizon in space and time endlessly recedes as we carry our adventure of exploration further; "still beyond the sea, there is more sea." What is more, Nature is always dependent; no part of it contains its complete explanation in itself; to explain why any part is what it is, we have always to take into account the relations of that part with some other, which in turn requires for explanation its relation to a third, and so on without end. And the fuller and richer our knowledge of the content of Nature becomes, the more, not the less, imperative do we find the necessity of explaining everything by reference to other things which, in their turn, call for explanation in the same way. Again, mutability is stamped on the face of every part of Nature. "All things pass and nothing abides." What was here in the past is now here no more, and what is here now will some day no longer be here. "There stood the rock where rolls the sea." Even what looks at first like permanence turns out on closer examination to be only slower birth and decay. Even the Christian Middle Ages thought of the "heavens" as persisting unchanged from the day of their creation to that of their coming dissolution in fiery heat and new creation; modern astronomy tells us of the gradual production and dissolution of whole "stellar systems." Thoughts like these suggested to the Greek mind from the very infancy of science the conclusion that Nature is no self-contained system which is its own *raison d'être*. Behind all temporality and change there must be something unchanging and eternal which is the source of all things mutable and the explanation why they are as they are. In the first instance this sense of mutability gave rise only to a desire to know what is the permanent stuff of which what we call "things" are only passing phases; is it water, or vapour, or fire, or perhaps something different from them all? The one question which was primary for the earliest men of science was just this question about the stuff of which everything is made. To us it seems a very different thing to say "all things are water," or to say "I believe in God," but at bottom the quest after the stuff of which things are made is a first uncertain and half-blind step in the same direction as Aristotle's famous argument, adopted by St. Thomas, for the existence of an "unmoved Mover" (who, remaining *immotus in se*, is the source of all the movement and life of this lower world), and as all the since familiar *a posteriori* proofs of the existence of God.

(2) It is but a further step in the same direction, which was soon taken by the early founders of science, when it is perceived that the persistence of an unchanged "stuff" is no complete explanation of the apparent facts of Nature, and that we have further to ask where the "motion" which is the life of all

natural processes comes from. This is the form in which the problem presented itself to Aristotle and his great follower St. Thomas. They believed that "Nature is uniform" in the sense that all the apparently irregular and lawless movements and changes with which life makes us familiar in the world around us issue from, and are the effects of, other movements (those of the "heavens"), which are absolutely regular and uniform. On this view, the supreme dominant uniform movement in Nature is naturally identified with the apparently absolutely regular diurnal revolution of the whole stellar heavens round the earth. But Aristotle could not be content to accept the mere fact of this supposed revolution as an ultimate fact needing no further explanation. No motion explains itself, and we have therefore to ask the "cause" or reason why the heavens should display this uniform continuous movement. That reason Aristotle and his followers could only explain in the language of imaginative myth. Since nothing can set itself going, the movement which pervades the whole universe of Nature must be set going by something which is not itself set going by anything else; not mutable and changeable therefore, but eternally selfsame and perfect, because it already is all that it can be, and so neither needs nor permits of development of any kind. "From such a principle depends the whole heaven."[2] And it follows from certain other presuppositions of Aristotle's philosophy that this "principle" must be thought of as a perfect and living intelligence. Thus in Aristotle's formulation of the principles of natural science we reach the explicit result that Nature is in its inmost structure only explicable as something which depends on a perfect and eternal source of life, and this source is not itself Nature nor any part of Nature; the "transcendence of God" has at last been explicitly affirmed as a truth suggested (Aristotle and St. Thomas would say demonstrated) by the rational analysis of Nature herself. In principle their argument is that of every later form of the "cosmological proof."

Meanwhile with the transference of interest from the question about the stuff of which things are made to the question of the source of their movement and life, another line of thought had become prominent. The connection between organ and function is one which naturally struck the far-away founders of the science of biology. For living things show adaptation to their environment, and the various organs of living beings show adaptation to the discharge of specific functions conducing to the maintenance of the individual or the kind. And again, the living creature is not equally adapted at all stages of its existence for the full discharge of these functions. We can see it adapting itself to one of the most important of these as we watch the series of changes it undergoes from infancy to puberty, and we see the same process more elaborately if we widen our horizon and study the pre-natal history of the embryo. From such considerations derives the further suggestion which ultimately becomes the "argument from design." Aristotle is convinced that the biological analogy may be applied to all processes of the organic or inorganic world. Every process has a final stage or "end" in which it culminates, as the whole process of conception, birth, post-natal growth culminates in the existence of the physically adult animal; and it is always the "end" to which a process is

---

[2] Aristotle, *Metaphysics*, 1072b, 14.

relative that determines the character of the earlier stages of the process. One seed grows into an apple-tree, another into a pear-tree, not because the two have been differently pulled or pushed, heated or cooled, wetted or dried, but because from the first the one was the sort of thing which was going, if not interfered with, to become an apple, the other the sort of thing which was going to become a pear. In the same way, there is definite order or plan everywhere in the structure of Nature, though Aristotle, unlike his master Plato, will not account for this orderliness by appeal to the conscious will and beneficent intention of his supreme Intelligence, but regards it rather, in the fashion of many modern biologists, as due to an unconscious and instinctive "quasi-purposiveness" in Nature herself.[3]

Let us look back at this line of thought, out of which the familiar "proofs of the existence of God" brought forward in popular works on Natural Theology have been developed, and ask ourselves what permanent value it retains for us to-day and how far it goes towards suggesting the real existence of a God whom a religious man can worship "in spirit and in truth." We must not suppose that the thought itself is necessarily antiquated because the language in which it is clothed strikes us as old-fashioned, or because those who gave it its first expression held certain views about the details of Nature's structure (notably the geocentric conception in astronomy) which are now obsolete. It may very well be that the substitution of contemporary for antiquated views about the structure of the "stellar universe" or the fixity of animal species will leave the force of the argument, whatever that force may be, unaffected. There are two criticisms in particular which it is as well to dispose of at once, since both sound plausible, and both, unless I am badly mistaken, go wide of the mark.

(a) The point of the argument about the necessity of an "unmoving source of motion" must not be missed. We shall grasp it better if we remember that "motion" in the vocabulary of Aristotle means change of every kind, so that what is being asserted is that there must be an unchanging cause or source of change. Also, we must not fancy that we have disposed of the argument by saying that there is no scientific presumption that the series of changes which make up the life of Nature may not have been without a beginning and destined to have no end. St. Thomas, whose famous five proofs of the existence of God are all of them variations on the argument from "motion," or, as we might say, the appeal to the principle of causality, was also the philosopher who created a sensation among the Christian thinkers of his day by insisting stiffly that, apart from the revelation given in Scripture, no reasons can be produced for holding that the world had a beginning or need have an end, as indeed Aristotle maintained that it has neither. The dependence meant in the argument has nothing to do with succession in time. What is really meant is that our knowledge of any event in Nature is not complete until we know the full reason for the event. So long as you only know that A is so because B is so,

---

[3] For an excellent summary account of the early Greek science referred to above see Burnet, *Greek Philosophy: Thales to Plato*, pp. 1–101; and for what has been said of Aristotle, W. D. Ross, *Aristotle*, chap. iii. pp. 62–111, chap. iv. pp. 112–128, and chap. vi. pp. 179–186; or, for a briefer summary, A. E. Taylor, *Aristotle* (Nelson & Sons, 1919), chaps. iii.–iv. pp. 49–93.

but cannot tell why B is so, your knowledge is incomplete. It only becomes complete when you are in a position to say that ultimately A is so because Z is so, Z being something which is its own *raison d'être*, and therefore such that it would be senseless to ask *why* Z is so. This at once leads to the conclusion that since we always have the right to ask about any event in Nature why that event is so, what are its conditions, the Z which is its own *raison d'être* cannot itself belong to Nature. The point of the reasoning is precisely that it is an argument from the fact that there is a "Nature" to the reality of a "Supernature," and this point is unaffected by the question whether there ever was a beginning of time, or a time when there were no "events."

Again, we must not be led off the track by the plausible but shallow remark that the whole problem about the "cause of motion" arose from the unnecessary assumption that things were once at rest and afterwards began to move, so that you have only to start, as the modern physicist does, with a plurality of moving particles, or atoms, or electrons to get rid of the whole question. Nor would it be relevant to remark that modern physics knows of no such absolutely uniform motions as those which Aristotle ascribes to "the heavens," but only of more or less stable motions. If you start, for example, with a system of "particles" all in uniform motion, you have still to account for the rise of "differential" motions. If you start, as Epicurus tried to do, with a rain of particles all moving in the same direction and with the same relative velocities, you cannot explain why these particles ever came together to form complexes. If you prefer, with Herbert Spencer, to start with a strictly "homogeneous" nebula, you have to explain, as Spencer does not, how "heterogeneity" ever got in. You must have individual variety, as well as "uniformity," in whatever you choose to take as your postulated original data if you are to get out of the data a world like ours, which, as Mill truly says, is not only uniform but also infinitely various. *Ex nihilo, nihil fit*, and equally out of blank uniformity nothing *fit* but a uniformity equally blank. Even if, *per impossibile*, you could exclude all individual variety from the initial data of a system of natural science, you might properly be asked to account for this singular absence of variety, and a naturalistic account of it could only take the form of deriving it from some more ultimate state of things which was not marked by absolute "uniformity." Neither uniformity nor variety is self-explanatory; whichever you start with, you are faced by the old dilemma. Either the initial data must simply be taken as brute "fact," for which there is no reason at all, or if there is a reason, it must be found outside Nature, in the "supernatural."

(b) Similarly, it does not dispose of the conception of natural processes as tending to an "end" and being at least "quasi-purposive" to say that the thought originated with men who knew nothing of "evolution" and falsely believed in the fixity of natural kinds. In point of fact the notion of the gradual development of existing natural species made its appearance at the very dawn of Greek science and was quite familiar to the great philosophers who gave the Greek tradition its definitive form, though they rejected it because, so far as they knew, the evidence of facts seemed against it. The admission of the reality of the "evolution" of fresh species has, however, no direct bearing on the question of "ends in Nature": it actually suggests the raising of that very question in a new form. Is there, or is there not, in organic evolution a general trend to the successive emergence of beings of increasing intelligence? And if so, must the process be supposed to have reached its culmination, so far as our planet is concerned, in man, or must man be regarded as a mere stage in the production of something better, a *Pfeil der Sehnsucht nach dem Uebermenschen*? There are questions which we are still asking ourselves to-day, and though the strict positivists among our scientific men may insist that they probably cannot be answered and that it is certainly not the business of natural science to answer them, it is at least curious that the scientific man not infrequently unconsciously betrays the fact that he has privately answered them to his own satisfaction by the very fact that he talks of "evolution" as "progress," a phrase which has no meaning except in relation to a goal or an end, or even, on occasion, permits himself to assume that what is "more fully evolved," i.e. comes later in the course of a development, must obviously be brighter and better than whatever went before it. Thus the old problem is still with us and we cannot take it for granted that the old answers have lost their meaning or value.

We may, for example, consider how the old-fashioned argument from "motion" to the "unmoving" source of motion, when stated in its most general form, might still be urged even to-day. As we have seen, the argument is simply from the temporal, conditioned and mutable to something eternal, unconditioned and immutable as its source. The nerve of the whole reasoning is that every explanation of given facts or events involves bringing in reference to further unexplained facts; a complete explanation of anything, if we could obtain one, would therefore require that we should trace the fact explained back to something which contains its own explanation within itself, a something which is and is what it is in its own right; such a something plainly is not an event or mere fact and therefore not included in "Nature," the complex of all events and facts, but "above" Nature. Any man has a right to say, if he pleases, that he personally does not care to spend his time in exercising this mode of thinking, but would rather occupy himself in discovering fresh facts or fresh and hitherto unsuspected relations between facts. We need not blame him for that; but we are entitled to ask those who are alive to the meaning of the old problem how they propose to deal with it, if they reject the inference from the unfinished and conditioned to the perfect and unconditioned. For my own part I can see only two alternatives.

(i) One is to say, as Hume[4] did in his "Dialogues on Natural Religion," that, though every "part" of Nature may be dependent on other parts for its explanation, the *whole* system of facts or events which we call Nature may as a whole be self-explanatory; the "world" itself may be that "necessary being" of which philosophers and divines have spoken. In other words, a complex system in which every member, taken singly, is temporal, may as a complex be eternal; every member may be incomplete, but the whole may be complete; every member mutable, but the whole unchanging. Thus, as many philosophers of yesterday and to-day have said, the "eternal" would just be the temporal fully understood; there would be no contrast between Nature and "supernature," but only between "Nature apprehended as a whole" and

---

[4] Or rather, the sceptical critic in the *Dialogues*. We cannot be sure of Hume's own agreement with the suggestion.

Nature as we have to apprehend her fragmentarily. The thought is a pretty one, but I cannot believe that it will stand criticism. The very first question suggested by the sort of formula I have just quoted is whether it is not actually self-contradictory to call Nature a "whole" at all; if it is, there can clearly be no apprehending of Nature as something which she is not. And I think it quite clear that Nature, in the sense of the complex of events, is, in virtue of her very structure, something incomplete and not a true whole. I can explain the point best, perhaps, by an absurdly simplified example. Let us suppose that Nature consists of just four constituents, A, B, C, D. We are supposed to "explain" the behavior of A by the structure of B, C, and D, and the interaction of B, C, and D with A, and similarly with each of the other three constituents. Obviously enough, with a set of "general laws" of some kind we can "explain" why A behaves as it does, if we know all about its structure and the structures of B, C, and D. But it still remains entirely unexplained why A should be there at all, or why, if it is there, it should have B, C, and D as its neighbors rather than others with a totally different structure of their own. That this is so has to be accepted as a "brute" fact which is not explained nor yet self-explanatory. Thus no amount of knowledge of "natural laws" will explain the present actual state of Nature unless we also assume it as a brute fact that the distribution of "matter" and "energy" (or whatever else we take as the ultimates of our system of physics) a hundred millions of years ago was such and such. With the same "laws" and a different "initial" distribution the actual state of the world to-day would be very different. "Collocations," to use Mill's terminology, as well as "laws of causation" have to enter into all our scientific explanations. And though it is true that as our knowledge grows, we are continually learning to assign causes for particular "collocations" originally accepted as bare facts, we only succeed in doing so by falling back on other anterior "collocations" which we have equally to take as unexplained bare facts. As M. Meyerson puts it, we only get rid of the "inexplicable" at one point at the price of introducing it again somewhere else. Now any attempt to treat the complex of facts we call Nature as something which will be found to be more nearly self-explanatory the more of them we know, and would become quite self-explanatory if we only knew them all, amounts to an attempt to eliminate "bare fact" altogether, and reduce Nature simply to a complex of "laws." In other words, it is an attempt to manufacture particular existents out of mere universals, and therefore must end in failure. And the actual progress of science bears witness to this. The more we advance to the reduction of the visible face of Nature to "law," the more, not the less, complex and baffling become the mass of characters which we have to attribute as bare unexplained fact to our ultimate constituents. An electron is a much stiffer dose of "brute" fact than one of Newton's hard impenetrable corpuscles.

Thus we may fairly say that to surrender ourselves to the suggestion that Nature, if we only knew enough, would be seen to be a self-explanatory whole is to follow a will-of-the-wisp. The duality of "law" and "fact" cannot be eliminated from natural science, and this means that in the end either Nature is not explicable at all, or, if she is, the explanation has to be sought in something "outside" on which Nature depends.

(ii) Hence it is not surprising that both among men of science and among philosophers there is just now a strong tendency to give up the attempt to "explain" Nature completely and to fall back on an "ultimate pluralism." This means that we resign ourselves to the admission of the duality of "law" and "fact." We assume that there are a plurality of ultimately different constituents of Nature, each with its own specific character and way of behaving, and our business in explanation is simply to show how to account for the world as we find it by the fewest and simplest laws of interaction between these different constituents. In other words we give up altogether the attempt to "explain Nature"; we are content to "explain" lesser "parts" of Nature in terms of their specific character and their relations to other "parts." This is clearly a completely justified mode of procedure for a man of science who is aiming at the solution of some particular problem such as, *e.g.*, the discovery of the conditions under which a permanent new "species" originates and maintains itself. But it is quite another question whether "ultimate pluralism" can be the last word of a "philosophy of Nature." If you take it so, it really means that in the end you have no reason to assign why there should be just so many ultimate constituents of "Nature" as you say there are, or why they should have the particular characters you say they have, except that "it happens to be the case." You are acquiescing in unexplained brute fact, not because in the present state of knowledge you do not see your way to do better, but on the plea that there is and can be no explanation. You are putting unintelligible mystery at the very heart of reality.

Perhaps it may be rejoined, "And why should we not acknowledge this, seeing that, whether we like it or not, we must come to this in the end?" Well, at least it may be retorted that to acquiesce in such a "final inexplicability" as final means that you have denied the validity of the very assumption on which all science is built. All through the history of scientific advance it has been taken for granted that we are not to acquiesce in inexplicable brute fact; whenever we come across what, with our present light, has to be accepted as merely fact, we have a right to ask for further explanation, and should be false to the spirit of science if we did not. Thus we inevitably reach the conclusion that either the very principles which inspire and guide scientific inquiry itself are an illusion, or Nature itself must be dependent on some reality which is self-explanatory, and therefore not Nature nor any part of Nature, but, in the strict sense of the words, "supernatural" or "transcendent"—transcendent, that is, in the sense that in it there is overcome that duality of "law" and "fact" which is characteristic of Nature and every part of Nature. It is not "brute" fact, and yet it is not an abstract universal law or complex of such laws, but a really existing self-luminous Being, such that you could see, if you only apprehended its true character, that to have that character and to be are the same thing. This is the way in which Nature, as it seems to me, inevitably points beyond itself as the temporal and mutable to an "other" which is eternal and immutable.

The "argument from design," rightly stated, seems to me to have a similar force. In our small region of the universe, at any rate, we can see for ourselves that the course of development has taken a very remarkable direction. It has led up, through a line of species which have had to adapt themselves to their "environment," to the emergence of an intelligent and moral creature who adapts his environment to himself and even to his ideals of what he is not yet but ought to be and hopes to be, and the environment of the species he "domesticates" to his own purposes. It is increasingly true as we pass from savagery to civilisation that men make their own environment and are not made by it. On the face of it, it at least looks as though, so far as our own region of Nature is concerned, this emergence of creatures who, being intelligent and moral, freely shape their own environment, is the culminating stage beyond which the development of new species cannot go, and that the whole anterior history of the inorganic and prehuman organic development of our planet has been controlled throughout by the requirements of this "end." I know it will be said that we have no proof that the same thing has happened anywhere else in the "universe"; our planet may, for all we know, not be a fair "average sample." Again, it may be urged that there are reasons for thinking that the history of our planet will end in its unfitness first to contain intelligent human life, and then to contain any form of life; consequently man and all his works cannot be the "end of evolution" even on this earth, but must be a mere passing phase in a process which is controlled by no "ends," and is therefore in no true sense of the term a "history." One would not wish to shirk any of these objections, and yet it is, I think, not too much to say that, to anyone but a fanatical atheist, it will always appear preposterous to regard the production of moral and intelligent masters of Nature as a mere by-product or accident of "evolution on this planet," or indeed as anything but the "end" which has all along determined the process. "Nature," we might say, really does show a "trend" or "bias" to the production of intelligence surpassing her own. And further, we must remember that if there is such a "trend," it will be necessary to include under the head of the processes it determines, not only the emergence of the various forms of prehuman life on our earth, but the "geological" preparation of the earth itself to be the scene of the ensuing development and the pre-preparation during the still remoter astronomical period of the formation of our solar system. Thus to recognise so-called "quasi-purposiveness" even in the course development has followed on "one tiny planet" inevitably involves finding the same quasi-purposiveness on a vaster scale, throughout the whole indefinite range of natural events.[5] The more we are alive to this simple consideration that "*de facto* determination by ends," once admitted anywhere in Nature, cannot be confined to any single region or part of Nature but inevitably

---

[5] This is not to say that man is the sole or chief end of Creation, a proposition which, in fact, no orthodox Christian theologian would make; at least not without very careful explanations and reservations. But it is worth while to remind ourselves that there is nothing in itself absurd in the view of the Middle Ages that human history is the central interest, the main plot, of the drama of the universe. For all we *know*, our planet may be the only home of beings "with immortal souls to be saved." If it is, then the fact that it is "*tiny*" is obviously irrelevant as a reason for denying its central importance. When I reflect on the capacities of a man for good and evil, I see nothing ludicrous in the supposition, which, however, I am not making, that it might have been the chief purpose of a wise Creator in making the solar system that the sun should give us men light and warmth.

All I seriously wish to insist on, however, is that to let in "purpose" *anywhere* into natural fact means letting it in *everywhere*. Give it an inch and it will rightly take infinite room. (This as a reply to the arguments based on the allegation that we cannot regard the part of things with which we are acquainted as a "fair average sample." What we are acquainted with is not a definite isolated "part" or "region," but has ramifications which extend indefinitely far.)

penetrates everywhere, the more impossible it becomes to be satisfied with such expressions as "quasi-purposive" or "*de facto*" teleology and the like.

The vaster the dominating "plan," the more vividly must it suggest a planning and guiding intelligence. Nature herself, we may suppose (if we allow ourselves to use the miserably misleading personification at all), may, as has been said, be like a sleep-walker who executes trains of purposive acts without knowing that he does so. But the plan itself cannot have originated without a wakeful and alert intelligence. (Even the sleep-walker, as we know, only performs trains of acts adjusted to ends in his sleep because he has first learnt consciously to adjust means to ends in his waking life.) Let "Nature" be as unconscious as you please: the stronger is the suggestion that the marvellous, and often comical, "adaptations" of a highly complex character which pervade "Nature" are the "artifices" of one who neither slumbers nor sleeps. What look like "accidents" may very well be deliberate designs of a master artist, or, as Plato says, contrary to the proverbial expression, it may be Nature which "imitates" Art. I will not attempt to estimate the amount of probative force which ought to be ascribed to these suggestions. It is enough for my purpose that they are there, and that their drawing has notoriously been felt with special intensity by so many of those who are best acquainted with the facts, even where their metaphysical bias has led them to withhold assent.

The spectacle of movement and change which we call "Nature" thus at least suggests the presence of some "transcendent" source of movement and change which is strictly eternal, being above all mutability and having no succession of phases within itself, and is omnipotent, since it is itself the source of *all* "becoming." The orderliness and apparent purposive "trend towards intelligence" in Nature similarly at least suggest that this omnipotent and eternal "supernatural" is a wholly intelligent Will. The force of the suggestion seems to have been felt by man in every stage of his history so far as that history is accessible to us. It is noteworthy that the more intimate our inquiries become with the "savages" who by our estimate stand nearest to a pre-civilised condition, the clearer it becomes that even those of them who have been set down on first acquaintance as wholly "godless" turn out, on better knowledge, to have their traditions of a "maker of life" and the like. And at the same time we are not dealing with anything which can be set aside as a "relic of primitive savagery." *Our* conception of "One God the Father Almighty, Creator of heaven and earth," has come to us from two immediate sources, Greek science and philosophy and Hebrew prophecy, and both science and prophecy, as cannot be too often repeated, began by a complete break with the "primitive superstition" of the past. Belief in God as the source of Nature is thus a "survival of primitive superstition" only in the same sense in which the same could be said of belief in causality[6] or, if you prefer it, in "laws of uniform sequence."

So far, however, our attention has been confined to what Bonaventura calls the "things around and below us," and they clearly have taken us a very

---

[6] It is significant that Witgenstein's penetrating though unbalanced *Tractatus logico-philosophicus* definitely *identifies* "superstition" with the belief in causality. *Op. cit.* 5:1361.

little way indeed in the direction of suggesting the reality of a God who is God in the religious man's sense, a being who can be loved and trusted utterly and without qualification. In the creatures we may have discerned the "footprints" of a Creator, but we have seen no token of his "likeness." Perhaps, if we turn our attention to "what is within us," we may find in our own moral being the suggestion of something further. We may get at any rate a hint that the creative intelligence we divine behind all things has also the character which makes adoration, love, and trust, as distinguished from mere wonder, possible. In man's moral being we may discern not the mere "footprints" but the "image" of God.

II. FROM MAN TO GOD

With the line of thought we have now to consider we can deal more briefly. If meditation on the creatures in general leads us by a circuitous route and an obscure light to the thought of their Maker, meditation on the moral being of man suggests God more directly and much less obscurely. For we are now starting a fresh stage of the "ascent" from a higher level, and it is with the road to God as with Dante's purgatorial mountain: the higher you have mounted, the easier it is to rise higher still. In Nature we at best see God under a disguise so heavy that it allows us to discern little more than that someone is there; within our own moral life we see Him with the mask, so to say, half fallen off.

Once more the general character of the ascent is the same; we begin with the temporal, and in a certain sense the natural, to end in the eternal and supernatural. But the line of thought, though kindred to the first, is independent, so that Nature and Man are like two witnesses who have had no opportunity of collusion. The clearer and more emphatic testimony of the latter to what was testified less unambiguously by the former affords a further confirmation of our hope that we have read the suggestions of Nature, so ambiguous in their purport, aright.

A single sentence will be enough to show both the analogy of the argument from Man to God with the argument from Nature and the real independence of the two lines of testimony. Nature, we have urged, on inspection points to the "supernatural" beyond itself as its own presupposition; if we look within ourselves we shall see that in man "Nature" and "supernature" meet; he has both within his own heart, and is a denizen at once of the temporal and of the eternal. He has not, like the animals, so far as we can judge of their inner life, one "environment" to which he must adapt himself but two, a secular and an eternal. Because he is designed ultimately to be at home with God in the eternal, he can never be really at home in this world, but at best is, like Abraham, a pilgrim to a promised but unseen land; at worst, like Cain, an aimless fugitive and wanderer on the face of the earth. The very "image" of his Maker which has been stamped on him is not only a sign of his rightful domination over the creatures; it is also "the mark of Cain" from which all creatures shrink. Hence among all the creatures, many of whom are comic enough, man is alone in being tragic. His life, at the very best, is a tragicomedy; at the worst, it is stark tragedy. And naturally enough this is so; for, if man has only the "environment" which is common to him with the beasts of the field, his whole life is no more than a perpetual attempt to find a rational solution of an equation all whose roots are surds. He can only achieve adjustment to one of his two "environments" by sacrifices of adjustment to the other; he can no more be equally in tune with the eternal and the secular at once than a piano can be exactly in tune for all keys. In practice we know how the difficulty is apparently solved in the best human lives; it is solved by cultivating our earthly attachments and yet also practising a high detachment, not "setting our hearts" too much on the best temporal goods, since "the best in this kind are but shadows," "using" the creatures, but always in the remembrance that the time will come when we can use them no more, loving them but loving them *ordinate*, with care not to lose our hearts to any of them. Wise men do not need to be reminded that the deliberate voluntary refusal of real good things is necessary, as a protection against the over-valuation of the secular, in any life they count worth living. And yet wise men know also that the renunciation of real good which they recommend is not recommended for the mere sake of some "better good." But the "better good" plainly cannot be any of the good things of this secular existence. For there is none of them whatever which it may not be a duty to renounce for some man and at some time.

I do not mean merely that occasions demand the sacrifice of the sort of thing the "average sensual man" calls good—comfort, wealth, influence, rank and the like. For no serious moralist would dream of regarding any of these as more, at best, than very inferior goods. I mean that the same thing holds true of the very things to which men of nobler mould are ready to sacrifice these obvious and secondary goods. For example, there are few, if any, earthly goods to compare with our personal affections. Yet a man must be prepared to sacrifice all his personal affections in the service of his country, or for what he honestly believes to be the one Church of God. But there are things to which the greater lover of his country or his Church must be prepared in turn to sacrifice what lies so near his heart. I may die for my country, I may, as so many a fighting man does, leave wife and young children to run the extreme hazards of fortune, but I must not purchase peace and safety for this country I love so much by procuring the privy murder of a dangerous and remorseless enemy. I may give my body to be burned for my faith, I may leave my little ones to beg their bread for its sake, but I must not help it in its need by a fraud or a forgery. It may be argued that for the good of the human race I ought to be prepared to sacrifice the very independence of my native land, but for no advantage to the whole body of mankind may I insult justice by knowingly giving sentence or verdict against the innocent. If these things are not true, the whole foundation of our morality is dissolved; if they are true, the greatest good, to which I must at need be prepared to sacrifice everything else, must be something which cannot even be appraised in the terms of a secular arithmetic, something incommensurable with the "welfare" of Church and State or even of the whole human race. If it is to be had in fruition at all, it must be had where the secular environment has finally and for ever fallen away, "yonder" as the Neo-Platonist would say, "in heaven" as the ordinary Christian says. If this world of time and passage were really our home and our only home, I own I should find it impossible to justify such a complete surrender of all temporal good as that I have spoken of; yet it is certain that the sacrifice is no more than what is demanded, when the need arises, by the most familiar principles of morality. Whoever says "ought," meaning "ought," is in the act bearing witness to the supernatural and supra-temporal as the destined home of man. No doubt we should all admit that there are very many rules of our conventional morality which are not of unconditional and universal obligation; we "ought" to conform to them under certain specified and understood conditions. I ought to be generous only when I have first satisfied the just claims of my creditors, just as I ought to abstain from redressing grievances with the high hand when society supplies me with the machinery for getting them redressed by the law. But whoever says "ought" at all, must mean that at least *when* the requisite conditions are fulfilled the obligation is absolute. There may be occasions when it is not binding on me to speak the truth to a questioner, but if there is one single occasion on which I ought to speak the truth, I ought to speak it then, "though the sky should fall."

Now, if there ever is a single occasion on which we ought to speak the truth, or to do anything else, "at all costs" as we say, what is the good in the name of which this unconditional demand is made of me? It cannot be any secular good that can be named, my own health or prosperity or life, nor even the prosperity and pleasurable existence of mankind. For I can never, since the consequences of my act are endless and unforeseeable, be sure that I may not be endangering these very goods by my act, and yet I am sure that the act is one which I ought to do. No doubt, you may fall back upon probability as the guide of life and say, "I ought to do this act because it seems to me most likely to conduce to the temporal well-being of myself, my family, my nation, and my kind." And in practice these are, no doubt, the sort of considerations by which we are constantly influenced. But it should be clear that they cannot be the ultimate grounds of obligation, unless all morality is to be reduced to the status of a convenient illusion. To say that the ultimate ground of an obligation is the mere fact that a man thinks he would further such a concrete tangible end by his act involves the consequence that no man is bound to do any act unless he thinks it will have these results, and that he may do anything he pleases so long as he thinks it will have them. At heart, I believe, even the writers who go furthest in professing to accept these conclusions do themselves a moral injustice. I am convinced that there is not one of them, whatever he may hold in theory, who would not in practice "draw the line" somewhere and say, "This thing I will not do, whatever the cost may be to myself or to anyone else or to everyone." Now an obligation wholly independent of all temporal "consequences" clearly cannot have justification in the temporal, nor oblige any creature constructed to find his good wholly in the temporal. Only to a being who has in his structure the adaptation to the eternal can you significantly say "You ought."[7]

It will be seen that the thought on which we have dwelt in the last paragraph is one of the underlying fundamental themes of Kant's principal ethical treatise, the "Critique of Practical Reason." It is characteristic of Kant that, wrongly as I think, he wholly distrusted the suggestions of the "super-

---

[7] I owe the expression to a report of a recent utterance of some Roman Catholic divine. I regret that I cannot give the precise reference.

natural" to be derived from the contemplation of Nature itself, and that, from an exaggerated dread of unregulated fanaticism and superstition, characteristic of his century, he was all but blind to the third source of suggestion of which we have yet to speak. Hence with him it is our knowledge of our own moral being, as creatures who have unconditional obligations, which has to bear the whole weight of the argument. Here, I own, he seems to me to be definitely wrong. The full force of the vindication of religion cannot be felt unless we recognise that its weight is supported not by one strand only but by a cord of three intertwined strands; we need to integrate Bonaventura and Thomas and Butler with Kant to appreciate the real strength of the believer's position. Yet Kant seems to me unquestionably right as far as this. Even were there nothing else to suggest to us that we are denizens at once of a natural and temporal and of a supernatural and eternal world, the revelation of our own inner division against ourselves afforded by Conscience, duly meditated, is enough to bear the strain. Or, to make my point rather differently, I would urge that of all the philosophical thinkers who have concerned themselves with the life of man as a moral being, the two who stand out, even in the estimation of those who dissent from them, as the great undying moralists of literature, Plato and Kant, are just the two who have insisted most vigorously on what the secularly-minded call, by way of depreciation, the "dualism" of "this world" and the "other world," or, in Kantian language, of "man as (natural) phenomenon" and "man as (supernatural) reality." To deny the reality of this antithesis is to eviscerate morality.

We see this at once if we compare Kant, for example, with Hume, or Plato with Aristotle. It is so obvious that Plato and Kant really "care" about moral practice and Aristotle and Hume do not care, or do not care as much as they ought. In Hume's hands moral goodness is put so completely on a level with mere respectability that our approval of virtue and disapproval of vice is said in so many words to be at bottom one in kind with our preference of a well-dressed man to a badly-dressed. Aristotle cares more than this. He reduces moral goodness to the discharge of the duties of a good citizen, family man, and neighbour in this secular life, and is careful to insist that these obligations are not to be shirked. But when he comes to speak of the true happiness of man and the kind of life which he lives "as a being with something divine in him," we find that the life of this "divine" part means nothing more than the promotion of science. To live near to God means to him not justice, mercy, and humility, as it does to Plato and the Hebrew prophets, but to be a metaphysician, a physicist, and an astronomer. Justice, mercy, and humility are to be practised, but only for a secular purpose, in order that the man of science may have an orderly and quiet social "environment" and so be free, as he would not be if he had to contend with disorderly passions in himself or his neighbours, to give a maximum of time and interest to things which really matter. We cannot say of Hume, nor of Aristotle, nor indeed of any moralist who makes morality merely a matter of right social adjustments in this temporal world, what you can say of Plato or Kant, *beati qui esuriunt et sitiunt justitiam.* "Otherworldliness" is as characteristic of the greatest theoretical moralists as it is of all the noblest livers, whatever their professed theories may be. . . .

We see that the general character of the argument from Nature and from our moral being to God is the same in both cases. In both we reason from the temporal to the eternal. But there is this difference, that the elusive being to which we reason is, in the second case, something richer. Reflexion on what is below and around us suggested only an eternal intelligent designer and source of Nature. Reflexion on the moral nature of man suggests a being who is more, the eternal something before whom we must not only bow in amazement, like Job, but kneel in reverence as the source of support of all moral goodness. This is as it should be, since in the one case we are attempting to see the cause in the effect, in the other to see the features of the father in his child. If Nature shows us only the footsteps of God, in man as a moral being we see His image.

III.B.   The Ontological Argument

III.B.1.   The Inconceivability of God's Nonexistence

ST. ANSELM AND GAUNILON

*St. Anselm (1033–1109) was a Benedictine monk who be-
came the Archbishop of Canterbury. Gaunilon, a contemporary of Anselm and also a monk, is remembered only because
of his attempt to refute Anselm's ontological argument for the
existence of God. Anselm argues that even David's fool (the
reference is to Psalm 15:1, supposedly a psalm of David)
understands the notion of God because he "had said in his
heart, there is no God." But since God, that being than which
no greater can be conceived, exists in the understanding, God
must also exist in reality. If God existed only in the understanding and not in reality, he would not be that being than
which no greater can be conceived, which is a contradiction.
Gaunilon, however, takes up the argument "in behalf of the
fool," maintaining that all sorts of nonexistent things exist in
the understanding in the sense that we understand the words
when such things are mentioned. He suggests that Anselm's
argument, if it were valid, would prove the existence of the
most idyllic island one could imagine, a patent absurdity.
Anselm attempts to answer the "fool's advocate," but scholarly opinion has been divided ever since on the success of his
answer.*

CHAPTER II

Truly there is a God, although the fool hath said in his heart,
There is no God.

And so, Lord, do thou, who dost give understanding to faith, give me, so far as
thou knowest it to be profitable, to understand that thou art as we believe; and

---

Reprinted from *St. Anselm: Basic Writings*, ed. and trans. S. N. Deane by permission of Open
Court Publishing Company, La Salle, Illinois. © 1962 Open Court Publishing Company.

that thou art that which we believe. And, indeed, we believe that thou art a being than which nothing greater can be conceived. Or is there no such nature, since the fool hath said in his heart, there is no God? (*Psalms* xiv. 1). But, at any rate, this very fool, when he hears of this being of which I speak—a being than which nothing greater can be conceived—understands what he hears, and what he understands is in his understanding; although he does not understand it to exist.

For, it is one thing for an object to be in the understanding, and another to understand that the object exists. When a painter first conceives of what he will afterwards perform, he has it in his understanding, but he does not yet understand it to be, because he has not yet performed it. But after he has made the painting, he both has it in his understanding, and he understands that it exists, because he has made it.

Hence, even the fool is convinced that something exists in the understanding, at least, than which nothing greater can be conceived. For, when he hears of this, he understands it. And whatever is understood, exists in the understanding. And assuredly that, than which nothing greater can be conceived, cannot exist in the understanding alone. For, suppose it exists in the understanding alone: then it can be conceived to exist in reality; which is greater.

Therefore, if that, than which nothing greater can be conceived, exists in the understanding alone, the very being, than which nothing greater can be conceived, is one, than which a greater can be conceived. But obviously this is impossible. Hence, there is no doubt that there exists a being, than which nothing greater can be conceived, and it exists both in the understanding and in reality.

CHAPTER III

God cannot be conceived not to exist —God is that, than which nothing greater can be conceived.—That which can be conceived not to exist is not God.

And it assuredly exists so truly, that it cannot be conceived not to exist. For, it is possible to conceive of a being which cannot be conceived not to exist; and this is greater than one which can be conceived not to exist. Hence, if that, than which nothing greater can be conceived can be conceived not to exist, it is not that, than which nothing greater can be conceived. But this is an irreconcilable contradiction. There is, then, so truly a being than which nothing greater can be conceived to exist, that it cannot even be conceived not to exist; and this being thou art, O Lord, our God.

So truly, therefore, dost thou exist, O Lord, my God, that thou canst not be conceived not to exist; and rightly. For, if a mind could conceive of a being better than thee, the creature would rise above the Creator; and this is most absurd. And, indeed, whatever else there is, except thee alone, can be conceived not to exist. To thee alone, therefore, it belongs to exist more truly than all other beings, and hence in a higher degree than all others. For, whatever else exists does not exist so truly, and hence in a less degree it belongs to it to exist. Why, then, has the fool said in his heart, there is no God (*Psalms* xiv. 1) since it is so evident, to a rational mind, that thou dost exist in the highest degree of all? Why, except that he is dull and a fool?

CHAPTER IV

How the fool has said in his heart what cannot be conceived.—
A thing may be conceived in two ways: (1) when the word
signifying it is conceived; (2) when the thing itself is
understood. As far as the word goes, God can be conceived not
to exist; in reality he cannot.

But how has the fool said in his heart what he could not conceive; or how is it that he could not conceive what he said in his heart, since it is the same to say in the heart, and to conceive?

But, if really, nay, since really, he both conceived, because he said in his heart; and did not say in his heart, because he could not conceive; there is more than one way in which a thing is said in the heart or conceived. For, in the one sense, an object is conceived, when the word signifying it is conceived; and in another, when the very entity, which the object is, is understood.

In the former sense, then, God can be conceived not to exist; but in the latter, not at all. For no one who understands what fire and water are can conceive fire to be water, in accordance with the nature of the facts themselves, although this is possible according to the words. So, then, no one who understands what God is can conceive that God does not exist; although he says these words in his heart, either without any, or with some foreign, signification. For, God is that than which a greater cannot be conceived. And he who thoroughly understands this, assuredly understands that this being so truly exists, that not even in concept can it be nonexistent. Therefore, he who understands that God so exists, cannot conceive that he does not exist.

I thank thee, gracious Lord, I thank thee; because what I formerly believed by thy bounty, I now so understand by thine illumination, that if I were unwilling to believe that thou dost exist, I should not be able to understand this to be true. . . .

IN BEHALF OF THE FOOL

An Answer to the argument of Anselm in the Proslogium, by
Gaunilon, a monk of Marmoutier

(1) If one doubts or denies the existence of a being of such a nature that nothing greater than it can be conceived, he receives this answer:

The existence of this being is proved, in the first place, by the fact that he himself, in his doubt or denial regarding this being, already has it in his understanding; for in hearing it spoken of he understands what is spoken of. It is proved, therefore, by the fact that what he understands must exist not only in his understanding, but in reality also.

And the proof of this is as follows: It is a greater thing to exist both in the understanding and in reality than to be in the understanding alone. And if this being is in the understanding alone, whatever has even in the past existed in reality will be greater than this being. And so that which was greater than all beings will be less than some being, and will not be greater than all: which is a manifest contradiction.

And hence, that which is greater than all, already proved to be in the understanding, must exist not only in the understanding, but also in reality: for otherwise it will not be greater than all other beings.

(2)The fool might make this reply:

This being is said to be in my understanding already, only because I understand what is said. Now could it not with equal justice be said that I have in my understanding all manner of unreal objects, having absolutely no existence in themselves, because I understand these things if one speaks of them, whatever they may be?

Unless indeed it is shown that this being is of such a character that it cannot be held in concept like all unreal objects, or objects whose existence is uncertain; and hence I am not able to conceive of it when I hear of it, or to hold it in concept; but I must understand it and have it in my understanding: because, it seems, I cannot conceive of it in any other way than by understanding it, that is, by comprehending in my knowledge its existence in reality.

But if this is the case, in the first place there will be no distinction between what has precedence in time—namely, the having of an object in the understanding—and what is subsequent in time—namely, the understanding that an object exists; as in the example of the picture, which exists first in the mind of the painter, and afterwards in his work.

Moreover, the following assertion can hardly be accepted: that this being, when it is spoken of and heard of, cannot be conceived not to exist in the way in which even God can be conceived not to exist. For if this is impossible, what was the object of this argument against one who doubts or denies the existence of such a being?

Finally, that this being so exists that it cannot be perceived by an understanding convinced of its own indubitable existence, unless this being is afterwards conceived of—this should be proved to me by an indisputable argument, but not by that which you have advanced: namely, that what I understand, when I hear it, already is in my understanding. For thus in my understanding, as I still think, could be all sorts of things whose existence is uncertain, or which do not exist at all, if some one whose words I should understand mentioned them. And so much the more if I should be deceived, as often happens, and believe in them: though I do not yet believe in the being whose existence you would prove.

(3) Hence, your example of the painter who already has in his understanding what he is to paint cannot agree with this argument. For the picture, before it is made, is contained in the artificer's art itself; and any such thing, existing in the art of an artificer, is nothing but a part of his understanding itself. A joiner, St. Augustine says, when he is about to make a box in fact, first has it in his art. The box which is made in fact is not life; but the box which exists in his art is life. For the artificer's soul lives, in which all these things are, before they are produced. Why, then, are these things life in the living soul of the artificer, unless because they are nothing else than the knowledge or understanding of the soul itself?

With the exception, however, of those facts which are known to pertain to the mental nature, whatever, on being heard and thought out by the understanding, is perceived to be real, undoubtedly that real object is one thing, and the understanding itself, by which the object is grasped, is another. Hence, even if it were true that there is a being than which a greater is inconceivable: yet to this being, when heard of and understood, the not yet created picture in the mind of the painter is not analogous.

(4) Let us notice also the point touched on above, with regard to this being which is greater than all which can be conceived, and which, it is said, can be none other than God himself. I, so far as actual knowledge of the object, either from its specific or general character, is concerned, am as little able to conceive of this being when I hear of it, or to have it in my understanding, as I am to conceive of or understand God himself: whom, indeed, for this very reason I can conceive not to exist. For I do not know that reality itself which God is, nor can I form a conjecture of that reality from some other like reality. For you yourself assert that that reality is such that there can be nothing else like it.

For, suppose that I should hear something said of a man absolutely unknown to me, of whose very existence I was unaware. Through that special or general knowledge by which I know what man is, or what men are, I could conceive of him also, according to the reality itself, which man is. And yet it would be possible, if the person who told me of him deceived me, that the man himself, of whom I conceived, did not exist; since that reality according to which I conceived of him, though a no less indisputable fact, was not that man, but any man.

Hence, I am not able, in the way in which I should have this unreal being in concept or in understanding, to have that being of which you speak in concept or in understanding, when I hear the word *God* or the words, *a being greater than all other beings*. For I can conceive of the man according to a fact that is real and familiar to me: but of God, or a being greater than all others, I could not conceive at all, except merely according to the word. And an object can hardly or never be conceived according to the word alone.

For when it is so conceived, it is not so much the word itself (which is, indeed, a real thing—that is, the sound of the letters and syllables) as the signification of the word, when heard, that is conceived. But it is not conceived as by one who knows what is generally signified by the word; by whom, that is, it is conceived according to reality and in true conception alone. It is conceived as by a man who does not know the object, and conceives of it only in accordance with the movement of his mind produced by hearing the word, the mind attempting to image for itself the signification of the word that is heard. And it would be surprising if in the reality of fact it could ever attain to this.

Thus, it appears, and in no other way, this being is also in my understanding, when I hear and understand a person who says that there is a being greater than all conceivable beings. So much for the assertion that this supreme nature already is in my understanding.

(5) But that this being must exist, not only in the understanding but also in reality, is thus proved to me:

If it did not so exist, whatever exists in reality would be greater than it.

And so the being which has been already proved to exist in my understanding, will not be greater than all other beings.

I still answer: if it should be said that a being which cannot be even conceived in terms of any fact, is in the understanding, I do not deny that this being is, accordingly, in my understanding. But since through this fact it can in no wise attain to real existence also, I do not yet concede to it that existence at all, until some certain proof of it shall be given.

For he who says that this being exists, because otherwise the being which is greater than all will not be greater than all, does not attend strictly enough to what he is saying. For I do not yet say, no, I even deny or doubt that this being is greater than any real object. Nor do I concede to it any other existence than this (if it should be called existence) which it has when the mind, according to a word merely heard, tries to form the image of an object absolutely unknown to it.

How, then, is the veritable existence of the being proved to me from the assumption, by hypothesis, that it is greater than all other beings? For I should still deny this, or doubt your demonstration of it, to this extent, that I should not admit that this being is in my understanding and concept even in the way in which many objects whose real existence is uncertain and doubtful, are in my understanding and concept. For it should be proved first that this being itself really exists somewhere; and then, from the fact that it is greater than all, we shall not hesitate to infer that it also subsists in itself.

(6) For example: it is said that somewhere in the ocean is an island, which, because of the difficulty, or rather the impossibility, of discovering what does not exist, is called the lost island. And they say that this island has an inestimable wealth of all manner of riches and delicacies in greater abundance than is told of the Islands of the Blest; and that having no owner or inhabitant, it is more excellent than all other countries, which are inhabited by mankind, in the abundance with which it is stored.

Now if some one should tell me that there is such an island, I should easily understand his words, in which there is no difficulty. But suppose that he went on to say, as if by a logical inference: "You can no longer doubt that this island which is more excellent than all lands exists somewhere, since you have no doubt that it is in your understanding. And since it is more excellent not to be in the understanding alone, but to exist both in the understanding and in reality, for this reason it must exist. For if it does not exist, any land which really exists will be more excellent than it; and so the island already understood by you to be more excellent will not be more excellent."

If a man should try to prove to me by such reasoning that this island truly exists, and that its existence should no longer be doubted, either I should believe that he was jesting, or I know not which I ought to regard as the greater fool: myself, supposing that I should allow this proof; or him, if he should suppose that he had established with any certainty the existence of this island. For he ought to show first that the hypothetical excellence of this island exists as a real and indubitable fact, and in no wise as any unreal object, or one whose existence is uncertain, in my understanding.

(7) This, in the mean time, is the answer the fool could make to the arguments urged against him. When he is assured in the first place that this

being is so great that its nonexistence is not even conceivable, and that this in turn is proved on no other ground than the fact that otherwise it will not be greater than all things, the fool may make the same answer, and say:

When did I say that any such being exists in reality, that is, a being greater than all others? that on this ground it should be proved to me that it also exists in reality to such a degree that it cannot even be conceived not to exist? Whereas in the first place it should be in some way proved that a nature which is higher, that is, greater and better, than all other natures, exists; in order that from this we may then be able to prove all attributes which necessarily the being that is greater and better than all possesses.

Moreover, it is said that the nonexistence of this being is inconceivable. It might better be said, perhaps, that its nonexistence, or the possibility of its nonexistence, is unintelligible. For according to the true meaning of the word, unreal objects are unintelligible. Yet their existence is conceivable in the way in which the fool conceived of the nonexistence of God. I am most certainly aware of my own existence; but I know, nevertheless, that my nonexistence is possible. As to that supreme being, moreover, which God is, I understand without any doubt both his existence, and the impossibility of his nonexistence. Whether, however, so long as I am most positively aware of my existence, I can conceive of my nonexistence, I am not sure. But if I can, why can I not conceive of the nonexistence of whatever else I know with the same certainty? If, however, I cannot, God will not be the only being of which it can be said, it is impossible to conceive of his nonexistence.

(8) The other parts of this book are argued with such truth, such brilliancy, such grandeur; and are so replete with usefulness, so fragrant with a certain perfume of devout and holy feeling, that though there are matters in the beginning which, however rightly sensed, are weakly presented, the rest of the work should not be rejected on this account. The rather ought these earlier matters to be reasoned more cogently, and the whole to be received with great respect and honor.

[The following is part of Anselm's reply to Gaunilon.]

It was a fool against whom the argument of my Proslogium was directed. Seeing, however, that the author of these objections is by no means a fool, and is a Catholic, speaking in behalf of the fool, I think it sufficient that I answer the Catholic.

CHAPTER I

A general refutation of Gaunilon's argument. It is shown that a
being than which a greater cannot be conceived exists in
reality.

You say—whosoever you may be, who say that a fool is capable of making these statements—that a being than which a greater cannot be conceived is not in the understanding in any other sense than that in which a being that is altogether inconceivable in terms of reality, is in the understanding. You say that the inference that this being exists in reality, from the fact that it is in the understanding, is no more just than the inference that a lost island most certainly exists, from the fact that when it is described the hearer does not doubt that it is in his understanding.

But I say: if a being than which a greater is inconceivable is not understood or conceived, and is not in the understanding or in concept, certainly either God is not a being than which a greater is inconceivable, or else he is not understood or conceived, and is not in the understanding or in concept. But I call on your faith and conscience to attest that this is most false. Hence, that than which a greater cannot be conceived is truly understood and conceived, and is in the understanding and in concept. Therefore either the grounds on which you try to controvert me are not true, or else the inference which you think to base logically on those grounds is not justified.

But you hold, moreover, that supposing that a being than which a greater cannot be conceived is understood, it does not follow that this being is in the understanding; nor, if it is in the understanding, does it therefore exist in reality.

In answer to this, I maintain positively: if that being can be even conceived to be, it must exist in reality. For that than which a greater is inconceivable cannot be conceived except as without beginning. But whatever can be conceived to exist, and does not exist, can be conceived to exist through a beginning. Hence what can be conceived to exist, but does not exist, is not the being than which a greater cannot be conceived. Therefore, if such a being can be conceived to exist, necessarily it does exist.

Furthermore: if it can be conceived at all, it must exist. For no one who denies or doubts the existence of a being than which a greater is inconceivable, denies or doubts that if it did exist, its nonexistence, either in reality or in the understanding, would be impossible. For otherwise it would not be a being than which a greater cannot be conceived. But as to whatever can be conceived, but does not exist—if there were such a being, its nonexistence, either in reality or in the understanding, would be possible. Therefore if a being than which a greater is inconceivable can be even conceived, it cannot be nonexistent.

But let us suppose that it does not exist, even if it can be conceived. Whatever can be conceived, but does not exist, if it existed, would not be a being than which a greater is inconceivable. If, then, there were a being a greater than which is inconceivable, it would not be a being than which a greater is inconceivable: which is most absurd. Hence, it is false to deny that a being than which a greater cannot be conceived exists, if it can be even conceived; much the more, therefore, if it can be understood or can be in the understanding.

Moreover, I will venture to make this assertion: without doubt, whatever at any place or at any time does not exist—even if it does exist at some place or at some time—can be conceived to exist nowhere and never, as at some place and at some time it does not exist. For what did not exist yesterday, and exists today, as it is understood not to have existed yesterday, so it can be apprehended by the intelligence that it never exists. And what is not here, and is elsewhere, can be conceived to be nowhere, just as it is not here. So with regard to an object of which the individual parts do not exist at the same places or times: all its parts and therefore its very whole can be conceived to exist nowhere or never.

For, although time is said to exist always, and the world everywhere, yet time does not as a whole exist always, nor the world as a whole everywhere. And as individual parts of time do not exist when others exist, so they can be conceived never to exist. And so it can be apprehended by the intelligence that individual parts of the world exist nowhere, as they do not exist where other parts exist. Moreover, what is composed of parts can be dissolved in concept, and be nonexistent. Therefore, whatever at any place or at any time does not exist as a whole, even if it is existent, can be conceived not to exist.

But that than which a greater cannot be conceived, if it exists, cannot be conceived not to exist. Otherwise, it is not a being than which a greater cannot be conceived: which is inconsistent. By no means, then, does it at any place or at any time fail to exist as a whole: but it exists as a whole everywhere and always.

Do you believe that this being can in some way be conceived or understood, or that the being with regard to which these things are understood can be in concept or in the understanding? For if it cannot, these things cannot be understood with reference to it. But if you say that it is not understood and that it is not in the understanding, because it is not thoroughly understood; you should say that a man who cannot face the direct rays of the sun does not see the light of day, which is none other than the sunlight. Assuredly a being than which a greater cannot be conceived exists, and is in the understanding, at least to this extent—that these statements regarding it are understood. . . .

CHAPTER V

A particular discussion of certain statements of Gaunilon's. In the first place, he misquoted the argument which he undertook to refute.

The nature of the other objections which you, in behalf of the fool, urge against me it is easy, even for a man of small wisdom, to detect; and I had therefore thought it unnecessary to show this. But since I hear that some readers of these objections think they have some weight against me, I will discuss them briefly.

In the first place, you often repeat that I assert that what is greater than all other beings is in the understanding; and if it is in the understanding, it exists also in reality, for otherwise the being which is greater than all would not be greater than all.

Nowhere in all my writings is such a demonstration found. For the real existence of a being which is said to be *greater than all other beings* cannot be demonstrated in the same way with the real existence of one that is said to be *a being than which a greater cannot be conceived*.

If it should be said that a being than which a greater cannot be conceived has no real existence, or that it is possible that it does not exist, or even that it can be conceived not to exist, such an assertion can be easily refuted. For the nonexistence of what does not exist is possible, and that whose nonexistence is possible can be conceived not to exist. But whatever can be conceived not to exist, if it exists, is not a being than which a greater cannot be conceived; but if it does not exist, it would not, even if it existed, be a being than which a greater cannot be conceived. But it cannot be said that a being than which a greater is inconceivable, if if exists, is not a being than which a greater is inconceivable; or that if it existed, it would not be a being than which a greater is inconceivable.

It is evident, then, that neither is it nonexistent, nor is it possible that it does not exist, nor can it be conceived not to exist. For otherwise, if it exists, it is not that which it is said to be in the hypothesis; and if it existed, it would not be what it is said to be in the hypothesis.

But this, it appears, cannot be so easily proved of a being which is said to be *greater than all other beings*. For it is not so evident that what can be conceived not to exist is not greater than all existing beings, as it is evident that it is not a being than which a greater cannot be conceived. Nor is it so indubitable that if a being greater than all other beings exists, it is no other than the being than which a greater cannot be conceived; or that if it were such a being, some other might not be this being in like manner; as it is certain with regard to a being which is hypothetically posited as one than which a greater cannot be conceived.

For consider: if one should say that there is a being greater than all other beings, and that this being can nevertheless be conceived not to exist; and that a being greater than this, although it does not exist, can be conceived to exist: can it be so clearly inferred in this case that this being is therefore not a being greater than all other existing beings, as it would be most positively affirmed in the other case, that the being under discussion is not, therefore, a being than which a greater cannot be conceived?

For the former conclusion requires another premise than the predication, *greater than all other beings*. In my argument, on the other hand, there is no need of any other than this very predication, *a being than which a greater cannot be conceived*.

If the same proof cannot be applied when the being in question is predicated to be greater than all others, which can be applied when it is predicated to be a being than which a greater cannot be conceived, you have unjustly censured me for saying what I did not say; since such a predication differs so greatly from that which I actually made. If, on the other hand, the other argument is valid, you ought not to blame me so for having said what can be proved.

Whether this can be proved, however, he will easily decide who recognises that this being than which a greater cannot be conceived is demonstrable. For by no means can this being than which a greater cannot be conceived be understood as any other than that which alone is greater than all. Hence, just as that than which a greater cannot be conceived is understood, and is in the understanding, and for that reason is asserted to exist in the reality of fact: so what is said to be greater than all other beings is understood and is in the understanding, and therefore it is necessarily inferred that it exists in reality.

You see, then, with how much justice you have compared me with your fool, who, on the sole ground that he understands what is described to him would affirm that a lost island exists. . . .

CHAPTER IX

The possibility of understanding and conceiving of the supremely great being. The argument advanced against the fool is confirmed.

But even if it were true that a being than which a greater is inconceivable cannot be conceived or understood; yet it would not be untrue that a being than which a greater cannot be conceived is conceivable and intelligible. There is nothing to prevent one's saying *ineffable*, although what is said to be ineffable cannot be spoken of. *Inconceivable* is conceivable, although that to which the word *inconceivable* can be applied is not conceivable. So when one says, *that than which nothing greater is conceivable*, undoubtedly what is heard is conceivable and intelligible, although that being itself, than which a greater is inconceivable, cannot be conceived or understood.

Or, though there is a man so foolish as to say that there is no being than which a greater is inconceivable, he will not be so shameless as to say that he cannot understand or conceive of what he says. Or, if such a man is found, not only ought his words to be rejected, but he himself should be contemned.

Whoever, then denies the existence of a being than which a greater cannot be conceived, at least understands and conceives of the denial which he makes. But this denial he cannot understand or conceive of without its component terms; and a term of this statement is *a being than which a greater cannot be conceived*. Whoever, then, makes this denial, understands and conceives of that than which a greater is inconceivable.

Moreover, it is evident that in the same way it is possible to conceive of and understand a being whose nonexistence is impossible; but he who conceives of this conceives of a greater being than one whose nonexistence is possible. Hence, when a being than which a greater is inconceivable is conceived, if it is a being whose nonexistence is possible that is conceived, it is not a being than which a greater cannot be conceived. But an object cannot be at once conceived and not conceived. Hence he who conceives of a being than which a greater is inconceivable, does not conceive of that whose nonexistence is possible, but of that whose nonexistence is impossible. Therefore, what he conceives of must exist; for anything whose nonexistence is possible, is not that of which he conceives.

III.B.2. Existence Is Inseparable from the Essence of God

RENÉ DESCARTES

René Descartes (1596–1650), often called the father of modern philosophy, set out to see whether human knowledge might be established on a firm foundation that would yield certainty. First, by the method of doubt, he resolved to rid himself of all false and even uncertain beliefs. Then, through the policy of accepting only those beliefs that have the clear and distinct support of reason in the sense that their negations involve contradictions, he resolved to reconstruct a system of beliefs to replace that which the method of doubt had pulled down. Descartes discovered that most of his beliefs could be doubted, but he found one the doubting of which was contradictory. To doubt his own existence was self-contradictory; in order to doubt, one must exist. Thus he arrived at the affirmation Cogito, ergo sum *(I think, therefore I am), the fundamental, indubitable truth on which the rest of his system would be built.*

Descartes argues here that existence is a part of the essence of God, just as having its internal angles equal to two right angles is part of the essence of a triangle. It is no more possible to separate the notion of existence from the notion of God, than it is to separate the notion of a triangle's having its internal angles equal to two right angles from the notion of a triangle, or the notion of a mountain from that of a valley. Though mountains or triangles might not exist—since existence is no part of their essence—they must still be conceived as having those features that are inseparable aspects of their essence. God, however, cannot even be conceived of as not existing, because existence is included in God's essence.

. . . This is what I believe most needs examination here: I find within me countless ideas of things, that, although perhaps not existing anywhere outside me, still cannot be said to be nothing. Although I somehow think them at will, nevertheless I have not put them together; rather, they have their own true and immutable natures. For example, when I imagine a triangle, although perhaps no such figure exists outside my thought anywhere in the world and never will, still its nature, essence, or form is

From *Meditations on First Philosophy,* trans. and ed. Donald A. Cress, *Discourse on Method with Meditations* (Indianapolis: Hackett, 1980), pp. 85–87. With the permission of Hackett Publishing Co., Inc. Indianapolis, IN & Cambridge, MA.

completely determined, unchangeable, and eternal. I did not produce it and it does not depend on my mind. This point is evident from the fact that many properties can be demonstrated regarding this triangle—namely that its three angles are equal to two right angles, that its longest side is opposite the largest angle, and so on; whether I want to or not, I now clearly acknowledge them, although I had not previously thought of them at all when I imagined a triangle. For this reason, then, I have not produced them.

It is irrelevant to say that perhaps the idea of a triangle came to me from external things through the sense organs, on the grounds that on occasion I have seen triangular-shaped bodies. For I can think of many other figures, concerning which there can be no suspicion of their ever having entered me through the senses, and yet the various properties of these figures, no less than those of the triangle, can be demonstrated. All of these are patently true because they are clearly known by me; thus they are something and not merely nothing. For it is evident that everything that is true is something; I have already demonstrated this, certainly the nature of my mind is such that I nevertheless must assent to them, at least while I perceive them clearly; I remember that even before now, when I adhered very closely to the objects of the senses, I always took this type of truth to be the most certain of every truth that I evidently knew regarding figures, numbers, or other things pertaining to arithmetic, geometry or, in general, to pure and abstract mathematics.

But if, from the mere fact that I can bring forth from my thought the idea of something, it follows that all that I clearly and distinctly perceive to pertain to something really does pertain to it, then is this not an argument by which to prove the existence of God? Certainly I discover within me an idea of God, that is, of a supremely perfect being, no less than the idea of some figure or number. And I understand clearly and distinctly that it pertains to his nature that he always exists, no less than whatever has been demonstrated about some figure or number also pertains to the nature of this figure or number. Thus, even if everything that I have meditated upon during these last few days were not true, I ought to be at least as certain of the existence of God as I have hitherto been about the truths of mathematics.

Nevertheless, this point is not wholly obvious at first glance, but has the appearance of a sophism. Since in all other matters I am accustomed to distinguishing existence from essence, I easily persuade myself that the essence of God can be separated off from his existence; thus God can be thought of as not existing. Be that as it may, it still becomes obvious to a very diligently attentive person that the existence of God can no more be separated from his essence than the essence of a triangle can be separated from the fact that its three internal angles equal two right angles, or the idea of a valley can be separated from the idea of a mountain. So it is no less repugnant to think of a God (that is, a supremely perfect being) lacking existence (that is, as lacking some perfection), than it is to think of a mountain lacking a valley.

But granted I could no more think of God as not existing than I can think of a mountain without a valley, still it does not follow that a mountain or a valley exists anywhere, but only that, whether they exist or not, a mountain and a valley cannot be separated from one another. But from the fact that I cannot think of God except as existing, it follows that existence is inseparable from God; for this reason he truly exists. Not because my thought brings this

situation about, or imposes any necessity on anything; but because the necessity of this thing, namely of the existence of God, forces me to entertain this
thought; for I am not free to think of God without existence (that is, the
supremely perfect being apart from the supreme perfection), as I am free to
imagine a horse with or without wings.

Further, it should not be said here that, having asserted that he has all
perfections, I needed to assert that God exists—since existence is one of these
perfections—but that my earlier assertion need not have been made. So, I need
not believe that all four-sided figures are inscribed in a circle; but assuming that
I do believe it, it would then be necessary for me to admit that a rhombus is
inscribed in a circle—this is plainly false. Although it is not necessary that I
happen upon any thought of God, nevertheless as often as I think of a being
first and supreme—and bring forth the idea of God as if from the storehouse of
my mind—I must of necessity ascribe all perfections to it, even though I do not
at any time enumerate them all, nor take note of them one by one. This
necessity plainly suffices so that afterwards, when I consider that existence is a
perfection, I rightly conclude that a first and supreme being exists. In the same
way, there is no necessity for me ever to imagine a triangle, but as often as I
wish to consider a rectilinear figure having but three internal angles, I must
ascribe to it those properties from which one rightly infers that the three
internal angles of this figure are not greater than two right angles, even though
I do not then take notice of this fact. But when I inquire which figures might be
inscribed in a circle, there is absolutely no need whatever for my believing that
all four-sided figures are of this sort; nor even, for that matter, can I possibly
imagine it, as long as I wish to admit only what I clearly and distinctly
understand. Consequently, there is a great difference between false benefits of
this sort and true ideas inborn in me, the first and principal of which is the idea
of God. For I plainly understand in many ways that it is not an invention
dependent upon my thought, but an image of a true and immutable nature.
First, because I cannot think of anything but God himself to whose essence
belongs existence; next, because I cannot understand two or more Gods of this
kind; because, having asserted that one God now exists, I plainly see that it is
necessarily the case that he has existed from eternity and will endure forever;
finally, because I perceive many other things in God, none of which I can
remove or change.

III.B.3. The Impossibility of an Ontological Proof

IMMANUEL KANT

Immanuel Kant (1724–1804), the great German critical philosopher denied the possibility of positive knowledge about metaphysical matters, including the existence of God, although he believed that the human moral sense provides some grounds for believing in God. He argues here that the unconditioned necessity of a judgment does not prove the absolute necessity or being of the thing to which the judgment refers. Kant is claiming that no existential proposition is logically necessary: Whatever can be conceived as existing can also be conceived as not existing. Thus the claim that the nonexistence of God is inconceivable is not acceptable.

Kant believes that the confusion on which the ontological argument rests is the mistaken assumption that existence is a real predicate—that is, that in saying of something that it exists, we are attributing to it a property in the same way that we do when we say that something is red or tall. The judgment that God is omnipotent is a necessary judgment because it involves a real predicate (omnipotence) that belongs necessarily to the subject (God), and its denial is self-contradictory. We cannot affirm that something might be God and at the same time deny that it is omnipotent. The claim that God exists, however, is not the same sort of judgment. To say that God exists is not to attribute some property or perfection to God, since existence is not a predicate or a perfection that anything might have or not have along with its other characteristics. To say that something exists is to claim that that something, with whatever predicates may characterize it, is actually manifest or present in the world— that there is such a thing. We can affirm that something might be God (an omnipotent being, for example) and at the same time deny that it exists. The claim that God is omnipotent amounts to saying that if anything is God, then it is an omnipotent being; this does not say, however, that anything really existing is omnipotent. If God is a being characterized by all the perfections, then God is characterized by omnipotence. But if God is a being characterized by all the perfections, this does not mean that God is characterized by exis-

From *Critique of Pure Reason*, trans. J. M. D. Meiklejohn (New York. P. F. Collier, 1900), pp. 331–337.

tence, since existence is not a perfection it is not even a characteristic at all.

It is evident from what has been said, that the conception of an absolutely necessary being is a mere idea, the objective reality of which is far from being established by the mere fact that it is a need of reason. On the contrary, this idea serves merely to indicate a certain unattainable perfection, and rather limits the operations than, by the presentation of new objects, extends the sphere of the understanding. But a strange anomaly meets us at the very threshold; for the inference from a given existence in general to an absolutely necessary existence, seems to be correct and unavoidable, while the conditions of the *understanding* refuse to aid us in forming any conception of such a being.

Philosophers have always talked of an *absolutely necessary* being, and have nevertheless declined to take the trouble of conceiving, whether—and how—a being of this nature is even cogitable, not to mention that its existence is actually demonstrable. A verbal definition of the conception is certainly easy enough; it is something, the non-existence of which is impossible. But does this definition throw any light upon the conditions which render it impossible to cogitate the non-existence of a thing—conditions which we wish to ascertain, that we may discover whether we think anything in the conception of such a being or not? For the mere fact that I throw away, by means of the word *Unconditioned*, all the conditions which the understanding habitually requires in order to regard anything as necessary, is very far from making clear whether by means of the conception of the unconditionally necessary I think of something, or really of nothing at all.

Nay, more this chance-conception, now become so current, many have endeavored to explain by examples, which seemed to render any inquiries regarding its intelligibility quite needless. Every geometrical proposition—a triangle has three angles—it was said, is absolutely necessary; and thus people talked of an object which lay out of the sphere of our understanding as if it were perfectly plain what the conception of such a being meant.

All the examples adduced have been drawn, without exception, from *judgments*, and not from *things*. But the unconditioned necessity of a judgment does not form the absolute necessity of a thing. On the contrary, the absolute necessity of a judgment is only a conditioned necessity of a thing, or of the predicate in a judgment. The proposition above-mentioned, does not enounce that three angles necessarily exist, but, upon condition that a triangle exists, three angles must necessarily exist—in it. And thus this logical necessity has been the source of the greatest delusions. Having formed an *à priori* conception of a thing, the content of which was made to embrace existence, we believed ourselves safe in concluding that, because existence belongs necessarily to the object of the conception (that is, under the condition of my positing this thing as given), the existence of the thing is also posited necessarily, and that it is therefore absolutely necessary—merely because its existence has been cogitated in the conception.

If, in an identical judgment, I annihilate the predicate in thought, and retain the subject, a contradiction is the result; and hence I say, the former belongs necessarily to the latter. But if I suppress both subject and predicate in thought, no contradiction arises; for there *is nothing* at all, and therefore no means of forming a contradiction. To suppose the existence of a triangle and not that of its three angles, is self-contradictory; but to suppose the non-existence of both triangle and angles is perfectly admissible. And so is it with the conception of an absolutely necessary being. Annihilate its existence in thought, and you annihilate the thing itself with all its predicates; how then can there be any room for contradiction? Externally, there is nothing to give rise to a contradiction, for a thing cannot be necessary externally; nor internally, for, by the annihilation or suppression of the thing itself, its internal properties are also annihilated. God is omnipotent—that is a necessary judgment. His omnipotence cannot be denied, if the existence of a Deity is posited—the existence, that is, of an infinite being, the two conceptions being identical. But when you say, *God does not exist*, neither omnipotence nor any other predicate is affirmed; they must all disappear with the subject, and in this judgment there cannot exist the least self-contradiction.

You have thus seen, that when the predicate of a judgment is annihilated in thought along with the subject, no internal contradiction can arise, be the predicate what it may. There is no possibility of evading the conclusion—you find yourselves compelled to declare: There are certain subjects which cannot be annihilated in thought. But this is nothing more than saying: There exist subjects which are absolutely necessary—the very hypothesis which you are called upon to establish. For I find myself unable to form the slightest conception of a thing which, when annihilated in thought with all its predicates, leaves behind a contradiction; and contradiction is the only criterion of impossibility, in the sphere of pure *à priori* conceptions.

Against these general considerations, the justice of which no one can dispute, one argument is adduced, which is regarded as furnishing a satisfactory demonstration from the fact. It is affirmed, that there is one and only one conception, in which the non-being or annihilation of the object is self-contradictory, and this is the conception of an *ens realissimum*. It possesses, you say, all reality, and you feel yourselves justified in admitting the possibility of such a being. (This I am willing to grant for the present, although the existence of a conception which is not self-contradictory, is far from being sufficient to prove the possibility of an object.[1]) Now the notion of all reality embraces in it that of existence; the notion of existence lies, therefore, in the conception of this possible thing. If this thing is annihilated in thought, the internal possibility of the thing is also annihilated, which is self-contradictory.

I answer: It is absurd to introduce—under whatever term disguised—into the conception of a thing, which is to be cogitated solely in reference to its possibility, the conception of its existence. If this is admitted, you will have

---

[1] A conception is always possible, if it is not self-contradictory. This is the logical criterion of possibility, distinguishing the object of such a conception from the *nihil negativum*. But it may be, notwithstanding, an empty conception, unless the objective reality of this synthesis, by which it is generated, is demonstrated; and a proof of this kind must be based upon principles of possible experience, and not upon the principle of analysis or contradiction. This remark may be serviceable as a warning against concluding, from the possibility of a conception—which is logical, the possibility of a thing—which is real.

apparently gained the day, but in reality have enounced nothing but a mere tautology. I ask, is the proposition *this or that thing* (which I am admitting to be possible) *exists*, an analytical or a synthetical proposition? If the former, there is no addition made to the subject of your thought by the affirmation of its existence; but then the conception in your minds is identical with the thing itself, or you have supposed the existence of a thing to be possible, and then inferred its existence from its internal possibility—which is but a miserable tautology. The word *reality* in the conception of the thing, and the word *existence* in the conception of the predicate, will not help you out of the difficulty. For, supposing you were to term all positing of a thing, reality, you have thereby posited the thing with all its predicates in the conception of the subject and assumed its actual existence, and this you merely repeat in the predicate. But if you confess, as every reasonable person must, that every existential proposition is synthetical, how can it be maintained that the predicate of existence cannot be denied without contradiction—a property which is the characteristic of analytical propositions, alone.

I should have a reasonable hope of putting an end forever to this sophistical mode of argumentation, by a strict definition of the conception of existence, did not my own experience teach me that the illusion arising from our confounding a logical with a real predicate (a predicate which aids in the determination of a thing) resists almost all the endeavors of explanation and illustration. A *logical predicate* may be what you please, even the subject may be predicated of itself; for logic pays no regard to the content of a judgment. But the determination of a conception is a predicate, which adds to and enlarges the conception. It must not, therefore, be contained in the conception.

Being is evidently not a real predicate, that is, a conception of something which is added to the conception of some other thing. It is merely the positing of a thing, or of certain determinations in it. Logically, it is merely the copula of a judgment. The proposition, *God is omnipotent*, contains two conceptions, which have a certain object or content; the word *is*, is no additional predicate—it merely indicates the relation of the predicate to the subject. Now, if I take the subject (God) with all its predicates (omnipotence being one), and say, *God is*, or, *There is a God*, I add no new predicate to the conception of God, I merely posit or affirm the existence of the subject with all its predicates—I posit the *object* in relation to my *conception*. The content of both is the same; and there is no addition made to the conception, which expresses merely the possibility of the object, by my cogitating the object—in the expression, it *is*— as absolutely given or existing. Thus the real contains no more than the possible. A hundred real dollars contain no more than a hundred possible dollars. For, as the latter indicate the conception, and the former the object, on the supposition that the content of the former was greater than that of the latter, my conception would not be an expression of the whole object, and would consequently be an inadequate conception of it. But in reckoning my wealth there may be said to be more in a hundred real dollars, than in a hundred possible dollars—that is, in the mere conception of them. For the real object—the dollars—is not analytically contained in my conception, but forms a synthetical addition to my conception (which is merely a determination of my mental state), although this objective reality—this existence—apart from my conception, does not in the least degree increase the aforesaid hundred dollars.

By whatever and by whatever number of predicates—even to the complete determination of it—I may cogitate a thing I do not in the least augment the object of my conception by the addition of the statement, this thing exists. Otherwise, not exactly the same, but something more than what was cogitated in my conception, would exist, and I could not affirm that the exact object of my conception had real existence. If I cogitate a thing as containing all modes of reality except one, the mode of reality which is absent is not added to the conception of the thing by the affirmation that the thing exists; on the contrary, the thing exists—if it exist at all—with the same defect as that cogitated in its conception; otherwise not that which was cogitated, but something different, exists. Now, if I cogitate a being as the highest reality, without defect or imperfection, the question still remains—whether this being exists or not? For although no element is wanting in the possible real content of my conception, there is a defect in its relation to my mental state, that is, I am ignorant whether the cognition of the object indicated by the conception is possible *à posteriori*. And here the cause of the present difficulty becomes apparent. If the question regarded an object of sense merely, it would be impossible for me to confound the conception with the existence of a thing. For the conception merely enables me to cogitate an object as according with the general conditions of experience; while the existence of the object permits me to cogitate it as contained in the sphere of actual experience. At the same time, this connection with the world of experience does not in the least augment the conception, although a possible perception has been added to the experience of the mind. But if we cogitate existence by the pure category alone, it is not to be wondered at, that we should find ourselves unable to present any criterion sufficient to distinguish it from mere possibility.

Whatever be the content of our conception of an object, it is necessary to go beyond it, if we wish to predicate existence of the object. In the case of sensuous objects, this is attained by their connection according to empirical laws with some one of my perceptions; but there is no means of cognizing the existence of objects of pure thought, because it must be cognized completely *à priori*. But all our knowledge of existence (be it immediately by perception, or by inferences connecting some object with a perception) belongs entirely to the sphere of experience—which is in perfect unity with itself—and although an existence out of this sphere cannot be absolutely declared to be impossible, it is a hypothesis the truth of which we have no means of ascertaining.

The notion of a supreme being is in many respects a highly useful idea; but for the very reason that it is an idea, it is incapable of enlarging our cognition with regard to the existence of things. It is not even sufficient to instruct us as to the possibility of a being which we do not know to exist. The analytical criterion of possibility, which consists in the absence of contradiction in propositions, cannot be denied it. But the connection of real properties in a thing is a synthesis of the possibility of which an *à priori* judgment cannot be formed, because these realities are not presented to us specifically; and even if this were to happen, a judgment would still be impossible, because the criterion of the possibility of synthetical cognitions must be sought for in the world of experience, to which the object of an idea cannot belong. And thus the celebrated Leibnitz has utterly failed in his attempt to establish upon *à priori* grounds the possibility of this sublime ideal being.

The celebrated ontological or Cartesian argument for the existence of a Supreme Being is therefore insufficient; and we may as well hope to increase our stock of knowledge by the aid of mere ideas, as the merchant to augment his wealth by the addition of noughts to his cash-account.

III.B.4. The Ontological Argument

BRIAN DAVIES

Brian Davies, a Dominican friar and lecturer in philosophy at Blackfriars, Oxford, offers a brief survey and critique of some of the major objections that have been raised against the ontological argument. In the process, he also provides a glimpse of the modal version of the ontological argument: Making use of the concept of possible worlds, this version of the argument attempts first to show that a being with maximal excellence is possible—that is, that in some possible world there is such a being. Then it undertakes to establish that a being that possesses maximal excellence in some but not all possible worlds would not actually be a being with maximal excellence and that therefore such a being must possess maximal excellence in every possible world. Because the actual world is a possible world, the argument moves on to claim that God (a being with maximal excellence) exists. The conclusion, however, seems not to follow.

To see why, consider the following argument: There is a possible world in which unicorns have only one horn. Indeed, in every possible world unicorns have only one horn. The actual world is a possible world. Thus, unicorns exist. The argument is parallel to the one about God, but it is not difficult to see that it does not establish its conclusion. God possesses maximal excellence in every possible world just as unicorns have only one horn in every possible world. But that no more means that God exists than it means that unicorns exist. To say that God possesses maximal excellence in every possible world amounts to saying not that God exists in every possible world, but that in every possible world whatever (if anything) is God has maximal excellence. The error lies in reasoning from a universal proposition, which is hypothetical, to an existential proposition. "God has maximal excellence" means "If anything is God, then it has maximal excellence," just as "Unicorns have one horn" means "If anything is a unicorn, it has one horn." It does not prove that anything that is God or anything that is a unicorn exists. Davies concludes that the ontological argument fails, but he hints that there are other types of theistic arguments that may be more successful.

From *An Introduction to the Philosophy of Religion* (New York: Oxford University Press, 1982), pp. 26–37.

'What's in a name?' asked Juliet. It could be said that defenders of the Ontological Argument think there can be quite a lot. Before we see why, however, I ought to point out that there is actually no single argument which alone deserves to be called 'The Ontological Argument'. For reasons of convention and convenience I retain the title as a chapter-heading. I also sometimes use the expression 'the ontological argument'. But 'the ontological argument' is best taken as referring to a group of related arguments.

ONTOLOGICAL ARGUMENTS

The most famous form of the ontological argument is to be found in St. Anselm's *Proslogion*, Chapter 2, where we find Anselm apparently offering a definition of God. God, he says, is 'something than which nothing greater can be thought' (*aliquid quo nihil maius cogitari possit*). Anselm's question is whether God, so understood, exists; and his reply takes the form of a *reductio ad absurdum* argument—an argument whose aim is to show that a proposition is true because its denial entails a contradiction or some other absurdity.

Anselm quotes the beginning of Psalm 52: 'The fool says in his heart "There is no God".' The fool, says Anselm, at least understands what it is whose existence he is denying. Thus, says Anselm, he has the idea of God 'in his mind' (*in intellectu*). But God, he continues, must be more than an idea in someone's mind if he is also something than which nothing greater can be thought, for otherwise he would not be something than which nothing greater can be thought. It follows, says Anselm, that God must exist in reality (*in re*) as well as in the mind.

> Even the Fool, then, is forced to agree that something-than-which-nothing-greater-can-be-thought exists in the mind, since he understands this when he hears it, and whatever is understood is in the mind. And surely that-than-which-a-greater-cannot-be-thought cannot exist in the mind alone. For if it exists solely in the mind even, it can be thought to exist in reality also, which is greater. If then that-than-which-a-greater-cannot-be-thought exists in the mind alone, this same that-than-which-a-greater-cannot-be-thought is that-than-which-a-greater-can-be-thought. But this is obviously impossible. Therefore there is absolutely no doubt that something-than-which-a-greater-cannot-be-thought exists both in the mind and in reality.[1]

Thus Anselm seems to be deducing the real existence of God from the concept of God, and, for this reason, his argument can be called *a priori*. In other words, it tries to reach its conclusion not by considering evidence of a tangible nature—as when one argues from a specimen that a patient has anaemia—but by considering meanings or ideas or definitions.

So much, then, for Anselm's version of the ontological argument. But the argument also has several other notable forms. In particular, there are those defended by René Descartes (1591–1650), Norman Malcolm, and Alvin Plantinga.

Descartes's argument comes in the fifth of his *Meditations*.[2] According to

Descartes, just as one can have a clear and distinct idea of numbers or figures so one can have a clear and distinct idea of God. And as Descartes sees it, the idea of God is the idea of supremely perfect being. Furthermore, this being can be seen to have 'an actual and eternal existence' just as some number or figures can be seen to have some kind of character or attribute.

> Existence can no more be separated from the essence of God than can its having its three angles equal to two right angles be separated from the essence of a rectilinear triangle, or the idea of a mountain from the idea of a valley; and so there is not any less repugnance to our conceiving a God (that is, a Being supremely perfect) to whom existence is lacking (that is to say, to whom a certain perfection is lacking), than to conceive of a mountain which has no valley.[3]

The idea here seems to be that from the notion of God one can deduce his existence. God is supremely perfect and must therefore exist.

Malcolm's version of the ontological argument[4] begins by trying to remove certain difficulties. Philosophers often object to the ontological argument by saying that it wrongly treats existence as a perfection which things may have or lack. Malcolm agrees with this criticism and he also allows that Anselm is subject to it. According to Malcolm, Anselm supposes that existence is a perfection in his statement of the ontological argument in *Proslogion* 2. But Malcolm also thinks that Anselm has an ontological argument that does not assume that existence is a perfection. In *Proslogion* 3 we come across the following passage:

> And this being (sc. God) so truly exists that it cannot be even thought not to exist. For something can be thought to exist that cannot be thought not to exist, and this is greater than that which can be thought not to exist. Hence, if that-than-which-a-greater-cannot-be-thought can be thought not to exist, then that-than-which-a-greater-cannot-be-thought is not the same as that-than-which-a-greater-cannot-be-thought, which is absurd. Something-than-which-a-greater-cannot-be-thought exists so truly then, that it cannot be even thought not to exist.

According to Malcolm, Anselm is saying here not that God must exist because existence is a perfection, but that God must exist because the concept of God is the concept of a being whose existence is necessary. As Malcolm sees it, Anselm's *Proslogion* 3 considers God as a being who, if he exists, has the property of necessary existence. Since, however, a being who has this property cannot fail to exist it follows that God actually exists.

> If God, a being a greater than which cannot be conceived, does not exist then He cannot *come* into existence. For if He did He would either have been *caused* to come into existence or have *happened* to come into existence, and in either case He would be a limited being, which by our conception of Him He is not. Since He cannot come into existence, if He does not exist His existence is impossible. If He does exist He cannot have come into existence . . . nor can He cease to exist, for nothing could cause him to cease to exist nor could it just happen that He ceased to exist. So if God exists His existence is necessary. Thus God's existence

is either impossible or necessary. It can be the former only if the concept of such a being is self-contradictory or in some way logically absurd. Assuming that this is not so, it follows that He necessarily exists.[5]

This argument is criticized by Plantinga, but Plantinga argues that it can be salvaged if restated with the help of the philosophical notion of possible worlds, a notion popularized through the writings of a group commonly known as modal logicians.[6] Roughly speaking, a possible world is a way things might have been. Our world is a possible world. So too is a world exactly like ours but where, for example, elephants have two trunks instead of one. Working with this notion of possible worlds, therefore, Plantinga first formulates Malcolm's argument in two propositions:

1. There is a world, W, in which there exists a being with maximal greatness, and

2. A being has maximal greatness in a world only if it exists in every world.[7]

According to Plantinga, this argument establishes that in some possible world there is a being with maximal greatness. And a world containing such a being contains an essence, E, which entails the property 'exists in every world'. Unfortunately, however, says Plantinga, the argument does not establish that there is a being who enjoys maximal greatness in our world. For, presumably, there would be more to being maximally great than just existing in every world, and Malcolm's argument only shows that in some world a being is maximally great.

But Plantinga thinks that the ontological argument can be defended and at this point he begins his defense. If he is right in his assessment of Malcolm's argument it follows that there is a possible world where a being has maximal greatness, which entails that the being exists in every world. But it does not entail that in every world the being is greater or more perfect than other inhabitants of those worlds. Plantinga therefore introduces the notion of maximal excellence. Maximal excellence is connected with maximal greatness.

> The property *has maximal greatness* entails the property *has maximal excellence in every possible world.*

> Maximal excellence entails *omniscience, omnipotence,* and *moral perfection.*[8]

Now, says Plantinga, maximal greatness is possibly exemplified. There is a possible world where there is a being who is maximally great. In that case, however, there is a world with a being who has maximal excellence, from which it follows that in any possible world there is a being who has maximal excellence, from which it follows that there is in our world a being who has maximal excellence, which is to say that there is actually a God whose existence follows from his essence and who can thus be thought to exist in reality by reasoning that counts as a form of the ontological argument.

HOW SUCCESSFUL IS THE ONTOLOGICAL ARGUMENT?

The argument of Anselm's *Proslogion* 2 has at least one point in its favour. People offer different accounts of the nature of God, but it would normally be accepted that God must be immeasurably superior to other things or to whatever is not God. Furthermore, it seems that God cannot merely happen to exist. That might be taken to imply that God's existence was somehow conditional on something, even that it was a sort of accident. It might also be taken to imply that at some future date God could cease to exist. Anselm maintains that God is something than which nothing greater can be thought, that he is necessary or ultimate in a way that nothing apart from God is. This suggestion seems reasonable in the context of an argument for God's existence. It seems fair to suggest that no argument can count as an argument for God as traditionally conceived unless it somehow allows that God is supremely great or in some way inevitable.

But is Anselm's argument cogent? After the appearance of the *Proslogion* a monk called Gaunilo replied to Anselm and virtually accused him of absurdity. According to Gaunilo, if Anselm is correct then it is not only God's existence that can be established by reasoning akin to Anselm's.

> For example: they say that there is in the ocean somewhere an island which, because of the difficulty (or rather the impossibility) of finding that which does not exist, some have called the 'Lost Island'. And the story goes that it is blessed with all manner of priceless riches and delights in abundance, much more even than the Happy Isles, and, having no owner or inhabitant, it is superior everywhere in abundance of riches to all those other lands that men inhabit. Now, if anyone tell me that it is like this, I shall easily understand what is said, since nothing is difficult about it. But if he should then go on to say, as though it were a logical consequence of this: You cannot any more doubt that this island that is more excellent than all other lands truly exists somewhere in reality than you can doubt that it is in your mind; and since it is more excellent to exist not only in the mind alone but also in reality, therefore it must needs be that it exists. For if it did not exist, any other land existing in reality would be more excellent than it, and so this island, already conceived by you to be more excellent than others, will not be more excellent. If, I say, someone wishes thus to persuade me that this island really exists beyond all doubt, I should either think that he was joking, or I should find it hard to decide which of us I ought to judge the bigger fool—I, if I agreed with him, or he, if he thought that he had proved the existence of this island with any certainty, unless he had first convinced me that its very excellence exists in my mind precisely as a thing existing truly and indubitably and not just as something unreal or doubtfully real.[9]

There is one reply that Anselm could make against this objection. For Anselm never talks about something that is in fact greater than anything else. He talks about God as something than which nothing greater can be conceived. Gaunilo refers to an island which might be better than all the islands that there are. But Anselm refers to God as something that cannot be surpassed in any respect. It might thus be suggested that to some extent Anselm and Gaunilo are talking at cross-purposes.

A defender of Gaunilo might, however, accept this point and still try to preserve the thrust of his argument. What if we take it as urging that if Anselm's argument works then it is possible to establish the existence not of the island which is better than all others, but of the island than which no more perfect island can be conceived?

The move has seemed plausible to many, but it need not really show that Anselm is talking nonsense. For it depends on assuming the coherence of the concept of an island than which no island more perfect can be conceived. Yet no matter what description of an island is provided, it is always possible that something could be added to it so as to give an account of a better island. As Plantinga puts it:

> No matter how great an island is, no matter how many Nubian maidens and dancing girls adorn it, there could always be a greater— one with twice as many, for example. The qualities that make for greatness in islands—number of palm trees, amount and quality of coconuts, for example—most of these qualities have no *intrinsic maximum*. That is, there is no degree of productivity or number of palm trees (or of dancing girls) such that it is impossible that an island display more of that quality. So the idea of a greatest possible island is an inconsistent or incoherent idea; it's not possible that there be such a thing.[10]

Perhaps, then, we might conclude that Anselm's position survives the attack of Gaunilo. The trouble now, however, is that there is a possible snag for Anselm in the very point which he might urge against Gaunilo. If the idea of the greatest possible island is incoherent, must not the same be true of the idea of the greatest possible being? Some of the attributes of a perfect being might be said to have an intrinsic maximum, but it is not at all clear that all of them do. Suppose, for example, it is said that a perfect being is totally loving. Might it not be replied that the idea of a perfectly loving being is incoherent if it is taken to imply that there can be a being who is loving such that nothing more loving can be imagined? The reader might like to think about this question, but perhaps I can now simply note that there is a possible difficulty here for Anselm and pass on to consider whether his argument in *Proslogion* 2 is vulnerable for reasons other than those so far introduced. And at this point it is worth referring to Kant, for it is commonly claimed that Kant provided absolutely decisive objections to Anselm's argument.

The substance of Kant's objection to the ontological argument can be briefly stated thus:

1. No existential proposition is logically necessary.

2. 'Existence' is not a real predicate.

In Kant's own words, 1 is expressed thus:

> If, in an identical proposition, I reject the predicate while retaining the subject, contradiction results; and I therefore say that the former belongs necessarily to the latter. But if we reject the subject and

predicate alike, there is no contradiction; for nothing is then left that can be contradicted. To posit triangle, and yet to reject its three angles, is self-contradictory; but there is no contradiction in rejecting the triangle together with its three angles. The same holds true of the concept of an absolutely necessary being. If its existence is rejected, we reject the thing itself with all its predicates; and no question of contradiction can then arise. There is nothing outside it that would be contradicted, since the necessity of the thing is not supposed to be derived from anything external; nor is there anything internal that would be contradicted, since in rejecting the thing itself we have at the same time rejected all its internal properties. . . . I cannot form the least concept of a thing which, should it be rejected with all its predicates, leaves behind a contradiction.[11]

But is this reasoning acceptable? Many writers find it impressive, but it is far from clear that they are right to do so. According to Kant, if one said 'God does not exist' then 'nothing outside' the concept of God would 'be contradicted.' But what does this mean? Kant might mean that 'God does not exist' cannot contradict 'God exists'. But 'God does not exist' and 'God exists' do seem to contradict each other. Perhaps Kant thinks that God need not exist since the notion of a necessary being would have to be contradicted by some object outside it. But, if this is Kant's argument, it is difficult to make sense of his proposal. It is normally propositions that contradict each other. People can be said to contradict each other, and they can also be said to contradict propositions; but if Kant is saying that people contradict the view that there is a necessary being then he is not saying anything of great philosophical importance. The question is whether people who contradict the view that there can be a necessary being can be right to do so. It might be replied that they can, since no existential proposition is logically necessary. But this view would be challenged by many philosophers. Thus, for example, Swinburne writes: 'Some things do exist of logical necessity. . . . There exists a number greater than one million—and it is a logically necessary truth that there does. There exist concepts which include other concepts. . . . Certain numbers and concepts and similar things (such as logical truths) have logically necessary existence.'[12]

In short, the first part of Kant's critique of the ontological argument does not seem unanswerable. Let us then proceed to Kant's second point, which is stated by him in the following passage:

'Being' is obviously not a real predicate; that is, it is not a concept of something which could be added to the concept of a thing. It is merely the positing of a thing, or of certain determinations, as existing in themselves. Logically, it is merely the copula of a judgment. . . . If, now, we take the subject (God) with all its predicates (among which is omnipotence), and say 'God is' or 'there is a God', we attach no new predicate to the concept of God, but only posit the subject in itself with all its predicates, and indeed posit it as being an *object* that stands in relation to my *concept*. The content of both must be one and the same. . . . Otherwise stated, the real contains no more than the merely possible. A hundred real thalers do not contain the least coin more than a hundred possible thalers.[13]

What does Kant mean by saying that 'Being' is not a real predicate? His point seems to be that when we say that something exists we are not ascribing to it some quality, attribute, or characteristic. And, although this suggestion is sometimes challenged, it seems to me to be correct. For, surely, to say that something exists is always to say that some concept of description is exemplified or instantiated. When I say that the Tower of London exists and that the man who assassinated Hitler does not exist I am not first talking about two things and then giving you more information about what they are like. I am saying that what is contained in two respective concepts is in the one case to be found in the real world and in the other not. Gottlob Frege (1848–1925) puts this point by saying that 'existence' is a second-order predicate. When one is dealing with a first-order predicate one is dealing with a term that tells one something about the nature of something. In 'The man in the house is bald', 'bald' is a first-order predicate. In the case of a second-order predicate, however, we are dealing with a term that tells us something about a concept rather than about the nature of some object. Thus in 'Horses are numerous', 'numerous' does not tell us what horses are like, as, for example, does 'are four-legged'; so 'numerous' functions here as a second-order predicate. It tells us that the concept 'horse' is instantiated many times.

And here, perhaps, we really do have an answer to the argument of *Proslogion* 2. For Anselm's argument does appear to take existence as an attribute, quality, or characteristic. It has been suggested that Anselm does not regard existence in this way; but this supposition is hard to square with his talk about greatness. His argument seems to be that God must exist *in re* if he is that than which nothing greater can be thought. So, as Anselm sees it, to exist must be to have some kind of great-making quality. And since a great-making quality must be some kind of attribute, quality, or characteristic, it follows that Anselm regards existence as a predicate in the sense covered by Frege's notion of a first-order predicate.

The above criticism of Anselm also applies to Descartes's argument. Certainly Descartes is right to say that there is a concept of God suggesting that 'God does not exist' is nonsense. There is indeed a sense in which we can regard 'God does not exist' as absurd in the way that 'This triangle has four sides' is absurd. For how can you have a non-existent God? But this argument does not show that there actually is a God. Descartes is treating existence as a property; he explicitly says that it is a perfection. Yet existence as actuality is not a perfection, not a predicate that tells one something about the nature of something. Even in Descartes's day the thrust of this point was recognized. Pierre Gassendi (1592–1655) replied to Descartes by saying: 'Existence is a perfection neither in God nor in anything else; it is rather that in the absence of which there is no perfection . . . in enumerating the perfections of God, you ought not to have put existence among them, in order to draw the conclusion that God exists, unless you wanted to beg the question.[14]

I suggest, then, that, because of their attempt to treat 'exists' as a first-order predicate, the argument of *Proslogion* 2 and the argument of Descartes are difficult to accept. This is not to say that 'exists' can *never* be used as a predicate.[15] But Anselm and Descartes seem to hold that something is a member of the real world, where 'being a member of the real world' is some kind of property that things can have or lack. And this suggestion is misguided.

Thus we come to the version of the ontological argument defended by Malcolm and Plantinga. It might be worth noting in advance that Malcolm is arguably wrong to read *Proslogion* 3 as a separate attempt to show that there is a God. It has, for instance, been plausibly maintained that *Proslogion* 3 is trying to show that something is true of the actual God, not that there is an actual God. But this exegetical point need not detain us. Malcolm's argument may not be Anselm's, but it is still an argument and we can ask if it is cogent.

The first thing to be said is that Malcolm has made a valid enough distinction in his account of existence and necessity. He holds that we can talk of necessary existence as a property, which seems true. Something like such talk was used in medieval discussions about necessary beings. According to many medieval thinkers there are beings which, as a matter of fact, could not be generated or made to corrupt. If, then, we use the word 'necessary' in the medieval sense meant in the expression 'necessary being' it is easy to see how necessary existence can be thought of as a property. A being will have necessary existence if it is a necessary being in the medieval sense, and since such beings were understood with reference to their inability to be generated or made to corrupt it seems that they were understood with reference to a very definite property or characteristic.

But having granted this point we can yet, I think, see that Malcolm's argument fails. One reason for saying so can be seen if we concentrate on its use of the term 'impossible'.

Remember that according to Malcolm: (1) since God cannot come into existence his existence is impossible if he does not exist; (2) if God does exist, his existence is necessary; (3) God's existence is either impossible or necessary. But 'impossible' here is being used in two senses. First it is being used to mean 'as a matter of fact unable to come about', for when Malcolm first talks about impossibility he is expressing the view that if God is in fact the sort of thing that cannot come into existence then if God does not exist he cannot in fact exist at all, for his existing depends on his not being brought into existence. In the second sense, however, 'impossible' is being used to mean 'unable to be thought without contradiction', for Malcolm explains that if God's existence is impossible, 'the concept of such a being is self-contradictory or in some way logically absurd." Now Malcolm's conclusion is that God's existence is necessary, i.e. the opposite of impossible. But as Malcolm presents this conclusion it must mean that the concept of God is the concept of something that is logically necessary. Thus, from 'God's non-existence is as a matter of fact impossible' Malcolm reaches the conclusion 'God's existence is logically necessary.' But that means that Malcolm's offering a very poor argument indeed. For the conclusion is presupposed by the very thing on which it is based, i.e. that there is a God whose non-existence is as a matter of fact impossible.

This point is well brought out by John Hick who, following Malcolm, distinguishes between something that cannot in fact be brought into existence and something whose non-existence is strictly inconceivable. The first kind of being Hick calls an 'ontologically necessary being'; the second he refers to as a 'logically necessary being'. Then he explains that:

> Whether there is an ontologically necessary being . . . is a question of fact, although of uniquely ultimate fact. Given this concept of an ontologically necessary being, it is a matter of logic that if there is such a being, his existence is necessary in the sense that he cannot cease to exist, and that if there is no such being, none can come to exist. This logical necessity and this logical impossibility are, however, dependent upon the hypotheses, respectively, that there is and that there is not an ontologically necessary being; apart from the hypotheses from which they follow they do not entail that there is or that there is not an eternal self-existent being. Hence, there is no substance to the dilemma. The existence of God is either logically necessary or logically absurd.[17]

Another way of seeing why Malcolm's argument will not do is to begin by considering the following argument:

> A pixie is a little man with pointed ears,
> Therefore there actually exists a pixie.

Now clearly we would not accept this as an argument for pixies. Why not? Because it seems to move from a definition of 'pixie' to the conclusion that there actually is a pixie. But suppose someone were to reply that if a pixie *is* a little man with pointed ears then he must *be* in some sense or he would not be there to have pointed ears. That too would be an unjustifiable (if unforgettable) argument. But why? Because it fails to acknowledge that 'is' can be used in at least two different ways. 'Is' can be used in giving a definition—as in 'A novel is a work of fiction.' Or it can be used to explain that there actually is something or other—as in 'There is an abominable snowman after all.' In the first use we are not really saying anything about something that exists: 'A novel is a work of fiction' does not, for example, say anything about any existent novel. It explains what the word 'novel' means. In the second use too there is a sense in which we are not saying anything about some existent thing. But nor are we explaining what something (which may or may not exist) is. In 'There is an abominable snowman after all' we are not describing anything; nor are we explaining what we should have found if we discovered it. We are saying that an abominable snowman is what something is, and in doing so we tacitly suppose that what we are talking about actually exists. In the above argument from 'A pixie is . . .' to 'There is a pixie . . .' the arguer would be moving from a premise containing the first sense of 'is' to a conclusion containing the second. Or, as some philosophers would put it, he would be moving from an 'is' of *definition* to an 'is' of *affirmative predication*. And his argument is unacceptable just because this cannot validly be done. If it could, we could define anything we like into existence.

Returning now to Malcolm, we can see at this point that he is arguing in the same way as the person whose argument about pixies was just discussed. He is saying that if God is (definitionally) necessarily existent, then there is something which can truly be said to be necessarily existent. And here lies Malcolm's error. We can certainly agree that if God is defined as a necessary being, then God is by definition a necessary being. And if we can get people to accept our definition, we can easily convict them of self-contradiction if they also say that God is not a necessary being. For then they would be saying that God is and that he is not by definition a necessary being. But we cannot move from this conclusion to the conclusion that our definition of God as a necessary being entails that there is anything that actually corresponds to our definition of him as necessary. In other words, we cannot infer from 'God is a necessary being' that 'is God' is affirmatively predictable of anything. It might seem that in that case we would have to end up saying 'The necessary being does not exist', which might be thought to involve the same mistake as that involved in saying 'My mother is not my mother,' But to deny Malcolm's conclusion all we have to say is 'Possibly nothing at all is a necessary being', which is certainly not self-contradictory and may even be true.

So Malcolm's version of the ontological argument is unsuccessful. But what of Plantinga's? His argument can be briefly stated thus:

1. There is a possible world containing a being with maximal greatness.

2. Any being with maximal greatness has the property of maximal excellence in every possible world.

3. Maximal excellence entails omniscience, omnipotence, and moral perfection.

4. There is therefore a possible world where there is a being who has maximal excellence.

5. If there is a possible world where a being has maximal excellence then that being has maximal excellence in every possible world.

6. This is a possible world.

7. Therefore God exists.

Some philosophers would challenge this argument by attacking the whole notion of possible worlds, but the intricacies of this debate cannot be entered into here. Let us instead concentrate on Plantinga's interpretation of 4. As Plantinga sees it, from the fact that it is possible for there to be something having the property of maximal excellence in every world it follows that there is actually a being with maximal excellence in our world. But is this inference correct?

Let us agree that our world is a possible world. Let us also agree that a being with maximal excellence is possible and that it is therefore possible that such a being exists in every possible world. But it does not follow that there is actually any being with maximal excellence. What follows is that maximal excellence is possible. But what is merely possible does not have any real existence—not at least in the sense in which God is normally thought to have existence. And a God who exists in all possible worlds does not have any real existence either. To show the existence of God it seems that one needs more than the possibility of God. From the fact that God is possible it follows only that he is possible; not that he is actual. And, for this reason, Plantinga's argument also seems to fail.

It might be worth adding that there is a further difficulty for someone disposed to accept Plantinga's version of the ontological argument. According to Plantinga, maximal excellence entails omniscience, omnipotence, and moral perfection. Thus Plantinga's argument is one for the existence of a being who is omniscient, omnipotent, and morally perfect. But is it not possible that the notion of such a being is incoherent, i.e. that it is impossible that there should be such a being? A critic, even one who believes in an omniscient, omnipotent, morally perfect God, might well argue that it is indeed possible that the notion of such a God is incoherent. Thus it might be urged that it is possible that the God Plantinga argues for is possibly impossible, in which case it would seem that even if maximal excellence is possibly exemplified, it is also possible that it is not, that it could not be, and that Plantinga's argument based on 4 above may therefore be regarded as undemonstrable.

CONCLUSION

Whole books have been written on the ontological argument and, like any major philosophical argument, it is not to be lightly dismissed. But it does seem unsuccessful—at least in the forms considered here. Why is this so? Basically because definitions can take one only so far; because we can say what we mean by something without its having to be true that what we are talking about really exists. Maybe a successful ontological argument for God's existence will one day be forthcoming; but that remains to be seen.

But this is not to say that belief in Gods' existence is unreasonable. There may be no good ontological argument for the existence of God, but this does not mean that a good *non*-ontological argument is impossible. And . . . it has been maintained that there actually is such an argument.

NOTES

1. Anselm, *Proslogion*, trans. M. J. Charlesworth (Oxford, 1965), chap. ii. It is most important to point out that scholarly interpretations of Anselm's whole programme in the *Proslogion* differ widely and that the interpretation presupposed here (which is probably the most common among philosophers of religion) is by no means indisputable and certainly calls for various qualifications which space here prohibits. For material on Anselm see the Bibliography.

2. In *The Philosophical Works of Descartes*, vol. I, trans. Elizabeth S. Haldane and G. R. T. Ross (Cambridge, 1911).

3. Descartes, op. cit. p. 181.

4. Norman Malcolm, 'Anselm's Ontological Arguments', reprinted in John Hick (ed.), *The Existence of God* (London and New York, 1964), pp. 48–70.

5. Malcolm, p. 56.

6. Cf. Robert C. Stalnaker, 'Possible Worlds' in Ted Honderich and Myles Burnyeat (ed.), *Philosophy As It Is* (London, 1979).

7. Alvin Plantinga, *The Nature of Necessity*, p. 213.

8. Plantinga, p. 214.

9. See Charlesworth, op. cit., p. 175.

10. Alvin Plantinga, *God, Freedom and Evil* (London, 1975), p. 91.

11. Immanuel Kant, *Critique of Pure Reason*, trans. Norman Kemp Smith (London, 1964), pp. 502f.

12. *The Coherence of Theism*, p. 264.

13. *Critique of Pure Reason*, pp. 504f.

14. *The Philosophical Works of Descartes*, vol. 2, trans. Elizabeth S. Haldane and G. R. T. Ross (Cambridge, 1912), p. 186.

15. Cf. Peter Geach, 'Form and Existence' in *God and the Soul* (London, 1969).

16. Cf. D. P. Henry, *Medieval Logic and Metaphysics* (London, 1972), III, 7.

17. John Hick, 'A Critique of the "Second Argument"', in John Hick and Arthur McGill (ed.), *The Many Faced Argument* (London, 1968), pp. 353f.

III.C. The Cosmological Argument

III.C.1. Only God Could Cause My Idea of Perfection

RENÉ DESCARTES

René Descartes (1596–1650), in his effort to found all his belief on firm rational grounds, examines each of the ideas he finds in his mind and asks himself what might be the cause of the idea. The idea he has of other humans, of angels, of material objects, and of animals he believes might actually be caused by himself, since they are all less perfect or at least not more perfect than himself. Yet he also finds the idea of God. Now he has discovered by rational reflection that the cause of anything must be at least as perfect, must have as much reality or power, as that which it causes. But surely he, an imperfect, doubt-filled human, could not be the cause of the idea he has of a supremely perfect being, God. Indeed, nothing short of a supremely perfect being possesses as much reality or perfection as his idea of God possesses. Thus God must exist as the cause of his idea of God. If we are tempted to suggest that perhaps we don't really possess an idea of God—that is, an idea of a supremely perfect being—Descartes argues that the fact that we can recognize ourselves and other things as imperfect proves that we do in fact have the idea of perfection.

Although one idea can perhaps come into being from another, nevertheless there is no infinite regress here; at length some first idea must be reached whose cause is a sort of archetype that formally contains all the reality that is in the idea only objectively. Thus it is evident to me by the light of nature that my ideas are like images that can easily fail to match the perfection of the things from which they have been drawn, but my ideas cannot contain anything better or more perfect.

But the longer and more attentively I examine all these points, the more clearly and distinctly I know they are true. But what do I finally conclude? Why, if the objective reality of one of my ideas is such that I am certain that the

From *Meditations on First Philosophy*, ed. and trans. Donald A. Cress, *Discourse on Method* with *Meditations* (Indianapolis: Hackett, 1980), pp. 85–87. With the permission of Hackett Publishing Co., Inc. Indianapolis, IN and Cambridge, MA.

same reality is not formally or eminently in me, or that I myself can [not] be the cause of the idea, then it necessarily follows that I am not alone in the world, and that something else—the cause of this idea—also exists. If in fact no such idea is found in me, I shall plainly have no argument to make me certain of the existence of something other than myself. For I have looked at all of these arguments most diligently and so far I have been unable to find any other.

Among my ideas, in addition to the one that represents me to myself—about which there can be no difficulty at this point—there are some that represent God, others that represent inanimate, corporeal objects, others that represent men like myself.

As to the ideas that represent other men, animals, or angels, I easily understand that they can be formed from the ideas that I have of myself, of corporeal things, and of God—even if no men except myself, no animals, and no angels were to exist in the world.

As to the ideas of corporeal things, there is nothing in them which is such that it seems unable to have come from me. For if I investigate thoroughly and if I examine each one individually in the same way that I examined the idea of wax yesterday, I notice that there are only a very few properties that I perceive in them clearly and distinctly: namely, magnitude, or extension in length, breadth, and depth; shape, which arises from the limit of this extension; position, which the various shaped things possess in relation to one another; and motion, or the alteration of this position; to these can be added substance, duration, and number. The remaining properties, however—such as light and colors, sounds, odors, tastes, heat and cold and other tactile qualities—are thought by me only in a very confused and obscure manner, with the result that I do not know whether they are true or false, that is, whether the ideas that I have of these things are ideas of certain things or are not ideas of things. For although a short time ago I noted that falsity properly so called ("formal" falsity) can be found only in judgments, nevertheless there is another kind of falsity (called "material" falsity) in ideas; it occurs whenever judgments present a non-thing as if it were a thing. For example, the ideas that I have of heat and cold fall so short of being clear and distinct that I cannot learn from them whether cold is only a privation of heat or whether heat is a privation of cold; whether both are real qualities or neither is. Because ideas can only be ideas of things, and if it is true that cold is nothing more than the privation of heat, then an idea such as this one, that repesents something real and positive to me, will not inappropriately be called false—and so too for the other ideas.

Assuredly it is not necessary for me to assign to these ideas an author distinct from me. For if they were false, that is, if they should represent no objects, I know by the light of nature that they proceed from nothing; that is, they are in me for no other reason than that something is lacking in my nature, that my nature is plainly not perfect. If, on the other hand, these ideas are true because they exhibit so little reality to me that I cannot distinguish them from a non-thing, then I see no reason why they cannot get their existence from myself.

As for those things that are the clear and distinct elements in the ideas of corporeal things, I seem able to have borrowed some from the idea of myself: namely, substance, duration, number, and whatever else there may be of this type. For when I think that a stone is a substance, that is to say, a thing that in its own right has an aptitude for existing, and that I too am a substance—although I conceive that I am a thing that thinks and not an extended thing, whereas a stone is an extended thing and not a thing that thinks—there is, accordingly, the greatest diversity between these two concepts, even though they seem to agree with one another when they are considered under the rubric of substance. Furthermore, when I perceive that I exist now and recall that I have previously existed for some time, and when I have several thoughts and know the number of these thoughts, I acquire the ideas of duration and number, which I then apply to everything else. However, all the other elements out of which the ideas of corporeal things are put together (namely extension, shape, position, and motion) are not contained in me formally, because I am only a thing that thinks. But because they are only modes of a substance, and I too am a substance, they seem capable of being contained in me eminently.

Thus there remains only the idea of God. We must consider whether there is in this idea something which could not have originated from me. I understand by the word "God" an infinite and independent substance, intelligent and powerful in the highest degree, who created me along with everything else—if in fact there is anything else. Indeed all these qualities are such that, the more diligently I attend to them, the less they seem capable of having arisen from myself alone. Thus, from what has been said above, we must conclude that God necessarily exists.

For although the idea of substance is in me by virtue of the fact that I am a substance, nevertheless it would not for that reason be the idea of an infinite substance, unless it proceeded from some substance which is in fact infinite, because I am finite.

Nor should I think that I do not perceive the infinite by means of a true idea, but only through a negation of the finite, just as I perceive rest and shadows by means of a negation of motion and light. On the contrary, I clearly understand that there is more reality in an infinite substance than there is in a finite one. Thus the perception of the infinite somehow exists in me prior to the perception of the finite, that is, the perception of God exists prior to the perception of myself. Why would I know that I doubt and I desire, that is, that I lack something and that I am not wholly perfect, if there were no idea in me of a more perfect being by comparison with which I might acknowledge my defects?

Nor can it be said that this idea of God is perhaps materially false, and therefore can be from nothing, as I pointed out just now regarding the ideas of heat and cold and the like. On the contrary, because it is the most clear and distinct of all ideas and because it contains more objective reality than any other idea, no idea is truer in its own right, and there is no idea in which less suspicion of falsity is to be found. I maintain that this idea of a being most perfect and infinite is true in the highest degree. Although such a being can perhaps be imagined not to exist, it nevertheless cannot be imagined that this idea shows me nothing real, as was the case with the idea of cold that I referred to earlier. It is also an idea that is clear and distinct in the highest degree; for whatever I clearly and distinctly perceive that is real and true and that contains some perfection is wholly contained in that idea. It is not inconsistent to say that I do not comprehend the infinite or that there are countless other things in

God that I can in no way either comprehend or perhaps even touch with thought. For the nature of the infinite is such that it is not comprehended by me, who am finite. And it is sufficient that I understand this very point and judge that all those things that I clearly perceive and that I know to contain some perfection—and perhaps even countless other things of which I am ignorant—are in God either formally or eminently. The result is that, of all those that are in me, the idea that I have of him is the most true, the most clear, and the most distinct.

But perhaps I am something greater than I take myself to be. Perhaps all these perfections that I attribute to God are somehow in me potentially, although they do not yet assert themselves and are not yet reduced to act. For I now observe that my knowledge is gradually being increased; I see nothing that stands in the way of my knowledge being increased more and more to infinity. I see no reason why, with my knowledge thus increased, I cannot acquire all the remaining perfections of God. And, finally, if the potential for producing these perfections is in me already, I see no reason why this potential does not suffice to produce the idea of these perfections.

Yet none of these things can be the case. First, while it is true that my knowledge is gradually increased and that in me there are many elements in potency which do not yet exist in act, nevertheless, none of these elements pertain to the idea of God, in which nothing whatever is potential; this gradual increase is itself a most certain argument for my imperfection. Moreover, although my knowledge might always increase more and more, nevertheless I understand this knowledge will never by this means be infinite in act, because it will never reach a point where it is incapable of greater increase. On the contrary, I judge God to be infinite in act, with the result that nothing can be added to his perfection. Finally, I perceive that the objective being of an idea cannot be produced by a merely potential being (which, properly speaking, is nothing), but only by an actual or formal being.

III.C.2. God

RICHARD TAYLOR

Richard Taylor (1919–), for many years professor of philoso-
phy at the University of Rochester and now visiting professor
at Union College, provides here a detailed exposition of the
cosmological argument. Taylor begins by referring to the
principle of sufficient reason, which, he concedes, cannot be
proved, but which seems too obvious to doubt seriously. He
further points out that the world and the things of which it
consists seem all to be contingent in the sense that their
existence is not self explanatory but requires reference to some-
thing else. Even if it could be shown that the world had
existed forever, that would not explain its existence. The world
seems to require something on which it depends for its exis-
tence, a creator, that is not itself dependent on something else.
The suggestion that God is the creator is supported by the
evidence, although this argument does not establish that God
has all the characteristics that religious persons are ac-
customed to attributing to God.

An active, living, and religious belief in the gods has
probably never arisen and been maintained on purely metaphysical grounds.
Such beliefs are found in every civilized land and time, and are often virtually
universal in a particular culture, yet relatively few men have much of a
conception of metaphysics. There are in fact entire cultures, such as ancient
Israel, to whom metaphysics is quite foreign, though these cultures may
nevertheless be religious.

Belief in the gods seems to have its roots in human desires and fears,
particularly those associated with self-preservation. Like all other creatures,
men have a profound will to live, which is what mainly gives one's existence a
meaning from one sunrise to the next. Unlike other creatures, however, men
are capable of the full and terrible realization of their own inevitable decay. A
man can bring before his mind the image of his own grave, and with it the
complete certainty of its ultimate reality, and against this his will naturally
recoils. It can hardly seem to him less than an absolute catastrophe, the very
end, so far as he is concerned, of everything, though he has no difficulty
viewing death, as it touches others more or less remote from himself, as a
perhaps puzzling, occasionally distressing, but nonetheless necessary aspect
of nature. It is probably partly in response to this fear that he turns to the gods,
as those beings of such power that they can overturn this verdict of nature.

The sources of religious belief are doubtless much more complex than this,
but they seem to lie in man's will rather than in his speculative intelligence,

Richard Taylor, *Metaphysics*, 3e, © 1983, pp. 90–99, 105. Reprinted by permission of Prentice-
Hall, Inc., Englewood Cliffs, New Jersey.

nevertheless. Men who possess such a belief seldom permit any metaphysical considerations to wrest it from them, while those who lack it are seldom turned toward it by other metaphysical considerations. Still, in every land in which philosophy has flourished, there have been some profound thinkers who have sought to discover some metaphysical basis for a rational belief in the existence of some supreme being or beings. Even though religion may properly be a matter of faith rather than reason, still, a philosophical person can hardly help wondering whether it might, at least in part, be also a matter of reason, and whether, in particular, the existence of God might be something that can be not merely believed but shown. It is this question that we want now to consider; that is, we want to see whether there are not strong metaphysical considerations from which the existence of some supreme and supranatural being might reasonably be inferred.

THE PRINCIPLE OF SUFFICIENT REASON

Suppose you were strolling in the woods and, in addition to the sticks, stones, and other accustomed litter of the forest floor, you one day came upon some quite unaccustomed object, something not quite like what you had ever seen before and would never expect to find in such a place. Suppose, for example, that it is a large ball, about your own height, perfectly smooth and translucent. You would deem this puzzling and mysterious, certainly, but if one considers the matter, it is no more inherently mysterious that such a thing should exist than that anything else should exist. If you were quite accustomed to finding such objects of various sizes around you most of the time, but had never seen an ordinary rock, then upon finding a large rock in the woods one day you would be just as puzzled and mystified. This illustrates the fact that something that is mysterious ceases to seem so simply by its accustomed presence. It is strange indeed, for example, that a world such as ours should exist; yet few men are very often struck by this strangeness, but simply take it for granted.

Suppose, then, that you have found this translucent ball and are mystified by it. Now whatever else you might wonder about it, there is one thing you would hardly question; namely, that it did not appear there all by itself, that it owes its existence to something. You might not have the remotest idea whence and how it came to be there, but you would hardly doubt that there was an explanation. The idea that it might have come from nothing at all, that it might exist without there being any explanation of its existence, is one that few people would consider worthy of entertaining.

This illustrates a metaphysical belief that seems to be almost a part of reason itself, even though few men ever think upon it; the belief, namely, that there is some explanation for the existence of anything whatever, some reason why it should exist rather than not. The sheer nonexistence of anything, which is not to be confused with the passing out of existence of something, never requires a reason; but existence does. That there should never have been any such ball in the forest does not require any explanation or reason, but that there should ever be such a ball does. If one were to look upon a barren plain and ask why there is not and never has been any large translucent ball there, the natural response would be to ask why there should be; but if one finds such a ball, and wonders why it is there, it is not quite so natural to ask why it should *not* be, as though existence should simply be taken for granted. That anything should not exist, then, and that, for instance, no such ball should exist in the forest, or that there should be no forest for it to occupy, or no continent containing a forest, or no earth, nor any world at all, do not seem to be things for which there needs to be any explanation or reason; but that such things should be, does seem to require a reason.

The principle involved here has been called the principle of sufficient reason. Actually, it is a very general principle, and is best expressed by saying that, in the case of any positive truth, there is some sufficient reason for it, something which, in this sense, makes it true—in short, that there is some sort of explanation, known or unknown, for everything.

Now some truths depend on something else, and are accordingly called *contingent*, while others depend only upon themselves, that is, are true by their very natures and are accordingly called *necessary*. There is, for example, a reason why the stone on my window sill is warm; namely, that the sun is shining upon it. This happens to be true, but not by its very nature. Hence, it is contingent, and depends upon something other than itself. It is also true that all the points of a circle are equidistant from the center, but this truth depends upon nothing but itself. No matter what happens, nothing can make it false. Similarly, it is a truth, and a necessary one, that if the stone on my window sill is a body, as it is, then it has a form, since this fact depends upon nothing but itself for its confirmation. Untruths are also, of course, either contingent or necessary, it being contingently false, for example, that the stone on my window sill is cold, and necessarily false that it is both a body and formless, since this is by its very nature impossible.

The principle of sufficient reason can be illustrated in various ways, as we have done, and if one thinks about it, he is apt to find that he presupposes it in his thinking about reality, but it cannot be proved. It does not appear to be itself a necessary truth, and at the same time it would be most odd to say it is contingent. If one were to try proving it, he would sooner or later have to appeal to considerations that are less plausible than the principle itself. Indeed, it is hard to see how one could even make an argument for it, without already assuming it. For this one reason it might properly be called a presupposition of reason itself. One can deny that it is true, without embarrassment or fear of refutation, but one is then apt to find that what he is denying is not really what the principle asserts. We shall, then, treat it here as a datum—not something that is provably true, but as something which all men, whether they ever reflect upon it or not, seem more or less to presuppose.

THE EXISTENCE OF A WORLD

It happens to be true that something exists, that there is, for example, a world, and while no one ever seriously supposes that this might not be so, that there might exist nothing at all, there still seems to be nothing the least necessary in this, considering it just by itself. That no world should ever exist at all is perfectly comprehensible and seems to express not the slightest absurdity. Considering any particular item in the world it seems not at all necessary in itself that it should ever have existed, nor does it appear any more necessary that the totality of these things, or any totality of things, should ever exist.

From the principle of sufficient reason it follows, of course, that there must be a reason, not only for the existence of everything in the world but for the world itself, meaning by "the world" simply everything that ever does exist, except God, in case there is a god. This principle does not imply that there must be some purpose or goal for everything, or for the totality of all things; for explanations need not, and in fact seldom are, teleological or purposeful. All the principle requires is that there be some sort of reason for everything. And it would certainly be odd to maintain that everything in the world owes its existence to something, that nothing in the world is either purely accidental, or such that it just bestows its own being upon itself, and then to deny this of the world itself. One can indeed *say* that the world is in some sense a pure accident, that there simply is no reason at all why this or any world should exist, and one can equally say that the world exists by its very nature, or is an inherently necessary being. But it is at least very odd and arbitrary to deny of this existing world the need for any sufficient reason, whether independent of itself or not, while presupposing that there is a reason for every other thing that ever exists.

Consider again the strange ball that we imagine has been found in the forest. Now we can hardly doubt that there must be an explanation for the existence of such a thing, though we may have no notion what the explanation is. It is not, moreover, the fact of its having been found in the forest rather than elsewhere that renders an explanation necessary. It matters not in the least where it happens to be, for our question is not how it happens to be *there* but how it happens to exist at all. If we in our imagination annihilate the forest, leaving only this ball in an open field, our conviction that it is a contingent thing and owes its existence to something other than itself is not reduced in the least. If we now imagine the field to be annihilated, and in fact everything else as well to vanish into nothingness, leaving only this ball to constitute the entire physical universe, then we cannot for a moment suppose that its existence has thereby been explained, or the need of any explanation eliminated, or that its existence is suddenly rendered self-explanatory. If we now carry this thought one step further and suppose that no other reality ever has existed or ever will exist, that this ball forever constitutes the entire physical universe, then we must still insist on there being some reason independent of itself why it should exist rather than not. If there must be a reason for the existence of any particular thing, then the necessity of such a reason is not eliminated by the mere supposition that certain other things do *not* exist. And again, it matters not at all what the thing in question is, whether it be large and complex, such as the world we actually find ourselves in, or whether it be something small, simple and insignificant, such as a ball, a bacterium, or the merest grain of sand. We do not avoid the necessity of a reason for the existence of something merely by describing it in this way or that. And it would, in any event, seem quite plainly absurd to say that if the world were comprised entirely of a single ball about six feet in diameter, or of a single grain of sand, then it would be contingent and there would have to be some explanation other than itself why such a thing exists, but that, since the actual world is vastly more complex than this, there is no need for an explanation of its existence, independent of itself.

BEGINNINGLESS EXISTENCE

It should now be noted that it is no answer to the question, why a thing exists, to state *how long* it has existed. A geologist does not suppose that he has explained why there should be rivers and mountains merely by pointing out that they are old. Similarly, if one were to ask, concerning the ball of which we have spoken, for some sufficient reason for its being, he would not receive any answer upon being told that it had been there since yesterday. Nor would it be any better answer to say that it had existed since before anyone could remember, or even that it had always existed; for the question was not one concerning its age but its existence. If, to be sure, one were to ask where a given thing came from, or how it came into being, then upon learning that it had always existed he would learn that it never really *came* into being at all; but he could still reasonably wonder why it should exist at all. If, accordingly, the world—that is, the totality of all things excepting God, in case there is a god—had really no beginning at all, but has always existed in some form or other, then there is clearly no answer to the question, where it came from and when; it did not, on this supposition, *come* from anything at all, at any time. But still, it can be asked why there is a world, why indeed there is a beginningless world, why there should have perhaps always been something rather than nothing. And, if the principle of sufficient reason is a good principle, there must be an answer to that question, an answer that is by no means supplied by giving the world an age, or even an infinite age.

CREATION

This brings out an important point with respect to the concept of creation that is often misunderstood, particularly by those whose thinking has been influenced by Christian ideas. People tend to think that creation—for example, the creation of the world by God—*means* creation *in time*, from which it of course logically follows that if the world had no beginning in time, then it cannot be the creation of God. This, however, is erroneous, for creation means essentially *dependence*, even in Christian theology. If one thing is the creation of another, then it depends for its existence on that other, and this is perfectly consistent with saying that both are eternal, that neither ever came into being, and hence, that neither was ever created at any point of time. Perhaps an analogy will help convey this point. Consider, then, a flame that is casting beams of light. Now there seems to be a clear sense in which the beams of light are dependent for their existence upon the flame, which is their source, while the flame, on the other hand, is not similarly dependent for its existence upon them. The beams of light arise from the flame, but the flame does not arise from them. In this sense, they are the creation of the flame; they derive their existence from it. And none of this has any reference to time; the relationship of dependence in such a case would not be altered in the slightest if we supposed that the flame, and with it the beams of light, had always existed, that neither had ever *come* into being.

Now if the world is the creation of God, its relationship to God should be thought of in this fashion; namely that the world depends for its existence upon God, and could not exist independently of God. If God is eternal, as those who believe in God generally assume, then the world may (though it need not) be eternal too, without that altering in the least its dependence upon God for its existence, and hence without altering its being the creation of God. The supposition of God's eternality, on the other hand, does not by itself imply that the world is eternal too; for there is not the least reason why something of finite duration might not depend for its existence upon something of infinite duration—though the reverse is, of course, impossible.

GOD

If we think of God as "the creator of heaven and earth," and if we consider heaven and earth to include everything that exists except God, then we appear to have, in the foregoing considerations, fairly strong reasons for asserting that God, as so conceived, exists. Now of course most people have much more in mind than this when they think of God, for religions have ascribed to God ever so many attributes that are not at all implied by describing him merely as the creator of the world; but that is not relevant here. Most religious persons do, in any case, think of God as being at least the creator, as that being upon which everything ultimately depends, no matter what else they may say about him in addition. It is, in fact, the first item in the creeds of Christianity that God is the "creator of heaven and earth." And, it seems, there are good metaphysical reasons, as distinguished from the persuasions of faith, for thinking that such a creative being exists.

If, as seems clearly implied by the principle of sufficient reason, there must be a reason for the existence of heaven and earth—i.e., for the world—then that reason must be found either in the world itself, or outside it, in something that is literally supranatural, or outside heaven and earth. Now if we suppose that the world—i.e., the totality of all things except God—contains within itself the reason for its existence, we are supposing that it exists by its very nature, that is, that it is a necessary being. In that case there would, of course, be no reason for saying that it must depend upon God or anything else for its existence; for if it exists by its very nature, then it depends upon nothing but itself, much as the sun depends upon nothing but itself for its heat. This, however, is implausible, for we find nothing about the world or anything in it to suggest that it exists by its own nature, and we do find, on the contrary, ever so many things to suggest that it does not. For in the first place, anything which exists by its very nature must necessarily be eternal and indestructible. It would be a self-contradiction to say of anything that it exists by its own nature, or is a necessarily existing thing, and at the same time to say that it comes into being or passes away, or that it ever could come into being or pass away. Nothing about the world seems at all like this, for concerning anything in the world, we can perfectly easily think of it as being annihilated, or as never having existed in the first place, without there being the slightest hint of any absurdity in such a supposition. Some of the things in the universe are, to be sure, very old; the moon, for example, or the stars and the planets. It is even possible to imagine that they have always existed. Yet it seems quite impossible to suppose that they owe their existence to nothing but themselves, that they bestow existence upon themselves by their very natures, or that they are in themselves things of such nature that it would be impossible for them not to exist. Even if we suppose that something, such as the sun, for instance, has existed forever, and will never cease, still we cannot conclude just from this that it exists by its own nature. If, as is of course very doubtful, the sun has existed forever and will never cease, then it is possible that its heat and light have also existed forever and will never cease; but that would not show that the heat and light of the sun exist by their own natures. They are obviously contingent and depend on the sun for their existence, whether they are beginningless and everlasting or not.

There seems to be nothing in the world, then, concerning which it is at all plausible to suppose that it exists by its own nature, or contains within itself the reason for its existence. In fact, everything in the world appears to be quite plainly the opposite, namely, something that not only need not exist, but at some time or other, past or future or both, does not in fact exist. Everything in the world seems to have finite duration, whether long or short. Most things, such as ourselves, exist only for a short while; they come into being, then soon cease. Other things, like the heavenly bodies, last longer, but they are still corruptible, and from all that we can gather about them, they too seem destined eventually to perish. We arrive at the conclusion, then, that while the world may contain some things which have always existed and are destined never to perish, it is nevertheless doubtful that it contains any such thing and, in any case, everything in the world is capable of perishing, and nothing in it, however long it may already have existed and however long it may yet remain, exists only by its own nature, but depends instead upon something else.

While this might be true of everything in the world, is it necessarily true of the world itself? That is, if we grant, as we seem forced to, that nothing in the world exists by its own nature, that everything in the world is contingent and perishable, must we also say that the world itself, or the totality of all these perishable things, is also contingent and perishable? Logically, we are not forced to, for it is logically possible that the totality of all perishable things might itself be imperishable, and hence, that the world might exist by its own nature, even though it is comprised exclusively of things which are contingent. It is not logically necessary that a totality should share the defects of its members. For example, even though every man is mortal, it does not follow from this that the human race, or the totality of all men, is also mortal; for it is possible that there will always be human beings, even though there are no human beings which will always exist. Similarly, it is possible that the world is in itself a necessary thing, even though it is comprised entirely of things that are contingent.

This is logically possible, but it is not plausible. For we find nothing whatever about the world, any more than in its parts, to suggest that it exists by its own nature. Concerning anything in the world, we have not the slightest difficulty in supposing that it should perish, or even, that it should never have existed in the first place. We have almost as little difficulty in supposing this of the world itself. It might be somewhat hard to think of everything as utterly perishing and leaving no trace whatever of its ever having been, but there seems to be not the slightest difficulty in imagining that the world should never have existed in the first place. We can, for instance, perfectly easily suppose that nothing in the world had ever existed except, let us suppose, a single grain of sand, and we can thus suppose that this grain of sand has forever constituted the whole universe. Now if we consider just this grain of sand, it is quite impossible for us to suppose that it exists by its very nature, and could never have failed to exist. It clearly depends for its existence upon something other than itself, if it depends on anything at all. The same will be true if we consider the world to consist, not of one grain of sand, but of two, or of a million, or, as we in fact find, of a vast number of stars and planets and all their minuter parts.

It would seem, then, that the world, in case it happens to exist at all—and this is quite beyond doubt—is contingent and thus dependent upon something other than itself for its existence, if it depends upon anything at all. And it must depend upon something, for otherwise there could be no reason why it exists in the first place. Now that upon which the world depends must be something that either exists by its own nature or does not. If it does not exist by its own nature, then it, in turn, depends for its existence upon something else, and so on. Now then, we can say either of two things; namely, (1) that the world depends for its existence upon something else, which in turn depends on still another thing, this depending upon still another, *ad infinitum*; or (2) that the world derives its existence from something that exists by its own nature and which is accordingly eternal and imperishable, and is the creator of heaven and earth. The first of these alternatives, however, is impossible, for it does not render a sufficient reason why anything should exist in the first place. Instead of supplying a reason why any world should exist, it repeatedly begs off giving a reason. It explains what is dependent and perishable in terms of what is itself dependent and perishable, leaving us still without a reason why perishable things should exist at all, which is what we are seeking. Ultimately, then, it would seem that the world, or the totality of contingent or perishable things, in case it exists at all, must depend upon something that is necessary and imperishable, and which accordingly exists, not in dependence upon something else, but by its own nature.

Self-Caused

What has been said thus far gives some intimation of what meaning should be attached to the concept of a self-caused being, a concept that is quite generally misunderstood, sometimes even by scholars. To say that something—God, for example—is self-caused, or is the cause of its own existence, does not mean that this being brings itself into existence, which is a perfectly absurd idea. Nothing can *bring* itself into existence. To say that something is self-caused (*causa sui*) means only that it exists, not contingently or in dependence upon something else, but by its own nature, which is only to say that it is a being which is such that it can neither come into being nor perish. Now whether such a being in fact exists or not, there is in any case no absurdity in the idea.

We have found, in fact, that the principle of sufficient reason seems to point to the existence of such a being, as that upon which the world, with everything in it, must ultimately depend for its existence.

Necessary Being

A being that depends for its existence upon nothing but itself, and is in this sense self-caused, can equally be described as a necessary being; that is to say, a being that is not contingent, and hence not perishable. For in the case of anything which exists by its own nature, and is dependent upon nothing else, it is impossible that it should not exist, which is equivalent to saying that it is necessary. Many persons have professed to find the gravest difficulties in this concept, too, but that is partly because it has been confused with other notions. If it makes sense to speak of anything as an *impossible* being, or something which by its very nature does not exist, then it is hard to see why the idea of a necessary being, or something which in its very nature exists, should not be just as comprehensible. And of course, we have not the slightest difficulty in speaking of something, such as a square circle or a formless body, as an impossible being. And if it makes sense to speak of something as being perishable, contingent, as it surely does, then there seems to be no difficulty in thinking of something as imperishable and dependent upon nothing other than itself for its existence.

First Cause

From these considerations we can see also what is properly meant by a first cause, an appellative that has often been applied to God by theologians, and which many persons have deemed an absurdity. It is a common criticism of this notion to say that there need not be any first cause, since the series of causes and effects which constitute the history of the universe might be infinite or beginningless and must, in fact, be infinite in case the universe itself had no beginning in time. This criticism, however, reflects a total misconception of what is meant by a first cause. *First* here does not mean first in time, and when God is spoken of as a first cause, he is not being described as a being which, at some time in the remote past, *started* everything. To describe God as a first cause is only to say that he is literally a *primary* rather than a secondary cause, an *ultimate* rather than a derived cause, or a being upon which all other things, heaven and earth, ultimately depend for their existence. It is, in short, only to say that God is the creator, in the sense of creation explained above. Now this, of course, is perfectly consistent with saying that the world is eternal or beginningless. As we have seen, one gives no reason for the existence of a world merely by giving it an age, even if it is supposed to have an infinite age. To use a helpful analogy, we can say that the sun is the first cause of daylight and, for that matter, of the moonlight of the night as well, which means only that daylight and moonlight ultimately depend upon the sun for their existence. The moon, on the other hand, is only a secondary or derivative cause of its light. This light would be no less dependent upon the sun if we affirmed that it had no beginning, for an ageless and beginningless light requires a source no less than an ephemeral one. If we supposed that the sun has always existed, and with it its light, then we would have to say that the sun has always been the first—i.e., the primary or ultimate—cause of its light. Such is precisely the manner in which God should be thought of, and is by theologians often thought of, as the first cause of heaven and earth. . . .

THE SIGNIFICANCE OF THESE ARGUMENTS

It would be extravagant indeed to suppose that these reflections amount to any sort of confirmation of religion, or even, that they have much to do with religion. They are purely metaphysical and philosophical considerations having implications of only a purely speculative kind. Even if they are utterly probative, which is of course controversial, it can still be pointed out, correctly, that they are consistent with ever so many views which are radically inconsistent with religion. They imply almost nothing with respect to any divine attributes, such as benevolence, and one could insist with some justification that even the word God, which is supposed to be the proper name of a personal being and not just a label to be attached to metaphysically inferred things, is out of place in them.

No more is claimed for these arguments, however, than that they are good arguments, and that they seem to yield the conclusions derived from them. If they are defective, the defects are not gross or obvious. The reader may suit himself whether they yield those conclusions, and if so, what their human significance might be.

III.C.3. First Cause

DAVID HUME

David Hume (1711–1776), a British empiricist philosopher, examines in his Dialogues Concerning Natural Religion *all the major arguments for theism and finds none of them sound. In the dialogue, Cleanthes is the philosophical rationalist and Philo, who comes nearest to reflecting Hume's view, is the skeptic. The following short selection presents the argument that the necessity of everything's having a cause or reason for its existence implies a necessary being, God, whose reason for existence is intrinsic to his nature rather than determined from outside by another. It is also argued that even if the succession of causes in the world is infinite, so that each one is explained by its antecedent, we still must have a cause for the whole succession. Hume concludes that it is unreasonable, when the cause for each item has been given, to add them all together and demand a cause for the whole. In explaining each one, the whole has been explained. Hume also argues that the concept of a necessary being is unintelligible. If everything that exists requires an explanation or cause, so must God. If God is said to be a self-existent being, why might not the same thing be said of the world?*

DEMEA: But if so many difficulties attend the argument *a posteriori*, said *Demea*, had we not better adhere to that simple and sublime argument *a priori* which, by offering to us infallible demonstration, cuts off at once all doubt and difficulty? By this argument, too, we may prove the *Infinity* of the Divine Attributes, which, I am afraid, can never be ascertained with certainty from any other topic. For how can an effect which either is finite or, for aught we know, may be so; how can such an effect, I say, prove an infinite cause? The unity, too, of the Divine Nature it is very difficult, if not absolutely impossible, to deduce merely from contemplating the works of Nature; nor will the uniformity alone of the plan, even were it allowed, give us any assurance of that attribute. Whereas the argument *a priori* . . .

CLEANTHES: You seem to reason, *Demea*, interposed *Cleanthes*, as if those advantages and conveniences in the abstract argument were full proofs of its solidity. But it is first proper, in my opinion, to determine what argument of this nature you choose to insist on; and we shall afterwards, from itself, better than from its *useful* consequences, endeavor to determine what value we ought to put upon it.

DEMEA: The argument, replied *Demea*, which I would insist on is the common one. Whatever exists must have a cause or reason of its existence, it being

From *Dialogues Concerning Natural Religion* ed. Richard H. Popkin. (Indianapolis: Hackett, 1980), pp. 54–57. With permission of Hackett Publishing Company, Inc., Indianapolis, IN and Cambridge, MA.

absolutely impossible for anything to produce itself or be the cause of its own existence. In mounting up, therefore, from effects to causes, we must either go on in tracing an infinite succession, without any ultimate cause at all, or must at last have recourse to some ultimate cause that is *necessarily* existent: Now, that the first supposition is absurd may be thus proved. In the infinite chain or succession of causes and effects, each single effect is determined to exist by the power and efficacy of that cause which immediately preceded; but the whole eternal chain or succession, taken together, is not determined or caused by anything: And yet it is evident that it requires a cause or reason, as much as any particular object which begins to exist in time. The question is still reasonable why this particular succession of causes existed from eternity, and not any other succession or no succession at all. If there be no necessarily existent being, any supposition which can be formed is equally possible; nor is there any more absurdity in nothing's having existed from eternity than there is in that succession of causes which constitutes the universe. What was it, then, which determined something to exist rather than nothing, and bestowed being on a particular possibility, exclusive of the rest? *External causes*, there are supposed to be none. *Chance* is a word without a meaning. Was it *nothing*? But that can never produce anything. We must, therefore, have recourse to a necessarily existent Being who carries the *reason* of his existence in himself; and who cannot be supposed not to exist, without an express contradiction. There is, consequently, such a Being—that is, there is a Deity.

CLEANTHES: I shall not leave it to *Philo*, said *Cleanthes* (though I know that the starting objections is his chief delight), to point out the weakness of this metaphysical reasoning. It seems to me so obviously ill-grounded, and at the same time of so little consequence to the cause of true piety and religion, that I shall myself venture to show the fallacy of it.

I shall begin with observing that there is an evident absurdity in pretending to demonstrate a matter of fact, or to prove it by any arguments *a priori*. Nothing is demonstrable unless the contrary implies a contradiction. Nothing that is distinctly conceivable implies a contradiction. Whatever we conceive as existent, we can also conceive as non-existent. There is no being, therefore, whose non-existence implies a contradiction. Consequently there is no being whose existence is demonstrable. I propose this argument as entirely decisive, and am willing to rest the whole controversy upon it.

It is pretended that the Deity is a necessarily existent being; and this necessity of his existence is attempted to be explained by asserting that, if we knew his whole essence or nature, we should perceive it to be as impossible for him not to exist, as for twice two not to be four. But it is evident that this can never happen, while our faculties remain the same as at present. It will still be possible for us, at any time, to conceive the non-existence of what we formerly conceived to exist; nor can the mind ever lie under a necessity of supposing any object to remain always in being; in the same manner as we lie under a necessity of always conceiving twice two to be four. The words, therefore, "necessary existence" have no meaning; or, which is the same thing, none that is consistent.

But further, why may not the material universe be the necessarily existent Being, according to this pretended explication of necessity? We dare not affirm that we know all the qualities of matter; and, for aught we can determine, it may contain some qualities which, were they known, would make its non-existence appear as great a contradiction as that twice two is five. I find only one argument employed to prove that the material world is not the necessarily existent Being; and this argument is derived from the contingency both of the matter and the form of the world. "Any particle of matter," it is said, "may be *conceived* to be annihilated; and any form may be *conceived* to be altered. Such an annihilation or alteration, therefore, is not impossible."[1] But it seems a great partiality not to perceive that the same argument extends equally to the Deity, so far as we have any conception of him; and that the mind can at least imagine him to be non-existent, or his attributes to be altered. It must be some unknown, inconceivable qualities which can make his non-existence appear impossible or his attributes unalterable: And no reason can be assigned why these qualities may not belong to matter. As they are altogether unknown and inconceivable, they can never be proved incompatible with it.

Add to this that in tracing an eternal succession of objects it seems absurd to inquire for a general cause or first author. How can anything that exists from eternity have a cause, since that relation implies a priority in time and a beginning of existence?

In such a chain, too, or succession of objects, each part is caused by that which preceded it, and causes that which succeeds it. Where then is the difficulty? But the *whole*, you say, wants a cause. I answer that the uniting of these parts into a whole, like the uniting of several distinct countries into one kingdom, or several distinct members into one body, is performed merely by an arbitrary act of the mind, and has no influence upon the nature of things. Did I show you the particular causes of each individual in a collection of twenty particles of matter, I should think it very unreasonable should you afterwards ask me what was the cause of the whole twenty. This is sufficiently explained in explaining the cause of the parts.

PHILO: Though the reasonings which you have urged, *Cleanthes*, may well excuse me, said *Philo*, from starting any further difficulties; yet I cannot forbear insisting still upon another topic. It is observed by arithmeticians that the products of 9 compose always either 9 or some lesser product of 9 if you add together all the characters of which any of the former products is composed. Thus of 18, 27, 36, which are products of 9, you make 9 by adding 1 to 8, 2 to 7, 3 to 6. Thus 369 is a product also of 9; and if you add 3, 6, and 9, you make 18, a lesser product of 9.[2] To a superficial observer so wonderful a regularity may be admired as the effect either of chance or design; but a skillful algebraist immediately concludes it to be the work of necessity, and demonstrates that it must forever result from the nature of these numbers. Is it not probable, I ask, that the whole economy of the universe is conducted by a like necessity, though no human algebra can furnish a key which solves the difficulty? And instead of admiring the order of natural beings, may it not happen that, could we penetrate into the intimate nature of bodies, we should clearly see why it

---

[1] Dr. Clarke. [Samuel Clarke, 1675–1729, leading English theologian and philosopher, a follower of Sir Isaac Newton.]

[2] *Republique des Lettres*, Aug. 1685. [The article referred to is by Fontenelle, and it appeared in Pierre Bayle's *Nouvelles de la Republique des Lettres*, Sept. 1685, art. II.]

was absolutely impossible they could ever admit of any other disposition? So dangerous is it to introduce this idea of necessity into the present question! And so naturally does it afford an inference directly opposite to the religious hypothesis!

But dropping all these abstractions, continued *Philo*, and confining ourselves to more familiar topics, I shall venture to add an observation that the argument *a priori* has seldom been found very convincing, except to people of a metaphysical head who have accustomed themselves to abstract reasoning, and who, finding from mathematics that the understanding frequently leads to truth through obscurity, and contrary to first appearances, have transferred the same habit of thinking to subjects where it ought not to have place. Other people, even of good sense and the best inclined to religion, feel always some deficiency in such arguments, though they are not perhaps able to explain distinctly where it lies, a certain proof that men ever did and ever will derive their religion from other sources than from this species of reasoning.

III.D.   The Teleological Argument

III.D.1.   The Cosmic Watchmaker

JOHN A. O'BRIEN

John A. O'Brien (1897–1963) offers what amounts to a retelling of William Paley's (1743–1805) celebrated story of the watch found on the seashore and the argument by analogy from that story to the existence of God. If even a simple mechanism such as a watch requires an intelligent planner and designer, the argument runs, it would strain credulity to suggest that anything so vast and pervaded by evidence of planning and design as the universe itself should have occurred otherwise than through the deliberate contrivance and creation of God.

Thus when Robinson Crusoe perceived a footprint on the island of Juan Fernandez, he rightly concluded that it had been made by a man. The clear imprint of the sole of the foot and five toes was enough to

---

From John A. O'Brien, *Truths Men Live By* (Huntington, Indiana: Our Sunday Visitor Press, 1946), pp. 8ff.

convince him that it had been made not by a bird or an elephant, or by the wind and the rain playing with the sand, but only by a man.

If a person walking along a seashore, comes suddenly upon a watch, he will conclude that there must be a watchmaker. Why? Because as he looks at the mechanism of the watch, with its springs and its cogwheels, its hour hand and its minute hand, with its crystal and its face, with the movement of the minute hand so coordinated that it travels precisely twelve times faster than the hour hand, he knows that this could not have happened by accident or by blind chance. The adaption of the parts and the coordination of movements reflect unmistakably the work of a thinking agent who arranged the whole to achieve a definite, previsioned end. There is a blinding evidence here of plan, purpose, order, and design, which leaves him no uncertainty.

Suppose you were to say to such a person: There is no evidence of a thinking agent behind that bit of mechanism. Those parts are simply an aggregation of bits of metal and glass, and were blown together by the winds of chance. Earth, sea, wind, sun, sky, air, and the blind forces of nature explain the makings of that watch. Would he not conclude that you were either joking or that you were a lunatic? Would he not say: Surely you cannot expect an intelligent person to believe so wild a fairy tale? Even a child of six would scorn such an explanation as an insult to his intelligence. There is woven into that watch an artistry of power and intelligence which convinces me that nothing on this planet could account for that watch except a human being who has mastered the craft of watchmaker.

Let us now glance at the marvelous universe in which our earth is a tiny speck. The whole is arranged with wonderful order and design. Our earth rotates on its axis once in twenty-four hours, bringing to us night and day. The earth revolves around the sun once in the course of a year, bringing to us with unfailing regularity the four seasons of the year. This planet of ours, with its great cities teeming with millions of inhabitants, with its lofty skyscrapers, with its vast emporiums of trade and commerce, with its mountains, rivers, and valleys, is shooting through space at the startling velocity of 68,400 miles per hour. Yet so smoothly does it move, that it disturbs not a babe in its cradle, nor brings a tremor to the wings of the bee nestling on the frail petals of the autumn rose.

The stars move in their appointed orbits with a regularity and precision which shames the most accurate chronometer made by human hands.

Inescapable then is the simple conclusion: As the watch implies a watchmaker, so the universe implies a God. As the watch demands adequate cause in the form of an intelligent horologist, so the universe, vastly great in size, complexity of organization, and adjustment of parts, demands an adequate cause in the form of a Being of vastly greater power and intelligence. This is the Being whom we call by the venerable name of God.

III.D.2. Problems with the Argument from Analogy

DAVID HUME

David Hume (1711–1776), a Scottish radical empiricist and skeptic, raises serious questions about the extent of human knowledge generally and particularly about knowledge in the realm of religion. His Dialogues Concerning Natural Religion, *from which the following selections are taken, is written with delightful wit and humor. The dialogue form provides Hume with the opportunity to present several sides of the argument. Demea represents the sanctimonious and naive believer who regards reason as presumptuous if it undertakes so much as to understand, much less to prove or disprove, religious claims. Cleanthes is the serious advocate of rational religion, patiently attempting to build up a theology on a foundation of reason. Philo, who probably comes the closest to representing Hume's own point of view, is the impish skeptic, pretending to be on the side of Demea and piety but actually taking roguish delight in demolishing every theistic argument Cleanthes is able to offer.*

In these selections Hume brings his formidable wit to bear on the teleological argument, or the argument from design. Despite the unmistakable tongue-in-cheek spirit of his speeches, he offers what philosophers ever since have considered to be some of the most formidable objections to the teleological argument.

CLEANTHES: Not to lose any time in circumlocutions, said *Cleanthes*, addressing himself to *Demea*, much less in replying to the pious declamations of *Philo*, I shall briefly explain how I conceive this matter. Look round the world: Contemplate the whole and every part of it: You will find it to be nothing but one great machine, subdivided into an infinite number of lesser machines, which again admit of subdivisions to a degree beyond what human senses and faculties can trace and explain. All these various machines, and even their most minute parts, are adjusted to each other with an accuracy which ravishes into admiration all men who have ever contemplated them. The curious adapting of means to ends, throughout all nature, resembles exactly, though it much exceeds, the productions of human contrivance; of human design, thought, wisdom, and intelligence. Since therefore the effects

From *Dialogues Concerning Natural Religion* ed. Richard H. Popkin. (Indianapolis: Hackett, 1980), pp. 15–21, 34–38. With permission of Hackett Publishing Company, Inc., Indianapolis, IN and Cambridge, MA.

resemble each other, we are led to infer, by all the rules of analogy, that the causes also resemble, and that the Author of Nature is somewhat similar to the mind of man, though possessed of much larger faculties, proportioned to the grandeur of the work which he has executed. By this argument *a posteriori*, and by this argument alone, do we prove at once the existence of a Deity and his similarity to human mind and intelligence.

DEMEA: I shall be so free, *Cleanthes*, said *Demea*, as to tell you that from the beginning I could not approve of your conclusion concerning the similarity of the Deity to men; still less can I approve of the mediums by which you endeavor to establish it. What! No demonstration of the Being of God! No abstract arguments! No proofs *a priori*! Are these which have hitherto been so much insisted on by philosophers all fallacy, all sophism? Can we reach no farther in this subject than experience and probability? I will say not that this is betraying the cause of a Deity; but surely, by this affected candor, you give advantages to atheists which they never could obtain by the mere dint of argument and reasoning.

PHILO: What I chiefly scruple in this subject, said *Philo*, is not so much that all religious arguments are by *Cleanthes* reduced to experience, as that they appear not be even the most certain and irrefragable of that inferior kind. That a stone will fall, that fire will burn, that the earth has solidity, we have observed a thousand and a thousand times; and when any new instance of this nature is presented, we draw without hesitation the accustomed inference. The exact similarity of the cases gives us a perfect assurance of a similar event, and a stronger evidence is never desired nor sought after. But wherever you depart, in the least, from the similarity of the cases, you diminish proportionably the evidence; and may at last bring it to a very weak *analogy*, which is confessedly liable to error and uncertainty. After having experienced the circulation of the blood in human creatures, we make no doubt that it takes place in *Titius* and *Maevius*; but from its circulation in frogs and fishes it is only a presumption, though a strong one, from analogy that it takes place in men and other animals. The analogical reasoning is much weaker when we infer the circulation of the sap in vegetables from our experience that the blood circulates in animals; and those who hastily followed that imperfect analogy are found, by more accurate experiments, to have been mistaken.

If we see a house, *Cleanthes*, we conclude, with the greatest certainty, that it had an architect or builder because this is precisely that species of effect which we have experienced to proceed from that species of cause. But surely you will not affirm that the universe bears such a resemblance to a house that we can with the same certainty infer a similar cause, or that the analogy is here entire and perfect. The dissimilitude is so striking that the utmost you can here pretend to is a guess, a conjecture, a presumption concerning a similar cause; and how that pretension will be received in the world, I leave you to consider.

CLEANTHES: It would surely be very ill received, replied *Cleanthes*; and I should be deservedly blamed and detested did I allow that the proofs of a Deity amounted to no more than a guess or conjecture. But is the whole adjustment of means to ends in a house and in the universe so slight a resemblance? The economy of final causes? The order, proportion, and arrangement of every part? Steps of a stair are plainly contrived that human legs may use them in mounting; and this inference is certain and infallible. Human legs are also contrived for walking and mounting; and this inference, I allow, is not altogether so certain because of the dissimilarity which you remark; but does it, therefore deserve the name only of presumption or conjecture?

DEMEA: Good God! cried *Demea*, interrupting him, where are we? Zealous defenders of religion allow that the proofs of a Deity fall short of perfect evidence! And you, *Philo*, on whose assistance I depended in proving the adorable mysteriousness of the Divine Nature, do you assent to all these extravagant opinions of *Cleanthes*? For what other name can I give them? or, why spare my censure when such principles are advanced, supported by such an authority, before so young a man as *Pamphilus*?

PHILO: You seem not to apprehend, replied *Philo*, that I argue with *Cleanthes* in his own way, and, by showing him the dangerous consequences of his tenets, hope at last to reduce him to our opinion. But what sticks most with you, I observe, is the representation which *Cleanthes* has made of the argument *a posteriori*; and, finding that that argument is likely to escape your hold and vanish into air, you think it so disguised that you can scarcely believe it to be set in its true light. Now, however much I may dissent, in other respects, from the dangerous principle of *Cleanthes*, I must allow that he has fairly represented that argument, and I shall endeavor so to state the matter to you that you will entertain no further scruples with regard to it.

Were a man to abstract from everything which he knows or has seen, he would be altogether incapable, merely from his own ideas, to determine what kind of scene the universe must be, or to give the preference to one state or situation of things above another. For as nothing which he clearly conceives could be esteemed impossible or implying a contradiction, every chimera of his fancy would be upon an equal footing; nor could he assign any just reason why he adheres to one idea or system, and rejects the others which are equally possible.

Again, after he opens his eyes and contemplates the world as it really is, it would be impossible for him at first to assign the cause of any one event, much less of the whole of things, or of the universe. He might set his fancy a rambling, and she might bring him in an infinite variety of reports and representations. These would all be possible; but, being all equally possible, he would never of himself give a satisfactory account for his preferring one of them to the rest. Experience alone can point out to him the true cause of any phenomenon.

Now, according to his method of reasoning, *Demea*, it follows (and is, indeed, tacitly allowed by *Cleanthes* himself) that order, arrangement, or the adjustment of final causes, is not of itself any proof of design, but only so far as it has been experienced to proceed from that principle. For aught we can know *a priori*, matter may contain the source or spring of order originally within itself, as well as mind does; and there is no more difficulty in conceiving that the several elements, from an internal unknown cause, may fall into the most exquisite arrangement, than to conceive that their ideas, in the great universal mind, from a like internal unknown cause, fall into that arrangement. The equal possibility of both these suppositions is allowed. But, by experience, we find, according to *Cleanthes*, that there is a difference between them. Throw several pieces of steel together, without shape or form; they will never arrange themselves so as to compose a watch. Stone and mortar and wood, without an architect, never erect a house. But the ideas in a human mind, we see, by an unknown, inexplicable economy, arrange themselves so as to form the plan of a watch or house. Experience, therefore, proves that there is an original principle of order in mind, not in matter. From similar effects we infer similar causes. The adjustment of means to ends is alike in the universe, as in a machine of human contrivance. The causes, therefore, must be resembling.

I was from the beginning scandalized, I must own, with this resemblance which is asserted between the Deity and human creatures, and must conceive it to imply such a degradation of the Supreme Being as no sound theist could endure. With your assistance, therefore, *Demea*, I shall endeavor to defend what you justly call the adorable mysteriousness of the Divine Nature, and shall refute this reasoning of *Cleanthes*, provided he allows that I have made a fair representation of it.

When *Cleanthes* had assented, *Philo*, after a short pause, proceeded in the following manner.

That all inferences, *Cleanthes*, concerning fact are founded on experience, and that all experimental reasonings are founded on the supposition that similar causes prove similar effects, and similar effects similar causes, I shall not at present much dispute with you. But observe, I entreat you, with what extreme caution all just reasoners proceed in the transferring of experiments to similar cases. Unless the cases be exactly similar, they repose no perfect confidence in applying their past observation to any particular phenomenon. Every alteration of circumstances occasions a doubt concerning the event; and it requires new experiments to prove certainly that the new circumstances are of no moment or importance. A change in bulk, situation, arrangement, age, disposition of the air, or surrounding bodies; any of these particulars may be attended with the most unexpected consequences. And unless the objects be quite familiar to us, it is the highest temerity to expect with assurance, after any of these changes, an event similar to that which before fell under our observation. The slow and deliberate steps of philosophers here, if anywhere, are distinguished from the precipitate march of the vulgar, who, hurried on by the smallest similitude, are incapable of all discernment or consideration.

But can you think, *Cleanthes*, that your usual phlegm and philosophy have been preserved in so wide a step as you have taken when you compared to the universe houses, ships, furniture, machines; and, from their similarity in some circumstances, inferred a similarity in their causes? Thought, design, intelligence, such as we discover in men and other animals, is no more than one of the springs and principles of the universe, as well as heat or cold, attraction or repulsion, and a hundred others which fall under daily observation. It is an active cause by which some particular parts of nature, we find, produce alterations on other parts. But can a conclusion, with any propriety, be transferred from parts to the whole? Does not the great disproportion bar all comparison and inference? From observing the growth of a hair, can we learn anything concerning the generation of a man? Would the manner of a leaf's blowing, even though perfectly known, afford us any instruction concerning the vegetation of a tree?

But allowing that we were to take the *operations* of one part of nature upon another for the foundation of our judgment concerning the *origin* of the whole (which never can be admitted), yet why select so minute, so weak, so bounded a principle as the reason and design of animals is found to be upon this planet? What peculiar privilege has this little agitation of the brain which we call "thought", that we must thus make it the model of the whole universe? Our partiality in our own favor does indeed present it on all occasions, but sound philosophy ought carefully to guard against so natural an illusion.

So far from admitting, continued *Philo*, that the operations of a part can afford us any just conclusion concerning the origin of the whole, I will not allow any one part to form a rule for another part if the latter be very remote from the former. Is there any reasonable ground to conclude that the inhabitants of other planets possess thought, intelligence, reason, or anything similar to these faculties in men? When nature has so extremely diversified her manner of operation on this small globe, can we imagine that she incessantly copies herself throughout so immense a universe? And if thought, as we may well suppose, be confined merely to this narrow corner, and has even here so limited a sphere of action, with what propriety can we assign it for the original cause of all things? The narrow views of a peasant who makes his domestic economy the rule for the government of kingdoms is in comparison a pardonable sophism.

But were we ever so much assured that a thought and reason resembling the human were to be found throughout the whole universe, and were its activity elsewhere vastly greater and more commanding than it appears in this globe; yet I cannot see why the operations of a world constituted, arranged, adjusted, can with any propriety be extended to a world which is in its embryo-state, and is advancing towards that constitution and arrangement. By observation we know somewhat of the economy, action, and nourishment of a finished animal; but we must transfer with great caution that observation to the growth of a foetus in the womb, and still more to the formation of an animalcule in the loins of its male parent. Nature, we find, even from our limited experience, possesses an infinite number of springs and principles which incessantly discover themselves on every change of her position and situation. And what new and unknown principles would actuate her in so new and unknown a situation as that of the formation of a universe, we cannot, without the utmost temerity, pretend to determine.

A very small part of this great system, during a very short time, is very imperfectly discovered to us; and do we thence pronounce decisively concerning the origin of the whole?

Admirable conclusion! Stone, wood, brick, iron, brass, have not, at this time, in this minute globe of earth, an order or arrangement without human art and contrivance; therefore, the universe could not originally attain its order and arrangement without something similar to human art. But is a part of nature a rule for another part very wide of the former? Is it a rule for the whole? Is a very small part a rule for the universe? Is nature in one situation a certain rule for nature in another situation vastly different from the former?

And can you blame me, *Cleanthes*, if I here imitate the prudent reserve of *Simonides*, who, according to the noted story, being asked by *Hiero*, *What God was?* desired a day to think of it, and then two days more; and after that manner continually prolonged the term, without ever bringing in his definition or description? Could you even blame me if I had answered, at first, *that I did not know*, and was sensible that this subject lay vastly beyond the reach of my faculties? You might cry out skeptic and raillier, as much as you pleased; but, having found in so many other subjects much more familiar the imperfections and even contradictions of human reason, I never should expect any success from its feeble conjectures in a subject so sublime and so remote from the sphere of our observation. When two *species* of objects have always been observed to be conjoined together, I can *infer*, by custom, the existence of one wherever I see the existence of the other; and this I call an argument from experience. But how this argument can have place where the objects, as in the present case, are single, individual, without parallel or specific resemblance, may be difficult to explain. And will any man tell me with a serious countenance that an orderly universe must arise from some thought and art like the human because we have experience of it? To ascertain this reasoning it were requisite that we had experience of the origin of worlds; and it is not sufficient, surely, that we have seen ships and cities arise from human art and contrivance. . . .

PHILO: But to show you still more inconveniences, continued *Philo*, in your anthropomorphism, please to take a new survey of your principles. *Like effects prove like causes.* This is the experimental argument; and this, you say too, is the sole theological argument. Now it is certain that the liker the effects are which are seen and the liker the causes which are inferred, the stronger is the argument. Every departure on either side diminishes the probability and renders the experiment less conclusive. You cannot doubt of the principle; neither ought you to reject its consequences.

All the new discoveries in astronomy which prove the immense grandeur and magnificence of the works of nature are so many additional arguments for a Deity, according to the true system of theism; but, according to your hypothesis of experimental theism, they become so many objections, by removing the effect still farther from all resemblance to the effects of human art and contrivance. For if *Lucretius*, even following the old system of the world, could exclaim:

> Who is strong enough to rule the sum, who to hold in hand and control the mighty bridle of the unfathomable deep? who to turn about all the heavens at one time, and warm the fruitful worlds with ethereal fires, or to be present in all places and at all times.[1]

If Tully[2] esteemed this reasoning so natural as to put it into the mouth of his Epicurean:

> What power of mental vision enabled your master Plato to descry the vast and elaborate architectural process which, as he makes out, the deity adopted in building the structure of the universe? What method of engineering was employed? What tools and levers and derricks? What

---

[1] [*On the Nature of Things*, II, 1096–1099 (trans. by W. D. Rouse).]

[2] [Tully was a common name for the Roman lawyer and philosopher, Marcus Tullius Cicero, 106–43 B.C.]

agents carried out so vast an understanding? And how were air, fire, water, and earth enabled to obey and execute the will of the architect?[3]

If this argument, I say, had any force in former ages, how much greater must it have at present when the bounds of nature are so infinitely enlarged and such a magnificent scene is opened to us? It is still more unreasonable to form our idea of so unlimited a cause from our experience of the narrow productions of human design and invention.

The discoveries by microscopes, as they open a new universe in miniature, are still objections, according to you; arguments, according to me. The farther we push our researches of this kind, we are still led to infer the universal cause of all to be vastly different from mankind, or from any object of human experience and observation.

And what say you to the discoveries in anatomy, chemistry, botany? . . .

CLEANTHES: These surely are no objections, replied *Cleanthes*; they only discover new instances of art and contrivance. It is still the image of mind reflected on us from innumerable objects.

PHILO: Add a mind *like the human*, said *Philo*.

CLEANTHES: I know of no other, replied *Cleanthes*.

PHILO: And the liker, the better, insisted *Philo*.

CLEANTHES: To be sure, said *Cleanthes*.

PHILO: Now, *Cleanthes*, said *Philo*, with an air of alacrity and triumph, mark the consequences. *First*, by this method of reasoning you renounce all claim to infinity in any of the attributes of the Deity. For, as the cause ought only to be proportioned to the effect, and the effect, so far as it falls under our cognizance, is not infinite: What pretensions have we, upon your suppositions, to ascribe that attribute to the Divine Being? You will still insist that, by removing him so much from all similarity to human creatures, we give in to the most arbitrary hypothesis, and at the same time weaken all proofs of his existence.

Secondly, you have no reason, on your theory, for ascribing perfection to the Deity, even in his finite capacity; or for supposing him free from every error, mistake, or incoherence, in his undertakings. There are many inexplicable difficulties in the works of Nature which, if we allow a perfect author to be proved *a priori*, are easily solved, and become only seeming difficulties from the narrow capacity of man, who cannot trace infinite relations. But according to your method of reasoning, these difficulties become all real; and, perhaps, will be insisted on as new instances of likeness to human art and contrivance. At least, you must acknowledge that it is impossible for us to tell, from our limited views, whether this system contains any great faults or deserves any considerable praise if compared to other possible and even real systems. Could a peasant, if the *Aeneid* were read to him, pronounce that poem to be absolutely faultless, or even assign to it its proper rank among the productions of human wit, he who had never seen any other production?

But were this world ever so perfect a production, it must still remain uncertain whether all the excellences of the work can justly be ascribed to the workman. If we survey a ship, what an exalted idea must we form of the

---

[3] [Cicero, *The Nature of the Gods*, I, viii, 19 (trans. by H. Rackham).]

ingenuity of the carpenter who framed so complicated, useful, and beautiful a machine? And what surprise must we feel when we find him a stupid mechanic who imitated others, and copied an art which, through a long succession of ages, after multiplied trials, mistakes, corrections, deliberations, and controversies, had been gradually improving? Many worlds might have been botched and bungled, throughout an eternity, ere this system was struck out; much labor lost; many fruitless trials made; and a slow but continued improvement carried on during infinite ages in the art of world-making. In such subjects, who can determine where the truth, nay, who can conjecture where the probability lies, amidst a great number of hypotheses which may be proposed, and a still greater which may be imagined?

And what shadow of an argument, continued *Philo*, can you produce from your hypothesis to prove the unity of the Deity? A great number of men join in building a house or ship, in rearing a city, in framing a commonwealth; why may not several deities combine in contriving and framing a world? This is only so much greater similarity to human affairs. By sharing the work among several, we may so much further limit the attributes of each, and get rid of that extensive power and knowledge which must be supposed in one deity, and which, according to you, can only serve to weaken the proof of his existence. And if such foolish, such vicious creatures as man can yet often unite in framing and executing one plan, how much more of those deities or demons, whom we may suppose several degrees more perfect?

To multiply causes without necessity is indeed contrary to true philosophy, but this principle applies not to the present case. Were one deity antecedently proved by your theory who were possessed of every attribute requisite to the production of the universe, it would be needless, I own (though not absurd), to suppose any other deity existent. But while it is still a question whether all these attributes are united in one subject or dispersed among several independent beings; by what phenomena in nature can we pretend to decide the controversy? Where we see a body raised in a scale, we are sure that there is in the opposite scale, however concealed from sight, some counterpoising weight equal to it; but it is still allowed to doubt whether that weight be an aggregate of several distinct bodies or one uniform united mass. And if the weight requisite very much exceeds anything which we have ever seen conjoined in any single body, the former supposition becomes still more probable and natural. An intelligent being of such vast power and capacity as is necessary to produce the universe, or, to speak in the language of ancient philosophy, so prodigious an animal, exceeds all analogy and even comprehension.

But further, *Cleanthes*, men are mortal, and renew their species by generation; and this is common to all living creatures. The two great sexes of male and female, says *Milton*, animate the world. Why must this circumstance, so universal, so essential, be excluded from those numerous and limited deities? Behold, then, the theogeny of ancient times brought back upon us.

And why not become a perfect anthropomorphite? Why not assert the deity or deities to be corporeal, and to have eyes, a nose, mouth, ears, etc.? *Epicurus* maintained that no man had ever seen reason but in a human figure; therefore, the gods must have a human figure. And this argument, which is deservedly so much ridiculed by *Cicero*, becomes, according to you, solid and philosophical.

In a word, *Cleanthes*, a man who follows your hypothesis is able, perhaps, to assert or conjecture that the universe sometime arose from something like design: But beyond that position he cannot ascertain one single circumstance, and is left afterwards to fix every point of his theology by the utmost license of fancy and hypothesis. This world, for aught he knows, is very faulty and imperfect, compared to a superior standard; and was only the first rude essay of some infant deity who afterwards abandoned it, ashamed of his lame performance: It is the work only of some dependent, inferior deity, and is the object of derision to his superiors: It is the production of old age and dotage in some superannuated deity; and ever since his death has run on at adventures, from the first impulse and active force which it received from him. . . . You justly give signs of horror, *Demea*, at these strange suppositions; but these, and a thousand more of the same kind, are *Cleanthes'* suppositions, not mine. From the moment the attributes of the Deity are supposed finite, all these have place. And I cannot, for my part, think that so wild and unsettled a system of theology is, in any respect, preferable to none at all.

CLEANTHES: These suppositions I absolutely disown, cried *Cleanthes*: They strike me, however, with no horror, especially when proposed in that rambling way in which they drop from you. On the contrary, they give me pleasure when I see that, by the utmost indulgence of your imagination, you never get rid of the hypothesis of design in the universe, but are obliged at every turn to have recourse to it. To this concession I adhere steadily; and this I regard as a sufficient foundation for religion.

III.E. The Moral Argument

III.E.1. The Moral Argument

IMMANUEL KANT

Immanuel Kant (1724–1804), one of the most important philosophers of the past two hundred years, undertook to bring together what he found to be sound in both the rationalist and the empiricist schools of modern philosophy. But he found the rationalistic ontological argument on one hand and the empiricist, cosmological, and teleological arguments on the other to be unsatisfactory. Indeed, Kant arrived at the conclusion that metaphysical matters such as the existence of God are beyond the reach of human cognitive power. Still, he was persuaded that human reason cannot be satisfied to think only of those matters that our understanding can grasp. Reason pushes us to formulate postulates that, if they should be true, would give coherence and completeness to our vision of reality. It is our moral sense that provides what constitutes the best grounds for theistic belief, according to Kant. We experience moral obligations in such a way to suggest an objective ground of the commandments of morality. Such experienced demands, however, make no sense unless it is possible for us to fulfill them. The conditions that Kant finds necessary to make our keen sense of moral obligation intelligible are that the human will be free, that the soul be immortal (so that wrongs not righted in this life can be made right in the next), and that there be a God who stands as the guarantor of these conditions. Kant explicitly states that this does not constitute a proof of the existence of God. God, freedom, and immortality are postulates of the practical reason and do not constitute knowledge properly so considered. Still, they are postulates that render our experience of morality intelligible and for that reason deserve our respect.

Reprinted with permission of Macmillan Publishing Company from *Critique of Practical Reason* translated by Lewis White Beck (Indianapolis: Bobbs-Merrill, 1956), v–viii, pp. 128–139; 147–151. Copyright © 1956 by Macmillan Publishing Company.

V. THE EXISTENCE OF GOD AS A POSTULATE OF PURE PRACTICAL REASON

The moral law led, in the foregoing analysis, to a practical problem which is assigned solely by pure reason and without any concurrence of sensuous incentives. It is the problem of the completeness of the first and principal part of the highest good, viz., morality; since this problem can be solved only in eternity, it led to the postulate of immortality. The same law must also lead us to affirm the possibility of the second element of the highest good, i.e., happiness proportional to that morality; it must do so just as disinterestedly as heretofore, by a purely impartial reason. This it can do on the supposition of the existence of a cause adequate to this effect, i.e., it must postulate the existence of God as necessarily belonging to the possibility of the highest good (the object of our will which is necessarily connected with the moral legislation of pure reason). We proceed to exhibit this connection in a convincing manner.

Happiness is the condition of a rational being in the world, in whose whole existence everything goes according to wish and will. It thus rests on the harmony of nature with his entire end and with the essential determining ground of his will. But the moral law commands as a law of freedom through motives wholly independent of nature and of its harmony with our faculty of desire (as incentives). Still, the acting rational being in the world is not at the same time the cause of the world and of nature itself. Hence there is not the slightest ground in the moral law for a necessary connection between the morality and proportionate happiness of a being which belongs to the world as one of its parts and as thus dependent on it. Not being nature's cause, his will cannot by its own strength bring nature, as it touches on his happiness, into complete harmony with his practical principles. Nevertheless, in the practical task of [125] pure reason, i.e., in the necessary endeavor after the highest good, such a connection is postulated as necessary: we *should* seek to further the highest good (which therefore must be at least possible). Therefore also the existence is postulated of a cause of the whole of nature, itself distinct from nature, which contains the ground of the exact coincidence of happiness with morality. This supreme cause, however, must contain the ground of the agreement of nature not merely with a law of the will of rational beings but with the idea of this law so far as they make it the supreme ground of determination of the will. Thus it contains the ground of the agreement of nature not merely with actions moral in their form but also with their morality as the motives to such actions, i.e., with their moral intention. Therefore, the highest good is possible in the world only on the supposition of a supreme cause of nature which has a causality corresponding to the moral intention. Now a being which is capable of actions by the idea of laws is an intelligence (a rational being), and the causality of such a being according to this idea of laws is his will. Therefore the supreme cause of nature, in so far as it must be presupposed for the highest good, is a being which is the cause (and consequently the author) of nature through understanding and will, i.e., God. As a consequence, the postulate of the possibility of a highest derived good (the best world) is at the same time the postulate of the reality of a highest original good, namely, the existence of God. Now it was our duty to promote the highest good; and it is not merely our privilege but a necessity connected with duty as a requisite to presuppose the possibility of this highest good. This presupposition is made only under the condition of the existence of God, and this condition inseparably connects this supposition with duty. Therefore, it is morally necessary to assume the existence of God.

It is well to notice here that this moral necessity is subjective, i.e., a need, and not objective, i.e., duty itself. For there cannot be any duty to assume the existence of a thing, because such a supposition concerns only the theoretical use of reason. It is also not to be understood that the assumption of the existence of God is necessary as a ground of all obligation in general (for this rests, as has been fully shown, solely on the autonomy [126] of reason itself). All that here belongs to duty is the endeavor to produce and to further the highest good in the world, the existence of which may thus be postulated though our reason cannot conceive it except by presupposing a highest intelligence. To assume its existence is thus connected with the consciousness of our duty, though this assumption itself belongs to the realm of theoretical reason. Considered only in reference to the latter, it is a hypothesis, i.e., a ground of explanation. But in reference to the comprehensibility of an object (the highest good) placed before us by the moral law, and thus as a practical need, it can be called *faith* and even pure *rational faith*, because pure reason alone (by its theoretical as well as practical employment) is the source from which it springs. . . .

The doctrine of Christianity,[1] even when not regarded as a religious doc-

---

[1] The view is commonly held that the Christian precept of morals has no advantage over the moral concept of the Stoics in respect to its purity; but the difference between them is nevertheless obvious. The Stoic system makes the consciousness of strength of mind the pivot around which all moral intentions should turn; and, if the followers of this system spoke of duties and even defined them accurately, they nevertheless placed the incentives and the real determining ground of the will in an elevation of character above the base incentives of the senses which have their power only through weakness of the mind. Virtue was, therefore, for them a certain heroism of the sage who, raising himself above the animal nature of man, was sufficient unto himself, subject to no temptation to transgress the moral law, and elevated above duties though he propounded duties to others. But all this they could not have done had they conceived this law in the same purity and rigor as does the precept of the Gospel. If I understand by "idea" a perfection to which the senses can give nothing adequate, the moral ideas are not transcendent, i.e., of such a kind that we cannot even sufficiently define the concept or of which we are uncertain whether there is a corresponding object (as are the ideas of speculative reason); rather, they serve as models of practical perfections, as an indispensable rule of moral conduct, and as a standard for comparison. If I now regard Christian morals from their philosophical side, it appears in comparison with the ideas of the Greek schools as follows: the ideas of the Cynics, Epicureans, Stoics, and Christians are, respectively, the simplicity of nature, prudence, wisdom, and holiness. In respect to the way they achieve them, the Greek schools differ in that the Cynics found common sense sufficient, while the others found it in the path of science, and thus all held it to lie in the mere use of man's natural powers. Christian ethics, because it formulated its precept as pure and uncompromising (as befits a moral precept), destroyed man's confidence of being wholly adequate to it, at least in this life; but it re-established it by enabling us to hope that, if we act as well as lies in our power, what is not in our power will come to our aid from another source, whether we know in what way or not. Aristotle and Plato differed only as to the origin of our moral concepts.

trine, gives at this point a concept of the highest [128] good (the Kingdom of God) which is alone sufficient to the strictest demand of practical reason. The moral law is holy (unyielding) and demands holiness of morals, although all moral perfection to which man can attain is only virtue, i.e., a law-abiding disposition resulting from respect for the law and thus implying consciousness of a continuous propensity to transgress it or at least to a defilement, i.e., to an admixture of many spurious (not moral) motives to obedience to the law; consequently, man can achieve only self-esteem combined with humility. And thus with respect to the holiness required by the Christian law, nothing remains to the creature but endless progress, though for the same reason hope of endless duration is justified. The worth of a character completely accordant with the moral law is infinite, because all possible happiness in the judgment of a wise and omnipotent dispenser of happiness has no other limitation than the lack of fitness of rational beings to their duty. But the moral law does not of itself promise happiness, for the latter is not, according to concepts of any order of nature, necessarily connected with obedience to the law. Christian ethics supplies this defect of the second indispensable component of the highest good by presenting a world wherein reasonable beings single-mindedly devote themselves to the moral law; this is the Kingdom of God, in which nature and morality come into a harmony, which is foreign to each as such, through a holy Author of the world, who makes possible the derived highest good. The holiness of morals is prescribed to them even in this life as a guide to conduct, but the well-being proportionate [129] to this, which is bliss, is thought of as attainable only in eternity. This is due to the fact that the former must always be the pattern of their conduct in every state, and progressing toward it is even in this life possible and necessary, whereas the latter, under the name of happiness, cannot (as far as our own capacity is concerned) be reached in this life and therefore is made only an object of hope. Nevertheless, the Christian principle of morality is not theological and thus heteronomous, being rather the autonomy of pure practical reason itself, because it does not make the knowledge of God and His will the basis of these laws but makes such knowledge the basis only of succeeding to the highest good on condition of obedience to these laws; it places the real incentive for obedience to the law not in the desired consequences of obedience but in the conception of duty alone, in true observance of which the worthiness to attain the latter alone consists.

In this manner, through the concept of the highest good as the object and final end of pure practical reason, the moral law leads to religion. Religion is the recognition of all duties as divine commands, not as sanctions, i.e., arbitrary and contingent ordinances of a foreign will, but as essential laws of any free will as such. Even as such, they must be regarded as commands of the Supreme Being because we can hope for the highest good (to strive for which is our duty under the moral law) only from a morally perfect (holy and beneficent) and omnipotent will; and, therefore, we can hope to attain it only through harmony with this will. But here again everything remains disinterested and based only on duty, without being based on fear or hope as incentives, which, if they became principles, would destroy the entire moral worth of the actions. The moral law commands us to make the highest possible good in a world the final object of all our conduct. This I cannot hope to effect except through the agreement of my will with that of a holy and beneficent Author of the world. And although my own happiness is included in the concept of the highest good as a whole wherein the greatest happiness is thought of as connected in exact proportion to the greatest degree of moral perfection [130] possible to creatures, still it is not happiness but the moral law (which, in fact, sternly places restricting conditions upon my boundless longing for happiness) which is proved to be the ground determining the will to further the highest good.

Therefore, morals is not really the doctrine of how to make ourselves happy but of how we are to be *worthy* of happiness. Only if religion is added to it can the hope arise of someday participating in happiness in proportion as we endeavored not to be unworthy of it.

One is worthy of possessing a thing or a state when his possession is harmonious with the highest good. We can easily see now that all worthiness is a matter of moral conduct, because this constitutes the condition of everything else (which belongs to one's state) in the concept of the highest good, i.e., participation in happiness. From this there follows that one must never consider morals itself as a doctrine of happiness, i.e., as an instruction in how to acquire happiness. For morals has to do only with the rational condition (*conditio sine qua non*) of happiness and not with means of achieving it. But when morals (which imposes only duties instead of providing rules for selfish wishes) is completely expounded, and a moral wish has been awakened to promote the highest good (to bring the Kingdom of God to us), which is a wish based on law and one to which no selfish mind could have aspired, and when for the sake of this wish the step to religion has been taken—then only can ethics be called a doctrine of happiness, because the *hope* for it first arises with religion.

From this it can also be seen that, if we inquire into God's final end in creating the world, we must name not the happiness of rational beings in the world but the highest good, which adds a further condition to the wish of rational beings to be happy, viz., the condition of being worthy of happiness, which is the morality of these beings, for this alone contains the standard by which they can hope to participate in happiness at the hand of a *wise* creator. For since wisdom, theoretically regarded, means the knowledge of the highest good and, practically, the [131] suitability of the will to the highest good, one cannot ascribe to a supreme independent wisdom an end based merely on benevolence. For we cannot conceive the action of this benevolence (with respect to the happiness of rational beings) except as conformable to the restrictive conditions of harmony with the holiness[2] of His will as the highest

---

[2] Incidentally, and in order to make the peculiarity of this concept clear, I make the following remark. Since we ascribe various attributes to God, whose quality we find suitable also to creatures (e.g., power, knowledge, presence, goodness, etc.), though in God they are present in a higher degree under such names as omnipotence, omniscience, omnipresence, and perfect goodness, etc., there are three which exclusively and without qualification of magnitude are ascribed to God, and they are all moral. He is the only holy, the only blessed, and the only wise being, because these concepts of themselves imply unlimitedness. By the arrangement of these He is thus the holy lawgiver (and creator), the beneficent ruler (and sustainer), and the just judge. These three attributes contain everything whereby God is the object of religion, and in conformity to them the metaphysical perfections of themselves arise in reason.

original good. Then perhaps those who have placed the end of creation in the glory of God, provided this is not thought of anthropomorphically as an inclination to be esteemed, have found the best term. For nothing glorifies God more than what is the most estimable thing in the world, namely, respect for His command, the observance of sacred duty which His law imposes on us, when there is added to this His glorious plan of crowning such excellent order with corresponding happiness. If the latter, to speak in human terms, makes Him worthy of love, by the former He is an object of adoration. Human beings can win love by doing good, but by this alone even they never win respect; the greatest well-doing does them honor only by being exercised according to worthiness.

It follows of itself that, in the order of ends, man (and every rational being) is an end-in-himself, i.e., he is never to be used merely as a means for someone (even for God) without at the same time being himself an end, and that thus the humanity in our person must itself be holy to us, because man is subject to the moral law and therefore subject to that which is of itself holy, and it is only on account of this and in agreement [132] with this that anything can be called holy. For this moral law is founded on the autonomy of his will as a free will, which by its universal laws must necessarily be able to agree with that to which it subjects itself.

VI. ON THE POSTULATES OF PURE PRACTICAL REASON IN GENERAL

The postulates of pure practical reason all proceed from the principle of morality, which is not a postulate but a law by which reason directly determines the will. This will, by the fact that it is so determined, as a pure will requires these necessary conditions for obedience to its precept. These postulates are not theoretical dogmas but presuppositions of necessarily practical import; thus, while they do not extend speculative knowledge, they give objective reality to the ideas of speculative reason in general (by means of their relation to the practical sphere), and they justify it in holding to concepts even the possibility of which it could not otherwise venture to affirm.

These postulates are those of immortality, of freedom affirmatively regarded (as the causality of a being so far as he belongs to the intelligible world), and of the existence of God. The first derives from the practically necessary condition of a duration adequate to the perfect fulfilment of the moral law. The second comes from the necessary presupposition of independence from the world of sense and of the capacity of determining man's will by the law of an intelligible world, i.e., the law of freedom itself; the third arises from the necessary condition of such an intelligible world by which it may be the highest good, through the presupposition of the highest independent good, i.e., the existence of God.

The prospect of the highest good, necessary through respect for the moral law and the consequent supposition of its objective reality, thus leads through postulates of practical reason to concepts which the speculative reason only exhibited as problems which it could not solve. It leads first to the problem of immortality, in the solution of which speculative reason [133] could only commit paralogisms, because the marks of permanence, by which the psy-chological concept of an ultimate subject necessarily ascribed to the soul in self-consciousness, were lacking though they were needed to complete the real conception of a substance. Practical reason, through the postulates of fitness to the moral law in the highest good as the whole end of practical reason, consigns to this subject the requisite duration. Secondly, it leads to the concept which speculative reason contained only as an antinomy, and the solution of which it could base only on a problematical, though thinkable, concept whose objective reality was not provable or determinable by speculative reason. This is the cosmological idea of an intelligible world and the consciousness of our existence in it. It leads to this by means of the postulate of freedom (the reality of which practical reason exhibits in the moral law, at the same time exhibiting the law of an intelligible world, which the speculative reason could only indicate but whose concept it could not define.) Thirdly, it gives significance to what speculative reason could indeed think but had to leave indeterminate as a mere transcendental ideal, i.e., to the theological concept of a First Being. This significance is given in a practical point of view, i.e., as a condition of the possibility of the object of a will determined by that law. It is that of a supreme principle of the highest good in an intelligible world having sovereign power in it by means of a moral legislation.

Is our knowledge really widened in such a way by pure practical reason, and is that which was transcendent for speculative reason immanent in practical reason? Certainly, but only from a practical point of view. For we thereby know neither the nature of our soul, nor the intelligible world, nor the Supreme Being as they are in themselves, but have only united the concepts of them in a practical concept of the highest good as the object of our will and have done so entirely a priori through pure reason. We have so united them only by means of the moral law and merely in relation to it, with respect to the object which it commands. But how freedom is possible, and how we should think theoretically and positively of this type of causality, is not thereby discovered. All that is comprehended is that such a causality is postulated through the moral law and for its sake. It is the same with the remaining ideas, whose possibility cannot be fathomed by human understanding, though no sophistry [134] will ever wrest from the conviction of even the most ordinary man an admission that they are not true. . . .

VIII. ON ASSENT ARISING FROM A NEED OF PURE REASON

A need of pure reason in its speculative use leads only to [142] hypotheses; that of pure practical reason, to postulates. For, in the first case, I may ascend from the result as far as I wish in the series of conditions, and I shall need an ultimate ground not in order to give objective reality to the result (e.g., the causal connection of things and changes in the world) but only in order completely to satisfy my inquiring reason with respect to them. Thus before me I see order and design in nature, and I do not need to go over to speculation in order to assure myself of their reality, though in order to explain them I need to presuppose a Deity as their cause; but since an inference from an effect to a definite cause, especially to one so exactly and perfectly defined as we have to think God to be, is always uncertain and fallible, such a presupposition cannot be brought to a higher degree of certainty than the acknowledgement that it is the most reasonable opinion for us men.[3]

A need of pure practical reason, on the other hand, is based on a duty to make something (the highest good) the object of my will so as to promote it with all my strength. In doing so, I must presuppose its possibility and also its conditions, which are God, freedom, and immortality; for these conditions I am not in a position to prove by my speculative reason, though I cannot disprove them either. This duty is based on an apodictic law, the moral law, which is independent of these presuppositions, and thus needs no further support from theoretical opinions [143] on the inner character of things, on the secret final end of the world order, or on a ruler presiding over it in order to bind us completely to actions unconditionally conformable to the law. But the subjective effect of this law, i.e., the intention which is suitable to this law and which is necessary because of it, the intention to promote the practically possible highest good at least presupposes that the latter is possible. Otherwise it would be practically impossible to strive for the object of a concept, which, at bottom, would be empty and without an object. Now the afore-mentioned postulates concern only the physical or metaphysical conditions (that is, those lying in the nature of things) of the possibility of the highest good, though not for the sake of some arbitrary speculative design but only for the sake of a practically necessary end of the pure rational will, which does not here choose but rather obeys an inexorable command of reason. This command of reason has its ground objectively in the character of things as they must be universally judged by pure reason and is not based on inclination, which would by no means justify us in assuming the means to be possible or the object to be real for the sake of that which we wish on merely subjective grounds. This is, therefore, an absolutely necessary need and justifies its presupposition not merely as an allowable hypothesis but as a practical postulate. Granted that the pure moral law inexorably binds every man as a command (not as a rule of prudence), the righteous man may say: I will that there be a God, that my existence in this world be also an existence in a pure world of the understanding outside the system of natural connections, and finally that my duration be endless. I stand by this and will not give up this belief, for this is the only case where my interest inevitably determines my judgment because I will not yield anything of this interest; I do so without any attention to sophistries, however

---

[3] But even here we could not allege a need of reason if there were not before us a problematical but inevitable concept of reason, that of an absolutely necessary being. This concept requires to be defined, and, when the tendency to extend [the competence of reason] is added, it is the objective ground of a need of speculative reason, which is the need to define more accurately the concept of a necessary being which will serve as the ultimate ground of others and thus to characterize this necessary being by a distinctive mark. Without such prior necessary problems there are no needs, at least none of pure reason, the others being needs of inclination.

little I may be able to answer them or oppose them with others more plausible.[4]

In order to avoid all misinterpretations of the use of [144] such an unusual concept as that of pure practical faith, I may add one more remark. It might almost seem as if this rational faith is here decreed as a command to assume as possible the highest good. But faith that is commanded is an absurdity. If one remembers from the preceding analysis what is needed to be presupposed in the concept of the highest good, one will realize that to assume this possibility cannot be commanded, and that no practical disposition to grant it can be demanded, but that speculative reason must admit it without being asked; for no one can affirm that it is impossible of itself that rational beings in the world should at the same time be worthy of happiness in conformity to the moral law and be in possession of happiness proportionate to this worthiness. Now with respect to the first component of the highest good, viz., morality, the moral law merely gives a command, and to doubt the possibility of that ingredient would be the same as to call the moral law itself into question. But with respect to the second component of that object, viz., happiness perfectly proportionate to that worthiness, the assumption of its possibility is not at all in need of a command, for theoretical reason has nothing to say against it. It is only in the way in which we are to think of this harmony of natural laws with laws of freedom that there is anything [145] about which we have a choice, because here theoretical reason does not decide with apodictic certainty, and in this respect there can be a moral interest which turns the scale.

I have said above that in the mere course of nature happiness exactly proportionate to moral worth is not to be expected and is indeed impossible and that therefore the possibility of the highest good from this side cannot be granted except under the presupposition of a moral Author of the world. I intentionally postponed restricting this judgment to the subjective conditions of our reason in order to make use of this restriction only when the manner of the assent had been more precisely defined. In fact, the impossibility men

---

[4] In the *Deutsches Museum* for February, 1787, there is a dissertation by a very subtle and clear-headed man, the late Wizenmann, whose early death is to be lamented. In this he disputes the right to argue from a need to the objective reality of the object of the need, and he illustrates his point by the example of a man in love, who has fooled himself with an idea of beauty which is merely a chimera of his own brain and who now tries to argue that such an object really exists somewhere. I concede that he is right in all cases where the need is based on inclination, which cannot postulate the existence of its object even for him who is beset by it, and which even less contains a demand valid for everyone, and which is therefore a merely subjective ground of wishes. Here we have to do, however, with a need of reason arising from an objective determining ground of the will, i.e., the moral law, which is necessarily binding on every rational being; this, therefore, justifies a priori the presupposition of suitable conditions in nature and makes them inseparable from the complete practical use of reason. It is a duty to realize the highest good as far as it lies within our power to do so; therefore, it must be possible to do so. Consequently, it is unavoidable for every rational being in the world to assume whatever is necessary to its objective possibility. The assumption is as necessary as the moral law, in relation to which alone it is valid.

tioned is merely subjective, i.e., our reason finds it impossible to conceive, in the mere course of nature, a connection so exactly proportioned and so thoroughly adapted to an end between natural events which occur according to laws so heterogeneous. But, as with every other purposive thing in nature, it still cannot prove that it is impossible according to universal laws of nature [only], i.e., show this by objectively sufficient reasons.

But now a determining factor of another kind comes into play to turn the scale in this indecision of speculative reason. The command to further the highest good is objectively grounded (in practical reason), and its possibility itself is likewise objectively grounded (in theoretical reason, which has nothing to say against it). But as to the manner in which this possibility is to be thought, reason cannot objectively decide whether it is by universal laws of nature without a wise Author presiding over nature or whether only on the assumption of such an Author. Now a subjective condition of reason enters which is the only way in which it is theoretically possible for it to conceive of the exact harmony of the realm of nature with the realm of morals as the condition of the possibility of the highest good; and it is the only way which is conducive to morality (which is under an objective law of reason). Since the promotion of the highest good and thus the presupposition of its possibility are objectively necessary (though only as a consequence of practical reason), and since the manner in which we are to think of it as possible is subject to our own choice, in which a free interest of pure practical reason is decisive for the assumption [146] of a wise Author of the world, it follows that the principle which here determines our judgment, while subjectively a need, is the ground of a maxim of moral assent, as a means to promoting that which is objectively (practically) necessary; that is, it is a faith of pure practical reason. As a voluntary decision of our judgment to assume that existence and to make it the foundation of further employment of reason, conducing to the moral (commanded) purpose and agreeing moreover with the theoretical need of reason, it is itself not commanded. It rather springs from the moral disposition itself. It can therefore often waver even in the well disposed but can never fall into unbelief.

III.E.2.   The Moral Argument

JOHN HICK

John Hick (1922–), a British-born philosopher of religion who has spent most of his professional life in American universities, holds a distinguished chair in religion at Claremont Graduate School. In the brief selection here he summarizes two forms of moral argument. Hick finds neither to be a convincing proof but concedes that the argument, carefully stated, has a limited validity.

The moral argument, in its various forms, claims that ethical experience, and particularly one's sense of an inalienable obligation to fellow human beings, presupposes the reality of God as in some way the source and ground of this obligation.

FIRST FORM

In one form the argument is presented as a logical inference from objective moral laws to a divine Law Giver; or from the objectivity of moral values or of values in general to a transcendent Ground of Values; or again, from the fact of conscience to a God whose "voice" conscience is—as in the following passage by Cardinal Newman:

> If, as is the case, we feel responsibility, are ashamed, are frightened, at transgressing the voice of conscience, this implies that there is One to whom we are responsible, before whom we are ashamed, whose claims upon us we fear. . . . If the cause of these emotions does not belong to this visible world, the Object to which [the conscientious person's] perception is directed must be Supernatural and Divine.[1]

The basic assumption of all arguments of this kind is that moral values are not capable of naturalistic explanation in terms of human needs and desires, self-interest, the structure of human nature or human society, or in any other way that does not involve appeal to the Supernatural. But to make such an assumption is to beg the question. Thus, an essential premise of the inference from axiology to God is in dispute, and from the point of view of the naturalistic skeptic nothing has been established.

From *Philosophy of Religion*, © 1983, pp. 28–29. Reprinted by permission of Prentice-Hall, Inc., Englewood Cliffs, NJ.

[1] J. H. Cardinal Newman, *A Grammar of Assent*, 1870, ed. C. F. Harrold (New York: David McKay Co., Inc., 1947), pp. 83–84.

SECOND FORM

The second kind of moral argument is not open to the same objection, for it is not strictly a proof at all. It consists of the claim that anyone seriously committed to respect moral values as exercising a sovereign claim upon his or her life must thereby implicitly believe in the reality of a transhuman source and basis for these values, which religion calls God. Thus, Immanuel Kant argues that both immortality and the existence of God are "postulates" of the moral life, i.e., beliefs which can legitimately be affirmed as presuppositions by one who recognizes duty as rightfully laying upon one an unconditional claim.[2] Again, a more recent theological writer asks:

> Is it too paradoxical in the modern world to say that faith in God is a very part of our moral consciousness, without which the latter becomes meaningless? . . . Either our moral values tell us something about the nature and purpose of reality (i.e., give us the germ of religious belief) or they are subjective and therefore meaningless.[3]

It seems to the present writer that so long as this contention is not overstated it has a certain limited validity. To recognize moral claims as taking precedence over all other interests is, in effect, to believe in a reality, other than the natural world, that is superior to oneself and entitled to one's obedience. This is at least a move in the direction of belief in God, who is known in the Judaic-Christian tradition as the supreme moral reality. But it cannot be presented as a proof of God's existence, for the sovereign authority of moral obligation can be questioned; and even if moral values are acknowledged as pointing toward a transcendent ground, they cannot be said to point all the way and with unerring aim to the infinite, omnipotent, self-existent, personal creator who is the object of biblical faith.

---

[2] *Critique of Practical Reason*, Book II, Chap. 2, Secs. 4 and 5.

[3] D. M. Baillie, *Faith in God and Its Christian Consummation* (Edinburgh: T. & T. Clark, 1927), pp. 172–73.

III.E.3. Moral Arguments for the Existence of God

J. L. MACKIE

J. L. Mackie (1917–1981), a reader in philosophy at Oxford University, was a skeptic and sharp critic of religion. The title of his book, The Miracle of Theism, *from which the following passage comes, is a tongue-in-cheek reference to David Hume's saying that it takes a miracle to allow anyone to believe the claims of religion. Mackie provides an exposition of Kant's position along with a variant of the moral argument that Henry Sidgwick offered but did not endorse. Mackie points out that the moral argument begins by asserting that morality is unintelligible unless certain factual propositions are true: that the human will is free, that the human soul is immortal, and that God exists. It then attempts to establish, on the basis of practical reason that these factual propositions must therefore be true. One cannot properly reason thus, says Mackie. If the factual claims are to be regarded as true, their truth must be established independently of the practical principle of morality. If this cannot be done, then the principle or postulate, as Kant calls it, is itself unjustified.*

(A) A POPULAR LINE OF THOUGHT

It is often suggested that morality requires and presupposes religion, and that moral thinking will therefore support theistic beliefs. A familiar line of popular thought runs somewhat like this. Moral principles tell us what we must do, whether we like it or not. That is, they are commands, and such commands must have a source, a commander. But the requirements of morality go beyond what any human authority demands of us, and they sometimes require us to resist all human authorities. Moral requirements go beyond, and sometimes against, what the law prescribes, or the state, or our friends, or any organized church, or the public opinion of any community, even a world-wide one. They must therefore be the commands of some more than human, and hence supernatural, authority. Also, if these commands are to overrule, as they claim to do, all other considerations, we must have an adequate motive for obeying them no matter what threats or temptations urge us to disobey. Such a motive can be supplied only by our knowing that there is a being who has both the will and the power to give rewards and to impose penalties which outweigh all worldly losses and gains. Morality needs a god, therefore, both as a supreme source of commands and as an all-powerful wielder of sanctions to enforce them. Besides, moral thinking includes a confident demand for justice, an assurance that what is unfair and unjust cannot in the end prevail, and justice requires that there should be some power which will somehow balance happiness with desert.

Such an argument has, perhaps, seldom served as an original ground of religious belief; but it has seemed to many to be a powerful reinforcement for that belief, and, in particular, a strong reason for continuing to adhere to it when it is threatened in some other way. It is felt that if theistic beliefs are given up, moral convictions will lose their point and their force, and also their determinacy. Religious beliefs that we see some ground for doubting are thus buttressed by the feeling that we can neither abandon morality nor leave it without religious support.

I shall come back later to this popular line of thought. But first I want to examine several different and even incompatible philosophical versions of the argument from morality, each of which can be seen as a development or refinement of some elements in the popular line of thought. These versions are ones put forward by Newman and by Kant, and one that is considered, but not endorsed, by Sidgwick. [The passage about Newman is omitted—Ed.] . . .

(C) KANT: GOD AS A PRESUPPOSITION OF MORALITY

In the *Critique of Pure Reason* Kant argues that there is no sound speculative proof of the existence of a god. We have already referred to his criticisms of the ontological and cosmological arguments. . . . But in the *Critique of Practical Reason* he suggests that moral reasoning can achieve what speculative reasoning cannot, and that the existence of a god, and also affirmative solutions to the other great metaphysical questions of the immortality of the soul and the freedom of the will, can be defended as being necessarily presupposed in moral consciousness.[1]

Kant's view is much further than Newman's from the popular line of thought with which we began. He stresses autonomy of morality, to which I appealed in the first horn of the dilemma used to criticize Newman's argument. What is morally right and obligatory is so, Kant holds, in itself, and can be rationally seen in itself to be so. Each rational being is, as such, competent to determine the moral law, to prescribe moral commands to himself, and therefore does not need God to command him—or even, it would seem, to advise him. 'Moreover, it is not meant by this that it is necessary to suppose the existence of God *as a basis of all obligation in general* (for this rests . . . simply on the autonomy of reason itself).' (267) Moral agents, or rational beings, are the

---

[1] I. Kant, *Critique of Practical Reason*, e.g. in T. K. Abbott, *Kant's Theory of Ethics* (Longmans, London, 1927), especially Part I, Book II, Chapter 2. References in the text to this work and to Kant's *Metaphysic of Morals* are to the pages in the German edition of Rosenkranz and Schubert, given at the top of each page in Abbott.

citizens of an ideal commonwealth, making universal laws for themselves and one another. Morality is corrupted if it is derived from prudence and self-interest: divine rewards and punishments, therefore, far from supplying a necessary motive for morality, would introduce heteronomy, substituting an alien and morally worthless motive for the only genuinely valuable one of respect for the moral law.

However, Kant finds another and more appropriate place for a god in the moral universe. His positive argument starts from the notion of the *summum bonum*, the highest good, which, he says, is not merely moral rectitude but also includes happiness. Virtue and happiness together constitute the highest good for a person, and the distribution of happiness in proportion to morality constitutes the highest good for a possible world. Whereas the Epicureans made the mistake of reducing morality to the pursuit of happiness, the Stoics made the opposite mistake of either leaving happiness out of their conception of the highest good, or what amounts to the same thing identifying happiness simply with the consciousness of virtue. In contrast with both these mistakes, an adequate conception of the highest good must include both virtue and happiness, but each in its own right. Now since these two elements in the highest good are independent of one another, there is no logical necessity that they should go together, and hence no *a priori* guarantee that the realization of this highest good is even possible. Equally, there is no natural, causal guarantee of this. Happiness (in this life) depends largely on what happens in the natural world, but the moral choices of rational beings are not to any great extent in control of this: our moral efforts cannot causally ensure that those who will and act rightly will be happy. Nor does nature as such conform to a moral standard. But, Kant says, moral thought tells us that we must take the highest good as a supreme end; that is, 'we ought to endeavor to promote the highest good, which must, therefore, be possible'. He infers that 'the existence of a cause of all nature, distinct from nature itself, and containing the principle...of the exact harmony of happiness with morality' is *postulated* in moral thought. 'The highest good is possible in the world only on the supposition of a Supreme Being having a causality corresponding to moral character'—that is, a god. Since it is for us a duty to promote the highest good, there is 'a necessity connected with duty as a requisite, that we should presuppose the possibility of this *summum bonum*; and as this is possible only on condition of the existence of God...it is morally necessary to assume the existence of God'. But since happiness in this life is pretty plainly not proportioned to morality, it is also necessary to assume that individuals survive in a life after death; Kant has also argued separately for such immortality, again as a presupposition of moral thought, as being necessary to allow for an indefinite progress towards perfection which is involved in the first half of the highest good, complete virtue or 'the *perfect accordance* of the mind with the moral law'. (265–7)

It is not easy to decide just how Kant meant these conclusions to be interpreted. On the one hand he argues for 'the primacy of pure practical reason in its union with the speculative reason', saying that when certain propositions 'are *inseparably* attached *to the practical interest* of pure reason', theoretical reason must accept them, and 'must try to compare and connect them with everything that it has in its power as speculative reason', and this is plainly intended to apply to the propositions asserting the immortality of the soul and the existence of a god, as well as the freedom of the will. But on the other hand, asking whether our knowledge is 'actually extended in this way by pure practical reason', and whether that is '*immanent* in practical reason which for the speculative was only *transcendent*', Kant replies 'Certainly, but *only in a practical point of view'*—which seems to take away what it gives. We do not in this way gain knowledge of our souls or of the Supreme Being as they are in themselves. Theoretical reason 'is compelled to admit *that there are such objects*, although it is not able to define them more closely'; knowledge of them has been given 'only for practical use'. In fact speculative reason will work with regard to these objects only 'in a negative manner', to remove '*anthropomorphism*, as the source of *superstition*, or seeming extension of these conceptions by supposed experience; and . . . *fanaticism*, which promises the same by means of supersensible intuition'. (276–9) He seems to be saying that the existence of a god and the immortality of the soul can be established as facts by the arguments from morality, but only in a highly indeterminate form. Yet he hints also at a more sceptical position, that the existence of a god, the freedom of the will, and the immortality of the soul cannot be established as facts, even by reasoning based on the moral consciousness, but can only be shown to be necessarily presupposed in that consciousness, to be, as it were, implicit in its content. In other words, we as rational beings cannot help thinking morally, and if we develop our moral thinking fully and coherently we cannot help supposing that there is a god; but whether in fact there is a god remains an open question. Kant says that 'the righteous man may say: I *will* that there be a God, that my existence in this world be also an existence outside the chain of physical causes, and in a pure world of the understanding, and lastly, that my duration be endless; I firmly abide by this, and will not let this faith be taken from me; for in this instance alone my interest, because I *must* not relax anything of it, inevitably determines my judgment', and he speaks of a *faith of pure practical reason*, which, he admits, is an 'unusual notion'. (289–92)

But in whichever of these ways we interpret his conclusion, Kant's argument is open to criticism. The most glaring weakness is in the step from the proposition that 'we ought to seek the highest good' to the claim that it 'must therefore be possible.' Even if, as Kant argues elsewhere, 'ought' implies 'can', the thesis that we ought to seek to promote the highest good implies only that we can *seek to promote* it, and perhaps, since rational seeking could not be completely fruitless, that we can to some extent actually *promote* it. But this does not require that the full realization of the highest good should be possible. For example, it is thoroughly rational to try to improve the condition of human life, provided that some improvement is possible; there is no need to entertain vain hopes for its perfection. And even for the *possibility* of that full realization the most that would be needed is the possible existence of a wholly good and all-powerful governor of the world; the actual existence of such a governor would ensure not merely the possibility but the actuality of the highest good. Kant might say that we can and should aspire to the ultimate realization of the highest good, and that a *hope* for such ultimate realization is necessarily involved in moral thought. But he cannot claim that even its possible realization is a necessary postulate of moral thought in general; it is not even a necessary postulate of that particular sort of moral theory which Kant himself developed. The willing of universal laws by and for all rational beings as such could be strictly autonomous activity.

There are, indeed, recurrent tensions between Kant's theism and his stress on the autonomy of morals. In sharp contrast with the popular view, and with Newman's, Kant holds that neither our knowledge of God and of his will, nor that will itself, is the foundation of the moral law. Yet because (as he thinks) we have to postulate a god who *also* wills these laws, as does every other free and rational will, he still calls them 'commands of the Supreme Being', but in a sense which is only a pale shadow of what is intended by most theological moralists. Again, Kant holds that no 'desired results' are 'the proper motive of obedience' to these laws, indeed that fear of punishment or hope of reward 'if taken as principles, would destroy the whole moral worth of actions'. Yet his belief that there is something appropriate about the *proportioning* of happiness to morality—a retributive thesis—again seems to be a pale shadow of the popular reliance on punishment and rewards. Is not this true also of his stress (after all) on happiness, whose conjunction with virtue we are to take not merely as a legitimate hope but as a *postulate* of moral thought? Would not a thoroughgoing recognition of the autonomy of morals lead rather to the Stoic view that morality needs no actual happiness beyond the consciousness of right action itself?

Kant himself seems to have been aware of these difficulties, and a passage in his *Metaphysics of Morals* suggests a quite different proof of God's existence: again a moral proof, but one which anticipates Newman's argument about conscience.

> Now this original intellectual and . . . moral capacity, called *conscience*, has this peculiarity in it, that although its business is a business of man with himself, yet he finds himself compelled by his reason to transact it as if at the command of *another person* . . . in all duties the conscience of the man must regard *another* than himself as the judge of his actions . . . Now this other may be an actual or a merely ideal person which reason frames to itself. Such an idealized person . . . must be one who knows the heart . . . at the same time he must also be *all-obliging*, that is, must be or be conceived as a person in respect of whom all duties are to be regarded as his commands . . . Now since such a moral being must at the same time possess all power (in heaven and earth), since otherwise he could not give his commands their proper effect, and since such a moral being possessing power over all is called God, hence conscience must be conceived as the subjective principle of a responsibility for one's deeds before God; nay, this latter concept is contained (though it be only obscurely) in every moral self-consciousness. (293-4)

Here Kant is vacillating between the recognition of the merely psychological phenomenon of the setting up of an ideal spectator (Adam Smith's 'man within the breast'[2]) and the suggestion that moral thought has at least to postulate the real existence of an outside authority—but how weak a reason he

---

[2] A. Smith, *The Theory of Moral Sentiments* (Edinburgh, 1808), Part III, Chapter 2, p. 308.

offers for the ascription of all power to this moral being! In any case, in so far as this argument anticipates Newman's, it is open to the same criticisms.

We need not labour these internal tensions and vacillations. What is important is that even if moral thought is as Kant describes it, it does not follow that such thought has even to postulate the existence of a god, let alone that we can infer the real existence of a god from the character of that thought.

(D) SIDGWICK: THE DUALITY OF PRACTICAL REASON

Another variant of the moral argument is clearly stated, but not endorsed, by Sidgwick.[3] This starts from 'the duality of practical reason', the fact that both prudential egotism and the commands of conscience are practically reasonable, each without qualification, and yet that, if there is neither a god nor anything like a god, they will not always coincide. Its premisses are:

1. What I have most reason to do is always what will best secure my own happiness in the long run.
2. What I have most reason to do is always what morality requires.
3. If there is no moral government of the universe, what will best secure my own happiness is not always what morality requires.

The first two of these premisses would indeed entail that prudence and morality always coincide; for if they required different choices in the same situation, it could not be true that each of these different choices was the one that I had most reason to make: that is, these premisses could not both be true. But then, if prudence and morality will always coincide only if there is a moral government of the universe, it follows that there must be such a government, that is, either a god or something like a god.

This argument is plainly valid, though its conclusion is not quite what traditional theism asserts: moral government would not need to include a personal god. But are the premisses true? Sidgwick, for one, regarded the first two as inescapable intuitions about what is reasonable in conduct—taking the second as prescribing social duty in a utilitarian sense. Also, if there is no moral government of the universe, then presumably the present life is all we have to take into account; and it is an easily established empirical truth that in this life the demands of utilitarian morality—the promotion of the general happiness—do not always coincide with what will best promote one's own happiness. This, then, establishes the third premiss.

But although Sidgwick, for these reasons, accepted all three premisses, he did not accept the conclusion. He preferred to admit that there is a fundamental and unresolved chaos in our practical reasoning, and that the human intellect cannot frame a fully satisfactory ideal of rational conduct: 'the mere fact that I cannot act rationally without assuming a certain proposition, does not appear to me,—as it does to some minds,— a sufficient ground for believing it to be true'. Equally he rejects what he calls 'the Kantian resource of

---

[3] H. Sidgwick, *The Methods of Ethics* (Macmillan, London, 1874), Book IV, Chapter VI.

thinking myself under a moral necessity to regard all my duties *as if they were* commandments of God, although not entitled to hold speculatively that any such Supreme Being exists "as Real"'. (In this reference to 'the Kantian resource', Sidgwick is clearly favouring the second of the two interpretations of Kant offered above; but the previous comment on what appears 'to some minds' would apply to the first.) Sidgwick adds: 'I am so far from feeling bound to believe for purposes of practice what I see no ground for holding as a speculative truth, that I cannot even conceive the state of mind which these words seem to describe, except as a momentary half-willful irrationality, committed in a violent access of philosophic despair'.

Is Sidgwick perverse in refusing to accept this conclusion? I think not. It is rather that he has put his finger on the basic weakness of almost every form of moral argument for the existence of a god. A set of beliefs, even if they are called 'intuitions', about how one ought to act cannot be a good reason for settling a factual issue, a way of determining what is the case, or even for deciding what to 'believe for practical purposes'. Practical choices must be based on factual beliefs, not the other way round, though beliefs *alone*, of course, will not determine choices.

To see this, let us take an analogous case. Most of those who have discussed imperative logic have assumed that such syllogisms as this are valid: 'Eat no animal fats; butter is an animal fat; so don't eat butter'. But if that syllogism is valid, so must this one be: 'Eat no animal fats; you may eat butter; so butter is not an animal fat'. That is, there can be a valid syllogism with one imperative and one permissive premiss, and this would still be valid if the permissive premiss were strengthened to an imperative—in our example, to 'Eat butter'. But such a pair of imperative premisses (or an imperative along with a permissive one) could not objectively establish the truth of the factual conclusion. They show only that anyone who coherently issues both imperatives (or the imperative and the permission) must *believe* the conclusion to be true. Again, what should we say about a general who accepted these three premisses:

1. If the enemy are advancing in overwhelming strength, then, if we do not withdraw, our army will be wiped out;

2. We must not allow our army to be wiped out;

3. We must not withdraw, because that would mean letting down our allies;

and concluded, on these grounds alone, that the enemy were not advancing in overwhelming strength?

In all such cases, what it is rational to do depends upon what the facts are; but we cannot take what we are inclined to think that it is rational to do as evidence about those facts. To use a conjunction of practical judgments to try to establish what the facts are would be to put the cart before the horse. We must rely on speculative reasoning first to determine what is the case, and then frame our practical and moral beliefs and attitudes in the light of these facts. There is a direction of supervenience: since what *is* morally and practically rational supervenes upon what is the case, what it is rational to *believe* with a view to practice, or to *choose* to do, must similarly supervene upon what it is rational to believe about what is the case.

But this is what Kant was denying when, as we saw, he maintained the primacy of pure practical reason. He refers, indeed, to Thomas Wizenmann, who had brought what is essentially our objection, or Sidgwick's, against his argument. Kant concedes that we cannot argue from a want founded merely on inclination to the reality of its object or of what is needed to satisfy it, but he thinks it is otherwise when we have 'a want of reason springing from an objective determining principle of the will, namely the moral law'. Since it is a duty to realize the *summum bonum* to the utmost of our power, it must be possible, and 'consequently it is unavoidable for every rational being... to assume what is necessary for its objective possibility. The assumption is as necessary as the moral law, in connection with which alone it is valid' (289, note). Kant admits that where practical reason 'merely regulat[es] the inclinations under the sensible principle of happiness, we could not require speculative reason to take its principles from such a source'. This, he sees, would lead to absurd fantasies. But he thinks that *pure* practical reason, which determines the moral law, is in a different position. 'But if pure reason of itself can be practical and is actually so, as the consciousness of the moral law proves, then it is still only one and the same reason which, whether in a theoretical or a practical point of view, judges according to *a priori* principles...' Propositions established in this way, he holds, 'are not additions to its [i.e. reason's] insight, but yet are extensions of its employment in another, namely a practical, aspect...' 'Nor', he says, 'could we reverse the order, and require pure practical reason to be subordinate to the speculative, since all interest is ultimately practical, and even that of speculative reason is conditional, and it is only in the practical employment that it is complete.' (261–2)

However, what this last remark can mean is unclear, and the reply to Wizenmann merely repeats the original argument. Nothing has been done to explain how pure practical reason could escape the constraints which, as Kant admits, apply to practical reason in general. If a certain practical principle presupposes certain factual propositions, then reason, however pure, cannot establish the validity of that practical principle without *independently* showing that those factual propositions are true. We cannot therefore use the practical principle to prove that these are truths of fact. This consideration is fatal to Kant's argument in the *Critique of Practical Reason*, just as it is to the argument which Sidgwick formulated, but rejected precisely on this account.

Whether there are other ways of resolving Sidgwick's paradox is not our present concern. It may be that his first two premises do not hold without qualification as principles of practical rationality. But if all such escape routes were blocked, the right conclusion to draw would be the one that Sidgwick himself drew, that there is no fully coherent ideal of practical reason.

III.F. The Pragmatic Argument

III.F.1. The Wager

BLAISE PASCAL

Blaise Pascal (1623–1662), a French mathematician and philosopher, found the divine beyond human understanding and thus conceded that we cannot know the nature of God. Yet we can conceive the existence of what we cannot know, as we do when we conceive that an infinite number exists. The arguments that reason generates to support a belief in God are not compelling; there are counterarguments, but they are not compelling, either. Thus reason is unable to decide whether God exists or not. Yet we cannot suspend judgment; we must either believe or not believe. We should therefore decide to believe and wager our life that God does exist, because the loss if we are wrong is trivial and the gain if we are right is infinite. Arguing against the resisting unbeliever's position, Pascal goes on to show how a mind not naturally ready to adopt belief can be induced to do so by behaving as if it did believe.

Infinity—nothing. Our soul is cast into the body where it finds number, time, dimensions; it reasons about these things and calls them natural, or necessary, and can believe nothing else.

Unity added to infinity does not increase it at all, any more than a foot added to an infinite measurement: the finite is annihilated in the presence of the infinite and becomes pure nothingness. So it is with our mind before God, with our justice before divine justice. There is not so great a disproportion between our justice and God's as between unity and infinity.

God's justice must be as vast as his mercy. Now his justice towards the damned is less vast and ought to be less startling to us than his mercy towards the elect.

We know that the infinite exists without knowing its nature, just as we know that it is untrue that numbers are finite. Thus it is true that there is an infinite number, but we do not know what it is. It is untrue that it is even, untrue that it is odd, for by adding a unit it does not change its nature. Yet it is a number, and every number is even or odd. (It is true that this applies to every finite number.)

Therefore we may well know that God exists without knowing what he is.

From *Pensées,* trans. and ed. A. J. Krailsheimer (New York: Penguin, 1966), pp. 149–153. Used by permission of David Campbell Publishers.

Is there no substantial truth, seeing that there are so many true things which are not truth itself?

Thus we know the existence and nature of the finite because we too are finite and extended in space.

We know the existence of the infinite without knowing its nature, because it too has extension but unlike us no limits.

But we do not know either the existence or the nature of God, because he has neither extension nor limits.

But by faith we know his existence, through glory we shall know his nature.

Now I have already proved that it is quite possible to know that something exists without knowing its nature.

Let us now speak according to our natural lights.

If there is a God, he is infinitely beyond our comprehension, since, being indivisible and without limits, he bears no relation to us. We are therefore incapable of knowing either what he is or whether he is. That being so, who would dare to attempt an answer to the question? Certainly not we, who bear no relation to him.

Who then will condemn Christians for being unable to give rational grounds for their belief, professing as they do a religion for which they cannot give rational grounds? They declare that it is a folly, *stultitiam*, in expounding it to the world, and then you complain that they do not prove it. If they did prove it they would not be keeping their word. It is by being without proof that they show they are not without sense. 'Yes, but although that excuses those who offer their religion as such, and absolves them from the criticism of producing it without rational grounds, it does not absolve those who accept it.' Let us then examine this point, and let us say: 'Either God is or he is not.' But to which view shall we be inclined? Reason cannot decide this question. Infinite chaos separates us. At the far end of this infinite distance a coin is being spun which will come down heads or tails. How will you wager? Reason cannot make you choose either, reason cannot prove either wrong.

Do not then condemn as wrong those who have made a choice, for you know nothing about it. 'No, but I will condemn them not for having made this particular choice, but any choice, for, although the one who calls heads and the other one are equally at fault, the fact is that they are both at fault: the right thing is not to wager at all.'

Yes, but you must wager. There is no choice, you are already committed. Which will you choose then? Let us see: since a choice must be made, let us see which offers you the least interest. You have two things to lose: the true and the good; and two things to stake: your reason and your will, your knowledge and your happiness; and your nature has two things to avoid: error and wretchedness. Since you must necessarily choose, your reason is no more affronted by choosing one rather than the other. That is one point cleared up. But your happiness? Let us weigh up the gain and the loss involved in calling heads that God exists. Let us assess the two cases: if you win you win everything, if you lose you lose nothing. Do not hesitate then; wager that he does exist. 'That is wonderful. Yes, I must wager, but perhaps I am wagering too much.' Let us see: since there is an equal chance of gain and loss, if you stood to win only two lives for one you could still wager, but supposing you stood to win three?

You would have to play (since you must necessarily play) and it would be unwise of you, once you are obliged to play, not to risk your life in order to win three lives at a game in which there is an equal chance of losing and winning. But there is an eternity of life and happiness. That being so, even though there were an infinite number of chances, of which only one were in your favour, you would still be right to wager one in order to win two; and you would be acting wrongly, being obliged to play, in refusing to stake one life against three in a game, where out of an infinite number of chances there is one in your favour, if there were an infinity of infinitely happy life to be won. But here there is an infinity of infinitely happy life to be won, one chance of winning against a finite number of chances of losing, and what you are staking is finite. That leaves no choice; wherever there is infinity, and where there are not infinite chances of losing against that of winning, there is no room for hesitation, you must give everything. And thus, since you are obliged to play, you must be renouncing reason if you hoard your life rather than risk it for an infinite gain, just as likely to occur as a loss amounting to nothing.

For it is no good saying that it is uncertain whether you will win, that it is certain that you are taking a risk, and that the infinite distance between the certainty of what you are risking and the uncertainty of what you may gain makes the finite good you are certainly risking equal to the infinite good that you are not certain to gain. This is not the case. Every gambler takes a certain risk for an uncertain gain, and yet he is taking a certain finite risk for an uncertain finite gain without sinning against reason. Here there is no infinite distance between the certain risk and the uncertain gain: that is not true. There is, indeed, an infinite distance between the certainty of winning and the certainty of losing, but the proportion between the uncertainty of winning and the certainty of what is being risked is in proportion to the chances of winning or losing. And hence if there are as many chances on the one side as on the other you are playing for even odds. And in that case the certainty of what you are risking is equal to the uncertainty of what you may win; it is by no means infinitely distant from it. Thus our argument carries infinite weight, when the stakes are finite in a game where there are even chances of winning and losing and an infinite prize to be won.

This is conclusive and if men are capable of any truth this is it.

'I confess, I admit it, but is there really no way of seeing what the cards are?'—'Yes. Scripture and the rest, etc.'—'Yes, but my hands are tied and my lips are sealed; I am being forced to wager and I am not free; I am being held fast and I am so made that I cannot believe. What do you want me to do then?'—'That is true, but at least get it into your head that, if you are unable to believe, it is because of your passions, since reason impels you to believe and yet you cannot do so. Concentrate then not on convincing yourself by multiplying proofs of God's existence but by diminishing your passions. You want to find faith and you do not know the road. You want to be cured of unbelief and you ask for the remedy: learn from those who were once bound like you and who now wager all they have. These are people who know the road you wish to follow, who have been cured of the affliction of which you wish to be cured; follow the way by which they began. They behaved just as if they did believe, taking holy water, having masses said, and so on. That will make you believe quite naturally, and will make you more docile.'[1] But that is what I am afraid of.'—'But why? What have you to lose? But to show you that this is the way, the fact is that this diminishes the passions which are your great obstacles. . . .'

III.F.2.   The Ethics of Belief

W. K. CLIFFORD

W. K. Clifford (1845–1879) was a religious believer, interested in the philosophy of Aquinas in his youth, but later in life an agnostic. In this essay he argues that we must be at least as conscientious in our beliefs as we are obliged to be in our actions. Believing is a moral matter and we are morally responsible for our beliefs as much as for our actions. What we believe affects our character, and our character determines our behavior. Ill-founded belief is likely to lead to morally questionable or irresponsible actions. And even if holding unjustified beliefs never did contribute to immoral behavior, merely adopting beliefs without rational justification is an act of dishonesty. Clifford is very strongly opposed to the kind of thought represented in Pascal's work, which attempts to excuse and authorize the holding of beliefs for which we do not have sufficient rational justification. His central conclusion here is that it is morally wrong for anyone under any conditions to adopt a belief lacking evidential warrant.

A shipowner was about to send to sea an emigrant-ship. He knew that she was old, and not over-well built at the first; that she had seen many seas and climes, and often had needed repairs. Doubts had been suggested to him that possibly she was not seaworthy. These doubts preyed upon his mind and made him unhappy; he thought that perhaps he ought to have her thoroughly overhauled and refitted, even though this should put him to great expense. Before the ship sailed, however, he succeeded in overcoming these melancholy reflections. He said to himself that she had gone safely through so many voyages and weathered so many storms that it was idle to suppose she would not come safely home from this trip also. He would put his

---

From *Lectures and Essays* (London: Macmillan, 1901), pp. 163–176.

[1] *abêtira.* That is, the unbeliever will act unthinkingly and mechanically, and in this become more like the beasts, from whom man was differentiated, according to contemporary philosophy, by his faculty of reason.

trust in Providence, which could hardly fail to protect all these unhappy families that were leaving their fatherland to seek for better times elsewhere. He would dismiss from his mind all ungenerous suspicions about the honesty of the builders and contractors. In such ways he acquired a sincere and comfortable conviction that his vessel was thoroughly safe and seaworthy; he watched her departure with a light heart, and benevolent wishes for the success of the exiles in their strange new home that was to be; and he got his insurance-money when she went down in mid-ocean and told no tales.

What shall we say of him? Surely this, that he was verily guilty of the death of those men. It is admitted that he did sincerely believe in the soundness of his ship; but the sincerity of his conviction can in no wise help him, *because he had no right to believe on such evidence as was before him*. He had acquired his belief not by honestly earning it in patient investigation, but by stifling his doubts. And although in the end he may have felt so sure about it that he could not think otherwise, yet inasmuch as he had knowingly and willingly worked himself into that frame of mind, he must be held responsible for it.

Let us alter the case a little, and suppose that the ship was not unsound after all; that she made her voyage safely, and many others after it. Will that diminish the guilt of her owner? Not one jot. When an action is once done, it is right or wrong for ever; no accidental failure of its good or evil fruits can possibly alter that The man would not have been innocent, he would only have been not found out. The question of right or wrong has to do with the origin of his belief, not the matter of it; not what it was, but how he got it; not whether it turned out to be true or false, but whether he had a right to believe on such evidence as was before him.

There was once an island in which some of the inhabitants professed a religion teaching neither the doctrine of original sin nor that of eternal punishment. A suspicion got abroad that the professors of this religion had made use of unfair means to get their doctrines taught to children. They were accused of wresting the laws of their country in such a way as to remove children from the care of their natural and legal guardians; and even of stealing them away and keeping them concealed from their friends and relations. A certain number of men formed themselves into a society for the purpose of agitating the public about this matter. They published grave accusations against individual citizens of the highest position and character, and did all in their power to injure these citizens in the exercise of their professions. So great was the noise they made, that a Commission was appointed to investigate the facts; but after the Commission had carefully inquired into all the evidence that could be got, it appeared that the accused were innocent. Not only had they been accused on insufficient evidence, but the evidence of their innocence was such as the agitators might easily have obtained, if they had attempted a fair inquiry. After these disclosures the inhabitants of that country looked upon the members of the agitating society, not only as persons whose judgment was to be distrusted, but also as no longer to be counted honourable men. For although they had sincerely and conscientiously believed in the charges they had made, *yet they had no right to believe on such evidence as was before them*. Their sincere convictions, instead of being honestly earned by patient inquiring, were stolen by listening to the voice of prejudice and passion.

Let us vary this case also, and suppose, other things remaining as before, that a still more accurate investigation proved the accused to have been really guilty. Would this make any difference in the guilt of the accusers? Clearly not; the question is not whether their belief was true or false, but whether they entertained it on wrong grounds. They would no doubt say, "Now you see that we were right after all; next time perhaps you will believe us." And they might be believed, but they would not thereby become honourable men. They would not be innocent, they would only be not found out. Every one of them, if he chose to examine himself *in foro conscientiæ*, would know that he had acquired and nourished a belief, when he had no right to believe on such evidence as was before him; and therein he would know that he had done a wrong thing.

It may be said, however, that in both of these supposed cases it is not the belief which is judged to be wrong, but the action following upon it. The shipowner might say, "I am perfectly certain that my ship is sound, but still I feel it my duty to have her examined, before trusting the lives of so many people to her." And it might be said to the agitator, "However convinced you were of the justice of your cause and the truth of your convictions, you ought not to have made a public attack upon any man's character until you had examined the evidence on both sides with the utmost patience and care."

In the first place, let us admit that, so far as it goes, this view of the case is right and necessary; right, because even when a man's belief is so fixed that he cannot think otherwise, he still has a choice in regard to the action suggested by it, and so cannot escape the duty of investigating on the ground of the strength of his convictions; and necessary, because those who are not yet capable of controlling their feelings and thoughts must have a plain rule dealing with overt acts.

But this being premised as necessary, it becomes clear that it is not sufficient, and that our previous judgment is required to supplement it. For it is not possible so to sever the belief from the action it suggests as to condemn the one without condemning the other. No man holding a strong belief on one side of a question, or even wishing to hold a belief on one side, can investigate it with such fairness and completeness as if he were really in doubt and unbiased; so that the existence of a belief not founded on fair inquiry unfits a man for the performance of this necessary duty.

Nor is that truly a belief at all which has not some influence upon the actions of him who holds it. He who truly believes that which prompts him to an action has looked upon the action to lust after it, he has committed it already in his heart. If a belief is not realised immediately in open deeds, it is stored up for the guidance of the future. It goes to make a part of that aggregate of beliefs which is the link between sensation and action at every moment of all our lives, and which is so organised and compacted together that no part of it can be isolated from the rest, but every new addition modifies the structure of the whole. No real belief, however trifling and fragmentary it may seem, is ever truly insignificant; it prepares us to receive more of its like, confirms those which resembled it before, and weakens others; and so gradually it lays a stealthy train in our inmost thoughts, which may some day explode into overt action, and leave its stamp upon our characters for ever.

And no one man's belief is in any case a private matter which concerns himself alone. Our lives are guided by that general conception of the course of things which has been created by society for social purposes. Our words, our phrases, our forms and processes and modes of thought, are common property, fashioned and perfected from age to age; an heirloom which every succeeding generation inherits as a precious deposit and a sacred trust to be handed on to the next one, not unchanged but enlarged and purified, with some clear marks of its proper handiwork. Into this, for good or ill, is woven every belief of every man who has speech of his fellows. An awful privilege, and an awful responsibility, that we should help to create the world in which posterity will live.

In the two supposed cases which have been considered, it has been judged wrong to believe on insufficient evidence, or to nourish belief by suppressing doubts and avoiding investigation. The reason of this judgment is not far to seek: it is that in both these cases the belief held by one man was of great importance to other men. But forasmuch as no belief held by one man, however seemingly trivial the belief, and however obscure the believer, is ever actually insignificant or without its effect on the fate of mankind, we have no choice but to extend our judgment to all cases of belief whatever. Belief, that sacred faculty which prompts the decisions of our will, and knits into harmonious working all the compacted energies of our being, is ours not for ourselves, but for humanity. It is rightly used on truths which have been established by long experience and waiting toil, and which have stood in the fierce light of free and fearless questioning. Then it helps to bind men together, and to strengthen and direct their common action. It is desecrated when given to unproved and unquestioned statements, for the solace and private pleasure of the believer; to add a tinsel splendour to the plain straight road of our life and display a bright mirage beyond it; or even to drown the common sorrows of our kind by a self-deception which allows them not only to cast down, but also to degrade us. Whoso would deserve well of his fellows in this matter will guard the purity of his belief with a very fanaticism of jealous care, lest at any time it should rest on an unworthy object, and catch a stain which can never be wiped away.

It is not only the leaders of men, statesman, philosopher, or poet, that owes this bounden duty to mankind. Every rustic who delivers in the alehouse his slow, infrequent sentences, may help to kill or keep alive the fatal superstitions which clog his race. Every hard-worked wife of an artisan may transmit to her children beliefs which shall knit society together, or rend it in pieces. No simplicity of mind, no obscurity of station, can escape the universal duty of questioning all that we believe.

It is true that this duty is a hard one, and the doubt which comes out of it is often a very bitter thing. It leaves us bare and powerless where we thought that we were safe and strong. To know all about anything is to know how to deal with it under all circumstances. We feel much happier and more secure when we think we know precisely what to do, no matter what happens, than when we have lost our way and do not know where to turn. And if we have supposed ourselves to know all about anything, and to be capable of doing what is fit in regard to it, we naturally do not like to find that we are really ignorant and powerless, that we have to begin again at the beginning and try to learn what the thing is and how it is to be dealt with—if indeed anything can be learnt about it. It is the sense of power attached to a sense of knowledge that makes men desirous of believing, and afraid of doubting.

This sense of power is the highest and best of pleasures when the belief on which it is founded is a true belief, and has been fairly earned by investigation. For then we may justly feel that it is common property, and holds good for others as well as for ourselves. Then we may be glad, not that *I* have learned secrets by which I am safer and stronger, but that *we men* have got mastery over more of the world; and we shall be strong, not for ourselves, but in the name of Man and in his strength. But if the belief has been accepted on insufficient evidence, the pleasure is a stolen one. Not only does it deceive ourselves by giving us a sense of power which we do not really possess, but it is sinful, because it is stolen in defiance of our duty to mankind. That duty is to guard ourselves from such beliefs as from a pestilence, which may shortly master our own body and then spread to the rest of the town. What would be thought of one who, for the sake of a sweet fruit, should deliberately run the risk of bringing a plague upon his family and his neighbors?

And, as in other such cases, it is not the risk only which has to be considered; for a bad action is always bad at the time when it is done, no matter what happens afterwards. Every time we let ourselves believe for unworthy reasons, we weaken our powers of self-control, of doubting, of judicially and fairly weighing evidence. We all suffer severely enough from the maintenance and support of false beliefs and the fatally wrong actions which they lead to, and the evil born when one such belief is entertained is great and wide. But a greater and wider evil arises when the credulous character is maintained and supported, when a habit of believing for unworthy reasons is fostered and made permanent. If I steal money from any person, there may be no harm done by the mere transfer of possession; he may not feel the loss, or it may prevent him from using the money badly. But I cannot help doing this great wrong towards Man, that I make myself dishonest. What hurts society is not that it should lose its property, but that it should become a den of thieves; for then it must cease to be society. This is why we ought not to do evil that good may come; for at any rate this great evil has come, that we have done evil and are made wicked thereby. In like manner, if I let myself believe anything on insufficient evidence, there may be no great harm done by the mere belief; it may be true after all, or I may never have occasion to exhibit it in outward acts. But I cannot help doing this great wrong towards Man, that I make myself credulous. The danger to society is not merely that it should believe wrong things, though that is great enough; but that it should become credulous, and lose the habit of testing things and inquiring into them; for then it must sink back into savagery.

The harm which is done by credulity in a man is not confined to the fostering of a credulous character in others, and consequent support of false beliefs. Habitual want of care about what I believe leads to habitual want of care in others about the truth of what is told to me. Men speak the truth to one another when each reveres the truth in his own mind and in the other's mind; but how shall my friend revere the truth in my mind when I myself am careless about it, when I believe things because I want to believe them, and because they are comforting and pleasant? Will he not learn to cry, "Peace," to me, when there is no peace? By such a course I shall surround myself with a thick atmosphere of falsehood and fraud, and in that I must live. It may matter little to me, in my cloud-castle of sweet illusions and darling lies; but it matters much to Man that I have made my neighbours ready to deceive. The credulous man is father to the liar and the cheat; he lives in the bosom of this his family, and it is no marvel if he should become even as they are. So closely are our duties knit together, that whoso shall keep the whole law, and yet offend at one point, he is guilty of all.

To sum up: it is wrong always, everywhere, and for any one, to believe anything upon insufficient evidence.

If a man, holding a belief which he was taught in childhood or persuaded of afterwards, keeps down and pushes away any doubts which arise about it in his mind, purposely avoids the reading of books and the company of men that call in question or discuss it, and regards as impious those questions which cannot easily be asked without disturbing it—the life of that man is one long sin against mankind.

If this judgment seems harsh when applied to those simple souls who have never known better, who have been brought up from the cradle with a horror of doubt, and taught that their eternal welfare depends on *what* they believe, then it leads to the very serious question, *Who hath made Israel to sin?*

It may be permitted me to fortify this judgment with the sentence of Milton[1]—

"A man may be a heretic in the truth; and if he believes things only because his pastor says so, or the assembly so determine, without knowing other reason, though his belief be true, yet the very truth he holds becomes his heresy."

And with this famous aphorism of Coleridge[2]—

"He who begins by loving Christianity better than Truth, will proceed by loving his own sect or Church better than Christianity, and end in loving himself better than all."

Inquiry into the evidence of a doctrine is not to be made once for all, and then taken as finally settled. It is never lawful to stifle a doubt; for either it can be honestly answered by means of the inquiry already made, or else it proves that the inquiry was not complete.

"But," says one, "I am a busy man; I have no time for the long course of study which would be necessary to make me in any degree a competent judge of certain questions, or even able to understand the nature of the arguments." Then he should have no time to believe.

---

[1] *Areopagitica.*

[2] *Aids to Reflection.*

III.F.3.   The Will to Believe

WILLIAM JAMES

*The American psychologist and philosopher William James
(1842–1910), along with Charles Saunders Peirce and John
Dewey, formulated pragmatism, a school of thought that has
been called the characteristically American philosophy.
Peirce, the acknowledged originator of pragmatism, was of a
mathematical bent and was devoted to logic. John Dewey's
version, called instrumentalism, concerned itself particularly
with education. James was the popularizer of pragmatism,
writing not primarily for other philosophers but for ordinary
men and women interested in finding a philosophy that could
guide their lives and give depth and meaning to their existence. Thus his doctrines are not expressed in technical language; neither are they as carefully formulated as the teachings of many other philosophers.*

*In his celebrated work on the will to believe, reproduced
in abridged form here, James argues that it is permissible to
adopt religious faith by an act of the will when belief is not
coerced one way or the other by decisive evidence or rational
proofs. He cites Pascal's wager along with Clifford's scruples,
concedes that Clifford's case sounds strong, but is led to
conclude that the latter is overly fastidious in his resolute
determination never to believe anything for which we do not
have sufficient evidence. Which is more important, James
challenges us to ask ourselves, the possibility that we will
believe something that is not true or the danger that we will
miss out on important truth by overscrupulous fear of error?
He counsels us to take a somewhat more light-hearted attitude toward potential error, recognizing that despite our best
efforts we will in any case inevitably believe many things that
will turn out not to be true.*

*Some of James's critics have suggested that his theory
authorizes our believing anything at all that makes us happy,
but these critics seem not to have read him carefully enough.
Where the evidence is decisive, or even where it is just slightly
stronger on one side than the other, we must follow the
evidence. We are not free to decide what to believe when there
is any preponderance of evidence to guide us. In the case of
what James calls* genuine *options—that is, those that are*

From *The Will to Believe and Other Essays* (New York: Longmans, Green & Co., 1897), pp. 2–4,
8–14, 17–20, 25.

*living, forced, and momentous—and when the evidence
for and against such beliefs is so evenly balanced that we
cannot decide on the basis of the evidence, we are entitled to
choose the belief that most contributes to our well-being.*

Let us give the name of *hypothesis* to anything that
may be proposed to our belief; and just as the electricians speak of live and
dead wires, let us speak of any hypothesis as either *live* or *dead*. A live hypothesis is one which appeals as a real possibility to him to whom it is proposed. If I
ask you to believe in the Mahdi, the notion makes no electric connection with
your nature—it refuses to scintillate with any credibility at all. As an hypothesis it is completely dead. To an Arab, however (even if he be not one of the
Mahdi's followers), the hypothesis is among the mind's possibilities: it is alive.
This shows that deadness and liveness in an hypothesis are not intrinsic
properties, but relations to the individual thinker. They are measured by his
willingness to act. The maximum of liveness in an hypothesis means willingness to act irrevocably. Practically, that means belief; but there is some believing tendency wherever there is willingness to act at all.

Next, let us call the decision between two hypotheses an *option*. Options
may be of several kinds. They may be—1, *living* or *dead*; 2, *forced* or *avoidable*; 3,
momentous or *trivial*; and for our purposes we may call an option a *genuine*
option when it is of the forced, living and momentous kind.

1. A living option is one in which both hypotheses are live ones. If I say to
you: "Be a theosophist or be a mahomedan," it is probably a dead option,
because for you neither hypothesis is likely to be alive. But if I say "Be an
agnostic or be a Christian," it is otherwise: trained as you are, each hypothesis
makes some appeal, however small, to your belief.

2. Next, if I say to you: "Choose between going out with your umbrella or
without it," I do not offer you a genuine option, for it is not forced. You can
easily avoid it by not going out at all. Similarly, if I say "Either love me or hate
me," "Either call my theory true or call it false," your option is avoidable. You
may remain indifferent to me, neither loving nor hating, and you may decline
to offer any judgment as to my theory. But if I say "Either accept this truth or go
without it," I put on you a forced option, for there is no standing place outside
of the alternative. Every dilemma based on a complete logical disjunction,
with no possibility of not choosing, is an option of this forced kind.

3. Finally, if I were Dr. Nansen and proposed to you to join my North Pole
expedition, your option would be momentous; for this would probably be
your only similar opportunity, and your choice now would either exclude you
from the North Pole sort of immortality altogether or put at least the chance of
it into your hands. He who refuses to embrace a unique opportunity loses the
prize as surely as if he tried and failed. . . .

Clifford writes: "Belief is desecrated when given to unproved and unquestioned statements, for the solace and private pleasure of the believer. . . .
Whoso would deserve well of his fellows in this matter will guard the purity of
his belief with a very fanaticism of jealous care, lest at any time it should rest
on an unworthy object, and catch a stain which can never be wiped away. . . .
If [a] belief has been accepted on insufficient evidence [even though the belief

be true, as Clifford on the same page explains], the pleasure is a stolen one. . . . It is sinful, because it is stolen in defiance of our duty to mankind. That duty is to guard ourselves from such beliefs as from a pestilence, which may shortly master our own body and then spread to the rest of the town. . . . It is wrong always, everywhere, and for anyone, to believe anything upon insufficient evidence."

III

All this strikes one as healthy, even when expressed, as by Clifford, with somewhat too much of robustious pathos in the voice. Free-will and simple wishing do seem, in the matter of our credences, to be only fifth wheels to the coach. Yet if anyone should thereupon assume that intellectual insight is what remains after wish and will and sentimental preference have taken wing, or that pure reason is what then settles our opinions, he would fly quite as directly in the teeth of the facts.

It is only our already dead hypotheses that our willing nature is unable to bring to life again. But what has made them dead for us is for the most part a previous action of our willing nature of an antagonistic kind. When I say "willing nature," I do not mean only such deliberate volitions as may have set up habits of belief that we cannot now escape from—I mean all such factors of belief as fear and hope, prejudice and passion, imitation and partisanship, the circumpressure of our caste and set. As a matter of fact we find ourselves believing, we hardly know how or why. Mr. Balfour gives the name of "authority" to all those influences, born of the intellectual climate, that make hypotheses possible or impossible for us, alive or dead. Here in this room, we all of us believe in molecules and the conservation of energy, in democracy and necessary progress, in Protestant Christianity and the duty of fighting for "the doctrine of the immortal Monroe," all for no reasons worthy of the name. We see into these matters with no more inner clearness, and probably with much less, than any disbeliever in them might possess. His unconventionality would probably have some grounds to show for its conclusions: but for us, not insight, but the *prestige* of the opinions, is what makes the spark shoot from them and light up our sleeping magazines of faith. Our reason is quite satisfied, in nine hundred and ninety-nine cases out of every thousand of us, if it can find a few arguments that will do to recite in case our credulity is criticized by someone else. Our faith is faith in someone else's faith, and in the greatest matters this is most the case. Our belief in truth itself, for instance, that there is a truth, and that our minds and it are made for each other—what is it but a passionate affirmation of desire, in which our social system backs us up? We want to have a truth; we want to believe that our experiments and studies and discussions must put us in a continually better and better position towards it; and on this line we agree to fight out our thinking lives. But if a pyrrhonistic sceptic asks us *how we know* all this, can our logic find a reply? No! Certainly it cannot. It is just one volition against another—we willing to go in for life upon a trust or assumption which he, for his part, does not care to make.[1]

---

[1] Compare the admirable page 310 in S. H. Hodgson's *Time and Space*, London, 1865.

As a rule we disbelieve all facts and theories for which we have no use. Clifford's cosmic emotions find no use for Christian feelings. Huxley belabors the bishops because there is no use for sacerdotalism in his scheme of life. Newman, on the contrary, goes over to Romanism, and finds all sorts of reasons good for staying there, because a priestly system is for him an organic need and delight. Why do so few "scientists" even look at the evidence for telepathy, so called? Because they think, as a leading biologist, now dead, once said to me, that even if such a thing were true, scientists ought to band together to keep it suppressed and concealed. It would undo the uniformity of Nature and all sorts of other things without which scientists cannot carry on their pursuits. But if this very man had been shown something which as a scientist he might *do* with telepathy, he might not only have examined the evidence, but even have found it good enough. This very law which the logicians would impose upon us—if I may give the name of logicians to those who would rule out our willing nature here—is based on nothing but their own natural wish to exclude all elements for which they, in their professional quality of logicians, can find no use.

Evidently, then, our non-intellectual nature does influence our convictions. There are passional tendencies and volitions which run before and others which come after belief, and it is only the latter that are too late for the fair, and they are not too late when the previous passional work has been already in their own direction. Pascal's argument, instead of being powerless, then seems a regular clincher, and is the last stroke needed to make our faith in masses and holy water complete. The state of things is evidently far from simple; and pure insight and logic, whatever they might do ideally, are not the only things that really do produce our creeds.

IV

Our next duty, having recognized this mixed-up state of affairs, is to ask whether it be simply reprehensible and pathological, or whether, on the contrary, we must treat it as a normal element in making up our minds. The thesis I defend is, briefly stated, this: *Our passional nature not only lawfully may, but must, decide an option between propositions, whenever it is a genuine option that cannot by its nature be decided on intellectual grounds; for to say, under such circumstances, "Do not decide, but leave the question open," is itself a passional decision—just like deciding yes or no—and is attended with the same risk of losing the truth.* The thesis thus abstractly expressed will, I trust, soon become quite clear. . . .

Objective evidence and certitude are doubtless very fine ideals to play with, but where on this moonlit and dream-visited planet are they found? I am, therefore, myself a complete empiricist so far as my theory of human knowledge goes. I live, to be sure, by the practical faith that we must go on experiencing and thinking over our experience, for only thus can our opinions grow more true; but to hold any one of them—I absolutely do not care which—as if it never could be re-interpretable or corrigible, I believe to be a tremendously mistaken attitude, and I think that the whole history of philosophy will bear me out. There is but one indefectibly certain truth, and that is the truth that pyrrhonistic scepticism itself leaves standing—the truth that the present phenomenon of consciousness exists. That, however, is the bare starting-point of knowledge, the mere admission of a stuff to be philosophized-about. The various philosophies are but so many attempts at expressing what this stuff really is.

One more point, small but important, and our preliminaries are done. There are two ways of looking at our duty in the matter of opinion—ways entirely different, and yet ways about whose difference the theory of knowledge seems hitherto to have shown very little concern. *We must know the truth*; and *we must avoid error*—these are our first and great commandments as would-be knowers; but they are not two ways of stating an identical commandment, they are two separable laws. Although it may indeed happen that when we believe the truth *A*, we escape as an incidental consequence from believing the falsehood *B*, it hardly ever happens that by merely disbelieving *B* we necessarily believe *A*. We may in escaping *B* fall into believing other falsehoods, *C* or *D*, just as bad as *B*; or we may escape *B* by not believing anything at all, not even *A*.

Believe truth! Shun error!—these, we see, are two materially different laws; and by choosing between them we may end by colouring differently our whole intellectual life. We may regard the chase for truth as paramount, and the avoidance of error as secondary; or we may, on the other hand, treat the avoidance of error as more imperative, and let truth take its chance. Clifford, in the instructive passage which I have quoted, exhorts us to the latter course. Believe nothing, he tells us, keep your mind in suspense forever, rather than by closing it on insufficient evidence incur the awful risk of believing lies. You, on the other hand, may think that the risk of being in error is a very small matter when compared with the blessings of real knowledge, and be ready to be duped many times in your investigation rather than postpone indefinitely the chance of guessing true. I myself find it impossible to go with Clifford. We must remember that these feelings of our duty about either truth or error are in any case only expressions of our passional life. Biologically considered, our minds are as ready to grind out falsehoods as veracity, and he who says "Better go without belief forever than believe a lie!" merely shows his own preponderant private horror of becoming a dupe. He may be critical of many of his desires and fears, but this fear he slavishly obeys. He cannot imagine anyone questioning its binding force. For my own part, I have also a horror of being duped; but I can believe that worse things than being duped may happen to a man in this world; so Clifford's exhortation has to my ears a thoroughly fantastic sound. It is like a general informing his soldiers that it is better to keep out of battle forever than to risk a single wound. Not so are victories either over enemies or over nature gained. Our errors are surely not such awfully solemn things. In a world where we are so certain to incur them in spite of all our caution, a certain lightness of heart seems healthier than this excessive nervousness on their behalf. At any rate, it seems the fittest thing for the empiricist philosopher.

VIII

And now, after all this introduction, let us go straight at our question. I have said, and now repeat it, that not only as a matter of fact do we find our passional nation influencing us in our opinions, but that there are some options between opinions in which this influence must be regarded both as an inevitable and as a lawful determinant of our choice.

I fear here that some of you my hearers will begin to scent danger, and lend an inhospitable ear. Two first steps of passion you have indeed had to admit as necessary—we must think so as to avoid dupery, and we must think so as to gain truth; but the surest path to those ideal consummations, you will probably consider, is from now onwards to take no farther passional step.

Well, of course I agree as far as the facts will allow. Wherever the option between losing truth and gaining it is not momentous, we can throw the chance of *gaining truth* away, and at any rate save ourselves from any chance of *believing falsehood*, by not making up our minds at all till objective evidence has come. In scientific questions, this is almost always the case; and even in human affairs in general, the need of acting is seldom so urgent that a false belief to act on is better than no belief at all. Law courts, indeed, have to decide on the best evidence attainable for the moment, because a judge's duty is to make law as well as to ascertain it, and (as a learned judge once said to me) few cases are worth spending much time over: the great thing is to have them decided on *any* acceptable principle, and got out of the way. But in our dealings with objective nature we obviously are recorders, not makers, of the truth; and decisions for the mere sake of deciding promptly and getting on to the next business would be wholly out of place. Throughout the breadth of physical nature facts are what they are quite independently of us, and seldom is there any such hurry about them that the risks of being duped by believing a premature theory need be faced. The questions here are always trivial options, the hypotheses are hardly living (at any rate not living for us spectators), the choice between believing truth or falsehood is seldom forced. The attitude of sceptical balance is therefore the absolutely wise one if we would escape mistakes. What difference, indeed, does it make to most of us whether we have or have not a theory of the Röntgen rays, whether we believe or not in mind-stuff, or have a conviction about the causality of conscious states? It makes no difference. Such options are not forced on us. On every account it is better not to make them, but still keep weighing reasons *pro et contra* with an indifferent hand. . . .

But now, it will be said, these are all childish human cases, and have nothing to do with great cosmical matters, like the question of religious faith. Let us then pass on to that. Religions differ so much in their accidents that in discussing the religious question we must make it very generic and broad. What then do we now mean by the religious hypothesis? Science says things are; morality says some things are better than other things; and religion says essentially two things.

First, she says that the best things are the more eternal things, the overlapping things, the things in the universe that throw the last stone, so to speak, and say the final word. "Perfection is eternal"—this phrase of Charles Secrétan seems a good way of putting this first affirmation of religion, an affirmation which obviously cannot yet be verified scientifically at all.

The second affirmation of religion is that we are better off even now if we believe her first affirmation to be true.

Now let us consider what the logical elements of this situation are *in case the religious hypothesis in both its branches be really true.* (Of course, we must admit that possibility at the outset. If we are to discuss the question at all, it must involve a living option. If for any of you religion be a hypothesis that cannot, by any living possibility be true, then you need go no farther. I speak to the "saving remnant" alone.) So proceeding, we see, first, that religion offers itself as a *momentous* option. We are supposed to gain, even now, by our belief, and to lose by our non-belief, a certain vital good. Secondly, religion is a *forced* option, so far as that good goes. We cannot escape the issue by remaining sceptical and waiting for more light, because, although we do avoid error in that way *if religion be untrue*, we lose the good, *if it be true*, just as certainly as if we positively chose to disbelieve. It is as if a man should hesitate indefinitely to ask a certain woman to marry him because he was not perfectly sure that she would prove an angel after he brought her home. Would he not cut himself off from that particular angel-possibility as decisively as if he went and married someone else? Scepticism, then, is not avoidance of option; it is option of a certain particular kind of risk. *Better risk loss of truth than chance of error*—that is your faith-vetoer's exact position. He is actively playing his stake as much as the believer is; he is backing the field against the religious hypothesis, just as the believer is backing the religious hypothesis against the field. To preach scepticism to us as a duty until "sufficient evidence" for religion be found, is tantamount therefore to telling us, when in presence of the religious hypothesis, that to yield to our fear of its being error is wiser and better than to yield to our hope that it may be true. It is not intellect against all passions, then; it is only intellect with one passion laying down its law. And by what, forsooth, is the supreme wisdom of this passion warranted? Dupery for dupery, what proof is there that dupery through hope is so much worse than dupery through fear? I, for one, can see no proof; and I simply refuse obedience to the scientist's command to imitate his kind of option, in a case where my own stake is important enough to give me the right to choose my own form of risk. If religion be true and the evidence for it be still insufficient, I do not wish, by putting your extinguisher upon my nature (which feels to me as if it had after all some business in this matter), to forfeit my sole chance in life of getting upon the winning side—that chance depending, of course, on my willingness to run the risk of acting as if my passional need of taking the world religiously might be prophetic and right.

All this is on the supposition that it really may be prophetic and right, and that, even to us who are discussing the matter, religion is a live hypothesis which may be true. Now to most of us religion comes in a still farther way that makes a veto on our active faith even more illogical. The more perfect and more eternal aspect of the universe is represented in our religions as having personal form. The universe is no longer a mere *It* to us, but a *Thou*, if we are religious; and any relation that may be possible from person to person might be possible here. For instance, although in one sense we are passive portions of the universe, in another we show a curious autonomy, as if we were small active centres on our own account. We feel, too, as if the appeal of religion to us were made to our own active good-will, as if evidence might be forever withheld from us unless we met the hypothesis half-way. To take a trivial illustration: just as a man who in a company of gentlemen made no advances, asked a warrant for every concession, and believed no one's word without proof, would cut himself off by such churlishness from all social rewards that a more trusting spirit would earn—so here, one who should shut himself up in snarling logicality and try to make the gods extort his recognition willy-nilly, or not get it at all, might cut himself off forever from his only opportunity of making the gods' acquaintance. This feeling, forced on us we know not whence, that by obstinately believing that there are gods (although not to do so would be so easy both for our logic and our life) we are doing the universe the deepest service we can, seems part of the living essence of the religious hypothesis. If the hypothesis *were* true in all its parts, including this one, then pure intellectualism, with its veto on our making willing advances, would be an absurdity; and some participation of our sympathetic nature would be logically required. I, therefore, for one, cannot see my way to accepting the agnostic rules for truth-seeking, or wilfully agree to keep my willing nature out of the game. I cannot do so for this plain reason, that *a rule of thinking which would absolutely prevent me from acknowledging certain kinds of truth if those kinds of truth were really there, would be an irrational rule.* That for me is the long and short of the formal logic of the situation, no matter what the kinds of truth might materially be.

I confess I do not see how this logic can be escaped. But sad experience makes me fear that some of you may still shrink from radically saying with me, *in abstracto*, that we have the right to believe at our own risk any hypothesis that is live enough to tempt our will. I suspect, however, that if this is so, it is because you have got away from the abstract logical point of view altogether, and are thinking (perhaps without realizing it) of some particular religious hypothesis which for you is dead. The freedom to "believe what we will" you apply to the case of some patent superstition; and the faith you think of is the faith defined by the schoolboy when he said, "Faith is when you believe something that you know ain't true." I can only repeat that this is a misapprehension. *In concreto*, the freedom to believe can only cover living options which the intellect of the individual cannot by itself resolve; and living options never seem absurdities to him who has them to consider. When I look at the religious question as it really puts itself to concrete men, and when I think of all the possibilities which both practically and theoretically it involves, then this command that we shall put a stopper on our heart, instincts and courage, and *wait*—acting of course meanwhile more or less as if religion were *not* true[2]—till doomsday, or till such time as our intellect and senses working together may have raked in evidence enough—this command, I say, seems to me the queerest idol ever manufactured in the philosophic cave. Were we scholastic

---

' Since belief is measured by action, he who forbids us to believe religion to be true, necessarily also forbids us to act as we should if we did believe it to be true. The whole defence of religious faith hinges upon action. If the action required or inspired by the religious hypothesis is in no way different from that dictated by the naturalistic hypothesis, then religious faith is a pure superfluity, better pruned away, and controversy about its legitimacy is a piece of idle trifling, unworthy of serious minds. I myself believe, of course, that the religious hypothesis gives to the world an expression which specifically determines our reactions, and makes them in a large part unlike what they might be on a purely naturalistic scheme of belief.

absolutists, there might be more excuse. If we had an infallible intellect with its objective certitudes, we might feel ourselves disloyal to such a perfect organ of knowledge in not trusting to it exclusively, in not waiting for its releasing word. But if we are empiricists, if we believe that no bell in us tolls to let us know for certain when truth is in our grasp, then it seems a piece of idle fantasticality to preach so solemnly our duty of waiting for the bell. Indeed we *may* wait if we will—I hope you do not think that I am denying that—but if we do so, we do so at our peril as much as if we believed. In either case we *act*, taking our life in our hands. No one of us ought to issue vetoes to the other, nor should we bandy words of abuse. We ought, on the contrary, delicately and profoundly to respect one another's mental freedom—then only shall we bring about the intellectual republic; then only shall we have that spirit of inner tolerance without which all our outer tolerance is soulless, and which is empiricism's glory; then only shall we live and let live, in speculative as well as in practical things.

I began by a reference to Fitzjames Stephen; let me end by a quotation from him. "What do you think of yourself? What do you think of the world? . . . These are questions with which all must deal as it seems good to them. They are riddles of the Sphinx, and in some way or other we must deal with them. . . . In all important transactions of life we have to take a leap in the dark. . . . If we decide to leave the riddles unanswered, that is a choice. If we waver in our answer, that too is a choice; but whatever choice we make, we make it at our peril. If a man chooses to turn his back altogether on God and the future, no one can prevent him. No one can show beyond a reasonable doubt that he is mistaken. If a man thinks otherwise, and acts as he thinks, I do not see how any one can prove that *he* is mistaken. Each must act as he thinks best, and if he is wrong so much the worse for him. We stand on a mountain pass in the midst of whirling snow and blinding mist, through which we get glimpses now and then of paths which may be deceptive. If we stand still, we shall be frozen to death. If we take the wrong road, we shall be dashed to pieces. We do not certainly know whether there is any right one. What must we do? 'Be strong and of a good courage.' Act for the best, hope for the best, and take what comes. . . . If death ends all, we cannot meet death better."[3]

---

[3] *Liberty, Equality, Fraternity,* p. 353, 2d edition. London, 1874.

Part IV

Objections to Theism

Those thinkers who have attempted to establish the existence of God by means of rational arguments have always had to face a cluster of counterarguments designed to undermine theism. Some of these counterarguments have been directed against the theistic arguments themselves. Several selections in Part III represent arguments of this kind, designed to weaken the traditional theistic proofs. Part IV includes several kinds of arguments that attack theism more directly.

It is generally agreed that the problem of evil constitutes the most threatening of the major antitheistic arguments. This is a problem that has troubled Western thinkers for more than two thousand years. Epicurus (341–270 B.C.E.) offered a formulation of the problem as early as the fourth century before the Common Era. During the early centuries of the Common Era, as Christianity worked out the details of its doctrine of creation, which depicted the world as created by a God who is all powerful and wholly good, the presence of evil in such a world became an increasingly urgent problem. Attempts were made again and again to work our arguments designed to show that God's goodness is not undermined by the existence of evil in the world. Milton characterized this enterprise as the task of "justifying the ways of God to men," and the arguments themselves are called *theodicies*.

The problem of evil can be stated in clear outline by means of four propositions, alleged to be mutually incompatible. This is the so-called inconsistent tretrad:

1. God is omnipotent.
2. God is omniscient.
3. God is omnibenevolent.
4. There is evil in the world.

The implication of proposition 1 seems to be that God should be able to prevent evil if he knows about it and wants to prevent it. The implication of proposition 2 is that God knows about evil. Proposition 3 implies that God would want to prevent evil if he could. But proposition 4 asserts that evil really does exist. All four propositions, taken singly, are highly plausible, and there are reasons that many thinkers would want to affirm all four. Taken together, however, they seem to imply a contradiction.

Another way of stating the problem is to point out that any three of the propositions can be shown to be mutually consistent but that any combination of three seems to imply the falsity of the remaining proposition. If we give up the first proposition the remaining three are consistent; if we give up the second, the others are consistent; and so on for all combinations. It seems to be impossible, however, to affirm all four without committing oneself to a contradiction. Those who use the problem of evil for advancing antitheistic arguments insist that the only real way to solve the problem is to recognize that at least one proposition must be false and to determine which one or ones that is.

Some thinkers, attempting this kind of solution, assert that proposition 4 is false. This is the position taken by certain monistic metaphysical systems. An example is the Advaita Vedanta doctrine, which calls the entire realm of material things *maya*, illusion. Such a view seems to make it possible to dismiss evil as a mere misunderstanding of the real nature of things. Everything real is good; our belief that there is real evil in the world results from *avidya*, ignorance. Advatia Vedanta teaches that the human soul or *atman* is identical with the World Soul, Brahman. Our salvation lies, not in getting rid of evil, which after all does not really exist, but in getting rid of ignorance by coming to understand the oneness of all reality and in particular that atman is Brahman.

In the West, such Christian thinkers as Augustine (354–430), though not embracing monism, asserted the ultimate unreality of evil. Augustine, using the metaphor of light and darkness, maintained that evil, like darkness, is nothing real but is merely absence of good, just as darkness is absence of light. In the modern era, Christian Science made an attempt to take the same path to a solution. Mary Baker Eddy, the founder of Christian Science, argued that evil and particularly disease is not ultimately real but simply a mistake, a misunderstanding of the fact that everything that exists is good.

But the attempt to deny or argue away all evil has not convinced most people. Even if the material world with its attendant evil and suffering is an illusion, even if ultimate reality is wholly good, the experiences of human beings, caught in the web of this illusion, are certainly not wholly good. In fact, evil looms so large in the world, so thoroughly pervades every department of human life, so firmly resists our efforts to control or remove it, and so ominously threatens the ultimate and final destruction of all values in the universe that the attempt to rationalize it away or call it unreal appears both false and callous. Suffering is pervasive; even the most fortunate escape it only during part of their lives. Death is all consuming, finally depriving every living thing of every good sought or cherished. Disease, war, famine, ignorance, cruelty, hatred lurk at every crossing, rampage through every place and path. Not even a cultivated optimism can blind us to the ever-present ills that all living things are heir to; nor the most persistent averting of the eye hide the blood and the tears shed around us everywhere. The fourth of the propositions cannot really be denied with any plausibility. Evil is real. Every sentient thing suffers. If the problem of evil is to be solved, the solution must be sought elsewhere than attempting to deny its reality.

Another example of trying to solve the problem of evil by giving up one of the four propositions may be found in the thought of those few philosophers and theologians in the West who concede that God is not omnipotent. If God is conceived as a being of great but limited power, then evil can be attributed to the limitations of God's power. Plato's (fifth century B.C.E.) account of creation depicts a god or demigod who did not create the substance of which the world is made, did not even create the patterns according to which individual things are made, but only imposed the preexisting forms on preexisting substance. In a world created by such a deity, imperfections can be attributed to the limitations in the nature of the substance with which the god had to work. John Stuart Mill (1806–1873) also depicts a creator of limited power in Selection II. F. 1, and Edgar S. Brightman (1919–1953), an advocate of the philosophy of personal idealism or personalism, attempts to deal with the problem of evil through a conception of what he calls a "finitely infinite" God.

Theism has not usually been willing to make such concessions. Thus, the major efforts to deal with the problem of evil have been attempts to show that the four propositions are after all not incompatible. Thinkers who have offered theodocies of this sort have usually distinguished two major kinds of evil: natural and moral. Moral evil is the evil that results from human actions—whether ignorant folly or wickedness. Natural evil includes such events as droughts, floods, famine, earthquakes, disease, and other natural calamities whose occurrence cannot be attributed to human acts.

Occasionally a theologian attempts to reduce all evil to moral evil, thus apparently shifting all blame away from God and onto humans. And it is true that the severity of the impact of many calamities on humans is often caused at least in part by human foolishness or perverseness. Floods are aggravated by deforestation; droughts by unwise water management; famines by foolish farming practices or perverse systems of economic distribution. War, perhaps the greatest single curse on human life, is surely to be blamed on human greed, prejudice, stubbornness, or hatred. Yet even when every disaster that can possibly be construed as humanly caused has been counted, a great many seem to be left over for which humans cannot really be blamed. Furthermore, many have argued that an omnipotent deity who created humans ought to be able to control them and is responsible if he does not prevent them from wreaking such havoc. Some have argued that an all-powerful God should have made humans in such a manner that they always do what is good.

The most popular theodocies have not denied the existence of evil, or accepted the notion of a limited deity, or tried to reduce all evil to moral evil. Rather, they have attempted to show how it is possible for an omnipotent, omniscient, loving God to be justified in allowing the existence of some evil. Some have argued that an orderly created world where invariable physical laws operate is a necessary condition for human knowledge and morality and that the existence of such invariable laws makes the occurrence of some evil likely or even inevitable. Others have suggested that evil makes greater goods possible or enhances our enjoyment of goods. The free will defense has maintained that the existence of free human agents is such a great value that it is worth the risk that some of these agents will make unwise choices and cause evil. When all the many and varied arguments are assessed, some thinkers believe that these arguments have turned back the force of the problem of evil. Others insist that the problem stands, after every attempt to answer it, as the death knell of theism.

Other objections to theism have been raised from different quarters and on very different grounds. One is the claim that our conception of God is a human fabrication, created unconsciously in an effort to make the world seem a safer place or to provide ourselves with a Great Protector against whom all the forces of evil would be powerless and ultimately unsuccessful. This position is also quite old in Western civilization, dating back at least to the sixth century before the Common Era, when Xenophanes (c. 570– 500 B.C.E.) suggested, by the following saying, that the gods are human fabrications made in our own image: "The Ethiopians make their gods black and stub-nosed; the Tracians say theirs have blue eyes and red hair."

The general charge of anthropomorphism—that humans give their gods their own human traits and characteristics—has been raised and pressed again and again through the centuries as evidence that the gods are simply imaginary inventions of human need and desire. In the twentieth century this position has been argued by the originator of psychoanalysis, Sigmund Freud (1856–1939), who regards theism as an attempt by insecure humans to provide for themselves a powerful father figure. Freud also calls religion a mass delusion shared by most individuals in a given society. Karl Marx (1818–1883) also offers a psychological or sociological criticism of theism and religion in general, calling it the opium of the masses. The rulers of oppressive societies, Marx argues, use religion as an instrument of control, inducing citizens to endure exploitation by claiming the authority of religion for the rulers and by holding out the promise of a heavenly reward to those who live obedient lives in this world.

It is perhaps worth noting that the arguments of thinkers such as Freud and Marx are often put forward with more rhetorical than logical force. These psychological and sociological theories offer what might be called hypotheses to explain how religious belief might have arisen or why people might accept such beliefs. The hypotheses may strike readers as plausible, but the question that has to be asked is why anyone should believe them. The best that can be said is that these theories *might* be true. It is questionable whether the arguments presented in their support suffice to establish that such theories are more plausible than theism itself.

A third type of objection to theism comes from those who assert an incompatibility between religious doctrines and the discoveries of science. Those who take the most extreme version of this position even claim that science has succeeded in proving that religion is illusory, the result of wishful thinking, or just plain false. These arguments focus particularly on scriptural teachings, which, taken literally, seem to be contradicted by scientific findings.

In the West, the awareness of a tension between science and religious doctrines began to agitate theologians as early as the sixteenth century, when the work of astronomers such as Copernicus (1473–1543) and Galileo (1564–1642) gave a picture of a world that seemed to clash with Christian teachings. The Church had accepted the Ptolemaic view of the world, which placed the earth at the center, and had elaborated a theology around this theory that made humans the focus of all creation. The implications of the new astronomy, particularly as it developed in later centuries was that the earth, far from being the center of the universe, is simply one of many planets circling a sun that is an ordinary star itself, one of billions in a galaxy that in its turn is also one of a multitude. Snatched from the cozy center of creation, humans suddenly had to recognize themselves as tiny inhabitants of a vast universe that awards them no special place.

In the nineteenth century, Charles Darwin argued for a theory of evolution that pictured humans evolving from lower forms of life, a position that flatly contradicts a literal understanding of the biblical account of creation. The further progress of science turned up more and more evidence that clashed with biblical materials and Church doctrines. As every department of the universe and human life comes increasingly under scientific scrutiny and scientific understanding, the effort to hold onto a literal belief in the crude pictures of the world found in the early scriptures of the great world religions becomes increasingly indefensible.

If science really is incompatible with theism, as many people now believe, then theism seems destined to lose out, because science grows ever more plausible. But some thinkers insist that the quarrel between science and religion is based on a complete misunderstanding of what each of these human concerns really is or is supposed to be. Science is concerned with a description of the regularities that can be detected in the phenomena of the material world. Theism, it is suggested, focuses on the value dimensions of human experience. As long as the two remain in their proper domains, they do not impinge competitively on each other. The alleged incompatibility relates rather to literal interpretations of ancient scriptures. When such documents were written, prevailing beliefs about the material world were certainly less well developed than scientific beliefs are today, and some of those crude beliefs about the world seeped into the sacred writings.

But, many would claim, it is the distinctively religious and not the protoscientific ingredients of the scriptures that are of central importance. If the scriptures say that rabbits chew a cud when we now know that rabbits do not chew a cud, this in no way impacts on the spiritual teachings that are the real point of the scriptures on which theism is grounded. Tillich and others insist that the truths that theism, or religion in general, attempt to convey are in any case beyond the power of language to express literally and must be expressed through symbols and myths. The scriptures understood in their true religious sense, in terms of myths, are not incompatible with science.

The progress of science is also said to have made it impossible any longer to believe in miracles. Miracles have often been regarded as important sources of evidence for the truth of religious doctrines in several religious traditions. The early Christians seem to have believed that Jesus performed miracles and that these miracles authenticated his teachings and his mission. Miracles are also attributed to Mohammed and to the Buddha, and even to various lesser holy men and women. Within the Catholic Christian tradition, the performance of miracles is one of the requirements for sainthood; thus all the saints are alleged to have performed miracles. During the nineteenth century, when deism became widespread in Europe and America, the appeal to miracles to prove the truth of the Christian faith was frequently made and the threat to the credibility of the claim that miracles even really happen was met with vigorous opposition by certain religious groups.

Miracles have usually been regarded as violations or interruptions of the laws of nature for a special purpose on certain occasions. The healing of the sick, the raising of the dead, the transformation of a few loaves and fishes into enough food to feed a great multitude are all examples of alleged miraculous violations of natural law. But the laws of nature describe the orderly regularity that has been observed to hold everywhere throughout the long history of human kind. The invariability of natural law is thus said to have the support of virtually the whole combined experience of the human race. That there should be exceptions to such order—particularly exceptions allegedly arranged by the deity on behalf of some favorite individual or tribe, and often to serve what appears to be rather trivial purposes—severely strains rational credulity. God, after all, does not miraculously heal all the sick or feed all the victims of a famine as a deed of mercy or loving kindness. Instead, the miracle is usually alleged to occur in a very local setting, to pertain to one or a small number of persons, to bear no discernible relationship to the merits of the recipient(s), and frequently to be performed as a way of displaying the prowess of the human miracle worker.

Those who attempt to support theism, or the doctrines of their own particular religious tradition, on the basis of miracle claims frequently argue that miracles are signs provided by the deity to show that the human representative of God really does have God's favor and commands God's power. The Christian scriptures report that a witness of Jesus' deeds said to him, "Rabbi, we know that you are a teacher come from God; for no one can do these signs [the word sometimes translated as "miracle" literally means "signs"] that you do, unless God is with him" (John 3:2). But even if deeds that violate the laws of nature were not inherently improbable in the highest degree, it hardly supports an admirably conceived theistic God to argue that this God performs miracles just to show a handful of people that a particular human teacher has God's favor, when God neglects to perform miracles to prevent calamity, famine, or widespread suffering.

Thus miracle claims, so frequently cited by supporters of theism, become, in the hands of opponents of theism, a source of denigration of theism. The progress of science in increasingly bringing the processes of nature under intelligible, invariable laws makes miracle claims even more difficult to support. In the adolescence of human knowledge, when our understanding of nature was vague and forces analogous to human volition were thought to be responsible for such things as disease, drought, floods, and the like, the notion of a miracle as a particular act of the divine will to counter such a force seemed not quite so unbelievable. But our growing scientific understanding of nature as a self-regulating system of cause and effect requiring no externally injected energy or guidance makes miracle claims not just superfluous but incredible. Doctrines that appeal to miracles do not merely lose the support that the authenticity of miracles would provide; they actually accrue negative credibility. The undermining of the plausibility of miracle claims by the progress of modern science counts, in the minds of some thinkers, not just as a weakening of one of the arguments in support of theism, but actually as an objection to theism. Some theists, however, continue to make and support miracle claims, convinced that the opponents of theism have failed to show either that miracles could not or do not occur, and confident both that miracles do occur and that they constitute a valid argument for the truth of theism.

ANNOTATED GUIDE TO FURTHER READINGS

The Problem of Evil

Mackie, J.L. *The Miracle of Theism.* Oxford: Clarendon Press, 1982.
Mackie treats the problem of evil as a serious challenge to the rationality of traditional theistic claims. (The title of the book is a humorous allusion to Hume's claim that nothing short of a miracle could engender belief.)

Pike, Nelson, ed. *God and Evil.* Englewood Cliffs, N.J.: Prentice-Hall, 1964.
An excellent source for the study of the problem of evil. An excerpt from Dostoevsky's novel The Brothers Karamazov *provides a particularly*

graphic illustration of the problem of evil. Selections by Hume, Mill, Mackie, and McCloskey conclude that the existence of evil seriously compromises the theistic God; in the final two sections Pike and Smart come to the defense of God.

Plantinga, Alvin. *God, Freedom, and Evil.* Grand Rapids, Mich.: William B. Eerdmans, 1977.
A sustained, somewhat technical examination of the problem of evil. The primary vehicle of Plantinga's case is the free will defense. Plantinga goes through his argument step by step, logically progressing to his conclusion that God and evil can indeed coexist.

Pojman, Louis P. *Philosophy of Religion: An Anthology.* Belmont, Calif.: Wadsworth, 1987.
Part III explains and outlines the problem of evil and then presents selections by Hume, Hick, and Swinburne, Leibniz, Edward Madden and Peter Hare, and D. Z. Phillips.

Swinburne, Richard. *The Existence of God.* Oxford: Clarendon Press, 1979.
Swinburne attempts to surmount the problem of evil by emphasizing the importance of human free will. The possibility of moral evil, he argues, is a necessary condition of genuine human freedom; natural evil is also needed because it allows human beings to learn about evil through experience and gives them true free choice.

Other Objections to Theism

Bonansea, Bernardino M. *God and Atheism.* Washington, D. C.: The Catholic University of America Press, 1979.
Bonansea defends religion from science on the issue of creation.

Freud, Sigmund. *The Future of an Illusion.* Garden City, N.Y.: Anchor Books, 1961.
This book, from which a selection is included in this Part, deserves to be read in its entirety. Freud construes religion as a form of psychopathology, a humanly created delusion in the form of an imaginary perfect heavenly father, invented in an attempt to tame the uncontrollable aspects of the environment and make the dangerous world seem safe.

Rolston, Holmes, *Science and Religion.* New York: Random House, 1987.
A thorough study of the relation of religion to science, with an interesting format: Rolston takes sepcific examples from various natural and social sciences and examines how they relate to religion.

Trueblood, David Elton. *Philosophy of Religion.* New York: Harper and Brothers, 1957.
Part III of this text, "Challenges to Faith," includes a section on the Marxian objections to religion.

IV.A.   The Problem of Evil

IV.A.1.   The Implications of Evil

DAVID HUME

David Hume (1711–1776) offers skeptical arguments in his Dialogues Concerning Natural Religion against virtually every portion of the structure of theism. In the following selection he uses graphic descriptions of suffering to suggest that rational theology cannot reconcile evil with its image of an all-powerful and all-loving God. Hume employs the dialogue format to present several sides of each argument. Demea is the pious believer who maintains that human reason is too feeble to understand God's ways; thus he urges us to eschew rational arguments and simply to adore the wondrous mystery of God's ways. Cleanthes is the rational theologian who attempts to justify every aspect of belief with argument. Philo, who most nearly represents Hume's own position, pretends to agree with Demea but in fact through sparkling wit and sarcasm subjects every doctrine and argument to sharp skeptical criticism.

Philo seems to suggest that the problem of evil is not necessarily fatal to theism itself but only to rational theology. A faith like that advocated by Demea and (as he pretends) himself, which acknowledges that human reason is too feeble to understand divine ways, might affirm theism and claim that evil is reconciled with the goodness of God in ways beyond our understanding. He goes on to argue, however, that none of the causes of evil that we can detect seem unavoidable. Our experience of the world suggests a blind nature operated by a creator or set of principles that, though not full of malice, is perhaps indifferent to the things that we humans value.

PART X

DEMEA: It is my opinion, I own, replied *Demea*, that each man feels, in a manner, the truth of religion within his own breast, and,

From *Dialogues Concerning Natural Religion* ed. Richard H. Popkin, (Indianapolis: Hackett, 1980), pp. 58–76. With permission of Hackett Publishing Company, Inc., Indianapolis, IN and Cambridge, MA.

from a consciousness of his imbecility and misery rather than from any reasoning, is led to seek protection from that Being on whom he and all nature are dependent. So anxious or so tedious are even the best scenes of life that futurity is still the object of all our hopes and fears. We incessantly look forward and endeavor, by prayers, adoration, and sacrifice, to appease those unknown powers whom we find, by experience, so able to afflict and oppress us. Wretched creatures that we are! What resource for us amidst the innumerable ills of life did not religion suggest some methods of atonement, and appease those terrors with which we are incessantly agitated and tormented?

PHILO: I am indeed persuaded, said *Philo*, that the best and indeed the only method of bringing everyone to a due sense of religion is by just representations of the misery and wickedness of men. And for that purpose a talent of eloquence and strong imagery is more requisite than that of reasoning and argument. For is it necessary to prove what everyone feels within himself? It is only necessary to make us feel it, if possible, more intimately and sensibly.

DEMEA: The people, indeed, replied *Demea*, are sufficiently convinced of this great and melancholy truth. The miseries of life, the unhappiness of man, the general corruptions of our nature, the unsatisfactory enjoyment of pleasures, riches, honors; these phrases have become almost proverbial in all languages. And who can doubt of what all men declare from their own immediate feeling and experience?

PHILO: In this point, said *Philo*, the learned are perfectly agreed with the vulgar; and in all letters, *sacred* and *profane*, the topic of human misery has been insisted on with the most pathetic eloquence that sorrow and melancholy could inspire. The poets, who speak from sentiment, without a system, and whose testimony has therefore the more authority, abound in images of this nature. From *Homer* down to *Dr. Young*,[1] the whole inspired tribe have ever been sensible that no other representation of things would suit the feeling and observation of each individual.

DEMEA: As to authorities, replied *Demea*, you need not seek them. Look round this library of *Cleanthes*. I shall venture to affirm that, except authors of particular sciences, such as chemistry or botany, who have no occasion to treat of human life, there is scarce one of those innumerable writers from whom the sense of human misery has not, in some passage or other, extorted a complaint and confession of it. At least, the chance is entirely on that side; and no one author has ever, so far as I can recollect, been so extravagant as to deny it.

PHILO: There you must excuse me, said *Philo: Leibniz* has denied it, and is perhaps the first[2] who ventured upon so bold and paradoxical an opinion; at least, the first who made it essential to his philosophical system.

DEMEA: And by being the first, replied *Demea*, might he not have been sensible of his error? For is this a subject in which philosophers can propose to make discoveries especially in so late an age? And can any man hope by a simple

---

[1] [Hume was apparently referring to the prolific poet, Edward Young, 1683–1765.]

[2] That sentiment had been maintained by *Dr. King* and some few others before Leibniz, though by none of so great fame as that German philosopher. [Dr. William King, 1650–1729, was the archbishop of Dublin. He wrote *De Origine Mali*, The Origins of Evil, published in 1702.]

denial (for the subject scarcely admits of reasoning) to bear down the united testimony of mankind, founded on sense and consciousness?

And why should man, added he, pretend to an exemption from the lot of all other animals? The whole earth, believe me, *Philo*, is cursed and polluted. A perpetual war is kindled amongst all living creatures. Necessity, hunger, want stimulate the strong and courageous: fear, anxiety, terror agitate the weak and infirm. The first entrance into life gives anguish to the new-born infant and to its wretched parent: weakness, impotence, distress attend each stage of that life, and it is, at last, finished in agony and horror.

PHILO: Observe, too, says *Philo*, the curious artifices of nature in order to embitter the life of every living being. The stronger prey upon the weaker and keep them in perpetual terror and anxiety. The weaker, too, in their turn, often prey upon the stronger, and vex and molest them without relaxation. Consider that innumerable race of insects, which either are bred on the body of each animal or, flying about, infix their stings in him. These insects have others still less than themselves which torment them. And thus on each hand, before and behind, above and below, every animal is surrounded with enemies which incessantly seek his misery and destruction.

DEMEA: Man alone, said *Demea*, seems to be, in part, an exception to this rule. For by combination in society he can easily master lions, tigers, and bears, whose greater strength and agility naturally enable them to prey upon him.

PHILO: On the contrary, it is here chiefly, cried *Philo*, that the uniform and equal maxims of nature are most apparent. Man, it is true, can, by combination, surmount all his *real* enemies and become master of the whole animal creation. But does he not immediately raise up to himself *imaginary* enemies, the demons of his fancy, who haunt him with superstitious terrors and blast every enjoyment of life? His pleasure, as he imagines, becomes in their eyes a crime: His food and repose give them umbrage and offence; his very sleep and dreams furnish new materials to anxious fear: And even death, his refuge from every other ill, presents only the dread of endless and innumerable woes. Nor does the wolf molest more the timid flock than superstition does the anxious breast of wretched mortals.

Besides, consider, *Demea*: This very society by which we surmount those wild beasts, our natural enemies, what new enemies does it not raise to us? What woe and misery does it not occasion? Man is the greatest enemy of man. Oppression, injustice, contempt, contumely, violence, sedition, war, calumny, treachery, fraud; by these they mutually torment each other, and they would soon dissolve that society which they had formed were it not for the dread of still greater ills which must attend their separation.

DEMEA: But though these external insults, said *Demea*, from animals, from men, from all the elements, which assault us from a frightful catalogue of woes, they are nothing in comparison of those which arise within ourselves, from the distempered condition of our mind and body. How many lie under the lingering torment of disease? Hear the pathetic enumeration of the great poet

> Intestine stone and ulcer, colic-pangs,
> Demoniac frenzy, moping melancholy,
> And moon-struck madness, pining atrophy,

Marasmus, and wide-wasting pestilence.
Dire was the tossing, deep the groans: *Despair*
Tended the sick, busiest from couch to couch.
And over them triumphant *Death* his dart
Shook: but delay'd to strike, though oft invok'd
With vows, as their chief good and final hope.[3]

The disorders of the mind, continued *Demea*, though more secret, are not perhaps less dismal and vexatious. Remorse, shame, anguish, rage, disappointment, anxiety, fear, dejection, despair: who has ever passed though life without cruel inroads from these tormentors? How many have scarcely ever felt any better sensations? Labor and poverty, so abhorred by everyone, are the certain lot of the far greater number: And those few privileged persons who enjoy ease and opulence never reach contentment or true felicity. All the goods of life united would not make a very happy man: But all the ills united would make a wretch indeed; and any one of them almost (and who can be free from every one), nay, often the absence of one good (and who can possess all) is sufficient to render life ineligible.

Were a stranger to drop on a sudden into this world, I would show him, as a specimen of its ills, a hospital full of diseases, a prison crowded with malefactors and debtors, a field of battle strewed with carcases, a fleet foundering in the ocean, a nation languishing under tyranny, famine, or pestilence. To turn the gay side of life to him and give him a notion of its pleasures; whither should I conduct him? to a ball, to an opera, to court? He might justly think that I was only showing him a diversity of distress and sorrow.

PHILO: There is no evading such striking instances, said *Philo*, but by apologies which still further aggravate the charge. Why have all men, I ask, in all ages, complained incessantly of the miseries of life? . . . They have no just reason, says one: These complaints proceed only from their discontented, repining, anxious disposition. . . . And can there possibly, I reply, be a more certain foundation of misery than such a wretched temper?

But if they were really as unhappy as they pretend, says my antagonist, why do they remain in life? . . .

Not satisfied with life, afraid of death.

This is the secret chain, say I, that holds us. We are terrified, not bribed to the continuance of our existence.

It is only a false delicacy, he may insist, which a few refined spirits indulge, and which has spread these complaints among the whole race of mankind. . . . And what is this delicacy, I ask, which you blame? Is it anything but a greater sensibility to all the pleasures and pains of life? And if the man of a delicate, refined temper, by being so much more alive than the rest of the world, is only so much more unhappy, what judgment must we form in general of human life?

Let men remain at rest, says our adversary, and they will be easy. They are willing artificers of their own misery. . . . No! reply I: An anxious languor

---

[3] [Milton: *Paradise Lost*, Bk. XI.]

follows their repose; disappointment, vexation, trouble, their activity and ambition.

CLEANTHES: I can observe something like what you mention in some others, replied *Cleanthes*; but I confess I feel little or nothing of it in myself, and hope that it is not so common as you represent it.

DEMEA: If you feel not human misery yourself, cried *Demea*, I congratulate you on so happy a singularity. Others, seemingly the most prosperous, have not been ashamed to vent their complaints in the most melancholy strains. Let us attend to the great, the fortunate emperor, *Charles V*,[4] when, tired with human grandeur, he resigned all his extensive dominions into the hands of his son. In the last harangue which he made on that memorable occasion, he publicly avowed *that the greatest prosperities which he had ever enjoyed had been mixed with so many adversities that he might truly say he had never enjoyed any satisfaction or contentment.* But did the retired life in which he sought for shelter afford him any greater happiness? If we may credit his son's account, his repentance commenced the very day of his resignation.

Cicero's fortune, from small beginnings, rose to the greatest luster and renown; yet what pathetic complaints of the ills of life do his familiar letters, as well as philosophical discourses, contain? And suitably to his own experience, he introduces *Cato*, the great, the fortunate *Cato* protesting in his old age that had he a new life in his offer he would reject the present.

Ask yourself, ask any of your acquaintance, whether they would live over again the last ten or twenty years of their life. No! but the next twenty, they say, will be better:

> And from the dregs of life, hope to receive
> What the first sprightly running could not give.[5]

Thus, at last, they find (such is the greatness of human misery, it reconciles even contradictions) that they complain at once of the shortness of life and of its vanity and sorrow.

PHILO: And is it possible, *Cleanthes*, said *Philo*, that after all these reflections, and infinitely more which might be suggested, you can still persevere in your anthropomorphism, and assert the moral attributes of the Deity, his justice, benevolence, mercy, and rectitude, to be of the same nature with these virtues in human creatures? His power, we allow, is infinite; whatever he wills is executed: But neither man nor any other animal is happy; therefore, he does not will their happiness. His wisdom is infinite; He is never mistaken in choosing the means to any end; But the course of nature tends not to human or animal felicity: Therefore, it is not established for that purpose. Through the whole compass of human knowledge there are no inferences more certain and infallible than these. In what respect, then, do his benevolence and mercy resemble the benevolence and mercy of men?

Epicurus' old questions are yet unanswered.

---

4 [Charles V, 1500–1558, was king of Spain and Holy Roman Emperor. He retired from his thrones in 1556 and 1558.]

5 [John Dryden, *Aureng-Zebe*, Act IV, sc. 1.]

Is he willing to prevent evil, but not able? then is he impotent. Is he able, but not willing? then is he malevolent. Is he both able and willing? whence then is evil?

You ascribe, *Cleanthes* (and I believe justly), a purpose and intention to nature. But what, I beseech you, is the object of that curious artifice and machinery which she had displayed in all animals? The preservation alone of individuals, and propagation of the species? It seems enough for her purpose, if such a rank be barely upheld in the universe, without any care or concern for the happiness of the members that compose it. No resource for this purpose: No machinery in order merely to give pleasure or ease: No fund of pure joy and contentment: No indulgence without some want or necessity accompanying it. At least, the few phenomena of this nature are overbalanced by opposite phenomena of still greater importance.

Our sense of music, harmony, and indeed beauty of all kinds, gives satisfaction, without being absolutely necessary to the preservation and propagation of the species. But what racking pains, on the other hand, arise from gouts, gravels, megrims, toothaches, rheumatisms, where the injury to the animal machinery is either small or incurable? Mirth, laughter, play, frolic seem gratuitous satisfactions which have no further tendency; spleen, melancholy, discontent, superstition are pains of the same nature. How then does the divine benevolence display itself, in the sense of you anthropomorphites? None but we mystics, as you were pleased to call us, can account for this strange mixture of phenomena, by deriving it from attributes infinitely perfect but incomprehensible.

CLEANTHES: And have you, at last, said *Cleanthes* smiling, betrayed your intentions, *Philo*? Your long agreement with *Demea* did indeed a little surprise me, but I find you were all the while erecting a concealed battery against me. And I must confess that you have now fallen upon a subject worthy of your noble spirit of opposition and controversy. If you can make out the present point, and prove mankind to be unhappy or corrupted, there is an end at once of all religion. For to what purpose establish the natural attributes of the Deity, while the moral are still doubtful and uncertain?

DEMEA: You take umbrage very easily, replied *Demea*, at opinions the most innocent and the most generally received, even amongst the religious and devout themselves; and nothing can be more surprising than to find a topic like this—concerning the wickedness and misery of man—charged with no less than atheism and profaneness. Have not all pious divines and preachers who have indulged their rhetoric on so fertile a subject; have they not easily, I say, given a solution of any difficulties which may attend it? This world is but a point in comparison of the universe; this life but a moment in comparison of eternity. The present evil phenomena, therefore, are rectified in other regions, and in some future period of existence. And the eyes of men, being then opened to large views of things, see the whole connection of general laws, and trace, with adoration, the benevolence and rectitude of the Deity through all the mazes and intricacies of his providence.

CLEANTHES: No! replied *Cleanthes*, no! These arbitrary suppositions can never be admitted, contrary to matter of fact, visible and uncontroverted. Whence can any cause be known but from its known effects? Whence can any hypothesis be proved but from the apparent phenomena? To establish one hypothesis upon another is building entirely in the air; and the utmost we ever attain by these conjectures and fictions is to ascertain the bare possibility of our opinion, but never can we, upon such terms, establish its reality.

The only method of supporting divine benevolence (and it is what I willingly embrace) is to deny absolutely the misery and wickedness of man. Your representations are exaggerated; your melancholy views mostly fictitious; your inference contrary to fact and experience. Health is more common than sickness: Pleasure than pain: Happiness than misery. And for one vexation which we meet with, we attain, upon computation, a hundred enjoyments.

PHILO: Admitting your position, replied *Philo*, which yet is extremely doubtful, you must at the same time allow that, if pain be less frequent than pleasure, it is infinitely more violent and durable. One hour of it is often able to outweigh a day, a week, a month of our common insipid enjoyments; and how many days, weeks, and months are passed by several in the most acute torments? Pleasure, scarcely in one instance, is ever able to reach ecstasy and rapture: And in no one instance can it continue for any time at its highest pitch and altitude. The spirits evaporate, the nerves relax, the fabric is disordered, and the enjoyment quickly degenerates into fatigue and uneasiness. But pain often, good God, how often! rises to torture and agony; and the longer it continues, it becomes still more genuine agony and torture. Patience is exhausted, courage languishes, melancholy seizes us, and nothing terminates our misery but the removal of its cause or another event which is the sole cure of all evil, but which, from our natural folly, we regard with still greater horror and consternation.

But not to insist upon these topics, continued *Philo*, though most obvious, certain, and important, I must use the freedom to admonish you, *Cleanthes*, that you have put the controversy upon a most dangerous issue, and are unawares introducing a total skepticism into the most essential articles of natural and revealed theology. What! no method of fixing a just foundation for religion unless we allow the happiness of human life, and maintain a continued existence even in this world, with all our present pains, infirmities, vexations, and follies, to be eligible and desirable! But this is contrary to everyone's feeling and experience; it is contrary to an authority so established as nothing can subvert. No decisive proofs can ever be produced against this authority; nor is it possible for you to compute, estimate, and compare all the pains and all the pleasures in the lives of all men and of all animals: And thus, by your resting the whole system of religion on a point which, from its very nature, must forever be uncertain, you tacitly confess that that system is equally uncertain.

But allowing you what never will be believed, at least, what you never possibly can prove, that animal or, at least, human happiness in this life exceeds its misery, you have yet done nothing; for this is not, by any means, what we expect from infinite power, infinite wisdom, and infinite goodness. Why is there any misery at all in the world? Not by chance, surely. From some cause then. Is it from the intention of the Deity? But he is perfectly benevolent. Is it contrary to his intention? But he is almighty. Nothing can shake the solidity of this reasoning, so short, so clear, so decisive, except we assert that these subjects exceed all human capacity, and that our common measures of truth and falsehood are not applicable to them; a topic which I have all along insisted on, but which you have, from the beginning, rejected with scorn and indignation.

But I will be contented to retire still from this retrenchment, for I deny that you can ever force me in it. I will allow that pain or misery in man is *compatible* with infinite power and goodness in the Deity, even in your sense of these attributes: what are you advanced by all these concessions? A mere possible compatibility is not sufficient. You must *prove* these pure, unmixed and uncontrollable attributes from the present mixed and confused phenomena, and from these alone. A hopeful undertaking! Were the phenomena ever so pure and unmixed, yet, being finite, they would be insufficient for the purpose. How much more, where they are also so jarring and discordant!

Here, *Cleanthes*, I find myself at ease in my argument. Here I triumph. Formerly, when we argued concerning the natural attributes of intelligence and design, I needed all my skeptical and metaphysical subtilty to elude your grasp. In many views of the universe and of its parts, particularly the latter, the beauty and fitness of final causes strike us with such irresistible force that all objections appear (what I believe they really are) mere cavils and sophisms; nor can we then imagine how it was ever possible for us to repose any weight on them. But there is no view of human life or of the condition of mankind from which, without the greatest violence, we can infer the moral attributes or learn that infinite benevolence, conjoined with infinite power and infinite wisdom, which we must discover by the eyes of faith alone. It is your turn now to tug the laboring oar, and to support your philosophical subtilties against the dictates of plain reason and experience.

PART XI

CLEANTHES: I scruple not to allow, said *Cleanthes*, that I have been apt to suspect the frequent repetition of the word "infinite," which we meet with in all theological writers, to savor more of panegyric than of philosophy, and that any purposes of reasoning, and even of religion, would be better served were we to rest contented with more accurate and more moderate expressions. The terms "admirable," "excellent," "superlatively great," "wise," and "holy"; these sufficiently fill the imaginations of men, and anything beyond, besides that it leads into absurdities, has no influence on the affections or sentiments. Thus, in the present subject, if we abandon all human analogy, as seems your intention, *Demea*, I am afraid we abandon all religion and retain no conception of the great object of our adoration. If we preserve human analogy, we must forever find it impossible to reconcile any mixture of evil in the universe with infinite attributes; much less can we ever prove the latter from the former. But supposing the Author of Nature to be finitely perfect, though far exceeding mankind, a satisfactory account may then be given to natural and moral evil, and every untoward phenomenon be explained and adjusted. A lesser evil may then be chosen in order to avoid a greater; inconveniences be submitted to in order to reach a desirable end; and, in a word, benevolence, regulated by wisdom and limited by necessity, may produce just such a world as the present. You, *Philo*, who are so prompt at starting views and reflections and analogies, I would gladly hear, at length, without interruption, your opinion of this new theory; and if it deserve our attention, we may afterwards, at more leisure, reduce it into form.

PHILO: My sentiments, replied *Philo*, are not worth being made a mystery of: and, therefore, without any ceremony, I shall deliver what occurs to me with regard to the present subject. It must, I think, be allowed that, if a very limited intelligence whom we shall suppose utterly unacquainted with the universe were assured that it were the production of a very good, wise, and powerful being, however finite, he would, from his conjectures, form *beforehand* a different notion of it from what we find it to be by experience; nor would he ever imagine, merely from these attributes of the cause of which he is informed, that the effect could be so full of vice and misery and disorder, as it appears in this life. Supposing now that this person were brought into the world, still assured that it was the workmanship of such a sublime and benevolent being, he might, perhaps, be surprised at the disappointment, but would never retract his former belief if founded on any very solid argument; since such a limited intelligence must be sensible of his own blindness and ignorance, and must allow that there may be many solutions of those phenomena which will forever escape his comprehension. But supposing, which is the real case with regard to man, that this creature is not antecedently convinced of a supreme intelligence, benevolent, and powerful, but is left to gather such a belief from the appearances of things; this entirely alters the case, nor will he ever find any reason for such a conclusion. He may be fully convinced of the narrow limits of his understanding, but this will not help him in forming an inference concerning the goodness of superior powers, since he must form that inference from what he knows, not from what he is ignorant of. The more you exaggerate his weakness and ignorance, the more diffident you render him, and give him the greater suspicion that such subjects are beyond the reach of his faculties. You are obliged, therefore, to reason with him merely from the known phenomena, and to drop every arbitrary supposition or conjecture.

Did I show you a house or place where there was not one apartment convenient or agreeable; where the windows, doors, fires, passages, stairs, and the whole economy of the building were the source of noise, confusion, fatigue, darkness, and the extremes of heat and cold, you would certainly blame the contrivance, without any further examination. The architect would in vain display his subtilty, and prove to you that, if this door or that window were altered, greater ills would ensue. What he says may be strictly true: The alternation of one particular, while the other parts of the building remain, may only augment the inconveniences. But still you would assert in general that, if the architect had had skill and good intentions, he might have formed such a plan of the whole, and might have adjusted the parts in such a manner as would have remedied all or most of these inconveniences. His ignorance, or even your own ignorance of such a plan, will never convince you of the impossibility of it. If you find any inconveniences and deformities in the building, you will always, without entering into any detail, condemn the architect.

In short, I repeat the question: Is the world, considered in general and as it appears to us in this life, different from what a man or such a limited being would *beforehand*, expect from a very powerful, wise, and benevolent Deity? It must be strange prejudice to assert the contrary. And from thence I conclude that, however, consistent the world may be, allowing certain suppositions and conjectures with the idea of such a Deity, it can never afford us an inference concerning his existence. The consistency is not absolutely denied, only the inference. Conjectures, especially where infinity is excluded from the divine attributes, may perhaps be sufficient to prove a consistency, but can never be foundations for any inference.

There seem to be *four* circumstances on which depend all or the greatest part of the ills that molest sensible creatures; and it is not impossible but all these circumstances may be necessary and unavoidable. We know so little beyond common life, or even of common life, that, with regard to the economy of a universe, there is no conjecture, however wild, which may not be just; nor any one, however plausible, which may not be erroneous. All that belongs to human understanding, in this deep ignorance and obscurity, is to be skeptical or at least cautious, and not to admit of any hypothesis whatever, much less of any which is supported by no appearance of probability. Now this I assert to be the case with regard to all the causes of evil and the circumstances on which it depends. None of them appear to human reason in the least degree necessary or unavoidable, nor can we suppose them such, without the utmost license of imagination.

The *first* circumstance which introduces evil is that contrivance or economy of the animal creation by which pains, as well as pleasures, are employed to excite all creatures to action, and make them vigilant in the great work of self-preservation. Now pleasure alone, in its various degrees, seems to human understanding sufficient for this purpose. All animals might be constantly in a state of enjoyment; but when urged by any of the necessities of nature, such as thirst, hunger, weariness; instead of pain, they might feel a diminution of pleasure by which they might be prompted to seek that object which is necessary to their subsistence. Men pursue pleasure as eagerly as they avoid pain; at least, they might have been so constituted. It seems, therefore, plainly possible to carry on the business of life without any pain. Why then is any animal ever rendered susceptible of such a sensation? If animals can be free from it an hour, they might enjoy a perpetual exemption from it, and it required as particular a contrivance of their organs to produce that feeling as to endow them with sight, hearing, or any of the senses. Shall we conjecture that such a contrivance was necessary, without any appearance of reason? And shall we build on that conjecture as on the most certain truth?

But a capacity of pain would not alone produce pain were it not for the *second* circumstance, viz., the conducting of the world by general laws; and this seems nowise necessary to a very perfect being. It is true, if everything were conducted by particular volitions, the course of nature would be perpetually broken, and no man could employ his reason in the conduct of life. But might not other particular volitions remedy this inconvenience? In short, might not the Deity exterminate all ill, wherever it were to be found, and produce all good, without any preparation or long progress of causes and effects?

Besides, we must consider that, according to the present economy of the world, the course of nature, though supposed exactly regular, yet to us appears not so, and many events are uncertain, and many disappoint our expectations. Health and sickness, calm and tempest, with an infinite number of other accidents whose causes are unknown and variable, have a great influence both on the fortunes of particular persons and on the prosperity of public societies: And indeed all human life, in a manner, depends on such accidents. A being, therefore, who knows the secret springs of the universe might easily, by particular volitions, turn all these accidents to the good of mankind and render the whole world happy, without discovering himself in any operation. A fleet whose purposes were salutary to society might always meet with a fair wind: Good princes enjoy sound health and long life: Persons born to power and authority be framed with good tempers and virtuous dispositions A few such events as these, regularly and wisely conducted, would change the face of the world; and yet would no more seem to disturb the course of nature or confound human conduct than the present economy of things, where the causes are secret and variable and compounded. Some small touches given to *Caligula's* brain in his infancy might have converted him into a *Trajan*. One wave, a little higher than the rest, by burying *Caesar* and his fortune in the bottom of the ocean, might have restored liberty to a considerable part of mankind. There may, for aught we know, be good reasons why Providence interposes not in this manner, but they are unknown to us; And, though the mere supposition that such reasons exist may be sufficient to *save* the conclusion concerning the divine attributes, yet surely it can never be sufficient to *establish* that conclusion.

If everything in the universe be conducted by general laws, and if animals be rendered susceptible of pain, it scarcely seems possible but some ill must arise in the various shocks of matter and the various concurrence and opposition of general laws; but this ill would be very rare were it not for the *third* circumstance which I proposed to mention, viz., the great frugality with which all powers and faculties are distributed to every particular being. So well adjusted are the organs and capacities of all animals, and so well fitted to their preservation, that as far as history or tradition reaches, there appears not to be any single species which has yet been extinguished in the universe. Every animal has the requisite endowments, but these endowments are bestowed with so scrupulous an economy that any considerable diminution must entirely destroy the creature Wherever one power is increased, there is a proportional abatement in the others. Animals which excel in swiftness are commonly defective in force. Those which possess both are either imperfect in some of their senses or are oppressed with the most craving wants. The human species, whose chief excellence is reason and sagacity, is of all others the most necessitous, and the most deficient in bodily advantages; without clothes, without arms, without food, without lodging, without any convenience of life, except what they owe to their own skill and industry In short, nature seems to have formed an exact calculation of the necessities of her creatures; and, like a *rigid master*, has afforded them little more powers or endowments than what are strictly sufficient to supply those necessities. An *indulgent parent* would have bestowed a large stock in order to guard against accidents, and secure the happiness and welfare of the creature in the most unfortunate concurrence of circumstances. Every course of life would not have been so surrounded with precipices that the least departure from the true path, by mistake or necessity, must involve us in misery and ruin. Some reserve, some fund, would have been provided to ensure happiness, nor would the powers and the necessities have been adjusted with so rigid an economy. The Author of Nature is inconceivably powerful; his force is supposed great, if not altogether inexhaustible nor is there any reason, as far as we can judge, to make him observe this strict frugality in his dealings with his creatures. It would have been better, were his power extremely limited, to have created fewer animals, and to have endowed these with more faculties for their happiness and preservation. A builder is never esteemed prudent who undertakes a plan beyond what his stock will enable him to finish.

In order to cure most of the ills of human life, I require not that man should have the wings of the eagle, the swiftness of the stag, the force of the ox, the arms of the lion, the scales of the crocodile or rhinoceros; much less do I demand the sagacity of an angel or cherubim. I am contented to take an increase in one single power or faculty of his soul. Let him be endowed with a greater propensity to industry and labor, a more vigorous spring and activity of mind, a more constant bent to business and application. Let the whole species possess naturally an equal diligence with that which many individuals are able to attain by habit and reflection, and the most beneficial consequences, without any allay of ill, is the immediate and necessary result of this endowment. Almost all the moral as well as natural evils of human life arise from idleness; and were our species, by the original constitution of their frame, exempt from this vice or infirmity, the perfect cultivation of land, the improvement of arts and manufactures, the exact execution of every office and duty, immediately follow; and men at once may fully reach that state of society which is so imperfectly attained by the best regulated government. But as industry is a power, and the most valuable of any, nature seems determined, suitably to her usual maxims, to bestow it on men with a very sparing hand; and rather to punish him severely for his deficiency in it than to reward him for his attainments. She has so contrived his frame that nothing but the most violent necessity can oblige him to labor; and she employs all his other wants to overcome, at least in part, the want of diligence, and to endow him with some share of a faculty of which she has thought fit naturally to bereave him. Here our demands may be allowed very humble, and therefore the more reasonable. If we required the endowments of superior penetration and judgment, of a more delicate taste of beauty, of a nicer sensibility to benevolence and friendship, we might be told that we impiously pretend to break the order of Nature, that we want to exalt ourselves into a higher rank of being, that the presents which we require, not being suitable to our state and condition, would only be pernicious to us. But it is hard, I dare to repeat it, it is hard that, being placed in a world so full of wants and necessities, where almost every being and element is either our foe or refuses its assistance; we should also have our own temper to struggle with, and should be deprived of that faculty which can alone fence against these multiplied evils.

The *fourth* circumstance whence arises the misery and ill of the universe is the inaccurate workmanship of all the springs and principles of the great machine of nature. It must be acknowledged that there are few parts of the universe which seem not to serve some purpose, and whose removal would not produce a visible defect and disorder in the whole. The parts hang all together, nor can one be touched without affecting the rest, in a greater or less degree. But at the same time, it must be observed that none of these parts or principles, however useful, are so accurately adjusted as to keep precisely within those bounds in which their utility consists; but they are, all of them apt, on every occasion, to run into the one extreme or the other. One would imagine that this grand production had not received the last hand of the maker; so little finished is every part, and so coarse are the strokes with which it is executed. Thus the winds are requisite to convey the vapors along the surface of the globe, and to assist men in navigation: But how often, rising up to tempests and hurricanes, do they become pernicious? Rains are necessary to nourish all the plants and animals of the earth: But how often are they defective? how often excessive? Heat is requisite to all life and vegetation, but is not always found in the due proportion. On the mixture and secretion of the humors and juices of the body depend the health and prosperity of the animal: But the parts perform not regularly their proper function. What more useful than all the passions of the mind, ambition, vanity, love, anger? But how often do they break their bounds and cause the greatest convulsions in society? There is nothing so advantageous in the universe but what frequently becomes pernicious, by its excess or defect; nor has nature guarded, with the requisite accuracy, against all disorder or confusion. The irregularity is never perhaps so great as to destroy any species, but is often sufficient to involve the individuals in ruin and misery.

On the concurrence, then, of these *four* circumstances does all or the greatest part of natural evil depend. Were all living creatures incapable of pain, or were the world administered by particular volitions, evil never could have found access into the universe: And were animals endowed with a large stock of powers and faculties, beyond what strict necessity requires, or were the several springs and principles of the universe so accurately framed as to preserve always the just temperament and medium, there must have been very little ill in comparison of what we feel at present. What then shall we pronounce on this occasion? Shall we say that these circumstances are not necessary, and that they might easily have been altered in the contrivance of the universe? This decision seems too presumptuous for creatures so blind and ignorant. Let us be more modest in our conclusions. Let us allow that, if the goodness of the Deity (I mean a goodness like the human) could be established on any tolerable reasons *a priori*, these phenomena, however untoward, would not be sufficient to subvert that principle, but might easily, in some unknown manner, be reconcilable to it. But let us still assert that, as this goodness is not antecedently established but must be inferred from the phenomena, there can be no grounds for such an inference while there are so many ills in the universe, and while these ills might easily have been remedied, as human understanding can be allowed to judge on such a subject. I am skeptic enough to allow that the bad appearances, notwithstanding all my reasonings, may be compatible with such attributes. Such a conclusion cannot result from skepticism, but must arise from the phenomena, and from our confidence in the reasonings which we deduce from these phenomena.

Look round this universe. What an immense profusion of beings, animated and organized, sensible and active! You admire this prodigious variety and fecundity. But inspect a little more narrowly these living existences, the only beings worth regarding. How hostile and destructive to each other! How insufficient all of them for their own happiness! How contemptible or odious to the spectator! The whole presents nothing but the idea of a blind nature, impregnated by a great vivifying principle, and pouring forth from her lap, without discernment or parental care, her maimed and abortive children!

Here the Manichaean system[6] occurs as a proper hypothesis to solve the difficulty; and no doubt, in some respects it is very specious and has more probability than the common hypothesis, by giving a plausible account of the strange mixture of good and ill which appears in life. But if we consider, on the other hand, the perfect uniformity and agreement of the parts of the universe, we shall not discover in it any marks of the combat of a malevolent with a benevolent being. There is indeed an opposition of pains and pleasures in the feelings of sensible creatures; But are not all the operations of nature carried on by an opposition of principles, of hot and cold, moist and dry, light and heavy? The true conclusion is that the original source of all things is entirely indifferent to all these principles, and has no more regard to good above ill than to heat above cold, or to drought above moisture, or to light above heavy.

There may *four* hypotheses be framed concerning the first causes of the universe: *that* they are endowed with perfect goodness; *that* they have perfect malice; *that* they are opposite and have both goodness and malice; *that* they have neither goodness nor malice. Mixed phenomena can never prove the two former unmixed principles; and the uniformity and steadiness of general laws seem to oppose the third. The fourth, therefore, seems by far the most probable.

What I have said concerning natural evil will apply to moral with little or no variation; and we have no more reason to infer that the rectitude of the Supreme Being resembles human rectitude than that his benevolence resembles the human. Nay, it will be thought that we have still greater cause to exclude from him moral sentiments, such as we feel them; since moral evil, in the opinion of many, is much more predominant above moral good than natural evil above natural good.

But even though this should not be allowed, and though the virtue which is in mankind should be acknowledged much superior to the vice; yet, so long as there is any vice at all in the universe, it will very much puzzle you anthropomorphites how to account for it. You must assign a cause for it, without having recourse to the first cause. But as every effect must have a cause, and that cause another, you must either carry on the progression *in infinitum*, or rest on that original principle, who is the ultimate cause of all things. . . .

DEMEA: Hold! hold! cried *Demea*: Whither does your imagination hurry you? I joined in alliance with you in order to prove the incomprehensible nature of the Divine Being, and refute the principles of *Cleanthes*, who would measure everything by human rule and standard. But I now find you running into all the topics of the greatest libertines and infidels, and betraying that holy cause which you seemingly espoused. Are you secretly, then a more dangerous enemy than *Cleanthes* himself?

---

[6] [The ancient Manichean view was that the world is run by both a good force and an evil one.]

CLEANTHES: And are you so late in perceiving it? replied *Cleanthes*. Believe me, *Demea*, your friend *Philo*, from the beginning, has been amusing himself at both our expense: and it must be confessed that the injudicious reasoning of our vulgar theology has given him but too just a handle of ridicule. The total infirmity of human reason, the absolute incomprehensibility of the Divine Nature, the great and universal misery, and still greater wickedness of men; these are strange topics, surely, to be so fondly cherished by orthodox divines and doctors. In ages of stupidity and ignorance, indeed, these principles may safely be espoused; and perhaps no views of things are more proper to promote superstition than such as encourage the blind amazement, the difference, and melancholy of mankind. But at present . . .

PHILO: Blame not so much, interposed *Philo*, the ignorance of these reverend gentlemen. They know how to change their style with the times. Formerly, it was a most popular theological topic to maintain that human life was vanity and misery, and to exaggerate all the ills and pains which are incident to men. But of late years, divines, we find, begin to retract this position and maintain, though still with some hesitation, that there are more goods than evils, more pleasures than pains, even in this life. When religion stood entirely upon temper and education, it was thought proper to encourage melancholy; as, indeed, mankind never have recourse to superior powers so readily as in that disposition. But as men have now learned to form principles and to draw consequences, it is necessary to change the batteries, and to make use of such arguments as will endure at least some scrutiny and examination. This variation is the same (and from the same causes) with that which I formerly remarked with regard to skepticism.

Thus *Philo* continued to the last his spirit of opposition, and his censure of established opinions. But I could observe that *Demea* did not at all relish the latter part of the discourse; and he took occasion soon after, on some pretence or other, to leave the company.

IV.A.2   Good and Evil

H. J. McCLOSKEY

H. J. McCloskey (1925–), professor of philosophy at La Trobe University in Australia, offers a powerful statement of the problem of evil, as well as a brief critical survey of many of the most popular attempted solutions. McCloskey arrives at the conclusion that an omnipotent and benevolent God should have been able to create a world in which there is no unnecessary or avoidable evil; that much unnecessary evil exists in the world; and thus that there cannot be an omnipotent, benevolent God.

THE PROBLEM STATED

Evil is a problem for the theist in that a contradiction is involved in the fact of evil on the one hand, and the belief in the omnipotence and perfection of God on the other. God cannot be both all-powerful and perfectly good if evil is real. This contradiction is well set out in its detail by Mackie in his discussion of the problem.[1] In his discussion Mackie seeks to show that this contradiction cannot be resolved in terms of man's free will. In arguing in this way Mackie neglects a large number of important points and concedes far too much to the theist. He implicitly allows that while physical evil creates a problem, this problem is reducible to the problem of moral evil and that therefore the satisfactoriness of solutions of the problem of evil turns on the compatibility of free will and absolute goodness. In fact physical evils create a number of distinct problems which are not reducible to the problem of moral evil. Further, the proposed solution of the problem of moral evil in terms of free will renders the attempt to account for physical evil in terms of moral good, and the attempt thereby to reduce the problem of evil to the problem of moral evil, completely untenable. Moreover, the account of moral evil in terms of free will breaks down on more obvious and less disputable grounds than those indicated by Mackie. Moral evil can be shown to remain a problem whether or not free will is compatible with absolute goodness. I therefore propose in this paper to reopen the discussion of "the problem of evil," by approaching it from a more general standpoint, examining a wider variety of solutions than those considered by Mackie and his critics.

The fact of evil creates a problem for the theist; but there are a number of simple solutions available to a theist who is content seriously to modify his theism. He can either admit a limit to God's power, or he can deny God's moral perfection. He can assert either (1) that God is not powerful enough to make a world that does not contain evil, or (2) that God created only the good in the

From *The Philosophical Quarterly* 10, no. 39 (1960): 97–114. Used by permission of the author.

[1] "Evil and Omnipotence."

universe and that some other power created the evil, or (3) that God is all-powerful but morally imperfect, and chose to create an imperfect universe. Few Christians accept these solutions, and this is no doubt partly because such "solutions" ignore the real inspiration of religious beliefs, and partly because they introduce embarrassing complications for the theist in his attempts to deal with other serious problems. However, if any one of these "solutions" is accepted, then the problem of evil is avoided, and a weakened version of theism is made secure from attacks based upon the fact of the occurrence of evil.

For more orthodox theism, according to which God is both omnipotent and perfectly good, evil creates a real problem; and this problem is well stated by the Jesuit, Father G. H. Joyce. Joyce writes:

> The existence of evil in the world must at all times be the greatest of all problems which the mind encounters when it reflects on God and His relation to the world. If He is, indeed, all-good and all-powerful, how has evil any place in the world which He has made? Whence came it? Why is it here? If He is all-good why did He allow it to arise? If all-powerful why does He not deliver us from the burden? Alike in the physical and moral order creation seems so grievously marred that we find it hard to understand how it can derive in its entirety from God.[2]

The facts which give rise to the problem are of two general kinds, and give rise to two distinct types of problem. These two general kinds of evil are usually referred to as "physical" and as "moral" evil. These terms are by no means apt—suffering for instance is not strictly physical evil—and they conceal significant differences. However, this terminology is too widely accepted, and too convenient to be dispensed with here, the more especially as the various kinds of evil, while important as distinct kinds, need not for our purposes be designated by separate names.

Physical evil and moral evil then are the two general forms of evil which independently and jointly constitute conclusive grounds for denying the existence of God in the sense defined, namely as an all-powerful, perfect Being. The acuteness of these two general problems is evident when we consider the nature and extent of the evils of which account must be given. To take physical evils, looking first at the less important of these.

(a) *Physical evils*: Physical evils are involved in the very constitution of the earth and animal kingdom. There are deserts and icebound areas; there are dangerous animals of prey, as well as creatures such as scorpions and snakes. There are also pests such as flies and fleas and the hosts of other insect pests, as well as the multitude of lower parasites such as tapeworms, hookworms and the like. Secondly, there are the various natural calamities and the immense human suffering that follows in their wake—fires, floods, tempests, tidal waves, volcanoes, earthquakes, droughts and famines. Thirdly, there are the vast numbers of disease that torment and ravage man. Diseases such as leprosy, cancer, poliomyelitis, appear *prima facie* not to be creations which are

---

[2] Joyce, *Principles of Natural Theology*, Chap. 17. All subsequent quotations from Joyce in this paper are from this chapter of this work.

to be expected of a benevolent Creator. Fourthly, there are the evils with which so many are born—the various physical deformities and defects such as misshapen limbs, blindness, deafness, dumbness, mental deficiency and insanity. Most of these evils contribute towards increasing human pain and suffering; but not all physical evils are reducible simply to pain. Many of these evils are evils whether or not they result in pain. This is important, for it means that, unless there is one solution to such diverse evils, it is both inaccurate and positively misleading to speak of *the* problem of physical evil. Shortly I shall be arguing that no one "solution" covers all these evils, so we shall have to conclude that physical evils create not one problem but a number of distinct problems for the theist.

The nature of the various difficulties referred to by the theist as the problem of physical evil is indicated by Joyce in a way not untypical among the more honest, philosophical theists, as follows:

> The actual amount of suffering which the human race endures is immense. Disease has store and to spare of torments for the body: and disease and death are the lot to which we must all look forward. At all times, too, great numbers of the race are pinched by want. Nor is the world ever free for very long from the terrible sufferings which follow in the track of war. If we concentrate our attention on human woes, to the exclusion of the joys of life, we gain an appalling picture of the ills to which the flesh is heir. So too if we fasten our attention on the sterner side of nature, on the pains which men endure from natural forces—on the storms which wreck their ships, the cold which freezes them to death, the fire which consumes them—if we contemplate this aspect of nature alone we may be led to wonder how God came to deal so harshly with His Creatures as to provide them with such a home.

Many such statements of the problem proceed by suggesting, if not by stating, that the problem arises at least in part by concentrating one's attention too exclusively on one aspect of the world. This is quite contrary to the facts. The problem is not one that results from looking at only one aspect of the universe. It may be the case that over-all pleasure predominates over pain, and that physical goods in general predominate over physical evils, but the opposite may equally well be the case. It is both practically impossible and logically impossible for this question to be resolved. However, it is not an unreasonable presumption, with the large bulk of mankind inadequately fed and housed and without adequate medical and health services, to suppose that physical evils at present predominate over physical goods. In the light of the facts at our disposal, this would seem to be a much more reasonable conclusion than the conclusion hinted at by Joyce and openly advanced by less cautious theists, namely, that physical goods in fact outweigh physical evils in the world.

However, the question is not "Which predominates, physical good or physical evil?" The problem of physical evil remains a problem whether the balance in the universe is on the side of physical good or not, because the problem is that of accounting for the fact that physical evil occurs at all.

(b) *Moral evil*: Physical evils create one of the groups of problems referred to by the theist as "the problem of evil." Moral evil creates quite a distinct problem. Moral evil is simply immorality—evils such as selfishness, envy, greed, deceit, cruelty, callousness, cowardice and the larger scale evils such as wars and the atrocities they involve.

Moral evil is commonly regarded as constituting an even more serious problem than physical evil. Joyce so regards it, observing:

> The man who sins thereby offends God. . . . We are called on to explain how God came to create an order of things in which rebellion and even final rejection have such a place. Since a choice from among an infinite number of possible worlds lay open to God, how came He to choose one in which these occur? Is not such a choice in flagrant opposition to the Divine Goodness?

Some theists seek a solution by denying the reality of evil or by describing it as a "privation" or absence of good. They hope thereby to explain it away as not needing a solution. This, in the case of most of the evils which require explanation, seems to amount to little more than an attempt to sidestep the problem simply by changing the name of that which has to be explained. It can be exposed for what it is simply by describing some of the evils which have to be explained. That is why a survey of the data to be accounted for is a most important part of the discussion of the problem of evil.

In *The Brothers Karamazov*, Dostoevski introduces a discussion of the problem of evil by reference to some then recently committed atrocities. Ivan states the problem:

> "By the way, a Bulgarian I met lately in Moscow," Ivan went on . . . "told me about the crimes committed by Turks in all parts of Bulgaria through fear of a general rising of the Slavs. They burn villages, murder, outrage women and children, and nail their prisoners by the ears to the fences, leave them till morning, and in the morning hang them—all sorts of things you can't imagine. People talk sometimes of bestial cruelty, but that's a great injustice and insult to the beasts; a beast can never be so cruel as a man, so artistically cruel. The tiger only tears and gnaws and that's all he can do. He would never think of nailing people by the ears, even if he were able to do it. These Turks took a pleasure in torturing children too; cutting the unborn child from the mother's womb and tossing babies up in the air and catching them on the points of their bayonets before their mothers' eyes. Doing it before the mother's eyes was what gave zest to the amusement. Here is another scene that I thought very interesting. Imagine a trembling mother with her baby in her arms, a circle of invading Turks around her. They've planned a diversion: they pet the baby to make it laugh. They succeed; the baby laughs. At the moment a Turk points a pistol four inches from the baby's face. The baby laughs with glee, holds out its little hands to the pistol, and he pulls the trigger in the baby's face and blows out its brains. Artistic, wasn't it?"[3]

Ivan's statement of the problem was based on historical events. Such

---

[3] Garnett translation (London: William Heinemann, Ltd., 1945).

happenings did not cease in the nineteenth century. *The Scourge of the Swastika* by Lord Russell of Liverpool contains little else than descriptions of such atrocities; and it is simply one of a host of writings giving documented lists of instances of evils, both physical and moral.

Thus the problem of evil is both real and acute. There is a clear *prima facie* case that evil and God are incompatible—both cannot exist. Most theists admit this, and that the onus is on them to show that the conflict is not fatal to theism; but a consequence is that a host of proposed solutions are advanced.

The mere fact of such a multiplicity of proposed solutions, and the widespread repudiation of each other's solutions by theists, in itself suggests that the fact of evil is an insuperable obstacle to theism as defined here. It also makes it impossible to treat of all proposed solutions, and all that can be attempted here is an examination of those proposed solutions which are most commonly invoked and most generally thought to be important by theists.

Some theists admit the reality of the problem of evil, and then seek to sidestep it, declaring it to be a great mystery we poor humans cannot hope to comprehend. Other theists adopt a rational approach and advance rational arguments to show that evil, properly understood, is compatible with, and even a consequence of God's goodness. The arguments to be advanced in this paper are directed against the arguments of the latter theists; but in so far as these arguments are successful against the rational theists, to that extent they are also effective in showing that the nonrational approach in terms of great mysteries is positively irrational.

PROPOSED SOLUTIONS TO THE PROBLEM OF PHYSICAL EVIL

Of the large variety of arguments advanced by theists as solutions to the problem of physical evil, five popularly used and philosophically significant solutions will be examined. They are, in brief: (1) Physical good (pleasure) requires physical evil (pain) to exist at all; (2) Physical evil is God's punishment of sinners; (3) Physical evil is God's warning and reminder to man; (4) Physical evil is the result of the natural laws, the operations of which are on the whole good; (5) Physical evil increases the total good.

1. *Physical Good Is Impossible without Physical Evil*: Pleasure is possible only by way of contrast with pain. Here the analogy of color is used. If everything were blue we should, it is argued, understand neither what color is nor what blue is. So with pleasure and pain.

The most obvious defect of such an argument is that it does not cover all physical goods and evils. It is an argument commonly invoked by those who think of physical evil as creating only one problem, namely the problem of human pain. However, the problems of physical evils are not reduced to the one problem of pain; hence the argument is simply irrelevant to much physical evil. Disease and insanity are evils, but health and sanity are possible in the total absence of disease and insanity. Further, if the argument were in any way valid even in respect of pain, it would imply the existence of only a speck of pain, and not the immense amount of pain in the universe. A speck of yellow is all that is needed for an appreciation of blueness and of color generally. The argument is therefore seen to be seriously defective on two counts even if its underlying principle is left unquestioned. If its underlying principle is questioned, the argument is seen to be essentially invalid. Can it seriously be maintained that if an individual were born crippled and deformed and never in his life experienced pleasure, that he could not experience pain, not even if he were severely injured? It is clear that pain is possible in the absence of pleasure. It is true that it might not be distinguished by a special name and called "pain," but the state we now describe as a painful state would nonetheless be possible in the total absence of pleasure. So too the converse would seem to apply. Plato brings this out very clearly in Book 9 of the *Republic* in respect of the pleasures of taste and smell. These pleasures seem not to depend for their existence on any prior experience of pain. Thus the argument is unsound in respect of its main contention; and in being unsound in this respect, it is at the same time ascribing a serious limitation to God's power. It maintains that God cannot create pleasure without creating pain, although as we have seen, pleasure and pain are not correlatives.

2. *Physical Evil Is God's Punishment for Sin*. This kind of explanation was advanced to explain the terrible Lisbon earthquake in the eighteenth century, in which 40,000 people were killed. There are many replies to this argument, for instance Voltaire's. Voltaire asked: "Did God in this earthquake select the 40,000 least virtuous of the Portuguese citizens?" The distribution of disease and pain is in no obvious way related to the virtue of the persons afflicted, and popular saying has it that the distribution is slanted in the opposite direction. The only way of meeting the fact that evils are not distributed proportionately to the evil of the sufferer is by suggesting that all human beings, including children, are such miserable sinners, that our offences are of such enormity, that God would be justified in punishing all of us as severely as it is possible for humans to be punished; but even then, God's apparent caprice in the selection of His victims requires explanation. In any case it is by no means clear that young children who very often suffer severely are guilty of sin of such an enormity as would be necessary to justify their sufferings as punishment.

Further, many physical evils are simultaneous with birth—insanity, mental defectiveness, blindness, deformities, as well as much disease. No crime or sin of *the child* can explain and justify these physical evils as punishment; and, for a parent's sin to be punished in the child is injustice or evil of another kind.

Similarly, the sufferings of animals cannot be accounted for as punishment. For these various reasons, therefore, this argument must be rejected. In fact it has dropped out of favor in philosophical and theological circles, but it continues to be invoked at the popular level.

3. *Physical Evil Is God's Warning to Men*: It is argued, for instance of physical calamities, that "they serve a moral end which compensates the physical evil which they cause. The awful nature of these phenomena, the overwhelming power of the forces at work, and man's utter helplessness before them, rouse him from the religious indifference to which he is so prone. They inspire a reverential awe of the Creator who made them, and controls them, and a salutary fear of violating the laws which He has imposed" (Joyce). This is where immortality is often alluded to as justifying evil.

This argument proceeds from a proposition that is plainly false; and that the proposition from which it proceeds is false is conceded implicitly by most theologians. Natural calamities do not necessarily turn people to God, but rather present the problem of evil in an acute form; and the problem of evil is said to account for more defections from religion than any other cause. Thus if God's object in bringing about natural calamities is to inspire reverence and awe, He is a bungler. There are many more reliable methods of achieving this end. Equally important, the use of physical evil to achieve this object is hardly the course one would expect a benevolent God to adopt when other, more effective, less evil methods are available to Him, for example, special revelation, etc.

4. *Evils Are the Results of the Operations of Laws of Nature*:[4] This fourth argument relates to most physical evil, but it is more usually used to account for animal suffering and physical calamities. These evils are said to result from the operation of the natural laws which govern these objects, the relevant natural laws being the various causal laws, the law of pleasure-pain as a law governing sentient beings, etc. The theist argues that the nonoccurrence of these evils would involve either the constant intervention by God in a miraculous way, and contrary to his own natural laws, or else the construction of a universe with different components subject to different laws of nature; for God, in creating a certain kind of being, must create it subject to its appropriate law; He cannot create it and subject it to any law of His own choosing. Hence He creates a world which has components and laws good in their total effect, although calamitous in some particular effects.

Against this argument three objections are to be urged. First, it does not cover all physical evil. Clearly not all disease can be accounted for along these lines. Secondly, it is not to give a reason against God's miraculous intervention simply to assert that it would be unreasonable for Him constantly to intervene in the operation of His own laws. Yet this is the only reason that theists seem to offer here. If, by intervening in respect to the operation of His laws, God could thereby eliminate an evil, it would seem to be unreasonable and evil of Him not to do so. Some theists seek a way out of this difficulty by denying that God has the power miraculously to intervene; but this is to ascribe a severe limitation to His power. It amounts to asserting that when His Creation has been effected, God can do nothing else except contemplate it. The third objection is related to this, and is to the effect that it is already to ascribe a serious limitation to God's omnipotence to suggest that He could not make sentient beings which did not experience pain, nor sentient beings without deformities and deficiencies, nor natural phenomena with different laws of nature governing them. There is no reason why better laws of nature governing the existing objects are not possible on the divine hypothesis. Surely, if God is all-powerful, He could have made a better universe in the first place, or one with better laws of nature governing it, so that the operation of its laws did not produce calamities and pain. To maintain this is not to suggest that an omnipotent God should be capable of achieving what is logically impossible. All that has been indicated

---

[4] For further discussion of the proposed solutions treated in this and the following section see my article "The Problem of Evil," *Journal of Bible and Religion*, Vol. XXX, No. 3 (1962), esp. 188ff.

Shube thinks this is disgusting and MISLEADING

here is logically possible, and therefore not beyond the powers of a being Who is really omnipotent.

This fourth argument seeks to exonerate God by explaining that He created a universe sound on the whole, but such that He had no direct control over the laws governing His creations, and had control only in His selection of His creations. The previous two arguments attribute the detailed results of the operations of these laws directly to God's will. Theists commonly use all three arguments. It is not without significance that they betray such uncertainty as to whether God is to be *commended* or *exonerated*.

5. *The Universe Is Better with Evil in It*: This is the important argument. One version of it runs:

> Just as the human artist has in view the beauty of his composition as a whole, not making it his aim to give to each several part the highest degree of brilliancy, but that the measure of adornment which most contributes to the combined effect, so it is with God (Joyce).

Another version of this general type of argument explains evil not so much as *a component* of a good whole, seen out of its context as a mere component, but rather as *a means* to a greater good. Different as these versions are, they may be treated here as one general type of argument, for the same criticisms are fatal to both versions.

This kind of argument if valid simply shows that some evil may enrich the Universe; it tells us nothing about *how much* evil will enrich this particular universe, and how much will be too much. So, even if valid in principle—and shortly I shall argue that it is not valid—such an argument does not in itself provide a justification for the evil in the universe. It shows simply that the evil which occurs might have a justification. In view of the immense amount of evil the probabilities are against it.

This is the main point made by Wisdom in his discussion of this argument. Wisdom sums up his criticism as follows:

> It remains to add that, unless there are independent arguments in favor of this world's being the best logically possible world, it is probable that some of the evils in it are not logically necessary to a compensating good; it is probable because there are so many evils.[5]

Wisdom's reply brings out that the person who relies upon this argument as a conclusive and complete argument is seriously mistaken. The argument, if valid, justifies only some evil. A belief that it justifies all the evil that occurs in the world is mistaken, for a second argument, by way of a supplement to it, is needed. This supplementary argument would take the form of a proof that all the evil that occurs is *in fact* valuable and necessary as a means to greater good. Such a supplementary proof is in principle impossible; so, at best, this fifth argument can be taken to show only that some evil *may be* necessary for the production of good, and that the evil in the world may perhaps have a

---

[5] *Mind*, Vol. XLIV, No. 173 (1931).

justification on this account. This is not to justify a physical evil, but simply to suggest that physical evil might nonetheless have a justification, although we may never come to know this justification.

Thus the argument even if it is valid as a general form of reasoning is unsatisfactory because inconclusive. It is, however, also unsatisfactory in that it follows on the principle of the argument that, just as it is possible that evil in the total context contributes to increasing the total ultimate good, so equally, it will hold that good in the total context may increase the ultimate evil. Thus if the principle of the argument were sound, we could never know whether evil is really evil, or good really good. (Aesthetic analogies may be used to illustrate this point.) By implication it follows that it would be dangerous to eliminate evil because we may thereby introduce a discordant element into the divine symphony of the universe; and, conversely, it may be wrong to condemn the elimination of what is good, because the latter may result in the production of more, higher goods.

So it follows that, even if the general principle of the argument is not questioned, it is still seen to be a defective argument. On the one hand, it proves too little—it justifies only some evil and not necessarily all the evil in the universe; on the other hand it proves too much because it creates doubts about the goodness of apparent goods. These criticisms in themselves are fatal to the argument as a solution to the problem of physical evil. However, because this is one of the most popular and plausible accounts of physical evil, it is worthwhile considering whether it can properly be claimed to establish even the very weak conclusion indicated above.

Why, and in what way, is it supposed that physical evils such as pain and misery, disease and deformity, will heighten the total effect and add to the value of the moral whole? The answer given is that physical evil enriches the whole by giving rise to moral goodness. Disease, insanity, physical suffering and the like are said to bring into being the noble moral virtues—courage, endurance, benevolence, sympathy and the like. This is what the talk about the enriched whole comes to. W. D. Niven makes this explicit in his version of the argument:

> Physical evil has been the good which has impelled men to most of those achievements which made the history of man so wonderful. Hardship is a stern but fecund parent of invention. Where life is easy because physical ills are at a minimum we find man degenerating in body, mind, and character.

And Niven concludes by asking:

> "Which is preferable—a grim fight with the possibility of splendid triumph; or no battle at all?"[6]

---

[6] W. D. Niven, "Good and Evil," *Encyclopedia of Religion and Ethics*, James Hastings, ed., Vol. VI (New York: Charles Scribner's Sons, 1927.)

Joyce's corresponding argument runs:

"Pain is the great stimulant to action. Man no less than animals is impelled to work by the sense of hunger. Experience shows that, were it not for this motive the majority of men would be content to live in indolent ease. Man must earn his bread.

"One reason plainly why God permits suffering is that man may rise to a height of heroism which would otherwise have been beyond his scope. Nor are these the only benefits which it

The argument is: Physical evil brings moral good into being, and in fact is an essential precondition for the existence of some moral goods. Further, it is sometimes argued in this context that those moral goods which are possible in the total absence of physical evils are more valuable in themselves if they are achieved as a result of a struggle. Hence physical evil is said to be justified on the grounds that moral good plus physical evil is better than the absence of physical evil.

A common reply, and an obvious one, is that urged by Mackie.[7] Mackie argues that whilst it is true that moral good plus physical evil together are better than physical good alone, the issue is not as simple as that, for physical evil also gives rise to and makes possible many moral evils that would not or could not occur in the absence of physical evil. It is then urged that it is not clear that physical evils (for example, disease and pain) plus some moral goods (for example, courage) plus some moral evil (for example, brutality) are better than physical good and those moral goods which are possible and which would occur in the absence of physical evil.

This sort of reply, however, is not completely satisfactory. The objection it raises is a sound one, but it proceeds by conceding too much to the theist, and by overlooking two more basic defects of the argument. It allows implicitly that the problem of physical evil may be reduced to the problem of moral evil; and it neglects the two objections which show that the problem of physical evil cannot be so reduced.

The theist therefore happily accepts this kind of reply, and argues that, if he can give a satisfactory account of moral evil he will then have accounted for both physical and moral evil. He then goes on to account for moral evil in terms of the value of free will and/or its goods. This general argument is deceptively plausible. It breaks down for the two reasons indicated here, but it breaks down at another point as well. If free will alone is used to justify moral evil, then even if no moral good occurred, moral evil would still be said to be justified; but physical evil would have no justification. Physical evil is not

---

confers. That sympathy for others which is one of the most precious parts of our experience, and one of the most fruitful sources of well-doing, has its origin in the fellow-feeling engendered by endurance of similar trials. Furthermore, were it not for these trials, man would think little enough of a future existence, and of the need of striving after his last end. He would be perfectly content with his existence, and would reck little of any higher good. These considerations here briefly advanced suffice at least to show how important is the office filled by pain in human life, and with what little reason it is asserted that the existence of so much suffering is irreconcilable with the wisdom of the Creator."
And:
"It may be asked whether the Creator could not have brought man to perfection without the use of suffering. Most certainly He could have conferred upon him a similar degree of virtue without requiring any effort on his part. Yet it is easy to see that there is a special value attaching to a conquest of difficulties such as man's actual demands, and that in God's eyes this may well be an adequate reason for assigning this life to us in preference to another. . . . Pain has value in respect to the next life, but also in respect to this. The advance of scientific discovery, the gradual improvement of the organization of the community, the growth of material civilization are due in no small degree to the stimulus afforded by pain."

[7] Mackie, "Evil and Omnipotence."

essential to free will; it is only justified if moral good actually occurs, and if the moral good which results from physical evils outweighs the moral evils. This means that the argument from free will cannot alone justify physical evil along these lines; and it means that the argument from free will and its goods does not justify physical evil, because such an argument is incomplete, and necessarily incomplete. It needs to be supplemented by factual evidence that it is logically and practically impossible to obtain.

The correct reply, therefore, is first that the argument is irrelevant to many instances of physical evil, and secondly that it is not true that physical evil plus the moral good it produces is better than physical good and its moral goods. Much pain and suffering, in fact much physical evil generally, for example in children who die in infancy, animals and the insane passes unnoticed; it therefore has no morally uplifting effects upon others, and cannot by virtue of the examples chosen have such effects on the sufferers. Further, there are physical evils such as insanity and much disease to which the argument is inapplicable. So there is a large group of significant cases not covered by the argument. And where the argument is relevant, its premise is plainly false. It can be shown to be false by exposing its implications in the following way:

We either have obligations to lessen physical evil or we have not. If we have obligations to lessen physical evil then we are thereby reducing the total good in the universe. If, on the other hand, our obligation is to increase the total good in the universe it is our duty to prevent the reduction of physical evil and possibly even to increase the total amount of physical evil. Theists usually hold that we are obliged to reduce the physical evil in the universe; but in maintaining this, the theist is, in terms of this account of physical evil, maintaining that it is his duty to reduce the total amount of real good in the universe, and thereby to make the universe worse. Conversely, if by eliminating the physical evil he is not making the universe worse, then that amount of evil which he eliminates was unnecessary and in need of justification. It is relevant to notice here that evil is not always eliminated for morally praiseworthy reasons. Some discoveries have been due to positively unworthy motives, and many other discoveries which have resulted in a lessening of the sufferings of mankind have been due to no higher a motive than a scientist's desire to earn a reasonable living wage.

This reply to the theist's argument brings out its untenability. The theist's argument is seen to imply that war plus courage plus the many other moral virtues war brings into play are better than peace and its virtues; that famine and its moral virtues are better than plenty; that disease and its moral virtues are better than health. Some Christians in the past, in consistency with this mode of reasoning, opposed the use of anesthetics to leave scope for the virtues of endurance and courage, and they opposed state aid to the sick and needy to leave scope for the virtues of charity and sympathy. Some have even contended that war is a good in disguise, again in consistency with this argument. Similarly the theist should, in terms of this fifth argument, in his heart, if not aloud, regret the discovery of the Salk polio vaccine because Dr. Salk has in one blow destroyed infinite possibilities of moral good.

There are three important points that need to be made concerning this kind of account of physical evil. (*a*) We are told, as by Niven, Joyce and others, that pain is a goad to action and that part of its justification lies in this fact. This claim is empirically false as a generalization about all people and all pain. Much pain frustrates action and wrecks people and personalities. On the other hand many men work and work well without being goaded by pain or discomfort. Further, to assert that men need goading is to ascribe another evil to God, for it is to claim that God made men naturally lazy. There is no reason why God should not have made men naturally industrious; the one is no more incompatible with free will than the other. Thus the argument from physical evil being a goad to man breaks down on three distinct counts. Pain often frustrates human endeavor, pain is not essential as a goad with many men, and where pain is a goad to higher endeavors, it is clear that less evil means to this same end are available to an omnipotent God. (*b*) The real fallacy in the argument is in the assumption that all or the highest moral excellence results from physical evil. As we have already seen, this assumption is completely false. Neither all moral goodness nor the highest moral goodness is triumph in the face of adversity or benevolence towards others in suffering. Christ Himself stressed this when He observed that the two great commandments were commandments to love. Love does not depend for its possibility on the existence and conquest of evil. (*c*) The "negative" moral virtues which are brought into play by the various evils—courage, endurance, charity, sympathy and the like—besides not representing the highest forms of moral virtue, are in fact commonly supposed by the theist and atheist alike not to have the value this fifth argument ascribes to them. We—theists and atheists alike—reveal our comparative valuations of these virtues and of physical evil when we insist on state aid for the needy: when we strive for peace, for plenty, and for harmony within the state.

In brief, the good man, the morally admirable man, is he who loves what is good knowing that it is good and preferring it because it is good. He does not need to be torn by suffering or by the spectacle of another's sufferings to be morally admirable. Fortitude in his own sufferings, and sympathetic kindness in others' may reveal to us his goodness; but his goodness is not necessarily increased by such things.

Five arguments concerning physical evil have now been examined. We have seen that the problem of physical evil is a problem in its own right, and one that cannot be reduced to the problem of moral evil; and further, we have seen that physical evil creates not one but a number of problems to which no one nor any combination of the arguments examined offers a solution.

PROPOSED SOLUTIONS TO THE PROBLEM OF MORAL EVIL

The problem of moral evil is commonly regarded as being the greater of the problems concerning evil. As we shall see, it does create what appears to be insuperable difficulties of the theist; but so too, apparently, do physical evils.

For the theist moral evil must be interpreted as a breach of God's law and as a rejection of God Himself. It may involve the eternal damnation of the sinner, and in many of its forms it involves the infliction of suffering on other persons. Thus it aggravates the problem of physical evil, but its own peculiar character consists in the fact of sin. How could a morally perfect, all-powerful

God create a universe in which occur such moral evils as cruelty, cowardice and hatred, the more especially as these evils constitute a rejection of God Himself by His creations, and as such involve them in eternal damnation?

The two main solutions advanced relate to free will and to the fact that moral evil is a consequence of free will. There is a third kind of solution more often invoked implicitly than as an explicit and serious argument, which need not be examined here as its weaknesses are plainly evident. This third solution is to the effect that moral evils and even the most brutal atrocities have their justification in the moral goodness they make possible or bring into being.

1. *Free will alone provides a justification for the moral evil*: This is perhaps the more popular of the serious attempts to explain moral evil. The argument in brief runs: men have free will; moral evil is a consequence of free will; a universe in which men exercise free will even with lapses into moral evil is better than a universe in which men become *automata* doing good always because predestined to do so. Thus on this argument it is the mere fact of the supreme value of free will itself that is taken to provide a justification for its corollary moral evil.

2. *The goods made possible by free will provides a basis for accounting for moral evil*: According to this second argument, it is not the mere fact of free will that is claimed to be of such value as to provide a justification of moral evil, but the fact that free will makes certain goods possible. Some indicate the various moral virtues as the goods that free will makes possible, whilst others point to beatitude, and others again to beatitude achieved by man's own efforts or the virtues achieved as a result of one's own efforts. What all these have in common is the claim that the good consequences of free will provide a justification of the bad consequences of free will, namely moral evil.

Each of these two proposed solutions encounters two specific criticisms, which are fatal to their claims to be real solutions.

1. To consider first the difficulties to which the former proposed solution is exposed. (*a*) A difficulty for the first argument—that it is free will alone that provides a justification for moral evil—lies in the fact that the theist who argues in this way has to allow that it is logically possible on the free will hypothesis that all men should always will what is evil, and that even so, a universe of completely evil men possessing free will is better than one in which men are predestined to virtuous living. It has to be contended that the value of free will itself is so immense that it more than outweighs the total moral evil, the eternal punishment of the wicked, and the sufferings inflicted on others by the sinners in their evilness. It is this paradox that leads to the formulation of the second argument; and it is to be noted that the explanation of moral evil switches to the second argument or to a combination of the first and second argument, immediately the theist refuses to face the logical possibility of complete wickedness, and insists instead that in fact men do not always choose what is evil.

(*b*) The second difficulty encountered by the first argument relates to the possibility that free will is compatible with less evil, and even with no evil, that is, with absolute goodness, or even with less moral evil than actually occurs, then all or at least some evil will be left unexplained by free will alone.

Mackie, in his recent paper, and Joyce, in his discussion of this argument, both contend that free will is compatible with absolute goodness. Mackie argues that if it is not possible for God to confer free will on men and at the same time ensure that no moral evil is committed He cannot really be omnipotent. Joyce directs his argument rather to fellow-theists, and it is more of an *ad hominem* argument addressed to them. He writes:

> Free will need not (as is often assumed) involve the power to choose wrong. Our ability to misuse the gift is due to the conditions under which it is exercised here. In our present state we are able to reject what is truly good, and exercise our power of preference in favor of some baser attraction. Yet it is not necessary that it should be so. And all who accept Christian revelation admit that those who attain their final beatitude exercise freedom of will, and yet cannot choose aught but what is truly good. They possess the knowledge of Essential Goodness; and to it, not simply to good in general, they refer every choice. Moreover, even in our present condition it is open to omnipotence so to order our circumstances and to confer on the will such instinctive impulses that we should in every election adopt the right course and not the wrong one.

To this objection, that free will is compatible with absolute goodness and that therefore a benevolent, omnipotent God would have given man free will and ensured his absolute virtue, it is replied that God is being required to perform what is logically impossible. It is logically impossible, so it is argued, for free will and absolute goodness to be combined, and hence, if God lacks omnipotence only in this respect, He cannot be claimed to lack omnipotence in any sense in which serious theists have ascribed it to Him.

Quite clearly, if free will and absolute goodness are logically incompatible, then God, in not being able to confer both on man, does not lack omnipotence in any important sense of the term. However, it is not clear that free will and absolute goodness are logically opposed; and Joyce does point to considerations which suggest that they are not logical incompatibles. For my own part I am uncertain on this point; but my uncertainty is not a factual one but one concerning a point of usage. It is clear that an omnipotent God could create rational agents predestined always to make virtuous "decisions"; what is not clear is whether we should describe such agents as having free will. The considerations to which Joyce points have something of the status of test cases, and they would suggest that we should describe such agents as having free will. However, no matter how we resolve the linguistic point, the question remains—Which is more desirable, free will and moral evil and the physical evil to which free will gives rise, or this special free will or pseudo-free will which goes with absolute goodness? I suggest that the latter is clearly preferable. Later I shall endeavor to defend this conclusion; for the moment I am content to indicate the nature of the value judgment on which the question turns at this point.

The second objection to the proposed solution of the problem of moral evil in terms of free will alone, is related to the contention that free will is compatible with less moral evil than occurs, and possibly with no moral evil. We have seen what is involved in the latter contention. We may now consider what is involved in the former. It may be argued that free will is compatible with less moral evil than in fact occurs on various grounds. (i) God, if He were all-powerful, could miraculously intervene to prevent some or perhaps all moral evil; and He is said to do so on occasions in answer to prayers (for example, to prevent wars) or of His own initiative (for instance, by producing calamities which serve as warnings, or by working miracles, etc.).

(ii) God has made man with a certain nature. This nature is often interpreted by theologians as having a bias to evil. Clearly God could have created man with a strong bias to good, whilst still leaving scope for a decision to act evilly. Such a bias to good would be compatible with freedom of the will. (iii) An omnipotent God could so have ordered the world that it was less conducive to the practice of evil.

These are all considerations advanced by Joyce, and separately and jointly, they establish that God could have conferred free will upon us, and at least very considerably *reduced* the amount of moral evil that would have resulted from the exercise of free will. This is sufficient to show that *not all* the moral evil that exists can be justified by reference to free will alone. This conclusion is fatal to the account of moral evil in terms of free will alone. The more extreme conclusion that Mackie seeks to establish—that absolute goodness is compatible with free will—is not essential as a basis for refuting the free will argument. The difficulty is as fatal to the claims of theism whether all moral evil or only some moral evil is unaccountable. However, whether Mackie's contentions are sound is still a matter of logical interest, although not of any real moment in the context of the case against theism, once the fact that less moral evil is compatible with free will has been established.

2. The second free will argument arises out of an attempt to circumvent these objections. It is not free will, but the value of the goods achieved through free will that is said to be so great as to provide a justification for moral evil.

(*a*) This second argument meets a difficulty in that it is now necessary for it to be supplemented by a proof that the number of people who practice moral virtue or who attain beatitude and/or virtue after a struggle is sufficient to outweigh the evilness of moral evil, the evilness of their eternal damnation and the physical evil they cause to others. This is a serious defect in the argument, because it means that the argument can at best show that moral evil *may have* a justification, and not that it has a justification. It is both logically and practically impossible to supplement and complete the argument. It is necessarily incomplete and inconclusive even if its general principle is sound.

(*b*) This second argument is designed also to avoid the other difficulty of the first argument—that free will may be compatible with no evil and certainly with less evil. It is argued that even if free will is compatible with absolute goodness it is still better that virtue and beatitude be attained after a genuine personal struggle; and this, it is said, would not occur if God in conferring free will nonetheless prevented moral evil or reduced the risk of it. Joyce argues in this way:

> To receive our final beatitude as the fruit of our labors, and as the recompense of a hard-won victory, is an incomparably higher destiny than to receive it without any effort on our part. And since God in His wisdom has seen fit to give us such a lot as this, it was inevitable that man should have the power to choose wrong. We could not be called to merit the reward due to victory without being exposed to the possibility of defeat.

There are various objections which may be urged here. First, this argument implies that the more intense the struggle, the greater is the triumph and resultant good, and the better the world; hence we should apparently, on this argument, court temptation and moral struggles to attain greater virtue and to be more worthy of our reward. Secondly, it may be urged that God is being said to be demanding too high a price for the goods produced. He is omniscient. He knows that many will sin and not attain the goods or the Good free will is said to make possible. He creates men with free will, with the natures men have, in the world as it is constituted, knowing that in His doing so He is committing many to moral evil and eternal damnation. He could avoid all this evil by creating men with rational wills predestined to virtue, or He could eliminate much of it by making men's natures and the conditions in the world more conducive to the practice of virtue. He is said not to choose to do this. Instead, at the cost of the sacrifice of the many, He is said to have ordered things so as to allow fewer men to attain this higher virtue and higher beatitude that result from the more intense struggle.

In attributing such behavior to God, and in attempting to account for moral evil along these lines, theists are, I suggest, attributing to God immoral behavior of a serious kind—of a kind we should all unhesitatingly condemn in a fellow human being.

We do not commend people for putting temptation in the way of others. On the contrary, anyone who today advocated, or even allowed where he could prevent it, the occurrence of evil and the sacrifice of the many—even as a result of their own freely chosen actions—for the sake of the higher virtue of the few, would be condemned as an immoralist. To put severe temptation in the way of the many, knowing that many and perhaps even most will succumb to the temptation, for the sake of the higher virtue of the few, would be blatant immorality; and it would be immoral whether or not those who yielded to the temptation possessed free will. This point can be brought out by considering how a conscientious moral agent would answer the question: Which should I choose for other people, a world in which there are intense moral struggles and the possibility of magnificent triumphs and the certainty of many defeats, or a world in which there are less intense struggles, less magnificent triumphs but more triumphs and fewer defeats, or a world in which there are no struggles, no triumphs and no defeats? We are constantly answering less easy questions than this in a way that conflicts with the theist's contentions. If by modifying our own behavior we can save someone else from an intense moral struggle and almost certain moral evil, for example if by refraining from gambling or excessive drinking ourselves we can help a weaker person not to become a confirmed gambler or an alcoholic, or if by locking our car and not leaving it unlocked and with the key in it we can prevent people yielding to the temptation to become car thieves, we feel obliged to act accordingly, even though the persons concerned would freely choose the evil course of conduct. How much clearer is the decision with which God is said to be faced—the choice between the higher virtue of some and the evil of others, or the higher but less high virtue of many more, and the evil of many fewer. Neither alternative denies free will to men.

These various difficulties dispose of each of the main arguments relating to moral evil. There are in addition to these difficulties two other objections that might be urged.

If it could be shown that man has not free will both arguments collapse; and even if it could be shown that God's omniscience is incompatible with free will they would still break down. The issues raised here are too great to be pursued in this paper; and they can simply be noted as possible additional grounds from which criticisms of the main proposed solutions of the problem of moral evil may be advanced.

The other general objection is by way of a follow-up to points made in objections (*b*) to both arguments (1) and (2). It concerns the relative value of free will and its goods and evils and the value of the best of the alternatives to free will and its goods. Are free will and its goods so much more valuable than the next best alternatives that their superior value can really justify the immense amount of evil that is introduced into the world by free will?

Theologians who discuss this issue ask, Which is better—men with free will striving to work out their own destinies, or automata-machinelike creatures, who never make mistakes because they never make decisions? When put in this form we naturally doubt whether free will plus moral evil plus the possibility of the eternal damnation of the many and the physical evil of untold billions are quite so unjustified after all; but the fact of the matter is that the question has not been fairly put. The real alternative is, on the one hand, rational agents with free wills making many bad and some good decisions on rational and nonrational grounds, and "rational" agents predestined always "to choose" the right things for the right reasons—that is, if the language of automata must be used, rational automata. Predestination does not imply the absence of rationality in all senses of the term. God, were He omnipotent, could preordain the decisions and the reasons upon which they were based; and such a mode of existence would seem to be in itself a worthy mode of existence, and one preferable to an existence with free will, irrationality and evil.

CONCLUSION

In this paper it has been maintained that God, were He all-powerful and perfectly good, would have created a world in which there was no unnecessary evil. It has not been argued that God ought to have created a perfect world, nor that He should have made one that is in any way logically impossible. It has simply been argued that a benevolent God could, and would, have created a world devoid of superfluous evil. It has been contended that there is evil in this world—unnecessary evil—and that the more popular and philosophically more significant of the many attempts to explain this evil are completely unsatisfactory. Hence we must conclude from the existence of evil that there cannot be an omnipotent benevolent God.

IV.A.3.   Omnipotence, Evil and Supermen

NINIAN SMART

Ninian Smart (1927–), professor of religious studies at the University of California at Santa Barbara, undertakes to answer the claim, put forward by a number of philosophers such as Antony Flew and J. L. Mackie, that God could have made humans wholly good—that is, he could have fashioned free human agents so that they always do good things and never do evil. Smart argues that such a position, plausible enough when superficially considered, turns out to be extremely implausible, perhaps even unintelligible, when closely examined.

It has in recent years been argued, by Professors Antony Flew and J. L. Mackie,[1] that God could have created men wholly good. For causal determinism being compatible with free will, men could have been made in such a way that, without loss of freedom, they would never have fallen (and would never fall) into sin. This if true would constitute a weighty anti-theistic argument. And yet intuitively it seems unconvincing. I wish here to uncover the roots of this intuitive suspicion.

There are in the argument two assertions to be distinguished. First, that causal determinism (i.e. the claim that all human actions are the results of prior causes) is compatible with free will.[2] I call this the Compatibility Thesis. Second, there is the assertion that God could have created men wholly good. This I shall call the Utopia Thesis. An apparent inference from the latter is that God cannot be both omnipotent and wholly good, since men are in fact wicked.

In the present discussion I shall concentrate on the Utopia Thesis. Clearly, of course, if the Compatibility Thesis is not established the Utopia Thesis loses its principal basis and becomes altogether doubtful. But I shall here merely try to show that the Utopia Thesis does not follow from the Compatibility Thesis, despite appearances. This may well indicate that there is something queer about the latter (and the Paradigm Case Argument, on which perhaps it principally rests, has lately come in for perspicacious criticisms).[3] In the

From *Philosophy* 36, no. 137 (1961): 188–195. Reprinted with permission of Cambridge University Press.

[1] See Antony Flew, "Divine Omnipotence and Human Freedom," in *New Essays in Philosophical Theology*, A. Flew and A. MacIntyre, eds. (New York: The Macmillan Company, 1955).

[2] See Flew, *op. cit.*, p. 151.

[3] See the article "Farewell to the Paradigm-Case Argument" by J. W. N. Watkins, and Flew's comments and Watkins' reply to the comments, all in *Analysis*, Vol. XVIII, No. 2 (1957), and the articles by R. Harré and H. G. Alexander in *Analysis*, Vol. XVIII, Nos. 4-5 (1958), respectively.

discussion I shall be assuming the truth of determinism; for if it is false, the Compatibility Thesis becomes irrelevant and the Utopia Thesis totters. The chief points in my reasoning are as follows:

The concept *good* as applied to humans connects with other concepts such as *temptation, courage, generosity*, etc. These concepts have no clear application if men were built wholly good. I bring this out by a piece of anthropological fiction, i.e. (*a*) let us conjure up a universe like ours, only where men are supposed to be wholly good; or (*b*) let us consider the possibility of Utopian universes quite unlike ours. Under (*a*), I try to show that it is unclear whether the "men" in such a universe are to be called wholly good or even good, and that it is unclear whether they should be called men. And under (*b*), I try to show that we have even stronger reasons for saying that these things are unclear. Thus the abstract possibility that men might have been created wholly good has no clearly assignable content. Hence, it is rational to be quite agnostic about such a possibility. It follows that it will be quite unclear whether a Utopian universe will be superior (in respect of moral goodness) to ours. So the Utopia Thesis cannot constitute an anti-theistic argument.

I

When we say that a man is good we are liable to render an account of why we say this, by giving reasons. For example, it might be because he has been heroic in resisting temptations, courageous in the face of difficulties, generous to his friends, etc. Thus *good* normally connects with concepts like *courage* and so forth.

Let us look first at *temptation*. It is clear (at least on the determinist assumption) that if two identical twins were in otherwise similar situations but where one has a temptation not to do what is right, while no such temptation is presented to the other twin, and other things being equal, the tempted twin will be less likely to do what is right than the untempted one. It is this fact that temptations are empirically discovered to affect conduct that doubtless makes it relevant to consider them when appraising character and encouraging virtue. Moreover, unless we were built in a certain way there would be no temptations: for example, unless we were built so that sexual gratification is normally very pleasant there would be no serious temptations to commit adultery, etc. It would appear then that the only way to ensure that people were wholly good would be to build them in such a way that they were never tempted or only tempted to a negligible extent. True, there are two other peculiar possibilities, which I shall go on to deal with, namely (*a*) through lucky combination of circumstances men might never sin: (*b*) frequent miraculous intervention might keep them on the straight and narrow path. However, for the moment, I consider the main possibility, that to ensure that *all* men were *always* good, men would have to possess a built-in resistance to all temptations.

Similar remarks apply to courage, generosity, etc., although in some cases the situation may be rather complex. It will, I think, be conceded that we credit people with courage on such grounds as that they have faced adverse situations with calm and disregard for danger. But the adversities arise because there are fears, desires for comfort, disinclinations to offend people, and so on. And it will be generally agreed, at least by determinists, that one twin faced with a situation where doing right inspires fear will be less likely to do what is right than the other twin not so faced with adversity, and similarly with regard to desires for comfort and so forth. Thus to ensure that men would never panic, never wilt, etc., it would be necessary, as the main possibility, to build them differently.

Perhaps generosity is a trickier case. But it is clear that a person is praised for generosity because very often there is a conflict of generosity and self-interest. Indeed, if there were not some such conflict, or thought to be, however remote, an action would not really count as generosity, perhaps; the slight qualification here is due to the possibility of situations where a person has so much money, say, that it makes no psychological difference whether he gives away a certain sum or not, but he does it out of sympathy—I shall deal with such cases below. And to say that generosity conflicts with self-interest is a short-hand way of saying that one's inclinations for comfort, etc. are liable to have a more restricted fulfilment than would otherwise be the case.

Then there are actions which exhibit such dispositions as pride, which seem remote from simple inclinations such as likings for certain sorts of food or for sexual gratification and from fairly simple impulses such as fear. But though the springs of pride are hard to fathom, it is doubtless true that people would not display pride, in the ordinary sense, if they did not live in a socially competitive atmosphere, if they did not have desires to assert themselves, etc. One would not be sure quite how men would have to be rebuilt to immunize them from pride, but rebuilding would surely be necessary, on the determinist view.

As for the peculiar cases mentioned above—generosity not involving sacrifice and similar examples—I do not think that such instances are at all serious ones, inasmuch as (a) virtues are dispositions, and so there is a point in calling such non-sacrificial generosity generosity, in that it exhibits a disposition whose basic exercise involves sacrifice; (b) without the occasions for basic exercise of the disposition it is obscure as to what could be meant by calling the non basic instances of generosity instances of generosity.

These examples, then, are meant to indicate that the concept *goodness* is applied to beings of a certain sort, beings who are liable to temptations, possess inclinations, have fears, tend to assert themselves and so forth; and that if they were to be immunized from evil they would have to be built in a different way. But it soon becomes apparent that to rebuild them would mean that the ascription of goodness would become unintelligible, for the reasons why men are called good and bad have a connection with human nature as it is empirically discovered to be. Moral utterance is embedded in the cosmic status quo.

II

Of course, God is not bound by synthetic necessities: He is in no way shackled by the causal laws of our universe, for example. But in a back-handed way, He is confined by meaninglessness. For to say that God might do such and-such where the "such-and-such" is meaningless or completely obscure is not to assert that God can *do* anything. I therefore hope to show that "God might have created men wholly good" is without intelligible content, and hence that this alleged possibility has no force as an anti-theistic argument.

"God might have created men wholly good" *appears* to have content because at least it does not seem self-contradictory and because we think we can imagine such a situation. But I shall bring out its emptiness by in fact trying to do this, by imagining other possible universes. Now it may well be objected that in doing this I am showing nothing. For example, one will be wanting to make imaginative causal inferences like "If men are never to panic they must be built in such-and-such a way". But since God is not bound by causal principles the inferences have no legitimacy.

But this objection misses the point of my procedure. For my argument is based on the following dilemma. *Either* we can hope to assign a reasonably clear meaning to the possibility that men might have been created wholly good by imagining a Utopia—in which case the paradox arises that it would be quite unclear as to whether such "men" could reasonably be called wholly good. *Or* we can refuse to assign such a reasonably clear meaning to the possibility by simply postulating an unimaginable alternative universe—in which case there are even stronger reasons for doubting whether the possibility has content. Or, to make the matter *ad hominem* as against Flew, I am saying that alleged possibilities as well as alleged facts can die the Death by a Thousand Qualifications.

I proceed then to imagine possible universes. In line with the above dilemma, I divide such universes into two classes. First, those which are cosmomorphic, i.e. those which are governed by physical laws at least roughly comparable to those found in our cosmos. Second, I consider non-cosmomorphic universes, i.e. ones with a quite different set-up from ours.

(a) Cosmomorphic Utopia A.—The first and main type of cosmomorphic utopia, where men are wholly good, can be described perhaps as follows, in line with the earlier remarks about temptation, etc.

Men will never be seriously tempted to harm or injure each other. For this reason: that no one has any serious desires liable to conflict with those of others. For instance, they would be so built that one and only one woman would attract any one man and conversely. Say: one would have an overriding infatuation for the first uninfatuated woman one met and vice versa. As for property: men might arrive in the world with an automatic supply of necessities and comforts, and the individual would have a built-in mechanism to ensure that the supplies of others were mysteriously distasteful (the other man's passion-fruit smells like dung). And what of danger? During, say, a thunderstorm no one would be so seriously perturbed that he would be likely to panic and harm others. Let us suppose that a signal would (so to speak) flash in the individual's brain, telling him to take cover. What if he was in the middle of an *al fresco* dinner? Perhaps the signal flashing would dry up the juices in his mouth. And so forth. (Admittedly this picture is not elaborated with much scientific expertize: of this I shall say more later.)

I think that none of the usual reasons for calling men good would apply in such a Utopia. Consider one of these harmless beings. He is wholly good, you say? Really? Has he been courageous? No, you reply, not exactly, for such creatures do not feel fear. Then he is generous to his friends perhaps? Not precisely, you respond, for there is no question of his being ungenerous. Has he resisted temptations? No, not really, for there are no temptations (nothing you could really *call* temptations). Then why call them good? Well, you say, these creatures never harm each other. . . . Yes, but the inhabitants of Alpha Centauri never harm *us*. Ah, you reply, Centaurians do not harm us because there are as yet no ways for them to impinge upon us. Quite so, I say; it is causally impossible for them to harm us. Similarly the set-up of the Cosmomorphic Utopians makes it causally impossible for them to harm each other. The fact that it is distance in the one case and inner structure in the other makes no odds.

Now admittedly in such a conversation we are not brought face to face with the Death by a Thousand Qualifications in the form described by Flew in regard to such statements as "God loves His children". For there the criticism of the theologian is that when counter-evidence is presented he takes refuge in increasingly recondite senses of "love". But in the present case one who claims that the inhabitants of Cosmomorphic Utopia A are wholly good is not precisely resisting counter-evidence (that is, he is not resisting evidence that these creatures are not good and so possibly bad). Rather he is failing to give the usual reasons for calling them bad. And the positive moves are up to him. It is not sufficient airily and vaguely to say that in such an alternative universe men can be said to be wholly good. Similarly the traveller from Jupiter who tells us that unicorns are to be found there, though queer unicorns for they possess neither horns nor feet, leaves us at a justifiable loss.

Hence it is so far obscure as to what is meant by the possibility that men might have been created wholly good. For the usual criteria, at least in Cosmomorphic Utopia A, do not seem to apply. And so, even if the Compatibility Thesis is correct, it does not appear so far evident that men might have been created wholly good. For an unintelligible assertion cannot either be said to follow or not to follow from some other. And in any case, are the Utopians described above properly to be called *men*? Perhaps we ought to invent a new name: let us dub them "sapients". The question for the theist now becomes: "Why did God create man rather than sapients?" I shall return to this question later.

(b) Cosmomorphic Utopia B.—Circumstances here combine always to make men good. Adolf Hitler would never in fact be foul. He might have incipient impulses of hatred towards Jews, but these would luckily never overwhelm him, because circumstances would prevent this: he would fall in love with a Jewess, he would never get into anti-Semitic company, he would not meet with miseries in his youth, and so forth. Whenever on the point of falling for some temptation, his attention would be distracted. The whole thing would be a very, very long story. And everyone, not just the Führer, would be consistently lucky with regard to virtue and vice.

The trouble about this Utopia is that it is more like a dream than a fantasy. A corresponding meteorological dream would be: since circumstances occasionally combine to make the sun shine, let us suppose that the sky would never be overcast. This does not seem self-contradictory, to say "The sky might never be overcast". But what would a cosmomorphic universe have to be like for this to happen? Clearly it is not just luck that makes the sun shine sometimes: it is because the weather operates in a certain way. For the weather so to operate that it was never cloudy meteorological laws would have to be rewritten (and physics and biology too)—unless you are thinking of a place like the moon. Similarly, in a cosmomorphic utopia where circumstances for ever combined in favour of virtue, the set-up would, according to the determinist, have to be different. Thus Cosmomorphic Utopia B is either a version of A (or of some other) or it is a mere dream masquerading as an alternative universe.

(c) *Cosmomorphic Utopia C.*—Suppose men were always virtuous, not because of the set-up (which would be as now) but because of frequent miraculous intervention.

It is hard to make sense of the supposition. But observationally in such a world we might discover situations like this. Causal factors C usually give rise to actions of a certain empirical type, type-A. But in some circumstances type-A actions are wrong, and in these cases C will not have type-A effects. But it will not be that some other empirical factor will be present in such exceptions, for *ex hypothesi* the non-occurrence of the type-A action is due to miraculous intervention. Hence either we have to count rightness and wrongness as empirical differences in order to formulate a causal law here or we must confess that no strict causal laws of human behavior could be formulated in this cosmos. The former alternative is baffling and unacceptable, while the latter is incompatible with determinism. Hence Cosmomorphic Utopia C provides no support for the Utopia Thesis.

(d) I now turn to the thought of a *Non-Cosmomorphic Utopia.* As had been insisted, God is not limited to a cosmomorphic alternative. My anthropological fictions are feeble in comparison with the possibilities contained in God's thoughts. He might have produced a cosmos utterly unlike ours.

But as we have no notion what sapients in such a world would be like, it is even unclearer in this case what would be meant by calling them good. We would have to remain completely agnostic about such a world; and all the difficulties there are in knowing what is meant by calling God a person and good would recur with extra force when we try to understand what "wholly good men" could mean here. *Extra* force, because whereas God's nature is perhaps revealed to a limited extent in the *actual* cosmos, the nature of an alternative *possible* and *non-cosmomorphic* universe can in no way be so revealed. Hence it follows that it is totally unclear what the possibility that God might have created a non-cosmomorphic utopia amounts to.

It is therefore also unclear as to whether it would be superior to this universe. Moreover, it is most doubtful as to whether the sapients of Cosmomorphic Utopia A are superior to ourselves. I am not sure, of course, how one judges such matters; but if we rely on native wit, in default of some new method of evaluating alternative universes, it seems by no means clear that such a utopia is a better place than ours here.

III

It may be complained that I have been unfair. My anthropological fiction has been crude and possibly biassed. And the thing has not been worked out with any scientific expertize. But no one, so far as I know, with the requisite physiological, psychological and biological knowledge has attempted to work out such a fictional alternative anthropology, doubtless there are enough problems in the real-life biological sciences without our going off into subtle fantasies. But until someone were to do so, it remains obscure as to what a determinist cosmomorphic utopia would amount to.

IV.B.   Psychological Objections: Religion as Opiate or Mass Delusion

IV.B.1.   God Created in Man's Image

SIGMUND FREUD

Sigmund Freud (1856–1939), a seminal thinker of modern psychology, is credited with discovering the so-called "talking cure" for hysteria and other forms of mental illness and with founding the school of psychoanalysis. While writing extensively about psychopathology and psychotherapy, he was not at all reticent about venturing into the realm of philosophy and offering speculative theories about religion. In his Future of an Illusion, *from which the following selection is taken, Freud characterizes religion as one of the ways in which humans cope with the threats of a dangerous world and delude themselves into believing that they are cared for by a loving Father who will reward them in heaven for any hardships endured in this life.*

Reprinted from *The Future of an Illusion* by Sigmund Freud, translated and edited by James Strachey (published in the British Commonwealth as *The Standard Edition of the Complete Works of Sigmund Freud*). By permission of W.W. Norton & Company, Inc. and Sigmund Freud Copyrights, The Institute of Psycho-Analysis, and the Hogarth Press. Copyright © 1961 by James Strachey. Copyright renewed 1989.

In what does the peculiar value of religious ideas lie?

We have spoken of the hostility to civilization which is produced by the pressure that civilization exercises, the renunciations of instinct which it demands. If one imagines its prohibitions lifted—if, then, one may take any woman one pleases as a sexual object, if one may without hesitation kill one's rival for her love or anyone else who stands in one's way, if, too, one can carry off any of the other man's belongings without asking leave—how splendid, what a string of satisfactions one's life would be! True, one soon comes across the first difficulty: everyone else has exactly the same wishes as I have and will treat me with no more consideration than I treat him. And so in reality only one person could be made unrestrictedly happy by such a removal of the restrictions of civilization, and he would be a tyrant, a dictator, who had seized all the means to power. And even he would have every reason to wish that the others would observe at least one cultural commandment: 'thou shalt not kill'.

But how ungrateful, how short-sighted after all, to strive for the abolition of civilization! What would then remain would be a state of nature, and that would be far harder to bear. It is true that nature would not demand any restrictions of instinct from us, she would let us do as we liked; but she has her own particularly effective method of restricting us. She destroys us—coldly, cruelly, relentlessly, as it seems to us, and possibly through the very things that occasioned our satisfaction. It was precisely because of these dangers with which nature threatens us that we came together and created civilization, which is also, among other things, intended to make our communal life possible. For the principle task of civilization, its actual *raison d'être*, is to defend us against nature.

We all know that in many ways civilization does this fairly well already, and clearly as time goes on it will do it much better. But no one is under the illusion that nature has already been vanquished; and few dare hope that she will ever be entirely subject to man. There are the elements, which seem to mock at all human control: the earth, which quakes and is torn apart and buries all human life and its works; water, which deluges and drowns everything in a turmoil; storms, which blow everything before them; there are diseases, which we have only recently recognized as attacks by other organisms; and finally there is the painful riddle of death, against which no medicine has yet been found, nor probably will be. With these forces nature rises up against us, majestic, cruel and inexorable; she brings to our mind once more our weakness and helplessness, which we thought to escape through the work of civilization. One of the few gratifying and exalting impressions which mankind can offer is when, in the face of an elemental catastrophe, it forgets the discordancies of its civilization and all its internal difficulties and animosities, and recalls the great common task of preserving itself against the superior power of nature.

For the individual, too, life is hard to bear, just as it is for mankind in general. The civilization in which he participates imposes some amount of privation on him, and other men bring him a measure of suffering, either in spite of the precepts of his civilization or because of its imperfections. To this are added the injuries which untamed nature—he calls it Fate—inflicts on him. One might suppose that this condition of things would result in a permanent state of anxious expectation in him and a severe injury to his natural narcissism. We know already how the individual reacts to the injuries which civilization and other men inflict on him: he develops a corresponding degree of resistance to the regulations of civilization and of hostility to it. But how does he defend himself against the superior powers of nature, of Fate, which threaten him as they threaten all the rest?

Civilization relieves him of this task; it performs it in the same way for all alike; and it is noteworthy that in this almost all civilizations act alike. Civilization does not call a halt in the task of defending man against nature, it merely pursues it by other means. The task is a manifold one. Man's self-regard, seriously menaced, calls for consolation; life and the universe must be robbed of their terrors; moreover his curiosity, moved, it is true, by the strongest practical interest, demands an answer.

A great deal is already gained with the first step: the humanization of nature. Impersonal forces and destinies cannot be approached; they remain eternally remote. But if the elements have passions that rage as they do in our own souls, if death itself is not something spontaneous but the violent act of an evil Will, if everywhere in nature there are Beings around us of a kind that we know in our own society, then we can breathe freely, can feel at home in the uncanny and can deal by psychical means with our senseless anxiety. We are still defenceless, perhaps, but we are no longer helplessly paralysed; we can at least react. Perhaps, indeed, we are not even defenceless. We can apply the same methods against these violent supermen outside that we employ in our own society; we can try to adjure them, to appease them, to bribe them, and, by so influencing them, we may rob them of a part of their power. A replacement like this of natural science by psychology not only provides immediate relief, but also points the way to a further mastering of the situation.

For this situation is nothing new. It has an infantile prototype, of which it is in fact only the continuation. For once before one has found oneself in a similar state of helplessness: as a small child, in relation to one's parents. One had reason to fear them, and especially one's father; and yet one was sure of his protection against the dangers one knew. Thus it was natural to assimilate the two situations. Here, too, wishing played its part, as it does in dream-life. The sleeper may be seized with a presentiment of death, which threatens to place him in the grave. But the dream-work knows how to select a condition that will turn even that dreaded event into a wish-fulfilment: the dreamer sees himself in an ancient Etruscan grave which he has climbed down into, happy to find his archaeological interests satisfied.[1] In the same way, a man makes the forces of nature not simply into persons with whom he can associate as he would with his equals —that would not do justice to the overpowering impression which those forces make on him—but he gives them the character of a father. He turns them into gods, following in this as I have tried to show,[2] not only an infantile prototype but a phylogenetic one.

In the course of time the first observations were made of regularity and conformity to law in natural phenomena, and with this the forces of nature

---

[1] [This was an actual dream of Freud's reported in Chapter VI (G) of *The Interpretation of Dreams* (1900a), *Standard Ed.*, 5, 454–5.]

[2] [See section 6 of the fourth essay in *Totem and Taboo* (1912–13) *Standard Ed.*, 13, 146ff.)]

lost their human traits. But man's helplessness remains and along with it his longing for his father, and the gods. The gods retain their threefold task: they must exorcize the terrors of nature, they must reconcile men to the cruelty of Fate, particularly as it is shown in death, and they must compensate them for the sufferings and privations which a civilized life in common has imposed on them.

But within these functions there is a gradual displacement of accent. It was observed that the phenomena of nature developed automatically according to internal necessities. Without doubt the gods were lords of nature; they had arranged it to be as it was and now they could leave it to itself. Only occasionally, in what are known as miracles, did they intervene in its course, as though to make it plain that they had relinquished nothing of their original sphere of power. As regards the apportioning of destinies, an unpleasant suspicion persisted that the perplexity and helplessness of the human race could not be remedied. It was here that the gods were most apt to fail. If they themselves created Fate, then their counsels must be deemed inscrutable. The notion dawned on the most gifted people of antiquity that Moira [Fate] stood above the gods and that the gods themselves had their own destinies. And the more autonomous nature became and the more the gods withdrew from it, the more earnestly were all expectations directed to the third function of the gods—the more did morality become their true domain. It now became the task of the gods to even out the defects and evils of civilization, to attend to the sufferings which men inflict on one another in their life together and to watch over the fulfilment of the precepts of civilization, which men obey so imperfectly. Those precepts themselves were credited with a divine origin; they were elevated beyond human society and were extended to nature and the universe.

And thus a store of ideas is created, born from man's need to make his helplessness tolerable and built up from the material of memories of the helplessness of his own childhood and the childhood of the human race. It can clearly be seen that the possession of these ideas protects him in two directions—against the dangers of nature and Fate, and against the injuries that threaten him from human society itself. Here is the gist of the matter. Life in this world serves a higher purpose; no doubt it is not easy to guess what that purpose is, but it certainly signifies a perfecting of man's nature. It is probably the spiritual part of man, the soul, which in the course of time has so slowly and unwillingly detached itself from the body, that is the object of this elevation and exaltation. Everything that happens in this world is an expression of the intentions of an intelligence superior to us, which in the end, though its ways and byways are difficult to follow, orders everything for the best—that is, to make it enjoyable for us. Over each one of us there watches a benevolent Providence which is only seemingly stern and which will not suffer us to become a plaything of the over-mighty and pitiless forces of nature. Death itself is not extinction, is not a return to inorganic lifelessness, but the beginning of a new kind of existence which lies on the path of development to something higher. And, looking in the other direction, this view announces that the same moral laws which our civilizations have set up govern the whole universe as well, except that they are maintained by a supreme court of justice with incomparably more power and consistency. In the end all good is rewarded and all evil punished, if not actually in this form of life then in the later existences that begin after death. In this way all the terrors, the sufferings and the hardships of life are destined to be obliterated. Life after death, which continues life on earth just as the invisible part of the spectrum joins on to the visible part, brings us all the perfection that we may perhaps have missed here. And the superior wisdom which directs this course of things, the infinite goodness that expresses itself in it, the justice that achieves its aim in it—these are the attributes of the divine beings who also created us and the world as a whole, or rather, of the one divine being into which, in our civilization, all the gods of antiquity have been condensed. The people which first succeeded in thus concentrating the divine attributes was not a little proud of the advance. It had laid open to view the father who had all along been hidden behind every divine figure as its nucleus. Fundamentally this was a return to the historical beginnings of the idea of God. Now that God was a single person, man's relations to him could recover the intimacy and intensity of the child's relation to his father. But if one had done so much for one's father, one wanted to have a reward, or at least to be his only beloved child, his Chosen People. Very much later, pious America laid claim to being 'God's own Country'; and, as regards one of the shapes in which men worship the deity, the claim is undoubtedly valid.

The religious ideas that have been summarized above have of course passed through a long process of development and have been adhered to in various phases by various civilizations. I have singled out one such phase, which roughly corresponds to the final form taken by our present-day white Christian civilization. It is easy to see that not all the parts of this picture tally equally well with one another, that not all the questions that press for an answer receive one, and that it is difficult to dismiss the contradiction of daily experience. Nevertheless, such as they are, those ideas—ideas which are religious in the widest sense— are prized as the most precious thing it has to offer its participants. It is far more highly prized than all the devices for winning treasures from the earth or providing men with sustenance or preventing their illnesses, and so forth. People feel that life would not be tolerable if they did not attach to these ideas the value that is claimed for them. And now the question arises: what are these ideas in the light of psychology? Whence do they derive the esteem in which they are held? And, to take a further timid step, what is their real worth?

IV.B.2 Religion as Mass Delusion

SIGMUND FREUD

Sigmund Freud (1856–1939), the originator of psycho-analysis, added to his scientific writings on psychology a number of speculative writings on philosophy, religion, and social issues. Freud does not really advance rational argu-ments against the truth of theism but offers conjectural theo-ries about how religious belief and practice might have arisen—although he seems to regard his speculations not as hypotheses but as truths that he has discovered or as beliefs so obvious once recognized as not to need the support of argu-ment. In Civilization and Its Discontents, *from which this selection comes, he characterizes the human religious impulse as infantile and religion itself as a mass delusion that saves many people from individual neuroses. Freud does not seem to be aware that, even if his speculations about the origins of religion should be correct, exposing these origins provides no evidence concerning the validity of the developed teachings of the religion. Any doubts that such writings may raise concerning theism or religion can be only of a psychologi-cal and not a logical sort.*

The programme of becoming happy, which the plea-sure principle imposes on us, cannot be fulfilled; yet we must not—indeed, we cannot—give up our efforts to bring it nearer to fulfilment by some means or other. Very different paths may be taken in that direction, and we may give priority either to positive aspect of the aim, that of gaining pleasure, or to its negative one, that of avoiding unpleasure. By none of these paths can we attain all that we desire. Happiness, in the reduced sense in which we recog-nize it as possible, is a problem of the economics of the individual's libido. There is no golden rule which applies to everyone: every man must find out for himself in what particular fashion he can be saved.[1] All kinds of different factors will operate to direct his choice. It is a question of how much real satisfaction he can expect to get from the external world, how far he is led to make himself independent of it, and, finally, how much strength he feels he has for altering the world to suit his wishes. In this, his psychical constitution will play a decisive part, irrespectively of the external circumstances. The man

Reprinted from *Civilization and Its Discontents* by Sigmund Freud, translated and edited by James Strachey, by permission of W. W. Norton & Company, Inc. Copyright © 1961 by James Strachey. Copyright renewed 1989. (New York: W. W. Norton, 1961), pp. 30–32.

[1] [The allusion is to a saying attributed to Frederick the Great: 'in my State every man can be saved after his own fashion.' Freud had quoted this a short time before, in *Lay Analysis* (1926e), *Standard Ed.*, 20, 236.]

who is predominantly erotic will give first preference to his emotional relationships to other people; the narcissistic man, who inclines to be self-sufficient, will seek his main satisfactions in his internal mental processes; the man of action will never give up the external world on which he can try out his strength.[2] As regards the second of these types, the nature of his talents and the amount of instinctual sublimation open to him will decide where he shall locate his interests. Any choice that is pushed to an extreme will be penalized by exposing the individual to the dangers which arise if a technique of living that has been chosen as an exclusive one should prove inadequate. Just as a cautious business-man avoids tying up all his capital in one concern, so, perhaps, worldly wisdom will advise us not to look for the whole of our satisfaction from a single aspiration. Its success is never certain, for that depends on the convergence of many factors, perhaps on none more than on the capacity of the psychical constitution to adapt its function to the environment and then to exploit that environment for a yield of pleasure. A person who is born with a specially unfavorable instinctual constitution, and who has not properly undergone the transformation and rearrangement of his libidinal components which is indispensable for later achievements, will find it hard to obtain happiness from his external situation, especially if he is faced with tasks of some difficulty. As a last technique of living, which will at least bring him substitutive satisfactions, he is offered that of a flight into neurotic illness—a flight which he usually accomplishes when he is still young. The man who sees his pursuit of happiness come to nothing in later years can still find consolation in the yield of pleasure of chronic intoxication; or he can embark on the desperate attempt at rebellion seen in a psychosis.

Religion restricts this play of choice and adaptation, since it imposes equally on everyone its own path to the acquisition of happiness and protection from suffering. Its technique consists in depressing the value of life and distorting the picture of the real world in a delusional manner—which presupposes an intimidation of the intelligence. At this price, by forcibly fixing them in a state of psychical infantilism and by drawing them into a mass-delusion, religion succeeds in sparing many people an individual neurosis. But hardly anything more. There are, as we have said, many paths which *may* lead to such happiness as is attainable by men, but there is none which does so for certain. Even religion cannot keep its promise. If the believer finally sees himself obliged to speak to God's 'inscrutable decrees', he is admitting that all that is left to him as a last possible consolation and source of pleasure in his sufferings is an unconditional submission. And if he is prepared for that, he could probably have spared himself the *détour* he has made.

---

[2] [Freud further develops his ideas on these different types in his paper on 'Libidinal Types' (1931a).]

IV.B.3. The Abolition of Religion

KARL MARX

Karl Marx (1818–1883), a German revolutionary thinker, formulated the version of socialism known as communism or Marxism. An essential ingredient in Marx's revolutionary social program was the elimination of religion, which, as he views it, pacifies humans, reconciles them to the oppression they suffer under capitalist society, and hinders their awareness of the urgent need of revolution. Because religion is the opium of the people, its abolition is necessary if people are to achieve not a drugged, illusory happiness but a real happiness. Like Freud, Marx is not offering an argument about the truth or falsity of the teachings of theism. Starting from an unargued presupposition that theism is false and religion is harmful, he uses rhetoric in an effort to convince people to renounce religion.

The basis of irreligious criticism is: *Man makes religion, religion does not make man.* In other words, religion is the self-consciousness and self-feeling of man, who either has not yet found himself or has already lost himself again. But *man* is no abstract being, squatting outside the world. Man is *the world* of man, the state, society. This state, this society produce religion, *a perverted world consciousness*, because they are *a perverted world*. Religion is the general theory of that world, its encyclopedic compendium, its logic is a popular form, its spiritualistic *point d' honneur*, its enthusiasm, its moral sanction, its solemn completion, its universal ground for consolation and justification. It is *the fantastic realization* of the human essence because the *human essence* has no true reality. The struggle against religion is therefore mediately the fight against *the other world*, of which religion is the *spiritual aroma*.

Religious distress is at the same time the *expression* of real distress and the *protest* against real distress. Religion is the sigh of the oppressed creature, the heart of a heartless world, just as it is the spirit of an unspiritual situation. It is the *opium* of the people.

The abolition of religion as the *illusory* happiness of the people is required for their *real* happiness. The demand to give up the illusions about its condition is the *demand to give up a condition which needs illusions*. The criticism of religion is therefore *in embryo the criticism of the vale of woe*, the *halo* of which is religion.

Criticism has plucked the imaginary flowers from the chain not so that man will wear the chain without any fantasy or consolation, but so that he will shake off the chain and cull the living flower. The criticism of religion disillusions man, to make him think and act and shape his reality like a man

From *Towards a Critique of Hegel's Philosophy of Right*, in Lewis S. Feuer: *Marx and Engels: Basic Writings on Politics and Philosophy* (Garden City, N.Y.: Doubleday, 1959), pp. 262–263.

who has been disillusioned and has come to reason, so that he will revolve round himself and therefore round his true sun. Religion is only the illusory sun, which revolves round man as long as he does not revolve round himself.

The task of history, therefore, once the *world beyond the truth* has disappeared is to establish the *truth of this world*. The immediate *task of philosophy*, which is at the service of history, once the *saintly form* of human self-alienation has been unmasked, is to unmask self-alienation in its *unholy forms*. Thus the criticism of heaven turns into the criticism of the earth, the *criticism of religion* into the *criticism of right*, and the *criticism of theology* into the *criticism of politics*. . . .

IV.C. Religion, Science, and Skepticism About Miracles

IV.C.1. The Problem of Creation

OSCAR RIDDLE

Oscar Riddle (1877–1968), a biologist, is concerned to show here that the progress of science in understanding the processes of nature, and particularly evolution, makes the notion of a divine creator superfluous and that of a miracle-working deity morally contemptible. The clear direction of change in the history of the world, Riddle finds, is from the simple toward the complex, and the complex always arises out of and depends on a relatively simple being. This argument implies that mind, the most complex and dependent living thing we know, is very much a latecomer in the world. To propose a superconscious and disembodied thinker, one not dependent on a body, as the earliest being is thus to violate all that our knowledge makes us responsible to believe. Riddle regards as hardly more than whimsy the notion of a deity who will intervene in human affairs and break natural law for trivial purposes to help his favorites, but who will not intervene to rescue the world from tyranny or natural calamity; certainly such a deity is neither admirable nor credible. Science does not prove that God does not exist—any more than it proves that ghosts or witches do not exist—but it does generate a system of knowledge that makes the world intelligible. Further, it is a system in which belief in God is no more justified and should be no more respectable than believing in witches and ghosts.

The philosophy of Naturalism which wholeheartedly accepts scientific methods as the only reliable way of reaching truths about man, society, and nature, does not decree what may or may not exist. It does not rule out on *a priori* grounds the existence of supernatural entities and forces. The existence of God, immortality, disembodied souls or spirits, cosmic purpose or design, as these have customarily been interpreted by the great institutional

From *The Unleashing of Evolutionary Thought* (New York: Vantage Press, 1954), pp. 41–65.

religions, are denied by naturalists for the same generic reasons that they deny the existence of fairies, elves, leprechauns and an invisible satellite revolving between the earth and the moon. There is no plausible evidence to warrant belief in them or to justify a probable inference on the basis of partial evidence.—*Sidney Hook*

The idea of God as a blesser, one who may bless and who may be appeased, is among the most ancient—and certainly still the most wide-spread—of human conceptions of Deity. That conception, however, is of secondary interest in this chapter, because, like the question of fairies, it is difficult to discuss from the point of view of science, and because it is already so extensively discredited among learned persons. Even some leaders of liberal religion have abandoned it. Nevertheless, elements of the idea of God as a Blesser are wedded to the minds of most present followers of practically all existing religions; indeed, these thin-worn elements continue to sustain nearly all of organized religion. To most of the "faithful" everywhere, God is still both Creator and Blesser, and a prayer or a gift is a prudent investment. In the Roman Catholic branch of Christianity, creation, placation and veneration are more or less nicely apportioned among God, the Son of God (Jesus), and the latter's virgin mother (Mary).

THE BROAD SCENE

Of chief interest here is the question—asked by learned persons of our day—whether the universe exists and operates solely under its own inherent properties, or whether an additional agency or immanence—God—created the universe of energy and matter and in one or another way gives evidence of his existence. This learned group gives now, and has given in the past, conflicting answers to that question. And this diversity of view partly reflects a central fact in the matter, namely, that *positive* proof can be supplied neither for the existence nor for the nonexistence of God as a Creator. It seems certain, however, that in greater proportion than in any previous generation the living members of this learned group now reject ideas both of Blesser and Creator. Also, within this learned group, a greater proportion of leading biologists and psychologists than of lawyers and writers now accept a Godless universe. Finally, there is evidence . . . that the proportion of atheists in the total present population of certain civilized countries is much higher in some (France, Holland) than in others (Brazil, United States, Australia).

The last three statements are made here not as evidence on the problem before us, but as factual background for the general reader, and because they relate to an associated question: How do advances in science, and very close or less close personal contact with those advances, affect the thought of men in regard to God? And here the author ventures to suggest that, at one or another time in their lives, intelligent people generally have as much (or more) live interest in evidence relating to the existence of God as have the scientists who must contribute the crucial evidence of the question.

Fitting into the point last mentioned is the fact that wherever religion prevails this fine initial human interest in questions of ultimate origins of the real nature of ourselves and surroundings—is rarely permitted to survive even to the tenth year of life. Before this age is reached, a soft and deadeningly unreasonable answer, closing the question and putting the inquiry to sleep, will have been provided by family, by associates, by church, or by school. Thus practically all those who later acquire the mental hardihood to review and revise this verdict, and so slough the imposed mental anaesthesia, must do so against the powerful "conditioning" influence of a view caressed through youth's tender years. Useful here are the observations of psychologist William James on the extent to which individual training may influence metaphysical speculation. These observations should rid us of surprise at finding that even some good scientists never succeed in making a thorough revision of the God of their youth.

The first chapter of this book scanned the long series of especially significant events and processes—the "creative" processes—as they relate to earth and man. The story began with earth-cloud substances which slowly achieved lodgment in a solid earth, and was continued through the building of the body and the consciousness of man. The field of knowledge thus drawn upon includes a fragment of astronomy, parts of physics and chemistry, geology, biology, psychology, and social science; in the matter of *time* the chronicle extends over an abyss of three to five billion years. Within the area, which dealt specifically with the origin of earth, life, man, and society, the "creative" processes were described as comprehensible in terms of inherent properties of matter, and nowhere was there found need for or evidence of God a Creator. The second chapter reviewed a series of principles and insights of science that seem to make all concepts of the supernatural unnecessary and even untenable.

External to the earth and sun, and hitherto largely disregarded in this survey, are the impressive spaces and the incalculable quantities of matter and energy of an incompletely observed universe. This expanse is surveyed by astronomy, mathematics and astrophysics. These sciences, through many triumphs of observation, measurement and analysis of the external universe, have made it evident that evolutionary changes—"creative" processes—are still in active progress there; but to many or most investigators—though not to all—those changes also seem comprehensible in terms of inherent properties of matter, and nowhere is God a Creator indicated or hinted.

This writer thinks that the principles and insights just mentioned above include the really important evidence relating to the existence or nonexistence of God a Creator. But he is under no illusion that discussion of the matter properly ends there. Any selected group of facts proves only what those facts prove, not what all facts taken together prove. Clearly, it is necessary to give further consideration to certain metaphysical and theological concepts relating to the existence of Deity. Still other facts of science also await attention.

Two Words—"Create" and "Evolve"

First, however, we define two words. The verb "to create" has a short staircase of meanings. To confuse these meanings is easy, but it would cheat all profitable discussion. In its relation to the Hebraic-Christian-Mohammedan Creator, the word "create" originally meant that He brought the world of things into being from nothing. Some, and only some, among these three large religious groups would *now* accept a lower step on the staircase of meanings, suggesting that energy and matter coexisted with the Creator and that even now He continues to "create" by merely molding and directing the forms still being assumed by energy and matter. This view is in full conflict with science, which marks out precisely the area for the reign of natural, not supernatural, law. Still more dilute meanings, unrelated to Deity, allow the word "create" to accommodate such things as the products of one's thoughts or imagination, or even an invention. The history of religious thought makes it misleading to apply the undefined word "create" to any succession of states of matter that occurs, or seems ever to have occurred, in the realm of nature (universe). "To change" is often the true and proper term. "To evolve" suitably applies to many broad areas of cumulative or formative change. The term "cosmic evolution" can cover the expansion of the material universe and the formation of chemical elements, nebulae, galaxies, suns and planets; "organic evolution," or simply "evolution," covers the formation of all living things—plants, animals and man.

Now current evolution may have begun with an "explosive" expansion of inconceivably condensed materials of the universe ("monobloc") five billion years ago, and with the rapid building of the ninety-eight or more elements from elemental neutrons, protons and electrons. Granted too that the still earlier states or phases of the universe are now wholly unapproachable. Within the entire space-time area covered by the two terms "cosmic evolution" and "organic evolution" the word "create" really has no place whatever except as a well-emphasized concession to the widespread use of a demoted meaning of this particular word. The gulf between the two words—"create" and "evolve"—is best indicated by an attempt to push beyond the elemental neutrons, protons and electrons. To derive these or minor components of the atom from *nothing*, an uninhibited layman, and perhaps an undeterred theologian, will say, "Create"; and then forthwith also say or shout, "Creator"— all on a basis not better than imagination, myth, or wishful thinking. Nevertheless, it is precisely here that a Creator's job is to be found if there is a Creator. Making all the neutrons, protons and electrons from nothing—and thus "creating" in an undiluted, distinct, and unrivaled sense—is the stupendous and rather absurd task that believers place upon God a Creator. Here and here only is the kind of "creation" that might need or could clearly imply a Creator.

But nowhere does science attempt to deal with this impossible barrier. Nothing that we know or meet in any area or discipline permits the slightest move in that direction. Probably the topmost meaning of the word "create" actually applies nowhere in nature, but only to this wisp of mystical thought. And it should be so, since this meaning was born of mysticism or of theology, not of science. When this point is granted, but only then, the word "create" may thereafter—with due reservation—be applied to the very different and lesser order of change that is indeed easily found in nature and is there much more properly called "evolution." The entire sweep of science, except mathematics and a segment of physics, *falls within the path and performance of evolution;* and the exceptions never attempt the derivation of matter or energy from nothing (creation). The "earliest" state of the universe is, indeed, quite unknown. Rather more than suspicion puts all matter of the known universe in an inconceivably concentrated "monobloc" occupying a fixed point in space, with an "explosion" of the monobloc providing what our ideas of time call a beginning of galaxy formation, and with the final exhaustion of its radioactive stores providing an eventual end in darkness. Probably only pseudo-science now debates whether the widening space between the outrushing galaxies is being refilled by new galaxies continuously formed from matter in that widening gulf—all with no beginning and no end in time. New aggregations of lifeless matter, new organisms, and new endowments of organisms do of course arise. To all this natural process and result, accomplished under natural, not supernatural, law, the term "evolution" is rightly applied. And this clean and precise term would not now be widely misunderstood if church and theology, aided by the occasional scientist, had not, since Darwin's day, put their own several head-chopping *mitigations* on the true meaning of this word.

Within the sphere of living things—from virus or gene to bee, man and society—the evolving and integrative processes are met on a scale so tremendous that the trained observer—untainted with the thought of the mystic—sometimes ventures to use the word "create" in its reduced and casual sense. And, curiously and rather magnificently, to many performances of man himself the word "create"—thus naturalized and dwarfed—may also justly apply. Man never gets something from nothing, but his best is perhaps as good as that of an Olympian god. Man gets from matter (and energy) things that are neither inevitably nor predictably inherent in it; and, further, no organism not endowed with speech—and thus with abstract thinking—could bring them into existence. Thus man creates our knowledge of the principles of relativity and evolution; man creates a watch; man creates symphonies and the Taj Mahal; man creates alphabets and undying literatures. With zeal and fervor, and with an untainted logic, man may here salute the "creative" best in his own species.

Before approaching a matter of uncertainty—the question of the existence of God a Creator, for example—it makes good sense to come face to face with some certainties that probably bear more directly on that uncertain matter. It is quite probable that the visible material universe has existed during some four to ten billions of years. And practically certain that during that entire period the parts, or many parts, of that material universe have been undergoing change—change in position, in temperature, in combination or dismemberment, in organization or integration. Such "end results" as may be seen by man today—whether they be heavier atoms, galaxies, planetary systems, living stuff, man or society—are observed only *after* the parts of the material universe have been involved in evolving and integrative processes during a few billions of years. It is certain too that both law and chance shared in those processes, and that they continue to do so. When some people, including scientists, say, "I cannot believe it is all chance or accident and therefore I can admit a God," they merely build a straw man to assist them to a personally preferred conclusion. Nobody assumes that chance alone built anything that we observe in nature. Nobody conceives of accident as an alternative to God. First and most certain is the reign of law, natural laws; and firmly included here, regardless of chance, is the superior principle of the building process—each new combination of matter, each integration, giving birth to properties not included in the uniting parts. Again, chance does not play an identical role in the nonliving and the living world; not even identical at the bottom and the top of the living world. The one who fits God a Creator into his scheme of thought must do so by first refusing to accept the view that the simplified state of the universe existed without a Creator; next he must accept the view that a Creator built the universe from nothing, or toy with uncommon efforts to escape that gross conclusion; and finally he must accept the view that such a Creator is the thing that had no Creator.

SOME SPECIAL RELIGIOUS CONCEPTS AND PLEAS

According to Hopkins,[1] "The general doctrine that faith surpasses science is common to all mystics. Faith is real knowledge." If this view of the mystics is true, they and their successors may have obtained and may continue to obtain the most convincing evidence for the existence of a God of sorts—whether creative or not. This assertion of the mystics, however, can be received in only one way by the scientist—that is, by one familiar with methods of arriving at truth and able variously and repeatedly to prove the validity of those methods. Psychologist Leuba[2] has made a penetrating analysis of religious faith, ecstasy and inspiration. He has shown that much more than the raw datum of "immediate experience," which may not be denied, is usually very clearly involved in these cases. He further calls attention to the contradictory revelations—presumably from the same God—that continue to be received by Christians on such subjects as the trinity and predestination, with the result that the Roman Church has declared itself to be the final court of appeal regarding the truth of revelations obtained during mystical ecstasy.

The scientist will grant the "reality" of these special mental states only as he would grant equal reality—along with unequally "satisfactory" results—to any delusion whatever. To these ripples in the consciousness of a few or many mortals, however convincing they may be to the individuals experiencing them, the scientist can attach nothing of cosmic importance; they are born in human consciousness and cannot transcend it. Theology today still sets a supreme value on the activity called intuition, which, a biologist may note, has its known home and kin only in the mental processes of man, where in turn it is one of evolution's newer and less reliable productions.

The higher religions—Brahmanic, later Buddhistic, Hebraic, Christian, Islamic—all teach that faith is superior to reasoned or scientific knowledge; and that we can know God only by intuition, meditation and revelation, through which we must find the proof both for his existence and his goodness. In addition to what was said above, it may be granted that when the resulting personal exaltation or ecstasy of the meditator is coupled with suitably advanced moral codes—and when all this is shared with large groups of men the product has high social importance; but it may be neither true nor socially advantageous. It is of interest to note further that this method of "knowing" God is historically very old. It was employed and apparently got its more

---

[1] E. W. Hopkins, *Origin and Evolution of Religion* (New Haven: Yale University Press, 1923).

[2] J. H. Leuba, *The Psychology of Religious Mysticism* (London: Kegan Paul, 1930). See also his *God or Man?* (New York: Henry Holt and Co., 1933).

conspicuous results—the various lengthily recorded revelations—many hundreds of years before man surmised or used the experimental method as a tool to truth.

This same group of higher religions, Judaism and Islam excepted, developed the intricate idea of "trinity," which seems to involve God a Creator and to give Him still other attributes through which perhaps His existence might be sensed or verified. Indeed, the three personalities, Krishna, Buddha in later times, and Jesus, are alleged by many to provide this evidence. Modern scholars may not be expected to accept any or all of these characters as evidence for the existence of a God of any type. Reason, history, and the higher criticism all contribute evidence that it was such things as legend, human credulity and illusion, invented miracles, virgin births, and resurrections, that later (or much later) induced followers to identify their leaders with Deity. Christian theology seems to have been, and even now to be, much preoccupied with the idea of trinity, although, according to E. W. Hopkins, the doctrine was apparently unknown (unmentioned, at least) to Jesus and Paul.

It is possible that an item of acceptable evidence for trinity, from the domain of religion, has been unintentionally overlooked in this review. The writer has not fully explored the jungle of mankind's Upanishads, where myth, legend, ecstasy, meditation and miracles fill volumes beyond the reach and patience of most truth-seeking men. The construction of a concept of trinity seems nearly impossible. But the fact that it has been done and *redone*— and even with quite *different* materials—compels both our admiration and liveliest curiosity. To a roving human intellect, it seems to say that theological architecture is whatever is wanted.

Alleged, Believed, and Examined

At this point it is well to bring together the four things that many learned people now find most persuasive to a belief in the existence of God. First, reason and logic seem to them to require a Creator for the physical universe. That this is a false, naïve and unfounded view is made evident in both earlier and later pages of this chapter. Second, one's feelings or intuitions point to the existence of a Creator. The unsubstantial, uncritical and spurious nature of this argument has been noted immediately above. Third, our probings and scrutiny of the natural world provide us with evidence for the existence of the supernatural. Let the answer to this be the words used in 1926, at a conference on religion, by Yale philosopher Charles A. Bennett: "The fate of the older rationalistic attempts to infer the supernatural from the natural shows clearly enough that the undertaking is hopeless." Fourth, life, or living matter, is a thing so complex and mysterious that its existence and its superlative products point to a still greater, external Directive Agency. That this view should be taken by those who have not devoted long years of technical study to the specific problem—and the training and daily work of many biologists and medical men barely touch this study—is in no way surprising. But such a view is rejected by an increasing number of persons more familiar with the processes associated with life (organism); and it is inconsistent with now established principles that provide a purely natural basis for organic evolution. . . . Thus not one of these four most commonly used props to what is termed an enlightened belief in God can find plausible support in the knowledge of our day.

Probably more than half of the persons met in the course of a day by a reader of this book think they are *reasoning* when they assert "a God *must* exist, because man and the universe are much too involved and complex to exist without a Creator." The reckless and shallow sophistry of this particular assertion should be evident, since one thus adds and forthrightly accepts a thing still more involved and complex than man and the universe as that which had no creator.

To believers in a "mitigated" evolution, any acceptance of the creation of life and of man through a succession of animal forms is usually coupled with what is regarded as an all-important gate of exit: "But the biologist does not *explain* what life is." This statement is hardly true, and again it is hardly necessary or philosophically important that anyone "explain" what life is. Biology and related sciences have provided evidence that certain organizations of matter show activities or properties called liveness or life, also that these properties seem to arise—as do those of all other compounds and integrative levels—from the elements and organization involved in the union. In other words, these properties arise under the unvarying rule, the *natural law*, that each new chemical combination or level of integration exhibits new properties. Moreover, the biologist has now identified and tagged the purely *natural* mechanisms by which living forms (species) arise and become diversified; and he has further clearly shown the important part played by the intangible conditions known as chance in the equipment of every human being with his several abilities and defects. . . . In a similar sense, the astronomer and philosopher do not "explain" what the universe is, but they possess more accurate and intimate knowledge of some distant parts of it than any human being had of the earth prior to five hundred years ago; the physicist does not "explain" what the electron is, but he can describe some of its varieties and properties; and the chemist does not yet fully "explain" the rather accessible thing called valence, though he now comes much nearer to doing so than was possible when this writer was a young student of chemistry. In a truer sense, however, the sciences do "explain" these things, since in larger or smaller measure they have reduced the multiplicity and variety of phenomena to simple and general laws. And science at its best merely completes the procedure.

Again, many theologians and other cultured people of our day *mitigate* their acceptance of the principles of organic evolution with the view that for certain special processes or stages, such as the origin of life or of self-consciousness, a nonphysical directive principle (vital force, prevision, purpose) enters into the creative process. Too, it is often postulated that this same vital force, or prevision, is expressed within and throughout the whole series of living things. This view—best known as vitalism in biology, but also a widespread and basic theological assumption—has tried persistently for a place in biology. But it is now more thoroughly discredited in biology than at any earlier hour in the history of that science. By way of evidence, a single but especially significant item from the field of genetics will be cited. Though the genetic adaptation of organisms is most meticulous and all embracing, and though both individual and species survival generally rest upon this adaptation, "yet close scrutiny shows it [adaptation] most wanting in those respects which would have involved distant prevision rather than short-range trial and error."[3] And here factual observation looks directly into the very foundation of both persistence and novelty in the living world.

Momentary attention may now be given to the undeniable fact that the picture of reality obtained through scientific investigation is not full, complete or wholly exclusive. But does this mean that another *equally* valid view actually exists, or that such other view can neglect all that our senses can contact, survey or measure? Two decades ago a brilliant biochemist presented the rather lonely philosophical view that "Science does not claim a *truer* account of the world than the organicism of the philosopher or the other interpretations, perhaps impossible to formulate, of the religious man and the poet or the artist." If one takes the latter part of this statement seriously, truth (and reality?) would appear to be whatever man, or perhaps groups of men, forcefully feel or think it to be. On such a basis, the snake religion of parts of our American scene—though poles apart from other religious thought—can match any other in its profound faith and in its ardent desire to show the domination of religious faith over a poisonous reptile. But here the making of a case for "equal truth" must be somewhat inconvenienced by the circumstance that now and again these intense believers are bitten and die.

Disregarding science and philosophy, the Western world, prompted by a logical paradox of Christian theology, has indulged in three centuries of rather barren discussion of "free will." Christian theology sought a way to justify the coexistence of two of its terrible doctrines; namely, that God has predetermined the fate of every man, and that He nevertheless holds every man responsible for his action, rewarding or punishing eternally. In more recent times, discussion has centered more specifically on whether volition (action behavior) is completely (one hundred per cent) determined (mechanistic), or whether a small degree of indeterminateness is involved. Many have assumed the existence of a certain small amount of indeterminateness, and—herein lies the reason for these paragraphs—have further assumed that this "small amount" is an area for supernatural maneuver (God). These assumptions are hard to treat in a rational way. But the way in which the relatively new "uncertainty principle" of physics might apply in this case is suitably recorded in the words of physicist Tolman:[4]

> I must caution you, however, that the opinion of one good physicist that the uncertainty principle brings free will and moral responsibility back into the world can hardly be regarded as sensible. As far as I know, moral responsibility has never left the world, and, indeed, could hardly be helped by a principle which makes physical happenings, to the extent that they are not determined, take place in accordance with the laws of pure chance.

The position of the life sciences on this question has been stated thus briefly by physiologist Smith:[5]

---

[3] Herman J. Muller, *The Harvey Lectures, 1947–1948* (Springfield, Ill.: Charles C. Thomas, Publisher).

[4] Richard C. Tolman, *Science*, vol. 106, 1947.

[5] Homer W. Smith, *Man and His Gods* (Boston: Little, Brown and Co., 1952).

For the naturalists, free will was a countersense, a verbal contradiction. To "will" is to choose a course of action in which more than one course is potentially presented, and to choose one course of action as opposed to another requires not only knowledge of alternatives, but reason for the choice. Decision without reference to cause or consequence of that which is rejected or accepted could only refer to an act occurring in a referential vacuum, and if such could be conceived it could only be designated as an action issuing from nothing at all, *ab nihilo*, from absolute ignorance. Since willing can never be free of knowledge of either cause or consequence, it can never be free at all.

From metaphysics one may of course obtain other less binding, and even free-wheeling, evaluations of this overworked conundrum.

In theology and in much popular thinking, it is rather widely claimed that the order or orderliness that we all observe in nature, though involving natural processes, also involves a Directive Force that acts not dynamically but persistently. This tenuous and elusive halo can be neither successfully supported nor speedily dissipated. The alleged role of a Directive Force in this sphere is part of the broad theological assumption that the supernatural can be inferred from the natural world, a point dismissed by philosophy in the words of Bennett, quoted above. It is notable, however, that the immense and obvious amount of order in the universe is itself widely acclaimed by the world's clergy as good or sufficient evidence of God's existence. Of course, man and the living world arose in conformity with and in adjustment to all such things as the daily rotation of the earth, the seasons, and the usual yields of land and sea. The very existence of living things—like the earlier disappointment of many a noble group of species—is adequate evidence of the prevalence and necessity of this adjustment. When priest and minister endlessly cite these orderly relationships as considerate gifts of God to man, or as evidence for God's existence, they merely insult the information and intelligence of learned people.

Actually, our problem is to account for the order and for the seeming disorder displayed in nature. In this connection one may give a brief thought to the disorder present now or earlier in our well-observed solar system and in the living world. As bordering the disorderly one may cite the movements of gases in the corona of the sun,[6] which (*a*) show both as irregular eruptive flashes and as long-continued storms, which (*b*) move 3,000 to 4,000 times more speedily than the winds of our own atmosphere, and which (*c*) may move outward to more than 250,000 miles—a distance exceeding that between the earth and the moon. Again, the repeated and irregular mountain-forming convulsions of an earlier earth and the earthquakes that still continue to shatter parts of our planet's slowly advancing growth are types of awesome disorder in the inorganic world.

Even more evident and more common is a variety of tolerable, though distressing, disorder in the living world. The daily survival of many or most animals, including man, is based on strife and struggle with, and even the

---

[6] Donald H. Menzel, *Our Sun* (Philadelphia: Blakiston Co., 1949).

death of, hosts of other animals. Again, the very origin of most forms of life (species) is based partly, though only in part, on a struggle for existence in which this type of disorder abounds, and from which the noxious, the nuisance, and the degenerate sometimes survive along with the progressive, the majestic, and the mimic. "The evolution that Darwin discovered was process, not progress," declares H. W. Smith. The process by which man himself is reproduced assures that a low but tragic percentage of pregnancies and births will yield the defective or the deformed—physically or mentally—including the occasional ghastly clumps of flesh that must at once be put aside. Probably every one of the 208 bones of the normal human body has been repeatedly observed to be absent from babes born of women. The disorder involved in disease is mentionable but not measurable; the animal and plant kingdoms are its crowded home. Family, tribal, social, economic, national and international disorders are parts of a new, man-made world; and there, too, we must deal with both order and disorder.

Science does in fact examine successfully both order and disorder in nature and in society. It is done without the use or aid of the supernatural Directive Force to which theology appeals. Indeed, if only one single instance of the exercise of such a Directive Force could be established, that solitary *miracle*[7] would provide firm evidence for the existence of a Directive Force. That one case has never been established, though the trail of most religions is traced in the hidden and open frauds that are offered in its stead. In stating that science can deal comprehensively with both order and disorder, it is not implied that astronomy has solved its problems, that geology is a completed story, that biology has either asked or answered its endless questions, or that medicine has mastered the many ills of man. What is meant is that these and other sciences have proved that, with the method of science, they can continually increase the area of our practical, serviceable and solid understanding. In all fields this advance is made on the basis of uncontradicted evidence that phenomena, events and processes—whether of order or disorder—proceed under the rule of *natural* law.

The miracles, and the sacred or healing relics, statues and monuments of religions, are rather clearly contributions to the history of human credulity, human yearning and desire—and sometimes doubtless baser human motives—but they are all false mirrors of cosmic law and reality. It requires some special consideration, however, to show that, along with a fragment of truth, an element of error or of fraud exists also in the "mental healing" practiced by both early and modern Christian priests and ministers, a practice asserted by some of them to prove Divine intervention, and therefore the existence of the Divine. There can be no doubt that the agents of various sects of the Christian and other religions have effected some "cures" as did medical (not priestly) agents in the Greek temple of Pergamon long before the Christian era, and as do *some* psychotherapists of today on a far better and broader scale than either of them. Here the element of fraud enters when priest or minister, all of whom should now know better, attribute the cure to a Divine source. The

---

[7] According to St. Thomas: "Miracle is a free interference of God; what has been done by God outside the regular course of Nature."

reader will find that psychologist Leuba[8] has treated this subject at length, and has indicated the purely psychological and physiological conditions that attend the valid instances of such cures.

One may not neglect the fact that a very few quite modern theologians and some less modern philosophers now speak of "divine immanence" with and without capitals. Here God is not put "outside" things in general but is postulated as being a process or presence within all parts of the universe, and sometimes even the quality of consciousness is not attributed to this presence.

This uncommon concept of God deserves notice here because of its modernity, and because His there alleged *intimacy* with the universe might, just might, at some time or in some nook, let Him become evident in science. Yet, to date, one could well apply to this view the exact words that Bertrand Russell applied to the concept of a supposedly highly intimate soul.[9]

> One of the "grand" conceptions which have proved scientifically useless is the soul. I do not mean that there is positive evidence showing that men have no souls. I only mean that the soul, if it exists, plays no part in any discoverable law.

Another argument commonly makes much of an "unseen world," a world said to be indicated by parts of our human consciousness, which, when followed up, provides a wholly different road from that of science to truth and reality. Within this "unseen world" one thus finds a basis for religion, and for a revealed God. This argument has been developed less by theologians than by some religious-minded physicists of our day. It provides a basis for much of the advanced thought of the moment on religious questions, and it will now be given further attention.

This argument was condensed and most ably presented as an address by astronomer-physicist Eddington[10] to the Society of Friends, London, in 1929. Its main features are to be found in the following quotation:

> We have learnt that the exploration of the external world by methods of physical science leads not to a concrete reality but to a shadow world of symbols, beneath which those methods are unadapted for penetrating. Feeling that there must be more behind, we return to our starting point in human consciousness, the one centre where more might become known. There we find other stirrings, and other revelations (true or false) than those conditioned by the world of symbols. Are not these too of significance? . . .
>
> Are we, in pursuing the mystical outlook, facing the hard facts of experience? Surely we are. I think that those who would wish to take cognizance of nothing but the measurements of the scientific world made by our sense organs are shirking one of the most immediate facts of experience, namely, that consciousness is not wholly, nor even

[8] *God or Man?*, op. cit.

[9] Bertrand Russell, *Unpopular Essays* (New York: Simon and Schuster, Inc., 1950).

[10] Arthur Stanley Eddington, in *The New York Times*, Sunday, June 16, 1929. See also his *The Nature of the Physical World* (New York: The Macmillan Co., 1928).

primarily, a device for receiving sense impressions. We may the more boldly insist that there is another outlook than the scientific one, because in practice a more transcendental outlook is almost universally admitted.

The first sentence of this quotation requires amendment. Our explorations of the external world are not in fact limited to "the methods of physical science"; or, if we are to infer that natural science—including biology, psychology, and sociology—is possibly included, the thing we call "common sense," as a first step in science, is certainly also involved in our arrival not at a "concrete reality" but in "a shadow world of symbols." And granting something technically short of concrete reality to all that we describe in science, the "shadow" we get in its stead has all the firmness (near-reality) of the existence of our friends and enemies, and also of our mates, who provide our chance to be physically represented in all future generations. Again, these friends, enemies and mates are and were similarly real, or near-real, for all the long line of animal kin that produced man. The maligned "shadow" does in fact represent the full kind of certainty, except that of arithmetic, which serves the common man to live out his years and to project himself and his species into the future. To attain these great ends man and his animal ancestors assuredly have not needed to go beyond common sense (or science) and search deep in consciousness for "the mystical outlook."

Amendment is necessary also in the sentence of the second paragraph that states that "those who would wish to take cognizance of nothing but the measurements of the scientific world made by our own sense organs are shirking one of the most immediate facts of experience, namely, that consciousness is not wholly, nor even primarily, a device for receiving sense impressions." Here the point for first notice and correction is that the contributions of biology and psychology to the scientific world are by no means limited to "measurements" and their associated symbols; they also include observations, tests and sequences that, though they do not measure, nevertheless illuminate and lead to comprehension. An example of this from the writer's own studies. . . relates to observations and tests that show that a particular gene and the hormone prolactin are necessary—as is also the attainment of a particular kind of ripening of the organism—to the production of the parental instinct. And that with suitable use of these agents—not measurements—the experimenter himself has called *this element of consciousness* to rats and fowl and pigeons that never before had it. To assume that biological science is restricted to "measurements" and to "symbols" emerging from measurements is both to falsify and to degrade that science—the particular science, indeed, that accounts for the very consciousness to which this excellent astronomer appeals but also subverts. The second point for examination in the quoted sentence relates to the nature and content of consciousness. It is said "that consciousness is not wholly, nor even primarily, a device for receiving sense impressions." We may next note the broad and religiously unhelpful sense in which this is true.

The biologist and the psychologist must regard *conscious* or *self-conscious awareness* as a recent arrival among the mental activities that slowly developed as inseparable and essential parts of evolving organisms—from the low to the highest.[11] Somewhere within the broad and rather dark dome of the mental in man, a small illuminated spot, or window, could represent the minor part of the mental that is involved in conscious awareness (consciousness). Surely it is the larger, darker spread of dome—not the smaller spot—that deserves first and most attention, for from it the smaller spot was born. And, most meaningful of all, the entire dome was built of the successful organismic reactions and adjustments of an indescribably long ancestry. To say that the mental activities, conscious and unconscious, are fitted and suited to the organism would be to falsify utterly by saying far too little—they are, one and all, the very *parts* of organism.

Now the entire above-described dome—the mentality as a whole—may be called "a device for receiving sense impressions" and for very much besides, since in ape or man its participations, awake or asleep, are innumerable. But, however much this mentality—even in its brighter window of consciousness—may have developed its services, it is against all known biological history, expectation and principle to presume that mentality should evolve a segment that is not part and parcel of organism. Organism, in its long march to man and indeed in each instant of its billion years, has been forced inexorably to build itself in full conformity to the physical world—that is, to the "seen" world of science—and nothing would seem innately less probable than the production and cultivation there—in the whole of the subhuman world—of bases for a "mystical outlook" that would someday enable some members of *one* superior species to find equal or deeper truth in an "unseen world."

A mystical outlook can indeed be achieved by a man. It appears, however, to be rooted largely in the twilight area of the fluid emotions rather than in the brightest area of reason. It is certain enough that "stirrings" other than those of reason are present in all now known humans. They may take forms such as fasting, sweating, self-torture and hysterical dancing. But the practical value of the mystical (or religious) outlook as a way to get truth that is beyond scientific truth is also largely denied by the historical fact that enormous masses of men—not just individuals—have been led by it to a belief in God and in no God (early Buddhism, for example), and in wholly unlike varieties of God. Such facts make it evident that something quite *outside* those "other stirrings, and other revelations (true or false)" of consciousness to which Eddington appeals, is in fact largely responsible for his own view of "truth in the unseen world." The nature of that outside influence should not be hard to find in an astronomer *religiously* nurtured in a country where tradition is so powerful and respectable.

Eddington further states: "Religion does not depend on the substitution of the word 'God' for the word 'nature.' The crucial point for us is not a conviction of the existence of a supreme God but a conviction of the revelation of a supreme God. . . . I confine myself to the revelation implied in the indwelling of the divine spirit in the mind of man." This last sentence needs attention. If the "divine spirit" exists it would seem to be a "thing," and needs to find a home somewhere or everywhere. The "mind of man," however, is not a

---

[11] William A. White. "The Frontier of the Mind," *Journal of the Washington Academy of Sciences*, vol. 23, no. 1, 1933.

"thing" and the mentation referred to is an activity, not a repository. Moreover, as noted above, mentation, like locomotion, surely developed as a part of organism; and just as surely some of this activity may look like good or God, and some of it may look like the Devil.

Various views of God do indeed exist. One such—of a God *independent* of nature—admits that attempts to reason about Him or to prove that God is the Creator of the Universe are doomed to failure; but, it adds, in the words of Stace, "To ask for a proof of the existence of God is on a par with asking for a proof of the existence of beauty." Again, some current "advanced" theological thought confidently cites the support of one or more philosophers—mostly those of an earlier day though occasionally one adopted as a living authority. The authorities thus cited were, or are, those having a serious regard for such things as subjective philosophy, intuition, and essence—items discounted or abandoned by leaders in modern philosophic thought. Helpful here are the observations of philosopher Reichenbach:[12]

> It has become a favorite argument of antiscientific philosophies that explanation must stop somewhere, that there remain unanswerable questions. But the questions so referred to are constructed by a misuse of words. Words meaningful in one combination may be meaningless in another. Could there be a father who never had a child? Everyone would ridicule a philosopher who regarded this question as a serious problem. The question of the cause of the first event, or of the cause of the universe as a whole, is not of a better type. The word "cause" denotes a relation between two things and is inapplicable if only one thing is concerned. The universe as a whole has no cause, since by definition, there is no thing outside it that could be its cause. Questions of this type are empty verbalisms rather than philosophic arguments.

And modern philosopher John Dewey[13] wrote as follows:

> The developments of the last century have gone so far that we are now aware of the shock and overturn in older beliefs. But the formation of a new, coherent view of nature and man based on facts consonant with science and actual social conditions is still to be had. . . . Faith in the divine authority in which Western civilization confided, inherited ideas of the soul and its destiny, of fixed revelations, of completely stable institutions, of automatic progress, have been made impossible for the cultivated mind of the Western world.

Individual stars and galaxies are indeed observed to be in various stages of organization—youth, age and death. Our own sun will slowly end its existence as an individual source of light and heat; and our earth is destined to cease its daily rotation and to disappear as earth. But such decay and death involve the dispersion and conversion, not the annihilation, of the ultimate

---

[12] Hans Reichenbach, *The Rise of Scientific Philosophy* (Berkeley and Los Angeles: University of California Press, 1951).

[13] John Dewey, *Living Philosophies* (New York: Simon and Schuster, Inc., 1931).

particles of the atom. On this question modern physicists are the highest authority. They indicate that with reference to the constituent corpuscles of the atom neither creation nor annihilation is admissible. For him who asks: "What or how much preceded our cosmos of energy and mass?" there is no profitable answer; and the emptiness of the question has been indicated above.

Although the social God disappeared in the scientific advances of the previous century, some scientists and philosophers still continued, until the recent advent of the concepts of relativity, to think and speak of the Absolute or the Ultimate in capitals. Indeed, such is the power of the past that clarity sometimes requires a capital letter. Following the general acceptance (at least within the physical sciences) of the principles of relativity and quantum mechanics, our earlier concepts of such things as time, space, matter, energy, complete determinism and the absolute—even of absolute truth—have undergone radical change.

It is now held that all our observations, measurements and deductions are tinged with uncertain and ineradicable elements of our human sensations and consciousness. This may mean, for example, that you can say that eventually your neighbor, Mr. X, will probably die, not that he will die. Philosophy makes a point of the doubt. In the matter of cause and effect we still have possibilities of prediction, though only on a statistical basis. In this changed viewpoint of science, where indeed obscurities still attach to the basic concepts, some opportunists among the liberal clergy of various countries are busily engaged in making the obscurities the basis for the assertion that the conflict between science and theology is approaching reconciliation. The difficulties and the vicious error of this claim are evident to logical thought. They are partly indicated by mathematician Danzig:[14]

> Is religion too prepared to sacrifice, waive, and renounce? Has it decided to give up its gospel of absolute truth? Renounce the absolute God? Substitute for its absolute world a floating and fleeting chaos? Announce that it has been the victim of anthropomorphic delusion? Or declare itself to be a mere emotional game of make-believe, played on human fears and hopes? Religion is not prepared to make such sacrifices; indeed it cannot make such sacrifices and survive.

And they are further covered by Harvard philosopher Perry:[15]

> It would be presumptuous and foolish to assume that there is a kindly indulgence at the seat of cosmic control: presumptuous because unsupported by evidence; foolish because it would weaken man's reliance upon himself.

Nature would seem to be the nearest thing to a God that man is likely ever to know. Majesty and terrifying power are hers forever. The equality she grants is unquestionable; she makes no distinction between promising ape and

---

[14] Tobias Danzig, *Aspects of Science* (New York. The Macmillan Co., 1937).

[15] Ralph Barton Perry, *Realms of Value* (Cambridge. Harvard University Press, 1954).

noxious weed. And those creatures that understand or respect her are often rewarded with such things as safety and longer life.

How account for the fact that many scientists and some philosophers believe in the supernatural and in God? By way of answer there is only evidence—certainly not logical proof—and parts of that evidence will be found elsewhere in this book. It is this writer's opinion that, for many of them, the core of the answer relates to their neglect of one or more of the outstanding insights attained by science. Chief of these insights . . . is the newly reinforced and vital conclusion that it is impossible for human thought and feeling to transcend the human reference point. That summit of accomplishment has been ignored or rejected by at least many of the scientists who have written their beliefs into a library of books and addresses. And after ignoring such heights of present scientific attainment, these men seem to have swung freely into the blue, in a personally prompted pursuit of a "something further," a spirit, a "purpose," a God.

For an occasional scientist, it is certain, the case is much worse. Surely and strangely, some trained people are able to keep their science and their religion in two separate and nonleaking mental compartments. A famous professor of botany in one of our great American universities privately told of a brilliant nun, who accomplished her doctorate under his guidance. Before leaving the university, the Sister called to pay her respects. In the course of a pleasant conversation, she was asked how she harmonized all that she had learned with what her robes symbolized. In a matter-of-fact way she replied that she never let the two things mix.

It seems that just preceding the year 1600, the inventor of logarithms, the Scotsman John Napier, calculated that the Second Coming of Christ would occur between 1668 and 1700, and the great Sir Isaac Newton, though non-committal as to date, declared his belief that the time was at hand. If history can prove anything, it proves that when science was less developed than it is now many good scientists accepted some or all of the most violently absurd theology of their particular age and place of birth.

Of course, science does not and cannot *prove* that God a Creator does not exist. Science cannot prove that a witch does not exist. And science cannot prove that a devil, or even a flock of devils, does not exist. But science can and does put natural law into many a dark corner of the universe and also deep into the crannies of consciousness. The nature of the world we are part of can be passably comprehended on the basis of natural law; "the eternal mystery of the world is its comprehensibility," says physicist Einstein. And from natural law it is clear enough that one can obtain a hint of neither God nor witch nor devil. Moreover, many things we do know are anything but innocent of bearing on the question of the existence of God a Creator, witches, and devils. These pages deal with a few such items that relate to God a Creator. Bearing directly on this question are the words of philosopher Hook, at the head of this chapter. They merit rereading at this point.

One may not neglect the meaningful fact that the evolutionary process still goes on; that is, the "creation" ascribed by some to God continues through the present moment. For those who assume they can believe that the natural processes of evolution are God's chosen methods of creation, there are some most awkward facts that deprive Him of the attribute of mercy. Thus volcanoes and earthquakes are parts of the age-long evolution of the earth's crust; yet throughout a long past they have killed, in an indiscriminate and whole-sale manner, all living things within the area of their effect, including large masses of babes, women and men. If a creative God operates through evolution, then an endless and frightful man-killing by volcanoes, earthquakes, famines, and like disasters are His work; and if He wishes also to be regarded as a *merciful* God, He absurdly blundered when He permitted man the fair intelligence that is now his. Or, in the words of mathematician-philosopher Bertrand Russell, "If indeed the world in which we live has been produced in accordance with a plan we shall have to reckon Nero a saint in comparison with the Author of the Plan."

Again, with reference to the religious type of Supreme Authority which often has not hesitated at breaking natural law—in order to slay the Philistines in a puny tribal war, to provide sixty-four kinds of miracles by Shiva, to convulse nature at the birth and death of Buddha, to provide loaves and fishes for an assembly that tarried beyond mealtime, to impregnate a virgin in an obscure village and epoch, and to bring a mountain to Mohammed—but which in our day refuses to rescue a man-filled world from tyrants who have devastated and killed by the millions, and who still choke the pulse of humanity while they threaten all civilization—*that* Authority is far too whimsical to be of the slightest use to struggling mankind.

A SOUVENIR FROM EARTH'S LONGEST TRAIL

It remains to point to a logical conclusion that may be drawn from one aspect of what seems to have been learned of the long trail of evolutionary processes. Phenomena, processes, and events—items of history—are, of course, usually better known and more easily studied in our immediate surroundings here on earth and in our solar system than in more distant parts of the universe. Within this restricted space, an enormous range of evolutionary change, which took place during three to five billion years, has been studied with considerable success. The *relative order* in which phenomena of lesser and greater molecular complexity, simple life, more and more complex life, and finally consciousness occurred or appeared within this long period supplies the basis for a meaningful conclusion.

Within this best-studied segment of time and space, the known facts indicate that, above the level of the atom, the primary *direction* of change has been—with rather minor or unclear exceptions (chiefly among Orders of animals)—*always from the simpler to the more complex.* Practically nowhere is the reverse of this observed if or when one properly rejects the quick, later, and transient processes of death, degeneration, disorder and decay which, essentially as by-products, inevitably accompany the central, expanding and enormously prolonged "creative" processes. In the inorganic sphere, the sequence is from split or single atoms to associated atoms of the same kind; from the simplest (hydrogen) to the more complex atoms; then to the simplest, and later to the more complex molecules; then to organic molecules of increasing complexity; then to the simplest living aggregates; then through less to more complicated living things—within which only the highest *animal* forms developed consciousness. Thus *thinking* comes as the highest and *most recent* development in the whole sweep of evolutionary change from the progenitors of the earth-cloud to man; and it then appears only in association with the most complex *animal* types—the most elaborate and intricate organizations of matter actually known in the universe.

To assume, or to propose, a Conscious Super-Thinker—God—as a first or *earliest* entity and to characterize that Thinker as devoid of all *molecular organization* is to violate both the sense and the spirit of much of the best that man has learned about himself and about that part of the universe that is most accessible to study and test.

IV.C.2 The Truth of Faith and Scientific Truth and The Truth of Faith and Historical Truth

PAUL TILLICH

Paul Tillich (1886-1965) was a German-born theologian who fled Hitler's Germany to pass the rest of his life and career in the United States. In the following selection he offers an account of the relationship between science and religion that he believes removes any possibility of conflict. Tillich points out that the purpose of science is to represent our understanding of the world by means of principles and theories that depict the orderly processes of the world of nature. The purpose of religion, or what he calls faith, is to express our experience of the world as we relate to it in terms of our grasp of its ultimate ground. The cause of what many have perceived as a conflict is a biblical literalism that regards the Bible not as the Word of God but as the words *of God. The truths that faith undertakes to express cannot, however, be contained in the literal meaning of any language. Because faith pertains to what is infinite, finite language can only symbolize and point toward its meanings. If the Bible and the traditions of religion are understood as mythological representations of what cannot be literally expressed—as symbols designed to put us in a position to experience, rather than just to hear about, the ultimate—then there can be no question of a conflict between these symbolic meanings and the literal theories of science.*

Similarly, Tillich holds, there can be no conflict between the truths of history and the truths of faith. History attempts to give an account of events taking place at specific times. Faith, in contrast, expresses in symbolic form the significance those events have in the relationship between humans and the ground of being. Thus discoveries that certain events believed to have occurred historically might not have cannot diminish the power of the myths associated with these events to express the content of faith. Even if there was no Garden of Eden, the truth conveyed in the story of the fall of Adam and Eve through disobedience of God communicates a valid insight into the human bent to sinning and need for a restored relationship to God. Thus the progress of scientific, historical, and philosophical discoveries need not be feared by persons of faith. Each of these disciplines has its own valuable role in the pursuit of truth, as faith has its own. Rightly understood, there is no possibility for conflict between these roles.

THE TRUTH OF FAITH AND SCIENTIFIC TRUTH

There is no conflict between faith in its true nature and reason in its true nature. This includes the assertion that there is no essential conflict between faith and the cognitive functions of reason. Cognition in all its forms was always considered as that function of man's reason which comes most easily into conflict with faith. This was especially so when faith was defined as a lower form of knowledge and was accepted because the divine authority guaranteed its truth. We have rejected this distortion of the meaning of faith, and in doing so have removed one of the most frequent causes for the conflicts between faith and knowledge. But we must show beyond this the concrete relation of faith to the several forms of cognitive reason: the scientific, the historical and the philosophical. The truth of faith is different from the meaning of truth in each of these ways of knowledge. Nevertheless, it is truth they all try to reach, truth in the sense of the "really real" received adequately by the cognitive function of the human mind. Error takes place if man's cognitive endeavor misses the really real and takes that which is only seemingly real for real; or if it hits the really real but expresses it in a distorted way. Often it is difficult to say whether the real is missed or whether its expression is inadequate, because the two forms of error are interdependent. In any case, where there is the attempt to know, there is truth or error or one of the many degrees of transition between truth and error. In faith man's cognitive function is at work. Therefore, we must ask what the meaning of truth in faith is, what its criteria are, and how it is related to other forms of truth with other kinds of criteria.

Science tries to describe and to explain the structures and relations in the universe, in so far as they can be tested by experiment and calculated in quantitative terms. The truth of a scientific statement is the adequacy of the description of the structural laws which determine reality, and it is the verification of this description by experimental repetitions. Every scientific truth is preliminary and subject to changes both in grasping reality and in expressing it adequately. This element of uncertainty does not diminish the truth value of a tested and verified scientific assertion. It only prevents scientific dogmatism and absolutism.

Therefore, it is a very poor method of defending the truth of faith against the truth of science, if theologians point to the preliminary character of every scientific statement in order to provide a place of retreat for the truth of faith. If tomorrow scientific progress reduced the sphere of uncertainty, faith would have to continue its retreat—an undignified and unnecessary procedure, for scientific truth and the truth of faith do not belong to the same dimension of meaning. Science has no right and no power to interfere with faith and faith has no power to interfere with science. One dimension of meaning is not able to interfere with another dimension.

If this is understood, the previous conflicts between faith and science appear in a quite different light. The conflict was actually not between faith and science but between a faith and a science each of which was not aware of its own valid dimension. When the representatives of faith impeded the beginning of modern astronomy they were not aware that the Christian symbols, although using the Aristotelian-Ptolemaic astronomy, were not tied up with this astronomy. Only if the symbols of "God in heaven" and "man on earth" and "demons below the earth" are taken as descriptions of places, populated by divine or demonic beings can modern astronomy conflict with the Christian faith. On the other hand, if representatives of modern physics reduce the whole of reality to the mechanical movement of the smallest particles of matter, denying the really real quality of life and mind, they express a faith, objectively as well as subjectively. Subjectively science is their ultimate concern—and they are ready to sacrifice everything, including their lives, for this ultimate. Objectively, they create a monstrous symbol of this concern, namely, a universe in which everything, including their own scientific passion, is swallowed by a meaningless mechanism. In opposing this symbol of faith Christian faith is right.

Science can conflict only with science, and faith only with faith; science which remains science cannot conflict with faith which remains faith. This is true also of other spheres of scientific research, such as biology and psychology. The famous struggle between the theory of evolution and the theology of some Christian groups was not a struggle between science and faith, but between a science whose faith deprived man of his humanity and a faith whose expression was distorted by Biblical literalism. It is obvious that the theology which interprets the Biblical story of creation as a scientific description of an event which happened once upon a time interferes with the methodologically controlled scientific work; and that a theory of evolution which interprets man's descendance from older forms of life in a way that removes the infinite, qualitative difference between man and animal is faith and not science.

The same consideration must be given to present and future conflicts between faith and contemporary psychology. Modern psychology is afraid of the concept of soul because it seems to establish a reality which is unapproachable by scientific methods and may interfere with their results. This fear is not unfounded; psychology should not accept any concept which is not produced by its own scientific work. Its function is to describe man's processes as adequately as possible, and to be open to replacement of these descriptions at any time. This is true of the modern concepts of ego, superego, self, personality, unconsciousness, mind, as well as of the concepts of soul, spirit, will, etc. Methodological psychology is subject to scientific verification, as is every other scientific endeavor. All its concepts and definitions, even those most validated, are preliminary.

When faith speaks of the ultimate dimension in which man lives, and in which he can win or lose his soul, or of the ultimate meaning of his existence, it is not interfering at all with the scientific rejection of the concept of the soul. A psychology without soul cannot deny this nor can a psychology with soul confirm it. The truth of man's eternal meaning lies in a dimension other than the truth of adequate psychological concepts. Contemporary analytic or depth psychology has in many instances conflicted with pre-theological and theological expressions of faith. It is, however, not difficult in the statements of depth psychology to distinguish the more or less verified observations and hypotheses from assertions about man's nature and destiny which are clearly expressions of faith. The naturalistic elements which Freud carried from the nineteenth into the twentieth century, his basic puritanism with respect to love, his pessimism about culture, and his reduction of religion to ideological projection are all expressions of faith and not the result of scientific analysis. There is no reason to deny to a scholar who deals with man and his predicament the right to introduce elements of faith. But if he attacks other forms of faith in the name of scientific psychology, as Freud and many of his followers do, he is confusing dimensions. In this case those who represent another kind of faith are justified in resisting these attacks. It is not always easy to distinguish the element of faith from the element of scientific hypothesis in a psychological assertion, but it is possible and often necessary.

The distinction between the truth of faith and the truth of science leads to a warning, directed to theologians, not to use recent scientific discoveries to confirm the truth of faith. Microphysics have undercut some scientific hypotheses concerning the calculability of the universe. The theory of quantum and the principle of indeterminacy have had this effect. Immediately religious writers use these insights for the confirmation of their own ideas of human freedom, divine creativity, and miracles. But there is no justification for such a procedure at all, neither from the point of view of physics nor from the point of view of religion. The physical theories referred to have no direct relation to the infinitely complex phenomenon of human freedom, and the emission of power in quantums has no direct relation to the meaning of miracles. Theology, in using physical theories in this way, confuses the dimension of science with the dimension of faith. The truth of faith cannot be confirmed by latest physical or biological or psychological discoveries—as it cannot be denied by them.

THE TRUTH OF FAITH AND HISTORICAL TRUTH

Historical truth has a character quite different from that of scientific truth. History reports unique events, not repetitious processes which can be tested again and again. Historical events are not subject to experiment. The only analogy in history to a physical experiment is the comparison of documents. If documents of an independent origin agree, a historical assertion is verified within its own limits. But history does not tell a series of facts. It also tries to understand these facts in their origins, their relations, their meaning. History describes, explains, and understands. And understanding presupposes participation. This is the difference between historical and scientific truth. In historical truth the interpreting subject is involved; in scientific truth it is detached. Since the truth of faith means total involvement, historical truth has often been compared with the truth of faith. A complete dependence of the historical truth on the truth of faith has been derived from such an identification. In this way it has been asserted that faith can guarantee the truth of a questionable historical statement. But he who makes such assertions forgets that in a genuine historical work detached and controlled observation is as much used as in the observation of physical or biological processes. Historical truth is first of all factual truth; in this it is distinguished from the poetic truth of epics or from the mythical truth of legend. This difference is decisive for the relation of the truth of faith to the truth of history. Faith cannot guarantee factual truth. But faith can and must interpret the meaning of facts from the point of view of man's ultimate concern. In doing so it transfers historical truth into the dimension of the truth of faith.

This problem has come into the foreground of much popular and theological thought since historical research has discovered the literary character of the Biblical writings. It has shown that in their narrative parts the Old and the New Testament combine historical, legendary and mythological elements and that in many cases it is impossible to separate these elements from each other with any degree of probability. Historical research has made it obvious that there is no way to get at the historical events which have produced the Biblical picture of Jesus who is called the Christ with more than a degree of probability. Similar research in the historical character of the holy writings and the legendary traditions of non-Christian religions has discovered the same situation. The truth of faith cannot be made dependent on the historical truth of the stories and legends in which faith has expressed itself. It is a disastrous distortion of the meaning of faith to identify it with the belief in the historical validity of the Biblical stories. This, however, happens on high as well as on low levels of sophistication. People say that others or they themselves are without Christian faith, because they do not believe that the New Testament miracle stories are reliably documented. Certainly they are not, and the search for the degree of probability or improbability of a Biblical story has to be made with all the tools of a solid philological and historical method. It is not a matter of faith to decide if the presently used edition of the Moslemic Koran is identical with the original text, although this is the fervent belief of most of the adherents of Mohammed. It is not a matter of faith to decide that large parts of the Pentateuch are priestly wisdom of the period after the Babylonic exile, or that the Book of Genesis contains more myths and sacred legend than actual history. It is not a matter of faith to decide whether or not the expectation of the final catastrophe of the universe as envisaged in the late books of the Old and in the New Testament originated in the Persian religion. It is not a matter of faith to decide how much legendary, mythological and historical material is amalgamated in the stories about the birth and the resurrection of the Christ. It is not a matter of faith to decide which version of the reports about the early days of the Church has the greatest probability. All these questions must be decided, in terms of more or less probability, by historical research. They are questions of historical truth, not of the truth of faith. Faith can say that something of ultimate concern has happened in history because the question of the ultimate in being and meaning is involved. Faith can say that the Old Testament law which is given as the law of Moses has unconditional validity for those who are grasped by it, no matter how much or how little can be traced to a historical figure of that name. Faith can say that the reality which is manifest in the New

Testament picture of Jesus as the Christ has saving power for those who are grasped by it, no matter how much or how little can be traced to the historical figure who is called Jesus of Nazareth. Faith can ascertain its own foundation, the Mosaic law, or Jesus as the Christ, Mohammed the prophet, or Buddha the illuminated. But faith cannot ascertain the historical conditions which made it possible for these men to become matters of ultimate concern for large sections of humanity. Faith includes certitude about its own foundation—for example, an event in history which has transformed history—for the faithful. But faith does not include historical knowledge about the way in which this event took place. Therefore, faith cannot be shaken by historical research even if its results are critical of the traditions in which the event is reported. This independence of historical truth is one of the most important consequences of the understanding of faith as the state of ultimate concern. It liberates the faithful from a burden they cannot carry after the demands of scholarly honesty have shaped their conscience. If such honesty were in a necessary conflict with what has been called the "obedience of faith," God would be seen as split in himself, as having demonic traits; and the concern about it would not be ultimate concern, but the conflict of two limited concerns. Such faith, in the last analysis, is idolatrous.

IV.C.3.   Of Miracles

DAVID HUME

David Hume (1711–1776) presents powerful and far reaching criticisms of virtually every aspect of both rational and revealed religion. The following selection from his Enquiry Concerning Human Understanding *offers one of the most sustained and uncompromising attacks on miracles in the history of Western thought. Insisting on an empiricist approach, Hume points out that all of our knowledge about matters of fact is grounded in human experience. In particular, our knowledge of the laws of nature is based on the accumulated observations of humankind.*

Hume regards miracles as violations of laws of nature. Thus the vested experience of the whole human race over the entire stretch of recorded history testifies to the extreme improbability of miracles. When a person reports that he has witnessed a miracle, says Hume, we must ask ourselves which is more likely: that the miracle occurred or that the person is either mistaken or lying? Because we know that mistakes and lies are common and we know of no authenticated instance of a miracle, we are not warranted in believing in the miracle on the basis of testimony. Indeed, testimony could justify believing in a miracle only if the falsehood of the testimony turns out to imply a greater miracle than the miracle alleged.

The testimony we have concerning miracles, Hume continues, comes always from the distant past, from primitive and often barbaric peoples; the miracles are often self-serving, involving prodigies performed by heroes of their own tribes or special favors conferred on their tribes by the gods. These testimonies have nothing to recommend them as reliable, even if well-attested testimony could establish miracles. Concluding in an ironic tone, Hume tells us that not only was Christianity attended initially by miracles; even today nothing short of a miracle could get a reasonable person to believe in it.

PART I

. . . A wise man . . . proportions his belief to the evidence. In such conclusions as are founded on an infallible experience, he

From *An Enquiry Concerning Human Understanding* edited by Eric Steinberg (Indianapolis: Hackett, 1977), pp. 73–80; 81–82; 87–90. With permission of Hackett Publishing Company Inc., Indianapolis, IN and Cambridge, MA.

expects the event with the last degree of assurance, and regards his past experience as a full *proof* of the future existence of that event. In other cases, he proceeds with more caution: He weighs the opposite experiments: He considers which side is supported by the greater number of experiments: To that side he inclines, with doubt and hesitation; and when at last he fixes his judgment, the evidence exceeds not what we properly call *probability*. All probability, then, supposes an opposition of experiments and observations, where the one side is found to overbalance the other, and to produce a degree of evidence, proportioned to the superiority. A hundred instances or experiments on one side, and fifty on another, afford a doubtful expectation of any event; though a hundred uniform experiments, with only one that is contradictory, reasonably beget a pretty strong degree of assurance. In all cases, we must balance the opposite experiments, where they are opposite, and deduct the smaller number from the greater, in order to know the exact force of the superior evidence.

To apply these principles to a particular instance; we may observe, that there is no species of reasoning more common, more useful, and even necessary to human life, than that which is derived from the testimony of men, and the reports of eye-witnesses and spectators. This species of reasoning, perhaps, one may deny to be founded on the relation of cause and effect. I shall not dispute about a word. It will be sufficient to observe, that our assurance in any argument of this kind is derived from no other principle than our observation of the veracity of human testimony, and of the usual conformity of facts to the reports of witnesses. It being a general maxim, that no objects have any discoverable connexion together, and that all the inferences, which we can draw from one to another, are founded merely on our experience of their constant and regular conjunction; it is evident, that we ought not to make an exception to this maxim in favour of human testimony, whose connexion with any event seems, in itself, as little necessary as any other. Were not the memory tenacious to a certain degree; had not men commonly an inclination to truth and a principle of probity; were they not sensible to shame, when detected in a falsehood: Were not these, I say, discovered by *experience* to be qualities, inherent in human nature, we should never repose the least confidence in human testimony. A man delirious, or noted for falsehood and villainy, has no matter of authority with us.

And as the evidence, derived from witnesses and human testimony, is founded on past experience, so it varies with the experience, and is regarded either as a *proof* or a *probability*, according as the conjunction between any particular kind of report and any kind of object has been found to be constant or variable. There are a number of circumstances to be taken into consideration in all judgments of this kind; and the ultimate standard, by which we determine all disputes, that may arise concerning them, is always derived from experience and observation. Where this experience is not entirely uniform on any side, it is attended with an unavoidable contrariety in our judgments, and with the same opposition and mutual destruction of argument as in every other kind of evidence. We frequently hesitate concerning the reports of others. We balance the opposite circumstances, which cause any doubt or uncertainty; and when we discover a superiority on any side, we incline to it; but still with a diminution of assurance, in proportion to the force of its antagonist.

This contrariety of evidence, in the present case, may be derived from several different causes; from the opposition of contrary testimony; from the character or number of the witnesses; from the manner of their delivering their testimony; or from the union of all these circumstances. We entertain a suspicion concerning any matter of fact, when the witnesses contradict each other; when they are but few, or of a doubtful character; when they have an interest in what they affirm; when they deliver their testimony with hesitation, or on the contrary, with too violent asseverations. There are many other particulars of the same kind, which may diminish or destroy the force of any argument, derived from human testimony.

Suppose, for instance, that the fact, which the testimony endeavours to establish, partakes of the extraordinary and the marvellous; in that case, the evidence, resulting from the testimony, admits of a diminution, greater or less, in proportion as the fact is more or less unusual. The reason, why we place any credit in witnesses and historians, is not derived from any *connexion*, which we perceive *a priori*, between testimony and reality, but because we are accustomed to find a conformity between them. But when the fact attested is such a one as has seldom fallen under our observation, here is a contest of two opposite experiences; of which the one destroys the other, as far as its force goes, and the superior can only operate on the mind by the force, which remains. The very same principle of experience, which gives us a certain degree of assurance in the testimony of witnesses, gives us also, in this case, another degree of assurance against the fact, which they endeavour to establish; from which contradiction there necessarily arises a counterpoise, and mutual destruction of belief and authority.

I should not believe such a story were it told me by Cato; was a proverbial saying in Rome, even during the lifetime of that philosophical patriot. The incredibility of a fact, it was allowed, might invalidate so great an authority.

The Indian prince, who refused to believe the first relations concerning the effects of frost, reasoned justly; and it naturally required very strong testimony to engage his assent to facts, that arose from a state of nature, with which he was unacquainted, and which bore so little analogy to those events, of which he had had constant and uniform experience. Though they were not contrary to his experience, they were not conformable to it.

But in order to increase the probability against the testimony of witnesses, let us suppose, that the fact, which they affirm, instead of being only marvellous, is really miraculous; and suppose also, that the testimony, considered apart and in itself, amounts to an entire proof; in that case, there is proof against proof, of which the strongest must prevail, but still with a diminution of its force, in proportion to that of its antagonist.

A miracle is a violation of the laws of nature; and as a firm and unalterable experience has established these laws, the proof against a miracle, from the very nature of the fact, is as entire as any argument from experience can possibly be imagined. Why is it more than probable, that all men must die; that lead cannot, of itself, remain suspended in the air; that fire consumes wood, and is extinguished by water; unless it be, that these events are found agreeable to the laws of nature, and there is required a violation of these laws, or in other words, a miracle to prevent them? Nothing is esteemed a miracle, if it ever happen in the common course of nature. It is no miracle that a man, seemingly in good health, should die on a sudden: because such a kind of death, though more unusual than any other, has yet been frequently observed to happen. But it is a miracle, that a dead man should come to life; because that has never been observed, in any age or country. There must, therefore, be a uniform experience against every miraculous event, otherwise the event would not merit that appellation, And as a uniform experience amounts to a proof, there is here a direct and full *proof*, from the nature of the fact, against the existence of any miracle; nor can such a proof be destroyed, or the miracle rendered credible, but by an opposite proof, which is superior.

The plain consequence is (and it is a general maxim worthy of our attention), 'That no testimony is sufficient to establish a miracle, unless the testimony be of such a kind, that its falsehood would be more miraculous, than the fact, which it endeavours to establish: And even in that case there is a mutual destruction of arguments, and the superior only gives us an assurance suitable to that degree of force, which remains, after deducting the inferior.' When any one tells me, that he saw a dead man restored to life, I immediately consider with myself, whether it be more probable, that this person should either deceive or be deceived, or that the fact, which he relates, should really have happened. I weigh the one miracle against the other; and according to the superiority, which I discover, I pronounce my decision, and always reject the greater miracle. If the falsehood of his testimony would be more miraculous, than the event which he relates; then, and not till then, can he pretend to command my belief or opinion.

PART II

In the foregoing reasoning we have supposed, that the testimony, upon which a miracle is founded, may possibly amount to an entire proof, and that the falsehood of that testimony would be a real prodigy: But it is easy to show, that we have been a great deal too liberal in our concession, and that there never was a miraculous event established on so full an evidence.

For *first*, there is not to be found, in all history, any miracle attested by a sufficient number of men, of such unquestioned good-sense, education, and learning, as to secure us against all delusion in themselves; of such undoubted integrity, as to place them beyond all suspicion of any design to deceive others; of such credit and reputation in the eyes of mankind, as to have a great deal to lose in case of their being detected in any falsehood; and at the same time, attesting facts, performed in such a public manner, and in so celebrated a part of the world, as to render the detection unavoidable: All which circumstances are requisite to give us a full assurance in the testimony of men.

Secondly. We may observe in human nature a principle, which, if strictly examined, will be found to diminish extremely the assurance, which we might, from human testimony, have, in any kind of prodigy. The maxim, by which we commonly conduct ourselves in our reasonings, is, that the objects, of which we have no experience, resemble those, of which we have; that what we have found to be most usual is always most probable; and that where there is an opposition of arguments, we ought to give the preference to such as are founded on the greatest number of past observations. But though, in proceeding by this rule, we readily reject any fact which is unusual and incredible in an ordinary degree; yet in advancing farther, the mind observes not always the same rule: but when anything is affirmed utterly absurd and miraculous, it rather the more readily admits of such a fact, upon account of that very circumstance, which ought to destroy all its authority. The passion of *surprise* and *wonder*, arising from miracles, being an agreeable emotion, gives a sensible tendency towards the belief of those events, from which it is derived. And this goes so far, that even those who cannot enjoy this pleasure immediately, nor can believe those miraculous events, of which they are informed, yet love to partake of the satisfaction at second-hand or by rebound, and place a pride and delight in exciting the admiration of others.

With what greediness are the miraculous accounts of travellers received, their descriptions of sea and land monsters, their relations of wonderful adventures, strange men, and uncouth manners? But if the spirit of religion join itself to the love of wonder, there is an end of common sense; and human testimony, in these circumstances, loses all pretensions to authority. A religionist may be an enthusiast, and imagine he sees what has no reality: He may know his narrative to be false, and yet persevere in it, with the best intentions in the world, for the sake of promoting so holy a cause: Or even where this delusion has not place, vanity, excited by so strong a temptation, operates on him more powerfully than on the rest of mankind in any other circumstances; and self-interest with equal force. His auditors may not have, and commonly have not, sufficient judgment to canvass his evidence: What judgment they have, they renounce by principle, in these sublime and mysterious subjects: Or if they were ever so willing to employ it, passion and a heated imagination disturb the regularity of its operations. Their credulity increases his impudence: And his impudence overpowers their credulity.

Eloquence, when at its highest pitch, leaves little room for reason or reflection; but addressing itself entirely to the fancy or the affections, captivates the willing hearers, and subdues their understanding. Happily, this pitch it seldom attains. But what a Tully or a Demosthenes could scarcely effect over a Roman or Athenian audience, every *Capuchin*, every itinerant or stationary teacher can perform over the generality of mankind, and in a higher degree, by touching such gross and vulgar passions.

The many instances of forged miracles, and prophecies, and supernatural events, which in all ages have either been detected by contrary evidence, or which detect themselves by their absurdity, prove sufficiently the strong propensity of mankind to the extraordinary and the marvellous, and ought reasonably to beget a suspicion against all relations of this kind. This is our natural way of thinking, even with regard to the most common and most credible events. For instance: There is no kind of report, which rises so easily, and spreads so quickly, especially in country places and provincial towns, as those concerning marriages; insomuch that two young persons of equal condition never see each other twice, but the whole neighborhood immediately join them together. The pleasure of telling a piece of news so interesting, of propagating it, and of being the first reporters of it, spreads the intelligence. And this is so well known, that no man of sense gives attention to these reports, till he find them confirmed by some greater evidence. Do not the same passions, and others still stronger, incline the generality of mankind to believe and report, with the greatest vehemence and assurance, all religious miracles?

Thirdly. It forms a strong presumption against all supernatural and miraculous relations, that they are observed chiefly to abound among ignorant and barbarous nations; or if a civilized people has ever given admission to any of them, that people will be found to have received them from ignorant and barbarous ancestors, who transmitted them with that inviolable sanction, and authority, which always attend received opinions. When we peruse the first histories of all nations, we are apt to imagine ourselves transported into some new world; where the whole frame of nature is disjointed, and every element performs its operations in a different manner, from what it does at present. Battles, revolutions, pestilence, famine, and death, are never the effort of those natural causes, which we experience. Prodigies, omens, oracles, judgments, quite obscure the few natural events, that are intermingled with them. But as the former grow thinner every page, in proportion as we advance nearer the enlightened ages, we soon learn, that there is nothing mysterious or supernatural in the case, but that all proceeds from the usual propensity of mankind towards the marvellous, and that, though this inclination may at intervals receive a check from sense and learning, it can never be thoroughly extirpated from human nature.

It is strange, a judicious reader is apt to say, upon the perusal of these wonderful historians, *that such prodigious events never happen in our days.* But it is nothing strange, I hope, that men should lie in all ages. You must surely have seen instances enough of that frailty. You have yourself heard many such marvellous relations started, which being treated with scorn by all the wise and judicious, have at last been abandoned even by the vulgar. Be assured, that those renowned lies, which have spread and flourished to such a monstrous height, arose from like beginnings; but being sown in a more proper soil, shot up at least into prodigies almost equal to those which they relate. . . .

I may add as a *fourth* reason, which diminishes the authority of prodigies, that there is no testimony for any, even those which have not been expressly detected, that is not opposed by an infinite number of witnesses; so that not only the miracle destroys the credit of testimony, but the testimony destroys itself. To make this the better understood, let us consider, that, in matters of religion, whatever is different is contrary; and that it is impossible the religions of ancient ROME, of TURKEY, of SIAM, and of CHINA should, all of them, be established on any solid foundation. Every miracle, therefore, pretended to have been wrought in any of these religions (and all of them abound in miracles), as its direct scope is to establish the particular system to which it is attributed; so has it the same force, though more indirectly, to overthrow every other system. In destroying a rival system, it likewise destroys the credit of those miracles, on which that system was established; so that all the prodigies of different religions are to be regarded as contrary facts, and the evidence of these prodigies, whether weak or strong, as opposite to each other. According to this method of reasoning, when we believe any miracle of MAHOMET or his successors, we have for our warrant the testimony of a few barbarous ARABIANS: And on the other hand, we are to regard the authority of TITUS

LIVIUS, PLUTARCH, TACITUS, and, in short, of all the authors and witnesses, GRECIAN, CHINESE, and ROMAN CATHOLIC, who have related any miracle in their particular religion; I say, we are to regard their testimony in the same light as if they had mentioned that MAHOMETAN miracle, and had in express terms contradicted it, with the same certainty as they have for the miracle they relate. This argument may appear over subtile and refined; but is not in reality different from the reasoning of a judge, who supposes, that the credit of two witnesses, maintaining a crime against any one, is destroyed by the testimony of two others, who affirm him to have been two hundred leagues distant, at the same instant when the crime is said to have been committed. . . .

In the infancy of new religions, the wise and learned commonly esteem the matter too inconsiderable to deserve their attention or regard. And when afterwards they would willingly detect the cheat, in order to undeceive the deluded multitude, the season is now past, and the records and witnesses, which might clear up the matter, have perished beyond recovery.

No means of detection remain, but those which must be drawn from the very testimony itself of the reporters: And these, though always sufficient with the judicious and knowing, are commonly too fine to fall under the comprehension of the vulgar.

Upon the whole, then, it appears, that no testimony for any kind of miracle has ever amounted to a probability, much less to a proof; and that, even supposing it amounted to a proof, it would be opposed by another proof; derived from the very nature of the fact, which it would endeavour to establish. It is experience only, which gives authority to human testimony; and it is the same experience, which assures us of the laws of nature. When, therefore, these two kinds of experience are contrary, we have nothing to do but subtract the one from the other, and embrace an opinion, either on one side or the other, with that assurance which arises from the remainder. But according to the principle here explained, this subtraction, with regard to all popular religions, amounts to an entire annihilation; and therefore we may establish it as a maxim, that no human testimony can have such force as to prove a miracle, and make it a just foundation for any such system of religion.

I beg the limitations here made may be remarked, when I say, that a miracle can never be proved, so as to be the foundation of a system of religion. For I own, that otherwise, there may possibly be miracles, or violations of the usual course of nature, of such a kind as to admit of proof from human testimony; though, perhaps, it will be impossible to find any such in all the records of history. Thus, suppose, all authors, in all languages, agree, that, from the first of JANUARY 1600, there was a total darkness over the whole earth for eight days: Suppose that the tradition of this extraordinary event is still strong and lively among the people: That all travellers, who return from foreign countries, bring us accounts of the same tradition, without the least variation or contradiction: it is evident, that our present philosophers, instead of doubting the fact, ought to receive it as certain, and ought to search for the causes whence it might be derived. The decay, corruption, and dissolution of nature, is an event rendered probable by so many analogies, that any phenomenon, which seems to have a tendency towards that catastrophe, comes within the reach of human testimony, if that testimony be very extensive and uniform.

But suppose, that all the historians who treat of ENGLAND, should agree, that, on the first of JANUARY 1600, Queen ELIZABETH died; that both before and after her death she was seen by her physicians and the whole court, as is usual with persons of her rank; that her successor was acknowledged and proclaimed by the parliament; and that, after being interred a month, she again appeared, resumed the throne, and governed ENGLAND for three years: I must confess that I should be surprised at the concurrence of so many odd circumstances, but should not doubt of her pretended death, and of those other public circumstances that followed it: I should only assert it to have been pretended, and that it neither was, nor possibly could be real. You would in vain object to me the difficulty, and almost impossibility of deceiving the world in an affair of such consequence; the wisdom and solid judgment of that renowned queen; with the little or no advantage which she could reap from so poor an artifice: All this might astonish me; but I would still reply, that the knavery and folly of men are such common phenomena, that I should rather believe the most extraordinary events to arise from their concurrence, than admit of so signal a violation of the laws of nature.

But should this miracle be ascribed to any new system of religion; men, in all ages, have been so much imposed on by ridiculous stories of that kind, that this very circumstance would be a full proof of a cheat, and sufficient, with all men of sense, not only to make them reject the fact, but even reject it without farther examination. Though the Being to whom the miracle is ascribed, be, in this case, Almighty, it does not, upon that account, become a whit more probable; since it is impossible for us to know the attributes or actions of such a Being, otherwise than from the experience which we have of his productions, in the usual course of nature. This still reduces us to past observation, and obliges us to compare the instances of the violation of truth in the testimony of men, with those of the violation of the laws of nature by miracles, in order to judge which of them is most likely and probable. As the violations of truth are more common in the testimony concerning religious miracles, than in that concerning any other matter of fact; this must diminish very much the authority of the former testimony, and make us form a general resolution, never to lend any attention to it, with whatever specious pretence it may be covered.

Lord BACON seems to have embraced the same principles of reasoning. 'We ought,' says he, 'to make a collection or particular history of all monsters and prodigious births or productions, and in a word of every thing new, rare, and extraordinary in nature. But this must be done with the most severe scrutiny, lest we depart from truth. Above all, every relation must be considered as suspicious, which depends in any degree upon religion, as the prodigies of LIVY: And no less so, every thing that is to be found in the writers of natural magic or alchimy, or such authors, who seem, all of them, to have an unconquerable appetite for falsehood and fable.'

I am the better pleased with the method of reasoning here delivered, as I think it may serve to confound those dangerous friends or disguised enemies to the *Christian Religion*, who have undertaken to defend it by the principles of human reason. Our most holy religion is founded on *Faith*, not on reason; and it is a sure method of exposing it to put it to such a trial as it is, by no means, fitted to endure. To make this more evident, let us examine those miracles, related in scripture; and not to lose ourselves in too wide a field, let us confine ourselves to such as we find in the *Pentateuch*, which we shall examine, according to the principles of these pretended Christians, not as the word or testimony of God himself, but as the production of a mere human writer and historian. Here then we are first to consider a book, presented to us by a barbarous and ignorant people, written in an age when they were still more barbarous, and in all probability long after the facts which it relates, corroborated by no concurring testimony, and resembling those fabulous accounts, which every nation gives of its origin. Upon reading this book, we find it full of prodigies and miracles. It gives an account of a state of the world and of human nature entirely different from the present: Of our fall from that state: Of the age of man, extended to near a thousand years: Of the destruction of the world by a deluge: Of the arbitrary choice of one people, as the favourites of heaven; and that people the countrymen of the author: Of their deliverance from bondage by prodigies the most astonishing imaginable: I desire any one to lay his hand upon his heart, and after a serious consideration declare, whether he thinks that the falsehood of such a book, supported by such a testimony, would be more extraordinary and miraculous than all the miracles it relates; which is, however, necessary to make it be received, according to the measures of probability above established.

What we have said of miracles may be applied, without any variation, to prophecies; and indeed, all prophecies are real miracles, and as such only, can be admitted as proofs of any revelation. If it did not exceed the capacity of human nature to foretell future events, it would be absurd to employ any prophecy as an argument for a divine mission or authority from heaven. So that, upon the whole, we may conclude, that the *Christian Religion* not only was at first attended with miracles, but even at this day cannot be believed by any reasonable person without one. Mere reason is insufficient to convince us of its veracity: And whoever is moved by *Faith* to assent to it, is conscious of a continued miracle in his own person, which subverts all the principles of his understanding, and gives him a determination to believe what is most contrary to custom and experience.

IV.C.4.   Miracle

ALASTAIR McKINNON

Alastair McKinnon (1925–) is MacDonald Professor of Moral Philosophy at McGill University and a member of the Canadian Senate. Here he argues that miracles can be understood in either of two ways and that both show that miracles are impossible. If we understand the phenomenon of miracle to mean a violation of the laws of nature, to claim that a miracle occurred would amount to saying that something in the actual course of events is outside the actual course of events, since laws of nature simply describe the actual course of events. If, however, we take miracle to mean an event that conflicts with our understanding of nature, we contradict ourselves again. To say that a miracle occurred is to admit the necessity of revising our understanding of nature; to refuse to do so is to deny that the miracle occurred.

There are two main supernaturalist senses of *miracle*. They are: (1) an event involving the suspension of natural law, and (2) an event conflicting with our understanding of nature. We begin with the first of these senses.

The core of our objection is quite simple: the idea of a suspension of natural law is self-contradictory. This follows from the meaning of the term. Natural law is not, as has been widely supposed, a kind of code for nature having legislative and, perhaps particularly, prohibitive force. This is an outdated, untenable, and completely unscientific view. Natural laws bear no similarities to civil codes and they do not in any way constrain the course of nature. They exert no opposition or resistance to anything, not even to the odd or exceptional. They are simply highly generalized shorthand descriptions of how things do in fact happen. (This is misleading but will do for the moment.) Hence there can be no suspensions of natural law rightly understood. Or, as here defined, *miracle* contains a contradiction in terms.

Once we understand natural law in this proper sense we see that such law, as distinct from our conception of it, is inherently inviolable. Hence anything which happens, even an apparent miracle, happens according to law. Or, negatively, no actual event could possibly violate a law of nature. Hence there can be no miracles in that sense of the term with which we are now concerned. Or, less misleadingly, it is in the nature of the case impossible that there should be an event which could be properly described by this term.

This contradiction may stand out more clearly if for *natural law* we substitute the expression *the actual course of events*. Miracle would then be defined as "an event involving the suspension of the actual course of events" And someone who insisted upon describing an event as a miracle would be in the rather

From *American Philosophical Quarterly* 4, no. 4 (October 1967): 309–310.

odd position of claiming that its occurrence was contrary to the actual course of events.

But miracle (1) is not merely a contradiction in terms. It is also what might be called a contradiction in use. We see this in the plight of one confronted with an event conceived as a miracle. Such a person is faced with a dilemma. He can affirm the reality of this event and repudiate the "laws" which it violates. Or he can affirm these "laws" and repudiate the event. What he cannot do is to affirm both the event and the "laws" of which it is a violation. And this is to say that he cannot affirm that the event is both real and miraculous.

This can be put in a slightly different way. Belief in an event is belief that it happened. Belief that an event is a miracle is belief that it violates natural law. But, as already seen, such violations are impossible. Hence in respect of any alleged event we must choose between believing that it was actual and that it was not even possible. What we cannot believe, what it makes no sense to believe, is that any real or alleged event is a miracle in this sense. This, of course, is not to legislate for the course of events in the empirical world: it is simply to draw out the consequences of the self-contradictory nature of this concept.

So much for sense (1). What now of the more sophisticated (2) ("an event conflicting with our understanding of nature")? The clash posited by this sense is not within nature, as in (1), but rather between an event and our conception of nature. The idea of such a clash is not contradictory. Nor are such clashes either infrequent or always illusory. Hence there might be occasions on which *miracle* could be legitimately used in this sense. For example, I might use "*x* is a miracle (2)" to mean "*x* baffles me" or "I know no laws which could account for *x*." And if this was all I wanted to say, if my only concern was to register my lack of comprehension, then I would be as invulnerable as when I describe my dog as brown. But there are two relevant points. The original statement, so intended, deals not with the event as such but rather with my reaction to it; here the term *miracle* is being used expressively rather than descriptively. Secondly, in fact people do not use this term merely in this limited way. They do not use it simply to say that they do not know the appropriate law: they use it also to express their belief that there is no such law. They use it not merely to indicate their lack of comprehension but at the same time to insinuate their belief that the event cannot, perhaps should not, be comprehended. And if they did not so use it, it would be difficult to see how this term could have any distinctive meaning, much less the peculiar "religious" force it obviously has.

Though innocent when used expressively, this sense is contradictory when used to describe an event. One who so uses it implicitly affirms a conception of nature with which this is at variance. But he cannot believe both that the event happened and that the conception of nature with which it conflicts is adequate. In attempting to do so he necessarily contradicts himself. He is like the man who says, "Yes, this cat is white" then blandly adds, ". . . but I still hold that all cats are black."

Such a person may reasonably be asked to surrender either the historicity of the event or the conception of nature with which it conflicts. But as the proponent of an allegedly historical event he cannot well do the former. Nor, if the evidence was ever adequate, should he do so. He must therefore admit the inadequacy of the conception of nature with which he has been working. To do this is to put brackets around it, to withdraw it from circulation: it is to void or cancel the check. But in so doing he has cut the thread by which the whole structure was suspended and has repudiated the ground upon which he originally urged this description. The moral is clear: to affirm the historicity of an event is to destroy the ground for regarding it as a miracle.

Of course there is one other move open to our victim. Instead of surrendering his conception of nature as inadequate he might instead proclaim it a true and faithful copy. In so doing he locates the clash once again within the sphere of nature. But this brings him back to sense (1) and the impossible contradictions with which it is afflicted.

It appears then that one who insists upon describing an event as a miracle is faced with two equally impossible alternatives. If he attempts to represent the event as an instance of (2) he is forced by the logic of his position to withdraw the term completely. If he attempts instead to represent it as a case of (1) he forces himself to say that the event in question both is and is not a part of the actual course of events. Such a person is like a fly in a spider's web, he has ways around but no way out.

The conclusion of this matter can be stated "paradoxically": all the properly descriptive senses of *miracle* are logically improper.

IV.C.5.   On Miracles

PAUL J. DIETL

Paul J. Dietl of Syracuse University takes issue here with Hume's claim that we can never be justified in believing that a miracle has occurred. Although it may (or may not) be true that no miracle has ever occurred, it is not possible—as Hume tries to do—to rule out the possibility ahead of time, nor is it possible—as the logical positivists attempted to do—to show that the concept is meaningless. Miracle is a perfectly intelligible concept and we can describe the conditions that would have to be satisfied for us to say with confidence whether or not a miracle has occurred. To discover whether these conditions have been satisfied is an empirical matter.

Some of the most remarkable turns in recent philosophical discussion have been the resurrection of issues original readers of *Language, Truth and Logic* would have thought forever dead. "Freewill" is no

From *American Philosophical Quarterly* 5 (1968): 130–134.

longer considered a pseudoproblem. There is serious controversy concerning the existence of God. Ethics is considered cognitively significant in respectable circles. In fact the concept of a miracle is probably the only concept left for resurrection. Here there is general agreement—among sophisticated theologians as well as militant atheists—that *a priori* rejection of claims is justified. Miracle claims, it is generally believed, could not be true because of the very nature of the concept of a miracle. Nonetheless I should like to argue for its vindication. The crucial issue is whether conditions could ever obtain which would justify one in applying "miracle" in any way resembling its standard historical use. I shall argue that there could be such conditions, that we could very well recognize them, so that we do know what miracles are, and therefore that miracle claims are at worst false.

Here as elsewhere Hume anticipated much later opinion, so it is reasonable to begin with his contribution. The difficulty is that in much of what he wrote on the subject Hume seemed to be arguing that the event which is supposed to have been an exception to a law of nature could not happen. The laws themselves are based on "a firm and unalterable experience" and "as a uniform experience amounts to a proof, there is here a direct and full proof, from the nature of the fact, against the existence of any miracle. . . ."[1] In at least one place, though, Hume does admit that bizarre events could occur.

> Suppose all authors, in all languages, agree that from the first of January, 1600, there was total darkness over the whole earth for eight days; suppose that the tradition of this extraordinary event is still strong and lively among the people; that all travelers who return from foreign countries, bring us accounts of the same tradition without the least variation or contradiction—it is evident that our present philosophers, instead of doubting the fact, ought to receive it as certain and ought to search for the causes from whence it might be derived.[2]

Apparently the bizarre cannot be ruled out on the grounds that it is bizarre. Indeed, given the right circumstances, even the second-hand *reports* of bizarre events are immune to the criticism that the claim must be false on the grounds that it goes against laws of nature. Nevertheless, even though it is possible that exceptions to established laws should occur, apparently we are never justified in describing the events as miraculous. One looks in vain for Hume's reasons for this latter thesis.

P.H. Nowell-Smith has tried to defend this second view.[3] Nowell-Smith repudiates the view that miracle-claims can be refuted on the grounds that they are exceptions to laws of nature, but he cannot understand the difference between the natural and the supernatural upon which the interpretation or explanation of a bizarre event as miraculous depends.[4] Science, he reminds us, has come to explain things which at an earlier date were beyond its very concept. He claims that no matter what happens, if it is explained at all, that explanation will take its place in some department of the university. Perhaps a new department will have to be created to accommodate it but that the new department will be among the natural-science faculties Nowell-Smith has no doubt. The point is that to describe an event as miraculous is to say that it could never be explained in any natural science whatsoever, and we can never say that. Not even science itself could show it.

> To say that it is inexplicable as a result of natural agents is already
> beyond the competence of any scientist as a scientist, and to say that it
> must be ascribed to supernatural agents is to say something that no one
> could possibly have the right to affirm on the evidence alone.[5]

Some would answer this charge by attempting to reconcile an event's being
miraculous with its eventually being naturally explainable but, say, highly
coincidental.[6] That there is such a usage for "miracle" I do not contest, but I am
interested in defending the concept Nowell-Smith is attacking. That there is
also a usage of "miracle" according to which to call an event a miracle is to
attribute it to the will of a supernatural agent and to claim that if the supernatural agent had not intervened that event would not have taken place is, I
think, equally clear. Indeed this latter usage is unquestionably more frequent
in the history of religion.

It follows that in the way in which I am using "miracle" miracle-claims do
have the implications Nowell-Smith envisages. "Supernatural" implies that
the agent be able to bring about events which are exceptions to physical laws.
Nothing else about the agent is at issue, however. For example, we are not
concerned with questions of whether he is all-good or all-powerful or eternal
or even with the question of whether there is more than one such being. But he
must be a being who can control the laws of nature. The question is whether or
not any event would ever be rationally described as a manifestation of power
of such a being. It will only be such if all causes other than such a being can be
ruled out—which is precisely what Nowell-Smith denied could be done.

Before I construct what I think is a counter example to Nowell-Smith's
thesis, I want to call attention to two features of miracles. The first is simply
that there is nothing amiss in one person having several miracles he can
perform. In the Book of Exodus, for example, Moses is given more than a
dozen miracles with which he attempts to melt the Pharaoh's heart. He brings
on several miraculous catastrophes and then stops them. The Pharaoh's heart
remains hard, and so Moses brings about several more. The second feature of
historical accounts to which I wish to call attention is the rather elaborate
circumstances in which they may take place. The people who wrote the Old
Testament quite obviously had some notion of how to tell the real thing from a
fake. Take the story about Elijah at Carmel (I Kings 18). Controversy had arisen
whether prayer should be directed to the Lord God of the Jews or to Baal.
Elijah took the people to Mt. Carmel and said: "Let them . . . give us two
bullocks; and let them choose one bullock for themselves, and cut it to pieces,
and lay it on wood." The minsters of Baal took the meat from one animal and
made a pile, and Elijah called upon the ministers of Baal to ask Baal to cook
their meat. "But there was no voice, nor any that answered. And they leaped
upon the altar which was made. And it came to pass at noon, that Elijah
mocked them, and said, Cry aloud; for he is a god; either he is talking, or he is
pursuing, or he is on a journey, or peradventure he sleepeth, and must be
awakened. And they cried aloud, and cut themselves after their manner with
knives and lances, till the blood gushed out upon them." But all this to no
avail. Then Elijah stepped up and said: "Fill four barrels with water, and pour
it on the burnt sacrifice, and on the wood." And he said, Do it the second time.
And they did it the second time. And he said, Do it the third time. And they did

it the third time. And the water ran round about the altar; and he filled the trench also with water. Then he called on God for fire and "Then the fire of the Lord fell, and consumed the burnt sacrifice, and the wood, and the stones, and the dust, and licked up the water that was in the trench."

We are given here, first of all, about as artificial a setting as any laboratory affords. The account also involves a random sampling of the material to be set on fire, a prediction that one pile will burn up and one will not, a prediction when the fire will start, and twelve barrels of precaution against earthly independent variables. There is obviously nothing wrong with applying somewhat sophisticated experimental design to miracles.

Now for the example. Its essential ingredients are simply a bundle of miracles no larger than Moses had and a randomizing technique just a little more complicated than Elijah's. Let us assume that a local prophet opens, or appears with the help of God to open, the mighty Schuylkill River. Two possibilities arise. The first is that the prophet does not figure causally in the natural explanation but that he notices a cue in the physical situation which indicates natural sufficient conditions. This is especially tempting because he might not be consciously aware of the cue and so might himself honestly believe in the miracle. This sort of explanation can be ruled out, however, if he is required to do miracles at random. Say he allows non-believers to pick twelve miracles and number them. Which one he will do will be determined by the roll of a pair of unloaded dice, and the hour of the day at which it will occur will be determined by a second roll. Rolling the dice without his prediction could establish that the dice had no efficacy and using the dice to randomize the predictions proves that the prophet does not predict on the basis of a natural cue.[7]

This randomizing also establishes that there is a cause at work other than would have operated if the prophet had not been there. But perhaps there is still some law covering the events. To see how vastly different this would be from an ordinary scientific law, however, one has only to realize that there would be no new scientific department on a par with, say, physics or chemistry, which dealt with all the other sciences and had no laws of its own, except that when this prophet spoke, all laws, or any one of an indefinitely large number, are broken.

Odd, you might say, but not yet miraculous. Such a prophet might require a new metascientific department, but we still have not been forced to admit supernatural explanation. But this is so only because we have not yet looked at the *explanans* in these supposed scientific explanations. What could possibly be the natural conditions which this new department will ascertain to be necessary and sufficient for the unexpected events?

If the prophet prayed we might think that the prayer was connected in some curious way with the exceptions. But what if he does not pray? What if he just requests? Could it be the sounds of his words which have the extraordinary effect? Then let him predict in different languages. Might we mention language-independent brain processes as the sufficient conditions? Let him predict what will happen later when he is asleep—even drugged or dead.

But surely it has become obvious that there is nothing which could be pinned down as the independent variable in a scientific explanation; for no conceivable candidate is necessary. The prophet asks God to do miracle No. 4

at midnight and then goes to sleep. Or he asks God to do whatever miracle turns up at whatever hour turns up and then dies. We are dealing with requests and answers—that is, thoughts, and thoughts not as psychological occurrences but as understood.

No natural law will do because only vehicles of thought could function as the natural *explanans* and no such vehicle is necessary. There would have to be one law connecting the acoustics of English with general law-breaking, another for French, and so on indefinitely—and when the prophet asks that whatever miracle turns upon the dice be performed and then goes to sleep before the dice are thrown, there just is not anything left except his request as understood.[8]

What is needed here is not a law but an understanding which can grasp the request and then bring it about that a physical law be broken. But an understanding physical-law breaker is a supernatural being, and that is why if a new department is set up it will not be with the science faculties at all. It will be a department of religion.

I should like here to attempt to forestall some foreseeable objections. The first one is that even if what I have said is all true, that still does not prove that there ever has been a miracle. Of course I agree with this objection. The sophistication of the experimental design of the Elijah account may be the progressive result of centuries of anxious parents' trying to convince doubting children of false stories. The point is that the concept of miracle allowed such sophistication. What they *meant* to say was ascertainable, or at least they meant to *say* that it was ascertainable, in principle. Whether or not their claims were actually true is another question.

A second criticism shows a hankering after a simple *a priori* disproof. Believing in miracles, it will be said, inevitably involves believing in the suspension of some physical law. We can always avoid this by doubting the data. Hallucinations do not rest on the suspension of such laws. The trouble with this sort of objection to the miraculous is that it can quickly be pushed to the point at which the very distinction between hallucinatory and veridical experiences break down. Faith, it has been said, can move mountains. Suppose that someone moved the Poconos to northern Minnesota. Thousands saw them flying through the air. Old maps showed them in Pennsylvania where we all remembered them to have been, and a thriving ski industry grows up where there had only been the exhausted open mines of the Mesabi Range. If that is a hallucination then everything is.

A third criticism is that the account of physical laws in this paper is hopelessly over-simple and crude. I agree. One must show, however, that the crudity and simplicity make a difference to the general thesis about miracles. As far as I can see, the introduction of statistics and probability, or the ideal nature of some or all laws, or of accounts of laws as models or inference tickets or as the designation of patterns we find intelligible, make no difference. Specifically, the account offered here does not rest on belief in metaphysical connections between causes and effects. Of course, physical laws are only descriptive. But I take it that they do serve as bases for predictions and also for contrary-to-fact conditionals. They are not ontological, but they must be nomological. As long as according to the natural laws operative (e.g., gravity) and the state of the world at one time (e.g., including a free body) another state can be predicted to occur (e.g., the body's fall), then, even though there may never have been an exactly true formulation of the law or a perfect instantiation of the initial conditions (no body ever quite free), as long as the denial of the predicted event is internally coherent, to speak of exceptions is meaningful.

A fourth rejoinder to my arguments might be that even if I have proved that there could be conditions which, if you experienced them, would justify your belief in a miracle, and even though we might have reason to believe second-hand reports of bizarre phenomena, we could still never have better reasons to believe a second-hand miracle claim than to doubt the veracity of the man reporting it; and surely this is really all that Hume, if not Nowell-Smith, set out to prove. In answer let me say first that if you had good reason to believe that what the report describes as happening really did happen—and happened as the reports describe, viz., with randomizing and predictions—then it seems to me that you have good reasons to believe in supernatural intervention as an explanation of the events. But in any case remember Exodus once more. Moses had brought several miraculous plagues, then called them off, then brought down a new batch. Now say that you happened into Egypt during the second batch of catastrophes. Could you rule out *a priori* the possibility that there had been a earlier set? I think not.

Fifthly, one might object that even if I have shown that there could be evidence for miracles and even in the sense in which "miracle" implies supernatural intervention, this is still of no religious significance unless "miracle" also implies *divine* intervention. Miracles, as defined here, in short, do not tend to prove the existence of God. My only answer is that to prove the existence of a being who deserves some of the predicates which "God" normally gets would be to go some way toward proving the existence of *God*. The question whether the comprehensibility of miracle claims strengthens the position of the theologians or whether the paucity of latter-day evidence has the opposite effect, I leave to the theologians and more militant atheists.

A final criticism might be that calling an event a miracle appears to be offering an explanation for it, but is really not an explanation at all since explanations must always rest on laws. In fact, it might be held, this is the real dilemma behind miracle hypotheses. Either there are laws covering miracles or not. If there are no laws then miracles cannot be explanations: they are not hypotheses at all. But if there are laws, then there is no difference between natural and supernatural explanations. Nowell-Smith's argument goes:

(A). Calling an event a miracle is apparently to explain it.

(B). Explanations must rest on laws.

(C). If one has laws one can predict the events they explain.

(D). We cannot predict miracles, therefore calling an event a miracle has no (explanatory) meaning over and above a mere (descriptive) statement of the phenomena to be explained.[9]

Now, a prediction was involved in the Elijah story, and I do not see how one could pin down God as the independent variable unless predictions like those were possible. These predictions, however, were not made possible by anything Nowell-Smith would call a law. Indeed, that the prediction did not rest on the knowledge of a regularity between initial conditions and effect was the reason for looking to the supernatural. In other words, it cannot be objected that miracles are not explanations because miracles are not lawful until it has been proved that all explanations are lawful. This is all the more pressing since part of the point of interpreting an event as a miracle is to see it not as a natural event but as an action, or the result of an action, of an intelligent being.[10] That all intelligible *actions* are subsumable under laws is even less credible than that all *events* are. An action can be made intelligible by showing its *point* (for example, to bring wayward children back to the truth, to reward the holy, to save the chosen people, etc.), and showing the good of an action is not automatically to subsume it under a law.

I conclude that "miracle" is perfectly meaningful. To call an event a miracle is to claim that it is the result of supernatural intervention into the natural course of events. We could know that the supernatural agent was intelligent, but little else (though when and for whom he did miracles would be evidence about his character).[11]

NOTES

1. David Hume, *An Enquiry Concerning Human Understanding*, sect. 10, pt. 1, p. 115 (references are to the L. A. Selby-Bigge edition entitled *Enquiries*).

2. *Ibid.*, p. 128.

3. In "Miracles," reprinted in *New Essays in Philosophical Theology*, edd. A. Flew and A. MacIntyre (London, 1955), pp. 243–253.

4. *Ibid.*, p. 244.

5. *Ibid.*, pp. 246–247.

6. For an interesting discussion of that concept of "miracle," see chapter 16.

7. One might object to "proves," but such procedures eliminate candidates with as much certainty as any non-logical procedures ever could.

8. Since in this case the prophet does not know what miracle will be asked for, precognition is also ruled out.

9. Nowell-Smith, p. 250.

10. This is the point of drawing an analogy between explanations in terms of miracles and human intervention into the course of nature. Whether or not such divine intervention would have to be in conformity to the laws of nature because human intervention apparently is would be a further question. Nowell-Smith seems to think that anyone who draws the analogy at all must admit that divine intervention would have to be in accordance with laws (p. 249).

11. This paper has profited from criticisms by Professors William Wisdom and Michael Scriven.

Part V

Alternatives to Theism: Naturalism and Humanism

The major religions of the West during the past two thousand years—Christianity, Judaism, and Islam—are theistic religions. So it is probably safe to say that most Westerners who have taken any interest in religious beliefs have been theists. Every age, however, has produced individuals who have found prevailing religious teachings unconvincing. Unbelief has been more widespread in some periods than in others, and our age may be a particularly skeptical time. Even so, there is a tendency to assume that those who reject theism are simply atheists, irreligious persons who reject all beliefs about matters ultimate.

To be sure, atheism is the most obvious alternative to theism, but atheism amounts simply to the denial of belief in God or the claim that there is no God. It is not as empty a stance, and thus not as irresponsible a position, as agnosticism, which refuses to take a stand either way. Atheists, however, are not usually persons whose beliefs stop with the denial of the existence of God. Atheism is often an ingredient in a carefully formulated set of beliefs that offers alternative answers to many of the questions addressed by theism. Part V briefly examines several belief systems that omit or reject belief in God in the theistic sense but offer systematic accounts of the nature of the world and the place of humans in it.

A major theoretical function that the concept of God has performed in theistic philosophical belief systems is to answer questions about the origin of the physical world and the order that humans believe that they detect in it as well as to explain what the purpose of human existence might be. Theism usually involves a doctrine of creation that depicts the world as deliberately designed and created by God to serve God's purposes, and the welfare of humans usually figures importantly in these doctrines of creation. Some philosophers, however, have argued that God is not the only possible nor the most plausible explanation of the world and the human race. To the extent that the various objections to theism, some of which were examined in Part IV, are weighty, the justification of theistic belief becomes problematic. Many of the nontheistic advocates of alternative philosophical systems argue that theism uses the concept of God, admitted to be beyond human comprehension, to explain processes in nature that seem not nearly so mysterious and that indeed we are on our way toward understanding. A naturalistic theory that restricts itself completely to the realm of nature and the principles of science seems much simpler and more plausible than a theory that postulates supernatural beings and supermundane processes. Thus a number of thinkers have argued that the world is self-intelligible—understandable in terms of principles and processes that are a part of the natural order of things.

One alternative to theism that has attempted a naturalistic account of the world and of humans is materialism. This philosophy is old in Western thought, dating back at least to the time of the ancient Greek atomists Leucippus and Democritus in the fifth century before the Common Era. The atomists attempted to explain the material world as a configuration of tiny material particles (the Greek word for atom means "uncuttable") that themselves do not change but that generate the variety of forms we encounter in the world by the different patterns in which they conjoin. They held the human soul to be the tiniest, smoothest particles that slither in the spaces between the grosser particles of which our bodies are composed. Not all of the Greek materialists were atheists in the strictest sense of the term; some resorted to theories about gods to account for human dreams and visions. They rejected the notion, however, that the gods were involved in creating or regulating the material world.

The progress of science in the postmedieval period contributed to the rise of more sophisticated versions of materialism based on a better under-standing of what matter is and how it works. Mate-rialism in all its forms, however, has always been vulnerable to the criticism that it is reductive. Critics claim that materialism is inadequate because it at-tempts to account for the complex in terms of the simple, offering no convincing explanation of how inert particles of matter could form themselves into structured bodies mutually interacting in intelligible patterns, or how dead, inorganic particles could ar-range themselves in such a way as to become living, metabolizing, reproducing organisms, or—greatest mystery of all—how unfeeling plants and unreason-ing animals could give rise to humans with reason, moral understanding, aesthetic judgment, and even loving and altruistic behavior. The materialism of the nineteenth and early twentieth century implies that life is "nothing but" inorganic matter rearranged; that rationality is "only" animal bodily processes of a complex sort. Many philosophers have found such theories unacceptable because they lack the essential ingredient of an explanatory hypothesis: a principle of change that can account not just for rearrangement of particles but for the appearance of genuinely new qualities such as life, feeling, and thought.

It is precisely in dealing with this problem that naturalism is thought to show its superiority over materialism. Aided by the concept of evolution—not just biological natural selection but more general pro-cesses of random variation resulting in the gradual accumulation of more complex organization—the naturalists claim that they can give an account of the world that is materialistic but not reductive. Evolu-tionary or emergent naturalism teaches that the natu-ral processes of motion characteristic of the ultimate constituents of the the world result, without super-natural guidance or intervention, in a gradually emerging complexity. Each new level of organization manifests new characteristics that could not have been predicted before they appeared. Thus the pro-ponents of naturalism argue that the charge leveled against materialism—that the higher features of the world are reduced to the lower so that life is regarded as "nothing but" a more complex arrangement of matter and mind "merely" more complicated or-ganic processes—does not apply to naturalism.

Emergent naturalism recognizes that genuinely new features appear and that these are not reducible to the old, less complex processes on which they rest.

A living organism has qualities unprecedented in the world. Before the first such organism appeared, it would have been impossible to predict, by extrapolation upon the features of inorganic matter, what these qualities would be. This means, contrary to the reductive views of the old materialism, that the laws of psychology cannot be reduced to, or translated into, the laws of biology and that those of biology cannot be reduced to those of physics. Emergent naturalism recognizes each new level of order as having features that require their own explanatory laws. But this does not mean that a supernatural being is required to create them, or a supermundane principle to explain them. It means that nature is richer than we had imagined, capable of innovation and creativity.

The humanists remind us that this conclusion should really come as no surprise. After all, humans are capable of innovation, imagination, invention, and creation, and humans are products of the natural evolutionary processes of the world. Humanism is a version of naturalism whose focus is turned toward understanding the unique qualities the world manifests in its most complex and highly evolved creature. Like naturalists, humanists point out that the mind is a very late arrival in the world, a feature whose existence depends on the whole hierarchy of material and organic beings and which therefore cannot plausibly be postulated as the antecedent condition or creator of the world. Humanists note—to borrow a term popularized by recent materialists writing about the philosophy of the mind—that the cognitive, rational, moral, and aesthetic qualities of humans "supervene" on the organic and neural processes of their animal bodies. Where physical organisms of an appropriate structure and level of complexity are not present, the qualities of mind do not appear. Once the world has generated those qualities by giving rise to human beings, humans find themselves not alien but at home in the environment that produced them, which offers opportunity for the realization of the new values these new creatures cherish. So hospitable is the world to humans and their ideals that many thinkers, the humanists say, have mistakenly imagined that it must have been created by a supernatural superhuman Being just to serve human purposes. Unfortunately, such thinking has negative rather than positive consequences. It encourages humans to assume an attitude of dependence, relying on the deity to do whatever is necessary to promote the progress of human ideals. One of the most positive effects of humanism is to bring humans to the realization that their destiny is in their own hands, to challenge them to use their reason and imagination to conceive, and their energies to build, the kind of world in which they can be fully human in the highest sense. The recognition that the world is a natural and a human world encourages human responsibility for protecting the values that have emerged and for fostering processes conducive to the fuller realization of the higher values. This activist strand in humanism has resulted in the formation of several organizations, some of them religious—but distinctly not theistic—to foster human efforts to create a more humane world. The humanist manifestos, included in this chapter, are products of such efforts.

Theism is one of the major arguments by which humans have attempted to account for the existence and order of the natural world; their own existence; and the values, ideals, hopes, and dreams that are an inseparable part of being human. It is not, however, the only way. Other theories have been put forward that have a certain plausibility and in some instances certain advantages over theism. In this part we sample only a few types. Not represented here is another alternative now becoming widely accepted: the new, nonreductive materialism, whose major focus is on the philosophy of the mind. Thoughtful persons must examine both theism and the best among the alternatives to theism and decide, as the selection from William Wainwright tries to help us to do, the most convincing world view.

ANNOTATED GUIDE TO FURTHER READINGS

Materialism

Armstrong, D. M. *A Materialist Theory of the Mind.* London: Routledge and Kegan Paul, 1968.
Argues that there are no adequate reasons to reject the central-state materialist claim that the mental activities of human beings are derived from entirely physical processes.

Campbell, Keith. *Body and Mind.* Notre Dame, Indiana: University of Notre Dame Press, 1984
Examines the major mind-body theories, such as dualism, behavior-

ism, central-state materialism, functionalism, and a new version of epiphenomenalism.

Margolis, Joseph. *Persons and Minds: The Prospects of Nonreductive Materialism.* Dordrecht: D. Reidel, 1978.
Margolis develops a nonreductivist materialist theory of the person as an emergent entity embodied in a sentient organism.

Naturalism

Alexander, Samuel. *Space, Time, and Deity.* New York: Dover Publications, 1966.
In this substantial two-volume work, from which a selection is included in this Part, Alexander develops his theory of evolutionary naturalism as a universal evolutionary progression toward higher and higher levels of being, culminating in deity.

Hartshorne, Charles. *Beyond Humanism.* New York: Willett, Clark and Company, 1937.
Presents the theory of naturalistic theism, in which the concepts of God and nature merge, providing an alternative way of looking at the divine.

Romanell, Patrick. *Toward a Critical Naturalism.* New York: Macmillan, 1958.
Naturalism stresses the unity of humankind and nature; the importance of the natural world comes from its own intrinsic value. Naturalism and ethics are also extensively examined.

Idealism

Aurobindo, Sri. *The Life Divine.* Pondicherry, India: Sri Aurobindo Ashram, 1977.
These comoprehensive writings offer the reader an alternate explanation of the nature of existence. Aurobindo teaches absolute idealism, a form of supernaturalism that holds that all being originated from one all-inclusive mind called the Absolute. Today, all being is evolving from its current state of separation to the higher level of oneness within the consciousness of the Absolute.

Hocking, William Ernest. *Types of Philosophy.* New York: Charles Scribner's Sons, 1959.
Chapters 19 through 29 of this text deal with idealism. Hocking defines and explains idealism; examines individual facets of idealism and their relation to specific issues.

Humanism

Auer, J. A. C. Fagginer, and Hartt, Julian. *Humanism versus Theism.* Ames, Iowa: Iowa State University Press, 1981.
A good source for gaining an understanding of the humanist perspective. The first section, by Auer, is an argument supporting humanism; it is followed by Hartt's rebuttal which defends theism from the humanistic claims.

Dewey, John. *A Common Faith*. New Haven: Yale University Press, 1934.
Dewey draws a distinction between religious values and religions them-selves, directing his religious faith towards human civilization and ideals rather than the supernatural.

Lamont, Corliss. *Humanism as a Philosophy*. New York: Philo-sophical Library, 1949.
A thorough introduction to humanism: definition, historical back-ground, and an examination of basic humanist contentions, such as the overriding importance of this life and this world.

V.A. Naturalism

V.A.1. Deity and God

SAMUEL ALEXANDER

Samuel Alexander (1859–1938), a Welsh philosopher who spent most of his professional career at Victoria University, Manchester, was one of the leading and most creative advocates of emergent naturalism. In his 1916–18 Gifford lectures, published as Space, Time, and Deity, *he elaborated a thoroughly worked-out metaphysical system that depicted the world as an evolving process characterized by creativity and ever-emerging newness. Beginning with the concepts of space and time and the dynamic interaction of these two, Alexander depicts a hierarchy of emergent beings, each with new and surprising features. As space-time vibrates in ever-new patterns, such things as electrons, protons, and atoms emerge, each endowed with new qualities that confer on them the capacity for further complexification; these entities interact in ways that give rise to molecules and compounds of matter, which constitute themselves into galaxies of stars and planets. Some of the new qualities that ever-complexifying matter evolves enable it to form organic matter able to duplicate itself, and so there arise organic molecules, bacteria, plants, animals, and creatures with complex nervous systems characterized by sensitivity, desire, perception, reason, morality, philosophy, religion.*

Alexander regards each of the newly emerged qualities as marvelous and thus uses the word "deity" to describe such new characteristics and capacities, as viewed from the next lower level. From the point of view of inorganic matter, then, life is deity; from the perspective of animals, mind is deity. Thus Alexander suggests, the natural world is pregnant with deity and is ever striving and evolving toward deity. Deity is not, as the theists have believed, a supernatural Being who existed before the world appeared and who created it. Rather, deity means the creative newness, the surprising richness, the inspiring value dimensions the world is forever generating. Humans are the highest beings thus far to emerge in the process though there is every reason to expect that the process is ongoing and that higher beings are yet to come. We cannot

From *Space, Time, and Deity* (New York: Macmillan, 1966), vol. 2, pp. 341–350.

imagine what new qualities these higher beings will have, but those qualities, whatever they are, are what we mean by deity from our perspective as humans.

In the following selection from his Gifford lectures, Alexander attempts to relate his naturalistic, nontheistic conception of Deity to the religious emotions of humans and their tendency toward worship.

In a universe so described, consisting of things which have developed within the one matrix of Space-Time; we ourselves being but the highest finite existences known to us because the empirical quality which is distinctive of conscious beings is based on finites of a lower empirical quality; what room is there for, and what place can be assigned to, God?

TWO WAYS OF DEFINING GOD

Primarily God must be defined as the object of religious emotion or of worship. He is correlative to that emotion or sentiment, as food is correlative to appetite. What we worship, that is God. This is the practical or religious approach to God. But it is insufficient for our theoretical needs. It labours under the defect that so far as religion itself is able to assure us, the object of religion, however vitally rooted in human nature, however responsive to its needs, may be disconnected with the rest of the world. God may be but an ennobling fancy, a being whom we project before us in our imagination, in whom to believe may sustain and inspire us and have its own sufficient justification in its effects on our happiness, but to whom no reality corresponds which can be co-ordinated with familiar realities of the world. The appetite for food arises from internal causes, but the food which satisfies it is external and independent of the organism, and it is known to us apart from the satisfaction which it gives to our hunger. The passion for God is no less a real appetite of our nature, but what if it creates the very object which satisfies it? Always, indeed, the religious emotion believes in the reality of its object, as something greater than man and independent of him, in whom the finite creature may even in some phases of feeling be submerged; and it would reject as preposterous the suggestion that God may be a fancy with which it plays, like a lover with a dream of perfection. But the religious sentiment itself can supply us with no such theoretical assurance of reality, and it needs to be supplemented with a metaphysical inquiry, what place if any the object of worship occupies in the general scheme of things.

On the other hand from the metaphysical approach, God must be defined as the being, if any, which possesses deity or the divine quality; or, if there are more Gods than one, the beings which possess deity. The defect of this definition (which is only apparently circular) is that the being which possesses deity need not necessarily, so far as the bare metaphysical description goes, be the object of religious sentiment. It has to be shown that the being which possesses deity coincides with the object of religious passion and is its food. Neither definition is therefore for theory complete in itself. The religious description wants authentic coherence with the system of things. The metaphysical one wants the touch of feeling which brings it within the circle of human interests. Were the passion towards God not already lit, no speculative contemplation or proof of the existence or attributes of a metaphysical God would make him worshipful.[1] Even the intellectual love of God which in Spinoza's system has the force of religion can do so, not as a mere passion for truth in its fullest form, but because it presupposes a religious passion. Were it not on the other hand for the speculative or reflective justification, the God of religious sentiment would have no sure root in things. Religion leans on metaphysics for the justification of its indefeasible conviction of the reality of its object; philosophy leans on religion to justify it in calling the possessor of deity by the religious name of God. The two methods of approach are therefore complementary.

METHOD

But whichever method of approach be adopted, in either case God is defined indirectly. Religion is not the sentiment which is directed upon God; but God is that upon which the religious sentiment is directed. The datum of experience is that sentiment, and what God is is known only by examining its deliverances. In metaphysics, deity is not so much the quality which belongs to God as God is the being which possesses deity. The quality of deity is here the datum of experience. It is idle to hope that by defining God in conceptual terms, whether as the sum of reality, or the perfect being, or the first cause, or by other device, we can establish the connection between such a being and the rest of our experience. We do but start with an abstraction and we do but end with one. Proofs of God's existence and nature there are none, if such a God is to be identified with the object of worship. Granted that there is a sum of reality; in what respect does it stir the religious passion? The answer must be: because of its deity, and on what this deity is the conception of a sum of reality offers no light. The same thing holds in different degrees of the conceptions of a first cause or a supreme designer.

Nor can we even prove the existence of a being called God, whether worshipful or not, except on the basis of experience. No one now is convinced by the traditional arguments for God's existence. The reason is that at some point or other they introduce conceptions which are *a priori* in the bad sense of that phrase, in which it means not something experienced which is pervasive of all things but something supplied by the mind; or in other words they desert the scientific interpretation of things, along the lines indicated by experience itself, by a rigidly limited use of analogy.[2] The only one of the three which at all

---

[1] Cp. James, *Varieties of Religious Experience* (London, 1902), p. 431.

[2] The famous ontological argument proves nothing more than that the totality of things is real; which is a bare tautology. The argument assumes the form that the idea of the universe cannot be a mere idea as the idea of a finite thing may be, but its object must be real. In truth the idea of all reality is nothing but all reality over again. Mr. Bradley accepts the argument but adds the proviso that the idea of the Absolute though it must exist need not exist as such,

persuades is the argument from design which is based on the wonderful adaptation of living forms to their surroundings and on "the hierarchy of ministration"[3] amongst the forms, by which the lower serves the purposes of the higher. Because such adaptation implies in human products the operation of a designing mind, the conception is extended from this particular case, by an illegitimate use of analogy, to experience as a whole. The easy conception of a designing mind was foisted upon nature as a whole, without considering whether it could be used under conditions which required it to be infinite and to create its own material.[4] Subsequent knowledge has shown that the experi ence which was thought unintelligible without such a conception points in the opposite direction. For adaptation to the surroundings, or the internal tele ology of forms, is the result of selection operating on variations; and the external teleology of ministration is not to be assigned to a force operating in the past but is an incident of passage to the future. Who does not see that sheep were not created for man, but that man survives because he is able to live on sheep? On the other hand, if for this external designer we substitute the notion of an immanent design, we do but name the fact that the world works out so as to produce a plan. We may call the world so conceived by the name of God, and forget or possibly explain the wastefulness and destruction involved in the process. But in what sense is such a God worshipful? He is worshipful only if we silently reintroduce into the notion of an immanent design, which in the end is a bare compendious description of certain facts, that of a designer, and fall back on the previous and invalid view.

What we can hope to do is something more modest, and more consistent with scientific procedure in other matters. Abandoning the attempt to define God directly, we may ask ourselves whether there is place in the world for the quality of deity; we may then verify the reality of the being which possesses it, that is of the Deity or God; and having done so, we may then consult the religious consciousness to see whether this being coincides with the object of worship. Where then, if at all, is deity in the scheme of things?

DEITY THE NEXT HIGHER EMPIRICAL QUALITY THAN MIND

Within the all-embracing stuff of Space-Time, the universe exhibits an emergence in Time of successive levels of finite existences, each with its

---

that is in the form of the idea. But if I am thinking of all reality, if it really is all reality I think of, my idea can be nothing but that reality, and there can be no difference between my object and the reality. This corresponds to the assertion . . . that a complete perspective of Space-Time taken both from the place and date of any point-instant is nothing but the universe itself. In other words there can be no perspectives consisting of the whole of reality, and so in the strict sense there is no such thing as an idea of it. For all ideas are perspectives of the things they are ideas of.

[3] The phrase is St. George Mivart's.

[4] Difficulties raised by Spinoza and Kant.

characteristic empirical quality. The highest of these empirical qualities known to us is mind or consciousness. Deity is the next higher empirical quality to the highest we know; and, as shall presently be observed, at any level of existence there is a next higher empirical quality which stands towards the lower quality as deity stands towards mind. Let us for the moment neglect this wider implication and confine our attention to ourselves. There is an empirical quality which is to succeed the distinctive empirical quality of our level; and that new empirical quality is deity. If Time were as some have thought a mere form of sense or understanding under which the mind envisages things, this conception would be meaningless and impossible. But Time is an element in the stuff of which the universe and all its parts are made, and has no special relation to mind, which is but the last complexity of Time that is known to us in finite existence. Bare Time in our hypothesis, whose verification has been in progress through each stage of the two preceding Books and will be completed by the conception of God—bare Time is the soul of its Space, or performs towards it the office of soul to its equivalent body or brain; and this elementary mind which is Time becomes in the course of time so complicated and refined in its internal grouping that there arise finite beings whose soul is materiality, or colour, or life, or in the end what is familiar as mind. Now since Time is the principle of growth and Time is infinite, the internal development of the world, which before was described in its simplest terms as the redistribution of moments of time among points of Space, cannot be regarded as ceasing with the emergence of those finite configurations of space-time which carry the empirical quality of mind. We have to think upon the lines already traced by experience of the emergence of higher qualities, also empirical. There is a nisus in Space-Time which, as it has borne its creatures forward through matter and life to mind, will bear them forward to some higher level of existence. There is nothing in mind which requires us to stop and say this is the highest empirical quality which Time can produce from now throughout the infinite time to come. It is only the last empirical quality which we who are minds happen to know. Time itself compels us to think of a later birth of Time. For this reason it was legitimate for us to follow up the series of empirical qualities and imagine finite beings which we called angels, who would enjoy their own angelic being but would contemplate minds as minds themselves cannot do, in the same way as mind contemplates life and lower levels of existence. This device was adopted half-playfully as a pictorial embodiment of the conception forced upon us by the fact that there is this series of levels of existence. It was used illustratively to point the distinction of enjoyment and contemplation. But we now can see that it is a serious conception. For the angelic quality of deity and our supposed angels are finite beings with this quality. We shall have to ask how such finite deities are related to the infinite God, for they themselves are finite gods.

Deity is thus the next higher empirical quality to mind, which the universe is engaged in bringing to birth. That the universe is pregnant with such a quality we are speculatively assured. What that quality is we cannot know; for we can neither enjoy nor still less contemplate it. Our human altars still are raised to the unknown God. If we could know what deity is, how it feels to be divine, we should first have to have become as gods. What we know of it is but its relation to the other empirical qualities which precede it in time. Its nature we cannot penetrate. We can present it to ourselves only by analogy. It is fitly described in this analogical manner as the colour of the universe. For colour, we have seen, is a new quality which emerges in material things in attendance on motions of a certain sort. Deity in its turn is a quality which attends upon, or more strictly is equivalent to, previous or lower existences of the order of mind which itself rests on a still lower basis of qualities, and emerges when certain complexities and refinements of arrangement have been reached. Once more I am leaning for help upon Meredith, in whose *Hymn to Colour*, colour takes for a moment the place of what elsewhere he calls Earth: a soul of things which is their last perfection; whose relation to our soul is that of bridegroom to bride. He figures the relation of our soul to colour under the metaphor of love; but as I read the poem, deity as the next higher empirical quality is not different from colour as he conceives it; save only that for him the spirit of the world is timeless, whereas for us deity is like all other empirical qualities a birth of Time and exists in Time, and timelessness is for us a nonentity, and merely a device for contrasting God's infinite deity with the relative imperfection of the finite things we know, a conception which shall appear in due course.

EXTENSION OF THE CONCEPTION OF DEITY

We have not yet asked what the being is which possesses deity. But before attempting to raise the question we may still linger over the quality of deity itself. In the first place it is clear that, while for us men deity is the next higher empirical quality to mind, the description of deity is perfectly general. For any level of existence, deity is the next higher empirical quality. It is therefore a variable quality, and as the world grows in time, deity changes with it. On each level a new quality looms ahead, awfully, which plays to it the part of deity. For us who live upon the level of mind deity is, we can but say, deity. To creatures upon the level of life, deity is still the quality in front, but to us who come later this quality has been revealed as mind. For creatures who possessed only the primary qualities,—mere empirical configurations of space-time,—deity was what afterwards appeared as materiality, and their God was matter, for I am supposing that there is no level of existence nearer to the spatio-temporal than matter. On each level of finite creatures deity is for them some 'unknown' (though not 'unexperienced') quality in front, the real nature of which is enjoyed by the creatures of the next level. I do not mean that a material being would in some way think or forecast life; for there is no thinking in the proper sense till we reach mind. I do not even mean that matter forecasts deity in the sense in which it is sometimes said that to a dog his master is God. For the dog though he may not think, does feel and imagine, and his master is a finite being presented to his senses, for whom he feels attachment. I mean only that corresponding to the sense of a mysterious something which is more than we are and yet is felt in feeling and is conceived by speculation, there is some quality in the purview of material things which lies ahead of material quality. If we think ourselves back into material existence, we should feel ourselves, though matter would be the highest that we know, still swept on in the movement of Time. A merely material universe would not be exhausted by materiality and its lower empirical qualities; there would still be that restless movement of Time, which is not the mere turning of a squirrel in its cage, but the nisus towards a higher birth. That it is so, events show. How its being so would be 'experienced' in the material 'soul' may need for its description a greater capacity to strip off human privileges and sympathise with lower experience than most persons, and certainly I, possess.

DEITY NOT SPIRIT

Having thus realised that the relation of deity to mind is not peculiar to us but arises at each level between the next higher quality and the distinctive quality of that level, we can at once pass to another observation. We cannot tell what is the nature of deity, of our deity, but we can be certain that it is not mind, or if we use the term spirit as equivalent to mind or any quality of the order of mind, deity is not spirit, but something different from it in kind. God, the being which possesses deity, must be *also* spirit, for according to analogy, deity presupposes spirit, just as spirit or mind presupposes in its possessor life, and life physico-chemical material processes. But though God must be spiritual in the same way as he must be living and material and spatio-temporal, his deity is not spirit. To think so would be like thinking that mind is purely life, or life purely physico-chemical. The neural complexity which is equivalent to mind is not merely physiological, but a selected physiological constellation which is the bearer of mind, though it is also physiological, because it has physiological relations to what is purely physiological. That complexity and refinement of spirit which is equivalent to deity is something new, and while it is also spirit it is not merely spirit. Deity is therefore, according to the pattern of the growth of things in time, not a mere enlargement of mind or spirit, but something which mere spirit subserves, and to which accordingly the conception of spirit as such is totally inadequate. Spirit, personality, mind, all these human or mental characters belong to God, but not to his deity. They belong as we must hold not to his deity but to his 'body.' Yet since it is through spirit that we become aware of God, whether in the practical shape of the object of religious feeling or philosophically as the possessor of deity, since what is beyond spirit is realised through spirit, and since more particularly spirit is the highest quality whose nature we know, and we are compelled to embody our perceptions in imaginative shapes, it is not strange that we should represent God in human terms. Instead of the shadowy quality of which we can only say that it is a higher quality than mind, God is made vivid to us as a greater spirit; and we conceal the difference in kind of the divine and the human nature under magnified representations of human attributes. These are the inevitable devices of our weakness and our pictorial craving. But, for philosophy, God's deity is not different from spirit in degree but in kind, as a novelty in the series of empirical qualities.

THEORIES OF GOD AS A SPIRIT

When on a former occasion I endeavored to explain the relation of the mind of total Space-Time to the minds of the separate point-instants, I referred . . . to a hypothesis that had been advanced as to the nature of God, which was founded on the coexistence of a superior mind with an inferior one within the same abnormal body or personality. I made use of the notion of co-conscious minds not aware of each other, in order to elucidate certain features in Space-Time when Time is regarded as the mind of Space. This hypothesis in its reference to God I am compelled to reject and the reason will now be clear. The sequel will show that the position adopted here as to God is not dissimilar, at least to the extent that God is also for us, ideally speaking, an individual within the world. But it would be difficult on this hypothesis to admit an infinite God;[5] and what is more important it would commit us to making of God a being not higher in kind than minds.

On the basis of the same data as were used in the above hypothesis, we might again be tempted to compare God with the total personality in which the separate personalities are merged when the hysteric patient is restored to health; and to conceive of God as a society of minds. There is, however, nothing to show that the minds of distinct bodies are actually connected together so as to constitute a single all-embracing mind. Where dissociated personalities within a single individual are reunited, their physiological connection is re-established. Between the separate minds supposed to be contained within the mind of God there is no such physiological connection. In its application to the supposed mind of God accordingly the reference to dissociated personalities fails of relevance.

Nor can we help ourselves to think of God as an inclusive mind by the current metaphors of the mind of a state or a crowd. Where many persons are grouped together in co-operation there is no real reason for imagining the whole society to possess a mind. It is sufficient that the persons communicate with one another, and that while on the one hand their gregarious instinct brings about their juxtaposition, their juxtaposition supplies thoughts and passions, which are not experienced by the persons in isolation. The mind of a crowd is not a new single mind; the phrase represents the contagious influence upon an individual of the presence of many others. An incendiary oration addressed to one person might leave him cold, but in a meeting each catches infection from his neighbour (just as patients in a hospital will fall into a hypnotic sleep from sympathy with another patient who is receiving suggestion) and the oration may produce a riot. The individuals gather together to hear the orator and then their assemblage fans the flame. The institution of the family arises out of the mutual needs of persons and in turn evokes fresh ones. But there is no new mind of the family; only the minds of its members are affected by their participation in the family. In the same way there is no mind of the state or the nation which includes the minds of its members. The state is

---

[5] For physiological bodies with minds are finite. An infinite mind would require for its body the whole universe (see later) and would not then be one mind subsisting along with others but inclusive of them all, and would thus come under the suggestion of the next paragraph. There may indeed be an infinite part of the universe, *e.g.* a line. But this would not be the bearer of the mind. In other words either God's mind is really a mind and then it is finite; or if it is infinite, it must either be an all-inclusive mind (which is merely Time), or not mind at all but deity.

not a new individual created by the union of isolated individuals. The individuals are driven by their own sociality into union, and the union alters their minds. It affects the individuals because it is in the first instance the issue of their instinctive gregariousness. The general will is not a new individual will which contains the individual wills; it is but the will of individuals as inspired by desire for the collective good. T. H. Green seems to me to have been right in insisting that a nation or a national spirit is as much an abstraction unless it exists in persons as the individual is an abstraction apart from the nation.[6] It is true that a state or nation has features not recognisable in any one individual; but this is only to say that groupings of persons are not merely personal.

In a later page I shall return to this matter when I attempt to show the bearing of the doctrine that God's distinctive character is not mind or spirit but something new, or deity, upon the current theory that the Absolute in which all finites are merged is spirit.

GOD AS UNIVERSE POSSESSING DEITY

In the religious emotion we have the direct experience of something higher than ourselves which we call God, which is not presented through the ways of sense but through this emotion. The emotion is our going out or endeavor or striving toward this object. Speculation enables us to say wherein the divine quality consists, and that it is an empirical quality the next in the series which the very nature of Time compels us to postulate, though we cannot tell what it is like. But besides assuring us of the place of the divine quality in the world, speculation has also to ask wherein this quality resides. What is the being which possesses deity? Our answer is to be a philosophical one; we are not concerned with the various forms which the conception of God had assumed in earlier or later religions. Ours is the modester (and let me add far less arduous) inquiry what conception of God is required if we think of the universe as Space-Time engendering within itself in the course of time the series of empirical qualities of which deity is the one next ahead of mind. God is the whole world as possessing the quality of deity. Of such a being the whole world is the 'body' and deity is the 'mind.' But this possessor of deity is not actual but ideal. As an actual existent, God is the infinite world with its nisus towards deity, or to adapt a phrase of Leibniz, as big or in travail with deity.

Since Space-Time is already a whole and one, why, it may be urged, should we seek to go beyond it? Why not identify God with Space-Time? Now, no one could worship Space-Time. It may excite speculative or mathematical enthusiasm and fill our minds with intellectual admiration, but it lights no spark of religious emotion. Worship is not the response which Space-Time evokes in us, but intuition. Even Kant's starry heavens are material systems, and he added the moral law to them in describing the source of our reverence. In one way this consideration is irrelevant; for if philosophy were forced to this conclusion that God is nothing but Space-Time, we should needs be content.

---

[6] *Prolegomena to Ethics*, sect. 184; taken from the table of contents, p. xxi.

But a philosophy which left one portion of human experience suspended without attachment to the world of truth is gravely open to suspicion; and its failure to make the religious emotion speculatively intelligible betrays a speculative weakness. For the religious emotion is one part of experience, and an empirical philosophy must include in one form or another the whole of experience. The speculative failure of the answer is patent. It neglects the developments within Space-Time of the series of empirical qualities in their increasing grades of perfection. The universe, though it can be expressed without remainder in terms of Space and Time, is not merely spatio-temporal. It exhibits materiality and life and mind. It compels us to forecast the next empirical quality or deity. On the one hand we have the totality of the world, which in the end is spatio-temporal; on the other the quality of deity engendered or rather being engendered, within that whole. These two features are united in the conception of the whole world as expressing itself in the character of deity, and it is this and not bare Space-Time which for speculation is the ideal conception of God.

Belief in God, though an act of experience, is not an act of sight, for neither deity nor even the world as tending to deity is revealed to the sense, but of speculative and religious faith. A word will be said later to compare the faith we have in God with the faith we have in the minds of other persons than ourselves. Any attempt, therefore, to conceive God in a more definite manner must involve a large element of speculative or reflexive imagination. Even the description of God as the whole universe, as possessing deity, or as in travail with deity, is full of figurative language. If we are to make our conception less abstract we must try to represent to ourselves some individual in whom deity is related to its basis in the lower levels of empirical quality as far down as the purely spatio-temporal; and a being of this kind is, as we shall see, rather an ideal of thought than something which can be realised in fact in the form of an individual. What we have to do is to be careful to conceive the ideal in conformity with the plan of what we know of things from experience.

PERSONIFICATION OF THIS CONCEPTION: (A) FINITE GOD

The simplest way of doing so is to forget for a moment that God being the whole world possessing deity is infinite, and, transporting ourselves in thought to the next level of existence, that of deity, to imagine a finite being with that quality, a god of a polytheistic system, or what we have called an angel. We must conceive such a being on the analogy of ourselves. In us a living body has one portion of itself specialised and set apart to be the bearer of the quality of mind. That specialised constellation of living processes, endowed with the quality of mind, is the concrete thing called mind. The rest of the body in its physiological, material, and spatio-temporal characters, sustains the life of this mind-bearing portion, which in its turn is said in the physiological sense to represent the rest of the body, because there is a general correspondence between the affections of the body and the excitements of the mind-bearing portion which are enjoyed as mental processes. In virtue of some of these mental enjoyments the mind contemplates the things outside its body, in virtue of others it contemplates its own bodily conditions in the form of organic sensa or sensibles, or of other sensibles of movement, touch, and the rest. In the superior finite which has deity, we must conceive the immediate basis of deity to be something of the nature of mind, just as the immediate basis of our mind is life, and the mind of the finite deity will rest on a substructure of life as with us. One part of the god's mind will be of such complexity and refinement as mind, as to be fitted to carry the new quality of deity. Thus whereas with us, a piece of Space-Time, a substance, which is alive, is differentiated in a part of its life so as to be mind, here a substance or piece of Space-Time which is mental is differentiated in a portion of its mental body so as to be divine, and this deity is sustained by all the space-time to which it belongs, with all those qualities lower than deity itself which belong to that substance. Moreover, as our mind represents and gathers up into itself its whole body, so does the finite god represent or gather up into its divine part its whole body, only in its body is included mind as well as the other characters of a body which has mind. Now for such a being, what for us are organic sensibles would include not merely the affections of its physiological body, but those of its mental 'body,' its mental affections. To speak more accurately, its mental affections, the acts of its mind-body, would take the place of our organic or motor sensa, while sensa, like hunger and thirst, which are the affections of its life-body, would fall into the class of sensa which with us are, like the feel and visual look of our bodies, contemplated by special senses. For such a being its specially differentiated mind takes the place of the brain or central nervous system with us. The body which is equivalent with the deity of the finite god, that is to say, whose processes are not parallel to but identical with the 'deisings' or enjoyments of the god, is of the nature of mind.

Only this proviso must be added. The mental structure of which a portion more complex and subtle is the bearer of deity, must not be thought necessarily to be a human mind or aggregation of such, but only to be of the mental order. To assume it to be of the nature of human mind would be as if a race of seaweeds were to hold that mind when it comes (the quality of deity for seaweeds) must be founded on the life of seaweeds, and minds the offspring of seaweeds. What form the finite god would assume we cannot know, and it is idle to guess. The picture has been drawn merely in order to give some kind of definiteness to the vague idea of a higher quality of existence, deity as founded upon the highest order of existence we know. There is always a danger that such attempts at definiteness where precise knowledge from the nature of the case is out of the question may seem a little ridiculous. Fortunately when we leave the finite god and endeavour to form a conception of the infinite God in his relation to things, we may avail ourselves of what is useful in the picture and avoid the danger of seeming to affect a prevision of how things in the future will come to be. We use the picture merely in order to understand how the whole world can be thought of as possessing deity.

(B) INFINITE GOD

We have now to think, not as before of a limited portion of Space-Time, but of the whole infinite Space-Time, with all its engendered levels of existence possessing their distinctive empirical qualities, as sustaining the deity of God. But when we imagine such an individual, we discover two differences which mark him off from all finites, including finite gods. The first is this. Our experience is partly internal and partly external; that is, the stimuli which provoke our enjoyments and through them are contemplated by us (and the same account applies with the proper extension of the terms to all finites) partly arise within our bodies and partly from external ones. The objects which we contemplate are partly organic or motor sensa and partly special sensa, in which are included our bodies as seen or touched or similarly apprehended. Now the body of God is the whole universe and there is no body outside his. For him, therefore, all objects are internal, and the distinction of organic and special sensa disappears. Our minds, therefore, and everything else in the world are 'organic sensa' of God. All we are the hunger and thirst, the heart-beats and sweat of God. This is what Rabbi ben Ezra says in Browning's poem, when he protests that he has never mistaken his end, to slake God's thirst.[7] For God there is still the distinction of enjoyment or deising and contemplation, for God's deity is equivalent only to a portion of his body. But it is only for the finites which belong to God's body, all the finites up to finites with mind, that the objects of contemplation are some organic and some external.

The second difference, and ultimately it is a repetition of the first, is this. God's deity is lodged in a portion of his body, and represents that body. But since his body is infinite, his deity (I allow myself to turn deity from a quality into a concrete thing just as I use mind sometimes for the mental quality, sometimes for the concrete thing, mental processes), which represents his body, is infinite. God includes the whole universe, but his deity, though infinite, belongs to, or is lodged in, only a portion of the universe. The importance of this for the problem of theism will appear later. I repeat that when God's deity is said to represent his body, that representation is physiological; like the representation on the brain of the different portions of the body which send nervous messages to the brain. Deity does not represent the universe in the mathematical sense, in which, for example, the odd numbers represent or are an image of the whole series of numbers. Such mathematical representation would require God's deity also to be represented in his deity; and it is not so represented in the same fashion as his body is represented.

GOD'S INFINITUDE

The infinitude of God's deity marks the difference between him and all other empirical beings. Deity is an empirical quality, but though it is located in a portion only of the universe, which universe of Space-Time with all its finites of lower order is God's body, yet that portion is itself infinite in extent and

---

[7] "Frances, when a little one, had been told by her parents that 'in God we live and move and have our being': and then was overheard one day, when she was five years old, explaining to her younger brother that God had a stomach *ever* so big—everything in the whole world was inside it." *The Dawn of Religion*, by Edith E. Read Mumford (London, 1915), p. 32.

duration. Not only is God infinite in extent and duration, but his deity is also infinite in both respects. God's body being the whole of Space-Time is omnipresent and eternal; but his deity, though not everywhere, is yet infinite in its extension, and though his time is a portion only of infinite Time his deity is, in virtue of what corresponds in deity to memory and expectation in ourselves, infinite in both directions. Thus empirical as deity is, the infinity of his distinctive character separates him from all finites. It is his deity which makes him continuous with the series of empirical characters of finites, but neither is his 'body' nor his 'mind' finite.

For clearness' sake I must linger a little over this important and difficult matter; for in one sense our minds and all finite things are infinite as well. We are, however, finitely infinite; while deity is infinitely infinite. We are finite because our minds, which are extended both in space and time, are limited pieces of Space-Time. We are infinite because we are in relation to all Space-Time and to all things in it. Our minds are infinite in so far as from our point of view, our place or date, we mirror the whole universe; we are compresent with everything in that universe. I need not repeat at length what has been said more than once. Though only a limited range of distinct things comes within our view, they are fringed with their relations to what is beyond them, and are but islands rising out of an infinite circumambient ocean. The whole of which they are parts may shrink in our apprehension into a vague object of feeling or be conceived more definitely as infinite. Still it is there. But this infinite world of Space-Time with its finite things engendered within it finds access to our minds only through our bodies and thence to our brains, and is cognised through our neuro-mental processes and the combinations of them. Our minds consist of our mental processes, which are also neural ones. If we follow a dangerous method of language, or of thinking, and fancy that the objects we know are the 'content' of our minds we may be led into the belief that, since our minds contain representations of all things in the universe, our minds are infinite, in the same way as God's deity. If, however, we recollect that our minds are nothing but the processes of mind and have no contents but their process-characters we shall avoid this danger. We shall then understand how our minds can be finite in extent and duration and yet be compresent with and correspond to an infinite world.

We may distinguish two sorts of infinity, which I will call internal and external. An inch is internally infinite in respect of the number of its parts and corresponds to an infinite line of which it forms only a part. But it is itself finite in length. In the same way our minds, though finite in space-time, may be infinite in respect of their correspondence with the whole of things in Space-Time.

We said that our minds represented our bodies, because to speak generally the various parts of our body were connected neurally with their corresponding places in the cortex. External objects excite our minds through first impinging on our organs of sense. As such representations of our body, our mind is infinite. But through that body it is brought into relation with the infinite world. Thus though finite in extent of space and time we are internally infinite. We are so as pieces of Space and Time. But also within the brain there is room for multitudinous combinations initiated from within and enjoyed as imaginations and thoughts, and, for all I know, these are infinitely numerous in their possibilities of combination. We have at least enough of them to comprehend the universe as a whole so far as such apprehension is open to our powers.[8] It is sufficient for our purposes of argument that our minds as spatio-temporal substances are like all spatio-temporal extents internally infinite. Externally we are finite.

But there is nothing whatever outside the body of God, and his deity represents the whole of his body, and all the lower ranges of finites are for him 'organic sensa.' The spatio-temporal organ of his deity is not only internally but externally infinite. Deity, unlike mind, is infinitely infinite.

Thus when we are said to represent the universe in our apprehensions we must be careful to distinguish this sense of representation, which in truth signifies only the fact of compresence, from the physiological sense in which the brain is said to represent the body, the sense in which I have used the term in this chapter, in which the mind represents the bodily organism in which it is placed. Failing to make this distinction we should conclude as Leibnitz did that the monad, since it represents the whole by standing in relation to every part of it, is in itself infinite and eternal. The mind is thus removed from the limitations of Time and Space. From our point of view, the mind exists both in time and space; and if it is true that Time is nothing without Space, it is difficult to understand speculatively how an eternal existence of the mind could be possible without that specialised complex of space which experience tells us is the basis of the mind. If convincing experiment should in the future demonstrate the persistence of mind without its body which here subserves it, I should have to admit that the doctrine of this work would require radical alteration and, so far as I can judge at present, destruction. But this is not the only word which I should wish to say on so tender and, to many persons so precious, a belief.

GOD AS ACTUAL

We are now led to a qualification of the greatest importance. The picture which has been drawn of the infinite God is a concession to our figurative or mythological tendency and to the habit of the religious consciousness to embody its conception of God in an individual shape. Its sole value lies in its indication of the relation that must be understood upon the lines traced by experience to subsist between deity and mind. This is adequate for finite gods, supposing the stage of deity to have been reached. But the infinite God is purely ideal or conceptual. The individual so sketched is not asserted to exist; the sketch merely gives body and shape, by a sort of anticipation, to the actual infinite God whom, on the basis of experience, speculation declares to exist. As

---

[8] To illustrate this qualification. If it is true that our enjoyment of the past is a past enjoyment. . .must our minds not then, it may be asked, be eternal? This would be so if we had memory of all the past and anticipation of all the future. But I do not remember the death of Julius Caesar, but only think of it as a past event. The past which I have not been present at, and the future at which I shall not be present shrink into a thought of past and future time, just as I think of the whole of Space without being sensible of all its parts.

actual, God does not possess the quality of deity but is the universe as tending to that quality. This nisus in the universe, though not present to sense, is yet present to reflection upon experience. Only in this sense of straining towards deity can there be an infinite actual God. For, again following the lines of experience, we can see that if the quality of deity were actually attained in the empirical development of the world in time, we should have not one infinite being possessing deity but many (at least potentially many) finite ones. Beyond these finite gods or angels there would be in turn a new empirical quality looming into view, which for them would be deity—that is, would be for them what deity is for us. Just as when mind emerges it is the distinctive quality of many finite individuals with minds, so when deity actually emerges it would be the distinctive quality of many finite individuals. If the possessor of deity were an existent individual he must be finite and not infinite. Thus there is no actual infinite being with the quality of deity; but there is an actual infinite, the whole universe, with a nisus to deity; and this is the God of the religious consciousness, though that consciousness habitually forecasts the divinity of its object as actually realised in an individual form.

GOD AND OTHER INFINITES

The reason why the universe as possessing deity is purely idea, is found in the contrast between God so described and other empirical infinites. God is not the only infinite. We have, in the first place, the infinite Space-Time itself which is *a priori*, and besides this we have infinites which are generated within Space-Time and are empirical. Instances are infinite lines in Space and infinite numbers. These are empirical determinations of categorial characters and belong to the class of existents with purely primary qualities. Hitherto in the preceding chapters we have confined ourselves to finites, but it now remains briefly to discuss these empirical infinites, which are always less than the *a priori* infinity of Space-Time itself. God is no exception to this statement, for though his body is the whole universe, his deity (and deity is what distinguishes him) is lodged in an infinite portion only of this whole infinitude. Empirical infinites with primary qualities were touched upon in a preceding chapter, and in view of this very question how far they were ideal and how far real. Along with the empirical infinites go the beings which are infinitely small.

In both cases there is an ideal or conceptual element involved as well as a sensible or, to speak more properly, an intuited one. Neither the infinitely great nor the infinitely small is presented to intuition without the help of reflective concepts. But since concepts are as real as percepts their presence does not destroy the actual reality of the thing into which they enter. I do not propose to discuss the status of the various kinds of infinite numbers and to consider how far, if at all, any of them are to be treated as on a level with the conceptual creations of mathematics such as imaginaries or n-dimensional 'Spaces.' I am speaking of such empirical infinites as infinite lines or the number of, say, the infinite system of integers. It might be thought that such infinites cannot be more than ideal because it is impossible to possess them completed. There seems, however, no reason to doubt the actuality of infinite lines, nor of the number of the integers, whether number is defined extensionally or, as we have preferred, intensionally. For infinite number is the number belonging to classes containing infinite members. The fact that an infinite system cannot be completed is irrelevant to its actuality. For infinity means only that the infinite system can be represented in the mathematical sense by a part of itself, and it is indifferent that we cannot in intuition complete an infinite line. To suppose that the infinitely great must be completed is to eliminate Time from its nature, just as to suppose that the infinitely small is an indivisible self-subsistent entity or infinitesimal is to eliminate Time from its nature. Infinites, whether of division or of composition, are actual, just because of the element in them which makes them conceptual for us. Points and instants are not fixed minima but the elements of things, and their characteristic is that we can never come to a stop with them. Hence it was said before that points and instants, or more properly point-instants, are real and actual just because they are ideal. If we could take them in at once they would not be continuous with one another. The same thing holds of empirical infinites. Lines are actual and infinite and can be selected from Space, and infinite numbers, or at least some of them, from actual Space-Time.

Now these infinites are without quality. God as the possessor of deity, on the other hand, is a qualitied infinite, and we learn from experience that quality is borne by finite complexes of space-time. There may be actual infinites with none but primary qualities, for these are not qualities at all, and the entities in question are infinite portions of the infinite Space or Time. But the qualitied infinite is not merely ideal as implying, like all infinites, a conceptual element, but it is ideal because it is not actual. At any level of existence there is a claimant to be a qualitied infinite, and that claimant is not actual. It is a projected picture of an actual infinite, in which that quality is being engendered but has not actually come to birth.

The qualitied infinite, if the quality could be actually realised, would present overwhelming difficulties, when we ask if it is subject to the categories. God's body, being the whole universe of Space-Time, is the source of the categories but not itself subject to them. Since his deity is realised in a portion only of the universe, it might be thought that deity at any rate, which is equivalent to some complex of mind, might be subject to the categories, and be a true individual substance. It is not however an individual, for an individual is the union of particular and universal. And realised deity is not universal, since, representing as it does the whole, it admits of no repetition, which is vital to a universal.[9] We can only say that, like Space-Time itself, it is singular. Neither is it a substance, for the same reason. Representing the whole in the physiological sense, it admits no relation to other substances, but is the whole of Space-Time on a reduced scale. In this breakdown of the attempt to apply to it the categories (for the same considerations can be advanced in the case of the other categories as well) it betrays its merely ideal character of a picture and nothing more. The picture is not the less eminently worth drawing. Only nothing actual corresponds to it. We have an individual forecasted which is not a real individual. The actual reality which has deity is the world of

---

[9] It is of course a 'concrete universal'; but that conception has been already examined. . . .

empiricals filling up all Space-Time and tending towards a higher quality. Deity is a nisus and not an accomplishment. This, as we shall note, is what prevents the conception from being wholly theistical. Finite gods, on the other hand, are of course subject to the categories.

FINITE GODS AND INFINITE GOD

Two different questions accordingly may be asked as to the existence of deity, to which different answers must be given. The first is, do finite beings exist with deity or are there finite gods? The answer is we do not know. If Time has by now actually brought them forth, they do exist; if not, their existence belongs to the future. If they do exist ("millions of spirits walk the earth") they are not recognisable in any form of material existence known to us; and material existence they must have; though conceivably there may be such material bodies, containing also life and mind as the basis of deity, in regions of the universe beyond our ken.

That is a scholastic and trivial question. The other question admits an answer. Does infinite deity exist? The answer is that the world in its infinity tends towards infinite deity, or is pregnant with it, but that infinite deity does not exist; and we may now add that if it did, God—the actual world possessing infinite deity—would cease to be infinite God and break up into a multiplicity of finite gods, which would be merely a higher race of creatures than ourselves with a God beyond.

Infinite deity then embodies the conception of the infinite world in its straining after deity. But the attainment of deity makes deity finite. Deity is an empirical quality like mind or life. Before there was mind the universe was straining towards infinite mind. But there is no existent infinite mind, but only many finite minds. Deity is subject to the same law as other empirical qualities, and is but the next member of the series. At first a presage, in the lapse of time the quality comes to actual existence, animates a new race of creatures, and is succeeded by a still higher quality. God as an actual existent is always becoming deity but never attains it. He is the ideal God in embryo. The ideal when fulfilled ceases to be God, and yet it gives shape and character to our conception of the actual God, and always tends to usurp its place in our fancy.

V.B. Humanism

V.B.1. Humanist Manifestos I and II

Humanism, which may be regarded as a specialized form of naturalism, places its greatest emphasis on the recognition and cultivation of the highest human values in a context that also recognizes no gods on which we may depend for our salvation. The manifestos reprinted here are documents produced by groups of like-minded individuals eager to foster the growth of humanism as a philosophy and religious movement. The first manifesto was written in 1933 by a group of thirty-four thinkers who wanted to enunciate ideals capable of guiding and inspiring human progress in an age when orthodox religious teachings were, in their judgment, becoming increasingly out of step with the progress of human knowledge. A radical document in its own time and one that still seems radical to many religious persons of today, this manifesto omitted reference to many then-current social problems and could not anticipate the issues that would become so important with the passing of time. Forty years later, a second manifesto was drafted to supplement and update the original manifesto. It was originally signed by 114 individuals, but many others have added their signatures during the intervening years. A longer and more comprehensive document, this manifesto speaks out on many issues, including civil liberties, equality, democracy, economic justice, ecology and population growth, and war and peace.

HUMANIST MANIFESTO I

The time has come for widespread recognition of the radical changes in religious beliefs throughout the modern world. The time is past for mere revision of traditional attitudes. Science and economic change have disrupted the old beliefs. Religions the world over are under the necessity of coming to terms with new conditions created by a vastly increased knowledge and experience. In every field of human activity, the vital movement is

From *Humanist Manifestos I and II* (Buffalo, N.Y.: Prometheus Books, 1973), pp. 7–10; 13–24.

now in the direction of a candid and explicit humanism. In order that religious humanism may be better understood we, the undersigned, desire to make certain affirmations which we believe the facts of our contemporary life demonstrate.

There is great danger of a final, and we believe fatal, identification of the word *religion* with doctrines and methods which have lost their significance and which are powerless to solve the problem of human living in the Twentieth Century. Religions have always been means for realizing the highest values of life. Their end has been accomplished through the interpretation of the total environing situation (theology or world view), the sense of values resulting therefrom (goal or ideal), and the technique (cult) established for realizing the satisfactory life. A change in any of these factors results in alteration of the outward forms of religion. This fact explains the changefulness of religions through the centuries. But through all changes religion itself remains constant in its quest for abiding values, an inseparable feature of human life.

Today man's larger understanding of the universe, his scientific achievements, and his deeper appreciation of brotherhood, have created a situation which requires a new statement of the means and purposes of religion. Such a vital, fearless, and frank religion capable of furnishing adequate social goals and personal satisfactions may appear to many people as a complete break with the past. While this age does owe a vast debt to traditional religions, it is none the less obvious that any religion that can hope to be a synthesizing and dynamic force for today must be shaped for the needs of this age. To establish such a religion is a major necessity of the present. It is a responsibility which rests upon this generation. We therefore affirm the following:

First: Religious humanists regard the universe as self-existing and not created.

Second: Humanism believes that man is a part of nature and that he has emerged as the result of a continuous process.

Third: Holding an organic view of life, humanists find that the traditional dualism of mind and body must be rejected.

Fourth: Humanism recognizes that man's religious culture and civilization, as clearly depicted by anthropology and history, are the product of a gradual development due to his interaction with his natural environment and with his social heritage. The individual born into a particular culture is largely molded to that culture.

Fifth: Humanism asserts that the nature of the universe depicted by modern science makes unacceptable any supernatural or cosmic guarantees of human values. Obviously humanism does not deny the possibility of realities as yet undiscovered, but it does insist that the way to determine the existence and value of any and all realities is by means of intelligent inquiry and by the assessment of their relation to human needs. Religion must formulate its hopes and plans in the light of the scientific spirit and method.

Sixth: We are convinced that the time has passed for theism, deism, modernism, and the several varieties of "new thought."

Seventh: Religion consists of those actions, purposes, and experiences which are humanly significant. Nothing human is alien to the religious. It includes labor, art, science, philosophy, love, friendship, recreation—all that is in its degree expressive of intelligently satisfying human living. The distinction between the sacred and the secular can no longer be maintained.

Eighth: Religious humanism considers the complete realization of human personality to be the end of man's life and seeks its development and fulfillment in the here and now. This is the explanation of the humanist's social passion.

Ninth: In place of the old attitudes involved in worship and prayer the humanist finds his religious emotions expressed in a heightened sense of personal life and in a cooperative effort to promote social well-being.

Tenth: It follows that there will be no uniquely religious emotions and attitudes of the kind hitherto associated with belief in the supernatural.

Eleventh: Man will learn to face the crises of life in terms of his knowledge of their naturalness and probability. Reasonable and manly attitudes will be fostered by education and supported by custom. We assume that humanism will take the path of social and mental hygiene and discourage sentimental and unreal hopes and wishful thinking.

Twelfth: Believing that religion must work increasingly for joy in living, religious humanists aim to foster the creative in man and to encourage achievements that add to the satisfaction of life.

Thirteenth: Religious humanism maintains that all associations and institutions exist for the fulfillment of human life. The intelligent evaluation, transformation, control, and direction of such associations and institutions with a view to the enhancement of human life is the purpose and program of humanism. Certainly religious institutions, their ritualistic forms, ecclesiastical methods, and communal activities must be reconstituted as rapidly as experience allows, in order to function effectively in the modern world.

Fourteenth: The humanists are firmly convinced that existing acquisitive and profit-motivated society has shown itself to be inadequate and that a radical change in methods, controls, and motives must be instituted. A socialized and cooperative economic order must be established to the end that the equitable distribution of the means of life be possible. The goal of humanism is a free and universal society in which people voluntarily and intelligently cooperate for the common good. Humanists demand a shared life in a shared world.

Fifteenth and last: We assert that humanism will: (a) affirm life rather than deny it; (b) seek to elicit the possibilities of life, not flee from it; and (c) endeavor to establish the conditions of a satisfactory life for all, not merely for the few. By this positive morale and intention humanism will be guided, and from this perspective and alignment the techniques and efforts of humanism will flow.

So stand the theses of religious humanism. Though we consider the religious forms and ideas of our fathers no longer adequate, the quest for the good life is still the central task for mankind. Man is at last becoming aware that he alone is responsible for the realization of the world of his dreams, that he has within himself the power for its achievement. He must set intelligence and will to the task.

J. A. C. Fagginer Auer	Harold P. Marley
E. Burdette Backus	R. Lester Mondale
Harry Elmer Barnes	Charles Francis Potter
L. M. Birkhead	John Herman Randall, Jr.
Raymond B. Bragg	Curtis W. Reese
Edwin Arthur Burtt	Oliver L. Reiser
Ernest Caldecott	Roy Wood Sellars
A. J. Carlson	Clinton Lee Scott
John Dewey	Maynard Shipley
Albert C. Dieffenbach	W. Frank Swift
John H. Dietrich	V. T. Thayer
Bernard Fantus	Eldred C. Vanderlaan
William Floyd	Joseph Walker
F. H. Hankins	Jacob J. Weinstein
A. Eustace Haydon	Frank S. C. Wicks
Llewellyn Jones	David Rhys Williams
Robert Morss Lovett	Edwin H. Wilson

HUMANIST MANIFESTO II

Preface

It is forty years since *Humanist Manifesto I* (1933) appeared. Events since then make that earlier statement seem far too optimistic. Nazism has shown the depths of brutality of which humanity is capable. Other totalitarian regimes have suppressed human rights without ending poverty. Science has sometimes brought evil as well as good. Recent decades have shown that inhuman wars can be made in the name of peace. The beginnings of police states, even in democratic societies, widespread government espionage, and other abuses of power by military, political, and industrial elites, and the continuance of unyielding racism, all present a different and difficult social outlook. In various societies, the demands of women and minority groups for equal rights effectively challenge our generation.

As we approach the twenty-first century, however, an affirmative and hopeful vision is needed. Faith, commensurate with advancing knowledge, is also necessary. In the choice between despair and hope, humanists respond in this *Humanist Manifesto II* with a positive declaration for times of uncertainty.

As in 1933, humanists still believe that traditional theism, especially faith in the prayer-hearing God, assumed to love and care for persons, to hear and understand their prayers, and to be able to do something about them, is an unproved and outmoded faith. Salvationism, based on mere affirmation, still appears as harmful, diverting people with false hopes of heaven hereafter. Reasonable minds look to other means for survival.

Those who sign *Humanist Manifesto II* disclaim that they are setting forth a binding credo; their individual views would be stated in widely varying ways. The statement is, however, reaching for vision in a time that needs direction. It is social analysis in an effort at consensus. New statements should be developed to supersede this, but for today it is our conviction that humanism offers an alternative that can serve present-day needs and guide humankind toward the future.

Paul Kurtz
Edwin H. Wilson

The next century can be and should be the humanistic century. Dramatic scientific, technological, and ever-accelerating social and political changes crowd our awareness. We have virtually conquered the planet, explored the moon, overcome the natural limits of travel and communication; we stand at the dawn of a new age, ready to move farther into space and perhaps inhabit other planets. Using technology wisely, we can control our environment, conquer poverty, markedly reduce disease, extend our life-span, significantly modify our behavior, alter the course of human evolution and cultural development, unlock vast new powers, and provide humankind with unparalleled opportunity for achieving an abundant and meaningful life.

The future is, however, filled with dangers. In learning to apply the scientific method to nature and human life, we have opened the door to ecological damage, overpopulation, dehumanizing institutions, totalitarian repression, and nuclear and biochemical disaster. Faced with apocalyptic prophesies and doomsday scenarios, many flee in despair from reason and embrace irrational cults and theologies of withdrawal and retreat.

Traditional moral codes and newer irrational cults both fail to meet the pressing needs of today and tomorrow. False "theologies of hope" and messianic ideologies, substituting new dogmas for old, cannot cope with existing world realities. They separate rather than unite peoples.

Humanity, to survive, requires bold and daring measures. We need to extend the uses of scientific method, not renounce them, to fuse reason with compassion in order to build constructive social and moral values. Confronted by many possible futures, we must decide which to pursue. The ultimate goal should be the fulfillment of the potential for growth in each human personality—not for the favored few, but for all of humankind. Only a shared world and global measures will suffice.

A humanist outlook will tap the creativity of each human being and provide the vision and courage for us to work together. This outlook emphasizes the role human beings can play in their own spheres of action. The decades ahead call for dedicated, clear-minded men and women able to marshal the will, intelligence, and cooperative skills for shaping a desirable future. Humanism can provide the purpose and inspiration that so many seek; it can give personal meaning and significance to human life.

Many kinds of humanism exist in the contemporary world. The varieties and emphases of naturalistic humanism include "scientific," "ethical," "democratic," "religious," and "Marxist" humanism. Free thought, atheism, agnosticism, skepticism, deism, rationalism, ethical culture, and liberal religion all claim to be heir to the humanist tradition. Humanism traces its roots from ancient China, classical Greece and Rome, through the Renaissance and the

Enlightenment, to the scientific revolution of the modern world. But views that merely reject theism are not equivalent to humanism. They lack commitment to the positive belief in the possibilities of human progress and to the values central to it. Many within religious groups, believing in the future of humanism, now claim humanist credentials. Humanism is an ethical process through which we all can move, above and beyond the divisive particulars, heroic personalities, dogmatic creeds, and ritual customs of past religions or their mere negation.

We affirm a set of common principles that can serve as a basis for united action—positive principles relevant to the present human condition. They are a design for a secular society on a planetary scale.

For these reasons, we submit this new *Humanist Manifesto* for the future of humankind; for us, it is a vision of hope, a direction for satisfying survival.

Religion

First: In the best sense, religion may inspire dedication to the highest ethical ideals. The cultivation of moral devotion and creative imagination is an expression of genuine "spiritual" experience and aspiration.

We believe, however, that traditional dogmatic or authoritarian religions that place revelation, God, ritual, or creed above human needs and experience do a disservice to the human species. Any account of nature should pass the tests of scientific evidence; in our judgment, the dogmas and myths of traditional religions do not do so. Even at this late date in human history, certain elementary facts based upon the critical use of scientific reason have to be restated. We find insufficient evidence for belief in the existence of a supernatural; it is either meaningless or irrelevant to the question of the survival and fulfillment of the human race. As nontheists, we begin with humans not God, nature not deity. Nature may indeed be broader and deeper than we now know; any new discoveries, however, will but enlarge our knowledge of the natural.

Some humanists believe we should reinterpret traditional religions and reinvest them with meanings appropriate to the current situation. Such redefinitions, however, often perpetuate old dependencies and escapisms; they easily become obscurantist, impeding the free use of the intellect. We need, instead, radically new human purposes and goals.

We appreciate the need to preserve the best ethical teachings in the religious traditions of humankind, many of which we share in common. But we reject those features of traditional religious morality that deny humans a full appreciation of their own potentialities and responsibilities. Traditional religions often offer solace to humans, but, as often, they inhibit humans from helping themselves or experiencing their full potentialities. Such institutions, creeds, and rituals often impede the will to serve others. Too often traditional faiths encourage dependence rather than independence, obedience rather than affirmation, fear rather than courage. More recently they have generated concerned social action, with many signs of relevance appearing in the wake of the "God Is Dead" theologies. But we can discover no divine purpose or providence for the human species. While there is much that we do not know, humans are responsible for what we are or will become. No deity will save us; we must save ourselves.

Second: Promises of immortal salvation or fear of eternal damnation are both illusory and harmful. They distract humans from present concerns, from self-actualization, and from rectifying social injustices. Modern science discredits such historic concepts as the "ghost in the machine" and the "separable soul." Rather, science affirms that the human species is an emergence from natural evolutionary forces. As far as we know, the total personality is a function of the biological organism transacting in a social and cultural context. There is no credible evidence that life survives the death of the body. We continue to exist in our progeny and in the way that our lives have influenced others in our culture.

Traditional religions are surely not the only obstacles to human progress. Other ideologies also impede human advance. Some forms of political doctrine, for instance, function religiously, reflecting the worst features of orthodoxy and authoritarianism, especially when they sacrifice individuals on the altar of Utopian promises. Purely economic and political viewpoints, whether capitalist or communist, often function as religious and ideological dogma. Although humans undoubtedly need economic and political goals, they also need creative values by which to live.

Ethics

Third: We affirm that moral values derive their source from human experience. Ethics is *autonomous* and *situational*, needing no theological or ideological sanction. Ethics stems from human need and interest. To deny this distorts the whole basis of life. Human life has meaning because we create and develop our futures. Happiness and the creative realization of human needs and desires, individually and in shared enjoyment, are continuous themes of humanism. We strive for the good life, here and now. The goal is to pursue life's enrichment despite debasing forces of vulgarization, commercialization, bureaucratization, and dehumanization.

Fourth: Reason and intelligence are the most effective instruments that humankind possesses. There is no substitute: neither faith nor passion suffices in itself. The controlled use of scientific methods, which have transformed the natural and social sciences since the Renaissance, must be extended further in the solution of human problems. But reason must be tempered by humility, since no group has a monopoly of wisdom or virtue. Nor is there any guarantee that all problems can be solved or all questions answered. Yet critical intelligence, infused by a sense of human caring, is the best method that humanity has for resolving problems. Reason should be balanced with compassion and empathy and the whole person fulfilled. Thus, we are not advocating the use of scientific intelligence independent of or in opposition to emotion, for we believe in the cultivation of feeling and love. As science pushes back the boundary of the known, one's sense of wonder is continually renewed, and art, poetry, and music find their places, along with religion and ethics.

The Individual

Fifth: The preciousness and dignity of the individual person is a central humanist value. Individuals should be encouraged to realize their own creative talents and desires. We reject all religious, ideological, or moral codes that denigrate the individual, suppress freedom, dull intellect, dehumanize personality. We believe in maximum individual autonomy consonant with social responsibility. Although science can account for the causes of behavior, the possibilities of individual freedom or choice exist in human life and should be increased.

Sixth: In the area of sexuality, we believe that intolerant attitudes, often cultivated by orthodox religions and puritanical cultures, unduly repress sexual conduct. The right to birth control, abortion, and divorce should be recognized. While we do not approve of exploitive, denigrating forms of sexual expression, neither do we wish to prohibit, by law or social sanction, sexual behavior between consenting adults. The many varieties of sexual exploration should not in themselves be considered "evil." Without countenancing mindless permissiveness or unbridled promiscuity, a civilized society should be a *tolerant* one. Short of harming others or compelling them to do likewise, individuals should be permitted to express their sexual proclivities and pursue their life-styles as they desire. We wish to cultivate the development of a responsible attitude toward sexuality, in which humans are not exploited as sexual objects, and in which intimacy, sensitivity, respect, and honesty in interpersonal relations are encouraged. Moral education for children and adults is an important way of developing awareness and sexual maturity.

Democratic Society

Seventh: To enhance freedom and dignity the individual must experience a full range of *civil liberties* in all societies. This includes freedom of speech and the press, political democracy, the legal right of opposition to governmental policies, fair judicial process, religious liberty, freedom of association, and artistic, scientific, and cultural freedom. It also includes a recognition of an individual's right to die with dignity, euthanasia, and the right to suicide. We oppose the increasing invasion of privacy, by whatever means, in both totalitarian and democratic societies. We would safeguard, extend, and implement the principles of human freedom evolved from the *Magna Carta* to the *Bill of Rights*, the *Rights of Man*, and the *Universal Declaration of Human Rights*.

Eighth: We are committed to an open and democratic society. We must extend *participatory democracy* in its true sense to the economy, the school, the family, the workplace, and voluntary associations. Decision-making must be decentralized to include widespread involvement of people at all levels— social, political, and economic. All persons should have a voice in developing the values and goals that determine their lives. Institutions should be responsive to expressed desires and needs. The conditions of work, education, devotion, and play should be humanized. Alienating forces should be modified or eradicated and bureaucratic structures should be held to a minimum. People are more important than decalogues, rules, proscriptions, or regulations.

Ninth: The separation of church and state and the separation of ideology and state are imperatives. The state should encourage maximum freedom for different moral, political, religious, and social values in society. It should not favor any particular religious bodies through the use of public monies, nor espouse a single ideology and function thereby as an instrument of propaganda or oppression, particularly against dissenters

Tenth: Humane societies should evaluate economic systems not by rhetoric or ideology, but by whether or not they *increase economic well-being* for all individuals and groups, minimize poverty and hardship, increase the sum of human satisfaction, and enhance the quality of life. Hence the door is open to alternative economic systems. We need to democratize the economy and judge it by its responsiveness to human needs, testing results in terms of the common good.

Eleventh: The principle of moral equality must be furthered through elimination of all discrimination based upon race, religion, sex, age, or national origin. This means equality of opportunity and recognition of talent and merit. Individuals should be encouraged to contribute to their own betterment. If unable, then society should provide means to satisfy their basic economic health, and cultural needs, including, wherever resources make possible, a minimum guaranteed annual income. We are concerned for the welfare of the aged, the infirm, the disadvantaged, and also for the outcasts—the mentally retarded, abandoned or abused children, the handicapped, prisoners, and addicts—for *all* who are neglected or ignored by society. Practicing humanists should make it their vocation to humanize personal relations.

We believe in the *right to universal education*. Everyone has a right to the cultural opportunity to fulfill his or her unique capacities and talents. The schools should foster satisfying and productive living. They should be open at all levels to any and all; the achievement of excellence should be encouraged. Innovative and experimental forms of education are to be welcomed. The energy and idealism of the young deserve to be appreciated and channeled to constructive purposes.

We deplore racial, religious, ethnic, or class antagonisms. Although we believe in cultural diversity and encourage racial and ethnic pride, we reject separations which promote alienation and set people and groups against each other; we envision an *integrated* community where people have a maximum opportunity for free and voluntary association.

We are *critical of sexism or sexual chauvinism*—male or female. We believe in equal rights for both women and men to fulfill their unique careers and potentialities as they see fit, free of invidious discrimination.

World Community

Twelfth: We deplore the division of humankind on nationalistic grounds. We have reached a turning point in human history where the best option is to *transcend the limits of national sovereignty* and to move toward the building of a world community in which all sectors of the human family can participate. Thus we look to the development of a system of world law and a world order based upon transnational federal government. This would appreciate cultural pluralism and diversity. It would not exclude pride in national origins and accomplishments nor the handling of regional problems on a regional basis. Human progress, however, can no longer be achieved by focusing on one section of the world, Western or Eastern, developed or underdeveloped. For the first time in human history, no part of humankind can be isolated from any other. Each person's future is in some way linked to all. We thus reaffirm a commitment to the building of world community, at the same time recognizing that this commits us to some hard choices.

Thirteenth: This world community must *renounce the resort to violence and force* as a method of solving international disputes. We believe in the peaceful adjudication of differences by international courts and by the development of the arts of negotiation and compromise. War is obsolete. So is the use of nuclear, biological, and chemical weapons. It is a planetary imperative to reduce the level of military expenditures and turn these savings to peaceful and people-oriented uses.

Fourteenth: the world community must engage in *cooperative planning* concerning the use of rapidly depleting resources. The planet earth must be considered a single *ecosystem*. Ecological damage, resource depletion, and excessive population growth must be checked by international concord. The cultivation and conservation of nature is a moral value; we should perceive ourselves as integral to the sources of our being in nature. We must free our world from needless pollution and waste, responsibly guarding and creating wealth, both natural and human. Exploitation of natural resources, uncurbed by social conscience, must end.

Fifteenth: The problems of *economic growth and development* can no longer be resolved by one nation alone; they are worldwide in scope. It is the moral obligation of the developed nations to provide—through an international authority that safeguards human rights—massive technical, agricultural, medical, and economic assistance, including birth control techniques, to the developing portions of the globe. World poverty must cease. Hence extreme disproportions in wealth, income, and economic growth should be reduced on a worldwide basis.

Sixteenth: Technology is a vital key to human progress and development. We deplore any neo-romantic efforts to condemn indiscriminately all technology and science or to counsel retreat from its further extension and use for the good of humankind. We would resist any moves to censor basic scientific research on moral, political, or social grounds. Technology must, however, be carefully judged by the consequences of its use; harmful and destructive changes should be avoided. We are particularly disturbed when technology and bureaucracy control, manipulate, or modify human beings without their consent. Technological feasibility does not imply social or cultural desirability.

Seventeenth: We must expand communication and transportation across frontiers. Travel restrictions must cease. The world must be open to diverse political, ideological, and moral viewpoints and evolve a worldwide system of television and radio for information and education. We thus call for full international cooperation in culture, science, the arts, and technology *across ideological borders*. We must learn to live openly together or we shall perish together.

Humanity as a Whole

In closing: The world cannot wait for a reconciliation of competing political or economic systems to solve its problems. These are the times for men and women of good will to further the building of a peaceful and prosperous world. We urge that parochial loyalties and inflexible moral and religious ideologies be transcended. We urge recognition of the common humanity of all people. We further urge the use of reason and compassion to produce the kind of world we want—a world in which peace, prosperity, freedom, and happiness are widely shared. Let us not abandon that vision in despair or cowardice. We are responsible for what we are or will be. Let us work together for a humane world by means commensurate with humane ends. Destructive ideological differences among communism, capitalism, socialism, conservatism, liberalism, and radicalism should be overcome. Let us call for an end to terror and hatred. We will survive and prosper only in a world of shared humane values. We can initiate new directions for humankind; ancient rivalries can be superseded by broad-based cooperative efforts. The commitment to tolerance, understanding, and peaceful negotiation does not necessitate acquiescence to the status quo nor the damming up of dynamic and revolutionary forces. The true revolution is occurring and can continue in countless non-violent adjustments. But this entails the willingness to step forward onto new and expanding plateaus. At the present juncture of history, commitment to all humankind is the highest commitment of which we are capable; it transcends the narrow allegiances of church, state, party, class, or race in moving toward a wider vision of human potentiality. What more daring a goal for humankind than for each person to become, in ideal as well as practice, a citizen of a world community. It is a classical vision; we can now give it new vitality. Humanism thus interpreted is a moral force that has time on its side. We believe that humankind has the potential intelligence, good will, and cooperative skill to implement this commitment in the decades ahead.

We, the undersigned, while not necessarily endorsing every detail of the above, pledge our general support to *Humanist Manifesto II* for the future of humankind. These affirmations are not a final credo or dogma but an expression of a living and growing faith. We invite others in all lands to join us in further developing and working for these goals.

Lionel Abel, *Prof. of English, State Univ. of New York at Buffalo*
Khoren Arisian, *Board of Leaders, NY Soc. for Ethical Culture*
Isaac Asimov, *author*
George Axtelle, *Prof. Emeritus, Southern Illinois Univ.*
Archie J. Bahm, *Prof. of Philosophy Emeritus, Univ. of N.M.*
Paul H. Beattie, *Pres., Fellowship of Religious Humanists*
Keith Beggs, *Exec. Dir., American Humanist Association*
Malcolm Bissell, *Prof. Emeritus, Univ. of Southern California*
H. J. Blackham, *Chm., Social Morality Council, Great Britain*
Brand Blanshard, *Prof. Emeritus, Yale University*
Paul Blanshard, *author*
Joseph L. Blau, *Prof. of Religion, Columbia University*
Sir Hermann Bondi, *Prof. of Math., King's Coll., Univ. of London*
Howard Box, *Leader, Brooklyn Society for Ethical Culture*
Raymond B. Bragg, *Minister Emer., Unitarian Ch., Kansas City*
Theodore Brameld, *Visiting Prof., C.U.N.Y.*
Lester R. Brown, *Senior Fellow, Overseas Development Council*

Bette Chambers, *Pres., American Humanist Association*
John Ciardi, *poet*
Francis Crick, *M.D., Great Britain*
Arthur Danto, *Prof. of Philosophy, Columbia University*
Lucien de Coninck, *Prof., University of Gand, Belgium*
Miriam Allen deFord, *author*
Edd Doerr, *Americans United for Separation of Church and State*
Peter Draper, *M.D., Guy's Hospital Medical School, London*
Paul Edwards, *Prof. of Philosophy, Brooklyn College*
Albert Ellis, *Exec. Dir., Inst. Adv. Study Rational Psychotherapy*
Edward L. Ericson, *Board of Leaders, NY Soc. for Ethical Culture*
H. J. Eysenck, *Prof. of Psychology, Univ. of London*
Roy P. Fairfield, *Coordinator, Union Graduate School*
Herbert Feigl, *Prof. Emeritus, Univ. of Minnesota*
Raymond Firth, *Prof. Emeritus of Anthropology, Univ. of London*
Antony Flew, *Prof. of Philosophy, The Univ., Reading, England*
Kenneth Furness, *Exec. Secy., British Humanist Association*
Erwin Gaede, *Minister, Unitarian Church, Ann Arbor, Mich.*
Richard S. Gilbert, *Minister, First Unitarian Ch., Rochester, N.Y.*
Charles Wesley Grady, *Minister, Unit. Univ. Ch., Arlington, Ma.*
Maxine Greene, *Prof., Teachers College, Columbia University*
Thomas C. Greening, *Editor,* Journal of Humanistic Psychology
Alan F. Guttmacher, *Pres., Planned Parenthood Fed. of America*
J. Harold Hadley, *Min., Unit. Univ. Ch., Pt. Washington, N.Y.*
Hector Hawton, *Editor,* Question, *Great Britain*
A. Eustace Haydon, *Prof. Emeritus of History of Religions*
James Hemming, *Psychologist, Great Britain*
Palmer A. Hilty, *Adm. Secy., Fellowship of Religious Humanists*
Hudson Hoagland, *Pres. Emeritus, Worcester Fdn. for Exper. Bio.*
Robert S. Hoagland, *Editor,* Religious Humanism
Sidney Hook, *Prof. Emeritus of Philosophy, New York University*
James F. Hornback, *Leader, Ethical Society of St. Louis*
James M. Hutchinson, *Minister Emer., First Unit. Ch., Cincinnati*
Mordecai M. Kaplan, *Rabbi, Fndr. of Jewish Reconstr. Movement*
John C. Kidneigh, *Prof. of Social Work., Univ. of Minnesota*
Lester A. Kirkendall, *Prof. Emeritus, Oregon State Univ.*
Margaret Knight, *Univ. of Aberdeen, Scotland*
Jean Kotkin, *Exec. Secy., American Ethical Union*
Richard Kostelanetz, *poet*
Paul Kurtz, *Editor,* The Humanist
Lawrence Lader, *Chm., Natl. Assn. for Repeal of Abortion Laws*
Edward Lamb, *Pres., Lamb Communications, Inc.*
Corliss Lamont, *Chm., Natl. Emergency Civil Liberties Comm.*
Chauncey D. Leake, *Prof., Univ. of California, San Francisco*
Alfred McC. Lee, *Prof. Emeritus, Soc.-Anthropology, C.U.N.Y.*
Elizabeth Briant Lee, *author*
Christopher Macy, *Dir., Rationalist Press Assn., Great Britain*
Clorinda Margolis, *Jefferson Comm. Mental Health Cen., Phila.*
Joseph Margolis, *Prof. of Philosophy, Temple Univ.*

Harold P. Marley, *Ret. Unitarian Minister*
Floyd W. Matson, *Prof. of American Studies, Univ. of Hawaii*
Lester Mondale, *former Pres., Fellowship of Religious Humanists*
Lloyd Morain, *Pres., Illinois Gas Company*
Mary Morain, *Editorial Bd., Intl. Soc. for General Semantics*
Charles Morris, *Prof. Emeritus, Univ. of Florida*
Henry Morgentaler, *M.D., Past Pres., Humanist Assn. of Canada*
Mary Mothersill, *Prof. of Philosophy, Barnard College*
Jerome Nathanson, *Chm. Bd. of Leaders, NY Soc. Ethical Culture*
Billy Joe Nichols, *Minister, Richardson Unitarian Church, Texas*
Kai Nielsen, *Prof. of Philosophy, Univ. of Calgary, Canada*
P. H. Nowell-Smith, *Prof. of Philosophy, York Univ., Canada*
Chaim Perelman, *Prof. of Philosophy, Univ. of Brussels, Belgium*
James W. Prescott, *Natl. Inst. of Child Health and Human Dev.*
Harold J. Quigley, *Leader, Ethical Humanist Society of Chicago*
Howard Radest, *Prof. of Philosophy, Ramapo College*
John Herman Randall, Jr., *Prof. Emeritus, Columbia Univ.*
Oliver L. Reiser, *Prof. Emeritus, Univ. of Pittsburgh*
Robert G. Risk, *Pres., Leadville Corp.*
Lord Ritchie-Calder, *Formerly Univ. of Edinburgh, Scotland*
B. T. Rocca, Jr., *Consultant, Intl. Trade and Commodities*
Andre D. Sakharov, *Academy of Sciences, Moscow, U.S.S.R.*
Sidney H. Scheuer, *Chm., Natl. Comm. for an Effective Congress*
Herbert W. Schneider, *Prof. Emeritus, Claremont Grad. School*
Clinton Lee Scott, *Universalist Minister, St. Petersburgh, Fla.*
Roy Wood Sellars, *Prof. Emeritus, Univ. of Michigan*
A. B. Shah, *Pres., Indian Secular Society*
B. F. Skinner, *Prof. of Psychology, Harvard Univ.*
Kenneth J. Smith, *Leader, Philadelphia Ethical Society*
Matthew Ies Spetter, *Chm., Dept. Ethics, Ethical Culture Schools*
Mark Starr, *Chm., Esperanto Info. Center*
Svetozar Stojanovic, *Prof. Philosophy, Univ. Belgrade, Yugoslavia*
Harold Taylor, *Project Director, World University Student Project*
V. T. Thayer, *author*
Herbert A. Tonne, *Ed. Board,* Journal of Business Education
Jack Tourin, *Pres., American Ethical Union*
F. C. Vanderlaan, *lecturer*
J. P. van Praag, *Chm., Intl. Humanist and Ethical Union, Utrecht*
Maurice B. Visscher, *M.D., Prof. Emeritus, Univ. of Minnesota*
Goodwin Watson, *Assn. Coordinator, Union Graduate School*
Gerald Wendt, *author*
Henry N. Wieman, *Prof. Emeritus, Univ. of Chicago*
Sherwin Wine, *Rabbi, Soc. for Humanistic Judaism*
Edwin H. Wilson, *Ex. Dir. Emeritus, American Humanist Assn.*
Bertram D. Wolfe, *Hoover Institution*
Alexander S. Yesenin-Volpin, *mathematician*
Marvin Zimmerman, *Prof. of Philosophy, State Univ. NY at Bflo.*

V.C. Axiarchism: "The Universe Exists Because It Ought To"

V.C.1. Replacements for God

J. L. MACKIE

J. L. Mackie (1917–1981) was a reader in philosophy at Oxford University. His book, The Miracle of Theism, *from which the following selection comes, is a sustained attack on theism. In it he also examines some of the proposed alternatives to theism, among them the theory of John Leslie, which Leslie calls axiarchism. The position is not new with Leslie; it can be found in Western thought as early as Plato's* Republic, *where Plato depicts the impersonal Form of Goodness as the cause both of the world's existence and of our knowledge of it. Leslie attempts to work out the details of this theory, and Mackie examines Leslie's position and finds it wanting, thus adding to his rejection of theism his rejection also of this alternative, which attempts to preserve, in an impersonal way, some of the features of theism.*

The forms of religion without factual belief . . . the view . . . that faith can and should dispense with reason, and even the emphasis on religious experience . . . can be seen as different ways in which traditional theism has retreated in the face of philosophical and scientific difficulties. Yet another possible move is to revise the concept of God, and in particular to give up the view of God as a person. This is the conclusion for which Hume's sceptic, Philo, was willing to settle: ' . . . the whole of natural theology . . . resolves itself into one simple, though somewhat ambiguous, at least undefined proposition, *that the cause or causes of order in the universe probably bear some remote analogy to human intelligence'.*[1] A somewhat different revision has recently been embraced by theologians; influential thinkers in this vein include Paul Tillich and, in a more popular style, J. A. T. Robinson.[2] When such writers identify God with 'Being-itself' or 'a depth at the centre of life' or 'the object of

[1] *Dialogues concerning Natural Religion*, Part XII. This passage was added by Hume in his final revision in 1776.

[2] P. Tillich, *Systematic Theology* (Nisbet, London, 1953-63), *The Shaking of the Foundations* (SCM Press, London, 1949); J. A. T. Robinson, *Honest to God* (SCM Press, London, 1963).

ultimate concern', it may seem that their claims have been so watered down as to be not only indisputable but uninteresting. If God is simply whatever you most care about, then not even St Anselm's fool will deny that God exists. But so easy a victory is not worth winning. However, this may be a misinterpretation. These writers may mean rather that some thing, or some principle, objectively *is* of ultimate concern and at the same time is *the* ultimate reality. If so, they are continuing a tradition that goes back at least to Plato.[3] Plato's Form of the Good is supposed to be an objective entity or principle which not only governs the universe but is creatively responsible for the existence of everything: 'you may say of the objects of knowledge that not only their being known comes from the good, but their existence and being also comes from it, though the good is not itself being but transcends even being in dignity and power'. Plato compares the Form of the Good with the sun, which provides not only the light which enables us to see things but also the creative energy which brings plants and animals to life; similarly, objective value not only makes everything intelligible but also brings everything into existence; but it is itself 'ἐπέκεινα τῆς οὐσίας, 'on the far side of being'.

This metaphysical theory is a real alternative to the doctrine that there is a personal creator, a divine mind or spirit. Its central idea, that objective value both explains things and creates them, has continued as a strand in philosophical and religious thinking, though often combined with or submerged within personal theism. But it deserves to be separated out and examined in its own right. It has been so separated, and not only clearly stated but also vigorously defended, by John Leslie.[4]

Leslie calls this theory *extreme axiarchism*: axiarchism would cover all theories that see the world as ruled largely or entirely by value (including both the belief in an omnipotent and benevolent creator and the view that all things are animated by desire for good), while extreme axiarchism is the view that 'some set of ethical needs is creatively powerful' (p. 6), or, more epigrammatically, that 'the universe exists because it ought to' (p. 1).

This theory plainly presupposes and requires the objectivity of value. It also interprets this value or goodness as ethical requiredness, or ought-to-be-ness. To say that something is good (in some respect) is to say that it is ethically required that it should be as it is. But, further, this theory proposes that this ethical feature also in another sense requires or necessitates existence, a sense related to that in which a cause requires or necessitates the existence of its effect—whatever that sense may be.[5] It cannot be exactly the same sense as this; for a cause normally, and perhaps necessarily, precedes its effect in time, and is an occurrent event or condition or state of affairs. But something's ethical requiredness, the need for it to be, could precede that thing in time only as a hypothetical fact, the fact that this item would be good, that its existence

---

[3] *Republic*, Book VI; the quotation is at 509.

[4] J. Leslie, *Value and Existence* (Basil Blackwell, Oxford, 1970); references are to this work, by page or by chapter. Articles which summarize Leslie's view are 'Efforts to explain all existence', in *Mind* 87 (1978), pp. 181–94, and 'The World's necessary existence', in *International Journal for the Philosophy of Religion* II (1980), pp. 207–24.

[5] See Chapter 8 of *The Cement of the Universe*.

or occurrence would be of value, whereas its continued non-existence would be a pity.

This notion, that the mere ethical *need* for something could *on its own* call that item into existence, without the operation of any person or mind that was aware of this need and acted so as to fulfill it, is, no doubt, initially strange and paradoxical. Yet in it lies also the greatest strength of extreme axiarchism. For Leslie argues that it offers the only possible answer to the question which underlies all forms of the cosmological argument, the question 'Why is there anything at all?' or "Why should there be any world rather than none?'. It is obvious that no causal explanation can answer this question. Many thinkers . . . have thought that the postulation of a god could answer it; but an answer of this kind encounters two radical difficulties. First, in giving what Swinburne calls a personal explanation, it has to assume that will alone, without any intermediary instrumentalities, can somehow bring about its own fulfillment, creating something out of nothing; but this notion has no empirical basis, but seems rather to result from an analogy with a mis-construal of what happens when a human agent's purpose is fulfilled by way of very complicated material intermediaries. Secondly, it invites the reply, 'But then why is there a god with this extraordinary power?' Then we are told that this question is out of order, that a god terminates the regress of explanation as nothing else could; but this requires the at least controversial concept of a necessary being, and, what is more, the concept, which I have argued to be indefensible, of something whose existence is self-explanatory; that is, it has to invoke the notions that provide the core of the ontological argument. But once we allow the (admittedly difficult) notion that something's value, its ethical requiredness, might both give rise to and explain its existence, we have a possible answer to this ultimate question which does not invite these objec-tions. The world's being good, its fulfilling of an ethical requirement, might be an ultimate, necessary, fact which does not itself call for any further explana-tion. Moreover, the availability of such an answer may make the question itself more respectable. 'The bare truth that there is any world could be thought to shout for explanation. If people have been deaf to the cry, then a main cause is their thinking it logically absurd to try to explain *absolutely all* existents. Through its sheer availability, however, extreme axiarchism may make this deafness, so often called anti-metaphysical, into metaphysics as speculative as axiarchism itself.' (p. 64)

Leslie does not claim that there is any analytic connection between ethical requirement and creative requirement. These are, he agrees, two quite dis-tinguishable features, two different ways in which something may be 'marked out for existence'. His suggestion is that there may be a synthetic but necessary connection between them. Necessary, but not *a priori*: he makes no claim that we can know with *a priori* certainty that ethical requiredness is creatively effective. Yet there is some analogy between an ethical requirement and a creative requirement—for example, in their like directedness towards exis-tence—which is enough to give some initial plausibility to the suggestion that they go together. And certainly it would be a gross error to argue *a priori* on the opposite side, that merely because ethical requirement and creative require-ment are conceptually or logically distinct there cannot be a real, and perhaps necessary, connection between them.

Although he commonly speaks of creative effectiveness, Leslie is as ready as, for example, Aquinas is to allow that nothing turns upon creation as a beginning of the universe in time. 'A deity would be a creator were a thing a necessary accompaniment of his wish for it, a wish which might be eternal. Similarly, that an ethical requirement "created" the universe says that had there been no such requirement, then the universe would not have existed, even if it has in fact existed always.' (p. 51)

Leslie sums up as follows what is, in effect, his variant of the cosmological argument. 'The choice then seems between (i) the universe, or some part bearing creative responsibility for the rest, just happening to be there, and (ii) the universe (perhaps including a divine person) existing thanks to its ethical requiredness. The one qualification which might be needed is that such requiredness might instead be responsible only for a divine person, leaving it up to him to create all else. . . .' (p. 79)

He also develops variants of the design argument and the argument from consciousness. The very occurrence of causal regularities calls for some further explanation. 'Of conceivable universes, the vast majority would be chaotic; what then persuades events in ours to conform to laws?' (p. 106) 'I agree that a universe ruled by chance, if sufficiently huge, would contain large patches easy to describe, much as monkeys with typewriters would in the end compose a few sonnets. But if taking seriously this means of explaining the orderliness which we have so far experienced, we should expect disorder to begin in the very next microsecond.' (p. 109) It is, therefore, not unreasonable to look for a further explanation of there being causal laws (Chapter VI). This explanation is particularly appropriate in that the specific laws by which our universe works are suited to the development of life and consciousness, when they might so easily have been otherwise (Chapter VII). But Leslie also considers the objection that value resides only in conscious states, so that it is difficult to appeal to value as an explanation of a universe of which consciousness is, so far as we can tell, only a very small part. He toys with phenomenalism as a possible way of answering this objection—for, if phenomenalism is correct, then minds alone are the fundamentally real substances that make up the universe (Chapter X)—but this is a very implausible way out of the difficulty.

Extreme axiarchism also faces its own variant of the problem of evil (Chapter V). One might not expect this difficulty to arise, since the ascription to God of omnipotence and omniscience is essential to the setting up of this problem for orthodox theism, and a radical revision of the concept of God might well dispense with these features. In particular, there is no reason why a non-personal principle of creative value should be encumbered with omniscience. Nevertheless, Leslie is right to confront this problem. For if goodness, ethical requiredness, is the *sole* creative principle and the only explanation why there is any world at all, we can indeed ask, Whence, then, is evil? It would obviously be less satisfactory, because less simple; to admit that value is, even in principle, only a partial explanation of what there is, that there is also an element of sheer unexplained brute fact, of things just happening to be there; for the recognition of such unexplained brute facts was the rejected alternative to the hypothesis that ethical requiredness is creative. Leslie's answer to the problem of evil is, in effect . . . to argue that there may well be no unabsorbed evils, when we take account of the value of lives that involve real choices against a background of discoverable causal regularities—whether those choices are causally determined or not, for Leslie allows for a compatibilist view of freedom.

This summary may be enough to show that extreme axiarchism is a formidable rival to the traditional theism which treats God as a person or mind or spirit. As I have noted, it leaves a place open for a personal god—or rather two alternative places. There might be such a god as one component among others of a universe whose ultimate source and explanation is its ethical requiredness; again, it might be that an omnipotent and benevolent spirit was himself the only immediate product of creative value, everything else being created in turn by him. But Leslie remarks that the latter 'looks both untidy and inessential to Christianity, for instance, which worships goodness and not sheer power—not even when it conceives God as a person' (p. 79). In fact, this could have been put more strongly. A divine person would be completely redundant within extreme axiarchism's scheme of explanation, since value alone, without conscious purpose, is supposed to be creative; and the postulation of a directly efficacious will, bringing about its own fulfilment without intermediaries, would . . . be an embarrassingly improbable addition to the theory. There is even less reason for allowing the hypothesized principle of creative value to be *called* God. That would be a device for slurring over a real change in belief, and, in all likelihood, an excuse for moving back and forth between traditional theism and this alternative, adhering in practice to the one while being prepared to defend only the other. Far from being honest to God, this is dishonest to both theism and extreme axiarchism. The latter should be seen and considered as what it is, a radically different alternative and rival to theism, with a distinguished ancestry of its own going back, as we have seen, to Plato's vision of the Form of the Good.

The availability of this alternative should tell against traditional theism with anyone who is dissatisfied, for whatever reason, with the naturalistic, sceptical, view of the world. If, with Leibniz and others, you demand an ultimate explanation, then this may well be a better one than the postulation of a divine mind or spirit. But for us the crucial question is how this suggestion fares in competition with the naturalistic or sceptical view.

As we have seen, extreme axiarchism still encounters the problem of evil. Indeed, it is specially exposed to this problem, in that it cannot shelter, as theism often tries to, behind the contra-causal development of the free will defence. It at first *seems* possible to detach the wrong choices of free agents from even an omnipotent god, whereas, if objective value is the sole creative principle, nothing that is real can be detached from it. (It is true that *in the end* theism is no better off, since . . . this method of defence fails.) That is, the extreme axiarchist must hold that there are no unabsorbed evils. Leslie does in effect hold this, so his position is at least consistent. Whether it can be thoroughly reconciled both with a realistic picture of the world as it is and with a plausible interpretation of ethical requiredness is another, more controversial, matter.

Paradoxically, however, extreme axiarchism may be embarrassed less by the problem of evil than by what we may call the problem of indifference. This has two aspects. Creative ethical requiredness, like Leibniz's God, could presumably do nothing without a sufficient reason. Leibniz argued that there could not be a Newtonian absolute space, because, if there were, God would have been faced with the choice of creating the universe just where it is or creating it somewhere else, 'preserving the same situations of bodies among themselves', that is, with all the same *relative* positions and motions, and he could have had no reasons for preferring one to the other.[6] Creative value, it seems, would be faced with innumerable equally embarrassing choices between alternatives of which neither was better than the other. The other aspect of the problem of indifference we have already noted: there seem to be vast tracts of space-time and material existents that have no value worth mentioning. This problem is acute for Leslie, because he believes that 'only experiences, conscious states, could have intrinsic value' (p. 153), and therefore agrees with Berkeley that to accept the ordinary view of the material world 'is to suppose that God has created innumerable beings that are entirely useless, and serve to no manner of purpose'.[7] To avoid, as he must, any corresponding supposition about creative value, he argues, as we have noted, for phenomenalism. But among hypotheses to explain the whole pattern of our experiences, phenomenalism is much less satisfactory than *some* kind of realism. Experiences, taken on their own, are fragmentary and disorderly, full of unexplained coincidences; it is only by supplementing their contents that we can reach any approximation to a coherent, orderly, world.[8] But further, among realisms, there is. . . a strong case for material realism as opposed to Berkeley's scheme of a divine mind which feeds into human minds small fragments of its own complete ideal world. If neither phenomenalism nor a Berkelian view is satisfactory, then we are forced to recognize the existence of innumerable beings that serve no sort of purpose, and this is a strong point against extreme axiarchism.

An even greater difficulty for this theory lies in the implausibility of its own central principle, the hypothesis that objective ethical requiredness is creative, that something's being valuable can in itself tend to bring that thing into existence or maintain its existence, and can therefore provide an ultimate explanation of its being there, independently of its being caused or created by any other existing things. Leslie is right both in renouncing any claim that this principle is analytic or otherwise *a priori* and in resisting the contrary prejudice that it can be known *a priori* to be impossible. Yet it remains a sheer speculation. This principle is equivalent to a doctrine of intrinsic immanent teleology (p. 25): things exist, and are as they are, for a goal or end or purpose or final cause; but the purpose is not located in any mind, nor is the goal or end made such by being taken as an end, by being desired or pursued, by any active being, nor even by the fact that it would be so taken as an end or would satisfy some desire. Thinkers have often believed in such pure immanent teleology; but it is a category which has no genuine ordinary applications. Explanations, for example of biological structures, of plant or animal behaviour, or of devices, like homing rockets, that are based on feedback, which are initially or superficially teleological can be shown to rest entirely on processes of efficient

---

[6] *The Leibniz-Clarke Correspondence*: e.g. Leibniz's Third Paper.

[7] *Principles of Human Knowledge*, Section 19.

[8] Hume, *Treatise*, Book I, Part IV, Section 2; cf. Chapter 2 of *Problems from Locke*

causation—either directly, or else mediately by way of reduction to conscious purposive action which itself reduces to a form of efficient causation.[9] Axiarchical creation, therefore, is modelled upon a *misunderstanding* of certain natural processes. Its proposed explanation of the world and its details is in the same position as Swinburne's personal explanation: this, too. . . is based on an analogy with a misleading abstraction from the ordinary process of the fulfillment of human intentions. In fact, what look at first like three rival, independent, kinds of explanations—causal, personal, and teleological—are, when their ordinary applications are properly understood, all forms of just one kind of explanation, that based on efficient causation. Ordinary 'personal' and 'teleological' explanations are only telescopings of somewhat complicated examples of causal explanation. We have, therefore, no sound empirical basis from which the axiarchical principle might be developed even by an enterprising extrapolation; it remains a pure, ungrounded, speculation.

Finally, extreme axiarchism rests essentially upon the assumption that there are objectively prescriptive values. And this assumption is false.[10] A thorough discussion of this topic would lead us into the foundations of ethics. I have argued elsewhere that the theological frontier of ethics remains open;[11] the same is true of the ethical frontier of theology. Just as we cannot finally settle various ethical questions without deciding whether there is, or is not, a god, so equally we cannot finally settle various theological questions, such as the viability of axiarchism, except with the help of a decision about the status of ethical values.

Leslie is right in arguing (Chapter XII) that neither ethical naturalism nor non-cognitivism (prescriptivism, emotivism, and the like), gives an adequate analysis of what we ordinarily mean when we use moral or in general evaluative language. These theories do not exhaustively interpret—either separately or in conjunction with one another—our ethical concepts. We do think of goodness as a supposedly objective ought-to-be-ness. In calling something good we do commonly imply that it is intrinsically and objectively required or marked out for existence, irrespective of whether any person, human or divine, or any group or society of persons, requires or demands or prescribes or admires it. Some thinkers hold that such a concept—even if we are inclined to use it—is incoherent, that requiring is something that only minds—or something constituted by minds, like a legal system—can do. I do not believe that it is incoherent: I can find no actual contradiction implicit within it. Nevertheless it cannot be denied that it is, when clearly distinguished from various concepts of relative or subjective value, a very strange concept.

Leslie's ontology of values is very like that of Samuel Clarke.[12] Some relations are fully secondary to the related terms. That one box is able to fit inside another does not involve or depend upon anything beyond the intrinsic

---

[9] This is argued at length in Chapter 11 of *The Cement of the Universe*.

[10] This is argued in Chapter 1 of *Ethics: Inventing Right and Wrong* and throughout *Hume's Moral Theory*.

[11] *Ethics: Inventing Right and Wrong*, Chapter 10.

[12] See, e.g., the extracts from S. Clarke, *The Being and Attributes of God*, in *British Moralists 1650–1800*, edited by D. D. Raphael (Oxford University Press, 1969).

characteristics (shape and size) of the two boxes, and the same is true of relations of comparative similarity between, for example, colours. Ethical requiredness is, he suggests, similarly a relation fully secondary to the intrinsic characteristics of whatever has it; thus, he argues, value can be connected synthetically but necessarily with the nature of what has value, though this relation need not be, and indeed is not, knowable *a priori*.

But this analogy is not very persuasive. Objective value seems very different from the other examples of secondary relations, which are less obviously synthetic, and seem far more open to *a priori* determination. We should hesitate to postulate that this strange concept has any real instantiations, provided that our inclination to use it can be explained adequately in some other way. And in fact we can explain this, in a manner that Hume, in particular, has indicated. Moral and evaluative thinking arises from human sentiments and purposes; it involves systems of attitudes developed particularly by interactions between people in societies, and the concept of intrinsic requiredness results from a projection of those attitudes upon their objects, by an abstraction of requiring from the persons—or institutions built out of persons—that really do the requiring.

This Humean style of explanation of our concept of goodness or objective requiredness is much more acceptable than the rival view that things or states of affairs actually have such objective requiredness as a secondary relation and that we are in some unexplained way able to detect it and respond to it. This approach also explains, or rather explains away, such plausibility as Leslie finds in the axiarchic principle, in the notion that what is ethically marked out for existence may *thereby* also be creatively marked out for existence. For if we require or demand something, we also necessarily have some tendency to bring it about if we can. The simultaneous projection of both of these into supposedly objective features will yield precisely the notion that there is an objective ethical requirement which, by a synthetic necessity, carries creative requirement with it, in other words that value must, at least to some extent, be creatively effective. Since the axiarchic cluster of ideas is so readily explicable in this alternative way, we must reject both the concept of objectively prescriptive value on which it rests and, *a fortiori*, the suggestion that such value is creative.

We cannot, therefore, soften our rejection of theism by the acceptance of this alternative, or by welcoming any less clearly stated views which hover between extreme axiarchism and traditional theism.

V.D. Theism and Metaphysics: Is Theism the Most Plausible World View?

V.D.1. Comparing Rival World-Views

WILLIAM J. WAINWRIGHT

William J. Wainwright (1935–), professor of philosophy and religious studies at the University of Wisconsin at Milwaukee, briefly enumerates and spells out here criteria that he believes are the necessary ones for comparing and judging competing world views. He applies his twelve criteria comparatively to naturalism and theism, concluding that both of these systems are highly plausible and that, in the final analysis, our adopting one over the other will depend on the weight we place on some of the criteria as contrasted with others—or perhaps on our own religious experiences, which we may feel offer overriding evidence.

A variety of criteria are used to assess rival metaphysical systems. We will discuss the most important ones and illustrate their application by examining the dispute between theism and naturalism.

THE CRITERIA

Good metaphysical systems must meet a number of criteria. For example, (1) *the facts that the system explains must actually exist.* Some metaphysical systems, for instance, offer explanations of the objectivity of moral and aesthetic values. If values *aren't* objective, these systems are defective.

In addition, (2) *a good metaphysical system should be compatible with well-established facts and theories.* For example, philosophical accounts of the mind-body relation mustn't contradict the findings of biology and psychology. Generally speaking, metaphysical systems should be compatible with accepted theories in other disciplines. If they aren't, the burden of proof is on the metaphysician to show why those theories are inadequate. Systems that are incompatible with the theory of biological evolution, for instance, begin with a strike against them.

From *The Philosophy of Religion* by William J. Wainwright. © 1988 by Wadsworth, Inc. Reprinted by permission of the publisher. Pp. 171–175.

An adequate system must also meet four formal criteria. (3) *it must be logically consistent*, and (4) *it shouldn't be "self-stultifying.* [1] While most world-views meet the first formal requirement, some seem to fail the second. A view is self-stultifying if its assertion implies that it can't be known to be true, or its assertion implies that it is false or can't be expressed. Madhyamika, for example, seems to assert that all views are false. But if *all* views are false, then its own view is false (that is, it is false that all views are false). Advaita maintains that reality is inexpressible. If reality is inexpressible, however, one can't *express* this by saying "Reality is inexpressible." (We will consider responses to these criticisms in the next section.)

(5) *Adequate metaphysical systems should also be coherent.* Their parts ought to "hang together." A system should thus display a certain amount of interconnectedness and systematic articulation. Monotheism, for example, seems more coherent than polytheisms that posit a number of gods but don't clearly explain the connections between them.

Other things being equal, (6) *simpler systems are preferable to complex ones.* A system may be simpler because it employs fewer basic concepts or makes fewer basic assumptions, or because it uses fewer explanatory principles or isn't committed to as many kinds of reality. For example, physicalism and idealism posit only one kind of reality (bodies and minds respectively). They are thus simpler than dualisms that assert that matter and mind are equally real and can't be reduced to each other. Monotheism is simpler than polytheism in the sense that it posits fewer explanatory principles.

But good metaphysical systems not only must meet formal criteria. They must also possess explanatory power. This involves several things—avoiding ad hoc hypotheses, precision, scope, fruitfulness, and a system's ability to "illuminate" the facts it explains.

(7) *Good metaphysical systems should avoid ad hoc hypotheses.* An ad hoc hypothesis has no independent plausibility and is neither implied by the theory nor naturally suggested by it. Its only function is to explain away apparent counter-evidence. For example, when confronted with evidence of geological and biological evolution, some nineteenth-century biblical literalists tried to preserve their version of Christianity by adding a hypothesis. They suggested that God had deliberately created a world containing fossil traces and other misleading indications of geological and biological evolution; the empirical evidence points to evolution but the evidence is deceptive.

(8) *Metaphysical explanations should be precise.* An explanation is more precise when it accounts for more features of a phenomenon or provides a more detailed explanation of the mechanisms responsible for them. For example, a theory of art that explains various kinds of aesthetic value (beauty, expressiveness, sublimity, and so on) is more precise than one that only accounts for aesthetic value in general. Or suppose two metaphysical theories trace phenomena back to an absolute mind. One is more precise than the other if it provides a more detailed account of the absolute spirit and its relation to other things.

---

[1] Keith Yandell, "Religious Experience and Rational Appraisal," *Religious Studies* 10 (1974): 186.

(9) *A system's scope is also important.* Other things being equal, metaphysical theories are better when they explain a wider range of phenomena. A system that illuminates humanity's scientific, moral, aesthetic, and religious experience, for example, is superior to one that only illuminates science.

Furthermore, (10) *one should consider a system's fruitfulness.* There are several ways in which theories can be fruitful. They may predict new phenomena or previously unnoticed aspects of known phenomena. They may also generate interesting new problems and solutions or suggest illuminating interpretations of facts the theories didn't anticipate. Metaphysical theories don't generate predictions. However, they can generate new problems and solutions and interesting interpretations of new facts. Platonism, for example, was used to illuminate the data of Christian revelation and romantic love, although it didn't anticipate either of these phenomena.

(11) *Good metaphysical systems provide illuminating explanations of the phenomena within their explanatory range.* There are several ways in which theories can illuminate facts. A puzzling phenomenon can sometimes be subsumed under general principles. The phenomenon is explained by showing how it follows from the system's postulates and theorems or from hypotheses that are either suggested by the system or are easily incorporated in it. For example, classical theists make sense of revelation by inferring the likelihood of a revelation from God's desire to enter into relations with His creatures and humanity's weakness and need for God. Theists frequently attempt to illuminate evil by showing how its occurrence follows from hypotheses that easily cohere with theism (the lawfulness of the created order, for instance, or the desirability of moral growth and independence). If the theist's postulates, theorems, and hypotheses are plausible, the puzzling phenomenon is "illuminated."

When a metaphysical theory integrates a set of apparently unrelated phenomena, it sometimes illuminates them. For example, a system may interpret historical, sociological, psychological, and moral facts as diverse expressions of humanity's drive toward transcendence. Other systems interpret the same facts as expressions of sinful self-reliance. Still others think it more helpful to view them as products of interaction between innately good human nature and a corrupt social environment.

One of the most effective ways of illuminating a phenomenon is by drawing analogies with phenomena that are better understood. Edward Schoen (1949–) discusses an important example of this. Many theistic explanations account for a pattern of phenomena by postulating the activity of an entity that is relevantly similar to entities that are known to be responsible for analogous patterns of phenomena. Thus, I may notice an apparently providential pattern in my life or in the history of a religious community. Noting similarities between those patterns and patterns in the lives of those who are cared for by others, I postulate a loving will to account for them.[2]

In short, a good metaphysical system explains real facts, is consistent with other things we know, meets formal criteria, and possesses explanatory power. It may also have to satisfy a pragmatic criterion.

Paul Tillich argues that (12) *philosophical theories should be judged by "their*

---

[2] Edward Schoen, *Religious Explanations* (Durham, N.C.: Duke University Press, 1985).

efficacy in the life-process of mankind. "[3] According to Frederick Ferre (1933–), an adequate metaphysical system must be "capable of 'coming to life' for individuals...becoming...a usable instrument for our coping with the total environment." It must have a "capacity for ringing true with respect to" those who use it, enabling them to "cope successfully with the challenges of life."[4] William James makes a similar point. Adequate metaphysical systems must meet practical as well as intellectual demands.

The best metaphysical system, then, is that which best satisfies these criteria. One should note that the criteria are comparative; they are used in deciding *between* competing theories. The question, therefore, is *"On the whole, does theory A satisfy the criteria better than theory B?"* Theory A might do this even if it doesn't fully satisfy *some* of the criteria (perhaps it includes some ad hoc hypotheses) and even if B satisfies a few criteria better than A. As an example of the complex issues involved in comparing systems, we will briefly look at theism and naturalism.

AN EXAMPLE: THEISM AND NATURALISM

Theists believe in a supernatural reality that transcends nature. Naturalists think that the space-time world is all there is. Theism and naturalism, then, are very different metaphysical systems. Does one satisfy our criteria better than the other?

Both systems are consistent and reasonably coherent. Neither is self-stultifying. Both can accommodate new knowledge and adapt themselves to new historical and cultural situations.

Gary Gutting thinks that naturalism is more precise.[5] However, this is doubtful. *Scientific* explanations may be more precise than theistic explanations, but naturalism isn't science; it is a metaphysical hypothesis like theism. Naturalists can *use* scientific explanations to fill out their picture of the world but so can theists. (Theists are only committed to rejecting *reductive* scientific accounts of things like religious experience.) Furthermore, many theistic explanations *are* precise. Some theological accounts of mystical experience, for instance, are as detailed as "scientific" ones.[6]

Naturalism is simpler in the sense that it denies the existence of transcen-

---

[3] Paul Tillich, *Systematic Theology*, vol. 1 (Chicago: University of Chicago Press, 1951), 105.

[4] Frederick Ferre and Kent Bedall, *Exploring the Logic of Faith* (New York: Association Press, 1963), 171.

[5] Garry Gutting, *Religious Belief and Religious Skepticism* (Notre Dame, Ind.: University of Notre Dame Press, 1982), chapter 5.

[6] See, for example, Albert Farges, *Mystical Phenomena*, trans. S. P. Jacques (New York: Benziger Bros., 1925), and Auguste Poulain, *The Graces of Interior Prayer*, trans. L. L. Yorke Smith (St. Louis: B. Herder, 1950). These accounts are as detailed as the "scientific" ones of atheists like James Leuba, *The Psychology of Religious Mysticism* (New York: Harcourt Brace, 1925) or Sigmund Freud—see, for example, *The Future of an Illusion*, trans. W. D. Robson-Scott (New York: Liveright, 1949).

dent reality and thus postulates fewer entities. On the other hand, theism seems superior in scope. The existence of contingent being falls within the explanatory range of any comprehensive metaphysical system.[7] Theism can explain it and naturalism can't.

The most significant question, probably, is, "Which system provides the most illuminating explanations and most effectively enables its adherents to come to terms with life?"

Theism may provide more illuminating accounts of apparent design, religious experience, and our dissatisfaction with temporal goods. Theists also believe that their world-view provides illuminating accounts of phenomena like sanctity and the apparent objectivity of moral value. For example, George Mavrodes (1926–) argues that objective values are more "at home" in a theistic universe than in the sort of world envisaged by naturalism. The existence of objective value is less surprising if maximal perfection exists and goodness is therefore embedded in the structure of things.[8]

On the other hand, naturalists think that their account of evil is more illuminating. The occurrence of suffering and wickedness isn't particularly surprising if the space-time world is all there is. It is regrettable that natural causes have this consequence but there is no reason why they shouldn't. If *God* had created the world, however, one wouldn't expect so much evil. Naturalists conclude that suffering and wickedness are more intelligible in their framework. The force of their point, of course, depends on the success or failure of theistic strategies.

Determining which system best satisfies the pragmatic criterion is also difficult. For one thing, assessments reflect people's values, and their values are influenced by their metaphysical commitments and predilections. Persons who are sympathetic with theism won't be happy with the systems that seem to frustrate our spiritual aspirations and deprive life of overall meaning. In deciding between theism and naturalism, however, they must be careful not to beg the question by appealing to values that couldn't be acknowledged by non-theists. For similar reasons, those who are sympathetic to naturalism shouldn't base their decision on claims that are plausible only if naturalism is true (for example, that the most important values are temporal).

Furthermore, secularization is a comparatively recent phenomenon. While every civilized society has included those who are indifferent or hostile to religion, the modern West may be the first in which some form of naturalism is held by many people in all walks of life. William James thinks that the relevant question is, "Which system best enables humanity to come to terms with life?" If it is, the verdict may still be out.

Our brief comparison of theism and naturalism illustrates the difficulty of

---

[7] Some naturalists think that the existence of the natural world is necessary. Others maintain that questions about its origins are meaningless. Nevertheless, most naturalists concede that, in their view, the existence of contingent being is simply a brute fact that has no explanation.

[8] George Mavrodes, "Religion and the Queerness of Morality," *Rationality, Religious Belief and Moral Commitment*, ed. Robert Audi and William J. Wainwright (Ithaca, N.Y.: Cornell University Press, 1968). For a theistic interpretation of sanctity see Patrick Sherry, *Spirits, Saints, and Immortality* (Albany: State University of New York Press, 1984).

applying our criteria. They aren't very precise, and there are disagreements concerning their relative weights. (Is scope, for example, more important than simplicity?) The relevant evidence is also complex, and much of it is "delicate." For example, a person who doesn't appreciate moral values or is insensitive to the richness and complexity of our moral life is a poor judge of explanations of moral value.

The application of the criteria thus calls for judgment. The quality of one's judgment is a function of knowledge, intelligence, and the care with which one has considered the issue. It is also a function of the depth of a person's experience and his or her sensitivity to the relevant evidence. It isn't surprising, then, that intelligent men and women apply these criteria and come to different conclusions. Each of us must nonetheless form the best judgment he or she can in the light of all the relevant considerations.

Part VI

Religious Experience and Mysticism

Certain medieval thinkers have been ridiculed for debating at length about how many teeth a horse has, based on various passages from Aristotle's writings, when they might simply have opened the mouths of a few horses and counted. Philosophers are perhaps guilty of the same folly, it has been suggested, when they resort to abstract reasoning in an attempt to find out about the religious dimension of reality that can be known directly through religious experience. "O taste and see that the Lord is good!" says the Psalmist, "Happy is the man who takes refuge in him!" (Psalm 34:8). Truths about the religious aspects of reality, according to those who argue this way, are not to be ascertained through abstract reason but rather by "tasting and seeing" through direct experience.

Thus, many for whom religion is of central importance would regard the abstract rational arguments about theism, and the other world views advocated as alternatives to theism, as somewhat like trying to decide by speculative thought which of two batches of soup is hotter or more highly seasoned. Although philosophers are preoccupied with argument and reasoning, the great founders and teachers of religion have nearly always claimed a much more experiential basis for their religious teachings. The burning bush experience of Moses set off the course of events that gave rise to Judaism (Exodus 3). The series of visions experienced by Muhammad and recorded in the Qur'an led to the founding of Islam. The enlightenment experience of Guatama inspired him to preach, teach, and establish Buddhism. These and many others were powerful experiences in which the person involved felt a direct relationship with deity or gained a supermundane insight into reality and truth. Although these experiences resulted in sets of teachings subsequently expounded on and reasoned for, it was not reason that originated the doctrines or ultimately established or authenticated them. The experiences themselves, according to believers, are grasped as self-certifying, indubitable, neither subject to nor in need of any outside credentials; at best, rational theology is a pale substitute. Ultimately, it is asserted, the person who seeks authentication of religious claims must seek it through such experiences.

Religious experiences are reported from every culture, major religious tradition, and era of history. Indeed, it is often claimed that a brother/sisterhood of saints and mystics encircles the world and encompasses every era of time, offering accounts of experienced human-divine encounters that are remarkably similar—much more similar than the conclusions of the rational argument of philosophers. On the basis of such experiential reports, it has been suggested that all persons who have religious experiences are in touch with the same reality. To be sure, there is not complete agreement about every detail, but that can be accounted for by pointing to differences of expectation raised by the religious training individuals receive in their differing cultures. What is remarkable, allegedly, is not differences in minutiae, but the great similarities in their broad outlines. This represents a version of what has been called the argument from religious experience, which attempts to infer, from the similar religious experiences of many individuals from many cultures and religious traditions, the one deity alleged to be the being encountered in such experiences.

The extent to which the experiences of persons from highly different backgrounds resemble one another has impressed many commentators. Yet these experiences are not by any means identical. Indeed, it is their variety that has seemed most striking to others. One of the great seminal studies of religious experience is a book by William James (1842–1910), *The Varieties of Religious Experience*, from which selections are included in this part. James devotes much attention to what we may call the phenomenology of religious experience—that is, the actual nature and content of the experiences themselves. Many such experiences have explicit religious content, involving visions or voices identified with God; Christ; the Blessed Virgin; the Buddha; Krishna; the goddess Kali; or some other saint, avatar, or religious personage.

Many religious experiences are explicitly colored by cultural beliefs and expectations; many clearly involve ingredients of a specific religious tradition. Others, however, are less culture specific, less anchored in any one religion. This is particularly true of the special type of religious experiences called *mystical*. Mystical experiences often involve nothing at all specific to a particular religion, and sometimes they do not seem even explicitly religious. Some mystics report merely a sense of oneness with the ultimate, with nature, with some segment of the world, or with the world itself.

The affinity of religious experience with aesthetic experience is also worth noting. These two kinds of human experiences seem to have a great deal in common. The feeling itself of awe, grandeur, wonder, and joy that characterizes many religious experiences is also frequently a central ingredient in aesthetic experience. A star-studded evening sky or the shimmering moon rising large and orange out of the ocean stirs keen aesthetic feelings, but often also inspires a sense of the presence of the divine. The stark ruggedness and lavish spread of color of a desert canyon or the wind-carved dunes of sand stretched out beyond the reach of the eye in every direction not only thrills us with a sense of beauty and vastness but also seem to speak of something which transcends the merely natural realm. The blending is even more evident in religious music. A stirring performance of a great piece of music, like the magnificent pageantry of a sacrament or religious liturgy, may fill us with aesthetic delight while it also sets our lofty thoughts on things holy and divine. Organized religions, always keenly aware of this affinity, have made explicit use of works of art to create settings conducive to religious experience. Indeed, a substantial proportion of the painting, sculpture, architecture, music, poetry, literature, stained glass work, and drama of most literate cultures has been addressed to religious themes, and the leaders of the various religions have always been great patrons of the arts.

The significance of these moving, often overwhelming, experiences has been appreciated by philosophers and theologians as well, and any satisfactory philosophical account of religion must include an examination of religious experience. Some thinkers have taken this experience as a primary source of information about the nature of ultimate reality and as a cognitive resource for establishing the truth or plausibility of claims made on behalf of religion in general or of a specific religion. Others, however, have seen in religious experience something more somber or less savory. An important charge often raised in connection with religious experience, particularly sudden, dramatic, or bizarre instances, is that religious experience is a form of psychopathology, or at least that mental disturbance tends to be characteristic of those persons given to having such experiences. William James and others admit the latter charge but argue that this tells us nothing about the authenticity of the experiences or the validity of the beliefs that grow out of them. Some mystics and other religious personages, like some great artists, have exhibited signs of psychopathology; but, James insists, religious experience, like art, science, and everything else, must be judged not by its origins or its least developed form but by its fruits. We judge the paintings of an artist on their own merits and do not dismiss those of artists whose psychological life may have been disturbed. We do not dismiss astronomy because it has its roots in astrology or chemistry because it originated in the attempts of the alchemists to transform base metals into gold. Similarly, we must ask not how religion originated or whether some of its advocates are psychologically disturbed, but whether in its most developed form it generates worthy fruits as astronomy and chemistry do.

By these standards James finds that religion does offer impressive and plausible interpretations of the nature of reality and programs for living meaningful and happy lives. He also concludes that religious experience, though not providing all that its most enthusiastic boosters have claimed, does offer some support for religious doctrines. James believes that religious experience justifies our believing that there is more to the nature of reality than simply the mundane dimension our ordinary sense experiences reveal to us.

Mystics themselves are confident beyond any doubt that their experiences put them in touch directly with the ultimate, whatever it may be. No rational argument can either strengthen their conviction or diminish its complete fullness in the slightest measure. The subject of the religious experience knows and enjoys internally what is beyond words and beyond doubt, and the philosopher cannot really disturb that luminous confidence. The philosopher, however, must examine critically the claims of those who enunciate doctrines based on such experiences. *If* these experiences really are direct encounters between human individuals and God, the divine, or ultimate reality, they must be regarded as our absolutely most valuable source of knowledge about things religious—even despite the frequent claim that what is experienced cannot be conveyed in language.

The question that looms large in the philosophical mind, however, is *whether* such experiences really are what they often claim to be. Religious experience is sometimes compared with sense experience and is thus alleged to be a primary source of data for our ordered systems of beliefs about the world. But we know well that some sense experiences are illusions. We cannot always tell by the fact that a sense experience seems vivid, clear, straightforward, and evident whether or not it is an illusion or a hallucination. The deliverances of sense experience must always stand before the judgment bar of reason; so also must the deliverances of any other kinds of human experience that claim to provide us with cognitive data. *Prima facie* religious experience appears to be a valuable source of information. The considered judgment of most philosophers is more cautious, but it is often conceded that in a context of reasoned beliefs, well supported by other evidence, religious experience can be regarded as a useful, perhaps even powerful, supplement.

ANNOTATED GUIDE TO FURTHER READINGS

Hume, David. "Of Miracles." In *Philosophy of Religion: Selected Readings*, 2nd ed., edited by William L. Rowe and William J. Wainwright. New York: Harcourt Brace Jovanovich, 1989.

Hume offers a skeptical view of miracles and revelations. The text also contains a section that deals exclusively with mysticism and religious experience.

James, William. *The Varieties of Religious Experience.* New York: Macmillan, 1961.
This definitive classic covers the topics of religious experience and mysticism thoroughly; it is an excellent source for further examination of these subjects.

Katz, Steven T., ed. *Mysticism and Philosophical Analysis.* New York. Oxford University Press, 1978.
Provides a variety of viewpoints on religious experience and mysticism.

Stace, Walter T. *Mysticism and Philosophy.* Philadelphia and New York: J. B. Lippincott, 1960.
An outstanding source for the study of mysticism.

Stace, Walter T. *The Teachings of the Mystics.* New York: Mentor Books, 1960.
Distinguishes two types of mysticism, introversive and extroversive; examines the occurrence of mystical experiences within the religions of Hinduism, Buddhism, Taoism, Christianity, Islam, and Judaism.

Swinburne, Richard. *The Existence of God.* Oxford: Clarendon Press, 1979.
Applies the principle of credulity to religious experience: that is, that an experience is innocent until proven guilty. The religious perceptions of mystics, like other perceptions, should be taken seriously and should be accepted as long as no evidence proves otherwise.

Tagore, Rabindranath. *The Religion of Man.* Boston: Beacon Press, 1961.
Tagore's exposition of what he calls a "poet's religion," a theistic/humanistic interpretation of Vedanta that teaches the "humanity of God," and the divinity of "man the eternal."

Wainwright, William J. *Mysticism.* Madison, Wisconsin: University of Wisconsin Press, 1981.
Provides the reader with a thorough and diverse study of mysticism. Standard topics are covered along with sections on drug-induced mysticism and the relationship between mysticism and morality.

Zaehner, R. C. *Mysticism: Sacred and Profane.* Oxford: Oxford University Press, 1961.
Rejecting the unanimity thesis, Zaehner emphasized the rich variety of types of religious experiences, giving particular attention to monistic and theistic mystical experiences.

VI.A. The Phenomenology of Religious Experience

VI.A.1. The Reality of the Unseen

WILLIAM JAMES

William James (1842–1910) began his career with the study of physiology and medicine, but soon shifted his attention to psychology and philosophy. He taught physiology and anatomy at Harvard and established there the first experimental psychology laboratory in the United States. Thus James brought to the study of religious phenomena the mind of a scientist and an empiricist, and he evolved his own philosophy of pragmatism, through the lenses of which he viewed religion.

His great work, The Varieties of Religious Experience, *first delivered as the Gifford Lectures at Edinburgh, is one of the classic works in the psychology of religion. An empirical study, it is copiously supported with case material scrutinized with the careful eye of a scientific psychologist fascinated by religion and convinced of its importance. James approaches his study with as few presuppositions as possible, resolved to follow where the evidence leads but eager to express his findings not in technical jargon but in terms ordinary intelligent persons would understand and find meaningful.*

In the most general sense, James points out, religion might be characterized as the belief that there is an unseen reality with which it is possible for humans to be in touch and that the supreme human good consists in relating appropriately to this reality. Here James begins with examples of the vague sense of a presence and proceeds to illustrate the gradation all the way through experiences involving highly detailed religious content.

Were one asked to characterize the life of religion in the broadest and most general terms possible, one might say that it consists of the belief that there is an unseen order, and that our supreme good lies in harmoniously adjusting ourselves thereto. This belief and this adjustment are

From *The Varieties of Religious Experience* (New York: Macmillan, 1961), pp. 59–60, 61–63, 66–72, 73–77.

the religious attitude in the soul. I wish during this hour to call your attention to some of the psychological peculiarities of such an attitude as this, or belief in an object which we cannot see. All our attitudes, moral, practical, or emotional, as well as religious, are due to the "objects" of our consciousness, the things which we believe to exist, whether really or ideally, along with ourselves. Such objects may be present to our senses, or they may be present only to our thought. In either case they elicit from us a *reaction*; and the reaction due to things of thought is notoriously in many cases as strong as that due to sensible presences. It may be even stronger. The memory of an insult may make us angrier than the insult did when we received it. We are frequently more ashamed of our blunders afterwards than we were at the moment of making them; and in general our whole higher prudential and moral life is based on the fact that material sensations actually present may have a weaker influence on our action than ideas of remoter facts.

The more concrete objects of most men's religion, the deities whom they worship, are known to them only in idea. It has been vouchsafed, for example, to very few Christian believers to have had a sensible vision of their Saviour; though enough appearances of this sort are on record, by way of miraculous exception, to merit our attention later. The whole force of the Christian religion, therefore, so far as belief in the divine personages determines the prevalent attitude of the believer, is in general exerted by the instrumentality of pure ideas, of which nothing in the individual's past experience directly serves as a model.

But in addition to these ideas of the more concrete religious objects, religion is full of abstract objects which prove to have equal power. God's attributes as such, his holiness, his justice, his mercy, his absoluteness, his infinity, his omniscience, his tri-unity, the various mysteries of the redemptive process, the operation of the sacraments, etc., have proved fertile wells of inspiring meditation for Christian believers.[1] We shall see later that the absence of definite sensible images is positively insisted on by the mystical authorities in all religions as the *sine qua non* of a successful orison, or contemplation of the higher divine truths. Such contemplations are expected (and abundantly verify the expectation, as we shall also see) to influence the believer's subsequent attitude very powerfully for good. . . .

This absolute determinability of our mind by abstractions is one of the cardinal facts in our human constitution. Polarizing and magnetizing us as they do, we turn towards them and from them, we seek them, hold them, hate them, bless them, just as if they were so many concrete beings. And beings they are, beings as real in the realm which they inhabit as the changing things of sense are in the realm of space.

Plato gave so brilliant and impressive a defense of this common human feeling, that the doctrine of the reality of abstract objects has been known as

---

[1] Example: "I have had much comfort lately in meditating on the passages which show the personality of the Holy Ghost, and his distinctness from the Father and Son. It is a subject that requires searching into to find out, but, when realized, gives one so much more true and lively a sense of the fullness of the Godhead, and its work in us, than when only thinking of the Spirit in its effect on us." Augustus Hare. Memorials, I, 244. Maria Hare to Lucy H. Hare.

the platonic theory of ideas ever since. Abstract Beauty, for example, is for Plato a perfectly definite individual being, of which the intellect is aware as of something additional to all the perishing beauties of the earth. "The true order of going," he says, in the often quoted passage in his "Banquet," "is to use the beauties of earth as steps along which one amounts upwards for the sake of that other Beauty, going from one to two, and from two to all fair forms, and from fair forms to fair actions, and from fair actions to fair notions, until from fair notions, he arrives at the notion of absolute Beauty, and at last knows what the essence of Beauty is."[2] In our last lecture we had a glimpse of the way in which a platonizing writer like Emerson may treat the abstract divineness of things, the moral structure of the universe, as a fact worthy of worship. In those various churches without a God which to-day are spreading through the world under the name of ethical societies, we have a similar worship of the abstract divine, the moral law believed in as an ultimate object. "Science" in many minds is genuinely taking the place of a religion. Where this is so, the scientist treats the "Laws of Nature" as objective facts to be revered. A brilliant school of interpretation of Greek mythology would have it that in their origin the Greek gods were only half-metaphoric personifications of those great spheres of abstract law and order into which the natural world falls apart—the sky-sphere, the ocean-sphere, the earth-sphere, and the like; just as even now we may speak of the smile of the morning, the kiss of the breeze, or the bite of the cold, without really meaning that these phenomena of nature actually wear a human face.[3]

As regards the origin of the Greek gods, we need not at present seek an opinion. But the whole array of our instances leads to a conclusion something like this: It is as if there were in the human consciousness a *sense of reality, a feeling of objective presence, a perception* of what we may call "something there," more deep and more general than any of the special and particular "senses" by which the current psychology supposes existent realities to be originally revealed. If this were so, we might suppose the senses to waken our attitudes and conduct as they so habitually do, by first exciting this sense of reality; but anything else, any idea, for example, that might similarly excite it, would have that same prerogative of appearing real which objects of sense normally possess. So far as religious conceptions were able to touch this reality-feeling, they would be believed in spite of criticism, even though they might be so vague and remote as to be almost unimaginable, even though they might be such non-entities in point of *whatness*, as Kant makes the objects of his moral theology to be. . . .

In an earlier book of mine I have cited at full length a curious case of presence felt by a blind man. The presence was that of the figure of a gray-bearded man dressed in a pepper and salt suit, squeezing himself under the crack of the door and moving across the floor of the room towards a sofa. The blind subject of this quasi-hallucination is an exceptionally intelligent re-

---

[2] Symposium, Jowett, 1871, i. 527.

[3] Example: "Nature is always so interesting, under whatever aspect she shows herself, that when it rains, I seem to see a beautiful woman weeping. She appears the more beautiful, the more afflicted she is." B. de St. Pierre.

porter. He is entirely without internal visual imagery and cannot represent light or colors to himself, and is positive that his other senses, hearing, etc., were not involved in this false perception. It seems to have been an abstract conception rather, with the feelings of reality and spatial outwardness directly attached to it—in other words, a fully objectified and exteriorized *idea*.

Such cases, taken along with others which would be too tedious for quotation, seem sufficiently to prove the existence in our mental machinery of a sense of present reality more diffused and general than that which our special senses yield. For the psychologists the tracing of the organic seat of such a feeling would form a pretty problem—nothing could be more natural than to connect it with the muscular sense, with the feeling that our muscles were innervating themselves for action. Whatsoever thus innervated our activity, or "made our flesh creep"—our senses are what do so oftenest might then appear real and present, even though it were but an abstract idea. But with such vague conjectures we have no concern at present, for our interest lies with the faculty rather than with its organic seat.

Like all positive affections of consciousness, the sense of reality has its negative counterpart in the shape of a feeling of unreality by which persons may be haunted, and of which one sometimes hears complaint:—

> "When I reflect on the fact that I have made my appearance by accident upon a globe itself whirled through space as the sport of the catastrophes of the heavens," says Madame Ackermann; "when I see myself surrounded by beings as ephemeral and incomprehensible as I am myself, and all excitedly pursuing pure chimeras, I experience a strange feeling of being in a dream. It seems to me as if I have loved and suffered and that erelong I shall die, in a dream. My last word will be, 'I have been dreaming.'"[4]

In another lecture we shall see how in morbid melancholy this sense of the unreality of things may become a carking pain, and even lead to suicide.

We may now lay it down as certain that in the distinctively religious sphere of experience, many persons (how many we cannot tell) possess the objects of their belief, not in the form of mere conceptions which their intellect accepts as true, but rather in the form of quasi-sensible realities directly apprehended. As his sense of the real presence of these objects fluctuates, so the believer alternates between warmth and coldness in his faith. Other examples will bring this home to one better than abstract description, so I proceed immediately to cite some. The first example is a negative one, deploring the loss of the sense in question. I have extracted it from an account given me by a scientific man of my acquaintance, of his religious life. It seems to me to show clearly that the feeling of reality may be something more like a sensation than an intellectual operation properly so-called.

> "Between twenty and thirty I gradually became more and more agnostic and irreligious, yet I cannot say that I ever lost that 'indefinite consciousness' which Herbert Spencer describes so well, of an Absolute

---

[4] *Pensées d'un Solitaire*, p. 66.

Reality behind phenomena. For me this Reality was not the pure Unknowable of Spencer's philosophy, for although I had ceased my childish prayers to God, and never prayed to *It* in a formal manner, yet my more recent experience shows me to have been in a relation to *It* which practically was the same thing as prayer. Whenever I had any trouble, especially when I had conflict with other people, either domestically or in the way of business, or when I was depressed in spirits or anxious about affairs, I now recognize that I used to fall back for support upon this curious relation I felt myself to be in to this fundamental cosmical *It*. It was on my side, or I was on Its side, however you please to term it, in the particular trouble, and it always strengthened me and seemed to give me endless vitality to feel its underlying and supporting presence. In fact, it was an unfailing fountain of living justice, truth, and strength, to which I instinctively turned at times of weakness, and it always brought me out. I know now that it was a personal relation I was in to it, because of late years the power of communicating with it has left me, and I am conscious of a perfectly definite loss. I used never to fail to find it when I turned to it. Then came a set of years when sometimes I found it, and then again I would be wholly unable to make connection with it. I remember many occasions on which at night in bed, I would be unable to get to sleep on account of worry. I turned this way and that in the darkness, and groped mentally for the familiar sense of that higher mind of my mind which had always seemed to be close at hand as it were, closing the passage, and yielding support, but there was no electric current. A blank was there instead of *It*: I couldn't find anything. Now, at the age of nearly fifty, my power of getting into connection with it has entirely left me; and I have to confess that a great help has gone out of my life. Life has become curiously dead and indifferent; and I can now see that my old experience was probably exactly the same thing as the prayers of the orthodox, only I did not call them by that name. What I have spoken of as 'It' was practically not Spencer's Unknowable, but just my own instinctive and individual God, whom I relied upon for higher sympathy, but whom somehow I have lost."

Nothing is more common in the pages of religious biography than the way in which seasons of lively and of difficult faith are described as alternating. Probably every religious person has the recollection of particular crisis in which a director vision of the truth, a direct perception, perhaps, of a living God's existence, swept in and overwhelmed the languor of the more ordinary belief. In James Russell Lowell's correspondence there is a brief memorandum of an experience of this kind:—

"I had a revelation last Friday evening. I was at Mary's, and happening to say something of the presence of spirits (of whom, I said, I was often dimly aware), Mr. Putnam entered into an argument with me on spiritual matters. As I was speaking, the whole system rose up before me like a vague destiny looming from the Abyss. I never before so clearly felt the Spirit of God in me and around me. The whole room seemed to me full of God. The air seemed to waver to and fro with the presence of Something I knew not what. I spoke with the calmness and clearness of a prophet. I cannot tell you what this revelation was. I have not yet studied it enough. But I shall perfect it one day, and then you shall hear it and acknowledge its grandeur."[5]

Here is a longer and more developed experience from a manuscript communication by a clergyman—I take it from Starbuck's manuscript collection:—

"I remember the night, and almost the very spot on the hilltop, where my soul opened out, as it were, into the Infinite, and there was a rushing together of the two worlds, the inner and the outer. It was deep calling unto deep—the deep that my own struggle had opened up within being answered by the unfathomable deep without, reaching beyond the stars. I stood alone with Him who had made me, and all the beauty of the world, and love, and sorrow, and even temptation. I did not seek Him, but felt the perfect unison of my spirit with His. The ordinary sense of things around me faded. For the moment nothing but an ineffable joy and exultation remained. it is impossible fully to describe the experience. It was like the effect of some great orchestra when all the separate notes have melted into one swelling harmony that leaves the listener conscious of nothing save that his soul is being wafted upwards, and almost bursting with its own emotion. The perfect stillness of the night was thrilled by a more solemn silence. The darkness held a presence that was all the more felt because it was not seen. I could not any more have doubted that *He* was there than that I was. Indeed, I felt myself to be, if possible, the less real of the two.

"My highest faith in God and truest idea of him were then born in me. I have stood upon the Mount of Vision since, and felt the Eternal round about me. But never since has there come quite the same stirring of the heart. Then, if ever, I believe, I stood face to face with God, and was born anew of his spirit. There was, as I recall it, no sudden change of thought or of belief, except that my early crude conception, had, as it were, burst into flower. There was no destruction of the old, but a rapid, wonderful unfolding. Since that time no discussion that I have heard of the proofs of God's existence has been able to shake my faith. Having once felt the presence of God's spirit, I have never lost it again for long. My most assuring evidence of his existence is deeply rooted in that hour of vision, in the memory of that supreme experience, and in the conviction, gained from reading and reflection, that something the same has come to all who have found God. I am aware that it may justly be called mystical. I am not enough acquainted with philosophy to defend it from that or any other charge. I feel that in writing of it I have overlaid it with words rather than put it clearly to your thought. But, such as it is, I have described it as carefully as I now am able to do."

---

[5] Letters of Lowell, i, 75.

Here is another document, even more definite in character, which, the writer being a Swiss, I translate from the French original.[6]

"I was in perfect health: we were on our sixth day of tramping, and in good training. We had come the day before from Sixt to Trient by Buet. I felt neither fatigue, hunger, nor thirst, and my state of mind was equally healthy. I had had at Forlaz good news from home; I was subject to no anxiety, either near or remote, for we had a good guide, and there was not a shadow of uncertainty about the road we should follow. I can best describe the condition in which I was by calling it a state of equilibrium. When all at once I experienced a feeling of being raised above myself, I felt the presence of God—I tell of the thing just as I was conscious of it—as if his goodness and his power were penetrating me altogether. The throb of emotion was so violent that I could barely tell the boys to pass on and not wait for me. I then sat down on a stone, unable to stand any longer, and my eyes overflowed with tears. I thanked God that in the course of my life he had taught me to know him, that he sustained my life and took pity both on the insignificant creature and on the sinner that I was. I begged him ardently that my life might be consecrated to the doing of his will. I felt his reply, which was that I should do his will from day to day, in humility and poverty, leaving him, the Almighty God, to be judge of whether I should some time be called to bear witness more conspicuously. Then, slowly, the ecstasy left my heart; that is, I felt that God had withdrawn the communion which he had granted, and I was able to walk on, but very slowly, so strongly was I still possessed by the interior emotion. Besides, I had wept uninterruptedly for several minutes, my eyes were swollen, and I did not wish my companions to see me. The state of ecstasy may have lasted for four or five minutes, although it seemed at the time to last much longer. My comrades waited for me ten minutes at the cross of Barine, but I took about twenty-five or thirty minutes to join them, for as well as I can remember, they said that I had kept them back for about half an hour. The impression had been so profound that in climbing slowly the slope I asked myself if it were possible that Moses on Sinai could have had a more intimate communication with God. I think it well to add that in this ecstasy of mine God had neither form, color, odor, nor taste; moreover, that the feeling of his presence was accompanied with no determinate localization. It was rather as if my personality had been transformed by the presence of a *spiritual spirit*. But the more I seek words to express this intimate intercourse, the more I feel the impossibility of describing the thing by any of our usual images. At bottom the expression most apt to render what I felt is this: God was present, though invisible; he fell under no one of my senses, yet my consciousness perceived him."

The adjective "mystical" is technically applied, most often, to states that

---

[6] I borrow it, with Professor Flournoy's permission, from his rich collection of psychological documents.

are of brief duration. Of course such hours of rapture as the last two persons describe are mystical experiences, of which in a later lecture I shall have much to say. Meanwhile here is the abridged record of another mystical or semi-mystical experience, in a mind evidently framed by nature for ardent piety. I owe it to Starbuck's collection. The lady who gives the account is the daughter of a man well known in his time as a writer against Christianity. The suddenness of her conversion shows well how native the sense of God's presence must be to certain minds. She relates that she was brought up in entire ignorance of Christian doctrine, but, when in Germany, after being talked to by Christian friends, she read the Bible and prayed, and finally the plan of salvation flashed upon her like a stream of light.

> "To this day," she writes, "I cannot understand dallying with religion and the commands of God. The very instant I heard my Father's cry calling unto me, my heart bounded in recognition. I ran, I stretched forth my arms, I cried aloud, 'Here, here I am, my Father.' Oh, happy child, what should I do? 'Love me,' answered my God. 'I do, I do,' I cried passionately. 'Come unto me,' called my Father. 'I will,' my heart panted. Did I stop to ask a single question? Not one. It never occurred to me to ask whether I was good enough, or to hesitate over my unfitness, or to find out what I thought of his church, or . . . to wait until I should be satisfied. Satisfied! I was satisfied. Had I not found my God and my Father? Did he not love me? Had he not called me? Was there not a Church into which I might enter? . . . Since then I have had direct answers to prayer—so significant as to be almost like talking with God and hearing his answer. The idea of God's reality has never left me for one moment."

Here is still another case, the writer being a man aged twenty-seven, in which the experience, probably almost as characteristic, is less vividly described:—

> "I have on a number of occasions felt that I had enjoyed a period of intimate communion with the divine. These meetings came unasked and unexpected, and seemed to consist merely in the temporary obliteration of the conventionalities which usually surround and cover my life. . . . Once it was when from the summit of a high mountain I looked over a gashed and corrugated landscape extending to a long convex of ocean that ascended to the horizon, and again from the same point when I could see nothing beneath me but a boundless expanse of white cloud, on the blown surface of which a few high peaks, including the one I was on, seemed plunging about as if they were dragging their anchors. What I felt on these occasions was a temporary loss of my identity, accompanied by an illumination which revealed to me a deeper significance than I had been wont to attach to life. It is in this that I find my justification for saying that I have enjoyed communication with God. Of course the absence of such a being as this would be chaos. I cannot conceive of life without its presence."

Of the more habitual and so to speak chronic sense of God's presence the following sample from Professor Starbuck's manuscript collection may serve to give an idea. It is from a man aged forty-nine—probably thousands of unpretending Christians would write an almost identical account.

> "God is more real to me than any thought or thing or person. I feel his presence positively, and the more as I live in closer harmony with his laws as written in my body and mind. I feel him in the sunshine or rain; and awe mingled with a delicious restfulness most nearly describes my feelings. I talk to him as to a companion in prayer and praise, and our communion is delightful. He answers me again and again, often in words so clearly spoken that it seems my outer ear must have carried the tone, but generally in strong mental impressions. Usually a text of Scripture, unfolding some new view of him and his love for me, and care for my safety. I could give hundreds of instances, in school matters, social problems, financial difficulties, etc. That he is mine and I am his never leaves me, it is an abiding joy. Without it life would be a blank, a desert, a shoreless, trackless waste."

. . . I spoke of the convincingness of these feelings of reality, and I must dwell a moment longer on that point. They are as convincing to those who have them as any direct sensible experience can be, and they are, as a rule, much more convincing than results established by mere logic ever are. One may indeed be entirely without them; probably more than one of you here present is without them in any marked degree; but if you do have them, and have them at all strongly, the probability is that you cannot help regarding them as genuine perceptions of truth, as revelations of a kind of reality which no adverse argument, however unanswerable by you in words, can expel from your belief. The opinion opposed to mysticism in philosophy is sometimes spoken of as *rationalism*. Rationalism insists that all our beliefs ought ultimately to find for themselves articulate grounds. Such grounds, for rationalism, must consist of four things: (1) definitely statable abstract principles; (2) definite facts of sensation; (3) definite hypotheses based on such facts; and (4) definite inferences logically drawn. Vague impressions of something indefinable have no place in the rationalistic system, which on its positive side is surely a splendid intellectual tendency, for not only are all our philosophies fruits of it, but physical science (amongst other good things) is its result.

Nevertheless, if we look on man's whole mental life as it exists, on the life of men that lies in them apart from their learning and science, and that they inwardly and privately follow, we have to confess that the part of it of which rationalism can give an account is relatively superficial. It is the part that has the *prestige* undoubtedly, for it has the loquacity, it can challenge you for proofs, and chop logic, and put you down with words. But it will fail to convince or convert you all the same, if your dumb intuitions are opposed to its conclusions. If you have intuitions at all, they come from a deeper level of your nature than the loquacious level which rationalism inhabits. Your whole subconscious life, your impulses, your faiths, your needs, your divinations, have prepared the premises, of which your consciousness now feels the weight of the result; and something in you absolutely *knows* that that result must be truer than any logic-chopping rationalistic talk, however clever, that may contradict it. This inferiority of the rationalistic level in founding belief is just as manifest when rationalism argues for religion as when it argues against it. That vast literature of the proofs of God's existence drawn from the order of nature, which a century ago seemed so overwhelmingly convincing, to-day does little more than gather dust in libraries, for the simple reason that our generation has ceased to believe in the kind of God it argued for. Whatever sort of a being God may be, we *know* to-day that he is nevermore that mere external inventor of "contrivances" intended to make manifest his "glory" in which our great-grandfathers took such satisfaction, though just how we know this we cannot possibly make clear by words either to others or to ourselves. I defy any of you here fully to account for your persuasion that if a God exist he must be a more cosmic and tragic personage than that Being.

The truth is that in the metaphysical or religious sphere, articulate reasons are cogent for us only when our inarticulate feelings of reality have already been impressed in favor of the same conclusion. Then, indeed, our intuitions and our reason work together, and great world-ruling systems, like that of the Buddhist or of the Catholic philosophy, may grow up. Our impulsive belief is here always what sets up the original body of truth, and our articulately verbalized philosophy is but its showy translation into formulas. The unreasoned and immediate assurance is the deep thing in us, the reasoned argument is but a surface exhibition. Instinct leads, intelligence does but follow. If a person feels the presence of a living God after the fashion shown by my quotations, your critical arguments, be they never so superior, will vainly set themselves to change his faith.

Please observe, however, that I do not yet say that it is *better* that the subconscious and non-rational should thus hold primacy in the religious realm. I confine myself to simply pointing out that they do so hold it as a matter of fact.

So much for our sense of the reality of the religious objects. Let me now say a brief word more about the attitudes they characteristically awaken.

We have already agreed that they are *solemn*; and we have seen reason to think that the most distinctive of them is the sort of joy which may result in extreme cases from absolute self-surrender. The sense of the kind of object to which the surrender is made has much to do with determining the precise complexion of the joy; and the whole phenomenon is more complex than any simple formula allows. In the literature of the subject, sadness and gladness have each been emphasized in turn. The ancient saying that the first maker of the Gods was fear receives voluminous corroboration from every age of religious history; but none the less does religious history show the part which joy has evermore tended to play. Sometimes the joy has been primary; sometimes secondary, being the gladness of deliverance from the fear. This latter state of things, being the more complex, is also the more complete; and as we proceed, I think we shall have abundant reason for refusing to leave out either the sadness or the gladness, if we look at religion with the breadth of view which it demands. Stated in the completest possible terms, a man's religion involves both moods of contraction and moods of expansion of his being. But the quantitative mixture and order of these moods vary so much from one age of the world, from one system of thought, and from one individual to another, that you may insist either on the dread and the submission, or on the peace and the freedom as the essence of the matter, and still remain materially within the limits of the truth. The constitutionally sombre and the constitutionally sanguine onlooker are bound to emphasize opposite aspects of what lies before their eyes.

The constitutionally sombre religious person makes even of his religious peace a very sober thing. Danger still hovers in the air about it. Flexion and contraction are not wholly checked. It were sparrowlike and childish after our deliverance to explode into twittering laughter and caper-cutting, and utterly to forget the imminent hawk on bough. Lie low, rather, lie low; for you are in the hands of a living God. In the Book of Job, for example, the impotence of man and the omnipotence of God is the exclusive burden of its author's mind. "It is as high as heaven; what canst thou do?—deeper than hell; what canst thou know?" There is an astringent relish about the truth of this conviction which some men can feel, and which for them is as near an approach as can be made to the feeling of religious joy.

> "In Job," says that coldly truthful writer, the author of Mark Rutherford, "God reminds us that man is not the measure of his creation. The world is immense, constructed on no plan or theory which the intellect of man can grasp. It is *transcendent* everywhere. This is the burden of every verse, and is the secret, if there be one, of the poem. Sufficient or insufficient, there is nothing more. . . . God is great, we know not his ways. He takes from us all we have, but yet if we possess our souls in patience, we *may* pass the valley of the shadow, and come out in sunlight again. We may or we may not! . . . What more have we to say now than God said from the whirlwind over two thousand five hundred years ago?"[7]

If we turn to the sanguine onlooker, on the other hand, we find that deliverance is felt as incomplete unless the burden be altogether overcome and the danger forgotten. Such onlookers give us definitions that seem to the sombre minds of whom we have just been speaking to leave out all the solemnity that makes religious peace so different from merely animal joys. In the opinion of some writers an attitude might be called religious, though no touch were left in it of sacrifice or submission, no tendency to flexion, no bowing of the head. Any "habitual and regulated admiration," says Professor J. R. Seeley,[8] "is worthy to be called a religion"; and accordingly he thinks that our Music, our Science, and our so-called "Civilization," as these things are now organized and admiringly believed in, form the more genuine religions of our time. Certainly the unhesitating and unreasoning way in which we feel that we must inflict our civilization upon "lower" races, by means of Hotchkiss guns, etc., reminds one of nothing so much as the early spirit of Islam spreading its religion by the sword.

---

[7] Mark Rutherford's Deliverance, London, 1885, pp. 196, 198.

[8] In his book (too little read, I fear), Natural Religion, 3d edition, Boston, 1886, pp. 91, 122.

VI.A.2. Religion and Neurology

WILLIAM JAMES

William James (1842–1910) brought to his examination of the phenomenology of religious experience a candid consideration of the charge that such experiences are symptoms of psychopathology. He found phenomenological similarities between psychosis and religious experience clear and undeniable. Great religious personages have often heard voices, seen visions, fallen into trances, and "presented all sorts of peculiarities which are ordinarily classed as pathological," and James cites instances. But he also found the arguments made on the basis of such observed similarities unconvincing. James gives the name "medical materialism" to the attempt to undermine the authenticity or authority of religious experience by attributing it to organic causes or disorders. He argues that every aspect of human experience, our lowliest urge to the highest flight of genius, is organically grounded. He insists that states of mind must be judged not by their origins but by their fruits. The products of science as much as those of religion have their origins in the bodily processes of individuals, and scientists also on occasion manifest morbid tendencies. Just as these tendencies are irrelevant to the value of their scientific discoveries, so also are the pathological conditions of mystics irrelevant to the value of their religious teachings.

The question, What are the religious propensities? and the question, What is their philosophic significance? are two entirely different orders of question from the logical point of view; and, as a failure to recognize this fact distinctly may breed confusion, I wish to insist upon the point a little before we enter into the documents and materials to which I have referred.

In recent books on logic, distinction is made between two orders of inquiry concerning anything. First, what is the nature of it? how did it come about? what is its constitution, origin, and history? And second, What is its importance, meaning, or significance, now that it is once here? The answer to the one question is given in an *existential judgment* or proposition. The answer to the other is a *proposition of value*, what the Germans call a *Werthurtheil*, or what we may, if we like, denominate a *spiritual judgment*. Neither judgment can be deduced immediately from the other. They proceed from diverse intellectual preoccupations, and the mind combines them only by making them first separately, and then adding them together.

From *The Varieties of Religious Experience* (New York: Macmillan, 1961), pp. 23–38

In the matter of religions it is particularly easy to distinguish the two orders of question. Every religious phenomenon has its history and its derivation from natural antecedents. What is nowadays called the higher criticism of the Bible is only a study of the Bible from this existential point of view, neglected too much by the earlier church. Under just what biographic conditions did the sacred writers bring forth their various contributions to the holy volume? And what had they exactly in their several individual minds, when they delivered their utterances? These are manifestly questions of historical fact, and one does not see how the answer to them can decide offhand the still further question: of what use should such a volume, with its manner of coming into existence so defined, be to us as a guide to life and a revelation? To answer this other question we must have already in our mind some sort of a general theory as to what the peculiarities in a thing should be which give it value for purposes of revelation; and this theory itself would be what I just called a spiritual judgment. Combining it with our existential judgment, we might indeed deduce another spiritual judgment as to the Bible's worth. Thus if our theory of revelation-value were to affirm that any book, to possess it, must have been composed automatically or not by the free caprice of the writer, or that it must exhibit no scientific and historic errors and express no local or personal passions, the Bible would probably fare ill at our hands. But if, on the other hand, our theory should allow that a book may well be a revelation in spite of errors and passions and deliberate human composition, if only it be a true record of the inner experiences of great-souled persons wrestling with the crises of their fate, then the verdict would be much more favorable. You see that the existential facts by themselves are insufficient for determining the value; and the best adepts of the higher criticism accordingly never confound the existential with the spiritual problem. With the same conclusions of fact before them, some take one view, and some another, of the Bible's value as a revelation, according as their spiritual judgment as to the foundation of values differs.

I make these general remarks about the two sorts of judgment, because there are many religious persons—some of you now present, possibly, are among them—who do not yet make a working use of the distinction, and who may therefore feel first a little startled at the purely existential point of view from which in the following lectures the phenomena of religious experience must be considered. When I handle them biologically and psychologically as if they were mere curious facts of individual history, some of you may think it a degradation of so sublime a subject, and may even suspect me, until my purpose gets more fully expressed, of deliberately seeking to discredit the religious side of life.

Such a result is of course absolutely alien to my intention; and since such a prejudice on your part would seriously obstruct the due effect of much of what I have to relate, I will devote a few more words to the point.

There can be no doubt that as a matter of fact a religious life, exclusively pursued, does tend to make the person exceptional and eccentric. I speak not now of your ordinary religious believer, who follows the conventional observances of his country, whether it be Buddhist, Christian, or Mohammedan. His religion has been made for him by others, communicated to him by tradition, determined to fixed forms by imitation, and retained by habit. It would profit us little to study this second-hand religious life. We must make search rather for the original experiences which were the pattern-setters to all this mass of suggested feeling and imitated conduct. These experiences we can only find in individuals for whom religion exists not as a dull habit, but as an acute fever rather. But such individuals are "geniuses" in the religious line; and like many other geniuses who have brought forth fruits effective enough for commemoration in the pages of biography, such religious geniuses have often shown symptoms of nervous instability. Even more perhaps than other kinds of genius, religious leaders have been subject to abnormal psychical visitations. Invariably they have been creatures of exalted emotional sensibility. Often they have led a discordant inner life, and had melancholy during a part of their career. They have known no measure, been liable to obsessions and fixed ideas; and frequently they have fallen into trances, heard voices, seen visions, and presented all sorts of peculiarities which are ordinarily classed as pathological. Often, moreover, these pathological features in their career have helped to give them their religious authority and influence.

If you ask for a concrete example, there can be no better one than is furnished by the person of George Fox. The Quaker religion which he founded is something which it is impossible to overpraise. In a day of shams, it was a religion of veracity rooted in spiritual inwardness, and a return to something more like the original gospel truth than men had ever known in England. So far as our Christian sects today are evolving into liberality, they are simply reverting in essence to the position which Fox and the early Quakers so long ago assumed. No one can pretend for a moment that in point of spiritual sagacity and capacity, Fox's mind was unsound. Everyone who confronted him personally, from Oliver Cromwell down to county magistrates and jailers, seems to have acknowledged his superior power. Yet from the point of view of his nervous constitution, Fox was a psychopath or *détraqué* of the deepest dye. His Journal abounds in entries of this sort:—

> "As I was walking with several friends, I lifted up my head, and saw three steeple-house spires, and they struck at my life. I asked them what place that was? They said, Lichfield. Immediately the word of the Lord came to me, that I must go thither. Being come to the house we were going to, I wished the friends to walk into the house, saying nothing to them of whither I was to go. As soon as they were gone I stept away, and went by my eye over hedge and ditch till I came within a mile of Lichfield; where, in a great field, shepherds were keeping their sheep. Then was I commanded by the Lord to pull off my shoes. I stood still, for it was winter: but the word of the Lord was like a fire in me. So I put off my shoes and left them with the shepherds; and the poor shepherds trembled, and were astonished. Then I walked on about a mile, and as soon as I was got within the city, the word of the Lord came to me again, saying: Cry, 'Wo to the bloody city of Lichfield!' So I went up and down the streets, crying with a loud voice, Wo to the bloody city of Lichfield! It being market day, I went into the market-place, and to and fro in the several parts of it, and made stands crying as before, Wo to the bloody city of Lichfield! And no one laid hands on

me. As I went thus crying through the streets, there seemed to me to be a channel of blood running down the streets, and the market-place appeared like a pool of blood. When I had declared what was upon me, and felt myself clear, I went out of the town in peace; and returning to the shepherds gave them some money, and took my shoes of them again. But the fire of the Lord was so on my feet, and all over me, that I did not matter to put on my shoes again, and was at a stand whether I should or no, till I felt freedom from the Lord so to do: then, after I had washed my feet, I put on my shoes again. After this a deep consideration came upon me, for what reason I should be sent to cry against that city, and call it The bloody city! For though the parliament had the minister one while, and the king another, and much blood had been shed in the town during the wars between them, yet there was no more than had befallen many other places. But afterwards I came to understand, that in the Emperor Diocletian's time a thousand Christians were martyr'd in Lichfield. So I was to go, without my shoes, through the channel of their blood, and into the pool of their blood in the market-place, that I might raise up the memorial of the blood of those martyrs, which had been shed above a thousand years before, and lay cold in their streets. So the sense of this blood was upon me, and I obeyed the word of the Lord."

Bent as we are on studying religion's existential conditions, we cannot possibly ignore these pathological aspects of the subject. We must describe and name them just as if they occurred in non-religious men. It is true that we instinctively recoil from seeing an object to which our emotions and affections are committed handled by the intellect as any other object is handled. The first thing the intellect does with an object is to class it along with something else. But any object that is infinitely important to us and awakens our devotion feels to us also as if it must be *sui generis* and unique. Probably a crab would be filled with a sense of personal outrage if it could hear us class it without ado or apology as a crustacean, and thus dispose of it. "I am no such thing," it would say; "I am MYSELF, MYSELF alone."

The next thing the intellect does is to lay bare the causes in which the thing originates. Spinoza says: "I will analyze the actions and appetites of men as if it were a question of lines, of planes, and of solids." And elsewhere he remarks that he will consider our passions and their properties with the same eye with which he looks on all other natural things, since the consequences of our affections flow from their nature with the same necessity as it results from the nature of a triangle that its three angles should be equal to two right angles. Similarly M. Taine, in the introduction to his history of English literature, has written: "Whether facts be moral or physical, it makes no matter. They always have their causes. There are causes for ambition, courage, veracity, just as there are for digestion, muscular movement, animal heat. Vice and virtue are products like vitriol and sugar." When we read such proclamations of the intellect bent on showing the existential conditions of absolutely everything we feel—quite apart from our legitimate impatience at the somewhat ridiculous swagger of the program, in view of what the authors are actually able to perform—menaced and negated in the springs of our innermost life.

Such cold-blooded assimilations threaten, we think, to undo our soul's vital secrets, as if the same breath which should succeed in explaining their origin would simultaneously explain away their significance, and make them appear of no more preciousness, either, than the useful groceries of which M. Taine speaks.

Perhaps the commonest expression of this assumption that spiritual value is undone if lowly origin be asserted is seen in those comments which unsentimental people so often pass on their more sentimental acquaintances. Alfred believes in immortality so strongly because his temperament is so emotional. Fanny's extraordinary conscientiousness is merely a matter of overinstigated nerves. William's melancholy about the universe is due to bad digestion—probably his liver is torpid. Eliza's delight in her church is a symptom of her hysterical constitution. Peter would be less troubled about his soul if he would take more exercise in the open air, etc. A more fully developed example of the same kind of reasoning is the fashion, quite common nowadays among certain writers, of criticizing the religious emotions by showing a connection between them and the sexual life. Conversion is a crisis of puberty and adolescence. The macerations of saints, and the devotion of missionaries, are only instances of parental instinct of self-sacrifice gone astray. For the hysterical nun, starving for natural life, Christ is but an imaginary substitute for a more earthly object of affection. And the like.[1]

---

[1] As with many ideas that float in the air of one's time, this notion shrinks from dogmatic general statement and expresses itself only partially and by innuendo. It seems to me that few conceptions are less instructive than this re-interpretation of religion as perverted sexuality. It reminds one, so crudely is it often employed, of the famous Catholic taunt, that the Reformation may be best understood by remembering that its *fons et origo* was Luther's wish to marry a nun:—the effects are infinitely wider than the alleged causes, and for the most part opposite in nature. It is true that in the vast collection of religious phenomena, some are undisguisedly amatory—e.g., sex-deities and obscene rites in polytheism, and ecstatic feelings of union with the Savior in a few Christian mystics. But then why not equally call religion an aberration of the digestive function, and prove one's point by the worship of Bacchus and Ceres, or by the ecstatic feelings of some other saints about the Eucharist? Religious language clothes itself in such poor symbols as our life affords, and the whole organism gives overtones of comment whenever the mind is strongly stirred to expression. Language drawn from eating and drinking is probably as common in religious literature as is language drawn from the sexual life. We "hunger and thirst" after righteousness; we "find the Lord a sweet savor;" we "taste and see that he is good." "Spiritual milk for American babes, drawn from the breasts of both testaments," is a subtitle of the once famous New England Primer, and Christian devotional literature indeed quite floats in milk, thought of from the point of view, not of the mother, but of the greedy babe.

Saint Francois de Sales, for instance, thus describes the "orison of quietude": "In this state the soul is like a little child still at the breast, whose mother, to caress him whilst he is still in her arms, makes her milk distill into his mouth without his even moving his lips. So it is here. . . . Our Lord desires that our will should be satisfied with sucking the milk which His Majesty pours into our mouth, and that we should relish the sweetness without even knowing that it cometh from the Lord." And again: "Consider the little infants, united and joined to the breasts of their nursing mothers, you will see that from time to time they press themselves closer by little starts to which the pleasure of sucking prompts them. Even so, during its orison, the heart united to its God oftentimes makes attempts at closer union by

We are surely all familiar in a general way with this method of discrediting states of mind for which we have an antipathy. We all use it to some degree in criticizing persons whose states of mind we regard as overstrained. But when other people criticize our own more exalted soul-flights by calling them 'nothing but' expressions of our organic disposition, we feel outraged and hurt, for we know that, whatever be our organism's peculiarities, our mental states have their substantive value as revelations of the living truth; and we wish that all this medical materialism could be made to hold its tongue.

Medical materialism seems indeed a good appellation for the too simple-minded system of thought which we are considering. Medical materialism finishes up Saint Paul by calling his vision on the road to Damascus a discharging lesion of the occipital cortex, he being an epileptic. It snuffs out Saint Teresa as an hysteric, Saint Francis of Assisi as an hereditary degenerate. George Fox's discontent with the shams of his age, and his pining for spiritual veracity, it treats as a symptom of a disordered colon. Carlyle's organ-tones of misery

---

movements during which it presses closer upon the divine sweetness." Chemin de la Perfection, ch. xxxi.; Amour de Dieu, vii., ch. i.

In fact, one might almost as well interpret religion as a perversion of the respiratory function. The Bible is full of the language of respiratory oppression: "Hide not thine ear at my breathing; my groaning is not hid from thee; my heart panteth, my strength faileth me; my bones are hot with my roaring all the night long; as the hart panteth after the water-brooks, so my soul panteth after thee, O my God." *God's Breath in Man* is the title of the chief work of our best known American mystic (Thomas Lake Harris); and in certain non-Christian countries the foundation of all religious discipline consists in regulation of the inspiration and expiration.

These arguments are as good as much of the reasoning one hears in favor of the sexual theory. But the champions of the latter will then say that their chief argument has no analogue elsewhere. The two main phenomena of religion, namely, melancholy and conversion, they will say, are essentially phenomena of adolescence, and therefore synchronous with the development of sexual life. To which the retort again is easy. Even were the asserted synchrony unrestrictedly true as a fact (which it is not), it is not only the sexual life, but the entire higher mental life which awakens during adolescence. One might then as well set up the thesis that the interest in mechanics, physics, chemistry, logic, philosophy, and sociology, which springs up during adolescent years along with that in poetry and religion, is also a perversion of the sexual instinct:—but that would be too absurd. Moreover, if the argument from synchrony is to decide, what is to be done with the fact that the religious age *par excellence* would seem to be old age, when the uproar of sexual life is past?

The plain truth is that to interpret religion one must in the end look at the immediate content of the religious consciousness. The moment one does this, one sees how wholly disconnected it is in the main from the content of the sexual consciousness. Everything about the two things differ, objects, moods, faculties concerned, and acts impelled to. Any *general* assimilation is simply impossible: what we find most often is complete hostility and contrast. If now the defenders of the sex-theory say that this makes no difference to their thesis; that without the chemical contributions which the sex-organs make to the blood, the brain would not be nourished so as to carry on religious activities, this final proposition may be true or not true; but at any rate it has become profoundly uninstructive: we can deduce no consequences from it which help us to interpret religion's meaning or value. In this sense the religious life depends just as much upon the spleen, the pancreas, and the kidneys as on the sexual apparatus, and the whole theory has lost its point in evaporating into a vague general assertion of the dependence, *somehow*, of the mind upon the body.

it accounts for by a gastro-duodenal catarrh. All such mental overtensions, it says, are, when you come to the bottom of the matter, mere affairs of diathesis (auto-intoxications most probably), due to the perverted action of various glands which physiology will yet discover.

And medical materialism then thinks that the spiritual authority of all such personages is successfully undermined [2]

Let us ourselves look at the matter in the largest possible way. Modern psychology, finding definite psycho-physical connections to hold good, assumes as a convenient hypothesis that the dependence of mental states upon bodily conditions must be thoroughgoing and complete. If we adopt the assumption, then of course what medical materialism insists on must be true in a general way, if not in every detail: Saint Paul certainly had once an epileptoid, if not an epileptic seizure; George Fox was an hereditary degenerate; Carlyle was undoubtedly auto-intoxicated by some organ or other, no matter which—and the rest. But now, I ask you, how can such an existential account of facts of mental history decide in one way or another upon their spiritual significance? According to the general postulate of psychology just referred to, there is not a single one of our states of mind, high or low, healthy or morbid, that has not some organic process as its condition. Scientific theories are organically conditioned just as much as religious emotions are; and if we only knew the facts intimately enough, we should doubtless see "the liver" determining the dicta of the sturdy atheist as decisively as it does those of the Methodist under conviction anxious about his soul. When it alters in one way the blood that percolates it, we get the methodist, when another way, we get the atheist form of mind. So of all our raptures and our drynesses, our longings and pantings, our questions and beliefs. They are equally organically founded, be they religious or of non-religious content.

To plead the organic causation of a religious state of mind, then, in refutation of its claim to possess superior spiritual value, is quite illogical and arbitrary, unless one has already worked out in advance some psycho-physical theory connecting spiritual values in general with determinate sorts of physiological change. Otherwise none of our thoughts and feelings, not even our scientific doctrines, not even our *dis*-beliefs, could retain any value as revelations of the truth, for every one of them without exception flows from the state of its possessor's body at the time.

It is needless to say that medical materialism draws in point of fact no such sweeping skeptical conclusion. It is sure, just as every simple man is sure, that some states of mind are inwardly superior to others, and reveal to us more truth, and in this it simply makes use of an ordinary spiritual judgment. It has no physiological theory of the production of these its favorite states, by which it may accredit them, and its attempt to discredit the states which it dislikes, by vaguely associating them with nerves and liver, and connecting them with names connoting bodily affliction, is altogether illogical and inconsistent.

Let us play fair in this whole matter, and be quite candid with ourselves and with the facts. When we think certain states of mind superior to others, is

---

it ever because of what we know concerning their organic antecedents? No! it is always for two entirely different reasons. It is either because we take an immediate delight in them; or else it is because we believe them to bring us good consequential fruits for life. When we speak disparagingly of "feverish fancies," surely the fever-process as such is not the ground of our disesteem—for aught we know to the contrary, 103° or 104° Fahrenheit might be a much more favorable temperature for truths to germinate and sprout in, than the more ordinary blood-heat of 97 or 98 degrees. It is either the disagreeableness itself of the fancies, or their inability to bear the criticisms of the convalescent hour. When we praise the thoughts which health brings, health's peculiar chemical metabolisms have nothing to do with determining our judgment. We know in fact almost nothing about these metabolisms. It is the character of inner happiness in the thoughts which stamps them as good, or else their consistency with our other opinions and their serviceability for our needs, which make them pass for true in our esteem.

Now the more intrinsic and the more remote of these criteria do not always hang together. Inner happiness and serviceability do not always agree. What immediately feels most "good" is not always most "true," when measured by the verdict of the rest of experience. The difference between Philip drunk and Philip sober is the classic instance in corroboration. If merely "feeling good" could decide, drunkenness would be the supremely valid human experience. But its revelations, however acutely satisfying at the moment, are inserted into an environment which refuses to bear them out for any length of time. The consequence of this discrepancy of the two criteria is the uncertainty which still prevails over so many of our spiritual judgments. There are moments of sentimental and mystical experience—we shall hereafter hear much of them—that carry an enormous sense of inner authority and illumination with them when they come. But they come seldom, and they do not come to everyone; and the rest of life makes either no connection with them, or tends to contradict them more than it confirms them. Some persons follow more the voice of the moment in these cases, some prefer to be guided by the average results. Hence the sad discordancy of so many of the spiritual judgments of human beings; a discordancy which will be brought home to us acutely enough before these lectures end.

It is, however, a discordancy that can never be resolved by any merely medical test. A good example of the impossibility of holding strictly to the medical tests is seen in the theory of the pathological causation of genius promulgated by recent authors. "Genius," said Dr. Moreau, "is but one of the many branches of the neuropathic tree." "Genius," says Dr. Lombroso, "is a symptom of hereditary degeneration of the epileptoid variety, and is allied to moral insanity." "Whenever a man's life," writes Mr. Nisbet, "is at once sufficiently illustrious and recorded with sufficient fullness to be a subject of profitable study, he inevitably falls into the morbid category. . . . And it is worthy of remark that, as a rule, the greater the genius, the greater the unsoundness."[3]

---

[3] J. F. Nisbet: The Insanity of Genius, 3d ed., London, 1893, pp. xvi, xxiv.

Now do these authors, after having succeeded in establishing to their own satisfaction that the works of genius are fruits of disease, consistently proceed thereupon to impugn the *value* of the fruits? Do they deduce a new spiritual judgment from their new doctrine of existential conditions? Do they frankly forbid us to admire the productions of genius from now onwards? and say outright that no neuropath can ever be a revealer of new truth?

No! their immediate spiritual instincts are too strong for them here, and hold their own against inferences which, in mere love of logical consistency, medical materialism ought to be only too glad to draw. One disciple of the school, indeed, has striven to impugn the value of works of genius in a wholesale way (such works of contemporary art, namely, as he himself is unable to enjoy, and they are many) by using medical arguments.[4] But for the most part the masterpieces are left unchallenged; and the medical line of attack either confines itself to such secular productions as everyone admits to be intrinsically eccentric, or else addresses itself exclusively to religious manifestations. And then it is because the religious manifestations have been already condemned because the critic dislikes them on internal or spiritual grounds.

In the natural sciences and industrial arts it never occurs to anyone to try to refute opinions by showing up their author's neurotic constitution. Opinions here are invariably tested by logic and by experiment, no matter what may be their author's neurological type. It should be no otherwise with religious opinions. Their value can only be ascertained by spiritual judgments directly passed upon them, judgments based on our own immediate feeling primarily; and secondarily on what we can ascertain of their experiential relations to our moral needs and to the rest of what we hold as true.

Immediate luminousness, in short, *philosophical reasonableness*, and *moral helpfulness* are the only available criteria. Saint Teresa might have had the nervous system of the placidest cow, and it would not now save her theology, if the trial of the theology by these other tests should show it to be contemptible. And conversely if her theology can stand these other tests, it will make no difference how hysterical or nervously off her balance Saint Teresa may have been when she was with us here below.

You see that at bottom we are thrown back upon the general principles by which the empirical philosophy has always contended that we must be guided in our search for truth. Dogmatic philosophies have sought for tests for truth which might dispense us from appealing to the future. Some direct mark, by noting which we can be protected immediately and absolutely, now and forever, against all mistake—such has been the darling dream of philosophic dogmatists. It is clear that the *origin* of the truth would be an admirable criterion of this sort, if only the various origins could be discriminated from one another from this point of view, and the history of dogmatic opinion shows that origin has always been a favorite test. Origin in immediate intuition; origin in pontifical authority; origin in supernatural revelation, as by vision, hearing, or unaccountable impression, origin in direct possession by a

---

[4] Max Nordau, in his bulky book entitled *Degeneration*.

higher spirit, expressing itself in prophecy and warning; origin in automatic utterance generally—these origins have been stock warrants for the truth of one opinion after another which we find represented in religious history. The medical materialists are therefore only so many belated dogmatists, neatly turning the tables on their predecessors by using the criterion of origin in a destructive instead of an accreditive way.

They are effective with their talk of pathological origin only so long as supernatural origin is pleaded by the other side, and nothing but the argument from origin is under discussion. But the argument from origin has seldom been used alone, for it is too obviously insufficient. Dr. Maudsley is perhaps the cleverest of the rebutters of supernatural religion on the grounds of origin. Yet he finds himself forced to write:—

"What right have we to believe Nature under any obligation to do her work by means of complete minds only? She may find an incomplete mind a more suitable instrument for a particular purpose. It is the work that is done, and the quality in the worker by which it was done, that is alone of moment; and it may be no great matter from a cosmical standpoint, if in other qualities of character he was singularly defective—if indeed he were hypocrite, adulterer, eccentric, or lunatic. . . . Home we come again, then, to the old and last resort of certitude—namely the common assent of mankind, or of the competent by instruction and training among mankind."[5]

In other words, not its origin, but *the way in which it works on the whole*, is Dr. Maudsley's final test of a belief. This is our own empiricist criterion; and this criterion the stoutest insisters on supernatural origin have also been forced to use in the end. Among the visions and messages some have always been too patently silly, among the trances and convulsive seizures some have been too fruitless for conduct and character, to pass themselves off as significant, still less as divine. In the history of Christian mysticism the problem how to discriminate between such messages and experiences as were really divine miracles, and such others as the demon in his malice was able to counterfeit, thus making the religious person twofold more the child of hell he was before, has always been a difficult one to solve, needing all the sagacity and experience of the best directors of conscience. In the end it had to come to our empiricist criterion: By their fruits ye shall know them, not by their roots. Jonathan Edwards' Treatise on Religious Affections is an elaborate working out of this thesis. The *roots* of a man's virtue are inaccessible to us. No appearances whatever are infallible proofs of grace. Our practice is the only sure evidence, even to ourselves, that we are genuinely Christians.

"In forming a judgment of ourselves now," Edwards writes, "we should certainly adopt that evidence which our supreme Judge will chiefly make use of when we come to stand before him at the last day. . . . There is not one grace of the Spirit of God, of the existence of which, in any professor of religion, Christian practice is not the most decisive evidence. . . . The degree in which our experience is productive of

---

[5] H. Maudsley: Natural Causes and Supernatural Seemings, 1886, pp. 257, 258.

practice shows the degree in which our experience is spiritual and divine."

Catholic writers are equally emphatic. The good dispositions which a vision, or voice, or other apparent heavenly favor leave behind them are the only marks by which we may be sure they are not possible deceptions of the tempter. Says Saint Teresa:—

"Like imperfect sleep which, instead of giving more strength to the head, doth but leave it the more exhausted, the result of mere operations of the imagination is but to weaken the soul. Instead of nourishment and energy she reaps only lassitude and disgust: whereas a genuine heavenly vision yields to her a harvest of ineffable spiritual riches, and an admirable renewal of bodily strength. I alleged these reasons to those who so often accused my visions of being the work of the enemy of mankind and the sport of my imagination. . . . I showed them the jewels which the divine hand had left with me:—they were my actual dispositions. All those who knew me saw that I was changed; my confessor bore witness to the fact; this improvement, palpable in all respects, far from being hidden, was brilliantly evident to all men. As for myself, it was impossible to believe that if the demon were its author, he could have used, in order to lose me and lead me to hell, an expedient so contrary to his own interests as that of uprooting my vices, and filling me with masculine courage and other virtues instead, for I saw clearly that a single one of these visions was enough to enrich me with all that wealth."[6]

I fear I may have made a longer excursus than was necessary, and that fewer words would have dispelled the uneasiness which may have arisen among some of you as I announced my pathological programme. At any rate you must all be ready now to judge the religious life by its results exclusively, and I shall assume that the bugaboo of morbid origin will scandalize your piety no more.

Still, you may ask me, if its results are to be the ground of our final spiritual estimate of a religious phenomenon, why threaten us at all with so much existential study of its conditions? Why not simply leave pathological questions out?

To this I reply in two ways: First, I say, irrepressible curiosity imperiously leads one on; and I say, secondly, that it always leads to a better understanding of a thing's significance to consider its exaggerations and perversions, its equivalents and substitutes and nearest relatives elsewhere. Not that we may thereby swamp the thing in the wholesale condemnation which we pass on its inferior congeners, but rather that we may by contrast ascertain the more precisely in what its merits consist, by learning at the same time to what particular dangers of corruption it may also be exposed.

Insane conditions have this advantage, that they isolate special factors of

---

[6] Autobiography, ch. xxviii.

the mental life, and enable us to inspect them unmasked by their more usual surroundings. They play the part in mental anatomy which the scalpel and the microscope play in the anatomy of the body. To understand a thing rightly we need to see it both out of its environment and in it, and to have acquaintance with the whole range of its variations. The study of hallucinations has in this way been for psychologists the key to their comprehension of normal sensation, that of illusions has been the key to the right comprehension of perception. Morbid impulses and imperative conceptions, "fixed ideas," so called, have thrown a flood of light on the psychology of the normal will; and obsessions and delusions have performed the same service for that of the normal faculty of belief.

Similarly, the nature of genius has been illuminated by the attempts, of which I already made mention, to class it with psychopathological phenomena. Borderland insanity, crankiness, insane temperament, loss of mental balance, psychopathic degeneration (to use a few of the many synonyms by which it has been called), has certain peculiarities and liabilities which, when combined with a superior quality of intellect in an individual, make it more probable that he will make his mark and affect his age, than if his temperament were less neurotic. There is of course no special affinity between crankiness as such and superior intellect,[7] for most psychopaths have feeble intellects, and superior intellects more commonly have normal nervous systems. But the psychopathic temperament, whatever be the intellect with which it finds itself paired, often brings with it ardor and excitability of character. The cranky person has extraordinary emotional susceptibility. He is liable to fixed ideas and obsessions. His conceptions tend to pass immediately into belief and action; and when he gets a new idea, he has no rest till he proclaims it, or in some way "works it off." "What shall I think of it?" a common person says to himself about a vexed question; but in a "cranky" mind "What must I do about it?" is the form the question tends to take. In the autobiography of that high-souled woman, Mrs. Annie Besant, I read the following passage: "Plenty of people wish well to any good cause, but very few care to exert themselves to help it, and still fewer will risk anything in its support. 'Someone ought to do it, but why should I?' is the ever reëchoed phrase of weak-kneed amiability. 'Someone ought to do it, so why not I?' is the cry of some earnest servant of man, eagerly forward springing to face some perilous duty. Between these two sentences lie whole centuries of moral evolution." True enough! and between these two sentences lie also the different destinies of the ordinary sluggard and the psychopathic man. Thus, when a superior intellect and a psychopathic temperament coalesce—as in the endless permutations and combinations of human faculty, they are bound to coalesce often enough—in the same individual, we have the best possible condition for the kind of effective genius that gets into the biographical dictionaries. Such men do not remain mere critics and understanders with their intellect. Their ideas possess them, they inflict them, for better or worse, upon their companions or their age. It is they who

---

[7] Superior intellect, as Professor Bain has admirably shown, seems to consist in nothing so much as in a large development of the faculty of association by similarity.

get counted when Messrs. Lombroso, Nisbet, and others invoke statistics to defend their paradox.

To pass now to religious phenomena, take the melancholy which, as we shall see, constitutes an essential moment in every complete religious evolution. Take the happiness which achieved religious belief confers. Take the trance-like states of insight into truth which all religious mystics report.[8] These are each and all of them special cases of kinds of human experience of much wider scope. Religious melancholy, whatever peculiarities it may have *qua* religious, is at any rate melancholy. Religious happiness is happiness. Religious trance is trance. And the moment we renounce the absurd notion that a thing is exploded away as soon as it is classed with others, or its origin is shown; the moment we agree to stand by experimental results and inner quality, in judging of values—who does not see that we are likely to ascertain the distinctive significance of religious melancholy and happiness, or of religious trances, far better by comparing them as conscientiously as we can with other varieties of melancholy, happiness, and trance, than by refusing to consider their place in any more general series, and treating them as if they were outside of nature's order altogether?

I hope that the course of these lectures will confirm us in this supposition. As regards the psychopathic origin of so many religious phenomena, that would not be in the least surprising or disconcerting, even were such phenomena certified from on high to be the most precious of human experiences. No one organism can possibly yield to its owner the whole body of truth. Few of us are not in some way infirm, or even diseased; and our very infirmities help us unexpectedly. In the psychopathic temperament we have the emotionality which is the *sine qua non* of moral perception; we have the intensity and tendency to emphasis which are the essence of practical moral vigor; and we have the love of metaphysics and mysticism which carry one's interests beyond the surface of the sensible world. What, then, is more natural than that this temperament should introduce one to regions of religious truth, to corners of the universe, which your robust Philistine type of nervous system, forever offering its biceps to be felt, thumping its breast, and thanking Heaven that it hasn't a single morbid fiber in its composition, would be sure to hide forever from its self-satisfied possessors?

If there were such a thing as inspiration from a higher realm, it might well be that the neurotic temperament would furnish the chief condition of the requisite receptivity. And having said thus much, I think that I may let the matter of religion and neuroticism drop.

---

[8] I may refer to a criticism of the insanity theory of genius in the Psychological Review, ii., 287 (1895).

VI.A.3. Belief and Delusion: Their Common Origin but Different Course of Development

HERMANN LENZ

Hermann Lenz (1913–), a medical doctor and professor of psychiatry at the University of Vienna, reports here on a comparative study of twenty-five victims of delusion and a number of artists and religious mystics. Dr. Lenz finds that the delusional experiences of all these persons and some scientists as well, in themselves, are so similar as to be indistinguishable, but important differences show up in the aftermath. Religious mystics, artists, and scientists experience both confidence and doubt, their sense of mission tends to be realistic, and their relations with other persons are normal and creative. Victims of delusion, on the other hand, experience no doubt whatever and seem to lose their personal freedom or ability to grow along with contact with their social and physical world.

Belief means believing something to be true. According to the German philosopher, Immanuel Kant, the thing in which a person believes is subjectively considered to be adequate and thus to be true. The thing believed in cannot be objectively proved by any other person, as in the case of scientific knowledge. It must therefore be presumed there is no difference between the belief of a healthy person and that of, for example, a person who is convinced of some delusory ideas. This has been pointed out often by psychiatrists. For example, K. Schneider says, "Belief, the only criterion of which is subjective certainty, cannot basically be distinguished psychologically from delusion."[1] He goes on to say that a mystical experience on the part of a healthy person has the same significance for the person in question as has a delusion for the mentally ill person.

In the first half of this essay I shall describe the similarities between belief and delusion by comparing short extracts from the autobiographies of two well-known mystics, similar statements by Zen Buddhists about *satori* experiences, and reports of artists speaking about their acts of creation with seven aspects of irrational experiences reported by a group of mentally ill patients examined by me in 1976. In all these groups the occurrence of the experience,

From *Zygon* 18, no. 2 (June 1983): 117–137.

its structure, and its meaning were to a great extent the same. Thus I shall suggest that it is impossible to distinguish phenomenologically mystical and delusionary experiences as they are originally reported. However, it is possible to make distinctions if one analyzes the subsequent course or life history of those having such experiences. In the second half of this paper I shall show there are significant differences between belief and delusion in terms of the kind of life led by people having religious or artistic creation experiences and by those suffering delusionary experiences.

THE EXPERIENCE OF WESTERN MYSTICS AND ZEN MASTERS

Theresa of Avila describes an experience of great significance for her in the ninth chapter of her autobiography written from 1563 to 1565. On gazing at an ecce homo picture in the oratorium she was struck down with grief and felt as if her heart were breaking, so she threw herself down in front of the picture weeping bitterly and begged for inner strength. This experience gave her a measureless feeling of clarity and truth—as she puts it—a truth above the knowledge of learned men. Again, she describes visions which she was able to recall in exact detail twenty-six years later. They had made such an impression on her that she says it was as if she necessarily had to see them, had to hear them regardless of her own volition or nonvolition.

She distinguishes very clearly between her experiences and illusions or hallucinations which she also knew existed; the deceptive character of such illusions is afterwards always known to the person in question. However, she also distinguishes her visions from intellectual visions, by which she appears to mean wishful thinking or autosuggestion. Her own visions she describes as follows, "an experience without images or words, which could be compared to knowing of the near presence of a second person in a pitch-dark cellar without being able to see, hear or touch him."[2] The intellect is not active in this: it is always a passive experience of short duration. The experience is a grace, and Theresa is emphatic that it is of a compelling force. She describes her state of mind during such experiences stating that overwhelming pain and indescribably great joy are commingled. In the chapter dealing with union and temptation she describes a changed feeling of time and space, the impression that the senses seem not to be functioning, and a sense of lost individuality. She also says that there is a feeling of shame with regard to what has been experienced and that one would prefer to be alone. Finally, she stresses that after experiences of this kind, the memory and intellect are for a time "confused, as in madness."

We can learn about similar experiences of a mystical nature in the account dictated many years later by Ignatius of Loyola to Gonzales de Camara.[3] Here again we read about such experiences of significance now in three modes, as in the Holy Trinity. They appear with a great clarity: everything subsequently appears in a completely different light. His visions are described in a manner similar to Theresa's—for example, "it was like a snake with a great number of points, like eyes,"—not with a concrete sensual image because the experience could not be put into concrete terms, but instead with "it was like." Here again we are told of the two extremities of state of mind, the pessimistic even approaching the suicidal during such mystical experiences and also the great "joy." He later fulfilled the sense of mission involved in these experiences by writing his "Rule" founding the Jesuit Order. In his own time Saint Ignatius was on one occasion even thought to be mad.

G. Schüttler interviewed on the spot great masters of Zen Buddhism about their experiences of enlightenment or satori.[4] Ten masters reported to him the different stages of their experiences which are very similar to the mystical events. Schüttler describes the preliminary stages, which are labelled as "piece of devilry" (makyo); hallucinations, levitations, itching sensation, and so on are experienced in these stages. They are similar to the stage of hallucination of Theresa of Avila. The Enlightenment occurs only in the last stage. Here the Zen master experiences spiritual relationships, inspiring him with great respect and new importance. The experience of great importance occurs suddenly, and the sense of time vanishes. The person changes into a new person characterized by inner harmony and peace; thus the master is highly blessed in a supernatural manner. The structure of the ego is not destroyed but is now open to the universe (god).

THE EXPERIENCE OF CREATIVITY IN ARTISTS

One can, however, also draw comparisons between these experiences and creative acts as they are described by artists or poets. For example, on 11 March 1829, Johann Wolfgang von Goethe said to J. P. Eckermann: "Any productivity of the highest kind, any important *aperçu*, any invention, any great thought which bears fruit and has results, lies beyond the power of any man and is loftier than all earthly authority. In the same way man receives all his unhoped for thoughts from above, these must be considered gifts of God pure and simple, to be accepted with grateful thanks and to be honoured. This experience is related to the demonic, which overpowers man as it likes, and to which he must surrender all unaware, while he thinks he is acting of his own free will."[5] Hence suddenly something (for example, an idea) gains enormous significance and, coming from outside a person, it inspires a sense of mission which cannot be shirked. The emotional tension between good and evil is also to be found here.

Another example appears in one of Wolfgang Mozart's letters, (quoted by O. Kankeleit):

> While composing a particular idea my heart grows warm. When I am not disturbed the idea becomes ever greater, spreading ever wider and brighter. When the composition is almost finished in my imagination, even if it is long, I can see it all at one glance, as if it were a beautiful picture in my mind and I cannot leave any part to be filled in later but must at once transcribe all that I have heard in my imagination. . . . All the discovering and working out goes on in me like in a wonderfully vivid dream, but hearing everything together is still the best.[6]

Mozart described how his experience is one in which he is passive, one in which everything happens at once and thus is independent of time, one which obviously fills him with a deep happiness and at the same time inspires him with a mission he must fulfill.

Alfred Kubin describes creative acts of this sort as follows: I was still feeling very moved when I wandered through the town. I went into a music hall in the evening as I was looking for neutral and yet noisy surroundings to offset an inner pressure which became stronger and stronger. Something spiritually very remarkable and decisive for me happened there, something which I cannot quite understand to this day although I have thought about it a great deal. When the orchestra began playing, my whole surroundings suddenly became brighter and clearer as in another light. In the faces of the people around me I suddenly saw something strangely animal and yet human, every noise was strangely different, freed from its origin. I heard a totality of language, jeering, moaning, booming, which I could not understand but which clearly seemed to have a quite spectral inner meaning. I grew sad although a strange feeling of wellbeing came over me and I thought again of the Klinger drawings wondering how I was now going to work. Then suddenly I was overcome by a whole whirlwind of visions of black-and-white pictures—it is quite impossible to describe the unending variety of ideas which came to my mind. I quickly left the theatre as the music and the lights disturbed me now and I wandered aimlessly through the dark streets while I was continually overcome, literally violated by a dark power which conjured up strange animals, houses, landscapes, grotesque figures and terrible situations before my eyes. I felt myself indescribably at ease in the world I had created for myself, and when I had walked for so long that I was tired I went into a little tearoom. Here, too, everything was quite strange. The moment I went in, the waitresses appeared to me to be wax dolls, animated by God knows what mechanisms. And the few customers seemed totally unreal, like shadows surprised at devilish tricks. The whole background, with a mechanical organ and bar, was suspect. It looked to me like a facade hiding the actual mystery, which was in all probability a dimly lit stable-like blood-filled cave. I made brief sketches of everything I could remember of these images which, to my surprise, kept changing, while I stayed absolutely passive. This inner turmoil lasted till I was on my way home. The Auguststrasse seemed to shrink of its own accord and a ring of mountains appeared to be growing up around our town. At home I sank as one dead onto my bed, and slept deep and dreamlessly until the evening of the next day.[7]

Here is a painter experiencing everything suddenly and unexpectedly in another clearer and brighter light, which made him happy but at the same time sad. He was completely passive; this experience broke over him like a hurricane and he felt he had to make a record of it. Everything had gained a new significance, another "face." The situation was "insubstantial," fabricated; it was no longer a representation of real life.

A CASE HISTORY OF DELUSION

In 1976 I described fifteen cases of patients who were the victims of delusion, adding to my own investigations two American cases and one Japanese case reported in psychiatric literature.[8] Since then I have been able to observe seven further cases of this kind so that the following remarks are based on twenty-five cases. Certainly these cases do not form a major part of the whole range of psychiatric illness; earlier I estimated them to be about 6 percent. This figure corresponds well to an estimate by W. Blankenburg of 5.7 percent of 405 schizophrenic patients.[9] I think it is feasible to make this comparison since Blankenburg was examining the frequency of introspection and speculation on philosophical matters in schizophrenic patients. It must not, however, be assumed that all seven symptoms of irrational thinking were to be found in all of my patients.

As a complete examination of all twenty-five cases would be far too comprehensive one case will be taken as a representative of all, and in conclusion some characteristic individual experiences of other cases will be added. Only then will the significance of the seven characteristic symptoms of delusion and their analogies to mysticism and satori be explored. In all probability mystics and people having delusions share the same basic experience. The personal accounts by artists of their creative activity also indicate an exactly similar basic experience.

Case history of U.Pr. She was the third child of an intact family with five children, her father being a graduate engineer. There was no particular evidence of a religious upbringing; however, her mother was rather strict. Once, as a small child, the patient refused to eat for a considerable length of time and was punished for this. At fifteen she became interested in Buddhism which was being studied in school. She reported having had periods of weakness at that time, and she experienced a disintegration of her feelings and believed herself to be in Nirvana. She only spoke about this years later; outwardly she merely made a somewhat dreamy impression. At sixteen, her schoolwork, which had been good up to then, suddenly deteriorated. When (in March 1973) she then told her parents about a spiritual development that enabled her to move mountains and bring mankind to the true faith, she was brought to us for in-patient treatment. Her accounts at that time were very hesitant; it was only with difficulty that she could find words for what she had experienced. She was not able to say when exactly she had had these experiences, although they all must have occurred in the previous few months. She said that everything had "come over her," "all doors were now open," she had "awoken and was in another world," she "could see through everybody," and "the measure of everything was in her." Later she said that during this first stay with us the Virgin Mary had appeared to her, "she had to gaze quite fixedly," and she had a very powerful impression of light. However, she had not wanted to speak about it at the time.

While these experiences made her very happy, there were also negative feelings. In this connection she said she "had experienced complete freedom," a freedom in which she could even have killed people, and she had been very frightened by this. She felt herself to be divided in her inmost being and spoke about an inner battle. She felt herself to be evil, and there was some indication of suicidal intention. A few days previously, on reading the word "flower," she immediately imagined a whole garden full of wonderful flowers and glorious scents and thought she had found her true personality, but now this all had disappeared. She felt she had lost her feelings; she said she was dead, no longer real; she was "only living in theory, like a machine."

Then, however, a hurricane of feeling seemed to overwhelm her. She had found "the way to God." Her previous ego had been another person; God was her spiritual father, and her parents were only her physical parents. She had experienced God without having seen or heard him; she had been "born again and could now help other people to come to the true faith." She believed herself to be saved and to have eternal life. Soon afterwards, however, there was a reversal: her "conscience-ego" was "dead," she was living apart from her true ego, she felt herself to be "an ordinary person" again, she had missed the only important thing in life and had very strong guilt feelings on this account.

In the months that followed, phases of "grace," in which she felt herself "to be one with the whole creation," alternated with much longer periods of constant depression with ideas of suicide when she felt herself to be like a machine or as if dead. Under neuroleptic therapy a considerable improvement was achieved, so that she was able to pass her exit examination at school, even though later than normal. However, she remained completely unaware that she was mentally ill. She said over a year later that the beautiful had outweighed the unpleasant, and she would gladly experience it all again. Yet this was not possible because the experience was not something you could bring about yourself, "it came over you." A few months later there was a further relapse when "everything was especially clear," her thoughts were "involved in God," her heart was burning. She later spoke of this as an experience of grace which consisted in knowing that "I am." By this she meant that through this experience she had been put in a position to receive God's thoughts and to transmit them to mankind. It seems as if, with this "I am," she wanted to proclaim her eternal being. She also said that during those months she was forced to lead a double life—a real one and a religious one. She said that her head no longer belonged to her heart and that she had lost parts of her ego. She said the same two years later during a further relapse, when she spoke of division and splintering.

In a follow-up examination four years later (early 1980), in a comparatively mentally healthy condition, she stated in connection with this that she had had the feeling in 1976 that something would remain with her that did not belong to her and yet, at the same time, she knew that, although it was something foreign to her, it was also a part of her own ego. She had been able to examine this element which was not her and yet belonged to her at close quarters and had suffered greatly. On being questioned further at this follow-up examination, she explained that her feelings, which she had transferred to her body, had burned out and her new, real ego had come from above but could not be united with her "inferior ego." Her new ego, however, had to support the other one, and so she "could not really live, only in theory." In the first two years of her psychosis she had a platonic relationship with a painter (an epilepsy sufferer, who seemed rather bigoted and made a somewhat slovenly impression). When the painter made his first shy advances, she broke off the relationship immediately and finally. Subsequently she said she was not able to reestablish a "harmony between body and soul," "nothing went deep anymore." "I cannot behave naturally any more." She felt religious thoughts as a compulsion. "If I let myself go, I could kill someone," she said at that time, smiling. The inner division remained at first, and she said she felt "blows to the soul" which she thought often lasted half an hour. In 1976 she said she felt afraid, hypnotized, and believed herself to be the "founder of Mondays." She obviously was ashamed to explain this in detail.

At the time of her last follow-up examination in 1980, still under continual narcoleptic therapy, she had already passed some minor examinations in a school of theology at a university. She believed she could have an influence on other people through television and radio, and thought the media was using her language. She said the letters of the alphabet had a very special meaning for her when they were connected with experiences of light. She only spoke about these things to me because I was the doctor in whom she had confidence; otherwise she made a relatively inconspicuous impression in everyday life.

This case history is a good example of how something gains very special significance, shuts out everything else, and transmits itself with unequalled clarity. An experience of this kind does not originate in normal sensual impressions or in wishful thinking; rather it is the interpretation of circumstances which may not be significant in themselves but which have a greater truth for the person experiencing them than what can be seen, heard, or touched. Experiences of this kind always include some feeling of vocation, a mission to be fulfilled. The patient described that she was in union with God, of whom all being was a part. She sometimes felt time was suspended for her, which she expressed in the words "I am," an expression which is reminiscent of Plotinus's concept of "is" and "always," in the meaning of eternity.[10] The emotional state during an experience of this sort is marked by either a feeling of supernatural bliss or the deepest guilt and depression. The experience is always felt to be a passive one which comes and goes suddenly, the feeling of happiness especially lasting only a very short time. The state of mind caused by such experiences cannot be considered to be the result of logical thinking. Finally, the person in question often has a feeling of shame when thinking of such experiences.

Thus the seven irrational symptoms of certain forms of delusion have been enumerated, and can be summarized as follows: (1) the experience of abnormal significance, (2) illusions or pseudohallucinations, (3) the sense of mission, (4) the suspension of time and place, (5) the extremes of mood, (6) the passive and sudden nature of such experiences, and (7) the feeling of shame.[11]

THE STRUCTURE OF DELUSION

Reflecting on autobiographies about mystically ecstatic states, satori experiences, and the act of creation in painting and poetry, one notices an amazing similarity between them and the seven symptoms of delusion in the case described above and the following case histories. Of course not all seven symptoms were present in all twenty-five cases of delusion examined. The following are individual, especially characteristic utterances of others of my patients on the subject of one or another of the symptoms.

The Experience of Abnormal Significance

3.AN.: "A light has been lit for me, I am bearing a child, that is my inner voice." The patient said this about the Bible, which had never interested him before, after a conversation with an uneducated man (a farmer). This patient was able to be almost totally cured.

DR.KO.: "He is the director of the Austrian and German television, he organizes the Salzburg Festival with my ideas; with my thoughts he wants to make decisions on world politics." A female patient said this about a university professor with whom she was obviously in love, without him having the faintest idea of this.

SCH.: "I am enlightened, the true Messiah, I possess supernatural powers." The patient came to this conclusion from harmless remarks made by people she knew, such as questions about what she thought of her colleagues or what the weather would be like the following day.

GLA.: When a mirror broke this was for him a sign from God that he had been guilty of some grievous sin.

BR.: "I am the cause of the evil in the world." "I am the cause of death." "I am the hub of the universe."

FO.: "I am inspired wholly by God, and cannot express this state in words."

SR.LE.: She believed she could take the sorrows of others onto herself, and thought she was a second Saint Theresa of Lisieux.

HUH.: "I am illuminated by thoughts of God. I was the greatest doubter, but I now know about everything."

LO.: "I am the brother of Jesus."

Pseudohallucinations (Apparitions)

GLA.: "I see myself as a sinner, God is always with me."

ZF.: "I have experienced being executed."

HO.: "I see walls and chains everywhere."

LO.: "I have the feeling that I have seen the devil." "You will possess a great kingdom one day." "The souls in torment have appeared to me."

These were never concrete sensual impressions, the words "seeing" and "hearing" were not to be taken literally. The patients mostly said they could not describe their experiences; it was "as if" they had had an experience with the above images and meaning. Furthermore, it is not always possible to make a sharp distinction between experiences of this sort and experiences with an abnormal significance.

The Sense of Mission

3.AN.: "I am given orders which I must carry out."

SCH.: "I have been commanded to relieve the Pope of a part of the burden of overcoming evil in the world."

GLA.: "I must go to the Pope in Rome to proclaim the salvation of the world." According to an inner vocation, he demanded from his superior that he "kiss the cross." In the same way he told his sister-in-law that she "must give away the million shillings she had been given," obviously according to an inner vocation to free oneself of material things.

FU.: He felt within himself continual instructions from God to pray for nights on end kneeling beside his bed. He "was not allowed to eat," according to his sense of mission.

LO.: "I have the vocation to become Saint Peter or Saint Paul."

The experiences of mission described here and the attempts to realize them were very frequently the reason for the admission into a hospital.

The Suspension of Time and Place

3.AN.: "Part of my body is dead, I am made of iron, my personality is empty and hollow." He also said that his mind was dead.

GLA.: He said he was "eternally damned," but then again "there is a wonderful eternity for everybody."

BR.: He said his mind was "on the moon."

STÖ.: "Everything is unreal," and his own "feelings were dead."

ZE.: He experienced himself as dead and thought time had stood still; there was no longer past or future.

GR.: "I live out of time."

HUKL.: He had no feeling for time any more, he believed himself sometimes in the future. He had a feeling of eternity. At that time he was looking for the Garden of Eden on the banks of the Danube river.

HO.: He entered his own death in his diary and added, "Hallelujah, what a liberating feeling!"

SCHI.: He has "lost himself," has had to keep saying to himself "I am I," because he felt he was losing himself in others. He always spoke of himself as well as of other people and things as being "in an amorphous state."

MEU.: "I am as if I were dead. Everything is empty, nothing is moving any more." "Life is put out." "My eyes are empty, my mouth is dead."

LO.: "Time has stood still, it is the transition to eternal life."

These were experiences of the suspension of the feeling for time and space. Space can be thought of as a function of time, and these patients speak in the main of a changed and mostly suspended time, expressed in such words as eternal, dead, nonexistence, unreality, and disintegration. A manic-depressive patient said the following: "We are not real. The world around us consists only of stereotypes, we are not on one of the planets going round the sun and revolving on its own axis, we are living on a planet taken out of circulation."

The Extremes of Mood

SCH.: "I can feel good and evil fighting in me. I am terribly happy, but then am plagued by terrible doubt."

GLA.: "I feel that the salvation of the world is here," but also "I feel Hell and the devil, I am damned forever."

FO.: He weeps and is at the same time supremely happy, and addressing the voice of God within, "if only you knew how much I love you."

GR.: She felt very happy through meditation and, for love, gave all her possessions away, but on the other hand she said that "it still burns in me," meaning terrible fear.

SR.LE.: She said she felt she was holy but then again thought she was damned eternally.

SEI.: He was at times the devil, then again a saint.

It will be readily understandable that when patients suffered from such extremes of mood, there was frequent mention of suicide. They experienced supernatural happiness on the one hand but on the other terrible suffering which was often described as torments of hell.

The Sudden and Passive Nature of Such Experiences

STÖ.: "It came over me like lightning."

ZE.: "It was as if my body had been struck by lightning."

LA.: "When the lightning struck," (it had in fact struck a nearby church tower) "I knew that I was Jesus."

SR.LE.: "It came over me suddenly, I could not do anything else."

LO.: "It came over me from outside myself."

These patients felt their experiences not only as sudden occurrences but also something which happened to them: they played no active part and much happened expressly against their will.

The Feeling of Shame

PR.: "I was ashamed of seeing Maria (mother of Jesu) and could not report about it."

FO.: He was ashamed of his weakness to shove god away, because he did not do his duty (to pray and to fast) as was ordered by god.

In conclusion it must be mentioned that the patients sometimes could not express themselves in words for fear of being misunderstood. However, they undoubtedly were at first silent for some time out of a feeling of shame, because their experiences were for them something quite extraordinary, touching their innermost selves.

What has been said here by patients suffering from schizophrenia or schizo-affective psychoses—even if it has been quoted out of context of the relevant complete psychopathological picture—points very impressively to the irrational basis of experiences of delusion. I wanted to describe the irrational aspect of these experiences as clearly as possible from a phenomenological point of view so that they could be compared; there are common and ever-recurring aspects to be found in each of them. However, it is important to consider the experiences which occur mainly at the outset of the delusion. In these cases the analogy with what is experienced in mystical ecstasy is evident as we can see by comparing them with the autobiographies of saints and with satori experiences as they have been described by Zen masters.[12] There also are similarities with experiences reported by artists.

THE DIFFERENCE OF DEVELOPMENT

Because there are such striking phenomenological similarities between the reported, original experiences of western mystics, Zen masters, and artistic creators on the one hand and the experiences of some psychiatric patients on the other, it is practically impossible to distinguish belief and delusion in their initial phases. However, it is possible to discover the difference between belief and delusion if we look at the ensuing course or life history of the person affected by the mystical or delusionary experience.

To bring this difference to the fore in the second half of this paper, we need to develop further the concept of belief by contrasting religious belief with scientific knowledge. When something is of such overwhelming importance for a person that he believes in it without the confirmation of other people and is convinced that it cannot be repeated at any time, then this experience cannot be considered a scientific fact. In science everything is founded on logic and causality: propositions are confirmable and observations can be repeated; things can be counted, measured, and weighed. Knowledge through belief—in the philosophical sense of "considered as true," or "to gain a way of thinking"—is more than knowledge through scientific reason, it is knowledge on another level than that of logical-empirical thinking. This concept of belief, also valid for religion, contains two further concepts: faith and hope. Faith means trusting oneself to a higher power and feeling oneself to be part of this power, even if only a very small part. Faith also is always a risk; a child trusts its parents; adults trust friends and the community in which they live; the believer trusts in God. In this trust there is always the hope or expectancy of a desired state. Our whole life consists of a daily hoping for the future, a hoping for the realization of ourself and our work, whether it be through our own children, through what we create in a material or spiritual sphere, or through the perfection of the world.

Faith and hope are open to their opposite, to doubt. Faith and hope on the one hand and perpetual doubt on the other are to be found in the experience of the mystics as well as in the coming into being of great works of art which, as we know, sometimes are destroyed by their creators. To some extent each of us is familiar with this oscillation between faith and hope on the one hand and doubt on the other, with being pulled in both directions between these two poles.

We must now examine to what extent these brief deliberations on the philosophical and religious concepts of belief are also valid for delusion. Does the victim of delusion also have faith and hope in the object of his delusion as well as doubt? Faith and hope presuppose a becoming, a future; in the same way doubt also has a future, a becoming. In faith and hope there are possibilities but no certainties. Sometimes, at the beginning of his illness and also occasionally later, the victim of delusion is not quite sure of the truth of what he has experienced. Usually, however, the opposite is the case, that is, the victim of delusion believes absolutely unshakably in the object of his delusion and is not prepared to discuss it. He is convinced of the object of his delusion even when this appears to contradict logical thinking.

Delusory belief thus appears to be paralyzed belief, no longer open to faith and hope, incapable of any further growth. This is at least undeniably true of acute cases of delusion. Only in those cases in which, for example, deeply religious people become victims of delusion, can fragments of "hoping in God" survive, while trust in other people is more or less extinguished. Only when contact with a "thou" begins to be reestablished, does hope and trust in the therapist show itself, as G. Benedetti reports about the psychotherapy of victims of delusion.[13] Likewise, in neuroleptic therapy, the hope of being able to master everyday life begins to be evident as in the case of U.Pi. described above. It should not be supposed that the victim of delusion has hope in the usual sense: for the victim what is hoped for is certainty and freedom from doubt, thus once again a rigid belief. A framework of delusion can be developed in a systematic way, but it is nevertheless basically delusion. The object of delusion is an end in itself, something finished, which cannot basically be altered. Delusory belief thus lacks the characteristics of philosophical and religious belief—faith, hope, and doubt. The believer is aware of his or her self "remaining open" to becoming. This naturally also includes uncertainty. However, the victim of delusion knows neither this "being open" nor this uncertainty; everything is established, final, clear, and irrefutable.

It is possible that a stated belief cannot always and immediately be recognized as delusory belief. This is especially the case when a statement of this sort is observed only from a short-term, sectional view. A longer term observation of a person declaring a belief will almost always show to what extent it is a rigid belief or a belief which fully includes faith, hope, and doubt. Almost everyone of us has experienced events which had a particular significance at one time and were the reason for seeing the world from that moment on with different eyes. Such experiences involve long-lasting effects for the whole life of the person concerned and result in a maturing of the personality, as exemplified in experiences associated with puberty. For the healthy person those experiences where something gains a special significance and thus becomes a guideline for the thinking and action of this person in the future are belief experiences in the extended meaning of the word. They are inseparably bound up with faith and hope but also with doubt and for the person concerned represent an orientation but not an irrevocable commitment for the future. A measure of uncertainty is present and in this very fact there is the possibility of growth. This growth can be due to the person himself but is often also the result of influences from outside. The victim of delusion, however, rigidly describes his belief as an experience of extraordinary significance which allows for no other interpretation, revealing to him only one single exclusive truth. Flexibility in matters of belief is impossible.

In both delusion and belief, then, there is always an experience of significance which at the outset is of irrational origin and which can be described in theological terms as suprarational or supramundane. It cannot be too strongly emphasized that experiences of this sort belong to the most profound events in a person's life, changing to a greater or lesser degree the personality and its social environment. The power of these experiences and their superiority over logical thought processes has been observed often in history. This is the case in individual delusion as well as in intuitive inspiration in art and science or in religious experience. Art, science, and religion affect the whole of a particular human society or culture.

In trying to distinguish the belief of the healthy person from the belief of the victim of delusion, the following compelling conclusion must be arrived at: the belief which includes faith, hope, and doubt has at the same time a measure of uncertainty as to the future of the person concerned, this belief is open to being and becoming. Delusory belief, on the other hand, is rigid, complete, final, and conclusive; it offers only an apparent safety.

FREEDOM AND CONSTRAINT

Hope and doubt are present in belief but absent in delusion. This leads to a second possible way of distinguishing between belief and delusion—involving the freedom of the human being. The freedom of the personality can only exist in connection with a belief that also includes faith and a possibility of growth, where there are still openings for change. Insofar as the content of belief is concerned, the personality of the victim of delusion is no longer free. His belief allows for no other interpretation, so that an abnormally significant but delusionary experience will result in a loss of freedom for the personality of the victim of delusion. An entire or partial loss of freedom is thus a decisive factor in distinguishing belief in delusion and belief which contains faith, hope, and doubt. This loss of freedom is, just as the concept of freedom itself, an irrational experience which cannot be grasped by causal thinking. As H. Ey so rightly says, psychiatry is the pathology of freedom: "If there were no human freedom, there would be no insanity."[14] The very fact of human existence implies insanity as the limitation of its freedom.

Sometimes such a loss of freedom is reported by the victim of delusion from his own experience, as in the following cases:

F.: stated that he had "a ring around my soul," "my will is limited," "I am unfree."

H.: said "There are walls and chains everywhere."

SCHI.: declared he had the feeling that his will was no longer free.

Even when patients such as U.Pr. speak of the "limitless freedom" they have experienced, this shows in fact a loss of freedom—in her case a loss of action. She said that in her limitless freedom she could kill anybody, and this frightened her. It is generally known how this loss of freedom is experienced by paranoics for they talk about being manipulated, hypnotized, limited, and influenced in their thinking and acting.

A limitation of freedom is known to exist in such states as pathological aggression and love sickness in the case of individuals, but it also exists in groups of people, for example, in psychic epidemics such as witch hunting. In delusion proper, this loss of freedom is, however, even greater and more far-reaching, because either it is not noticed by the person in question or it is accepted as inevitable. The loss of personal freedom in delusion was known as early as the classical period. In one of the many laws of the Lex Cornelia, we hear that a victim of furor is not to be considered a criminal and is not capable of conducting business. The victim of delusion is just not capable of taking advantage of the various possibilities for realizing himself, but is only aware of what he has experienced in his delusion. The ego is bogged down in its relationship to its surroundings, and every possibility of different emotional and intentional behavior is lacking. There is a rigidity not allowing for any other possibility, which one can compare with a mask having only one possible expression. The way "from being to meaning," says G. Huber, is closed to the victim of delusion because there is no longer a possibility of choice for him; the delusory belief prescribes the only apparent way.[15] The loss of personal freedom also can be described as a loss of time for the person in question. In personal time lies the possibility of a "liberation from spatial localization and causal constraint," for "the freedom of the personality . . . has its roots in time and grows out of time."[16]

This paper cannot describe in detail how the freedom of the personality is not adversely affected in corresponding experiences of artistic acts of creation, in the inspiration of great thinkers and researchers, or in mystical experience. History in fact proves it is not limited as with the victims of delusion. A person active in a cultural field will, through his activity, not only become freer himself, but also he will convey greater freedom to other people through what he does. The finding of meaning in sorrow, which the Christian doctrine teaches, is an example of this.

EFFECTIVENESS IN OR ISOLATION FROM SOCIETY

The loss of freedom of the personality in delusion is only one difference between delusory belief and belief in the philosophical and religious sense. Another is the loss of the world on the part of the personality in delusion. L. Binswanger has pointed to the fact that the victim of delusion can no longer step outside his or her own circle of experience, his or her personal world cannot be compared to the world of others, and communication is no longer possible with the outside world.[17] The ill person in a paranoic state rejects the world even when he or she is in fact very dependent on it. His or her "other world" is no longer the real world of other people with their friends and enemies; it is an anonymous threatening power which cannot be grasped and which remains obscure. So the patient becomes isolated and adopts an autistic way of behavior. G. Benedetti and U. Rauchfleisch, for example, have indicated this limited pattern of social behavior.[18] The impossibility of human community leads to a loss of naturalness and originality in the behavior of the ill person within society.[19] G. Huber and G. Gross have created the expression, "Wir-Krüppelhaftigkeit" (the crippled relationship between the "I" and the "thou") for this state of rupture of human contact.[20] In the Japanese attitude towards delusion, this changing in the personality and its surroundings is expressed in a slightly different way. B. Kimura demonstrated this very well etymologically by pointing to the Japanese word for schizophrenia, *Kichigai* meaning nothing other than in a state of delusion it is relationships which are altered.[21]

So-called normal people behave quite differently in their creative acts and in their religious life. After days, weeks, or months of reflection and introversion, a normal person can return to the community without difficulty. The thou, the other person, is never what it is for the victim of delusion—a blurred, threatening power; rather the thou remains what it always was, and the normal person's contact with the thou was only less intensive during the time of withdrawal. In fact, when he returns to the community, his relationship with it will be particularly strong. Only in this way can we explain how cultural achievements come about. The era of mysticism showed us the significance of the return to the world. Saint Theresa of Avila, along with Saint John of the Cross, reformed the order of the Carmelites and became one of the most important persons in Roman Catholic church reform.[22] Saint Ignatius of Loyola founded the order of the Society of Jesus; his laws formed the basis of the rules of the order.[23] The Jesuits also became very important for the reformation of the Catholic church. It would be within the scope of a cultural anthropologist's work to show the growth of these mystics and their reintegration into and impact on the society.

The above mystics are only two examples of the creative impact of mysticism on religion. Sidney S. Furst and his coauthors are of the opinion that Jesus and the apostles were the first Christian mystics.[24] Further, mysticism has been frequently the origin of renovation of belief in times of pronounced establishment of religious institutions and their officials not only in Christianity but also in other religions. Like Jesus of Nazareth, Siddhartha Gautama, the Buddha, exemplifies the mystical origins of a religious reform movement that evolved into a great new world religion. Finally, even scientists testify regarding the creative impact of mysticism. For example, Albert Einstein says, "the most beautiful and far-reaching experience is [that of] the Mystic. It is a fundamental experience, which stand[s] at the beginning of all real art and science."[25] All this illustrates how mystics become and act in the society in a way that would be totally impossible for patients with delusions.

The efficaciousness of great cultural creations—and the work of mystics are cultural creations—is based on the fact that they are not the work of only *one* human being. This is supported by Teilhard de Chardin, who is of the opinion that with humanity evolution is finished and an involution has begun.[26] This involution is a spiritual reflexiveness and is the start of a common—not individual—unity among humans. The external characteristics of the new unity are speech and script. However this new unity, which survives many generations, is not just sounds or markings on paper. It is the information of human culture, what Sir Karl Popper calls "World 3" in contrast to the material substrates of "World 1" and the subjective states of consciousness of "World 2."[27] The culture includes permanent changes in the areas of social structure, art, science, and also belief. The changes are based on the interaction between important human beings and the rest of society. However, it can be supposed that the great significance of a particular person may not be recognizable in his or her lifetime. For the full impact of a person's creative work to occur, the interaction between the creative person and the rest of society requires a longer time than the short life of the individual person. As frequently happens, the great importance of mystics as well as of artists and scientists is recognized in later times. Creations in art, science, and religion do not remain the property of one person, not even when they have been created in solitude. They become what we call culture only when they come in contact with the thou, with other persons in the human community.

Let us return to our starting point, to the concept of belief and the different course this can take in human life. From what has been said above it can be seen that belief involves the experience of significance described by G. Huber and G. Gross among other things as *Anmutungserlebnis* (the experience of being stuck in a particular way).[28] In the imagination of the victim of delusion this event acquires the same significance as that of a mystical experience. However, the course taken by delusion is different, consisting in the loss of personal freedom and in a fundamental disturbance of human relationships, indeed in a loss of the surrounding world. The man with delusionary experiences has no persistent significance for the human society or culture. The distinguishing feature of delusion therefore can be said to be a limitation and a paralysis which is experienced but of which the ill person is often not aware. This is the complete opposite of the breadth, depth, and height experienced in creative acts, which in effect do not convey an absolutely complete message and in which there is always a possibility of growth.

As a result of the changes described above, there is also a different course of development in the sense of mission. Artists or scientists return with what was created and offer it to the community. It will then be corrected or modified by society or by the creator. An act of creation of this sort consequently can contribute to a greater or lesser degree to the dominant culture. It is similar for the *homo religiosus* who returns to human society after a time of retreat in order to bring help and salvation to people in their spiritual needs or who is consulted by others hoping for help.

However, this return to human society and being accepted by it, as well as influencing society according to the directions received during the experience of mission is not possible for the victim of delusion. It might be thought that this is so because the ill person is not accepted by the community. However, a return to the community is primarily impossible because the natural relationship to the thou of the environment has been lost. The sick person can no longer understand his environment, can no longer put himself in another person's place; the world around him is no longer familiar. In addition, the changes in the personality as a result of the experiences of delusion more or less severely limit the effectiveness of this personality. The part emotions will play is just as affected as is logical thinking. The victim of delusion is incapable of plausibly transmitting his "new knowledge" or "observed truth" to his social environment.

CONCLUSION

This essay is based on the analysis of the psychopathological case histories of twenty-five victims of delusion juxtaposed with autobiographical statements of two mystics, reports of satori by Zen masters, and descriptions by three artists of their creative experience. It was shown that initially in all these groups there is the same kind of experience. In this type of experience the feeling for time and space can be suspended, and extreme oscillations of mood as well as the suddenness and passivity of the experience are likely. Also possible are feelings of shame. But most important, this is an experience of special significance that affects the person deeply and fills his or her life with a new purpose and a sense of mission.

What then is the difference between the experiences of the artist or the mystic on the one hand and those of the victim of delusion on the other? It is only its course of development which shows how these experiences are differently structured. In the creative or religious experience, faith and hope but also doubt are involved; various possibilities of growth thus remain open. In the experience of delusion, however, there is no faith and no doubt; the delusion is irrefutable and final. In other words, only in creative experiences is there a possibility of becoming, a state of being open to growth. This implies personal freedom, but in delusion there is a limitation of freedom. The delusion paralyzes the person in his belief; it is final. In this way, the victim of delusion is more or less robbed of personal freedom.

Every form of creative activity consists in building up a new relationship between one person and his or her peers, and in what he says about this new relationship. The ego of the victim of delusion is limited in its personal freedom and will be doubly handicapped in building up a relationship to a thou, or in other words, to another person. First, he will himself lack the capacity and necessary flexibility. Second, this thou will seem to the victim of delusion to be no longer familiar; in fact the thou will appear strangely unfamiliar, unreachable, often frightening. It is impossible for the mentally ill person to make use of what he or she has experienced. Finally, the sense of mission in delusion will be more or less impossible to realize. The change in the personality and the alienation from other people will make any far-reaching and lasting effectiveness impossible. All this is in direct contrast to those people who, as a result of creative experiences in the field of art, science and religion, have found an extension to their personal freedom and have been able to convey this through their works to a thou, to other people, to their surroundings. The creative person never loses contact with other people. He or she is more closely bound than before to them and their actions, which are in fact the result of this close relationship or union. It will be readily understood that the sense of mission which is related to the creative experience is also easier to realize and that works of art, important new ideas in science, and new movements in religion may thus well become a part of our human culture.

NOTES

1. Kurt Schneider, *Zur Einführung in die Religionspsychopathologie* (Tübingen: Mohr, 1975).

2. See Saint Theresa of Avila's account to Father Rodrigo Alvarez in the German translation by Father Aloisius Alkofer in *Leben der heiligen Theresia von Jesu*, 3rd ed., vol. 1 (Munich: Kösel, 1960), pp. 251ff.

3. Saint Ignatius of Loyola, *Der Bericht des Pilgers*, in the German translation by R. Schneider, 2nd ed. (Freiburg, Germany: Herder, 1963).

4. Günter Schüttler, *Die Erleuchtung in Zen-Buddhismus* (Freiburg, Germany: K. Alber, 1975).

5. Johann P. Eckermann, *Gespräche mit Goethe*, 11 March 1828 (Leipzig: Franz Deubel, 1908).

6. Otto Kankeleit, *Das Unbewusste als Keimstatte des Schöpferischen* (Munich: Ernst Reinhardt, 1959), pp. 18–19.

7. Alfred Kubin, *Aus Meinem Leben*, quoted in Wolfgang K. Müller-Thalheim, *Erotik und Dämonie im Werke Alfred Kubins* (Wiesbaden: Fourier und Fertig, 1970), p. 75.

8. Hermann Lenz, *Wahnsinn, Das Irrationale im Wahngeschehen* (Vienna: Herder, 1976).

9. Walter Blankenburg, "Philosophie als Gegenstand der Psychiatrie," in *Psychiatrie der Gegenwart, Forschung und Praxis*, vol. 1, no. 1, 2nd ed. (Berlin: Springer, 1979)

10. Plotinus, *Über Ewigkeit und Zeit*, trans. W. Beierwalter (Frankfurt am Main: Klostermann, 1967).

11. Hermann Lenz, "The Element of the Irrational at the Beginning and During the Course of Delusion," *Confinia Psychiatrica* 22 (1979): 183–90.

12. Schüttler.

13. Gaetano Benedetti, "Ausdruckspsychopathologie psychotischen Leidens im psychotherapeutischen Geschehen," presented at the International Kolloquium der Deutschsprachigen Gessellschaft für Psychopathologie des Ausdrucks, Cologne, Germany 2–4 October 1980.

14. Henry Ey, *Das Bewusstsein*, trans. from the French by K. P. Kisker (Berlin: Walter de Gruyter, 1967), pp. 196–199.

15. Gerd Huber, "Forschungsrichtungen und Lehrmeinungen in der Psychologie," in *Handbuch der forensischen Psychiatrie*, ed. 11, Göppinger and H. Witter (Berlin: Springer, 1972), 1:633–751.

16. See Bernhard Pauleikhoff, *Person und Zeit* (Heidelberg: Hüthig, 1979), p. 147.

17. Ludwig Binswanger, *Wahn* (Pfüllingen, Germany: Neske, 1965).

18. Gaetano Benedetti and Udo Rauchfleisch, *Der Schizophrene in unserer Gesellschaft* (Stuttgart: Thieme, 1975).

19. W. Blankenburg, "Ansätze zu einer Psychopathologie des commonsense," *Confinia Psychiatrica* 12 (1969): 144–63.

20. Gerd Huber and Gisela Gross, *Wahn* (Stuttgart: Enke, 1977).

21. Bin Kimura, "Schizophrenie als Geschehen des Zwischen-sein's," *Nervenarzt* 46 (1975): 434–39.

22. See n. 2 above.

23. See n. 3 above.

24. Sidney S. Furst, *Mysticism: Spiritual Quest or Psychic Disorder*, Group for the Advancement of Psychiatry, vol. 9, no. 97 (New York: Mental Health Materials Center, 1976).

25. Albert Einstein, *Ideas and Opinions* (New York: Crown Publishers, 1954).

26. Teilhard de Chardin, *Die Zukunft des Menschen*, 2nd ed. (Freiburg, Germany: Olten, 1966).

27. Karl R. Popper, cited in John C. Eccles, *The Human Mystery* (Edinburgh: Springer International, 1979), p. 98.

28. Huber and Gross.

VI.B. The Phenomenology of Mysticism

VI.B.1. Mysticism

WILLIAM JAMES

William James (1842–1910) brings the perspective of an empiricist to bear on his examination of mystical experience, taking care to base his interpretation on an abundance of actual cases and drawing on mystics from many different religious traditions. In the following excerpts from The Varieties of Religious Experience, *he begins by setting forth what he takes to be the central common features of mystical experience. Then he leads us through a wide range of types of such experiences, beginning with the vague sense of a suddenly apprehended significance of a saying or verse of scripture and proceeding through an examination of examples of what we might call "nature mysticism," the sensation of oneness with nature, and on to experiences in which the individual senses a unity with reality, God, or the Absolute.*

The words "mysticism" and "mystical" are often used as terms of mere reproach, to throw at any opinion which we regard as vague and vast and sentimental, and without a base in either facts or logic. For some writers a "mystic" is any person who believes in thought-transference, or spirit-return. Employed in this way the word has little value: there are too many less ambiguous synonyms. So, to keep it useful by restricting it, I will do what I did in the case of the word "religion," and simply propose to you four marks which, when an experience has them, may justify us in calling it mystical for the purpose of the present lectures. In this way we shall save verbal disputation, and the recriminations that generally go therewith.

1. *Ineffability.*—The handiest of the marks by which I classify a state of mind as mystical is negative. The subject of it immediately says that it defies expression, that no adequate report of its contents can be given in words. It follows from this that its quality must be directly experienced; it cannot be imparted or transferred to others. In this peculiarity mystical states are more like states of feeling than like states of intellect. No one can make clear to another who has never had a certain feeling, in what the quality or worth of it consists. One must have musical ears to know the value of a symphony; one

From *The Varieties of Religious Experience* (New York: Macmillan, 1961), pp. 299–305, 310–318, 329–331.

must have been in love one's self to understand a lover's state of mind. Lacking the heart or ear, we cannot interpret the musician or the lover justly, and are even likely to consider him weak-minded or absurd. The mystic finds that most of us accord to his experiences an equally incompetent treatment.

2. *Noetic quality.*—Although so similar to states of feeling, mystical states seem to those who experience them to be also states of knowledge. They are states of insight into depths of truth unplumbed by the discursive intellect. They are illuminations, revelations, full of significance and importance, all inarticulate though they remain; and as a rule they carry with them a curious sense of authority for aftertime.

These two characters will entitle any state to be called mystical, in the sense in which I use the word. Two other qualities are less sharply marked, but are usually found. These are:—

3. *Transiency.*—Mystical states cannot be sustained for long. Except in rare instances, half an hour, or at most an hour or two, seems to be the limit beyond which they fade into the light of common day. Often, when faded, their quality can but imperfectly be reproduced in memory; but when they recur it is recognized; and from one recurrence to another it is susceptible of continuous development in what is felt as inner richness and importance.

4. *Passivity.*—Although the oncoming of mystical states may be facilitated by preliminary voluntary operations, as by fixing the attention, or going through certain bodily performances, or in other ways which manuals of mysticism prescribe; yet when the characteristic sort of consciousness once has set in, the mystic feels as if his own will were in abeyance, and indeed sometimes as if he were grasped and held by a superior power. This latter peculiarity connects mystical states with certain definite phenomena of secondary or alternative personality, such as prophetic speech, automatic writing, or the mediumistic trance. When these latter conditions are well pronounced, however, there may be no recollection whatever of the phenomenon, and it may have no significance for the subject's usual inner life, to which, as it were, it makes a mere interruption. Mystical states, strictly so-called, are never merely interruptive. Some memory of their content always remains, and a profound sense of their importance. They modify the inner life of the subject between the times of their recurrence. Sharp divisions in this region are, however, difficult to make, and we find all sorts of gradations and mixtures.

These four characteristics are sufficient to mark out a group of states of consciousness peculiar enough to deserve a special name and to call for careful study. Let it then be called the mystical group.

Our next step should be to gain acquaintance with some typical examples. Professional mystics at the height of their development have often elaborately organized experiences and a philosophy based thereupon. But you remember what I said in my first lecture: phenomena are best understood when placed within their series, studied in their germ and in their over-ripe decay, and compared with their exaggerated and degenerated kindred. The range of mystical experience is very wide, much too wide for us to cover in the time at our disposal. Yet the method of serial study is so essential for interpretation that if we really wish to reach conclusions we must use it. I will begin, therefore, with phenomena which claim no special religious significance, and end with those of which the religious pretentions are extreme.

The simplest rudiment of mystical experience would seem to be that deepened sense of the significance of a maxim or formula which occasionally sweeps over one. "I've heard that said all my life," we exclaim, "but I never realized its full meaning until now." "When a fellow-monk," said Luther, "one day repeated the words of the Creed: 'I believe in the forgiveness of sins,' I saw the Scripture in an entirely new light; and straightway I felt as if I were born anew. It was as if I had found the door of paradise thrown wide open."[1] This sense of deeper significance is not confined to rational propositions. Single words,[2] and conjunctions of words, effects of light on land and sea, odors and musical sounds, all bring it when the mind is tuned aright. Most of us can remember the strangely moving power of passages in certain poems read when we were young, irrational doorways as they were through which the mystery of fact, the wildness and the pang of life, stole into our hearts and thrilled them. The words have now perhaps become mere polished surfaces for us; but lyric poetry and music are alive and significant only in proportion as they fetch these vague vistas of a life continuous with our own, beckoning and inviting, yet ever eluding our pursuit. We are alive or dead to the eternal inner message of the arts according as we have kept or lost this mystical susceptibility.

A more pronounced step forward on the mystical ladder is found in an extremely frequent phenomenon, that sudden feeling, namely, which sometimes sweeps over us, of having "been there before," as if at some indefinite past time, in just this place, with just these people, we were already saying just these things. As Tennyson writes:

"Moreover, something is or seems
　That touches me with mystic gleams,
　Like glimpses of forgotten dreams—

"Of something felt, like something here;
　Of something done, I know not where;
　Such as no language may declare."[3]

---

[1] Newman's *Securus judicat orbis terrarum* is another instance.

[2] "Mesopotamia" is the stock comic instance.—An excellent old German lady, who had done some traveling in her day, used to describe to me her *Sehnsucht* that she might yet visit "Philadelphia," whose wondrous name had always haunted her imagination. Of John Foster it is said that "single words (as *chalcedony*), or the names of ancient heroes, had a mighty fascination over him. 'At any time the word *hermit* was enough to transport him.' The words *woods* and *forests* would produce the most powerful emotion." Foster's Life, by Ryland, New York, 1846, p. 3.

[3] The Two Voices. In a letter to Mr. B. P. Blood, Tennyson reports of himself as follows:—

"I have never had any revelations through anæsthetics, but a kind of waking trance—this for lack of a better word—I have frequently had, quite up from boyhood, when I have been all alone. This has come upon me through repeating my own name to myself silently, till all at once, as it were out of the intensity of the consciousness of individuality, individuality itself seemed to dissolve and fade away into boundless being, and this not a confused state but the

Sir James Crichton-Browne has given the technical name of "dreamy states" to these sudden invasions of vaguely reminiscent consciousness.[4] They bring a sense of mystery and of the metaphysical duality of things, and the feeling of an enlargement of perception which seems imminent but which never completes itself. In Dr. Crichton-Browne's opinion they connect themselves with the perplexed and scared disturbances of self-consciousness which occasionally precede epileptic attacks. I think that this learned alienist takes a rather absurdly alarmist view of an intrinsically insignificant phenomenon. He follows it along the downward ladder, to insanity; our path pursues the upward ladder chiefly. The divergence shows how important it is to neglect no part of a phenomenon's connections, for we make it appear admirable or dreadful according to the context by which we set it off.

Somewhat deeper plunges into mystical consciousness are met with in yet other dreamy states. Such feelings as these which Charles Kingsley describes are surely far from being uncommon, especially in youth:—

> When I walk the fields, I am oppressed now and then with an innate feeling that everything I see has a meaning, if I could but understand it. And this feeling of being surrounded with truths which I cannot grasp amounts to indescribable awe sometimes. . . . Have you not felt that your real soul was imperceptible to your mental vision, except in a few hallowed moments?"[5]

A much more extreme state of mystical consciousness is described by J. A. Symonds; and probably more persons than we suspect could give parallels to it from their own experience.

> "Suddenly," writes Symonds, "at church, or in company, or when I was reading, and always, I think, when my muscles were at rest, I felt the approach of the mood. Irresistibly it took possession of my mind and will, lasted what seemed an eternity, and disappeared in a series of rapid sensations which resembled the awakening from anæsthetic influence. One reason why I disliked this kind of trance was that I could not describe it to myself. I cannot even now find words to render it intelligible. It consisted in a gradual but swiftly progressive obliteration of space, time, sensation, and the multitudinous factors of experience which seem to qualify what we are pleased to call our Self.

---

clearest, the surest of the surest, utterly beyond words—where death was an almost laughable impossibility—the loss of personality (if so it were) seeming no extinction, but the only true life. I am ashamed of my feeble description. Have I not said the state is utterly beyond words?"

Professor Tyndall, in a letter, recalls Tennyson saying of this condition: "By God Almighty! there is no delusion in the matter! It is no nebulous ecstasy, but a state of transcendent wonder, associated with absolute clearness of mind." Memoirs of Alfred Tennyson, ii, 473.

[4] The Lancet, July 6 and 13, 1895, reprinted as the Cavendish Lecture, on Dreamy Mental States, London, Baillière, 1895. They have been a good deal discussed of late by psychologists. See, for example, Bernard-Lerot: L'Illusion de Fausse Reconnaissance, Paris, 1898.

[5] Charles Kingsley's Life, i, 55, quoted by Inge: Christian Mysticism, London, 1899, p. 341.

In proportion as these conditions of ordinary consciousness were subtracted, the sense of an underlying or essential consciousness acquired intensity. At last nothing remained but a pure, absolute, abstract Self. The universe became without form and void of content. But Self persisted, formidable in its vivid keenness, feeling the most poignant doubt about reality, ready, as it seemed, to find existence break as breaks a bubble round about it. And what then? The apprehension of a coming dissolution, the grim conviction that this state was the last state of the conscious Self, the sense that I had followed the last thread of being to the verge of the abyss, and had arrived at demonstration of eternal Maya or illusion, stirred or seemed to stir me up again. The return to ordinary conditions of sentient existence began by my first recovering the power of touch, and then by the gradual though rapid influx of familiar impressions and diurnal interests. At last I felt myself once more a human being; and though the riddle of what is meant by life remained unsolved, I was thankful for this return from the abyss—this deliverance from so awful an initiation into the mysteries of skepticism.

"This trance recurred with diminishing frequency until I reached the age of twenty-eight. It served to impress upon my growing nature the phantasmal unreality of all the circumstances which contribute to a merely phenomenal consciousness. Often have I asked myself with anguish, on waking from that formless state of denuded, keenly sentient being, Which is the unreality—the trance of fiery, vacant, apprehensive, skeptical Self from which I issue, or these surrounding phenomena and habits which veil that inner Self and build a self of flesh-and-blood conventionality? Again, are men the factors of some dream, the dream-like unsubstantiality of which they comprehend at such eventful moments? What would happen if the final stage of the trance were reached?"[6]

In a recital like this there is certainly something suggestive of pathology.[7] The next step into mystical states carries us into a realm that public opinion and ethical philosophy have long since branded as pathological, though private practice and certain lyric strains of poetry seem still to bear witness to its ideality. I refer to the consciousness produced by intoxicants and anaesthetics, especially by alcohol. The sway of alcohol over mankind is unquestionably due to its power to stimulate the mystical faculties of human nature, usually crushed to earth by the cold facts and dry criticisms of the sober hour. Sobriety diminishes, discriminates, and says no; drunkenness expands, unites, and

---

[6] H. G. Brown: J. A. Symonds, a Biography, London, 1895, pp. 29–31, abridged.

[7] Crichton-Browne expressly says that Symonds's "highest" nerve centres were in some degree enfeebled or damaged by these dreamy mental states which afflicted him so grievously." Symonds was, however, a perfect monster of many-sided cerebral efficiency, and his critic gives no objective grounds whatever for his strange opinion, save that Symonds complained occasionally, as all susceptible and ambitious men complain, of lassitude and uncertainty as to his life's mission.

says yes. It is in fact the great exciter of the *Yes* function in man. It brings its votary from the chill periphery of things to the radiant core. It makes him for the moment one with truth. Not through mere perversity do men run after it. To the poor and the unlettered it stands in the place of symphony concerts and of literature; and it is part of the deeper mystery and tragedy of life that whiffs and gleams of something that we immediately recognize as excellent should be vouchsafed to so many of us only in the fleeting earlier phases of what in its totality is so degrading a poisoning. The drunken consciousness is one bit of the mystic consciousness, and our total opinion of it must find its place in our opinion of that larger whole.

Certain aspects of nature seem to have a peculiar power of awakening such mystical moods.[8] Most of the striking cases which I have collected have occurred out of doors. Literature has commemorated this fact in many passages of great beauty—this extract, for example, from Amiel's Journal Intime:—

> "Shall I ever again have any of those prodigious reveries which sometimes came to me in former days? One day, in youth, at sunrise, sitting in the ruins of the castle of Faucigny; and again in the mountains, under the noonday sun, above Lavey, lying at the foot of a tree and visited by three butterflies; once more at night upon the shingly shore of the Northern Ocean, my back upon the sand and my vision ranging through the milky way;—such grand and spacious, immortal, cosmogonic reveries, when one reaches to the stars, when one owns the infinite! Moments divine, ecstatic hours; in which our

---

[8] The larger God may then swallow up the smaller one. I take this from Starbuck's manuscript collection:—

"I never lost the consciousness of the presence of God until I stood at the foot of the Horseshoe Falls, Niagara. Then I lost him in the immensity of what I saw. I also lost myself, feeling that I was an atom too small for the notice of Almighty God."

I subjoin another similar case from Starbuck's collection:—

"In that time the consciousness of God's nearness came to me sometimes. I say God, to describe what is indescribable. A presence, I might say, yet that is too suggestive of personality, and the moments of which I speak did not hold the consciousness of a personality, but something in myself made me feel myself a part of something bigger than I, that was controlling. I felt myself one with the grass, the trees, birds, insects, everything in Nature. I exulted in the mere fact of existence, of being a part of it all—the drizzling rain, the shadows of the clouds, the tree-trunks, and so on. In the years following, such moments continued to come, but I wanted them constantly. I knew so well the satisfaction of losing self in a perception of supreme power and love, that I was unhappy because that perception was not constant." The cases quoted in my third lecture are still better ones of this type. In her essay, The Loss of Personality, in the Atlantic Monthly (vol. lxxxv, p. 195), Miss Ethel D. Puffer explains that the vanishing of the sense of self, and the feeling of immediate unity with the object, is due to the disappearance, in these rapturous experiences, of the motor adjustments which habitually intermediate between the constant background of consciousness (which is the Self) and the object in the foreground, whatever it may be. I must refer the reader to the highly instructive article, which seems to me to throw light upon the psychological conditions, though it fails to account for the rapture or the revelation-value of the experience in the Subject's eyes.

thought flies from world to world, pierces the great enigma, breathes with a respiration broad, tranquil, and deep as the respiration of the ocean, serene and limitless as the blue firmament; . . . instants of irresistible intuition in which one feels one's self great as the universe, and calm as a god. . . . What hours, what memories! The vestiges they leave behind are enough to fill us with belief and enthusiasm, as if they were visits of the Holy Ghost."[9]

Here is a similar record from the memoirs of that interesting German idealist, Malwida von Meysenbug:—

"I was alone upon the seashore as all these thoughts flowed over me, liberating and reconciling; and now again, as once before in distant days in the Alps of Dauphiné, I was impelled to kneel down, this time before the illimitable ocean, symbol of the Infinite. I felt that I prayed as I had never prayed before, and knew now what prayer really is: to return from the solitude of individuation into the consciousness of unity with all that is, to kneel down as one that passes away, and to rise up as one imperishable. Earth, heaven, and sea resounded as in one vast world-encircling harmony. It was as if the chorus of all the great who had ever lived were about me. I felt myself one with them, and it appeared as if I heard their greeting: 'Thou too belongest to the company of those who overcome.'"[10]

The well known passage from Walt Whitman is a classical expression of this sporadic type of mystical experience.

"I believe in you, my Soul . . .
Loaf with me on the grass, loose the stop from your throat; . . .
Only the lull I like, the hum of your valved voice.
I mind how once we lay, such a transparent summer morning.
Swiftly arose and spread around me the peace and knowledge that pass all the argument of the earth,
And I know that the hand of God is the promise of my own,
And I know that the spirit of God is the brother of my own,
And that all the men ever born are also my brothers and the women my sisters and lovers,
And that a kelson of the creation is love."[11]

---

[9] Op. cit., i, 43–44.

[10] Memoiren einer Idealistin, 5te Auflage, 1900, iii. 166. For years she had been unable to pray, owing to materialistic belief.

[11] Whitman in another place expresses in a quieter way what was probably with him a chronic mystical perception: "There is," he writes, "apart from mere intellect, in the make-up of every superior human identity, a wondrous something that realizes without argument, frequently without what is called education (though I think it the goal and apex of all education deserving the name), an intuition of the absolute balance, in time and space, of the whole of this multifariousness, this revel of fools, and incredible make-believe and general

I could easily give more instances, but one will suffice. I take it from the Autobiography of J. Trevor.[12]

"One brilliant Sunday morning, my wife and boys went to the Unitarian Chapel in Macclesfield. I felt it impossible to accompany them—as though to leave the sunshine on the hills, and go down there to the chapel, would be for the time an act of spiritual suicide. And I felt such need for new inspiration and expansion in my life. So, very reluctantly and sadly, I left my wife and boys to go down into the town, while I went further up into the hills with my stick and my dog. In the loveliness of the morning, and the beauty of the hills and valleys, I soon lost my sense of sadness and regret. For nearly an hour I walked along the road to the 'Cat and Fiddle,' and then returned. On the way back, suddenly, without warning, I felt that I was in Heaven—an inward state of peace and joy and assurance indescribably intense, accompanied with a sense of being bathed in a warm glow of light, as though the external condition had brought about the internal effect—a feeling of having passed beyond the body, though the scene around me stood out more clearly and as if nearer to me than before, by reason of the illumination in the midst of which I seemed to be placed. This deep emotion lasted, though with decreasing strength, until I reached home, and for some time after, only gradually passing away."

The writer adds that having had further experiences of a similar sort, he now knows them well.

"The spiritual life," he writes, "justifies itself to those who live it; but what can we say to those who do not understand? This, at least, we can say, that it is a life whose experiences are proved real to their possessor, because they remain with him when brought closest into contact with the objective realities of life. Dreams cannot stand this test. We wake from them to find that they are but dreams. Wanderings of an overwrought brain do not stand this test. These highest experiences that I have had of God's presence have been rare and brief—flashes of consciousness which have compelled me to exclaim with surprise—God is *here*!— or conditions of exaltation and insight, less intense, and only gradually passing away. I have severely questioned the worth of these moments. To no soul have I named them, lest I should be building my life and work on mere phantasies of the brain. But I find that, after every questioning and test, they stand out to-day as the most real

---

unsettledness, we call *the world*; a soul-sight of that divine clue and unseen thread which holds the whole congeries of things, all history and time, and all events, however trivial, however momentous, like a leashed dog in the hand of the hunter. [Of] such soul-sight and root-centre for the mind mere optimism explains only the surface." Whitman charges it against Carlyle that he lacked this perception. Specimen Days and Collect, Philadelphia, 1882, p. 174.

[12] My Quest for God, London, 1897, pp. 268, 269, abridged.

experiences of my life, and experiences which have explained and justified and unified all past experiences and all past growth. Indeed, their reality and their far-reaching significance are ever becoming more clear and evident. When they came, I was living the fullest, strongest, sanest, deepest life. I was not seeking them. What I was seeking, with resolute determination, was to live more intensely my own life, as against what I knew would be the adverse judgment of the world. It was in the most real seasons that the Real Presence came, and I was aware that I was immersed in the infinite ocean of God."[13]

Even the least mystical of you must by this time be convinced of the existence of mystical moments as states of consciousness of an entirely specific quality, and of the deep impression which they make on those who have them. A Canadian psychiatrist, Dr. R. M. Bucke, gives to the more distinctly characterized of these phenomena the name of cosmic consciousness. "Cosmic consciousness in its more striking instances is not," Dr. Bucke says, "simply an expansion or extension of the self-conscious mind with which we are all familiar, but the superaddition of a function as distinct from any possessed by the average man as *self*-consciousness is distinct from any function possessed by one of the higher animals."

"The prime characteristic of cosmic consciousness is a consciousness of the cosmos, that is, of the life and order of the universe. Along with the consciousness of the cosmos there occurs an intellectual enlightenment which alone would place the individual on a new plane of existence— would make him almost a member of a new species. To this is added a state of moral exaltation, an indescribable feeling of elevation, elation, and joyousness, and a quickening of the moral sense, which is fully as striking, and more important than is the enhanced intellectual power. With these come what may be called a sense of immortality, a consciousness of eternal life, not a conviction that he shall have this, but the consciousness that he has it already."[14]

It was Dr. Bucke's own experience of a typical onset of cosmic consciousness in his own person which led him to investigate it in others. He has printed his conclusions in a highly interesting volume, from which I take the following account of what occurred to him:—

"I had spent the evening in a great city, with two friends, reading and discussing poetry and philosophy. We parted at midnight. I had a long drive in a hansom to my lodging. My mind, deeply under the influence of the ideas, images, and emotions called up by the reading and talk, was calm and peaceful. I was in a state of quiet, almost passive enjoyment, not actually thinking, but letting ideas, images, and emotions flow of themselves, as it were, through my mind. All at once,

---

[13] Op. cit., pp. 256, 257, abridged.

[14] Cosmic Consciousness: a study in the evolution of the human Mind, Philadelphia, 1901, p. 2.

without warning of any kind, I found myself wrapped in a flame-colored cloud. For an instant I thought of fire, an immense conflagration somewhere close by in that great city; the next, I knew that the fire was within myself. Directly afterward there came upon me a sense of exultation, of immense joyousness accompanied or immediately followed by an intellectual illumination impossible to describe. Among other things, I did not merely come to believe, but I saw that the universe is not composed of dead matter, but is, on the contrary, a living Presence; I became conscious in myself of eternal life. It was not a conviction that I would have eternal life, but a consciousness that I possessed eternal life then; I saw that all men are immortal; that the cosmic order is such that without any peradventure all things work together for the good of each and all; that the foundation principle of the world, of all the worlds, is what we call love, and that the happiness of each and all is in the long run absolutely certain. The vision lasted a few seconds and was gone; but the memory of it and the sense of the reality of what it taught has remained during the quarter of a century which has since elapsed. I knew that what the vision showed was true. I had attained to a point of view from which I saw that it must be true. That view, that conviction, I may say that consciousness, has never, even during periods of the deepest depression, been lost."[15]

We have now seen enough of this cosmic or mystic consciousness, as it comes sporadically. We must next pass to its methodical cultivation as an element of the religious life. Hindus, Buddhists, Mohammedans, and Christians all have cultivated it methodically.

In India, training in mystical insight has been known from time immemorial under the name of yoga. Yoga means the experimental union of the individual with the divine. It is based on persevering exercise; and the diet, posture, breathing, intellectual concentration, and moral discipline vary slightly in the different systems which teach it. The yogi, or disciple, who has by these means overcome the obscurations of his lower nature sufficiently, enters into the condition termed *samâdhi*, "and comes face to face with facts which no instinct or reason can ever know." He learns—

"That the mind itself has a higher state of existence, beyond reason, a superconscious state, and that when the mind gets to that higher state, then this knowledge beyond reasoning comes. . . . All the different steps in yoga are intended to bring us scientifically to the superconscious state or Samâdhi. . . . Just as unconscious work is beneath consciousness, so there is another work which is above consciousness, and which, also, is not accompanied with the feeling of egoism. . . . There is no feeling of *I*, and yet the mind works, desireless, free from restlessness, objectless, bodiless. Then the Truth shines in its full effulgence, and we know ourselves—for Samâdhi lies potential in us

---

[15] Loc. cit., pp. 7, 8. My quotation follows the privately printed pamphlet which preceded Dr. Bucke's larger work, and differs verbally a little from the text of the latter.

all—for what we truly are, free, immortal, omnipotent, loosed from the finite, and its contrasts of good and evil altogether, and identical with the Atman or Universal Soul."[16]

The Vedantists say that one may stumble into superconsciousness sporadically, without the previous discipline, but it is then impure. Their test of its purity, like our test of religion's value, is empirical; its fruits must be good for life. When a man comes out of Samâdhi, they assure us that he remains "enlightened, a sage, a prophet, a saint, his whole character changed, his life changed, illumined."[17]

The Buddhists use the word "samâdhi" as well as the Hindus; but "dhyâna" is their special word for higher states of contemplation. There seem to be four stages recognized in dyhâna. The first stage comes through concentration of the mind upon one point. It excludes desire, but not discernment or judgment: it is still intellectual. In the second stage the intellectual functions drop off, and the satisfied sense of unity remains. In the third stage the satisfaction departs, and indifference begins, along with memory and self-consciousness. In the fourth stage the indifference, memory, and self-consciousness are perfected. [Just what "memory" and "self-consciousness" mean in this connection is doubtful. They cannot be the faculties familiar to us in the lower life.] Higher stages still of contemplation are mentioned—a region where there exists nothing, and where the mediator says: "There exists absolutely nothing," and stops. Then he reaches another region where he says: "There are neither ideas nor absence of ideas," and stops again. Then another region where, "having reached the end of both idea and perception, he stops finally." This would seem to be, not yet Nirvâna, but as close an approach to it as this life affords.[18]

In the Mohammedan world the Sufi sect and various dervish bodies are the possessors of the mystical tradition. The Sufis have existed in Persia from the earliest times, and as their pantheism is so at variance with the hot and rigid monotheism of the Arab mind, it has been suggested that Sufism must have been inoculated into Islam by Hindu influences. We Christians know little of Sufism, for its secrets are disclosed only to those initiated. To give its existence a certain liveliness in your minds, I will quote a Moslem document, and pass away from the subject.

Al-Ghazzali, a Persian philosopher and theologian, who flourished in the

---

[16] My quotations are from Vivekananda, Raja Yoga, London, 1896. The completest source of information on Yoga is the work translated by Vihari Lala Mitra: Yoga Vasishta Maha Ramayana, 4 vols. Calcutta, 1891–99.

[17] A European witness, after carefully comparing the results of Yoga with those of the hypnotic or dreamy states artificially producible by us, says: "It makes of its true disciples good, healthy, and happy men. . . . Through the mastery which the yogi attains over his thoughts and his body, he grows into a 'character.' By the subjection of his impulses and propensities to his will, and the fixing of the latter upon the ideal of goodness, he becomes a 'personality' hard to influence by others, and thus almost the opposite of what we usually imagine a 'medium' so-called, or 'psychic subject' to be." Karl Kellner: Yoga: Eine Skizze, München, 1896, p. 21.

[18] I follow the account in C. F. Koeppen: Die Religion des Buddha, Berlin, 1857, i. 585 ff.

eleventh century, and ranks as one of the greatest doctors of the Moslem church, has left us one of the few autobiographies to be found outside of Christian literature. Strange that a species of book so abundant among ourselves should be so little represented elsewhere—the absence of strictly personal confessions is the chief difficulty to the purely literary student who would like to become acquainted with the inwardness of religions other than the Christian.

M. Schmölders has translated a part of Al-Ghazzali's autobiography into French:—[19]

> "The Science of the Sufis," says the Moslem author, "aims at detaching the heart from all that is not God, and at giving to it for sole occupation the meditation of the divine being. Theory being more easy for me than practice, I read [certain books] until I understood all that can be learned by study and hearsay. Then I recognized that what pertains most exclusively to their method is just what no study can grasp, but only transport, ecstasy, and the transformation of the soul. How great, for example, is the difference between knowing the definitions of health, of satiety, with their causes and conditions, and being really healthy or filled. How different to know in what drunkenness consists—as being a state occasioned by a vapor that rises from the stomach—and *being* drunk effectively. Without doubt, the drunken man knows neither the definition of drunkenness nor what makes it interesting for science. Being drunk, he knows nothing; whilst the physician, although not drunk, knows well in what drunkenness consists, and what are its predisposing conditions. Similarly there is a difference between knowing the nature of abstinence, and *being* abstinent or having one's soul detached from the world.—Thus I had learned what words could teach of Sufism, but what was left could be learned neither by study nor through the ears, but solely by giving one's self up to ecstasy and leading a pious life.
>
> "Reflecting on my situation, I found myself tied down by a multitude of bonds—temptation on every side. Considering my teaching, I found it was impure before God. I saw myself struggling with all my might to achieve glory and to spread my name. [Here follows an account of his six months' hesitation to break away from the conditions of his life at Bagdad, at the end of which he fell ill with a paralysis of the tongue.] Then, feeling my own weakness, and having entirely given up my own will, I repaired to God like a man in distress who has no more resources. He answered, as he answers the wretch who invokes him. My heart no longer felt any difficulty in renouncing glory, wealth, and my children. So I quitted Bagdad, and reserving from my fortune only what was indispensable for my subsistence, I distributed the rest. I went to Syria, where I remained about two years, with no other occupation than living in retreat and solitude, conquering

---

[19] For a full account of him, see D. B. Macdonald: The Life of Al-Ghazzali, in the Journal of the American Oriental Society, 1899, vol. xx., p. 71.

my desires, combating my passions, training myself to purify my soul, to make my character perfect, to prepare my heart for meditating on God—all according to the methods of the Sufis, as I had read of them.

"This retreat only increased my desire to live in solitude, and to complete the purification of my heart and fit it for meditation. But the vicissitudes of the times, the affairs of the family, the need of subsistence, changed in some respects my primitive resolve, and interfered with my plans for a purely solitary life. I had never yet found myself completely in ecstasy, save in a few single hours; nevertheless, I kept the hope of attaining this state. Every time that the accidents led me astray, I sought to return; and in this situation I spent ten years. During this solitary state things were revealed to me which it is impossible either to describe or to point out. I recognized for certain that the Sufis are assuredly walking in the path of God. Both in their acts and in their inaction, whether internal or external, they are illumined by the light which proceeds from the prophetic source. The first condition for a Sufi is to purge his heart entirely of all that is not God. The next key of the contemplative life consists in the humble prayers which escape from the fervent soul, and in the meditations on God in which the heart is swallowed up entirely. But in reality this is only the beginning of the Sufi life, the end of Sufism being total absorption in God. The intuitions and all that precede are, so to speak, only the threshold for those who enter. From the beginning, revelations take place in so flagrant a shape that the Sufis see before them, whilst wide awake, the angels and the souls of the prophets. They hear their voices and obtain their favors. Then the transport rises from the perception of forms and figures to a degree which escapes all expression, and which no man may seek to give an account of without his words involving sin.

"Whosoever has had no experience of the transport knows of the true nature of prophetism nothing but the name. He may meanwhile be sure of its existence, both by experience and by what he hears the Sufis say. As there are men endowed only with the sensitive faculty who reject what is offered them in the way of objects of the pure understanding, so there are intellectual men who reject and avoid the things perceived by the prophetic faculty. A blind man can understand nothing of colors save what he has learned by narration and hearsay. Yet God has brought prophetism near to men in giving them all a state analogous to it in its principal characters. This state is sleep. If you were to tell a man who was himself without experience of such a phenomenon that there are people who at times swoon away so as to resemble dead men, and who [in dreams] yet perceive things that are hidden, he would deny it [and give his reasons]. Nevertheless, his arguments would be refuted by actual experience. Wherefore, just as the understanding is a stage of human life in which an eye opens to discern various intellectual objects uncomprehended by sensation; just so in the prophetic the sight is illumined by a light which uncovers hidden things and objects which the intellect fails to reach. The chief properties of prophetism are perceptible only during the transport, by those who embrace the Sufi life. The prophet is endowed with qualities to which you possess nothing analogous, and which consequently you cannot possibly understand. How should you know their true nature, since one knows only what one can comprehend? But the transport which one attains by the method of the Sufis is like an immediate perception, as if one touched the objects with one's hand."[20]

This incommunicableness of the transport is the keynote of all mysticism. Mystical truth exists for the individual who has the transport, but for no one else. In this, as I have said, it resembles the knowledge given to us in sensations more than that given by conceptual thought. Thought, with its remoteness and abstractness, has often enough in the history of philosophy been contrasted unfavorably with sensation. It is a commonplace of metaphysics that God's knowledge cannot be discursive but must be intuitive, that is, must be constructed more after the pattern of what in ourselves is called immediate feeling, that after that of proposition and judgment.

This overcoming of all the usual barriers between the individual and the Absolute is the great mystic achievement. In mystic states we both become one with the Absolute and we become aware of our oneness. This is the everlasting and triumphant mystical tradition, hardly altered by differences of clime or creed. In Hinduism, in Neoplatonism, in Sufism, in Christian mysticism, in Whitmanism, we find the same recurring note, so that there is about mystical utterances an eternal unanimity which ought to make a critic stop and think, and which brings it about that the mystical classics have, as has been said, neither birthday nor native land. Perpetually telling of the unity of man with God, their speech antedates languages, and they do not grow old.[21]

"That are Thou!" says the Upanishads, and the Vedantists add: "Not a part, not a mode of That, but identically That, that absolute Spirit of the World." "As pure water poured into pure water remains the same, thus, O Gautama, is the Self of a thinker who knows. Water in water, fire in fire, ether in ether, no one can distinguish them: likewise a man whose mind has entered into the self."[22] "'Every man,' says the Sufi Gulshan-Râz, whose heart is no longer shaken by any doubts, knows with certainty that there is no being save only One. . . . In his divine majesty the *me*, and *we*, the *thou*, are not found, for in the One there can be no distinction. Every being who is annulled and entirely separated from himself, hears resound outside of him this voice and this echo: *I am God*: he has an eternal way of existing, and is no longer subject to death.'"[23] In the vision of God, says Plotinus, "what sees is not our reason, but something prior and superior to our reason. . . . He who thus sees does not properly see, does not distinguish or imagine two things. He changes, he ceases to be himself, preserves nothing of himself. Absorbed in God, he makes

---

[20] A. Schmölders: Essai sur les écoles philosophiquez chez les Arabes, Paris 1842, pp. 54–68, abridged.

[21] Compare M. Maeterlinck: L'Ornement de Noces spirituelles de Ruysbroeck, Bruxelles, 1891, Introduction, p. XIX.

[22] Upanishads, M. Müller's translation, ii. 17, 334.

[23] Schmölders: Op. cit., p. 210.

but one with him, like a centre of a circle coinciding with another centre."[24] "Here," writes Suso, "the spirit dies, and yet is all alive in the marvels of the Godhead . . . and is lost in the stillness of the glorious dazzling obscurity and of the naked simple unity. It is in this modeless *where* that the highest bliss is to be found."[25] "Ich bin so gross als Gott," sings Angelus Silesius again, "Er ist als ich so klein; Er kann nicht über mich, ich unter ihm nicht sein."[26]

In mystical literature such self-contradictory phrases as "dazzling obscurity," "whispering silence," "teeming desert," are continually met with. They prove that not conceptual speech, but music rather, is the element through which we are best spoken to by mystical truth. Many mystical scriptures are indeed little more than musical compositions.

> "He who would hear the voice of Nada, 'the Soundless Sound,' and comprehend it, he has to learn the nature of Dhârânâ. . . . When to himself his form appears unreal, as do on waking all the forms he sees in dreams; when he has ceased to hear the many, he may discern the ONE—the inner sound which kills the outer. . . . For then the soul will hear, and will remember. And then to the inner ear will speak THE VOICE OF THE SILENCE. . . . And now thy *Self* is lost in SELF, *thyself* unto SELF, merged in that SELF from which thou first didst radiate. . . . Behold! thou has become the Light, thou hast become the Sound, thou art thy Master and thy God. Thou are THYSELF the object of thy search: the VOICE unbroken, that resounds throughout eternities, exempt from change, from sin exempt, the seven sounds in one, the VOICE OF THE SILENCE. *Om tat Sat*."[27]

These words, if they do not awaken laughter as you receive them, probably stir chords within you which music and language touch in common. Music gives us ontological messages which non-musical criticism is unable to contradict, though it may laugh at our foolishness in minding them. There is a verge of the mind which these things haunt; and whispers therefrom mingle with the operations of our understanding, even as the waters of the infinite ocean send their waves to break among the pebbles that lie upon our shores.

> "Here begins the sea that ends not till the world's end. Where we stand,
> Could we know the next high sea-mark set beyond these waves that gleam,
> We should know what never man hath known, nor eye of man hath scanned. . . .
> Ah, but here man's heart leaps, yearning towards the gloom with venturous glee,
> From the shore that hath no shore beyond it, set in all the seas."[28]

---

[24] Enneads, Bouillier's translation, Paris, 1861, iii. 561. Compare pp. 473–477, and vol. i. p. 27.

[25] Autobiography, pp. 309, 310.

[26] Op. cit., Strophe 10.

[27] H. P. Blavatsky: The Voice of the Silence.

[28] Swinburne: On the Verge, in "A Midsummer Vacation."

That doctrine, for example, that eternity is timeless, that our "immortality," if we live in the eternal, is not so much future as already now and here, which we find so often expressed to-day in certain philosophical circles, finds its support in a "hear, hear!" or an "amen," which floats up from that mysteriously deeper level.[29] We recognize the passwords to the mystical region as we hear them, but we cannot use them ourselves: it alone has the keeping of "the password primeval."[30]

I have now sketched with extreme brevity and insufficiency, but as fairly as I am able in the time allowed, the general traits of the mystic range of consciousness. *It is on the whole pantheistic and optimistic, or at least the opposite of pessimistic. It is anti-naturalistic, and harmonizes best with twice-bornness and so-called other-worldly states of mind.*

---

[29] Compare the extracts from Dr. Bucke, quoted on pp. 470–471.

[30] As serious an attempt as I know to mediate between the mystical region and the discursive life is contained in an article on Aristotle's Unmoved Mover, by F. C. S. Shiller, in Mind, vol. ix, 1900.

VI.B.2.   Our Experience of the Ultimate

NINIAN SMART

Ninian Smart (1927–), is a professor of religious studies at the University of California at Santa Barbara. Here he explores the intuitionist interpretation of religious experience and its relation to our theological beliefs about whatever we take to be the source or object of these experiences. Smart's contrast of the Christian and Buddhist traditions is concerned particularly with the personal and impersonal ways of conceiving the divine, ways that he concludes are complementary.

My title is of course a variation on Professor II. D. Lewis' well-known *Our Experience of God.*[1] There he expounded a variety of

---

From *Religious Studies* 20, no. 1, (March 1984): 19–26. Reprinted with the permission of Cambridge University Press.

[1] I take this opportunity of expressing my gratitude for the five years I spent at the University of London, working in the history and philosophy of religion under Professor Lewis' direction. It was a fruitful time for me, and this was in no small measure due to his solicitude

religious intuitionism, which stands in the line of Schleiermacher, Rudolf Otto and Martin Buber. These and other writers have characteristically made 'the move to experience', as a new blend of natural and revealed theology. The move makes a great deal of sense. On the one hand it grounds belief at a time when the older natural theology apparently had crumbled. On the other hand, it points to the dynamics of religious inspiration and gave a new perspective on revelation. It softens both reason and faith, of course, but it also provides a defence against skepticism. It fits well with a liberal attitude to scriptures and tradition. So there are manifest advantages of the move to experience, for those who wish to make it in the context of the Western theistic tradition. The writers I cited above, and Professor Lewis himself, have discussed religious experience from a mainly Western and theistic angle—even Otto with his great comparative concerns did so; and more needs to be said about the nature of religious experience in the broader context of Eastern and other religions. Lewis, however, paid attention to this wider problem, for instance in his 1963 article 'Buddha and God'.[2] In some respects this issue of the relationship of apparently non-theistic religions to theism is the most important one in contemporary crosscultural philosophy of religion.

There is another strand of experientialism, rather different from the intuitionist tradition, namely those who make use of notions such as 'seeing as' and 'experiencing as', of whom John Hick is the most systematic. This tradition is more propositional, because content has to be specified after the 'as. . . '. The most complex presentation of this position, and one which also makes use of performative analysis is that of Donald Evans' *The Logic of Self-Involvement*. But though these theories are important, it seems to me that intuitionism is nearer to the source of religion, in that it makes the models and words flow so far as possible out of the enigmatic character of religious experience, whereas aspectualists tend to have their models given by the tradition. Of course, both tradition and experience have to be held together if we are to be realistic about the religions: no prophets, converts or mystics spring unheralded from the general mass of human beings: rather, they develop or subvert a tradition and so one way or another are influenced by the particularities of their background. I wish then to explore the consequences of the apparent distance between non-personal and personalistic accounts of the experience of the ultimate. Before doing this, though, let me expand briefly the point that intuitionism as I have classified it is relatively realistic in regard to actual religions.

Obviously a key function is performed by people who one way or another have intense spiritual experiences: consider shamans, mediums, prophets, mystics, oracles. . . . Many of the founders or reformers of traditions have had dramatic and profound experiences: the Hebrew Prophets, Moses probably, Jesus doubtless, Paul, Augustine, Luther, Joseph Smith, the Buddha, Bodhidharma probably, Shankara probably, Nichiren, Kabir, Muhammad, Rumi, and so on. It is reasonable to think of these depth experiences as representing significant turning points which, together with the concepts

---

[2] *The Monist* (1963).

drawn from the preceding or surrounding, are the roots of new doctrines and written revelations.

Now of course modern history and sociology remind us of the economic, social, political and other 'non-religious' factors which shape the rise and spread of a religion. It is silly to isolate religion from other aspects of human life. Often, because religious experience may occur in a time of social or individual stress, the 'non-religious' causes of such stress may lead us to think of the experience merely as epiphenomenal: but since experience can shape new teachings and rituals that have far-reaching effects, it is unwise to be thus reductionists. Reductionism after all is undervaluing one sort of phenomenon in relation to others, and this may for certain purposes be justified. But all the phenomena are woven together and play their part in unwinding the fabric of the universe, and included among them are those which we classify as depth experiences in religion. It seems, empirically, that some of these are dynamic and others more resultant than causative. But some at least are powerful, and in any event most are treated seriously by those who are in the relevant traditions.

The main issue between East and West can be stated most clearly of all by contrasting Christianity and Theravada (and many other forms of Buddhism). There is the conception of God as personal in the three great Western monotheisms; but Christianity has this sense of the personhood of God even more intensely because Christ is God and Christ is a human being, a person in quite a literal way. By contrast the Theravada does not treat the Ultimate as creator, or even as Ground of Being, nor as something to pray to or worship. It is true that, chiefly through Mahayana influence, there are Buddha-statutes. But it would be wrong to see the Buddha in any strict sense as an object of worship. He has transcended processes whether of this world or the world beyond; just as the state of *nibbāna* is transcendent (but in the Theravada it is not immanent in the world at large, and only, so to speak in the liberated lives of the saints, who having realized *nibbāna* live luminously in and yet not of the world). Moreover, the Buddha's Enlightenment is a contemplative apex: it is not being seized by the Lord. The Buddha is not a prophet.

It seems reasonable therefore to distinguish between differing types of religious experience—between the numinous and the mystical, for instance.[3] Shamanistic experiences and spirit-possession have affinities to both, which may therefore be later developments out of a common archaic cluster of psychological states. Numinous experience typically involves a sense of the presence of the Other seen as 'out there' either in the world or in dream-like vision, a sense of power and mystery and of fascination, and in it all a sense of a Person. Here I fill out Otto's account. Spirits may be sub-personal or supra-personal, but these include personal quality to some degree. Mystical experience may sometimes include some of these elements, but it need not: it is often imageless, non-dual, empty, luminous, like pure consciousness.

Once we make this distinction it provides of course a ready explanation of religious differences. The one helps to generate the idea of a powerful God,

---

[3] For a bibliography of this distinction see my *Beyond Ideology* (1981), pp. 317–18.

who though mysteriously powerful confers holiness by his presence and so exhibits spiritual love as well as numinous wrath. The other helps to explain the idea of an imageless transcendence—*nibbāna*, the Void, *nirgunaṃ Brahman*, Deitas, the One. . . . It helps too to place the experience of the numinous within the context of worship, for that is the 'natural' reaction to Power and holiness and helps to express the converse smallness and unholiness of the individual confronted with the Other. And the experience of the mystical is placed within a different context, of contemplation, and of feelings of non-luminous ignorance and worldly turbulence which need to be overcome. Obviously religions often combine the paths—making contemplation take on the appearance of a form of worship, just as labor can be seen as a form of prayer (so *contemplare est laudare* just as *laborare est orare*). But as you can work without intending it as prayer so you can practice yoga[4] without seeing it as worshipping any God.

Should we therefore say—in the light of these two paths—that the one Ultimate can be experienced in two major ways? Recently John Hick has argued, in a manner reminiscent of some Vedantin teachers, that God has both a personal and a non-personal aspect.[5] Or it could be that God is so mysterious and elusive that the experience of Him (It, Her?) sometimes is expressed in minimalist ways, as with the Buddha. Thus Professor Lewis wrote:

> A more subtle analysis of the relevant texts, however, will disclose that the Buddha seems to have been anxious, not to dispense with God in the true sense, but to get rid of crude notions of God and come to a very subtle understanding of what it is really like to encounter God in the way set out by those who stress the elusiveness and mystery of God today.[6]

The two positions are a bit different. Hick argues that we should conceive of the Ultimate as noumenal X of which the various religious experiences as filtered through and expressed by the traditions are so many phenomenal apprehensions. But Lewis thinks of the Ultimate as God, though mysteriously and rather minimally described. But he obviously packs more into the word than the Buddhist does with terms such as *nibbāna* and *Tathatā*. Of course there is no reason why a person who is a Christian personalist should not begin at the theistic end and see other religions in the light of God; every religion has to have theory or theology about the others. But what about the converse move, by the non-theist who sees God as a human projection of at best ethical and practical significance?

A third position is taken up in my *Beyond Ideology*, namely that Buddhism and Christianity are complementary traditions, giving alternative views of the transcendent X that can nourish and criticize one another.

Though Lewis does not use Hick's model of the Ultimate as noumenal, because God is characterizable, if dimly, in a way in which the noumen is not,

---

[4] In the general sense: I am thinking of varieties of Buddhist and Jain yoga as well as Hindu.

[5] In his *God Has Many Names* (1983).

[6] *Philosophy of Religion* (1975), p. 328.

he holds that there is no direct knowledge of God, and so rejects what he takes to be one interpretation of mysticism—which he sees as sometimes claiming direct knowledge of God. This suggests we might see what happens if we modify his stated views in the direction of Hick: namely the Ultimate presents itself in differing ways, and one of the presentations—indeed the central presentation—is that personal but minimally described God which people can come to be aware of intuitionally. Since the problem of the religious noumenon is a complex and interesting one, it is worth exploring further here: and in the discussion I shall consider mystical non-dual experience about which Lewis has important and controversial things to say.

It may be useful to discuss the issue with some concrete examples. Let us take Arjuna's experience of Vishnu in the *Gītā* and Job's of Yahweh towards the end of *Job*. Let us assume that Arjuna and Job are historical persons (they may have been). The image content is rather different; but in both cases the divine presence is fearful, majestic, befitting a Creator; in both God speaks. Let us call these appearances (including speech) the Vishnu phenomenon and the Yahweh phenomenon. By the theory of the noumenon, the noumenal Ultimate is not Vishnu or Yahweh, but is perceived as such. Even saying that the Ultimate is *one* may be open to question, or there are religions in which what is divine is seen as plural. So we should perhaps say that the noumen is neither one nor many. One might go further and ask questions about the impression given (by using a noun and one indeed which is connected with Kant and 'things-in-themselves') that the Ultimate is a Being. Could it not be equally a process or processes? Perhaps we should call it 'X-ing'—an unknown Beyond. . . . If it has definition it is as that which so to say gives rise to revelatory experiences, such as the Yahweh phenomenon and the Vishnu phenomenon.

Why however should we pick out *these* events rather than others as pointing to what lies Beyond? Perhaps we do not need to make any hard distinction. After all every event potentially might point to the Ultimate, and doubtless a saintly or enlightened person is one who sees the Beyond in everything. Presumably, however, in seeing the Beyond in the grass or the sky I schematize it in some way—e.g. as permeated with the divine inner presence. In doing this I am linking the 'ordinary' world to the theophanies of Yahweh or of Vishnu.

Here, however, there is a tangle of problems. If I see the grass *as* the work of God, I am treating it in a different way from the theophany am I not? The theophany of God to Job I treat, being Christian, as a specially revelatory phenomenon, as being directly revelatory of God. In seeing green grass I see a phenomenon produced as it were by things in themselves; but in seeing God (or hearing him) I am perceiving a phenomenon given rise to not by things in themselves but by the divine X.

But of course it is possible to identify the noumena behind the grass and the sky with Suchness. This is a move made by T. R. V. Murti, in his exposition of the 'central philosophy' of Buddhism (i.e. the Madhyamika) [7] Maybe we do not wish to use the Kantian apparatus, of course, for the grass and the sky. But it is a useful 'hypothesis' for the present discussion since something like

---

[7] T. R. V. Murti, *The Central Philosophy of Buddhism* (1955).

the idea of an underlying 'invisible' material cause or indefinable reality or Suchness is in fact used in Indian religious philosophies; and it raises questions as to whether something like a noumenal X underlying the world of appearance has a different placement from the divine-type noumenon.

Let me try and put this last point plainly. We might think of the cosmos in the following way: it is a reality out there (so to speak) which impinges on our consciousness, and we describe it in various ways, including by complex theories. It is as if science were a kind of struggle between ourselves as seekers and Nature which progressively yields her secrets to us, but in such a manner that we notice how theory-laden and perception-laden are our descriptions. What is it like in itself? All we can speak about by definition is the interface between our knowledge and consciousness on the one hand and an indescribable X—maybe we could call it Process in Itself, the other side of sensuous flux. This Process in Itself might even be better described by some mass word, to prevent us asking how many (processes, things, etc.) there are. We might call it Energy in Itself. The picture I have drawn is, incidentally, reminiscent of Schopenhauer's.[8] Now what is the status of this Cosmic Energy? Maybe we think we get insight into it in mystical experience, so it becomes a fluctuating Emptiness; or through action, for this conveys the 'insideness' of Energy (and the Cosmos becomes the World as Will and Representation). But from a theist's point of view, we would be inclined to be dualistic about it and to say therefore that this Energy is a creation by God. Even if we were to agree with some Hindu systems and claim that the world is God's body, we would still distinguish between the Cosmic Energy as God's 'subtle body' and God's consciousness: he has a doubly transcendent aspect.[9] In brief, do we not require a double decker structure of the noumenal? The first level would be for Energy in Itself, the second for God as Creator. If we adopted a Theravadin or Sankhya view of nature and liberation we might have a similar double decker structure, with the liberated state as lying beyond Energy, which would be merely the natural substratum of the phenomenal flux.

After all the theist does not want to treat the Vishnu phenomenon or the Yahweh phenomenon as reflecting an underlying part of Energy in Itself, a process or event or thing which is part of the general fabric of the cosmos. That would reduce Vishnu and Yahweh to finite and shortlived flashes of the numinous, mere gods, not the grand and unspeakable Creator of everything else, including the whole of the unseen flux of the world. And though the Buddhist might use Kantian terminology, we do not, if we take it seriously and in its original context, necessarily wish to identify it with Emptiness or Brahman as Being, Consciousness and Bliss. So it might be useful to invent a different term to use of the noumenal Focus of religion which so to say lies behind the phenomenal Foci of religious experience and practice. I shall use the term transfocal. I am thinking that the believer is oriented towards a being or state which represents the focus of her faith, and that this focus presents

---

[8] See Bryan Magee, *The Philosophy of Schopenhauer* (1983), appendix on Buddhism.

[9] See my article 'God's body', *Union Seminary Quarterly Review* xxxvii, 1 and 2 (Fall/Winter 1981–2).

itself in experience, ritual, conscience and so on, and that yet we have the notion that the Ultimate lies beyond such presentational foci [10]

Now it is easy enough to understand the idea that God lies beyond the experiences of him—that beyond the phenomenon encountered by Job or Arjuna there lies a Divine Being in Itself, a transfocal Reality. This is part of what Lewis means by the indirectness of the knowledge of God: we do not as it were see into His essence. (Though I would add as an aside that the resistance among most theists to the supposition that we could know God's essence derives mainly, I think, from honorific sentiments—not to keep God beyond us is to belittle Him.) But is it easy to understand the same concept of the transfocal X in the case of non-dual mystical experience?

For if the non-dual experience of a focus involves that there is transfocal X beyond or behind the non-dual, then it is something other, and there is a duality. This argument might well appeal of course to theists who dislike all this talk of non-duality. But the notion of a non-dual experience (advaya, advaita) is a well attested and important one in some religious traditions. It may have its difficulties, but so does theism; and we should exercise at least a certain charity in trying to make sense of it. One might abandon the idea of the transfocal in this case: the experience is what it is, non-dual and nothing lies as it were behind it or beyond it. Now personally I think that people in fact have non-dual experiences in which the distinction between subject and object disappears, and they think of them as giving them insight into the true nature of the world. But they are in a strange predicament. To treat the experience as an isolated one, in which by chance the distinction between subject and object is overcome, is to treat it as dualistically, or rather pluralistically, separated from other experiences. But still, the experience could be a kind of knowledge of the non-duality of things: in which case it does involve going beyond mere experience as an isolable phenomenon. Because all other experiences than that of the non-dual mystic are dualistic, there is an important sense in which he knows directly the non-dual nature of the world. If, that is, the world is like that. Theism and non-dualism are actually competing doctrines and have differing consequences.

It is partly because of this that I prefer to think of theistic and non-dualist positions as complementary: that is they partially contradict one another but provide, positively, alternative insights and good mutual criticism. I am not sure that the Copernican image of Hick, of the religious presentations of the Real as being in orbit round one ultimate Sun, quite works out. But it is a good way of looking at world religions from a theistic point of view and in full recognition of the soft and experience-based character of revelation as perceived in a comparative context. Similarly we might say that Lewis' intuitionism in a numinous-oriented mode is an important way of explaining revelations and looking positively to other religious traditions.

He helps us to answer the question 'What would God have to be like if we are to count other religions' central experiences as indeed being experiences of

---

[10] For the phenomenological theory of foci see my *The Science of Religion and the Sociology of Knowledge* (1973) and *The Phenomenon of Religion* (1973).

God?' On this basis his account of Buddhism works. But there are questions from the other direction, as I have pointed out—such as 'What does the world have to be like if Theravada is true and Christianity has something positive to offer?' Maybe it is that theistic experience is a kind of Freudian projection; or maybe it is that Mahayana Buddhism is right in allowing *bhakti* and numinous experience a certain transitional validity. Perhaps Christ is to be seen as a Bodhisattva. All this is part of a continuing debate between the great cultural traditions.

I have made more of the distinction between the numinous and the mystical, especially that type of the mystical which is non-dual, than Lewis would like. But there is a certain metaphysical attraction in the polarity, for the numinous draws us outwards to strange reflections about the ultimate explanation of this cosmos in which we are immersed; while mysticism draws us inwards towards pure consciousness and so the mysterious role of conscious beings in a cosmos drenched in colours and feelings and yet noumenally quite alien. If the questions of why anything exists at all and how any consciousness exists are the root speculations of metaphysics, then the differing modes of experience of the ultimate reflect well the searches in which we are as humans involved.

I have, then, in this article suggested that there are different ways of looking at the nature of religious experience. It is an attempt to amplify Lewis's theory, and through him those of other perceptive members of the intuitionist tradition from Schleiermacher onwards.

VI.C. Has Religious Experience Epistemic Value for Religious Belief?

VI.C.1. The Cognitive Status of Mystical Experience

WILLIAM J. WAINWRIGHT

William J. Wainwright (1935–) is professor of philosophy and religious studies at the University of Wisconsin at Milwaukee. His book, Mysticism, *from which the following selection is taken, is an important contribution from a contemporary supporter of theism to the discussion of whether religious experience is a valid source of cognitive support for religious belief. Carefully examining the analogies between sense experience and mystical experience and the objections based on alleged disanalogies, Wainwright argues that both sense experience and mystical experience are noetic and the cognitive claims based on these experiences are independently checkable. He finds the analogies close enough to provide strong support for the epistemic claims of mystical experiences and the objections not very strong at all.*

I

Mystical experience is often said to involve a kind of 'seeing' or 'tasting' or 'touching'. We are told that mystical experience is an 'experimental knowledge' of the divine. Mystical experiences are believed to involve a direct or immediate awareness of reality or some aspect of reality which is normally hidden from us. It is clear that an analogy with sense experience is intended and that part of what is implied in ascribing cognitive value to mystical experience is that these experiences are, in some important respects, like ordinary perceptual experience. In the opposite camp we find critics like C. B. Martin[1] who assume that ordinary perceptual experiences provide us with the paradigm of a cognitive or perceptual experience and go on to argue that religious experiences cannot be cognitive or perceptual because they deviate in certain important ways from that paradigm.

From *Mysticism* (Madison, Wisc.: University of Wisconsin Press, 1981), pp. 82–96, 100–110.

The analogy (or lack of it) between mystical experience and sense experience appears, then, to be critically important both to those who ascribe cognitive value to mystical experiences and to those who refuse to do so.

A

Mystical experiences and sense experiences are alike in two important respects. (1) Both types of experience are noetic. (2) On the basis of both types of experience claims are made about something other than the experience itself. These claims are corrigible and independently checkable. In each case there are tests for determining whether or not the object of the experience is real and tests for determining whether or not an apparent perception of that object is a genuine one.

(1) Sense experiences (whether veridical or not) have a noetic quality. This involves two things. (a) The experiences have an object, i.e. they are experiences of something (real or imagined). In this respect sense experiences are unlike pains, feelings of depression and so on. The latter may have causes. They may be aroused or occasioned by certain kinds of events or objects but (in spite of certain continental philosophers) they are not experiences of these events or objects. (To the question 'What is the object of a visual [auditory] experience?' we can reply 'Colours and shapes [sounds]'. The question 'What is the object of a dull pain [a feeling of depression]?' cannot be answered so easily.) (b) Sense experience typically involves the conviction that the object on which the experience is focused is 'really there', that it exists and that one 'experimentally' apprehends it. To use Berkeley's language, the experience has 'outness'. This conviction is not an interpretation which is placed upon the experience, but part of the experience itself.

In spite of the fact that some mystics speak as if their experiences transcended the subject-object structure of ordinary perceptual experience, many mystical experiences (and perhaps all of them) are noetic in this sense. (For example, monistic mystics by and large agree that they experience something which transcends space and time, is devoid of distinctions and is supremely valuable. Theistic mystics believe that they experimentally perceive God.)

(2) No type of experience can be called cognitive if it induces those who have it to make false claims. Thus, the experience of a mirage or the experiences one obtains by pressing one's eyeball and seeing double are called delusive because they are inherently misleading—the very nature of these experiences is such that (until one learns better) one is likely to base false claims upon them, (that water is really present or that there are two candles rather than one). There is no conclusive reason to suppose that mystical experiences are delusive in this sense. The mystic does not make false empirical statements on the basis of his experiences because he does not make empirical statements. Rather he claims to know, on the basis of his experience, that God is real and present to him or that there is an 'uncreated, imperishable Beyond', or something of the sort. It would therefore seem that we are entitled to assert that these experiences are delusive only if we have good independent reasons for believing that claims of this kind are false. It is by no means clear that we do.

But the fact that experiences are not delusive does not imply that they are cognitive. Pains are not delusive, but they are not cognitive either. One of the reasons for calling sense experiences cognitive is that not only do they not induce *false* claims, they also provide a basis for making *true* claims about something other than the experience itself. This involves two things. First, sense experiences are means of apprehending (some aspect) of reality. Those who have them are more likely to discern certain truths than those who do not, or can at least discern them more easily. Second, sense experiences can be appealed to, to justify the truths which have been made out by their means. For example, people with normal vision are more likely to discern truths about colours and shapes, and can do so more easily, than those who are blind, and they are entitled to appeal to their visual experiences to justify their claims.

Are mystical experiences like sense experiences in this respect? We can at least say this: on the basis of their experiences, mystics make claims about something other than their own experiences. They believe that they have directly apprehended a reality which others accept on faith, or on the basis of certain arguments, and they appeal to their experiences to justify their claims.[2] Furthermore (assuming that there is no disproof of God's existence, or of the reality of the One, etc.) these claims are not known to be false. We seem therefore to have found a respect in which sense experiences and mystical experiences are like each other and unlike pains.

The analogy extends further. When a person claims to see, hear or touch something, his claim is not self-certifying. Things other than his own experience are relevant to a determination of the truth or falsity of his claim. C. B. Martin and others have asserted that sense experiences are radically unlike mystical experiences in this respect, for (they say) when the mystic claims to experience God or the Brahman, his claims are not corrigible—there are (to use Martin's phrase) no independent tests and check-up procedures which he and others would regard as relevant to a determination of the truth or falsity of the claims he makes. His claims are therefore private (like first person psychological reports), not public (like ordinary perceptual claims).

This is simply false. Misled by the fact that certain familiar tests (for example, the appeal to the agreement of others) play at most a minor role in the evaluation of mystical experiences, critics like Martin have illicitly concluded that mystics, therefore, dismiss all tests and check-up procedures as irrelevant and regard their claims as incorrigible.

Suppose someone claims to have seen an elephant in his backyard. There are at least two ways in which his claim might be attacked. One might try to show that no elephant was there at all, or one might try to show that he could not have seen it because, for example, he was not in a position to observe it, or his sensory equipment was defective. When we turn to mystical experience we find both sorts of test and check-up procedure (at least in a rough and ready way), that is, we find independent procedures for determining whether the experience is a genuine perception of its object.

Even when claims about such things as God or Nibbāna are grounded in mystical consciousness, they are not self-certifying. Things other than the experience itself are relevant to an evaluation of their truth. For example, considerations of logic are relevant. *Pace* Stace, these claims cannot be true if the concepts of God or Nibbāna are self-contradictory. Again, considerations adduced in arguments for and against the existence of God have some bearing on the truth of the claims made by theistic mystics. Even the statement that there is a One beyond distinctions does not appear to be self-certifying though, since what is claimed is relatively minimal, it would be harder to disprove. (Considerations of logic, and considerations adduced by positivists and naturalists, might count against it.) When the mystic asserts that he has experienced God (or Nibbāna, or Brahman) he implies that what he has experienced is real. He should therefore recognise that things besides his own experience are relevant to an evaluation of his claim. It is true that mystics are usually certain of the truth of the claims that they make, but this is no more incompatible with their corrigibility than the fact that I am certain that there is a red pen in front of me is incompatible with the fact that that claim is corrigible. In short, claims about God, or Nibbāna and other things of that kind are not self-certifying, and we have some idea of the sorts of things which count for and against them.

There are, then, independent tests for determining whether the object of mystical experience is real. There are also independent tests for determining whether an experience of this object is a genuine perception of it. Consider theistic mystical experiences, for example. Even if God exists and a direct experience of Him is possible, it does not follow that every claim to be immediately aware of God is justified. How, though, do we distinguish experiences of God which are veridical from those which are not? If we turn our attention to the communities in which theistic mysticism has flourished we find that various tests have been used to distinguish the experiences which genuinely involve a perception of God from those which do not. Each of the following six criteria is employed in the Christian (particularly the Catholic) community. Similar criteria are used in other communities.

(1) The consequences of the experience must be good for the mystic. The experience must lead to, produce, or reinforce, a new life marked by such virtues as wisdom, humility and charity. (Sanity should be subsumed under this criterion. A genuine experience of God is believed to have a tendency to produce a life of rather extraordinary goodness. It seems reasonable to suppose that sanity is a necessary condition of such a life.) This criterion helps to explain why people are bothered by the presence of certain kinds of causes. Many people find it impossible to believe that the use of drugs, nervous and physical disorders and so on, can play a part in the best sort of life. Consequently, if they find that these things play a major role in the life of a mystic, they will tend to discount his experience.

(2) One must consider the effect which the experience has on others. For instance, one should ask whether the mystic's words, actions and example tend to build up the community or weaken it.

(3) The depth, the profundity and the 'sweetness' (Jonathan Edwards) of what the mystic says on the basis of his experience counts in favour of the genuineness of that experience. On the other hand, the insignificance, or the silliness, of what he says counts against it. (On the basis of this criterion many would reject the claims of Margery Kempe.[3])

(4) We must examine what the mystic says on the basis of his experience and see whether it agrees or disagrees with orthodox talk. (It should be noted that this test is not circular. The statement being tested is a statement like

'Teresa saw God', or 'John received heavenly consolations'. Statements of this kind are not Christian dogmas.)

(5) It will be helpful to determine whether the experience in question resembles other mystical experiences regarded as paradigmatic by the religious community. (In the Roman Catholic church, experiences are often compared with the experiences of Teresa of Avila or of John of the Cross.)

(6) We must also consider the pronouncements of authority. In some communities (for example, Zen) the word of the spiritual director, guru or master is final. In other religious communities, the voice of the spiritual director is important though not conclusive. In some cases the relevant authority may be the community as a whole, or some special organ of it. (For example, the standing enjoyed by the experiences of John of the Cross and Teresa in the Roman Catholic community is largely a consequence of their acceptance by that community and its official representatives.) In some cases all of these authorities may be relevant.

If I am correct, these criteria are similar to the tests which we employ in ordinary perceptual cases to determine whether an apparent perception of an object is a genuine perception of it, that is, they are similar to the tests which take things into account like the position of the observer and the condition of his sensory equipment. Of course, the *nature* of the tests is not much alike. Nevertheless, the point of them is, viz, to show not that the object of the experience is real or unreal but that there is or is not a genuine perception of it. (One would not expect the nature of the tests to be much alike. For example, in the case of introvertive mystical experience there is no sensory equipment which can go awry because sense organs are not involved. Nor does there appear to be anything which clearly corresponds to the position of the observer in the sense experience.)

B

Among the more important tests and check-up procedures which are used to evaluate ordinary perceptual claims are (1) the agreement and disagreement of others occupying similar positions, and (2) the success or failure of predictions which have been based upon the experience whose claims are in question. Are similar tests used to assess the cognitive status of mystical experience?

(1) The claim that mystical experience is cognitive is frequently supported by appealing to the rather surprising amount of agreement that exists. Extrovertive mystics, monistic mystics and theistic mystics can be found in radically different cultures, in places which have had little or no contact with each other, and in all periods of history. Not only are their experiences alike, they base remarkably similar claims upon them. But some kinds of agreement are irrelevant. The visual and auditory experiences of persons from different cultures, with diverse social backgrounds and different psychological makeups, are often quite similar. Analogously mystics from different cultures, with diverse social backgrounds and different psychological makeups often have similar experiences. It is also the case that people suffering from migraines or indigestion undergo similar experiences in spite of the differences in culture, social background, psychological makeup and many other factors. Sense

experiences are widespread and so are mystical experiences, but so also are migraines and stomachaches. Since migraines and stomachaches are paradigm cases of non-cognitive experience, the presence of this sort of agreement has little tendency to show that a mode of experience is cognitive.

There are other sorts of agreement. People who make visual (or auditory or tactual) observations are normally able to describe conditions under which others can make similar observations. ('If you go into the room on the left, you will see the body.' 'If the telescope is trained on such and such a place at such and such a time, you will obtain a sighting of the moons of Jupiter.') Now mystics are able to do something like this. For example, they can prescribe procedures which are likely to lead to introvertive experiences. (These include the special postures, breathing techniques, a deliberate withdrawal of the attention from sense objects, mental concentration and so on. Sometimes these procedures are specified in detail. Furthermore, in spite of some variation—particularly in the emphasis placed upon physical techniques—there is a great deal of agreement as to just what these procedures involve.)

Now the only agreement or disagreement which is directly relevant to the cognitive value of a sense experience, is agreement or disagreement among those who use the procedures associated with that type of experience, and try to make the relevant observation under the prescribed conditions. Agreement among people who fail to follow these procedures is not expected, and its absence is therefore regarded as beside the point. If sense experience provides the model for all cognitive modes of experience, then the fact that most of us have never had a mystical experience is irrelevant, for most of us have made no attempt to use the mystic's techniques.

Nevertheless, agreement among those who employ a set of prescribed techniques is not decisive. This kind of agreement is characteristic of a sense experience, but it is also characteristic of subjective experiences. (For example, it can be safely asserted that people eating ten *bratwurst* sandwiches within twenty minutes will undergo strikingly similar and equally unpleasant digestive experiences.)[4] What sort of agreement, then, is relevant? People who see, hear and touch, base claims about the world upon their experiences, and a lack of agreement among those following the appropriate procedures is believed to have an important bearing on the truth of their claims. People suffering from headaches or indigestion, on the other hand, do not base claims about the world upon their experiences and hence do not consider the agreement or disagreement of others to be relevant to the *truth* of such claims.

Mystics base claims about 'objective' reality upon their experiences. They differ in this respect from people suffering from headaches and indigestion. But do they believe that the agreement or disagreement of others is relevant to the truth of their claims? Do they take the fact that some people have similar experiences when following the appropriate procedures as counting *for* their claims? And do they take the fact that there are others who do not have similar experiences when following these procedures as counting *against* their claims? If they do, then we have discovered what may be an important analogy between mystical experience and sense experience. If they do not, we have uncovered what many would regard as a significant disanalogy. Unfortunately, the situation is ambiguous.

I am inclined to think that at least some mystics believe that the fact that others have had similar experiences, and have made similar claims, supports the claims which they base upon their own experiences, and that because of this agreement these mystics are more confident of the cognitive value of their experiences than they would otherwise be. However, no distinction appears to be made between those experiences which are obtained by employing techniques of prayer and meditation and those which occur spontaneously. *All* similar experiences are thought to confirm (equally) the claims which are made or (which comes to more or less the same thing) the cognitive value of the experiences upon which those claims are based.

It is not clear whether mystics believe that disagreement has any bearing upon the cognitive value of their experiences.[5] Mystics are clearly not disturbed by the fact that most people never enjoy mystical experiences. Nor do they seem to be bothered by the fact that some people earnestly employ the appropriate techniques but never achieve illumination or union. These points are not decisive, however, for it might nonetheless be true that if there *was* more disagreement than in fact obtains, the mystic would withdraw or qualify his claim. The mystic regards disagreement as relevant if there is *any* degree of disagreement which *would* be taken as counting against his claim if it *were* to occur. Suppose, for example, that the mystic were to discover that those whom he thought had achieved a unitive experience by employing the standard techniques had not really done so. Would he regard this discovery as counting against the cognitive value of his own experiences? Of course he might (particularly if he had used these techniques himself) but he might only conclude that the techniques were not as effective as he had believed them to be. Suppose, however, the mystic stood alone. While it is by no means clear that the mystic would (or should) repudiate his experience under these conditions (it is, perhaps, too impressive for that) he might nevertheless be bothered by the absence of supporting claims. (There is some evidence that those who believe that their religious experiences are comparatively unique are more suspicious of them than those who are aware of the fact that others have had similar experiences.[6]) If he would, then perhaps the mystic does regard disagreement as having at least *some* relevance to the evaluation of his experiences.

What emerges from these considerations is this. The mystic bases ontological statements upon his experiences and seems to believe that the fact that others have similar experiences confirms those claims (or the veridical nature of his own experience). It is *possible* that if others were to fail altogether to have similar experiences, he would take this fact as counting against the veridical character of his own experience. In these respects mystical experience appears to be more like sense experience than like feelings of nausea or depression.

On the other hand there are significant disanalogies. (i) *All* similar experiences are believed to confirm the mystic's claim. The fact that some of these experiences were not obtained by employing the appropriate procedures but occurred spontaneously is ignored. (ii) Furthermore, it is not clear that a breakdown of the procedures for obtaining these experiences would induce the mystic to hedge his claims. In both respects mystical experience differs from sense experience. In the case of the latter, the only *relevant* agreement is that which is found among those who satisfy certain appropriate conditions, and a failure to obtain similar experiences after meeting those conditions casts serious doubts upon the experience's validity.

What is perhaps most significant is the fact that the presence of agreement or disagreement is not regarded as a crucial consideration by those who have had mystical experiences. It is not even clear that it is considered to be important. In the case of sense experience, on the other hand, the presence or absence of agreement (among those who employ the appropriate procedures) is always important, and often crucial.

(2) In evaluating a particular instance of sense experience, we consider predictions which have been based upon that experience. Successful predictions count for its veridicality and unsuccessful predictions count against it. Furthermore, if anyone were to attempt to justify the claim that sense experience in general is a cognitive mode of experience, he would undoubtedly appeal to the fact that a very large number of successful predictions about the course of external events have been based upon experiences of that type.

A few predictions do appear to be based upon mystical experience. On the basis of their experience mystics frequently assert that the soul is immortal and, of course, this involves a prediction.[7] Furthermore, mystics occasionally claim that their experiences confirm theological systems which include certain predictions as an integral part. Thus, Christian mystics have sometimes regarded their experiences as confirmations of the truth of Christian dogma, and Christian dogma includes a belief in the general resurrection and the transfiguration of heaven and earth.[8] A mystic may also, on the basis of his experience, predict that if one subjects oneself to the appropriate discipline (for example, practises the Jesus prayer or follows the noble eight-fold path) he will obtain a vision of God or pass into Nibbāna or something of the sort.[9]

Now many, perhaps most, of the predictions made by those who can see or hear (etc.) can be checked *both* by others who can see or hear *and* by those who cannot. Suppose, for example, that I see thunderclouds approaching and predict it will rain. A blind man cannot do this (though he might predict rain on the basis of other factors). He can, however, *check* this prediction. If it rains he will not see it, but he will (if suitably situated) feel, hear, and perhaps even taste the rain. If he does not, he is entitled to conclude that my prediction was a failure.

The claim that we are immortal and the claim that human beings will be resurrected are, I think, verifiable (though not falsifiable). However, the experiences which would justify them are (in the first case) post-mortem experiences, and (in the second case) post-Advent experiences. Neither mystics nor non-mystics can verify these claims in this life, or before the second Advent. If one verified the third prediction one would be a mystic. The conclusion then is that none of these predictions can be checked in this life by the non-mystic, and the first two predictions cannot be checked in this life by anyone.

Since these predictions cannot be checked, they cannot be appealed to in order to establish the cognitive value of mystical experience as such, or to establish the cognitive value of a particular instance of mystical experience. It would thus appear that a blind man may have a reason for ascribing cognitive value to visual experience (*qua* mode of experience) or to a particular visual experience, viz, that the blind man knows that visual experiences in general, or a particular visual experience, have led to successful predictions, whereas the non-mystic does not know that mystical experiences in general, or a particular mystical experience, have led to successful predictions. This difference is striking and perhaps significant.

(3) A consideration of the presence of agreement or disagreement, and of the success or failure of predictions which have been based upon the experience play an important role in the evaluation of the cognitive status of sense consciousness but not in the evaluation of the cognitive status of mystical consciousness. These differences are intelligible if sense experiences are cognitive and mystical experiences are not. However, there is another way to account for them. The differences can be explained by the fact that the *objects* of these two kinds of experience are radically different.

Suppose[10] that God is the object of a mystical experience (rather than Nibbāna or the Ātman, etc.). If God is what He is supposed to be (omnipotent, omniscient, mysterious, other, transcendent and so on), then whether or not one has an experience of Him will, in the last analysis, depend upon His will; there will be no set of procedures the correct use of which invariably results in illumination or union. Hence, while these experiences may be repeatable in the weak sense that given *exactly* the same conditions (including God's gracious activity), the same experience will occur, there is no reason to suppose that they will be repeatable in the strong sense, viz, that certain procedures or methods can be described which are such that (almost) all who correctly employ them will obtain the experience in question.

God is radically unlike physical objects in this respect. Physical objects exhibit spatio-temporal continuity, are relatively accessible and behave in law-like and regular ways. Given the nature of physical objects, one reasonably supposes that if one's experience of the object is veridical, others will enjoy similar experiences under similar conditions.[11] One expects experiences of these objects to cohere and mutually support one another in certain familiar ways. If the nature of physical objects were different, however, these expectations would not be reasonable; experiences of these objects would not be repeatable in the strong sense, *even though the objects were real and experiences of them were veridical.* Suppose, for example, that mountains jumped about in a discontinuous fashion, randomly appeared and disappeared, and behaved in other lawless and unpredictable ways. If these conditions obtained, observation under similar conditions would not normally yield similar results even if mountains were real and experiences of them were veridical. There would be no reason to expect experiences in this area to cohere and support one another in the way they do.

The general point is this. The nature of an object should (at least partly) determine the tests for its presence.[12] Given the nature of *physical* objects it is reasonable to suppose that genuine experiences of those objects can be confirmed by employing appropriate procedures and obtaining similar experiences, and that non-genuine experiences can be disconfirmed by employing the same procedures and obtaining different experiences. God's nature, on the other hand, is radically different from the nature of physical objects. It is therefore not clearly reasonable to suppose that (apparent) experiences of God can be confirmed or disconfirmed in the same fashion.

The difference in the nature of their respective objects thus explains why the presence or absence of agreement is an important test in the one case, but not in the other. This difference also explains other disanalogies. (1) God bestows His grace upon whom he pleases and is therefore not bound by our techniques. One person may employ mental prayer and fail to obtain the desired experience, while another who does not practise contemplation may experience (some degree) of illumination. It is therefore only to be expected that little distinction is made between similar experiences which are obtained by these techniques and similar experiences which occur spontaneously. In so far as agreement is considered to be relevant, *both* are regarded as confirmatory. (2) Since God freely bestows the experience upon whom He will, we have no idea of how many of these experiences to expect. Hence it is not clear at just what point (if any) a mystic should begin to be bothered by the *absence of agreement*. We should, therefore, not be surprised if we find it difficult to specify a degree of disagreement which is so great that in the face of it a mystic would or should withdraw his claim.

Similar considerations show that, in the case of theistic mystical experiences, the demand for successful predictions may be inappropriate. It is reasonable to insist on successful predictions when the type of experience which is involved is supposed to provide access to ordinary empirical objects—objects which exhibit spatial-temporal continuity, which are accessible, and which behave in law-like and regular ways—for the nature of these objects is such that testable predictions can be made about them.[13] However, it is not clear that the demand for successful predictions is reasonable when the object in question is (like God) a-spatial, a-temporal (?), and neither accessible in the way in which ordinary objects are accessible nor law-like and regular in its behaviour.

In short, there is no reason to believe that genuine experiences of God will be supported by the experience of others in the way in which veridical sense experiences are supported by the experience of others, or that veridical experiences of God will provide data which can be used to predict the future. The fact that mystical experiences are not supported by the agreement of others in the way in which veridical sense experiences are supported by the agreement of others, and that they afford no glimpse of the future, is therefore not decisive.

But suppose that the object of a mystical experience is Nibbāna, the nirguṇa Brahman, or one's own puruṣa rather than God. These realities do not dispense favours, but are impersonal and inactive. Since they do not act, their 'behaviour' cannot be irregular and unpredictable. Nor do they appear to have any other features which would make it unreasonable to include agreement and disagreement among the tests and check-up procedures that are used to assess experiences of them.[14] However, there is a reason for disregarding the lack of successful predictions. By definition, predictions are concerned with the temporal order; their content is the future. Nibbāna, the nirguṇa Brahman, and one's puruṣa are non-temporal realities. They are neither in time nor do they intervene in the temporal order. There is thus no reason to suppose that veridical experiences of these things will lead to successful predictions. . . .

D

Are there, then, reasons for supposing that mystical experiences are cognitive? I believe that there are. Consider the following argument:

(1) If the analogy between mystical experience and sense experience is very close,[15] then we are entitled to regard mystical experience as a mode of cognitive experience.[16]

(2) The analogy is very close. (Both experiences are noetic. Both are the basis of corrigible and independently checkable claims about something other than the experience itself In both cases there are tests for determining the reality of the object of experience as well as tests for determining the genuineness of an apparent perception of that object. (The tests are different in the two cases but the differences can be explained by differences in the nature of the objects of the two experiences.) The tests are relevant in both cases, and their application yields positive results in a large number of instances.[17])

(3) Therefore, we are entitled to regard mystical experience as a mode of cognitive experience.

A variant of this argument may be more persuasive:

(4) The analogy between mystical experience and sense experience is close enough to warrant the conclusion that mystical experiences are cognitive *provided that* we have independent reasons for believing mystics when they assert that they have directly experienced some transcendent aspect of reality.

(5) We have independent reasons for believing mystics when they assert that they have experienced a transcendent aspect of reality. (For example, arguments for God's existence, and for the sanity, sanctity and intelligence of the great mystics.[18])

(6) We are therefore warranted in concluding that mystical experiences are cognitive.

Sense experience is the paradigm case of cognitive experience. (1) therefore seems plausible. The plausibility of (5) largely depends upon the success or failure of natural theology, and here opinions can and do differ. (2) and (4) involve the same problem. One's opinion of these premises will be determined not only by one's estimate of the number or respects in which sense experience and mystical experience are like and unlike each other, but also by one's judgment as to the relative importance of these resemblances and differences. (Thus, when evaluating sense experiences the presence or absence of agreement is regarded as vitally important; when evaluating mystical experiences, as relatively unimportant. One's assessment of the significance of this fact will depend upon whether or not one believes that the appeal to the presence or absence of agreement is an appropriate test for the evaluation of mystical experience, upon whether or not one thinks that this test must be among the tests used to determine the cognitive value of an experience, and so on.) No mechanical decision procedures are available which can be used to determine the truth value of these premises, just as there are no mechanical decision procedures which can be appealed to, to determine what one should do when moral obligations conflict, or how one should appraise a new style of art, or the general plausibility of a world view. These cases call for judgment and reasonable people may differ. (There are criteria, but it is sometimes difficult to see whether or not they have been applied correctly. For example, in choosing a world view, we should attempt to determine which view has the most explanatory power. But this itself calls for judgment.) In spite of these considerations, I submit that, if the argument of the preceding sections has been correct, the analogy between mystical experience and sense experience is sufficiently striking to justify (4) and, somewhat less clearly, (2).

Although I believe that the two arguments being considered in this section are good arguments, their failure would not show that mystical experiences are non-cognitive. It is often assumed that no experience can be cognitive which is unlike sense experience in very many important respects. This is, of course, quite vague. (What deviations are *important* and how many deviations are *very many*?) More significantly, it is not clear that the assumption is true. As far as I can see, all that we *mean* when we say that an experience is cognitive or perceptual is that through this experience we come to know something which we could not know, or could not know as easily, in other ways, and (probably) that the knowledge in question is noninferential. If this is even roughly correct, then 'x is a cognitive experience' does not entail 'x is very much like sense experiences'. Of course sense experiences clearly are cognitive experiences. Therefore, if we can show that mystical experience is very much like sense experience, we have provided a good (if not conclusive) reason for supposing that mystical experience is cognitive. On the other hand, if the analysis I have provided is correct, then, even if mystical experience and sense experience were radically dissimilar, this dissimilarity would not be decisive. (Even if mystical experiences were radically unlike such objective experiences as seeing or hearing, it would not follow that they were like paradigmatic subjective experiences. They might—as Stace suggests—be like neither.[19])

II

But the conclusion that mystical experiences are cognitive, may be premature. There are several substantial objections to mysticism's cognitive pretensions. These must be shown to be inconclusive before we are entitled to assert that mystical consciousness is a means of knowledge.

A

Antony Flew, Paul Schmidt and Ronald Hepburn maintain that the cognitive claims which are made for praeternatural experiences must be certified by independent checks.[20] Schmidt's argument is typical. He asks us to look at a case in which we judge that we have a cavity because we have a toothache. He suggests that this judgment is warranted only because we have independent criteria (criteria other than the toothache) by which we can establish the existence of a cavity and because we know (on the basis of past experience) that toothaches and cavities are correlated. Schmidt concludes that, in general, we can move from a first person psychological report about feelings (or some other kind of private experience) to a claim about a non-psychological entity or event only if we have independent criteria for determining the truth or falsity of the claim and have discovered by experience that a correlation exists between the occurrence of that sort of feeling and the existence of that type of entity or event.[21]

The implication, of course, is that the mystic is only entitled to base religious and metaphysical claims upon his experience if he has independent criteria for establishing the existence (or presence) of the alleged object of his experience, and if he can show that experiences of that type and objects of that type are correlated.

What exactly is being demanded? We must distinguish (1) the demand that independent checks be provided for claims based on an instance of mystical experience from (2), the demand that one be given an independent certification of the claim that mystical experience as such provides an adequate basis for cognitive claims of a certain kind. In the latter case one is asking for a justification of the cognitive validity of an entire mode of experience.

The first demand is rather easily met. Just as there are tests other than the visual experiences of a person who bases a cognitive claim upon one of those experiences (for example, his own auditory and tactual experience, the sense experiences of others, etc.) so there are tests other than the mystical experiences of a person who bases cognitive claims on *those* particular experiences (for example, his sanity, the similarity of his experiences to those of other mystics, etc.). But this is clearly not what is at issue. What is at issue is the cognitive status of mystical experience in general. It is the second demand which is being made rather than the first, and Schmidt's argument is designed to show that this demand cannot be met.

Is Schmidt's argument convincing? There are reasons for thinking that it is not. (1) It is wrong to suppose that 'having certain feelings and sensations' is an adequate description of the subjective side of mystical experience. No description of these experiences is adequate which neglects their intentional character. As we have seen, these experiences are noetic. They have an object and incorporate the conviction that one is in the presence of that object. Having a mystical experience is not like feeling pain or being depressed.

(2) In the second place there may be independent reasons for thinking that (for example) God exists and that there is a correlation between the presence of God and the occurrence of certain kinds of religious experience. (These reasons might be provided by natural theology, tradition or authority.) Critics like Schmidt would not accept these reasons but it is not clear that this is significant. Again (though this is obviously not what Schmidt was looking for) one might suppose that a kind of independent certification of the cognitive character of mystical experience is provided by the arguments of the last section.

(3) Perhaps some other kind of experience can be used to confirm the claims made for mystical experience (by showing that judgments based on mystical experience cohere with judgments based on this other sort of experience). For example, it might be suggested that numinous experience corroborates theistic mystical experience in the way in which auditory and tactual experience corroborates visual experience, or (and this is essentially the same point) that theistic mystical experiences and numinous experiences support and reinforce one another in the way in which the various kinds of sense experience support and reinforce one another. Of course Schmidt would not accept this. In his view numinous and mystical experiences are equally suspect. What Schmidt is demanding is that we justify the claim that religious

experience of any kind involves an awareness of the presence of God (or some transcendent being or state) in precisely the same way in which we would justify the claim that toothaches are a sign of cavities.

(4) It is not clear that this demand is reasonable. Suppose we were asked to justify the claim that sense experiences involve an awareness of something distinct from those experiences, viz, physical objects. It is not clear that we would know how to satisfy this request. In particular, it should be noticed that we cannot independently (of those experiences) establish the existence of physical objects and the occurrence of sense experiences, and observe that the two are correlated. (To suppose that we could, would be to suppose that there are tests for ascertaining the presence of physical objects which neither directly nor indirectly appeal to our own sense experiences, or the sense experiences of other people, and there are no tests of this kind.) In short, while the connection between mystical experiences and a transcendental object cannot be justified in the manner which Schmidt demands, the connection between sense experiences and physical objects cannot be justified in that manner either. Since the latter hardly entitles us to conclude that sense experiences do not provide cognitive access to physical objects, it is unclear why the former should entitle us to conclude that mystical experiences do not provide cognitive access to a transcendent object. Schmidt's demand *might* be in order when we are dealing with experiences which are not 'perception-like', for example, toothaches, twinges, depression, etc. It is not clear that it is in order when the experiences in question are 'perception-like', for example, visual experiences and mystical experiences.[22]

One might object, however, that the two cases differ in the following important respect. When we learn the meaning of a physical object word like 'tree' we learn what trees look like, what they feel like, what they sound like when the wind blows through their branches, etc. That is, in learning the meaning of the word 'tree' we learn the connection between the presence of trees and experiences of this type. On the other hand numinous and mystical experiences are not connected in this way with the meaning of 'God' or 'Brahman'.[23] A person who has never had numinous or mystical experiences and has no idea of what they are like can learn the meaning of 'God' or 'Brahman'. On the basis of these considerations it might seem reasonable to conclude that tree experiences and trees are analytically connected, whereas mystical or numinous experiences and God (Brahman) are not, and that therefore while some kind of independent justification must be provided to connect mystical or numinous experiences and God (or Brahman), no such justification is needed to connect tree experiences and trees.

This move would be plausible if statements about trees and other physical objects could be translated into statements about sense experiences (i.e. if phenomenalism were true) and if statements about God (or Brahman) could not be translated into statements about mystical and numinous experiences. It is reasonably clear that statements about God (or Brahman) cannot be translated into statements about religious experience.[24] A number of good philosophers have thought that statements about physical objects could be translated into statements about sense experiences but it is by no means clear that they are correct.

Consider the following: (1) There is a gap between the phenomenological object of mystical experience and its apparent object. For example, although the phenomenological object of theistic mystical experience is a loving will, theistic mystics typically experience or interpret this object as God. But there is also a gap between the phenomenological object of sense experience and its apparent object. When I look at my desk, the phenomenological object of my experience is a desk-like surface seen from a particular point of view. However, its apparent object is the desk itself. There is another gap between the claim that one appears to be confronted with a loving will and the claim that this loving will is real but, similarly, there is a gap between the claim that one is appeared to in a desk-like way and the claim that there really is something which appears to one in that fashion.

(2) It is logically possible for physical objects to exist and for no one to have sense experiences, just as it is logically possible for God (or Brahman) to exist and for there to be no mystical or numinous experiences. As far as I can see, it is also logically possible for there to be sense experiences even though independent physical objects do not exist just as it is logically possible for there to be religious experiences even though God (or Brahman) does not exist.[25]

(3) Nevertheless, while there is no necessary connection between the existence of physical objects and the occurrence of sense experiences, there may be a necessary connection between the existence of physical objects and the *possibility* of sense experiences, e.g. it may be necessarily true that if a tree exists, then, if a normal observer is present under standard conditions, he will enjoy sense experiences of a certain type. But it should be noticed that a similar claim can be made about God and mystical experiences, viz, that it is necessarily true that, if God exists, then if there is an adequately prepared mystic whom God chooses to visit, he will enjoy mystical experiences.

The point is this. It is by no means clear that the logical relations between sense experiences and physical objects are significantly different from the logical relations between mystical or numinous experiences and an object like God.[26] It is thus not clear that some sort of special justification is needed in the one case which is not needed in the other. If a special justification is not needed in the case of sense experience, and it does not seem to be, then it is not needed in the case of mystical experience. I conclude therefore that the first objection is unsuccessful.

B

It is sometimes argued that religious experiences cannot be cognitively valid because they support conflicting claims (about Allah, Jesus, Nibbāna, etc.).[27] As it stands, this argument is unconvincing. 'Religious experience' is an umbrella term covering many different types of experience—charismatic phenomena, numinous feelings, possession, conversion experiences, mystical consciousness, visions, voices, and so on. Religious experience in general may indeed support conflicting claims, but the most that follows is that not all of these experiences or types of experience can be cognitive. In particular, it does not follow that mystical consciousness (or numinous feeling) is delusive.

But even if we were to restrict our attention to types of experience which are not known to be delusive,[28] and thus have some legitimate cognitive pretensions, the argument would still be unsound. Visual experiences support conflicting claims, for people hallucinate and misperceive in other ways, but it is surely wrong to conclude that visual experience is not cognitive. Our attention should be confined not only to types of experience with legitimate cognitive pretensions, but to instances of those types that pass the tests which are used to distinguish veridical experiences of that type from those which are not veridical. No cognitive claims are being made for the latter.

Finally, the only relevant conflicts are conflicts between propositions which are *immediately* based upon the experiences in question. Claims which are indirectly based upon veridical experiences can be infected with error from other sources. Thus, if I claim that the hat I see in front of me is Jack's, I may be mistaken, not because my visual experience is in error, but because I am wrong in thinking it belongs to Jack. If someone standing nearby says that he sees Tom's hat, then his claim conflicts with mine, but this conflict has no tendency to show either of us that our visual experiences are delusive.[29]

Nevertheless, the argument can be reformulated to take account of these objections:

(1) If the criteria which are used to sort out veridical experiences from those which are not veridical are adequate, then all the experiences which meet those criteria are veridical.

(2) If an experience is veridical, then the claims which are immediately based upon it are true. Therefore,

(3) If the criteria which are used to sort out veridical experiences from those which are not veridical are adequate, then the claims which are immediately based upon an experience which meets those criteria are true. (From 1 and 2.) Therefore,

(4) If the criteria which are used to sort out veridical, mystical or numinous experiences[30] from those which are not veridical are adequate, then the claims which are immediately based upon an experience which meets those criteria are true. (From 3.)

(5) Conflicting claims are immediately based upon mystical and numinous experiences which meet the criteria that are used to sort out veridical experiences of that type from those which are not veridical. (Among these claims are the claim that God exists and is the supreme reality, the claim that Nibbāna is the supreme reality, and so on.) Therefore,

(6) If the criteria which are used to sort out veridical mystical and numinous experiences from those which are not veridical are adequate, then conflicting claims are true. (From 4 and 5.)

(7) Conflicting claims cannot be true. Therefore,

(8) The criteria which are used to sort out veridical mystical and numinous experiences from those which are not veridical cannot be adequate. (From 6 and 7.)

(8) has significant implications for the cognitive status of mystical consciousness and numinous feeling, for if the criteria of validity which are actually used *cannot* be adequate, one suspects that

(9) Adequate criteria cannot be provided.

But it is plausible to suppose that

(10) For any cognitive mode of experience, there are (adequate) criteria for distinguishing veridical instances of that mode of experience from those which are not veridical. Hence,

(11) Mystical consciousness and numinous feeling are not cognitive modes of experience. (From 9 and 10.)

Although one might question (10), this line of response is not particularly promising, since the only type of cognitive experience for which there seem to be no criteria of this sort is the immediate awareness of some of our own mental states.[31] For example, while there are criteria for determining whether others are in pain, our awareness of our own pain is self-certifying; there are no criteria by which we distinguish those cases in which we really feel pain from those in which we only think we do. As you have seen, the mystic's claims are not private and they are not self-certifying. There is therefore no reason to suppose that they constitute an exception to the general rule.

However, it is by no means clear that (5) is true. We must remember that the only relevant conflicts are conflicts between claims which are *immediately* supported by religious experience. Many of the conflicting claims which people try to support by appealing to mystical or numinous experience are not *immediately* supported by it. For example, that God (as defined by Anselm) exists, or that the Ātman-Brahman is the ground of being, or that Nibbāna is real. None of these propositions would appear to be immediately warranted by the religious experiences upon which they are (partly) based.[32] If all the conflicting claims which people attempt to support by appealing to mystical experience or numinous feeling fall into this category, then premise (5) is false.

It is true that nature mysticism, monistic mysticism, theistic mysticism and numinous experience (immediately?) support *different* claims—that nature is one and sacred, that there is an undifferentiated unity transcending space and time, that an overwhelming love consciousness exists, that there is a holy Other. But it is not clear that these claims *conflict*. (Monistic and theistic experiences might be experiences of different objects, for example.) In order to establish (5), one must show that claims immediately supported by mystical experience or numinous feeling are not only different but incompatible, and it is by no means clear that this can be done.[33]

I therefore conclude that the objection from conflicting religious experiences or intuitions is inconclusive.

NOTES

1. C. B. Martin, *Religious Belief*, Ithaca, New York, 1959, chapter 5.

2. I do not wish to be understood as implying that mystics appeal to their experiences to demonstrate (e.g.) God's reality or the reality of Brahman, or that they are uncertain of God's reality or the reality of Brahman before they have their experiences. Nevertheless, mystics do appeal to their experiences to support the claim that they taste God or experience Brahman, and these claims entail that God exists or Brahman is real. Furthermore, mystics do seem to believe that their experiences confirm the latter although they usually think that there are

other grounds (e.g. scripture) on the basis of which one can be justifiably certain of their truth.

3. David Knowles, *The English Mystical Tradition*, London, 1960, chapter VIII.

4. R. M. Gale makes a similar point in the last section of 'Mysticism and Philosophy', (*The Journal of Philosophy* LVII (1960), pp. 471–81); Walter Stace makes a similar point in *Mysticism and Philosophy, op cit*, pp. 135–9.

5. The fact that the mystic believes that agreement is relevant does not entail that he believes (or should believe) that disagreement is relevant. True, if he thinks that the presence of agreement strengthens his claim, he must acknowledge that in its absence his claim would not be as strong as it is. It does not follow that he should concede that its absence counts *against* his claim. In general, that A recognises that e counts from p and that in the absence of e the case for p is not as strong as it would otherwise be, does not imply that A should take the absence of e as counting against p. For example, the fact that Smith helps Jones with whom he is barely acquainted and to whom he has no obligation, supports the claim that Smith is a good man, and if this fact did not obtain, the evidence for that claim. In general, that A recognises that e counts for p and that in the man who has no claim on him and whom he hardly knows would not count against his goodness.

6. J. A. Symonds and Richard Jefferies *may* be cases in point.

7. Stace (*Mysticism and Philosophy*, pp. 308–10) suggests that perhaps these claims ought to be taken at face value: (1) He points out that the conviction is not universal. Bucke refers to a case of cosmic consciousness in which the subject remained convinced that the self does not survive death. (Or consider the case of Richard Jefferies.) (2) As he says, not all mystics express the conviction that the soul is immortal. (Though of course, it does not follow that they do not possess that conviction.) (3) He suggests that it is possible that those who express this conviction are only speaking of an aspect of their experience (e.g. the feeling that time drops away) and not of survival after death. (However, there is no compelling reason to believe that this is the case.)

8. Though, again, one should probably be careful. I am not aware of any instance in which a Christian mystic claimed that his experience confirmed the doctrine of a general resurrection. Any confirmation of this doctrine which is provided by mystical experience is at best indirect. (These experiences allegedly confirm problematic elements of a 'theory' which includes certain predictions as an integral part. By providing new 'evidence' for these elements, the mystic's experiences confirm the theory as a whole, and thereby confirm its consequences. Whether the experiences of Christian mystics actually do confirm such peculiarly Christian doctrines as the doctrine of the Trinity is, of course, debatable.)

9. This should be regarded as a kind of prediction of the course of 'external' events. The vision of God or passing into Nibbāna are not just inner experiences. Neither can occur if God or Nibbāna are unreal, and the vision of God depends upon God's causal activity. The events referred to by 'a vision of God' or 'passing into Nibbāna' have a non-psychological dimension.

10. I am indebted to William Alston for the main point of the next three paragraphs. (See his *Religious Belief and Philosophical Thought*, New York, 1963, pp. 124–5.)

11. Or similar experiences under certain conditions. (If the object is moving, we can sometimes predict its future locations.) Or dissimilar but connected experiences under certain conditions. (If the object is rapidly changing, similar experiences cannot be obtained but we can often specify conditions under which related experiences can be obtained.) I shall continue to ignore these complications.

12. As H. P. Owen asserts in various places in *The Christian Knowledge of God*, (London, 1960).

13. Thus, since psychic experiences, like clairvoyance, purport to provide extraordinary knowledge about perfectly ordinary events and objects, the demand for a large number of successful predictions is entirely appropriate.

14. One might therefore expect to find more emphasis placed upon agreement (and disagreement) by monists and pantheists than by theists. But as far as I can determine, there is no evidence that this is the case. (One might argue that because these objects are 'incomprehensible', agreement and disagreement is an unreliable test. If Brahman, for example, is neti, neti [not this, not that], there is no reason to suppose that veridical experience of Brahman will be repeatable. However, this argument suffers from two defects. In the first place, the object is usually described with some precision. Thus, though Brahman is said to be neti, neti, it is characterised as pure, blissful, empty consciousness. In the second place, if the argument were sound, it would prove that *all* tests are unreliable; it would not show that there was any *special* problem with the test of [dis]agreement.)

15. At this point we might add 'with respect to those features which lead us to speak of the latter as cognitive'. I have not done so because it is not entirely clear just what those features are. Of course we are not entirely in the dark. In my opinion, they would include the presence of tests and check-up procedures, but not the fact that sense experiences are bound up with certain bodily organs. (The latter has recently been denied by Peter Donovan. [*Interpreting Religious Experience*, London, 1979, pp. 51–3.] As far as I can determine, Donovan has only two reasons for his denial: (1) the importance of the fact that we have several senses which can be used to check one another, and (2) our scientific understanding of the 'processes involved in the production of our sense experiences'. Neither is convincing. While it is true that our confidence in our senses is partly based upon the fact that they corroborate one another, I fail to see how the possibility of mutual corroboration depends upon the existence of different *physical organs* [as distinguished from the existence of different modes of experience]. [Notice, too, that an appeal to such things as agreement or successful predictions would seem to be relevant to the evaluation of visual or auditory experiences even if no physical organs were involved.] Donovan is undoubtedly correct in asserting that our scientific knowledge of sense experience is largely made possible by the fact that it is intimately bound up with physical organs. But how relevant is this knowledge to an appreciation of sense perception's cognitive validity? It is certainly not necessary, for, if it were, it would follow that sense experiences and the criteria used to evaluate them were not known to be reliable until quite recently.)

It is unclear whether the special *character* of the tests (the emphasis upon agreement and successful predictions) is among the features which lead us to speak of sense experiences as cognitive. Though I cannot prove it, I believe that, with one exception, I have considered all of the features one might reasonably suppose to be logically bound up with the cognitive status of sense experience. The exception is causality. Some would argue that in order for a sense experience to be veridical, its object must be among its causes. It is not certain that this is correct. In any case, if theism is true, this condition is met by theistic mystical experiences, since God is a cause of everything that exists. Similarly, although the Ātman-Brahman is not strictly a cause, it is believed to be the ground of all experience. (It is the awareness or consciousness in any act of awareness or consciousness.) It follows that if Advaita Vedānta is true, this condition is met by experiences of the Brahman. Again, nature (or some part of it) is a partial cause of extrovertive mystical experiences, and so on. Whether crucial or not, the condition in question may be met (in a rough and ready way) by mystical experiences. It is true, however, that (with the possible exception of extrovertive mystical experience) one cannot determine *whether* the condition is met independently of metaphysical and theological considerations. The practical value of an appeal to this consideration is therefore limited.

16. Or perhaps more accurately (since there are different types of mystical experience), as a *cluster* of modes of cognitive experience. Sense experience, too, is a cluster of modes of cognitive experience, although there is a difference, since different modes of sense experience ultimately have the same object, viz, physical reality, whereas the different modes of mystical experience *may* have different objects (God, nature, one's own soul, etc.).

17. In addition, there are less significant similarities. For example, in both cases agreement is sometimes appealed to, to support the claim that the experience is authentic.

18. The first consideration provides us with a reason for believing the *claims* which the (theistic) mystic makes. The second consideration provides us with a reason for believing *the mystic* when he makes those claims.

19. But not for the reason Stace gives. According to Stace, ordinary visual or auditory experiences cohere with our other experiences and are hence objective. Hallucinatory experiences conflict with the rest of our experience and are therefore subjective. Since mystical experience excludes multiplicity, it neither coheres nor conflicts with experience as a whole. It is therefore neither objective nor subjective. . . . Even if it were sound, [Stace's argument] would not show that mystical experience is not subjective in the sense in which headaches and feelings of depression are subjective. Stace fails to distinguish 'non-cognitive', i.e. 'providing *no* information' from 'delusive', i.e. 'providing *false* information'. Both can be meant by 'subjective'. That mystical experience does not conflict with the rest of our experiences shows that it is not delusive and is therefore not subjective in that sense. It does not show that it is not non-cognitive. For all Stace has shown to the contrary, mystical experience may be subjective in the same sense in which pains are subjective. (Cf Ninian Smart, 'Mystical Experience', *op cit.*)

20. Antony Flew, *God and Philosophy*, London, New York, 1966, chapter 6; Paul Schmidt, *Religious Knowledge*, Glencoe, Illinois, 1961, chapter 8; Ronald Hepburn, *Christianity and Paradox*, London, 1958, p. 37.

21. I am slightly modifying Schmidt's argument, but not weakening it. Schmidt's argument is rather more lucid than the arguments of Flew and Hepburn, but all three make essentially the same point. For example, Hepburn argues that even if we (and no one else?) saw a red circle in the air whenever John was angry, we would be entitled to claim that John was angry on the basis of this experience only if we had learned by ordinary procedures that the 'code' was reliable (i.e. to justify these claims we would have to show that a correlation obtained between seeing a red circle and John's anger, the latter being established by normal criteria).

22. H. P. Owen has made a similar point (*The Christian Knowledge of God, op cit*, pp. 276–80). The demand for pragmatic justification leads to similar difficulties. People sometimes attempt to justify the cognitive validity of sense experience by appealing to the fact that it enables us successfully to deal with the external world. Whether religious experiences assist successful adaptation depends upon the nature of the external world. If supernaturalism is true, it is reasonable to suppose that they do. If it is objected that supernaturalism is only reasonable upon the assumption that religious experiences are veridical, one may reply that (1) this is not obviously true (since there are other reasons for believing in supernaturalism), and that (2), in any case, the pragmatic justification of sense experience involves a similar circularity. That sense experience leads to successful adaptation can only be justified by appealing to statements about human beings and their environment which are ultimately supported by sense experience.

23. Though mystical experience *might* be connected with the meanings of 'Ātman' and 'Nibbāna'.

24. *Pace* Schleiermacher as sometimes interpreted. (See *The Christian Faith*, Edinburgh, 1928.) John Wilson also attempted a reduction of this kind. (*Language and Christian Belief*, London, New York, 1958; *Philosophy of Religion*, London and New York, 1961.)

25. This might be doubted but it seems to me to be logically possible for God to annihilate the physical world without annihilating particular minds, and for Him to produce impressions in those minds which are similar to those which they would have had if the physical world had continued to exist. And if this is possible, it would seem to be possible for God to have created particular minds without having created a physical world at all, but instead to have produced impressions in those minds which are similar to those which they would have enjoyed if He had chosen to create a physical world. An idealism of this sort *may* be incoherent, but that it *is* incoherent is at least controversial.

26. Though I would admit that the fact that phenomenalism is more attractive in the one case than in the other, *might* indicate some underlying logical difference.

27. John Hospers offers an argument of this kind in *An Introduction to Philosophical Analysis*, 2nd ed., Englewood Cliffs, New Jersey, 1967, pp. 444–8.

28. Or which are such that there is no compelling reason to believe that they are delusive. It should be pointed out in this connection that experiences of God or Nibbāna cannot be as easily discounted as visions of Thor, since there are better reasons for doubting the existence of Thor than for doubting the existence of God or the reality of Nibbāna. Again, mystical experience is less suspect than visionary experience for the contents of the latter do seem to conflict, and are more obviously culturally conditioned. (Though one must be careful. While the content of Teresa's visionary experiences of Christ seems to conflict with the content of a Norseman's vision of Odin, the existence of Christ and the existence of Odin are not logically incompatible. The conflict appears to be between the value and importance, the existential meaning and significance, of the visionary objects [which is itself part of the visionary content] rather than between the visionary objects as such.)

29. Strictly speaking, what is immediately warranted by a veridical noetic experience is the claim to have perceived its phenomenological object. When an experience's phenomenological object (e.g. a desk-like surface) is distinct from its apparent object (e.g. a desk), two types of perceptual error are possible; one's claim to have perceived the experience's apparent object may be mistaken, or one's claim to have perceived its phenomenological object may be mistaken. Although both mistakes are perceptual mistakes, they have very different implications. A claim to have perceived an experience's apparent object not only reflects the subject's experience and his linguistic competence (e.g. his understanding of the concept of a desk), but also reflects (true or false) beliefs which he brings to his experience (e.g. that desk-like surfaces normally belong to desks). Perceptual error may be due to these beliefs and not to any defect in the experience upon which his perceptual claim was based. By contrast, when a claim to have perceived an experience's phenomenological object is mistaken, the experience itself is delusive. Suppose, for example, that I claim to see a desk-like surface because I am having the sort of visual experiences which I would have had if a desk-like surface had been present, but that in fact there is no desk-like surface in front of me. In this instance, my *experience* has misled me, not my beliefs about how things are.

30. It seems to me that numinous experience is the other type of religious experience with legitimate cognitive pretensions. If other modes of religious experience have legitimate cognitive pretensions, then they too should be included. (Remember that the point of the original argument is that apparently valid religious 'intuitions' conflict.)

31. Or at least this is the only type of experience which is (*pace* Wittgenstein) non-controversially cognitive and of which this is true. Self-evident intuitions of moral truths and rules of logic might also be experiences of this type, but their cognitive value is controversial.

32. To be in a position to make these claims one must not only have mystical or numinous experiences, and be linguistically or conceptually competent, one must also know or believe certain things about God, or the Brahman or Nibbāna. One must know, for example, that an invisible loving presence is probably God, or that empty consciousness is an aspect of Brahman, or that Nibbāna is cessation ('stopping').

33. There is another objection to (5). One of the criteria which in practice is used to distinguish veridical religious experiences from those which are not is the compatibility of the claims that are immediately based upon a religious experience with orthodox talk. Because this is the case, the adherent of a religious tradition can argue that the only mystical or numinous experiences which meet *all* of the appropriate criteria are experiences which are such that the claims which are immediately based upon them are compatible with orthodoxy. Since the only experiences which will pass the tests are those which are compatible with orthodoxy, it is unlikely that there will be serious conflicts between the claims which are immediately based on mystical or numinous experiences meeting the appropriate criteria. The only possible conflicts will be between claims neither of which are unorthodox, and it is difficult to find clear examples of this type.

Part VII

Religion and Ethics

The central ingredients of Western civilization, particularly its legal and moral beliefs, are so closely associated with the teachings of Judaism and Christianity that many Westerners assume without raising any question that a necessary connection exists between morality and religion. If God is conceived as our creator and a being supremely wise and good, then his will must also be the source of moral commandments and it must be to God that we are answerable for how we behave. Judaism depicts God as the lawgiver, preoccupied with justice and righteousness; Christianity emphasizes obedience, holiness, and brotherly love. Rabbis and priests are looked up to as moral guides; the Bible is cited to settle questions of morality; even legislative actions and judicial judgments are often discussed and justified by reference to Judeo-Christian teachings or Biblical passages.

Thus the so-called "divine command" theory of ethics seems natural and obvious to many people. According to this view, it is God who determines what is right and wrong. "Wrong" means forbidden by God; "right" means commanded or permitted by God. It is often asserted that we must look to divine revelation to find out what morality requires of us. When reason is said to play a part in determining the dictates of morality, it is said to be because it is a gift of God provided to us for that purpose, and the holy scriptures are cited as major authoritative sources from which to begin our reasoning. According to the divine command theory, what makes an action right or wrong is simply that God commands or forbids it.

Because the divine command theory is so completely intertwined with Judeo-Christian theology about God's power, wisdom, and righteousness and the belief that God created and therefore rightfully governs every aspect of the world, it appears natural and correct that God also determines right and wrong by his own decrees or commandments. But when we examine the divine command theory a bit more closely, it turns out not to be so plausible after all. There are two major problems. The first is that the divine command theory implies that morality is arbitrary, the result merely of divine whim. And the second problem is that the theory undermines the claim that God is good. Let us briefly examine each of these problems.

If "right" simply means whatever God commands and "wrong" means what God happens to forbid, the implication is that God might have commanded lying or cruelty and then these acts would have been right, or he might have forbidden charity or respect for the elderly and then these acts would have been wrong. But surely this is quite implausible. When we stop to think about it, we can see clearly that inflicting gratuitous suffering on innocent persons is wrong and would still be wrong even if God were to command it. Our immediate reaction to such a suggestion tends to be, "But God would never command torture of innocents!" But why not? According to the divine command theory, if he did, it would not be wrong; indeed, it would be good. We see clearly, however, that it would not be good. Our keen feeling about this—what might properly be called our moral intuition about it—reveals our clear if heretofore unrecognized sense that morality is not really arbitrary. Objective human reason recognizes as a fact that inflicting gratuitous suffering on innocent persons is wrong. It may be true that God forbids such behavior, but it would continue to be wrong even if God did not forbid it. And this shows quite clearly that the divine command theory is mistaken. Morality is *not* just a matter of divine whim. Certain things are morally wrong and others morally right independent of what anyone might think—even God. Morality, like logic and mathematics, is an objective matter ascertained by reason. God could no more make torture morally right than he could make $2 + 2 = 7$.

The other major problem with the divine command theory is that it renders meaningless the claim that God is good. If "good" just means what God wills, if to be good only means to do what God wills should be done or what pleases God, then the claim that God is good only means that God is a being who does whatever he wills, or simply that God does as he pleases. It makes no sense to call God good if that is all that is involved. We call God good because we sense that there is such a thing as good that is objective and independent and that God conforms to that good. This awareness involves the implicit recognition that if God did not live up to that standard of goodness, it would be false to say that God is good. According to the divine command theory, one could never intelligibly say that God is not good, because that would mean that God did not do what God willed—an absurdity. To say that God *is* good, however, is empty because it is only a confusing way of saying that God does as he pleases. The implication again is that the divine command theory is false. Contrary to that theory, it does make sense to say that God is good because goodness is something independent of God's will, and thus the claim means that God recognizes the objective standard of goodness and conforms to it. This point is illustrated by Plato's dialogue *The Euthyphro*, included here.

The belief has been widespread in the West during much of the twentieth century that there is no such thing as objective rational morality. Moral relativism, the belief that morality is determined by the beliefs and customs of each society, has been accepted by a great many educated and open-minded persons. The reading in this part by Yeager Hudson addresses this serious confusion, pointing out that faith in relativism was initially driven by the commendable desire to promote an attitude of tolerance and to overcome ethnocentrism. Thus the differences of moral practices from one society to another were emphasized by anthropologists. More careful and sophisticated anthropological study, however, has uncovered underlying similarities of moral beliefs and attitudes among cultures that shows cultural relativism to be a superficial view. Differences of actual moral practices turn out to be the result not of basically different moral beliefs, but rather of different beliefs about facts of the natural world and human social life. Beneath the seemingly drastic moral differences, we find a basic similarity that might be seen as supporting the hope for diminishing the differences and increasing understanding among peoples of all cultures.

Another implication of the divine command theory, and a point that has also been taken for granted in Western civilization, is that because morality is determined by God's will, there may be occasions when God might command certain individuals to violate its standing rules. Søren Kierkegaard called this phenomenon the "teleological suspension of the ethical," that is, the setting aside of moral rules in order to achieve a special objective. Judaism and Christianity have often taught that obedience to God is more important than following moral rules and that God might occasionally require individuals to do what otherwise would be immoral. This notion gives rise to the belief that the teachings of religious morality take precedence over those of secular or rational morality. Thus the leaders of religion presume to pronounce judgment on which laws may properly be enacted and which court rulings are correct or mistaken, and even to authorize their faithful ones to disobey laws or otherwise accepted moral practices when they run counter to the religious teaching. The biblical story about the behavior of Abraham in undertaking to kill and present his son as a burnt offering to God is often cited as the paradigm of such piety and obedience.

The implication of the independence of ethics, however, is that religious morality can never overrule rational morality. Rational ethics reveals the moral obligations that reason imposes on every rational creature, human or divine. The sectarian teachings of a single religious tradition can no more overrule the requirements of universal rational morality than its religious claims can overrule the reasoned findings of science—the attempt of the Christian church to silence Galileo illustrates this point, to the considerable embarrassment of Christians today. Because all human beings belong to one family and share the faculty of rationality, they are all under the same system of morality discovered by human reason. Where the circumstances under which groups of persons live differ in important ways, the same underlying moral rules may authorize different details of moral behavior. But these differences are also discovered by human reason, not by reference to those pronouncements that claim to be divine revelations.

These serious problems with divine command

theory come as a surprise to many. Another fact surprising to many Christians is that the divine command theory has not been a standard doctrine of the Christian church. Indeed, Saint Thomas Aquinas explicitly rejects it, advocating a doctrine of universal rational morality grounded in the concept of natural law.

What perhaps provokes most surprise of all, however, is the fact that, in many if not most cultures during the stretch of human history, there has usually been little or no connection between morality and religion. In primitive cultures, the gods were concerned with rites and sacrifices; they were not thought to care about how humans treated one another. The ancient Greek and Roman gods paid little heed to human morality and were themselves often quite immoral by rational standards, and the same is true of the gods and spirits of many ancient and contemporary primitive societies.

Religion, in fact, has traditionally been concerned primarily with the vertical relationship between humans and their gods, not with the horizontal relationships among mere humans. In its early stages, religion was not clearly distinguished from magic, a process of spells and divinations that, when properly performed, was thought to force supernatural powers to do the required thing. The business of religion was the rituals, incantations, and sacrifices by which humans could win the favor of the gods, persuade them to withhold their wrath, badger them to give fertility to women and the fields, and implore them to grant their protection to human shades or ghosts after death. The gods were thought to be impressed by the correctness of the cult and the generosity of the sacrifices. Why should they care how we treat our brothers, our sisters, or our neighbors?

Thus the close association assumed in Western culture to obtain between ethics and religion is not at all typical. Neither, it turns out, is it philosophically defensible. Just as science, mathematics, and logic, each in its own proper realm, are independent of religion (and religion in the performance of its own proper function is independent of science, etc.), so also is ethics independent of religion. We discover the truths of logic and mathematics through the use of reason, and what we discover applies to all rational beings. The same is true of morality. Ethics, like logic, is a rational discipline that is only accidentally connected with religion in one era and one culture. Torture is wrong and truthfulness is right, not because God forbids the one and commands the other, rather, God commands what is right *because* it is right and forbids what is wrong *because* it is wrong. Consequently, there is no legitimate teleological suspension of the ethical. If God is good, as theism teaches, then God would never command persons to violate the requirements of rational morality, and any claim to that effect by any representative of a given religious tradition must be recognized as a mistake.

ANNOTATED GUIDE TO FURTHER READINGS

Nielsen, Kai. *Ethics Without God.* London: Pemberton Books, 1973.

In this interesting and thought-provoking book, Nielsen contends that there can be meaning to our moral lives without God. He shows that ethics can be separated from religion, then develops and explains his own humanistic system of ethics.

Outka, Gene, and Reeder, John P., Jr., eds. *Religion and Morality.* Garden City, N.Y.: Anchor Books, 1973.

Essays dealing exclusively with the relationship between religion and morality.

Pojman, Louis P., ed. *Philosophy of Religion: An Anthology.* Belmont, Calif.: Wadsworth, 1987.

Part 8 offers a selection of readings focusing largely on the divine command theory. In the initial piece, Socrates poses the classic question: Is it God who defines what is good, or is goodness a standard independent of God's will? The opposing positions are defended and attacked by four thinkers.

Rachels, James. *The Elements of Moral Philosophy.* New York: Random House, 1986.

An excellent introduction to some of the basic concepts of moral philosophy. Rachels discusses the connection between religion and morality, the divine command theory, and natural law, with relevant modern examples such as abortion, homosexuality, and famine relief.

Stewart, David. *Exploring the Philosophy of Religion.* Englewood Cliffs, N.J.: Prentice-Hall, 1980.

Chapter 7 offers a wide range of viewpoints dealing with the relationship of ethics and religion, including selections by Nietzche, Kai Nielsen and Paul Tillich, and Reinhold Neibuhr.

VII.A. The Divine Command Theory of Ethics

VII.A.1. *The Euthyphro* (Goodness and What the Gods Love)

PLATO

The relationship of morality to the will of the gods has been discussed by Western philosophers for well over two thousand years. Plato (c. 428–347 B.C.E.) addresses this issue in his dialogue, The Euthyphro. *In the conversation between Socrates and Euthyphro, the famous Socratic irony is evident as Socrates assumes the attitude of the inquirer, making no pretense to knowledge while actually applying with powerful effect his sharp faculty of reason to discern fallacious argument. Socrates refers in passing to the immoral behavior of the gods as depicted in the religious teachings of his time and argues that what is pleasing to the gods cannot be the same thing as piety or, in other words, right and wrong. He presents his arguments in connection with a question: "Is piety good because the gods love it, or do they love it because it is good?" If piety is good only because the gods love it, then it is arbitrary; if there are multiple gods, moreover, some will love what others hate. Although the discussion in* The Euthyphro *ends inconclusively, it is clear that Socrates believes that piety or morality is independent of the gods.*

EUTHYPHRO[1]: What's new, Socrates, to make you leave your usual haunts in the Lyceum and spend your time here by the king-archon's court? Surely you are not prosecuting any one before the king archon as I am?

From *The Euthyphro*, translated by G. M. A. Grube, in Plato, *The Trial and Death of Socrates*, 1975 Hackett Publishing Company, Inc., pp. 4–20.

[1] We know nothing about Euthyphro except what we can gather from this dialogue. He is obviously a professional priest who considers himself an expert on ritual and on piety generally, and, it seems, is generally so considered. One Euthyphro is mentioned in Plato's *Cratylus* (396 d) who is given to *enthousiasmos*, inspiration or possession, but we cannot be sure that it is the same person—Trans.

SOCRATES: The Athenians do not call this a prosecution but an indictment, Euthyphro.

EUTHYPHRO: What is this you say? Someone must have indicted you, for you are not going to tell me that you have indicted someone else.

SOCRATES: No indeed.

EUTHYPHRO: But some else has indicted you?

SOCRATES: Quite so.

EUTHYPHRO: Who is he?

SOCRATES: I do not really know him myself, Euthyphro. He is apparently young and unknown. They call him Meletus, I believe. He belongs to the Pitthean deme, if you know anyone from that deme called Meletus with long hair, not much of a beard, and a rather aquiline nose.

EUTHYPHRO: I don't know him, Socrates. What charge does he bring against you?

SOCRATES: What charge? A not ignoble one I think, for it is no small thing for a young man to have knowledge of such an important subject. He says he knows how our young men are corrupted and who corrupts them. He is likely to be wise, and when he sees my ignorance corrupting his contemporaries, he proceeds to accuse me to the city as to their mother. I think he is the only one of our public men to start out the right way, for it is right to care first that the young should be as good as possible, just as a good farmer is likely to take care of the young plants first, and of the others later. So, too, Meletus first gets rid of us who corrupt the growth of the young, as he says, and then afterwards he will obviously take care of the older and become a source of great blessings for the city, as seems likely to happen to one who started out this way.

EUTHYPHRO: I could wish this were true, Socrates, but I fear the opposite may happen. He seems to me to start out by harming the very heart of the city by attempting to wrong you. Tell me, what does he say you do to corrupt the young?

SOCRATES: Strange things, to hear him tell it, for he says that I am a maker of gods, that I create new gods while not believing in the old gods, and he has indicted me for this very reason, as he puts it.

EUTHYPHRO: I understand, Socrates. This is because you say that the divine sign keeps coming to you.[2] So he has written this indictment against you as one who makes innovations in religious matters, and he comes to court to slander you, knowing that such things are easily misrepresented to the crowd. The same is true in my case. Whenever I speak of divine matters in the assembly and foretell the future, they laugh me down as if I were crazy; and yet I have foretold nothing that did not happen. Nevertheless, they envy all of us who do this. One need not give them any thought, but carry on just the same.

SOCRATES: My dear Euthyphro, to be laughed at does not matter perhaps, for the Athenians do not mind anyone they think clever, as long as he does not

---

[2] In Plato, Socrates always speaks of his divine sign or voice as intervening to prevent him from doing or saying something (e.g., *Apology* 31 d), but never positively. The popular view was that it enabled him to foretell the future, and Euthyphro here represents that view. Note, however, that Socrates dissociates himself from "you prophets."—Trans.

teach his own wisdom, but if they think that he makes others to be like himself they get angry, whether through envy, as you say, or for some other reason.

EUTHYPHRO: I have certainly no desire to test their feelings towards me in this matter.

SOCRATES: Perhaps you seem to make yourself but rarely available, and not to be willing to teach your own wisdom, but my liking for people makes them think that I pour out to anybody anything I have to say, not only without charging a fee but appearing glad to reward anyone who is willing to listen. If then they were intending to laugh at me, as you say they laugh at you, there would be nothing unpleasant in their spending their time in court laughing and jesting, but if they are going to be serious, the outcome is not clear except to you prophets.

EUTHYPHRO: Perhaps it will come to nothing, Socrates, and you will fight your case as you think best, as I think I will mine.

SOCRATES: What is your case, Euthyphro? Are you the defendant or the prosecutor?

EUTHYPHRO: The prosecutor.

SOCRATES: Whom do you prosecute?

EUTHYPHRO: One whom I am thought crazy to prosecute.

SOCRATES: Are you pursuing someone who will easily escape you?

EUTHYPHRO: Far from it, for he is quite old.

SOCRATES: Who is it?

EUTHYPHRO: My father.

SOCRATES: My dear sir! Your own father?

EUTHYPHRO: Certainly.

SOCRATES: What is the charge? What is the case about?

EUTHYPHRO: Murder, Socrates.

SOCRATES: Good heavens! Certainly Euthyphro, most men would not know how they could do this and be right. It is not the part of anyone to do this, but of one who is far advanced in wisdom.

EUTHYPHRO: Yes by Zeus, Socrates, that is so.

SOCRATES: Is then the man your father killed one of your relatives? Or is that obvious, for you would not prosecute your father for the murder of a stranger.

EUTHYPHRO: It is ridiculous, Socrates, for you to think that it makes any difference whether the victim is a stranger or a relative. One should only watch whether the killer acted justly or not; if he acted justly, let him go, but if not, one should prosecute, even if the killer shares your hearth and table. The pollution is the same if you knowingly keep company with such a man and do not cleanse yourself and him by bringing him to justice. The victim was a dependent of mine, and when we were farming in Naxos he was a servant of ours. He killed one of our household slaves in drunken anger, so my father bound him hand and foot and threw him in a ditch, then sent a man here to enquire from the priest what should be done. During that time he gave no thought or care to the bound man, as being a killer, and it was no matter if he died, which he did. Hunger and cold and his bonds caused his death before the messenger came back from the seer. Both my father and my other relatives are angry that I am prosecuting my father for murder on behalf of a murderer, as he did not even kill him. They say that such a victim does not deserve a thought and that it is impious for a son to prosecute his father for murder. But their ideas of the divine attitude to piety and impiety are wrong, Socrates.

SOCRATES: Whereas, by Zeus, Euthyphro, you think that your knowledge of the divine, and of piety and impiety, is so accurate that, when those things happened as you say, you have no fear of having acted impiously in bringing your father to trial?

EUTHYPHRO: I should be of no use, Socrates, and Euthyphro would not be superior to the majority of men, if I did not have accurate knowledge of all such things.

SOCRATES: It is indeed most important, my admirable Euthyphro, that I should become your pupil, and as regards this indictment challenge Meletus about these very things and say to him: that in the past too I considered knowledge about the divine to be most important, and that now that he says that I improvise and innovate about the gods I have become your pupil. I would say to him: "If, Meletus, you agree that Euthyphro is wise in these matters, consider me, too, to have the right beliefs and do not bring me to trial. If you do not think so, then prosecute that teacher of mine for corrupting the older men, me and his own father, by teaching me and by exhorting and punishing him." If he is not convinced, does not discharge me, or indicts you instead of me, I shall repeat the same challenge in court.

EUTHYPHRO: Yes by Zeus, Socrates, and, if he should try to indict me, I think I would find his weak spots and the talk in court would be about him rather than about me.

SOCRATES: It is because I realize this that I am eager to become your pupil, my dear friend. I know that other people as well as this Meletus do not even seem to notice you, whereas he sees me so sharply and clearly that he indicts me for ungodliness. So tell me now, by Zeus, what you just now maintained you clearly knew: what kind of thing do you say that godliness and ungodliness are, both as regards murder and other things; or is the pious not the same and alike in every action, and the impious the opposite of all that is pious and like itself, and everything that is to be impious presents us with one form[3] or appearance in so far as it is impious.

EUTHYPHRO: Most certainly, Socrates.

SOCRATES: Tell me then, what is the pious, and what the impious, do you say?

EUTHYPHRO: I say that the pious is to do what I am doing now, to prosecute the wrongdoer, be it about murder or temple robbery or anything else, whether the wrongdoer is your father or your mother or anyone else; not to prosecute is impious. And observe, Socrates, that I can quote the law as a great proof that

---

[3] This is the kind of passage that makes it easier for us to follow the transition from Socrates' universal definitions to the Platonic theory of separately existent eternal universal Forms. The words *eidos* and *idea*, the technical terms for the Platonic Forms, commonly mean physical stature or bodily appearance. As we apply a common epithet, in this case pious, to different actions or things, these must have a common characteristic, present a common appearance or form, to justify the use of the same term, but in the early dialogues, as here, it seems to be thought of as immanent in the particulars and without separate existence. The same is true of 6 d where the word "Form" is also used.—Trans.

this is so. I have already said to others that such actions are right, not to favour the ungodly, whoever they are. These people themselves believe that Zeus is the best and most just of the gods, yet they agree that he bound his father because he unjustly swallowed his sons, and that he in turn castrated his father for similar reasons. But they are angry with me because I am prosecuting my father for his wrongdoing. They contradict themselves in what they say about the gods and about me.

SOCRATES: Indeed, Euthyphro, this is the reason why I am a defendant in the case, because I find it hard to accept things like that being said about the gods, and it is likely to be the reason why I shall be told I do wrong. Now, however, if you, who have full knowledge of such things, share their opinions, then we must agree with them too, it would seem. For what are we to say, we who agree that we ourselves have no knowledge? Tell me, by the god of friendship, do you really believe these things are true?

EUTHYPHRO: Yes, Socrates, and so are even more surprising things, of which the majority has no knowledge.

SOCRATES: And do you believe that there really is war among the gods, and terrible enmities and battles, and other such things as are told by the poets, and other sacred stories such as are embroidered by good writers and by representations of which the robe of the goddess is adorned when it is carried up to the Acropolis. Are we to say these things are true, Euthyphro?

EUTHYPHRO: Not only these, Socrates, but as I was saying just now, I will, if you wish, relate many other things about the gods which I know will amaze you.

SOCRATES: I should not be surprised, but you will tell me these at leisure some other time. For now, try to tell me more clearly what I was asking just now, for, my friend, you did not teach me adequately when I asked you what the pious was, but you told me that what you are doing now, to prosecute your father for murder, is pious.

EUTHYPHRO: And I told the truth, Socrates.

SOCRATES: Perhaps. You agree, however, that there are many other pious actions.

EUTHYPHRO: There are.

SOCRATES: Bear in mind then that I did not bid you tell me one or two of the many pious actions but that form itself that makes all pious actions pious, for you agreed that all impious actions are impious and all pious actions pious through one form, or don't you remember?

EUTHYPHRO: I do.

SOCRATES: Tell me then what form itself is, so that I may look upon it, and using it as a model, say that any action of yours or another's that is of that kind is pious, and if it is not that it is not.

EUTHYPHRO: If that is how you want it, Socrates, that is how I will tell you.

SOCRATES: That is what I want.

EUTHYPHRO: Well then, what is dear to the gods is pious, what is not is impious.

SOCRATES: Splendid, Euthyphro! You have now answered in the way I wanted. Whether your answer is true I do not know yet, but you will obviously show me that what you say is true.

EUTHYPHRO: Certainly.

SOCRATES: Come then, let us examine what we mean. An action or a man dear to the gods is pious, but an action or a man hated by the gods is impious. They are not the same, but opposites, the pious and the impious. Is that not so?

EUTHYPHRO: It is indeed.

SOCRATES: And that seems to be a good statement?

EUTHYPHRO: I think so, Socrates.

SOCRATES: We have also stated that the gods are in a state of discord, that they are at odds with each other, Euthyphro, and that they are at enmity with each other. That too has been said.

EUTHYPHRO: It has.

SOCRATES: What are the subjects of difference that cause hatred and anger? Let us look at it this way. If you and I were to differ about numbers as to which is the greater, would this difference make us enemies and angry with each other, or would we proceed to count and soon resolve our difference about this?

EUTHYPHRO: We would certainly do so.

SOCRATES: Again, if we differed about the larger and the smaller, we would turn to measurement and soon cease to differ.

EUTHYPHRO: That is so.

SOCRATES: And about the heavier and the lighter, we would resort to weighing and be reconciled.

EUTHYPHRO: Of course.

SOCRATES: What subject of difference would make us angry and hostile to each other if we were unable to come to a decision? Perhaps you do not have an answer ready, but examine as I tell you whether these subjects are the just and the unjust, the beautiful and the ugly, the good and the bad. Are these not the subjects of difference about which, when we are unable to come to satisfactory decision, you and I and other men become hostile to each other whenever we do.

EUTHYPHRO: That is the difference, Socrates, about those subjects.

SOCRATES: What about the gods, Euthyphro? If indeed they have differences, will it not be about these same subjects?

EUTHYPHRO: It certainly must be so.

SOCRATES: Then according to your argument, my good Euthyphro, different gods consider different things to be just, beautiful, ugly, good and bad, for they would not be at odds with one another unless they differed about these subjects, would they?

EUTHYPHRO: You are right.

SOCRATES: And they like what each of them considers beautiful, good, and just, and hate the opposites of these?

EUTHYPHRO: Certainly.

SOCRATES: But you say that the same things are considered just by some gods and unjust by others, and as they dispute about these things they are at odds and at war with each other. Is that not so?

EUTHYPHRO: It is.

SOCRATES: The same things then are loved by the gods and hated by the gods, both god-loved and god-hated.

EUTHYPHRO: It seems likely.

SOCRATES: And the same things would be both pious and impious, according to this argument?

EUTHYPHRO: I'm afraid so.

SOCRATES: So you did not answer my question, you surprising man. I did not ask you what same thing is both pious and impious, and it appears that what is loved by the gods is also hated by them. So it is in no way surprising if your present action, namely punishing your father, may be pleasing to Zeus but displeasing to Kronos and Ouranos, pleasing to Hephaestus but displeasing to Hera, and so with any other gods who differ from each other on this subject.

EUTHYPHRO: I think, Socrates, that on this subject no gods would differ from one another, that whoever has killed anyone unjustly should pay the penalty.

SOCRATES: Well now, Euthyphro, have you ever heard any man maintaining that one who has killed or done anything else unjustly should not pay the penalty?

EUTHYPHRO: They never cease to dispute on this subject, both elsewhere and in the courts, for when they have committed many wrongs they do and say anything to avoid the penalty.

SOCRATES: Do they agree they have done wrong, Euthyphro, and in spite of so agreeing do they nevertheless say they should not be punished?

EUTHYPHRO: No, they do not agree on that point.

SOCRATES: So they do not say or do anything. For they do not venture to say this, or dispute that they must not pay the penalty if they have done wrong, but I think they deny doing wrong. Is that not so?

EUTHYPHRO: That is true.

SOCRATES: Then they do not dispute that the wrongdoer must be punished, but they may disagree as to who the wrongdoer is, what he did and when.

EUTHYPHRO: You are right.

SOCRATES: Do not the gods have the same experience, if indeed they are at odds with each other about the just and the unjust, as your argument maintains? Some assert that they wrong one another, while others deny it, but no one among gods or men ventures to say that the wrongdoer must not be punished.

EUTHYPHRO: Yes, that is true, Socrates, as to the main point.

SOCRATES: And those who disagree, whether men or gods, dispute about each action, if indeed the gods disagree. Some say it is done justly, others unjustly. Is that not so?

EUTHYPHRO: Yes indeed.

SOCRATES: Come now, my dear Euthyphro, tell me, too, that I may become wiser, what proof you have that all the gods consider that man to have been killed unjustly who became a murderer while in your service, was bound by the master of his victim, and died in his bonds before the one who bound him found out from the seers what was to be done with him, and that it is right for a son to denounce and to prosecute his father on behalf of such a man. Come, try to show me a clear sign that all the gods definitely believe this action to be right. If you can give me adequate proof of this, I shall never cease to extol your wisdom.

EUTHYPHRO: This is perhaps no light task, Socrates, though I could show you very clearly.

SOCRATES: I understand that you think me more dull-witted than the jury, as you will obviously show them that these actions were unjust and that all the gods hate such actions.

EUTHYPHRO· I will show it to them clearly, Socrates, if only they will listen to me.

SOCRATES: They will listen if they think you show them well. But this thought came to me as I was speaking, and I am examining it, saying to myself: "If Euthyphro shows me conclusively that all the gods consider such a death unjust, to what greater extent have I learned from him the nature of piety and impiety? This action would then, it seems, be hated by the gods, but the pious and the impious were not thereby now defined, for what is hated by the gods has also been shown to be loved by them." So I will not insist on this point: let us assume, if you wish, that all the gods consider this unjust and that they all hate it. However, is this the correction we are making in our discussion, that what all the gods hate is impious, and what they all love is pious, and that what some gods love and others hate is neither or both? Is that how you now wish us to define piety and impiety?

EUTHYPHRO: What prevents us from doing so, Socrates?

SOCRATES: For my part nothing, Euthyphro, but you look whether on your part this proposal will enable you to teach me most easily what you promised.

EUTHYPHRO: I would certainly say that pious is what all the gods love, and the opposite, which all the gods hate, is the impious.

SOCRATES: Then let us again examine whether that is a sound statement, or do we let it pass, and if one of us, or someone else, merely says that this is so, do we accept that it is so? Or should we examine what the speaker means?

EUTHYPHRO: We must examine it, but I certainly think that this is now a fine statement.

SOCRATES: We shall soon know better whether it is. Consider this: Is the pious loved by the gods because it is pious, or is it pious because it is loved by the gods?

EUTHYPHRO: I don't know what you mean, Socrates.

SOCRATES.: I shall try to explain more clearly; we speak of something being carried[4] and something carrying, of something being led and something leading, of something being seen and something seeing, and you understand that these things are all different from one another and how they differ?

EUTHYPHRO: I think I do.

SOCRATES: So there is something being loved and something loving, and the loving is a different thing.

EUTHYPHRO: Of course.

SOCRATES: Tell me then whether that which it is (said to be) being carried is being carried because someone carries it or for some other reason.

---

[4] This is the present participle form of the verb *pheromenon*, literally *being-carried*. The following passage is somewhat obscure, especially in translation, but the general meaning is clear. Plato points out that this participle simply indicates the object of an action of carrying, seeing, loving, etc. It follows from the action and adds nothing new, the action being prior to it, not following from it, and a thing is said to be loved because someone loves it, not vice versa. To say therefore that the pious is being loved by the gods says no more than that the gods love it. Euthyphro, however, also agrees that the pious is loved by the gods because of its nature (because it is pious), but the fact of its being loved by the gods does not define that nature, and as a definition is therefore unsatisfactory. It only indicates a quality or affect of the pious, and the pious is therefore still to be defined.—Trans.

EUTHYPHRO: No, that is the reason.

SOCRATES: And that which is being led is so because someone leads it, and that which is being seen because someone sees it?

EUTHYPHRO: Certainly.

SOCRATES: It is not seen by someone because it is being seen but on the contrary it is being seen because someone sees it, nor is it because it is being led that someone leads it but because someone leads it that it is being led; it is not because it is being seen that someone sees it, but it is being seen because someone sees it; nor does someone carry an object because it is being carried, but it is being carried because someone carries it. Is what I want to say clear, Euthyphro? I want to say this, namely, that if anything comes to be, or is affected, it does not come to be because it is coming to be, but it is coming to be because it comes to be; nor is it affected because it is being affected but because something affects it. Or do you not agree?

EUTHYPHRO: I do.

SOCRATES: What is being loved is either something that comes to be or something that is affected by something?

EUTHYPHRO: Certainly.

SOCRATES: So it is in the same case as the things just mentioned; it is not loved by those who love it because it is being loved, but it is being loved because they love it?

EUTHYPHRO: Necessarily.

SOCRATES: What then do we say about the pious, Euthyphro? Surely that it is loved by all the gods, according to what you say?

EUTHYPHRO: Yes.

SOCRATES: Is it loved because it is pious, or for some other reason?

EUTHYPHRO: For no other reason.

SOCRATES: It is loved then because it is pious, but it is not pious because it is loved?[5]

EUTHYPHRO: Apparently.

SOCRATES: And because it is loved by the gods it is being loved and is dear to the gods?

EUTHYPHRO: Of course.

SOCRATES: The god-beloved is then not the same as the pious, Euthyphro, nor the pious the same as the god-beloved, as you say it is, but one differs from the other.

EUTHYPHRO: How so, Socrates?

SOCRATES: Because we agree that the pious is beloved for the reason that it is pious, but it is not pious because it is loved. Is that not so?

---

[5] I quote an earlier comment of mine on this passage: " . . . it gives in a nutshell a point of view from which Plato never departed. Whatever the gods may be, they must by their very nature love the right because it is right." They have no choice in the matter. "This separation of the dynamic power of the gods from the ultimate reality, this setting up of absolute values above the gods themselves was not as unnatural to a Greek as it would be to us . . . The gods who ruled on Olympus . . . were not creators but created beings. As in Homer, Zeus must obey the balance of Necessity, so the Platonic gods must conform to an eternal scale of values. They did not create them, cannot alter them, cannot indeed wish to do so."(*Plato's Thought*, Boston: Beacon Press, 1958, pp. 152–9.)—Trans.

EUTHYPHRO: Yes.

SOCRATES: And that the god beloved, on the other hand, is so because it is loved by the gods, by the very fact of being loved, but it is not loved because it is god-beloved.

EUTHYPHRO: True.

SOCRATES: But if the god-beloved and the pious were the same, my dear Euthyphro, and the pious were loved because it was pious, then the god-beloved would be loved because it was god-beloved, and if the god-beloved was god-beloved because it was loved by the gods, then the pious would also be pious because it was loved by the gods; but now you see that they are in opposite cases as being altogether different from each other: the one is of a nature to be loved because, it is loved, the other is loved because it is of a nature to be loved. I'm afraid, Euthyphro, that when you were asked what piety is, you did not wish to make its nature clear to me, but you told me an affect or quality of it, that the pious has the quality of being loved by all the gods, but you have not yet told me what the pious is. Now, if you will, do not hide things from me but tell me again from the beginning what piety is, whether loved by the gods or having some other quality—we shall not quarrel about that—but be keen to tell me what the pious and the impious are.

EUTHYPHRO: But Socrates, I have no way of telling you what I have in mind, for whatever proposition we put forward goes around and refuses to stay put where we establish it.

SOCRATES: Your statements, Euthyphro, seem to belong to my ancestor, Daedalus. If I were stating them and putting them forward, you would perhaps be making fun of me and say that because of my kinship with him my conclusions in discussion run away and will not stay where one puts them. As these propositions are yours, however, we need some other jest, for they will not stay put for you, as you say yourself.

EUTHYPHRO: I think the same jest will do for our discussion, Socrates, for I am not the one who makes them go round and not remain in the same place; it is you who are the Daedalus; for as far as I am concerned they would remain as they were.

SOCRATES: It looks as if I was cleverer than Daedalus in using my skill, my friend, in so far as he could only cause to move the things he made himself, but I can make other people's move as well as my own. And the smartest part of my skill is that I am clever without wanting to be, for I would rather have my arguments remain unmoved than possess the wealth of Tantalus as well as the cleverness of Daedalus. But enough of this. Since I think you are making unnecessary difficulties, I am as eager as you are to find a way to teach me about piety, and do not give up before you do. See whether you think all that is pious is of necessity just.

EUTHYPHRO: I think so.

SOCRATES: And is then all that is just pious? Or is all that is pious just, but not all that is just pious, but some of it is and some is not?

EUTHYPHRO: I do not follow what you are saying, Socrates.

SOCRATES: Yet you are younger than I by as much as you are wiser. As I say, you are making difficulties because of your wealth of wisdom. Pull yourself together, my dear sir, what I am saying is not difficult to grasp. I am saying the opposite of what the poet said who wrote:

> You do not wish to name Zeus, who had done it, and who made all
> things grow, for where there is fear there is also shame.

I disagree with the poet. Shall I tell you why?

EUTHYPHRO: Please do.

SOCRATES: I do not think that "where there is fear there is also shame," for I think that many people who fear disease and poverty and many other such things feel fear, but are not ashamed of the things they fear. Do you not think so?

EUTHYPHRO: I do indeed.

SOCRATES: But where there is shame there is also fear. Does anyone feel shame at something who is not also afraid at the same time of a reputation for wickedness?

EUTHYPHRO: He is certainly afraid.

SOCRATES: It is then not right to say "where there is fear there is also shame," but that where there is shame there is also fear, for fear covers a larger area than shame. Shame is a part of fear just as odd is a part of number, with the result that it is not true where there is a number there is also oddness, but that where there is oddness there is also number. Do you follow me now?

EUTHYPHRO: Surely.

SOCRATES: This is the kind of thing I was asking before, whether where there is piety there is also justice, but where there is justice there is not always piety, for the pious is a part of justice. Shall we say that, or do you think otherwise?

EUTHYPHRO: No, but like that, for what you say appears to be right.

SOCRATES: See what comes next; if the pious is a part of the just, we must, it seems, find out what part of the just it is. Now if you asked me something of what we mentioned just now, such as what part of number is the even, and what number that is, I would say it is the number that is divisible into two equal, not unequal parts. Or do you not think so?

EUTHYPHRO: I do.

SOCRATES: Try in this way to tell me what part of the just the pious is, in order to tell Meletus not to wrong us any more and not to indict me for ungodliness, since I have learned from you sufficiently what is godly and pious and what is not.

EUTHYPHRO: I think, Socrates, that the godly and pious is the part of the just that is concerned with the care of the gods, while that concerned with the care of men is the remaining part of justice.

SOCRATES: You seem to me to put that very well, but I still need a bit of information. I do not know yet what you mean by care, for you do not mean it in the same sense as the care of other things, as, for example, not everyone knows how to care for horses, but the horse breeder does.

EUTHYPHRO: Yes, I do mean it that way.

SOCRATES: So horse breeding is the care of horses.

EUTHYPHRO: Yes.

SOCRATES: Nor does everyone know how to care for dogs, but the hunter does.

EUTHYPHRO: That is so.

SOCRATES: So hunting is the care of dogs.

EUTHYPHRO: Yes.

SOCRATES: And cattle raising is the care of cattle.

EUTHYPHRO: Quite so.

SOCRATES: While piety and godliness is the care of the gods, Euthyphro. Is that what you mean?

EUTHYPHRO: It is.

SOCRATES: Now care in each case has the same effect; it aims at the good and the benefit of the object cared for, as you see that horses cared for by horse breeders are benefited and become better. Or do you not think so?

EUTHYPHRO: I do.

SOCRATES: So dogs are benefited by dog breeding, cattle by cattle raising, and so with all the others. Or do you think that care aims to harm the object of its care?

EUTHYPHRO: By Zeus, no.

SOCRATES: It aims to benefit the object of its care.

EUTHYPHRO: Of course.

SOCRATES: Is piety then, which is the care of the gods, also to benefit the gods and make them better? Would you agree that when you do something pious you make someone of the gods better?

EUTHYPHRO: By Zeus, no.

SOCRATES: Nor do I think that this is what you mean—far from it—but that is why I asked you what you meant by the care of gods, because I did not believe you meant this kind of care.

EUTHYPHRO: Quite right, Socrates, that is not the kind of care I mean.

SOCRATES: Very well, but what kind of care of the gods would piety be?

EUTHYPHRO: The kind of care, Socrates, that slaves take of their masters.

SOCRATES: I understand. It is likely to be the service of the gods.

EUTHYPHRO: Quite so.

SOCRATES: Could you tell me to the achievement of what goal service to doctors tends? Is is not, do you think, to achieving health?

EUTHYPHRO: I think so.

SOCRATES: What about service to shipbuilders? To what achievement is it directed?

EUTHYPHRO: Clearly, Socrates, to the building of a ship.

SOCRATES: And service to housebuilders to the building of a house?

EUTHYPHRO: Yes.

SOCRATES: Tell me then, my good sir, to the achievement of what aim does service to the gods tend? You obviously know since you say that you, of all men, have the best knowledge of the divine.

EUTHYPHRO: And I am telling the truth, Socrates.

SOCRATES: Tell me then, by Zeus, what is that excellent aim that the gods achieve, using us as their servants?

EUTHYPHRO: Many fine things, Socrates.

SOCRATES: So do generals, my friend. Nevertheless you could tell me their main concern, which is to achieve victory in war, is it not?

EUTHYPHRO: Of course.

SOCRATES: The farmers too, I think, achieve many fine things, but the main point of their efforts is to produce food from the earth.

EUTHYPHRO: Quite so.

SOCRATES: Well then, how would you sum up the many fine things that the gods achieve?

EUTHYPHRO: I told you a short while ago, Socrates, that it is a considerable task to acquire any precise knowledge of these things, but, to put it simply, I say that if a man knows how to say and do what is pleasing to the gods at prayer and sacrifice, those are pious actions such as preserve both private houses and public affairs of state. The opposite of these pleasing actions are impious and overturn and destroy everything.

SOCRATES: You could tell me in far fewer words, if you were willing, the sum of what I asked, Euthyphro, but you are not keen to teach me, that is clear. You were on the point of doing so, but you turned away. If you had given the answer, I should now have acquired from you sufficient knowledge of the nature of piety. As it is, the lover of inquiry must follow it wherever it may lead him. Once more then, what do you say that piety and the pious are, and also impiety? Are they a knowledge of how to sacrifice and pray?

EUTHYPHRO: They are.

SOCRATES: To sacrifice is to make a gift to the gods, whereas to pray is to beg from the gods?

EUTHYPHRO: Definitely, Socrates.

SOCRATES: It would follow from this statement that piety would be a knowledge of how to give to, and beg from, the gods.

EUTHYPHRO: You understood what I said very well, Socrates.

SOCRATES: That is because I am so desirous of your wisdom, and I concentrate my mind on it, so that no word of yours may fall to the ground. But tell me, what is this service to the gods? You say it is to beg from them and to give to them?

EUTHYPHRO: I do.

SOCRATES: And to beg correctly would be to ask from them things that we need?

EUTHYPHRO: What else?

SOCRATES: And to give correctly is to give them what they need from us, for it would not be skillful to bring gifts to anyone that are in no way needed.

EUTHYPHRO: True, Socrates.

SOCRATES: Piety would then be a sort of trading skill between gods and men?

EUTHYPHRO: Trading yes, if you prefer to call it that.

SOCRATES: I prefer nothing, unless it is true. But tell me, what benefit do the gods derive from the gifts they receive from us? What they give us is obvious to all. There is for us no good that we do not receive from them, but how are they benefited by what they receive from us? Or do we have such an advantage over them in the trade that we receive all our blessings from them and they receive nothing from us?

EUTHYPHRO: Do you suppose, Socrates, that the gods are benefited by what they receive from us?

SOCRATES: What could those gifts from us to the gods be, Euthyphro?

EUTHYPHRO: What else, you think, than honour, reverence, and what I mentioned before, gratitude.

SOCRATES: The pious is then, Euthyphro, pleasing to the gods, but not beneficial or dear to them?

EUTHYPHRO: I think it is of all things most dear to them.

SOCRATES: So the pious is once again what is dear to the gods.

EUTHYPHRO: Most certainly.

SOCRATES: When you say this, will you be surprised if your arguments seem to move about instead of staying put? And will you accuse me of being Daedalus who makes them move, though you are yourself much more skillful than Daedalus and make them go round in a circle? Or do you not realize that our argument has moved around and come again to the same place? You surely remember that earlier the pious and the god-beloved were shown not to be the same but different from each other. Or do you not remember?

EUTHYPHRO: I do.

SOCRATES: Do you then not realize that when you say now that that what is dear to the gods is the pious? Is this not the same as the god-beloved? Or is it not?

EUTHYPHRO: It certainly is.

SOCRATES: Either we were wrong when we agreed before, or, if we were right then, we are wrong now.

EUTHYPHRO: That seems to be so.

SOCRATES: So we must investigate again from the beginning what piety is, as I shall not willingly give up before I learn this. Do not think me unworthy, but concentrate your attention and tell the truth. For you know it, if any man does, and I must not let you go, like Proteus, before you tell me. If you had no clear knowledge of piety and impiety you would never have ventured to prosecute your father for murder on behalf of a servant. For fear of the gods you would have been afraid to take the risk lest you should not be acting rightly, and would have been ashamed before men, but now I know well that you believe you have clear knowledge of piety and impiety. So tell me, my good Euthyphro, and do not hide what you believe.

EUTHYPHRO: Some other time, Socrates, for I am in a hurry now, and it is time for me to go.

SOCRATES: What a thing to do, my friend! By going you have cast me down from a great hope I had, that I would learn from you the nature of the pious and the impious and so escape Meletus' indictment by showing that I had acquired wisdom in divine matters from Euthyphro, and my ignorance would no longer cause me to be careless and inventive about such things, and that I would be better for the rest of my life.

VII.A.2. God's Command to Abraham (The Teleological Suspension of the Ethical)

The following passage from the book of Genesis, a part of the Hebrew Bible, tells the celebrated story of God's testing of Abraham by commanding him to kill his beloved only son Isaac and make of him a burnt offering to God. The passage is frequently cited by Jews and Christians alike as the paradigm of faith and the exemplification of morality as obedience to God.

After these things God tested Abraham, and said to him, "Abraham!" And he said, "Here am I." He said, "Take your son, your only son Isaac, whom you love, and go to the land of Mori'ah, and offer him there as a burnt offering upon one of the mountains of which I shall tell you." So Abraham rose early in the morning, saddled his ass, and took two of his young men with him, and his son Isaac; and he cut the wood for the burnt offering, and arose and went to the place of which God had told him. On the third day Abraham lifted up his eyes and saw the place afar off. Then Abraham said to his young men, "Stay here with the ass; and I and the lad will go yonder and worship, and come again to you." And Abraham took the wood of the burnt offering, and laid it on Isaac his son; and he took in his hand the fire and the knife. So they went both of them together. And Isaac said to his father Abraham, "My father." And he said, "Here am I, my son." He said, "Behold, the fire and the wood; but where is the lamb for the burnt offering?" Abraham said, "God will provide himself the lamb for a burnt offering, my son." So they went both of them together.

When they came to the place of which God had told him, Abraham built an altar there, and laid wood in order, and bound Isaac his son, and laid him on the altar, upon the wood. Then Abraham put forth his hand, and took the knife to slay his son. But the angel of the Lord called to him from heaven, and said, "Abraham, Abraham!" And he said, "Here am I." He said, "Do not lay your hand on the lad or do anything to him; for now I know that you fear God, seeing you have not withheld your son, your only son, from me." And Abraham lifted up his eyes and looked and behold him was a ram caught in the thicket by his horns; and Abraham went and took the ram, and offered it as a burnt offering instead of his son. So Abraham called the name of this place

The Lord will provide; as it is said to this day, "On the mount of the Lord it shall be provided."

And the angel of the Lord called to Abraham a second time from heaven, and said, "By myself I have sworn, says the Lord, because you have done this, and have not withheld your son, your only son, I will indeed bless you, and I will multiply your descendants as the stars of heaven and as the sand which is on the seashore. And your descendants shall possess the gate of their enemies, and by your descendants shall the nations of the earth bless themselves, because you have obeyed my voice."

VII.A.3. Abraham and Isaac

SØREN KIERKEGAARD

Søren Kierkegaard (1813–1855), the Danish philosopher and religious thinker often called the grandfather of existentialism, was the first to define the concept of the teleological suspension of the ethical. By this term he meant the setting aside of what morality normally requires in response to a specific command from God for a higher purpose. The story of Abraham and Isaac is supposed to exemplify this principle, but Kierkegaard found such a notion profoundly disturbing. In the following brief selection, he offers four alternative interpretations of the famous story, interpretations that raise disquieting questions indeed about the notion of faith as the unquestioning performance of acts one becomes convinced God has commanded one to do.

PRELUDE

Once upon a time there was a man who as a child had heard the beautiful story about how God tempted Abraham, and how he endured temptation, kept the faith, and a second time received again a son contrary to expectation. When the child became older he read the same story

From *Fear and Trembling and The Sickness unto Death*, trans. with Introductions and Notes by Walter Lowrie. Copyright 1941, 1954, © 1982 renewed by Princeton University Press. Pp. 26–29.

with even greater admiration, for life had separated what was united in the pious simplicity of the child. The older he became, the more frequently his mind reverted to that story, his enthusiasm became greater and greater, and yet he was less and less able to understand the story. At last in his interest for that he forgot everything else; his soul had only one wish, to see Abraham, one longing, to have been witness to that event. His desire was not to behold the beautiful countries of the Orient, or the earthly glory of the Promised Land, or that godfearing couple whose old age God had blessed, or the venerable figure of the aged patriarch, or the vigorous young manhood of Isaac whom God had bestowed upon Abraham—he saw no reason why the same thing might not have taken place on a barren heath in Denmark. His yearning was to accompany them on the three days' journey when Abraham rode with sorrow before him and with Isaac by his side. His only wish was to be present at the time when Abraham lifted up his eyes and saw Mount Moriah afar off, at the time when he left the asses behind and went alone with Isaac up unto the mountain; for what his mind was intent upon was not the ingenious web of imagination but the shudder of thought.

That man was not a thinker, he felt no need of getting beyond faith; he deemed it the most glorious thing to be remembered as the father of it, an enviable lot to possess it, even though no one else were to know it.

That man was not a learned exegete, he didn't know Hebrew, if he had known Hebrew, he perhaps would easily have understood the story and Abraham.

I

"And God tempted Abraham and said unto him, Take Isaac, thine only son, whom thou lovest, and get thee into the land of Moriah, and offer him there for a burnt offering upon the mountain which I will show thee."

It was early in the morning, Abraham arose betimes, he had the asses saddled, left his tent, and Isaac with him, but Sarah looked out of the window after them until they had passed down the valley and she could see them no more. They rode in silence for three days. On the morning of the fourth day Abraham said never a word, but he lifted up his eyes and saw Mount Moriah afar off. He left the young men behind and went on alone with Isaac beside him up to the mountain. But Abraham said to himself, "I will not conceal from Isaac whither this course leads him." He stood still, he laid his hand upon the head of Isaac in benediction, and Isaac bowed to receive the blessing. And Abraham's face was fatherliness, his look was mild, his speech encouraging. But Isaac was unable to understand him, his soul could not be exalted; he embraced Abraham's knees, he fell on his knees imploringly, he begged for his young life, for the fair hope of his future, he called to mind the joy in Abraham's house, he called to mind the sorrow and loneliness. Then Abraham lifted up the boy, he walked with him by his side, and his talk was full of comfort and exhortation. But Isaac could not understand him. He climbed Mount Moriah, but Isaac understood him not. Then for an instant he turned away from him, and when Isaac saw Abraham's face it was changed, his glance was wild, his form was horror. He seized Isaac by the throat, threw him to the ground and said, "Stupid boy, dost thou then suppose that I am thy father? I am an idolater. Dost thou suppose that this is God's bidding? No, it is my desire." Then Isaac trembled and cried out in terror, "O God in heaven, have compassion upon me. God of Abraham, have compassion upon me. If I have no father upon earth, be Thou my father!" But Abraham in a low voice said to himself, "O Lord in heaven, I thank Thee. After all it is better for him to believe that I am a monster, rather than that he should lose faith in Thee."

When the child must be weaned, the mother blackens her breast, it would indeed be a shame that the breast should look delicious when the child must not have it. So the child believes that the breast has changed, but the mother is the same, her glance is as loving and tender as ever. Happy the person who had no need of more dreadful expedients for weaning the child!

II

It was early in the morning, Abraham arose betimes, he embraced Sarah, the bride of his old age, and Sarah kissed Isaac, who had taken away her reproach, who was her pride, her hope for all time. So they rode on in silence along the way and Abraham's glance was fixed upon the ground until the fourth day when he lifted up his eyes and saw afar off Mount Moriah, but his glance turned again to the ground. Silently he laid the wood in order, he bound Isaac, in silence he drew the knife—then he saw the ram which God had prepared. Then he offered that and returned home. . . . From that time on Abraham became old, he could not forget that God had required this of him. Isaac throve as before, but Abraham's eyes were darkened and knew joy no more.

When the child has grown up and must be weaned, the mother virginally hides her breast, so the child has no more mother. Happy the child which did not in another way lose its mother.

III

It was early in the morning, Abraham arose betimes, he kissed Sarah, the young mother, and Sarah kissed Isaac, her delight, her joy at all times. And Abraham rode pensively along the way, he thought of Hagar and of the son whom he drove out into the wilderness, he climbed Mount Moriah, he drew the knife.

It was a quiet evening when Abraham rode out alone, and he rode out to Mount Moriah; he threw himself upon his face, he prayed God to forgive his sin, that he had been willing to offer Isaac, that the father had forgotten the duty toward the son. Often he rode his lonely way, but he found no rest. He could not comprehend that it was a sin to be willing to offer to God the best thing he possessed, that for which he would many times have given his life; and if it was a sin, if he had not loved Isaac as he did, then he could not understand that it might be forgiven. For what sin could be more dreadful?

When the child must be weaned, the mother too is not without sorrow at the thought that she and the child are separated more and more, that the child first lay under her heart and later reposed upon her breast will be so near to her no more. So they mourn together for the brief period of mourning. Happy the person who has kept the child as near and needed not to sorrow any more!

IV

It was early in the morning, everything was prepared for the journey in Abraham's house. He bade Sarah farewell, and Eleazer, the faithful servant, followed him along the way. They rode together in harmony, Abraham and Isaac, until they came to Mount Moriah. But Abraham prepared everything for the sacrifice, calmly and quietly; but when he turned and drew the knife, Isaac saw that his left hand was clenched in despair, that a tremor passed through his body—but Abraham drew the knife.

Then they turned again home, Sarah hastened to meet them, but Isaac had lost his faith. No word of this had ever been spoken in the world, and Isaac never talked about what he had seen and Abraham did not suspect that anyone had seen it.

When the child must be weaned, the mother has stronger food in readiness, lest the child should perish. Happy the person who has stronger food in readiness!

Thus and in many like ways that man of whom we are speaking thought concerning this event. Every time he returned home after wandering to Mount Moriah, he sank down with weariness, he folded his hands and said, "No one is so great as Abraham! Who is capable of understanding him?"

VII.A.4. The Red Sea Scrolls

WOODY ALLEN

Woody Allen (1935–) is a contemporary humorist, actor, author, and filmmaker. The following piece, purporting tongue-in-cheek to be fragments of ancient scrolls, offers rather unorthodox interpretations of the biblical book of Job and, in fragment two, of the Abraham and Isaac story. The clear implication seems to be that humans often mistake their own ideas for divine commandments, and that we must be extremely cautious about going against established morality because we think that God has commanded us to do so.

Scholars will recall that several years ago a shepherd, wandering in the Gulf of Aqaba, stumbled upon a cave containing several large clay jars and also two tickets to the ice show. Inside the jars were discovered six parchment scrolls with ancient incomprehensible writing which the shepherd, in his ignorance, sold to the museum for $750,000 apiece. Two years later the jars turned up in a pawnshop in Philadelphia. One year later the shepherd turned up in a pawnshop in Philadelphia and neither was claimed.

Archaeologists originally set the date of the scrolls at 4000 B.C., or just after the massacre of the Israelites by their benefactors. The writing is a mixture of Sumerian, Aramaic, and Babylonian and seems to have been done by either one man over a long period of time, or several men who shared the same suit. The authenticity of the scrolls is currently in great doubt, particularly since the word "Oldsmobile" appears several times in the text, and the few fragments that have finally been translated deal with familiar religious themes in a more than dubious way. Still, excavationist A. H. Bauer has noted that even though the fragments seem totally fraudulent, this is probably the greatest archeological find in history with the exception of the recovery of his cuff links from a tomb in Jerusalem. The following are the translated fragments.

One . . . And the Lord made an bet with Satan to test Job's loyalty and the Lord, for no apparent reason to Job, smote him on the head and again on the ear and pushed him into an thick sauce so as to make Job sticky and vile and then He slew a tenth part of Job's kine and Job calleth out: "Why doth thou slay my kine? Kine are hard to come by. Now I am short kine and I 'm not even sure what kine are." And the Lord produced two stone tablets and snapped them closed on Job's nose. And when Job's wife saw this she wept and the Lord sent an angel of mercy who anointed her head with a polo mallet and of the ten plagues, the Lord sent one through six, inclusive, and Job was sore and his wife angry and she rent her garment and then raised the rent but refused to paint

And soon Job's pastures dried up and his tongue cleaved to the roof of his mouth so he could not pronounce the word "frankincense" without getting big laughs.

And once the Lord, while wreaking havoc upon his faithful servant, came too close and Job grabbed him around the neck and said, "Aha! Now I got you! Why art thou giving Job a hard time, eh? Eh? Speak up!"

And the Lord said, "Er, look—that's my neck you have . . . Could you let me go?"

But Job showed no mercy and said, "I was doing very well till you came along. I had myrrh and fig trees in abundance and a coat of many colors with two pairs of pants of many colors. Now look."

And the Lord spake and his voice thundered: "Must I who created heaven and earth explain my ways to thee? What hath thou created that thou doth dare question me?"

"That's no answer," Job said. "And for someone who's supposed to be omnipotent, let me tell you, 'tabernacle' has only one *l*." Then Job fell to his knees and cried to the Lord, "Thine is the kingdom and the power and the glory. Thou hast a good job. Don't blow it."

Two . . . And Abraham awoke in the middle of the night and said to his only son, Isaac, "I have had a dream where the voice of the Lord sayeth that I must sacrifice my only son, so put your pants on." And Isaac trembled and said, "So what did you say? I mean when He brought this whole thing up?"

"What am I going to say" Abraham said. "I'm standing there at two A.M. in my underwear with the Creator of the Universe. Should I argue?"

"Well, did he say why he wants me sacrificed?" Isaac asked his father.

But Abraham said, "The faithful do not question. Now let's go because I have a heavy day tomorrow."

And Sarah who heard Abraham's plan grew vexed and said, "How doth thou know it was the Lord and not, say, thy friend who loveth practical jokes, for the Lord hateth practical jokes and whosoever shall pull one shall be delivered into the hands of his enemies whether they can pay the delivery charges or not." And Abraham answered, "Because I know it was the Lord. It was a deep, resonant voice, well modulated, and nobody in the desert can get a rumble in it like that."

And Sarah said, "And thou art willing to carry out this senseless act?" But Abraham told her, "Frankly, yes, for to question the Lord's word is one of the worst things a person can do, particularly with the economy in the state it's in."

And so he took Isaac to a certain place and prepared to sacrifice him but at the last minute the Lord stayed Abraham's hand and said, "How could thou doest such a thing?"

And Abraham said, "But thou said—"

"Never mind what I said," the Lord spake. "Doth thou listen to every crazy idea that comes thy way?" And Abraham grew ashamed "Er—not really . . . no."

"I jokingly suggest thou sacrifice Isaac and thou immediately runs out to do it."

And Abraham fell to his knees, "See, I never know when you're kidding."

And the Lord thundered, "No sense of humor. I can't believe it."

"But doth this not prove I love thee. I was willing to donate mine only son on thy whim?"

And the Lord said, "It proves that some men will follow any order no matter how asinine as long as it comes from a resonant, well-modulated voice."

And with that, the Lord bid Abraham get some rest and check with him tomorrow.

Three. . . And it came to pass that a man who sold shirts was smitten by hard times. Neither did any of his merchandise move nor did he prosper. And he prayed and said, "Lord, why hast thou left me to suffer thus? All mine enemies sell their goods except I. And it's the height of the season. My shirts are good shirts. Take a look at this rayon. I got button-downs, flare collars, nothing sells. Yet I have kept thy commandments. Why can I not earn a living when mine younger brother cleans up in children's ready-to-wear?"

And the Lord heard the man and said, "About thy shirts . . . "

"Yes, Lord," the man said, falling to his knees.

"Put an alligator over the pocket."

"Pardon me, Lord?"

"Just do what I'm telling you. You won't be sorry."

And the man sewed on to all his shirts a small alligator symbol and lo and behold, suddenly his merchandise moved like gangbusters, and there was much rejoicing while amongst his enemies there was wailing and gnashing of teeth, and one said, "The Lord is merciful. He maketh me to lie down in green pastures. The problem is, I can't get up."

LAWS AND PROVERBS

Doing abominations is against the law, particularly if the abominations are done while wearing a lobster bib.

The lion and the calf shall lie down together but the calf won't get much sleep.

Whosoever shall not fall by the sword or by famine, shall fall by pestilence so why bother shaving?

The wicked at heart probably know something.

Whosoever loveth wisdom is righteous but he that keepeth company with fowl is weird.

My Lord, my Lord! What hast Thou done, lately?

VII.B. The Relation of Religion to Ethics

VII.B.1. The Independence of Ethics from Religion

YEAGER HUDSON

Yeager Hudson (1931-), the editor of this volume, is professor of philosophy at Colby College. The following selection attempts to document the actual independence of ethics from religion in most societies and argues for the objectivity of morality based on the universal human faculty of reason. It also argues that rational morality, applicable to all humans without regard to culture or religion, must necessarily take precedence over the narrower, sectarian ethical commandments of individual religions whenever they conflict.

Many religious people, particularly those who have come under the influence of Judaism and Christianity, seem to feel that for religious reasons the divine command theory is required of the devout or the faithful. After all, if God is the creator, a being worthy of love, and worship, he must also be the source of moral rules. Furthermore, since so many Westerners tend to assume that actual moral systems originated in and evolved out of religion, the divine command theory even appears—until the problems with the theory become apparent—too obvious to question. It is important, however, to pay attention to the extent to which these assumptions are unjustified.

RELIGION AND ETHICS IN PRIMITIVE SOCIETIES

The close connection between religion and morality, so widely taken for granted among Christian and Jews, does not by any means characterize all religions. It is particularly absent from most pretechnological societies, both ancient and contemporary.[1] Western Christian thought about the evolution of moral systems, based on the assumption of a necessary dependence of morality on religion, surmised that primitives derived their beliefs about right and

From *The Philosophy of Religion* (Mountain View, Calif.: Mayfield, 1991), pp. 237–247.

wrong from their priests and shamans, spokespersons for the deities. The inference was that humans initially developed religious beliefs intertwined with moral teachings, that these gradually became more sophisticated, and that only quite late, when a society reached a complex level of development, did morality begin to be explored apart from religious teachings and eventually formulated in a freestanding, secular fashion that obscured its former (presumed) dependence on religion.

So firm was the assumption of the dependence of morality on religion that early explorers and even some anthropologists tended not to notice that in fact religion has little to do with morality among contemporary primitives. Instead, religion functions primarily to placate the gods and the spirit forces through rites and sacrifices. The purpose of these religious practices is twofold: to ward off disasters thought to come from the wrath of the gods and to make provisions for the safety of the human spirit or shade after death. The favor of the gods is not thought to be won by living a life of moral goodness or righteousness. The gods are quite indifferent to the human practice of morality and, indeed, are not themselves beings of high moral character. What the gods want is worship, reverence, and sacrifices. Morality is a matter to be settled among humans.

This attitude about religion seems to have been as characteristic of the ancient Greeks and Romans as it was of both ancient and contemporary primitives. It is to be seen in the religions of the Vikings and early Scandinavians, in the Druid practices of Britain, among some Native American tribes, and in the contemporary primitive societies of the South Pacific. Religion pertains largely to what is not understood—natural disasters, sickness, infertility of cattle or wives—which is to be dealt with by rites performed by the priests. The gods are not concerned with human behavior except as it relates to the faithful performance of religious rituals.

MORALITY DEVELOPED INDEPENDENTLY OF RELIGION

The widespread belief that all religions included a preoccupation with morality turns out in fact to be mistaken. So also does the assumption that all great moral systems have evolved out of religions. Two of the greatest systems of moral philosophy in the West, Plato's and Aristotle's, were worked out philosophically by the use of reason, with virtually no concern for religion. Confucianism in ancient China is another example: Often called one of the great world religions—involving as it does the notion of piety toward the spirits of one's ancestors—Confucianism is actually almost entirely concerned with human morality and what might be called human etiquette. It is not theistic; there is no element of revelation or any sense of gods as moral lawgivers. Similarly, in the modern period, systems of ethics such as those of Immanuel Kant in the eighteenth, John Stuart Mill in the nineteenth, and the humanists in the twentieth centuries have been developed independently of religion. Of course, Kant, Mill, and the humanists were affected in some measure by the Judeo-Christian religious tradition because they were a part of a culture saturated with its influence. Their moral theories, however, were grounded in rational human principles and not derived from alleged revelation or religious teachings.

But even faced with these historical facts—the absence of moral concern in the religions of primitive peoples and the origin of sophisticated moral systems completely apart from religion—many people still feel that proper morality must ultimately be rooted in religion. They believe so not merely because most developed religious traditions include moral teachings as major ingredients of their theology, but also from a sense that a being whose power is so great, whose wisdom is supreme, and who exemplifies moral perfection uniquely has the right to command our obedience in matters of right and wrong. The clinching point in the minds of many, we may note, is the belief that the divine command theory belongs to orthodox Jewish and Christian theology.

MORALITY AND NATURAL LAW

It comes as a great surprise to some to learn that during much of the history of the West, even in the Christian tradition, the divine command theory has not been the standard or accepted position. Among the ancient Greeks, as we have said, morality was believed to be grounded in human rationality and had nothing to do with religion or the gods. The Romans developed a concept of law that recognized the objectivity of the principles of government as well as those of the detailed legislative regulations enacted and enforced by governments. The Romans also seem to be the originators of the concept of natural law, not only as a term to describe the regularities in the operation of the material world but also to name the principles recognized by human reason as valid for the regulation of human moral and political life. These principles have nothing to do with the gods or religion, but are written, as it were, into the very structure of reality itself and are discoverable by any humans who take the trouble to reason carefully. This, according to the Romans, is the reason that fundamental moral and social values are so similar from one culture to another despite their great differences in details.

This concept of natural law as the source both of political and moral law came to be incorporated into the thinking of the West and eventually found its way into Christian theology, where it was called the law of God. This view was refined and elaborated in detail by the great Catholic theologian of the Middle Ages, Thomas Aquinas (1224–1274). And though Thomas taught that Christian revelation is a source of knowledge about what God commands, he explicitly rejected the divine command theory of morality, teaching instead that an eternal law provides the foundation both of God's commandments and of the insights about morality that come from human reason.

According to Thomas, natural law is universal, the same for all time and place. Local variations in human law and in moral prescriptions (apart from inattention to, or misunderstanding of, what natural law requires) arise from the differences of circumstances to which natural law comes to be applied. Civil law is thus the result of applying natural law to the specific circumstances of a society. Lawmaking in human parliaments is not actually a process of *making* laws; rather, it is a process of *discovering* what natural law, applied to these local conditions, requires. Thomas says that legislating is like the use of a syllogism, whose first premise is natural law (and thus identical for all times and places), whose second premise is a description of the conditions to which the law is to apply, and whose conclusion is the piece of civil legislation. An example may serve to make his point clearer: When we legislate such matters as speed limits, the stable, unchanging natural law (the first premise) is a dictate about concern for the safety of all persons, but the specific application of that concern differs because the hazards vary from place to place. If we legislate for a congested area or an area near a school (second premise), then the conclusion (civil law) is a slow speed limit. But if we legislate for open countryside, where persons are not likely to be walking in the road, this different second premise, along with the same first premise of natural law, permits a faster speed. In every case, however, what makes the specific law right (assuming that it is properly made) is its foundation in natural law.

Now natural law as a source for civil legislation and for moral rules is valid for all societies alike and is accessible to all rational persons in whatever time or place; it is not connected with any one religion. This means that morality is founded on principles independent of religion and of God. Its laws are rather like the laws of logic and mathematics, which are similarly universal and binding on all rational beings, human and divine. . . .

Some philosophers, such as Descartes, insisted that the omnipotence of God requires what we might call a divine command theory of logic and mathematics—that is, they claimed that the principles of reasoning are created by God and derive their truth from the fact that God prescribes them. This amounts to saying that $2 + 2 = 4$ is true because God says it is, not that God says it is because it is true. It also implies that if God had said that $2 + 2 = 7$, this would have been true instead. But we argued that such a situation clearly renders all meaning and understanding impossible. Not even God himself could actually *think* such things, for they are simply impossible—they destroy the conditions under which thinking can occur or claims can have meaning. There seem to be overwhelming reasons to believe that even an omnipotent deity must conform to the principles of logic and mathematics if such a deity wishes to think or to create a world. What we have playfully called a divine command theory of logic and mathematics is, in the final reckoning, unintelligible and must be rejected. Logic and mathematics are in a sense antecedent to the will of God and govern that will so that even God cannot violate these principles.

The argument is much the same for the principles of morality. It amounts to saying that God forbids inflicting gratuitous suffering on the innocent because to do so is wrong, and not that it is wrong because God forbids it. This means that moral right and wrong are independent of God's will. Like the principles of mathematics, those of morality are objective, binding even on God, and thus not changeable by divine decree. If God declared that $3 + 3 = 7$, God would be wrong; if God declared that torturing the innocent is a moral duty, God would also be wrong. Of course, if God is omniscient in any proper sense of the word, he would never assert such a mathematical claim; similarly, if God is morally good, he would never make any such moral claim. There is an objective natural law from which morality can be inferred by any rational person, whether as religious believer or not. At least in principle, everyone who reasons carefully enough and succeeds in transcending the biases of his or her culture should arrive at the same set of fundamental moral principles binding for all.

INDEPENDENCE OF ETHICS FROM RELIGION

If there is indeed a natural law, valid for all time, written so to speak into the structure of reality and detectable by any carefully thinking rational being, why is it that moral beliefs seem to differ so drastically from one generation to another and from one culture to another? Should we not expect that reasonable persons would come to the same conclusions about what morality requires?

The belief that moral principles differ greatly from culture to culture and from age to age has been widespread, especially in the twentieth century, and has been buttressed by the campaign of anthropology against intolerant ethnocentrism. The efforts of anthropologists to engender a spirit of tolerance toward the beliefs and practices of other cultures was certainly justified by Westerners' arrogant, unthinking assumption of superiority and their attempts to impose their own beliefs and practices on the rest of the world. The result of these anthropologists' efforts was the spread of the concept of cultural relativism during the early years of this century. As anthropology matured, however, and as studies of non-Western cultures became more careful and detailed, the moral differences that had seemed so drastic at first came to be seen as differences in details; underlying moral principles were, in fact, remarkably similar across cultures.

A celebrated instance, often cited in anthropological literature on the controversy over relativism, is the custom among certain Eskimo groups of leaving the elderly to die once they become frail and unable to keep up with the migrations of the group. This practice was initially thought to imply a disrespect, even a moral disregard, for the elderly and was cited as a radical contrast to the veneration of the elderly in certain Asian societies and the respectful care for the aged in Western culture. Closer study revealed that the practice was grounded not in different beliefs about what is morally right, but in different beliefs about human afterlife. The Eskimos regard respect and care for the elderly to be an important moral value just as Asians and Westerners do. Leaving the aged to die is in fact an expression of their esteem because they believe that life in the next world begins at precisely the level of physical strength and health the individual possesses at the time of death. From this point of view, to keep old persons alive until they are bedridden and helpless would condemn them to an eternity of weakness and wretchedness.

Dramatic surface differences in moral beliefs, then, often prove to reflect differences in beliefs about situations to which moral principles are applied, not differences about the principles themselves. Another example closer to home may further serve to illustrate the point. In contemporary Western societies, there is a heated controversy about abortion.[2] One group maintains that abortion is morally unacceptable because it is an abominable act of murder; another holds that during the early weeks of pregnancy abortion is morally permissible under certain circumstances. There might seem to be sharp disagreement here about fundamental principles of morality, with one group holding human life to be sacrosanct and the other (as it is sometimes accused) disregarding this sanctity. The difference, however, has nothing to do with basic moral principles; both groups regard human life as sacred and murder as wrong. They differ only on the issue of whether or not the fertilized ovum is a human being during the early stages of its development. If it is, then to kill it (without strong justification, such as saving the mother's life) is clearly morally wrong. If it is not yet a human being, however, then removing it is not murder and is sometimes morally justifiable.

Many moral disputes seem to be of this sort. What appears to be a radical disagreement about a moral principle is actually a disagreement about the facts to which the principle is being applied. Rational, conscientious people seem nearly always to agree about the basic principles of morality: that murder, lying, stealing, cheating, torture and such things are wrong. Most disagreement seems to involve the definition of these moral terms and whether a particular instance is or is not a case of murder, lying, and so on. Other differences relate to cases where the demands of morality conflict—a murder can be prevented only by lying; the killing of a large number of persons can be prevented only by killing a crazed fanatic, and so on—and value judgments have to be made about which principle is the more pressing. Differences of this sort, however, are also to be decided by the exercise of human reason, and although there will often be room for conscientious, rational disagreement, careful and open-minded reasoning should lead at least to mutual understanding and, in principle, to a narrowing of differences.

Probably the greatest hindrance of such a meeting of minds is prejudice and closed-mindedness. Humans are prone to hold to the beliefs they have been taught and refuse to listen to reason. We are apt to be so convinced that what we already believe is beyond doubt that we dismiss evidence and refuse to consider changing our minds. This regrettable tendency of ours is nurtured and aggravated by the propaganda efforts of groups similarly convinced of the unshakable truth of their views and eager to bring emotion to bear in preventing their members from listening to any evidence or argument that might not support the received belief. Patriotism is a lamentable case in point. Pride in one's nation and one's cultural traditions is an entirely appropriate attitude, but when it leads to the total denigration of all other nations and cultures it is vicious and despicable. Time and time again, inflamed patriotism has led to cruelty, ruthlessness, and war. Another case in point is religious fervor, which sometimes clouds human judgment and leads people to refuse to listen to evidence or reason that contradicts precious beliefs thought to be essential to the faith. This is what results in the clash between religions on points of morality and the clash of religious teachings with those of secular rational morality.

What we have discovered about the relationship of human rationality to moral understanding implies that ultimately there is no place for conflict about the basic requirements of morality. When differences appear, they must be understood as arising from different perspectives on the situations to which the principles apply (assuming that preconceived positions have been set aside and open rational discussion is joined). Morality is a matter of rational inquiry. It involves the exercise of a faculty—reason—that is the same in all normal human persons without regard to culture, religion, or time in history. Like the laws of logic and mathematics, the principles of morality bind every rational being, human and divine; they are not the product of divine command. This fact implies that religious believers do not have greater access to morality than anyone else and that religious leaders are in no better position to make pronouncements about morality than any other rational persons—just as they are in no better position to know what logic or mathematics implies or what scientific truth involves. Religion and ethics, like religion and science, are entirely separate and independent enterprises.

Thus the notion that morality would collapse if belief in God or practice of religion disappeared is totally misguided. The statements by Nietzsche and Dostoevsky that the death of God means that all things are permitted reflect a childish understanding of morality. Such a notion resembles the idea that the only reason why the child should keep out of the cookie jar is that his mother will slap his hand if she catches him; when Mother is not looking, everything is permitted. But there is a reason for what morality requires and forbids, and that reason remains valid and binding on rational persons whether Mother is watching or not, and whether there is a God to enforce it or not. We should stay out of the cookie jar because eating too many sweets is harmful to our health; we should refrain from lying because lying undermines the social intercourse on which a good life is dependent. In other words, we should refrain from what morality forbids because such things really are wrong and their being wrong has nothing to do with whether or not they are commanded by God.

THE RELATIONSHIP OF RATIONAL TO RELIGIOUS ETHICS

Notwithstanding, many developed religions consider the teaching of morality—and the attempt to enforce on their members the practice of their sanctioned moral rules—to be one of their major functions. An appeal to divine command theory is sometimes made to reinforce the religion's claim to exercise authority over the moral behavior of its members—and sometimes to extend its moral power to matters of legislation binding even on persons who are not members. Thus many laypersons, who may not be knowledgeable about the relationship between religion and morality—that is, about the independence of morality from religion—feel obliged to obey the moral pronouncements of their religious leaders even when their own better judgment suggests that these pronouncements may not be right.[3] For example, many Catholics and Jews may feel obliged to refrain from the use of contraceptives, or a few Moslems may feel obliged to engage in acts of violence against non-Moslems, because some leaders of these religious groups say that such an obligation exists. Thus, even though philosophers discover that in principle there is no place for a conflict between what rational morality requires and what religions legitimately teach, because some religious leaders take it on themselves to make moral pronouncements they claim are authoritative, the philosopher must analyze the question of the proper relationship between rational (secular) morality and the moral sanctions of the various religions.

One of the problems with any moral scheme based in a specific religion or grounded on a divine command theory is that it is binding only on members of the religious tradition or persons who believe in the god alleged to have commanded it. Christian moral teachings are not obligatory for Buddhists, and morality commanded by God does not reach to atheists. But clearly morality applies to all human beings. Just as no one can claim to be above the laws of the society to which he or she belongs, so also no one can claim exemption from the principles of morality, because morality pertains to humans as humans. If murder is wrong—as it clearly is—it is just as wrong for Hindus as it is for Christians and just as wrong for atheists as for religious believers.

These insights imply that any teaching that contradicts the properly reasoned-out requirements of rational morality must be rejected. The person who claims the right to kill because he believes the voice of spirits told him to is not thereby justified. The person who claims the right to lie and cheat because she believes her government told her to is not thereby justified. The person who claims the right to kidnap or torture because he believes his religion tells him to is not thereby justified. The only thing that can justify acting contrary to a rational moral injunction is a rational argument showing that some other course of action takes moral precedence in the particular case. For example, the only justification I have for killing another human being is the clear realization that I have no other way to stop that person from killing others. Nothing takes precedence over rational moral commandments except other rational moral commandments supported by even stronger moral arguments, or arguments showing that the alternative course of action is even more urgent morally. In many cases, of course, what is required is difficult to ascertain. Sometimes there will be very good moral reasons supporting more than one incompatible course of action and no definitive way of deciding among these courses. These are the kinds of practical difficulties that accompany any kind of moral judgment, and in dealing with them one must proceed with considerable humility, recognizing one's fallibility and acting on one's most conscientious best judgment.

The principle, however, remains clear. When the requirement of rational morality can be ascertained, nothing else (except a more pressing moral requirement) can overrule it. This means that if a religion or a religious leader commands what rational morality forbids or forbids what rational morality commands, the requirement of rational morality must prevail. We have seen already that this should never happen provided those who speak on behalf of religion make open-minded and conscientious use of their reasoning faculty. But we know that sometimes the teachings of an earlier era, based on an underdeveloped science or an incomplete understanding of the world, become enshrined even when the advancement of human knowledge has shown them to be inadequate. When pronouncements from religious authorities clash with the discoveries of science, a conflict may ensue. This was the case with the church's condemnation of Galileo's scientific findings (a matter of some embarrassment to the Church today) and continues today in some sects' positions concerning evolution.

This may sound like an attempt to drive religion out of the moral arena altogether. Actually, it is nothing of the sort—any more than the recognition of the independence of science from religion in an attempt to enjoin religions from having anything to say about the findings of science or the world to which those findings pertain. Science offers descriptions and explanations of how phenomena occur in the material world. These descriptions and explanations make no reference to gods and no pronouncements about the significance of the findings for the human spirit. But persons who believe in God are likely to believe that the world that science describes is a realm of divine creation and that the order scientists discover in the world is the result of God's orderly plan. Religious persons may also interpret the facts that science discovers as evidence of God's love and care for his human creatures and may find in them great significance for the worth of human existence. They may also sense the appropriateness of our taking an attitude of reverence for the world because they regard it as God's creation. None of these factors clashed with science nor suggests any area of conflict between the legitimate work of science and that of religion.

In a similar way, religion may interpret the requirements of rationality as commanded and supported by God. We have seen that the validity of these requirements does not derive from God's command, but it is entirely likely that a wise and loving God would command that we behave in accordance with the rules of morality. Religion can offer incentives for living moral lives that may supplement for believers the incentive that reasonable persons already recognize in the nature of moral situations.

Furthermore, religions can place additional obligations on believers beyond those required by secular morality, provided they do not contradict anything required by universal human morality. Morality forbids gratuitous cruelty and requires truth telling of all persons; these injunctions may very well be a part of religious morality as well. But Christianity may also require believers to attend mass or to say certain prayers. Rational morality does not require such things, but neither does it forbid them, so there is no inconsistency between the two moral codes. If a religious group, however, forbids the use of blood transfusions to save the life of a child, there may be situations where this conflicts with rational morality, which requires taking appropriate measures to save the life, in which case the religious injunction must yield.

We conclude, then, that religion and ethics are separate realms independent of each other. Morality is not derived from the teachings of religion nor from the will of God. Rather, it is discovered, like the laws of logic and mathematics, by the proper use of human reason. It applies to all human beings alike, whether they are devotees of one religion or another, or of none. Because religion in the past has often been active in teaching morality and promoting moral behavior, however, we hope and expect that it will continue to do so in the future.

Although we have taken into account in some measure the teaching of non-Western religions up to this point, we have not examined in any detail the philosophy of any of those other religions. This is not the place to undertake the comparative study of religion. But just as an understanding of the history, politics, economics, and culture of other societies contributes in invaluable ways to our understanding of our own, so also an understanding of the philosophical teachings of other religions can give us a valuable perspective on those religions most familiar to us. Just as it is undesirable to be provincial in cultural outlook, it is likewise undesirable—even dangerous—to be uninformed about other religions. It is time now to turn our attention away from our customary preoccupation with the religions of the West to consider briefly the philosophies of several of the other great world religions.

NOTES

1. This claim is discussed and documented by Patrick H. Nowell-Smith in his article, "Religion and Morality," in *The Encyclopedia of Philosophy*, ed. Paul Edwards (New York: Macmillan, 1967), vol 7, pp 150–158. This article concludes with a good bibliography on the topic.

2. James Rachels offers a helpful examination of the relationship of morality to religion and an illuminating discussion of the abortion issue. He points out that Thomas Aquinas taught that the human embryo does not have a soul until several weeks into the pregnancy and that Aquinas's view was officially sanctioned by the Catholic Church at the Council of Vienna in 1312, an action that has not to this day been officially changed. See his book, *The Elements of Moral Philosophy* (New York: Random House, 1986). pp. 47–52.

3. Rachels points out that Thomas Aquinas teaches that it is a Christian's obligation to obey his conscience, which Thomas calls the "dictate of reason," in every case, even when it may run contrary to what the Church teaches. See ibid., p.46.

Part VIII

Philosophy and
Comparative Religion

There is good reason to believe that what modern Western philosophers call religion has been an important ingredient of every human culture past and present. In many cases the term *religion* may have been absent; many of the peoples may not have thought of those beliefs and practices we would call religious as anything distinct from the daily routines of their lives or deserving of being singled out by name as a special activity. Some of these beliefs and practices were directed to a deity or supreme being; others to many superbeings; others still to spirits, demons, and occult forces. Some practices were hardly distinguishable from magic. In every case, however, we seem to see evidence of an effort to fulfill what we take to be several functions of religion: to provide an explanation of the world and human life or some aspects thereof, and to offer guidance about what humans can do to relate better to the forces that control their destiny.

At first glance, the variety of teachings and behaviors that are labeled religious is so great and bewildering that one might wonder whether it makes sense to treat them collectively. Many anthropologists and philosophers who have examined them carefully claim to find much that is common, and some even claim that all are driven by the same human traits or reflect an apprehension of the same objective reality.

Until fairly recently, the various human cultures

and religions have existed in relative isolation. In-formed persons in all cultures have long held a vague awareness that peoples in other parts of the world hold differing religious beliefs and worship differ-ently. Because communication was slow and few people traveled widely, however, these differences attracted relatively little attention. The traveler might bring back exotic tales about strange customs, or the missionary on furlough might detail the quaint be-liefs and doings of the "heathens" he or she went out to convert. The accounts offered by such returning travelers did not embue these far-away religions with much reality; in any case, they seemed to have little concrete bearing on the daily lives, political rela-tions, or economic forces that seem always so impor-tant to most people.

The situation in our day has changed radically. No longer are the practitioners of other religions to be found only in some distant land the ordinary person never expects to visit. With only a few exceptions, there are no longer any countries where only a single religion is practiced; religious pluralism within so-cieties has become the rule rather than the exception. Nearly every major city in the world has places of worship representing virtually all the major re-ligions, and this is becoming true even of small towns. The followers of one religion thus find them-selves directly confronted, as never before, with se-rious and conscientious followers of other religions, and the assumption of exclusive validity for one's own faith can no longer be taken for granted.

Once we get beyond our mystified reaction to other religions as alien quantities—and the accom-panying assumption that their followers must be ig-norant or benighted—we find ourselves interacting with persons who are obviously intelligent, sincere, conscientious, educated, and just as devoted to their religious tradition as we are to ours. And once we get beyond the vague sense that other religions are crude, heathen, superstitious, and unintelligible to a more adequate understanding of what they actually teach, we find ourselves recognizing that these re-ligions have sophisticated theologies and moral teachings, that they promote in their followers high ideals for human life and high standards of moral practice. Thus the chauvinism that has been a central ingredient in most religious traditions, along with the parochialism characteristic particularly of Western religious thought, becomes all too apparent. No longer can we dismiss other religious traditions as unenlightened, or simply assume that they are mistaken or inferior. Any attitude of superiority on our part now requires explicit justification, which proves to be a formidable task.

The central problem that the nearly universal religious pluralism raises for the philosopher of religion concerns the evaluation of the cognitive claims of the various religions. Most religions offer sets of teachings that amount to comprehensive attempts to account for the world and the place of humans in it—what we might call metaphysical doctrines or world views. In fact, it is this aspect of the religious teachings, not their liturgical dimensions, that is of particular interest to philosophers. These different world views are often claimed to be mutually incompatible. If the claim is correct, it follows that they cannot all be true; indeed, one of them at most can be true. The problem is, therefore, to test these theories and see which, if any, is correct.

Other thinkers argue that the appearance of radical diversity and thus of incompatibility is illusory, that a closer examination reveals basic similarities hidden under the multicolored dress of different cultural accretions, and that it is reasonable to infer that all religions are attempting to get into touch with, and to communicate truths about, the same supermundane reality. From this approach some argue that a syncretic merging—one that preserved all that is essential and abandoned points of disagreement that pertain to the unessential—could generate a "religion of humankind" that might promote mutual understanding and cooperation to replace the bickering and fighting of the past. Others, beginning from the same basic premise, argue for the value of a rich diversity of traditions, each preserving its unique features while all recognize the legitimacy of the others.

Both of these major interpretations of religious diversity show considerable merit. On one hand, mutually irreconcilable claims do seem to be made by advocates of different religious traditions. Some religions make the explicitly exclusivist claims that their teachings are direct revelations of divine truth from which, they assert, it follows that any claims that disagree with them are necessarily false. Such extreme exclusivist claims tend to be characteristic particularly of the Western monotheistic religions Judaism, Christianity, and Islam, and especially of the latter two. Even where no such explicit, chauvinistic assertions are made, there are teachings about the nature of the world, of humans, of whatever is conceived as ultimate, and of what morality requires or forbids that, when juxtaposed with seemingly parallel teachings from other traditions, appear incompatible.

Of course, disagreements abound as well within each tradition about how the teachings of the tradition should be understood. Hard-liners, often called "fundamentalists," usually insist on a literal interpretation of the scriptures and doctrinal statements. More liberal practitioners tend to be willing to accept figurative interpretations, recognizing that the metaphorical meaning might be more profound and important than a literal understanding. Some suggest that because the scriptures of the various traditions were written long ago, when our knowledge of science was in a rather primitive state, our crude (mis)understandings of how nature works found their way into the holy writings. These naive notions, blended with the spiritual and moral teachings that are the more essential aspects of scripture, contribute the appearance of drastic disagreement. By separating the outmoded protoscience from the explicitly religious teachings, so we are told, we arrive at spiritual insights that not only escape the charge of conflict with science but that also no longer appear so blatantly inconsistent with the similarly purified teachings of other religious traditions.

The increasing encounter of religion with religion has resulted, especially in our times, in thoughtful reflection about the apparent incompatibilities of their teachings and in dialogue among leading proponents of the various traditions in an effort to promote mutual understanding. What better way to understand even one's own religion, some have pointed out, than by attempting to communicate its essence to persons from other traditions and to understand what they take to be essential in their own beliefs? And many who have made the effort, even when they remain convinced that their own religion is the true one or the best, have found a new respect for persons of different persuasions. Whatever else happens, one fact is clear: Practitioners of all the major religions will live now and henceforth in close association with one another. If there is to be peace, there will have to be understanding and at least a measure of mutual respect. The world has become much too small a place for attitudes of chauvinism. Even if proponents of the different religions agree to disagree, they must also agree to behave in tolerant ways toward one another. Better yet, they might strive after mutual understanding, sharing, cooperation, and respect.

ANNOTATED GUIDE TO FURTHER READINGS

The Religions

Ellwood, Robert S., and Wiggins, James B. *Christianity: A Cultural Perspective*. Englewood Cliffs, N.J.: Prentice-Hall, 1988.
Reads easily, almost like a story at times, and offers a good exposure to the basic principles of Christianity, Christian society and culture.

Hopfe, Lewis M. *Religions of the World*, 3rd ed. New York: Macmillan, 1983.
An excellent introductory text, with a chapter on each of the major religions. Of special interest to some may be specific chapters devoted entirely to Native American religions and African religions. Includes excerpts from the scriptures of each religion.

Jacobson, Nolan Pliny. *Understanding Buddhism*. Carbondale, Ill.: Southern Illinois University Press, 1986.
Relates Buddhism to Western philosophical thought, combining a scholarly presentation of the basic facts of Buddhism with a lucid writing style that transcends these facts.

Martin, Richard C. *Islam: A Cultural Perspective*. Englewood Cliffs, N.J.: Prentice-Hall, 1982.
A useful introductory text that deals with more than just the basic principles of Islam; examines life within the Muslim culture, art, and the Islamic community.

Morgan, Kenneth W., ed. *The Religion of the Hindus*. New York: The Ronald Press, 1953.
Six chapters, each written by a different Indian scholar, provide the reader with a good introduction to the Hindu religion. Also contains selections from the Hindu scriptures.

Neusner, Jacob. *From Testament to Torah: An Introduction to Judaism in Its Formative Age*. Englewood Cliffs, N.J.: Prentice-Hall, 1988.
The focus is basically historical, namely, three pivotal stages in the history of Judaism: the fall of the temple of Jerusalem, the fall of the second temple of Jerusalem, and Constantine's Christianization of Rome.

Noss, David S., and Noss, John B. *Man's Religions*, 7th ed. New York: Macmillan, 1984.
A basic resource in the study of religion, this text is notable for its extensive use of primary sources. Focuses on Buddhism, Christianity, Confucianism, Hinduism, Islam, Jainism, Judaism, Shinto, Sikhism, Taoism, and Zoroastrianism.

Comparative

Cobb, John B., Jr. *Beyond Dialogue*. Philadelphia: Fortress Press, 1982.
Through dialogue the differing world religions can transform one another. Cobb focuses on the interaction between Christianity and Buddhism.

Dharmasiri, Gunapala. *A Buddhist Critique of the Christian Concept of God*. Antioch, Calif.: Golden Leaves, 1988.
A valuable resource for the Western reader because of its Eastern point of view. The author considers the Christian religion to be primitive, perhaps even dangerous. Dharmasiri feels strongly that we must not blindly surrender our individual freedom to the self-proclaimed authority of religion.

Hick, John, and Meltzer, Edmund S., eds. *Three Faiths: One God*. Albany: State University of New York Press, 1989.
An interpretation of the common heritage of Judaism, Christianity, and Islam including chapters on God, the world, and humankind by major thinkers from the three religions.

Oxtoby, Willard G. *The Meaning of Other Faiths*. Philadelphia: Westminster Press, 1983.
Provides a useful basic discussion of the relationship of the world religions. Oxtoby, coming from a Christian background, examines his faith's view of other religions from both historical and contemporary perspectives.

Peters, F. E. *Children of Abraham*. Princeton, N.J.: Princeton University Press, 1982.
Islam, Judaism, and Christianity have a special relationship with one another because they share a common ancestry. Peters examines the link between these three great world religions by comparing their scriptures, traditions, and theologies.

Smart, Ninian. *A Dialogue of Religions*. London: SCM Press, 1960.
An original and interesting work. Smart adopts the format of a dialogue in which characters from the world religions address one another and discuss such topics as revelation, rebirth, and theism.

Smith, Wilfred Cantwell. *Towards a World Theology*. Philadelphia: Westminster Press, 1981.
Focuses on the historical aspect of the religions of Christianity, Judaism, Islam, Hinduism, and Buddhism, emphasizing the unity rather than the separateness of humankind's religious life.

VIII.1. The New Map of the Universe of Faith

JOHN HICK

John Hick (1922–), a British-born philosopher of religion who has spent most of his professional life in American universities, holds a distinguished chair in religion at Claremont Graduate School and is a major contributor to the contemporary discussion of interreligious issues. In the following selection, he proposes the idea that God or ultimate reality revealed himself or itself on numerous occasions through many individuals in a situation where geographic isolation made a single revelation to all humankind impossible. Over the centuries between that time and the present, human cultures have elaborated their understandings of the revelation in ways that grow increasingly diverse. Hick suggests that each of the major religions has been a path to salvation or enlightenment for generations of persons. And he is convinced that, in a world where isolation has vanished and all peoples must live together in a single global community, it is urgent that the many religious traditions communicate and share with one another to the end of diminishing their differences. Hick envisions a unity of faiths in which the highest visions of each tradition will be both fulfilled and transcended.

Let me begin by proposing a working definition of religion as an understanding of the universe, together with an appropriate way of living within it, which involves reference beyond the natural world to God or gods or to the Absolute or to a transcendent order or process. Such a definition includes such theistic faiths as Judaism, Christianity, Islam, Sikhism; the theistic Hinduism of the Bhagavad Gītā; the semi-theistic faith of Mahayana Buddhism and the non-theistic faiths of Theravada Buddhism and non-theistic Hinduism. It does not however include purely naturalistic systems of belief, such as communism and humanism, immensely important though these are today as alternatives to religious faith.

When we look back into the past we find that religion has been a virtually universal dimension of human life—so much so that man has been defined as the religious animal. For he has displayed an innate tendency to experience his environment as being religiously as well as naturally significant, and to feel required to live in it as such. To quote the anthropologist, Raymond Firth, "religion is universal in human societies."[1] "In every human community on

---

From *God and the Universe of Faiths* (London and Basingstoke: Macmillan, 1973), pp. 278–290. Used by permission of the publisher.

[1] *Elements of Social Organization*, 3rd ed. (London: Tavistock Publications, 1969), p. 216.

earth today," says Wilfred Cantwell Smith, "there exists something that we, as sophisticated observers, may term religion, or a religion. And we are able to see it in each case as the latest development in a continuous tradition that goes back, we can now affirm, for at least one hundred thousand years."[2] In the life of primitive man this religious tendency is expressed in a belief in sacred objects endowed with *mana*, and in a multitude of nature and ancestral spirits needing to be carefully propitiated. The divine was here crudely apprehended as a plurality of quasi-animal forces which could to some extent be controlled by ritualistic and magical procedures. This represents the simplest beginning of man's awareness of the transcendent in the infancy of the human race—an infancy which is also to some extent still available for study in the life of primitive tribes today.

The development of religion and religions begins to emerge into the light of recorded history as the third millennium B.C. moves towards the period around 2000 B.C. There are two main regions of the earth in which civilisation seems first to have arisen and in which religions first took a shape that is at least dimly discernible to us as we peer back through the mists of time—these being Mesopotamia in the Near East and the Indus valley of northern India. In Mesopotamia men lived in nomadic shepherd tribes, each worshipping its own god. Then the tribes gradually coalesced into nation states, the former tribal gods becoming ranked in hierarchies (some however being lost by amalgamation in the process) dominated by great national deities such as Marduk of Babylon, the Sumerian Ishtar, Amon of Thebes, Jahweh of Israel, the Greek Zeus, and so on. Further east in the Indus valley there was likewise a wealth of gods and goddesses, though apparently not so much tribal or national in character as expressive of the basic forces of nature, above all fertility. The many deities of the Near East and of India expressed man's awareness of the divine at the dawn of documentary history, some four thousand years ago. It is perhaps worth stressing that the picture was by no means a wholly pleasant one. The tribal and national gods were often martial and cruel, sometimes requiring human sacrifices. And although rather little is known about the very early, pre-Aryan Indian deities, it is certain that later Indian deities have vividly symbolised the cruel and destructive as well as the beneficent aspects of nature.

These early developments in the two cradles of civilisation, Mesopotamia and the Indus valley, can be described as the growth of natural religion, prior to any special intrusions of divine revelation or illumination. Primitive spirit-worship expressed man's fears of unknown forces; his reverence for nature deities expressed his sense of dependence upon realities greater than himself; and his tribal gods expressed the unity and continuity of his group over against other groups. One can in fact discern all sorts of causal connections between the forms which early religion took and the material circumstances of man's life, indicating the large part played by the human element within the history of religion. For example, Trevor Ling points out that life in ancient India (apart from the Punjab immediately prior to the Aryan invasions) was agricultural and was organised in small village units; and suggests that "among agri-

---

[2] *The Meaning and End of Religion* (New York: Mentor Books, 1963) p. 22.

cultural peoples, aware of the fertile earth which brings forth from itself and nourishes its progeny upon its broad bosom, it is the mother-principle which seems important."³ Accordingly God the Mother, and a variety of more specialised female deities, have always held a prominent place in Indian religious thought and mythology. This contrasts with the characteristically male expression of deity in the Semitic religions, which had their origins among nomadic, pastoral, herd-keeping peoples in the Near East. The divine was known to the desert-dwelling herdsmen who founded the Israelite tradition as God the King and Father; and this conception has continued both in later Judaism and in Christianity, and was renewed out of the desert experience of Mohammed in the Islamic religion. Such regional variations in our human ways of conceiving the divine have persisted through time into the developed world faiths that we know today. The typical western conception of God is still predominantly in terms of the male principle of power and authority; and in the typical Indian conceptions of deity the female principle still plays a distinctly larger part than in the west.

Here then was the natural condition of man's religious life: religion without revelation. But sometime around 800 B.C. there began what has been called the golden age of religious creativity. This consisted in a remarkable series of revelatory experiences occurring during the next five hundred or so years in different parts of the world, experiences which deepened and purified men's conception of the ultimate, and which religious faith can only attribute to the pressure of the divine Spirit upon the human spirit. First came the early Jewish prophets, Amos, Hosea and first Isaiah, declaring that they had heard the Word of the Lord claiming their obedience and demanding a new level of righteousness and justice in the life of Israel. Then in Persia the great prophet Zoroaster appeared; China produced Lao-tzu and then Confucius; in India the Upanishads were written, and Gotama the Buddha lived, and Mahavira, the founder of the Jain religion and, probably about the end of this period, the writing of the Bhagavad Gītā,⁴ and Greece produced Pythagoras and then, ending this golden age, Socrates and Plato. Then after the gap of some three hundred years came Jesus of Nazareth and the emergence of Christianity; and after another gap the prophet Mohammed and the rise of Islam.

The suggestion that we must consider is that these were all moments of divine revelation. But let us ask, in order to test this thought, whether we should not expect God to make his revelation in a single mighty act, rather than to produce a number of different, and therefore presumably partial, revelations at different times and places? I think that in seeing the answer to this question we receive an important clue to the place of the religions of the world in the divine purpose. For when we remember the facts of history and geography we realise that in the period we are speaking of, between two and

---

³ *A History of Religion: East and West* (London: Macmillan and New York: St. Martin's Press, 1968) p. 27.

⁴ The dating of the Bhagavad Gītā has been a matter of much debate; but R. C. Zaehner in his recent monumental critical edition says that "One would probably not be going far wrong if one dated it as some time between the fifth and second centuries B.C.." *The Bhagavad Gītā* (Oxford: Clarendon Press, 1969) p. 7.

three thousand years ago, it was not possible for God to reveal himself through any human mediation to all mankind. A world-wide revelation might be possible today, thanks to the inventions of printing, and even more of radio, TV and communication satellites. But in the technology of the ancient world this was not possible. Although on a time scale of centuries and millennia there has been a slow diffusion and interaction of cultures, particularly within the vast Euro-Asian land mass, yet the more striking fact for our present purpose is the fragmented character of the ancient world. Communications between the different groups of humanity was then so limited and slow that for all practical purposes men inhabited different worlds. For the most part people in Europe, in India, in Arabia, in Africa, in China were unaware of the others' existence. And as the world was fragmented, so was its religious life. If there was to be a revelation of the divine reality to mankind it had to be a pluriform revelation, a series of revealing experiences occurring independently within the different streams of human history. And since religion and culture were one, the great creative moments of revelation and illumination have influenced the development of the various cultures, giving them the coherence and impetus to expand into larger units, thus creating the vast, many-sided historical entities which we call the world religions.

Each of these religio-cultural complexes has expanded until it touched the boundaries of another such complex spreading out from another centre. Thus each major occasion of divine revelation has slowly transformed the primitive and national religions within the sphere of its influence into what we now know as the world faiths. The early Dravidian and Aryan polytheisms of India were drawn through the religious experience and thought of the Brahmins into what the west calls Hinduism. The national and mystery cults of the mediterranean world and then of northern Europe were drawn by influences stemming from the life and teaching of Christ into what has become Christianity. The early polytheism of the Arab peoples has been transformed under the influence of Mohammed and his message into Islam. Great areas of South-East Asia, of China, Tibet and Japan were drawn into the spreading Buddhist movement. None of these expansions from different centres of revelation has of course been simple and uncontested, and a number of alternatives which proved less durable have perished or been absorbed in the process—for example, Mithraism has disappeared altogether; and Zoroastrianism, whilst it greatly influenced the development of the Judaic-Christian tradition, and has to that extent been absorbed, only survives directly today on a small scale in Parseeism.

Seen in this historical context these movements of faith—the Judaic-Christian, the Buddhist, the Hindu, the Muslim—are not essentially rivals. They began at different times and in different places, and each expanded outwards into the surrounding world of primitive natural religion until most of the world was drawn up into one or other of the great revealed faiths. And once this global pattern had become established it has ever since remained fairly stable. It is true that the process of establishment involved conflict in the case of Islam's entry into India and the virtual expulsion of Buddhism from India in the medieval period, and in the case of Islam's advance into Europe and then its retreat at the end of the medieval period. But since the frontiers of the different world faiths became more or less fixed there has been little penetration of one faith into societies moulded by another. The most successful missionary efforts of the great faiths continue to this day to be "downwards" into the remaining world of relatively primitive religions rather than "sideways" into territories dominated by another world faith. For example, as between Christianity and Islam there has been little more than rather rare individual conversions; but both faiths have successful missions in Africa. Again, the Christian population of the Indian subcontinent, after more than two centuries of missionary effort, is only about 2.7 per cent; but on the other hand the Christian missions in the South Pacific are fairly successful. Thus the general picture, so far as the great world religions is concerned, is that each has gone through an early period of geographical expansion, converting a region of the world from its more primitive religious state, and has thereafter continued in a comparatively settled condition within more or less stable boundaries.

Now it is of course possible to see this entire development from the primitive forms of religion up to and including the great world faiths as the history of man's most persistent illusion, growing from crude fantasies into sophisticated metaphysical speculations. But from the standpoint of religious faith the only reasonable hypothesis is that this historical picture represents a movement of divine self-revelation to mankind. This hypothesis offers a general answer to the question of the relation between the different world religions and of the truths which they embody. It suggests to us that the same divine reality has always been self-revealingly active towards mankind, and that the differences of human response are related to different human circumstances. These circumstances—ethnic, geographical, climatic, economic, sociological, historical—have produced the existing differentiations of human culture, and within each main cultural region the response to the divine has taken its own characteristic forms. In each case the post-primitive response has been initiated by some spiritually outstanding individual or succession of individuals, developing in the course of time into one of the great religio-cultural phenomena which we call the world religions. Thus Islam embodies the main response of the Arabic peoples to the divine reality; Hinduism, the main (though not the only) response of the peoples of India; Buddhism, the main response of the peoples of South-East Asia and parts of northern Asia; Christianity, the main response of the European peoples, both within Europe itself and in their emigrations to the Americas and Australasia.

Thus it is, I think, intelligible historically why the revelation of the divine reality to man, and the disclosure of the divine will for human life, had to occur separately within the different streams of human life. We can see how these revelations took different forms related to the different mentalities of the peoples to whom they came, and developed within these different cultures into the vast and many-sided historical phenomena of the world religions.

But let us now ask whether this is intelligible theologically. What about the conflicting truth-claims of the different faiths? Is the divine nature personal or non-personal; does deity become incarnate in the world; are human beings born again and again on earth; is the Bible, or the Koran, or the Bhagavad Gītā the Word of God? If what Christianity says in answer to these questions is true, must not what Hinduism says be to a large extent false? If what Buddhism says is true, must not what Islam says be largely false?

Let us begin with the recognition, which is made in all the main religious traditions, that the ultimate divine reality is infinite and as such transcends the grasp of the human mind. God, to use our Christian term, is infinite. He is not a thing, a part of the universe, existing alongside other things; nor is he a being falling under a certain kind. And therefore he cannot be defined or encompassed by human thought. We cannot draw boundaries round his nature and say that he is this and no more. If we could fully define God, describing his inner being and his outer limits, this would not be God. The God whom our minds can penetrate and whom our thoughts can circumnavigate is merely a finite and partial image of God.

From this it follows that the different encounters with the transcendent within the different religious traditions may all be encounters with the one infinite reality; though with partially different and overlapping aspects of that reality. This is a very familiar thought in Indian religious literature. We read, for example, in the ancient Rig-Vedas, dating back to perhaps as much as a thousand years before Christ:

> They call it Indra, Mitra, Varuna, and Agni
> And also heavenly, beautiful Garutman;
> The real is one, though sages name it variously.[5]

We might translate this thought into the terms of the faiths represented today in Britain:

> They call it Jahweh, Allah, Krishna, Param Atma,
> And also holy, blessed Trinity:
> The real is one, though sages name it differently.

And in the Bhagavad Gītā the Lord Krishna, the personal God of love, says, "However men approach me, even so do I accept them: for, on all sides, whatever path they may choose is mine."[6]

Again, there is the parable of the blind men and the elephant, said to have been told by the Buddha. An elephant was brought to a group of blind men who had never encountered such an animal before. One felt a leg and reported that an elephant is a great living pillar. Another felt the trunk and reported that an elephant is a great snake. Another felt the tusk and reported that an elephant is like a sharp ploughshare. And so on. And then they all quarrelled together, each claiming that his own account was the truth and therefore all the others false. In fact of course they were all true, but each referring only to one aspect of the total reality and all expressed in very imperfect analogies.

Now the possibility, indeed the probability, that we have seriously to consider is that many different accounts of the divine reality may be true, though all expressed in imperfect human analogies, but that none is "the truth, the whole truth, and nothing but the truth." May it not be that the different concepts of God, as Jahweh, Allah, Krishna, Param Atma, Holy Trinity, and so on: and likewise the different concepts of the hidden structure

---

[5] I 164.

[6] IV II.

of reality, as the eternal emanation of Brahman or as an immense cosmic process culminating in Nirvana, are all images of the divine, each expressing some aspect or range of aspects and yet none by itself fully and exhaustively corresponding to the infinite nature of the ultimate reality?

Two immediate qualifications however to this hypothesis. First, the idea that we are considering is not that any and every conception of God or of the transcendent is valid, still less all equally valid; but that every conception of the divine which has come out of a great revelatory religious experience and has been tested through a long tradition of worship, and has sustained human faith over centuries of time and in millions of lives, is likely to represent a genuine encounter with the divine reality. And second, the parable of the blind men and the elephant is of course only a parable and like most parables it is designed to make one point and must not be pressed as an analogy at other points. The suggestion is not that the different encounters with the divine which lie at the basis of the great religious traditions are responses to different *parts* of the divine. They are rather encounters from different historical and cultural standpoints with the same infinite divine reality and as such they lead to differently focused awareness of the reality. The indications of this are most evident in worship and prayer. What is said about God in the theological treatises of the different faiths is indeed often widely different. But it is in prayer that a belief in God comes alive and does its main work. And when we turn from abstract theology to the living stuff of worship we meet again and again the overlap and confluence of faiths.

Here, for example, is a Muslim prayer at the feast of Ramadan:

> Praise be to God, Lord of creation, Source of all livelihood, who orders the morning, Lord of majesty and honour, of grace and beneficence. He who is so far that he may not be seen and so near that he witnesses the secret things. Blessed be he and for ever exalted.[7]

And here is a Sikh creed used at the morning prayer:

> There is but one God. He is all that is.
> He is the Creator of all things and He is all-pervasive.
> He is without fear and without enmity.
> He is timeless, unborn and self-existent.
> He is the Enlightener
> And can be realised by grace of Himself alone.
> He was in the beginning; He was in all ages.
> The True One is, was, O Nanak, and shall forever be.[8]

And here again is a verse from the Koran:

---

[7] Kenneth Cragg, *Alive to God: Muslim and Christian Prayer* (London and New York: Oxford University Press, 1970) p.65.

[8] Harbans Singh, *Guru Nanak and Origins of the Sikh Faith* (Bombay, London and New York: Asia Publishing House, 1969), pp. 96-7.

To God belongs the praise. Lord of the heavens and Lord of the earth, the Lord of all being. His is the dominion in the heavens and in the earth: he is the Almighty, the All-wise.[9]

Turning now to the Hindu idea of the many incarnations of God, here is a verse from the Rāmāyaṇa:

Seers and sages, saints and hermits, fix on Him their reverent gaze,
And in faint and trembling accents, holy scripture hymns His praise.
He the omnipresent spirit, lord of heaven and earth and hell,
To redeem His people, freely has vouchsafed with men to dwell.[10]

And from the rich literature of devotional song here is a Bhakti hymn of the Vaishnavite branch of Hinduism:

Now all my days with joy I'll fill, full to the brim
With all my heart to Vitthal cling, and only Him.

He will sweep utterly away all dole and care;
And all in sunder shall I rend illusion's snare.

O altogether dear is He, and He alone,
For all my burden He will take to be His own.

Lo, all the sorrow of the world will straightway cease,
And all unending now shall be the reign of peace.[11]

And a Muslim mystical verse:

Love came a guest
Within my breast,
My soul was spread,
Love banqueted.[12]

And finally another Hindu (Vaishnavite) devotional hymn:

O save me, save me, Mightiest,
    Save me and set me free.
O let the love that fills my breast
    Cling to thee lovingly.

Grant me to taste how sweet thou art;
    Grant me but this, I pray.
And never shall my love depart
    Or turn from thee away.

---

[9] *Alive to God*, p. 61 (Surah of the Kneeling, v. 35)

[10] *Sacred Books of the World*, edited by A. C. Bouquet (London: Pelican Books, 1954) p. 226 (The Rāmāyaṇa of Tulsi Das, Canto 1, Chandha 2, translated by F. S. Growse).

[11] Ibid., p. 245 (A Hymn of Namdev, translated by Nicol MacNicol).

[12] *Alive to God*, p. 79 (From Ibn Hazm, "The Ring of the Dove").

Then I thy name shall magnify
    And tell thy praise abroad,
For very love and gladness I
    Shall dance before my God.[13]

Such prayers and hymns as these must express, surely, diverse encounters with the same divine reality. These encounters have taken place within different human cultures by people of different ways of thought and feeling, with different histories and different frameworks of philosophical thought, and have developed into different systems of theology embodied in different religious structures and organisations. These resulting large-scale religio-cultural phenomena are what we call the religions of the world. But must there not lie behind them the same infinite divine reality, and may not our divisions into Christian, Hindu, Muslim, Jew, and so on, and all that goes with them, accordingly represent secondary, human, historical developments?

There is a further problem, however, which now arises. I have been speaking so far of the ultimate reality in a variety of terms—the Father, Son and Spirit of Christianity, the Jahweh of Judaism, the Allah of Islam, and so on—but always thus far in theistic terms, as a personal God under one name or another. But what of the non-theistic religions? What of the non-theistic Hinduism according to which the ultimate reality, Brahman, is not He but It; and what about Buddhism, which in one form is agnostic concerning the existence of God even though in another form it has come to worship the Buddha himself? Can these non-theistic faiths be seen as encounters with the same divine reality that is encountered in theistic religion?

Speaking very tentatively, I think it is possible that the sense of the divine as non-personal may indeed reflect an aspect of the same infinite reality that is encountered as personal in theistic religious experience. The question can be pursued both as a matter of pure theology and in relation to religious experience. Theologically, the Hindu distinction between Nirguna Brahman and Saguna Brahman is important and should be adopted into western religious thought. Detaching the distinction, then from its Hindu context we may say that Nirguna God is the eternal self-existent divine reality, beyond the scope of all human categories, including personality; and Saguna God is God in relation to his creation and with the attributes which express this relationship, such as personality, omnipotence, goodness, love and omniscience. Thus the one ultimate reality is both Nirguna and non-personal, and Saguna and personal, in a duality which is in principle acceptable to human understanding. When we turn to men's religious awareness of God we are speaking of Saguna God, God in relation to man. And here the larger traditions of both east and west report a dual experience of the divine as personal and as other than personal. It will be a sufficient reminder of the strand of personal relationship with the divine in Hinduism to mention Iswaru, the personal God who represents the Absolute as known and worshipped by finite persons. It should also be remembered that the characterisation of Brahman as *satcitananda*, absolute being, consciousness and bliss, is not far from the conception of infinitely

---

[13] *Sacred Books of the World*, p. 246 (A Hymn of Tukaram).

possible to treat seriously the whole gallery of theologies, then at least a selection of them. However, the very fact (if it is so) that the focus of faith transcends theologies means that the theological traditions can never be fixed. What is to preclude a new theology being devised, to set alongside the others? In this case, though, there is one sort of identification question which can profitably be asked, namely what is the norm whereby some new theology is adjudged to be *Christian*? Some resemblance, presumably, to earlier theologies. But how much? These things seem to be settled by an informal method of acceptance in the community. For example, Paul van Buren's *The Secular Meaning of the Gospel* expresses an atheistic Christology; but a number of Christians took this with sufficient seriousness to deem it as genuinely a *Christian* theology, despite its formal atheism.

Since new theologies await us over the horizon, it is also necessary to recall that the very situation of interplay between religions, which so markedly characterizes contemporary religious culture, may itself have an impact on theologizing: so that a new theology now beyond the horizon might in theory dissolve some of the incompatibilities between earlier theologies and received non-Christian theologies. For instance, there seems to be a conflict of *Weltanschauung* between theistic Christianity and non-theistic Buddhism; but the incompatibility is less obvious the more existentialist Christian theology becomes. So new syntheses may await us over the horizon; and they cannot be ruled out a priori.

However, there is another check upon indiscriminate synthesizing; this arises from the relation between truth-claims and practice-claims (to put it crudely). It is very obvious that the ritual, experiential and institutional aspects of a religion, and its ethical prescriptions, are not always well coordinated to the theologies being purveyed within it. For example, the meaning of the Eucharist, in Anglicanism, is shaped by the milieu of liturgy, architecture, custom, style of life of those engaged: it is not merely determined theologically, still less by the most avant theology. Attitudes to the Buddha in Theravāda Buddhism are not simply determined by doctrines, but by the whole temple-cultus, etc. Thus there is always the possibility of a lack of co-ordination between truth-claims, and actual practice-claims. In one way, this is doubtless a good thing, for it might be held to be the task of the theologian to criticize, where necessary, the actual practices of the church. But how is this legitimate critical tension to be preserved while at the same time theology is to escape the charge of disingenuousness? For it is a cheat if the theologian does not relate the ideal church to the actual church—if he recommends a faith that has no purchase on the received tradition.

For these and other reasons, the question of incompatibilities between one faith and another is a complex matter. In a way we are concerned with the elasticity of a faith—whether certain kinds of stretching the concepts and practices result in a snap. Let us try out a thought-experiment here, by considering what is to be said about Hindu attitudes to Christianity.

The modern Hindu ideology, if one may so dub it, consists in a neo-Sankaran theology in which all religions, albeit existing at different levels, ultimately point to the one truth. This is an appealing doctrine to many; for it suggests that religions are held apart by externals, institutional narrownesses, rather than by any essential conflict. It is the obverse of the conclusion sometimes drawn from conflicts of revelations and teachings, namely that they are all false; the modern Hindu ideology declares that they are all true. The best religion, however, is one which is explicitly synthesizing, all embracing (this being the merit of Hinduism). It follows from the modern Hindu ideology that there is no incompatibility between Hinduism and Christianity: they both ultimately have the same focus, though symbolized and concretized differently (Christ and Krishna, for example, are different manifestations of the one God). Should Christianity resist this synthesis? Not just on the ground that the Christian tradition is unique—for every tradition is. Let us consider some of the reasons for resisting the synthesis that might be advanced.

"The Hindu conception of deity is different from that revealed to the Christian tradition." *Comment*: it is true that God in the main Christian tradition is conceived in a more personal way than is the neo-Advaitin *Brahman*: but in *this* respect the ultimate reality of Tillich and John Robinson is similarly "impersonal" (compare also pseudo-Dionysius, Meister Eckhart, Dean Mansel). The anti-synthesis argument thus becomes a means of shutting off certain kinds of theological development within Christianity.

"Christ is uniquely Son of God: there are no other incarnations." *Comment*: this point can be stated if there is a prior monotheism and an identification of sorts of Christ with the one God; but the anti-synthesis argument here will not work in the following conditions (i) if Christ is seen as a "window on ultimate reality" (for there can be many windows); (ii) if Christ is seen, liberal theology-wise, as an exemplar of moral values (for there could be other exemplars, such as the Buddha); (iii) if Christ is simply the preached Christ—the historical anchor of an imperative *kerygma* (for there could be a variety of other historical and mystical anchors of existential challenge). In brief, the appeal to the uniqueness of the incarnation implies a rather conservative ontology. But can't it somehow be done by making a practice-claim? Thus:

"Christ alone is to be worshipped." The Hindu synthesis here seems to be rejected (unless secretly Krishna and others can be *identified* with Christ: to this sort of identification theme we shall return). *Comment*: the practice-claim could simply be a surd imperative, like a surd revelation. But it is usual in the Christian tradition to advance some grounds for the claim—that the risen Christ provides the key to liberation; that it is through sacramental participation in the death and resurrection of Christ that sin and death are overcome; and negatively that other gods do not have liberating power, are phantasms leading men astray, do not exist. It is thus difficult to give grounds for the practice-claim which does not imply some ontology: some account of the human predicament and of the way in which it is overcome. Historically, moreover, the worship of Christ in part arises from the background of worship of the one God. Here is another respect in which the Christian rejection of synthesis rests upon a particular theism. But as I said earlier, there is no knowing what the future may bring: yet at the present time it seems that Christianity, to maintain its incompatibility with Hinduism, would have to appeal to a particular theism as constituting part of its essence. I shall return to this point after a brief excursus on the paradox of a situation in which incompatibility is regarded as a good thing.

Why should there be a motive for standing out against the noble Hindu synthesis? It is partly a matter of having a *raison d'être*. A movement, religious or otherwise, which does not have a distinctive message tends (rightly) to wither. Still, couldn't Christianity have a more modest *raison d'être*—to nurture those within it and those who find that it chimes in with their spiritual and moral condition? It could be, so to speak, a loosely knit tribal religion, but where the tribe is a new Israel, not ethnically determined (although well rooted in certain, mainly western cultures). One must here, however, understand the logical and cultural predicament of a tribal religion in an intercultural situation (this too will cast light upon the reason for the evolution of the new Hindu ideology).

A tribal religion, like other religions, contains a doctrinal element, woven into the whole practical side: a certain picture of the world and of spirit is drawn. Consider the predicament of the tribal folk when it is faced with a new culture, with a transethnic religion. Is it possible for the tribal folk long to maintain that their world-picture is for them, the other world-picture for others? It is hard to say (from a logical point of view) that *P* is true for one group and not-*P* for another, unless all that is meant is that the one group *believes P* and the other believes not-*P*. Various devices have to be employed if the tribal picture is to remain itself at all. One option is hard—to claim that the tribal picture is of universal validity, for it was always meant for those initiated into tribal lore, and wasn't meant at all for other tribes. This secretive non-universalism could be carried with equanimity when the tribe constituted the real world, the values of other men being a mere shadowy penumbra. Even very big groups have felt like this: for the Chinese, barbarian values were shadowy until Buddhism crept in and destroyed the illusion; for expansionist Europe, the beliefs of colonized folk tended to be curiosities, oddities; in India over a long period the real world was the subcontinent, until Buddhism began to flicker outwards. So then our tribal folk will find the universalist option hard to maintain, because of the tight connection between the picture of the world and the secret sacraments of the tribe. Another option it may not want to face—namely to abandon entirely its own picture and assimilate that of the new culture, though even here unconsciously the old gods can be smuggled in. A *via media* is called for: one in which an adjusted world-picture is seen as a contribution to the store of myths and insights which point towards the transcendent. We may call this option: unity through conscious pluralism, or in short "the pluralistic solution."

We can now return to the question of whether Christianity can regard itself modestly as a loosely-knit tribal religion, nurturing those who participate in its sacraments. Faced with other trans-cultural faiths, it would be essentially in the tribal predicament, if so; and truth is no respecter of groups. To retain its modesty, without losing its *raison d'être*, it would have itself to adopt the pluralistic solution, and this would be virtually to accept the Hindu synthesis. In the context of the variety of faiths and of the virtual certainty that they will continue substantially in a plural world, the pluralistic solution seems sound common sense. Hence its appeal (a wide appeal, even among many Christians, who express this pluralism through a scepticism about missions, though not about hospitals in alien climes).

I have made something in this argument of the tightness of the connection between the tribal world-picture and their secret sacraments. This point is highly relevant to problems of meaning and understanding. Crudely one can distinguish between an initiatory and a non-initiatory view of understanding religious concepts. From the initiatory point of view, understanding God can only be approached via the sacramental or analogous activities, or can only be gained by the initiation constituted by the experience of grace. Full-bloodedly, the initiatory view is a sort of conceptual fideism: only those who can say "I know that my redeemer liveth" know what "redeemer" means. A thin-blooded view would be that we can imaginatively enter into initiations (hence the possibility of coming to understand something of other faiths). Those espousing a hardheaded natural theology would hold that at least some key concepts in religion could be understood metaphysically, without specific religious initiation.

There is a tension here. The more conceptually initiatory a religion is, the more it takes on the character of a tribal religion, except that it may be the religion of an open rather than a closed tribe, adding new members as it can. But though it could be thus universal evangelically, in the sense that any man or all men might join the faith-community, it could, if thus conceptually initiatory, give no reasons why men should join, save "Come and see" maybe. In *practice*, of course, men who join use reasons: the fruits are good—you can see peace on their faces, and so forth. This is a kind of practical natural theology, adding some rationality to the otherwise surd initiation. But by contrast, if a religion seems to be hardly initiatory at all, for the understanding of its concepts, it takes on the guise of a metaphysics, and the link between belief and sacrament is ruptured.

Extreme conceptual fideism as an account of the Christian faith does, I think, have to be rejected, if the aim at any rate is to avoid the pluralistic solution. For paradoxically conceptual fideism can give no account of what other faiths mean (e.g. the Hindu synthesis): for it is implied that initiation is necessary for understanding. Given the further premise that one cannot be initiated properly into more than one faith (*pace* Ramakrishna), then the Christian conceptual fideist can have no ground for rejecting any other faith. All faiths have this rather negative equal status. This being so, there can be no reason to reject the Hindu claim that all faiths point to the same Truth. Initiatory conceptional fideism slides in to acceptance of a polytheism, or rather a polyfideism, if one may coin so barbarous a hybrid.

But *should* the extra premise, that one cannot be properly initiated into more than one faith, be accepted? Is it that no man can serve two masters? But how are we to know that they *are* two masters? Is it that a person cannot be converted from one faith to another? We know that this happens empirically, so to speak; but could he really have had his earlier faith if he were converted? These are questions which extreme conceptual fideism is not in a position to answer.

As a postscript to the discussion of extreme conceptual fideism, it is worth noting that whereas truth and falsity do not admit, in any straightforward way, at least, of degrees, understanding does. One person can show greater, deeper, etc., understanding than another. It may be that a very deep under-standing of the concepts of a given faith is not accessible to the adherent of another faith; but this does not at all show that *some* level of understanding is impossible for him; and it can of course well be that the adherent of a faith has a less profound understanding of it than some person of another faith.

The pluralistic solution, as we have outlined it, is not absolute pluralism: there is at least the notion that there is a single truth towards which different religions point—in line with the modern Hindu ideology, which itself constitutes the response of a sophisticated, variegated cultural tradition faced by an incoming transethnic faith, accompanied by aggressive European values. This attempt at making differing traditions compatible by postulating a single focus of aspiration does, however, depend on identifications—identifying one divine focus of faith with another. Can such identifications be justified?

Let us begin with a relatively simply example. What justifies one in saying that the Christian and Muslim worship the same God? As far as the concepts and practices go, the two foci of faith are different. Among other things, the Christian worships Christ as a person of the Trinity: the Christian concept of God is thus organically related to God's manifestation in history and to his representation of himself in the sacraments. These are elements not present in the Muslim's conception of Allah. Thus conceptually the Christian God and Allah are different. This does not entail that the concepts do not refer to the same Being: far from it, a major point about identity statements is that the concepts are different (not all identity statements, but many, e.g., "Tomorrow is Friday"). The statement "The Christian and Muslim worship the same God" is not just to be interpreted intentionally, with phenomenological brackets as it were: rather, it is itself a theological statement, assuming the existence of a single God for both Christians and Muslims to worship. But if it is a theological claim, then from within which tradition? Or does it stand outside both? It could do, e.g., if it is part of the expression of the modern Hindu ideology. But let us consider more narrowly the reasons that a *Christian* theologian might give for the assertion. Let us assume too that he here as elsewhere is presenting a glass through which one can look on the focus of faith—there being no independent access to that focus. The only ground, one supposes, for the identification is that there is a sufficient degree of resemblance between the Christian and Muslim conceptions of God. Since, however, there is a certain degree of elasticity in Christian theology itself, for the focus of faith is theology-transcending, it is unlikely that it would take very strict account of what constitutes a sufficient degree of resemblance.

However, this way of discussing the issue might seem overly conceptual. After all, is it not largely upon the practical side of religion that the theologian feeds? Does his concept of God not articulate what is given in experience, ritual, history? Not suprisingly, those who espouse the pluralistic solution tend to stress the unity of religious *experience*. Thus an important part of the task of trying to establish a sufficient degree of resemblance is the attempt to evaluate the existential and experiential impact of different foci of faith. Strictly, there are two things to do: first, to arrive at a sensible and sensitive phenomenology of religious experience (basically a descriptive task this, though not without its conceptual pitfalls); and second, to see whether the results contribute to the judgement that there is a sufficient degree of resemblance to justify the identification of one focus of faith with another.

The phenomenological judgement as to whether there is a basic common core of religious experience must be based on the facts, and not determined a priori by theology. I do not wish to argue the point here: but my own view is that there is no such common core, but rather that there are different sorts of religious experience which recur in different traditions, though not univer-sally. From a phenomenological point of view it is not possible to base the judgement that all religions point to the same truth upon religious *experience*. Nor is it reasonable to think that there is sufficient conceptual resemblance between God and nirvānā (as conceived in Theravāda Buddhism) to aver that the Theravādin and the Christian are worshipping the same God (for one thing, the Theravādin is not basically *worshipping*). Thus it is hard to justify the pluralistic solution, at least as elaborated in the modern Hindu ideology—save by saying that Christians and Buddhists are really aspiring towards the same focus of faith, even though they cannot know that they are. But what then are the criteria of identity of aspiration? Is there a conceptual baptism of desire?

In brief, there are problems about the pluralistic solution, mainly prob-lems of identification of the religious ultimate. It still remains, however, that there is something to commend the solution: to put the matter in a nasty nutshell, the more evangelical Christianity is, the more it approximates to an open tribal faith, for the truth has to be experienced through the forms of Christian faith; but by the same token there is less ground for dismissing the truth of other initiations. On the other hand, the less evangelical Christianity becomes, the less motive it will have for resisting the pluralistic solution.

But *still* the argument may be over-conceptual, over-theological. Can the practical natural theology mentioned earlier come in to provide the test? It would be something of an irony if human fruits were invoked to decide the interpretation of divinity. But this is not a simple affair, as can be imagined; for what counts as fruits is in part determined by the theologies and the institu-tions. For example, a Christian might bring sustenance to villagers by getting things done, notably by getting folk to hunt birds; but the fruits of Christian dynamism have to be judged by attitudes to animal life. The Buddhist might not be unqualified in his praise of the dynamism. This indicates that the problem of compatibility is not just to do with the religious ultimate, but with the diagnosis of the worldly situation, including importantly the human situation.

The pluralistic situation is attractive, but it is doubtful whether it could work in the present state of religious traditions, because it is phenomenologi-cally unsound. In an important way, then there is incompatibility (at present) between religious truth-claims. There is also divergence in practice-claims. It is a further question as to the *criteria* for resolving questions of truth and practice. There are, however, certainly grounds for arguing both for and against the monotheism which makes sense of Christ's exclusive claim as liberator. As I have attempted to argue elsewhere, these criteria importantly have to do with religious experience and cultus. For the rest, we must accept that every religion has a given starting point, each unique. The pictures in the gallery are different, have different atmospheres and messages; they cannot be aligned in the same pictorial perspective. And for most men only one picture can be a real focus of loyalty.

VIII.3. Do Different Religions Share Moral Common Ground?

PETER DONOVAN

Peter Donovan, on the faculty of Massey University, New Zealand, cites here a claim made by the fourteenth Dalai Lama that all the major world religions teach similar moral principles of not lying, not stealing, not killing, and loving one's fellow human beings. Donovan asks how one might go about testing such a claim and points to such similarities as versions of the Golden Rule in many religions as well as myths, parables, allegories, and legends that seem to teach strikingly similar principles. But, Donovan argues, it is overly simplistic to claim that, because different religions teach some of the same moral rules, they share in a significant way a common moral ground or that this sharing of moral rules implies the existence of universal, culture-independent moral laws.

Do followers of different religions share common ground at the level of their morality, despite their disagreements over doctrine and metaphysical beliefs?

A typical statement of this view was made recently by the Dalai Lama.

I maintain that every major religion of the world—Buddhism, Christianity, Confucianism, Hinduism, Islam, Jainism, Judaism, Sikhism, Taoism, Zoroastrianism —has similar ideals of love, the same goal of benefiting humanity through spiritual practice, and the same effects of making their followers into better human beings. All religions teach moral precepts for perfecting the functions of mind, body, and speech. All teach us not to lie or steal or take others' lives, and so on.

All religions agree upon the necessity to control the undisciplined mind that harbours selfishness and other roots of trouble, and each teaches a path leading to a spiritual state that is peaceful, disciplined, ethical, and wise. It is in this sense that I believe all religions have essentially the same message. Differences of dogma may be ascribed to differences of time and circumstance as well as cultural influences; indeed, there is no end to scholastic argument when we consider the purely metaphysical side of religion. However, it is much more beneficial to try to implement in daily life the shared precepts for

From *Religious Studies* 22 (March 1986): 307–375. Reprinted with the permission of Cambridge University Press.

goodness taught by all religions rather than to argue about minor differences in approach.[1]

What kind of investigation is appropriate, for putting to the test such a claim or exploring such a possibility? Present-day seekers of common ground, concerned as they generally are about international peace and security and the pursuit of a global civilized society, have a right to expect some guidance from religious studies where there is, presumably, expertise to be found in this area. How is the comparative religionist to respond? And what guidance can the philosopher give, in making sense of the question being posed?

The obvious place to begin is where the moral dimension of religions becomes most explicit; i.e. in the form of teachings or precepts. Here we find lists of rules, commandments, laws, codes of conduct, models and paradigms, by which ideals and principles are illustrated and virtue and vices exemplified. Sayings, maxims, proverbs teach these principles, and when filled out with narrative they form myths, parables, allegories and legends, all aiming to reinforce certain kinds of behavior and discourage others, by cultivating appropriate attitudes and emotions.

The discovery of a number of shared moral precepts (e.g. versions of the Golden Rule) amongst different religions seems to offer *prima facie* evidence, at least, for moral common ground as a reality. Moreover, the modern history of religions shows that the sharing of similar material is often not accidental. Religious moralities appear to draw on an international pool of resources, including law-codes, heroic legends, moralistic fables and wisdom literature, gathered throughout history amongst a variety of races and cultures. Wilfred Cantwell Smith has recently illustrated his view of a 'world process of religious convergence' with a moral tale which can be shown to have passed through several Indian traditions, as well as Manichaeism and Islam, before entering Christian folklore as the Baalam and Josaphat legend and reaching modern thought through its influence on Tolstoy and Gandhi.[2]

The demonstration that moral codes and precepts are common property in religious history might well be taken to support the contention that a universal morality is there to be seen, at least in an emerging form, by the unprejudiced observer who takes a broad, cross-cultural view.

It is clearly too simple, however, to think that because followers of different religions assent, on occasion, to similar sets of moral precepts, they therefore must share moral common ground in some significant way. What is important in comparing moralities is not merely the rules people assent to in principle, but why and to what extent they follow them in particular cases, especially in cases of moral conflict or dilemma. Only when these details are appreciated can an observer be said to understand the moralities in question and be in a position to make reliable comparisons between them. To assume that once differing religious beliefs are down-played a common moral code will emerge is to ignore the fact that similar rules and precepts may be adopted

---

[1] *A Human Approach to World Peace*, by His Holiness Tenzin Gyatso, The Fourteenth Dalai Lama (Wisdom Publications, 1984), p. 13.

[2] *Towards a World Theology* (Macmillan, 1981), pp. 7–11.

as means to different ends. The nature of those ends will determine the scene in which the precepts are understood and applied by those who follow them.

Stewart Sutherland, in a recent paper, argues against the view that holders of different beliefs can be said to 'share an ethic' whenever they are observed to be following similar moral precepts.[3] Sutherland does not deny that there is *prima facie* common ground across the frontiers of religious belief. But genuine sameness of action cannot be established, as in the case of physical objects, by mere observation or comparison. Moral actions have to be individuated with reference to the intentions of those who do them. And as intentions entail beliefs, we are not entitled simply to assume that people 'may agree about what ought to be done without necessarily agreeing about the way the world is'.[4]

In Sutherland's example two men, Barry (a Marxist) and Brendan (a Christian) do appear, superficially, to be carrying out the same moral action—in this case lorryloads of food to a refugee camp. But when fuller descriptions of their intentions are given, involving on the one hand Marxist world-view, goals and values, and on the other hand Christian ones, it becomes apparent that what they are each doing is not in fact the same action in a moral sense, at all, and so they cannot be said to 'share an ethic' at that point.

From this it would seem to follow that adherents of different faiths—say, a Buddhist, a Christian, and a traditional Maori—may not in a moral sense be doing the same action at all when each for instance, gives food to a starving enemy or, for that matter, kills a brother or robs a neighbor. For it will be according to quite different systems of belief, involving such diverse concepts as *karma, sin* and *tapu* respectively, that the parties will explain their motives, characterize their intentions, or lament their misdoings.

Such common maxims, then, as may be found in various religions (Tell the truth, do not kill, respect the property of others, feed the starving) do not necessarily reveal any underlying commonalty. Like shared items of devotional practice (rosaries, candles, bodily postures) or like architecturally similar buildings (temples, synagogues, churches, mosques) what they reflect may not be any essential common factor, but only a coincidental similarity of means to quite different moral ends.

Sutherland's argument, extended along these lines, throws considerable doubt on the likely success of any attempt to demonstrate the existence of natural moral laws, or a shared basic morality, by appealing to similarities in teaching or practice amongst followers of different religions.

The problem lies not only with the notion of an action, but with the word *moral* itself. As Sutherland uses the word (and here he reflects modern philosophical usage) morality is necessarily associated with certain kinds of intentionality. The identifying and characterizing of actions as moral involves reference to aims and intentions, beliefs and explanations, on the part of the agents in question. A rule, precept or law becomes a *moral* action-guide for a

---

[3] 'Religion, Ethics and Action', in *The Philosophical Frontiers of Christian Theology*, edited by Brian Hebblethwaite and Stewart Sutherland (Cambridge University Press, 1982), pp.153–67.

[4] *Ibid.* p. 164.

particular piece of conduct only when it is adopted with the appropriate kind of intention in mind.

Comparisons of rule or precept-following in order to discover moral common ground will of necessity involve comparisons of intentionality. A demonstration of shared rules or precepts, or even of similar behaviour, will not be sufficient, for it fails to take account of the variety of differing intentions which may accompany those regularities. This is even more true of the attempt to demonstrate common ground simply by selecting from religious moralities the shared precepts and practices, and deliberately discarding 'differences at the theoretical level'.

For all that, it is undoubtedly the case that from time to time people who hold different and conflicting religious beliefs do nonetheless find themselves, like Sutherland's Barry and Brendan, disposed to act according to similar maxims and to involve themselves in common patterns of behaviour. Is this to be considered as morally of no significance at all—a matter of sheer coincidence? Sutherland admits that his argument does not preclude what he calls 'partial overlap' in descriptions of the actions of holders of different ultimate beliefs. But the overlap, he says, 'may turn out to be very limited indeed both in extent and significance'.[5]

It is here that Sutherland's argument, cogent though it is in theory, may well be felt by the historian of religions to do less than justice to the phenomena of religions themselves and of morality in religious contexts. It is remarkable, for instance, that while emphasizing the need for adequate criteria to individuate and describe actions, Sutherland says so little about how to identify, and distinguish between, the systems of belief in terms of which, on his argument, the moral intentions of different agents are to be defined. He refers variously to 'different theological or metaphysical positions', patterns of belief', 'view-point', views about 'the way the world is', 'habits and rules of thinking', and so on. But no clear way is offered for aligning these abstractions with the living world of religious belief and action.

At one point, Sutherland says his thesis does not commit one to the view that there are as many 'ethics' as there are thinking human beings, and admits that 'an elucidation of the reasons for this would be instructive'.[6] But he gives no hint of what those reasons might be. Yet if we are going to give the sense which he suggests to the notion of 'sharing an ethic', we must have criteria for estimating appropriate degrees of sameness (i.e. similarity) between two or more belief-systems.

Reliance on commonly-used names or labels is obviously inadequate, given the reality of religious diversity. Do all Hindus share a common ethic; or only Shaivite with Shaivite, Vaishnavite with Vaishnavite? Do the trinitarian beliefs of Catholic, Lutheran, and Kimbanguist Christians unite them on a moral common ground, while excluding Unitarians and Latterday Saints? No doubt some theological beliefs will be more relevant than others to the moral outlook of adherents. Does the traditionalist Christian who expects a 'literal Day of Judgement' adhere to the same belief-system, for moral purposes, as

---

[5] *Ibid.*

[6] *Ibid.* p. 166.

the modernist who does not? Or might the traditional Christian in fact have more in common, on this score, with the orthodox Muslim, who similarly undergirds his conduct with a belief in 'That Which Is To Come'? Questions like these reflect the growing awareness in modern religious studies of the inadequacy of thinking of religious faiths as clearly distinguishable by reference to static, named systems of belief with clear boundaries.[7]

Studies of religious change and interaction show that when followers of theoretically quite distinct faiths are thrown together in situations of practical necessity, implicit adjustments are made, priorities reassembled, compromises accepted, in the interests of common well-being. Thus over a period of time basic doctrines can come to be related in quite different ways to the moral outcomes and sensitivities they are believed to entail. Even religious belief systems containing such diverse concepts as *karma, sin,* and *tapu* which earlier were given as instances of distinctly different beliefs, may turn out to be capable of undergoing mutual influence through the pressure of a moral concern for dialogue, cultural interaction and the like.[8] The existence, nowadays, of a vigorous Christian/Marxist dialogue may even raise the question whether the two systems Sutherland takes to be obviously incompatible must necessarily be so under all possible interpretations.

It would, of course, be quite unjustified to conclude from the evidence of inter-religious dialogue, that all differences of religious belief can in the end be adjusted to meet common moral interests. But to rule out any significant or substantial common ground because of incompatibility of beliefs at the most general or ultimate level seems to remove moral theorizing too far from the experience of moral agents in practice.

People holding divergent ultimate beliefs about 'the way the world is' do commonly, nowadays, in multi-cultural societies especially, find themselves acting side-by-side in situations of common concern.[9] Discoveries like this are part of the experience of life by which one's ultimate beliefs themselves are put to the test. Religious ideologies which down-grade immediate personal and communal concerns in the interests of some long-term or supposedly ultimate ideal seem likely, sooner or later, to arouse a sense of their own moral inadequacy. It is to this sense that reformers of religions commonly appeal; as is illustrated, for instance, by Jesus's story of the Good Samaritan, by Muhammad's denunciation of the Meccan cult, or by Mahatma Gandhi's rejection of the caste system.

Common ground sought between different peoples today, moreover, is

---

[7] See W. Cantwell Smith, *The Meaning and End of Religion*, first published in 1962. On the limitations of the concept 'religious system' see Trevor Ling, 'Communalism and the Social Structure of Religion', in *Truth and Dialogue*, edited by John Hick (Sheldon Press, 1974).

[8] In the contemporary theology of Melanesian, Maori and Pacific Island Christianity, indigenous concepts such as *mana* and *tapu* are freely used to help interpret Biblical morality and soteriology. On compatibilities between Hindu and Christian moralities see *Christian and Hindu Ethics*, by Shivesh Thakur (George Allen and Unwin, 1969).

[9] For an introduction to the range of inter-religious activities in modern Britain, see appendix to *God Has Many Names*, by John Hick (Macmillan, 1980). See also *Religious Co-operation in the Pacific*, edited by Emiliana Afeaki and others (University of the South Pacific, 1983).

likely to be related to issues on which long-established religious belief-systems have little specific to say. The uses of nuclear energy, the control of environmental pollution, genetic engineering, information storage, and so on, raise questions about human life and the world itself which are not easily answered from within any of the existing ideologies. There may well be situations, then, in which divergent ultimate beliefs are neither determinate enough, nor play an immediate enough part in the thinking of the people in question to stand in the way of their genuinely sharing concerns at the moral level. The here-and-now benefits of arriving at similar moral conclusions, in other words, may carry greater conviction and be a truer expression of religious commitment than is loyalty to some more remote interpretation of an ultimate theology or ideology.

This possibility is well illustrated from the situation in which world religions have found themselves, in recent years, with the emergence of international agreements regarding human rights. In its Universal Declaration of Human Rights, the General Assembly of the United Nations in December 1948 proclaimed as 'a common standard of achievement for all people and all nations' a number of rights and fundamental freedoms. These include the right to life, liberty and the security of person; freedom from slavery, torture, cruel, inhuman or degrading treatment or punishment; equal and fair treatment before the law; freedom of movement; rights to nationality, family life, ownership of property; freedom of thought, conscience and religion, expression, peaceful assembly and association, and a variety of others. The Declaration has served as a model for subsequent international conventions, and for numerous Bills of Rights entrenched in constitutions of many countries.

While 'human rights' have legal and political implications as well as moral ones, the U.N. Declaration may nonetheless be viewed as a global affirmation of moral common ground. It is offered without theological or ideological justification, yet it reflects ethical norms defined by common consent amongst nations whose members include the widest possible range of religious affiliations. Can these adherents of different religious faiths genuinely affirm an intention to be bound by the Declaration, as a set of common moral precepts, despite the differences and incompatibilities amongst their ultimate beliefs?

In a recently-published discussion of human rights by representatives of world religions, there is a clear concern that the resources of religious belief should be drawn upon, in a combined effort to make the U.N. Declaration universally effective. As one contributor puts it:

> In this new world of intercultural bonds and international communications, there is splendid opportunity to stimulate common effort for the support of human rights. Not only is there an opportunity through theology as a discipline to take an expanded role in fostering intellectual support for these rights . . . but religiously formed persons also have a greatly expanded opportunity to insist upon and campaign for the strengthening of the supportive social processes and institutions which shape cultural mores with respect to rights.[10]

---

[10] 'Human Rights in Religious Traditions', in *Journal of Ecumenical Studies*, xix, 3 (Summer 1982), p. 86.

There is also frank admission that in certain respects the world religions themselves, in their own histories and institutions, do not meet the moral standards proclaimed in the Declaration. For instance, in areas such as sexual equality, freedom of speech and conscience, and religious toleration, it is admitted that the religions left to themselves have failed both in theory and in practice to attain to anything like the universality of scope which the Declaration proclaims. Some serious reinterpretation of belief-systems will be needed, it is recognized, to make genuine assent to the Declaration possible. As the Hindu contributor comments:

> It is evident that the establishment of human rights among Hindus demands not only social reform movements, but also exploration, investigation, and reinterpretation of the theoretical foundations underlying the social hierarchy of Hinduism.[11]

Other writers (e.g. Buddhist and Jewish) seem more confident that human rights as defined by the Declaration are already encompassed, implicitly or explicitly, by their ultimate beliefs, and that in their affirming these common moral principles, only practice, not ultimate ideology, will need to be brought into line.

There is a clear impression created, of theologians casting about in their respective traditions for concepts and arguments by which to justify and reinforce commitment to a common morality the content of which, in today's world, they find compelling in itself. A Catholic scholar, for instance, appears to have little doubt about the primacy of shared moral commitment over ultimate theoretical justification. He writes,

> A very good case can be made that the appeal of human rights norms themselves is really far broader than the appeal of any philosophical or theological foundation which may be offered for them.[12]

In describing the process of justifying this prior moral conviction as 'casting about for concepts and arguments' I do not wish to imply that such rationalization is a spurious activity, intended only to save the appearances. Rather, it is an indication of the open texture even of ultimate belief-systems, and the two-way relation between them and the immediate moral and religious experiences of adherents. Were this not the case, it would be difficult to account for the change and reform of religious ideologies which takes place continually, in the light of wider encounters at the moral and social levels.

There are reasons for thinking, then, that Sutherland's argument too lightly dismisses the significance of common moral intentions, shared by followers of different religions at a level less than that of ultimate beliefs about 'what the world is like'. In practice, when asked to give reasons for their moral actions, representatives of a religion may well express themselves in the concepts of the official ideology, with reference to its ultimate goal and world-view. Yet this may not be the best guide as to what for them personally, in a

---

[11] *Ibid.* p. 84.

[12] *Ibid.* pp. 26–7.

particular situation, are the most relevant moral considerations. (This must be still more true for adherents who are inarticulate or barely aware of the official world-view. Suppose, for instance, Sutherland's 'Brendan' is a convert from a freshly-evangelized hill tribe, and 'Barry' a peasant, newly-recruited into the Vietnamese army. Neither will have much grasp of the ultimate principles of their new-found belief-systems.

There will, undoubtedly, also be situations such as those Sutherland envisages, in which the apparent similarity of behaviour and even of precepts will in no way count as a genuine moral sharing, because the ultimate beliefs and intentions on the part of one or more of the parties will explicitly exclude that interpretation. (Christians holding firmly to a Calvinist theology, for instance, may reject 'universal human rights' as an unscriptural product of secular thought. They may still, however, find themselves able to affirm many of the same principles as those of the U.N. Declaration, on the basis of a belief in Divine covenants of grace.[13]) Given the difficulty of individuating belief-systems, and of determining which, in the minds of the moral agents themselves, are incompatible with which, confidently identifying situations where moral common ground is excluded will not be as straightforward a task as Sutherland's argument suggests.

According to the argument so far, then, moral teachings found by inspection to be shared by many religions will not in themselves count as evidence for a common morality existing by some natural necessity, in the way that natural law theories supposed. What inspection can reveal will be contingent, though perhaps quite widely-occurring, similarities in recommended moral conduct, resulting from commitment to similar principles and ideals. This can be said to amount to a genuinely shared ethic when, for the parties concerned, the intention to regard those principles as matters of moral agreement is not consciously excluded through adherence to incompatible ultimate beliefs.

Among the factors which open the way for such inclusive intentions may, of course, be the presence of beliefs about universal moral principles, carried in the scriptures of religious traditions or enshrined in their dogmas. (No doubt the availability of scholastic natural law theory assisted in Pope John XXIII's endorsement of the U.N declaration of human rights in the encyclical *Pacem in Terris*.)

From the fact that representatives of different religions may proclaim 'Despite our theological differences we all acknowledge the same basic moral precepts' it does not follow that they do. What may follow, however, is that through proclaiming that belief, they increase the likelihood that their followers will, in situations of potential common moral concern, adjust their own intentions so as to identify them with those of others holding different ultimate beliefs.

Pronouncements like that of the Dalai Lama ('All religions teach common moral precepts') are not to be taken, then, as descriptions of an actual state of affairs. They are, rather, pleas for religions to make common cause (in the interests, in this case, of world peace), interpreting and adjusting their traditions of belief so as to be able intentionally to affirm such common concerns as

---

[13] *Ibid.* pp. 11–12.

moral. What is offered, in other words, is encouragement for a creative theological enterprise; not a description of an already-existing universal moral bedrock, there to be uncovered once religious differences are set aside.[14]

In reply, then, to the question, Do different religions share moral common ground, the answer must be: Yes, from time to time they do, when their belief-systems are found to be sufficiently flexible of interpretation to permit believers to have inclusive moral intentions in situations involving common action. But this in itself does little to show that universal moral laws, independent of culturally-borne religious beliefs and intentions, are waiting to be discovered at the level of common human nature.

---

[14] Whether the proposal is capable of being implemented, by whom, for how long, at what cost to other beliefs, and so on, are other matters entirely.

VIII.4.   The Way to the Realization of a Universal Religion

SWAMI VIVEKANANDA

Swami Vivekananda, whose birth name was Narendranath Dutt (1863–1902), was a disciple of the nineteenth-century Hindu saint, Ramakrishna (1836–1886). Although Ramakrishna was born a Hindu and spent most of his life as priest of a temple dedicated to the goddess Kali, he made a conscious effort to understand and experience the truths of all world religions. He had mystical visions of Muhammad and Jesus that convinced him that all religions teach essentially the same truth, each in its own culturally colored way. Vivekananda learned from his master the ideal of religious understanding and inclusiveness. He became a major modern interpreter of the nondualist Hindu tradition derived from the medieval Hindu teacher Sankara and known as Advaita Vedanta.

In 1893, Vivekananda attended the World Parliament of Religions in Chicago and began to enunciate his universalism. In the following selection, a talk that he gave in California in 1900, he does not urge the merging of all sects into one single religion, for that would mean the loss of the great richness of the many traditions. The separate traditions should continue, but they should all recognize one another as different forces in the economy of God. They are many paths, each appropriate to its own people, to the same destination; many alternate ways of apprehending and having commerce with the deity, the divine dimension of reality. Vivekananda urges not toleration, a negative notion implying putting up with what you do not accept, but acceptance and mutual respect. In another of his writings he makes use of the image of the lake and the people coming to draw water, one with a jar, one with a pitcher, one with a pot, one with a bucket. The water takes the shape of the vessel in which it is carried, but it is all the same water. Similarly, the divine truth takes the shape of the cultural tradition in which it is expressed, but it is ultimately one and the same truth.

From "The Way to the Realization of the Universal Religion" in *Jnana-Yoga* by Swami Vivekananda, edited by Swami Nikhilananda, copyright 1955, published by the Ramakrishna-Vivekananda Center of New York, pp. 290–292, 294–295, 297–299, 301–302, 302–303, 304–308. Delivered in the Universalist Church, Pasadena, California, January 28, 1900.

No search has been dearer to the human heart than that which brings to us light from God. No study has taken so much of human energy, whether in times past or present, as the study of the soul, of God, and of human destiny. However deeply immersed we are in our daily occupations, in our ambitions, in our work, sometimes in the midst of the greatest of our struggles, there comes a pause; the mind stops and wants to know something beyond this world. Sometimes it catches glimpses of a realm beyond the senses, and a struggle to get at it is the result. Thus it has been throughout the ages in all countries. Man has wanted to look beyond, wanted to expand himself; and all that we call progress, evolution, has always been measured by that one search, the search for human destiny, the search for God.

As our social struggles are represented, among different nations, by different social organizations, so man's spiritual struggles are represented by various religions. And as different social organizations are constantly quarrelling, are constantly at war with each other, so these spiritual organizations have been constantly at war with each other, constantly quarrelling. Men belonging to a particular social organization claim that the right to live belongs only to them, and so long as they can, they want to exercise that right at the cost of the weak. We know that just now there is a fierce struggle of that sort going on in South Africa.[1] Similarly each religious sect has claimed the exclusive right to live. And thus we find that though nothing has brought man more blessings than religion, yet at the same time, there is nothing that has brought him more horror than religion. Nothing has made more for peace and love than religion; nothing has engendered fiercer hatred than religion. Nothing has made the brotherhood of man more tangible than religion; nothing has bred more bitter enmity between man and man than religion. Nothing has built more charitable institutions, more hospitals for men and even for animals, than religion; nothing has deluged the world with more blood than religion.

We know, at the same time, that there has always been an opposing undercurrent of thought; there have always been parties of men, philosophers, students of comparative religion, who have tried and are still trying to bring about harmony in the midst of all these jarring and discordant sects. As regards certain countries these attempts have succeeded, but as regards the whole world they have failed. Then again, there are some religions, which have come down to us from the remotest antiquity, imbued with the idea that all sects should be allowed to live--that every sect has a meaning, a great idea, imbedded in it, and therefore all sects are necessary for the good of the world and ought to be helped. In modern times the same idea is prevalent, and attempts are made from time to time to reduce it to practice. But these attempts do not always come up to our expectations, up to the required efficiency. Nay, to our great disappointment, we sometimes find that we are quarrelling all the more. . . .

Sects are multiplying all the time. If the claim of any one religion that it has all the truth, and that God has given it all that truth in a certain book, be true, why then are there so many sects? Not fifty years pass before there are twenty

---

[1] A reference to the Boer War.

sects founded upon the same book. If God has put all the truth in certain books, He does not give us those books in order that we may quarrel over texts. That seems to be the fact. Why is this? Even if a book were given by God which contained all the truth about religion, it would not serve the purpose, because nobody could understand the book. Take the Bible, for instance, and all the sects that exist among the Christians. Each one puts its own interpretation upon the same text, and each says that it alone understands that text and all the rest are wrong. So with every religion. There are many sects among the Mohammedans and among the Buddhists, and hundreds among the Hindus.

Now, I place these facts before you in order to show you that any attempt to bring all humanity to one method of thinking in spiritual things has been a failure and always will be a failure. Every man who starts a theory, even at the present day, finds that if he goes twenty miles away from his followers they will make twenty sects. You see that happening all the time. You cannot make all conform to the same ideas; that is a fact, and I thank God that it is so. I am not against any sect. I am glad that sects exist, and I only wish they may go on multiplying more and more. Why? Simply because of this: If you and I and all who are present here were to think exactly the same thoughts, there would be no thoughts for us to think. We know that two or more forces must come into collision in order to produce motion. It is the clash of thought, the differentiation of thought, that awakes thought. Now, if we all thought alike, we should be like Egyptian mummies in a museum, looking vacantly at one another's faces—no more than that! Whirls and eddies occur only in a rushing, living stream. There are no whirlpools in stagnant, dead water.

When religions are dead, there will be no more sects; it will be the perfect peace and harmony of the grave. . . .

Then arises the question: How can all this variety be true? If one thing is true, its negation is false. How can contradictory opinions be true at the same time? This is the question which I intend to answer. But I shall first ask you: Are all the religions of the world really contradictory? I do not mean the external forms in which great thoughts are clad. I do not mean the different buildings, languages, rituals, books, and so forth, employed in various religions, but I mean the internal soul of every religion. Every religion has a soul behind it, and that soul may differ from the soul of another religion; but are they contradictory? Do they contradict or supplement each other?—that is the question.

I took up this question when I was quite a boy, and have been studying it all my life. Thinking that my conclusion may be of some help to you, I place it before you. I believe that they are not contradictory; they are supplementary. Each religion, as it were, takes up one part of the great, universal truth and spends its whole force in embodying and typifying that part of the great truth. It is, therefore addition, not exclusion. That is the idea. System after system arises, each one embodying a great idea; ideals must be added to ideals. And this is how humanity marches on.

Man never progresses from error to truth, but from truth to truth—from lesser truth to higher truth, but never from error to truth. The child may develop more than the father; but was the father inane? The child is the father plus something else. If your present stage of knowledge is much greater than the stage you were in when you were a child, would you look down upon that earlier stage now? Will you look back and call it inanity? Your present stage is the knowledge of childhood plus something more.

Then again, we know that there may be almost contradictory points of view of a thing, but they all point to the same thing. Suppose a man is journeying towards the sun and as he advances he takes a photograph of the sun at every stage. When he comes back, he has many photographs of the sun, which he places before us. We see that no two are alike; and yet who will deny that all these are photographs of the same sun, from different standpoints? Take four photographs of this church from different corners. How different they would look! And yet they would all represent this church. In the same way, we are all looking at truth from different standpoints, which vary according to our birth, education, surroundings, and so on. We are viewing truth, getting as much of it as these circumstances will permit, colouring it with our own feelings, understanding it with our own intellects and grasping it with our own minds. We can know only as much of truth as is related to us, as much of it as we are able to receive. This makes the difference between man and man, and sometimes even occasions contradictory ideas. Yet we all belong to the same great universal truth.

My idea, therefore, is that all these religions are different forces in the economy of God, working for the good of mankind, and that not one can become dead, not one can be killed. Just as you cannot kill any force in nature, so you cannot kill any one of these spiritual forces. You have seen that each religion is living. From time to time it may retrogress or go forward. At one time it may be shorn of a good many of its trappings; at another time it may be covered with all sorts of trappings. But all the same, the soul is ever there, it can never be lost. The ideal which every religion represents is never lost, and so every religion is intelligently on the march.

And that universal religion about which philosophers and others have dreamt in every country already exists. It is here. As the universal brotherhood of man already exists, so also does the universal religion. Which of you that have travelled far and wide have not found brothers and sisters in every nation? I have found them all over the world. Brotherhood already exists; only there are numbers of persons who fail to see this and upset it by crying for new brotherhoods. The universal religion, too, already exists. If the priests and other people who have taken upon themselves the task of preaching different religions simply cease preaching for a few moments, we shall see it is there. . . .

We can eat only in our own way. For instance, we Hindus eat with our fingers. Our fingers are suppler than yours; you cannot use your fingers the same way. Not only should the food be supplied; it should also be taken in your own particular way. Not only must you have the spiritual ideas; they must also come to you according to your own method. They must speak your own language, the language of your soul, and then alone will they satisfy you. When the man comes who speaks my language and gives me the truth in my language, I at once understand it and receive it for ever. This is a great fact.

Now, from this we see that there are various grades and types of human minds—and what a task the religions take upon themselves! A man brings forth two or three doctrines and claims that his religion ought to satisfy all humanity. He goes out into the world, God's menagerie, with a little cage in hand, and says, "Man and the elephant and everybody has to go into this.". . . They never try to make their sect large enough to embrace everyone.

Therefore, we at once see why there has been so much narrow-mindedness, the part always claiming to be the whole, the little, finite unit always laying claim to the infinite. Think of little sects, born only a few hundred years ago, out of fallible human brains, making this arrogant claim of knowing the whole of God's infinite truth! Think of the arrogance of it! If it shows anything, it shows how vain human beings are. And it is no wonder that such claims have always failed, and by the mercy of the Lord are always destined to fail. In this line the Mohammedans were the best off. Every step forward was made with the sword—the Koran in the one hand and the sword in the other: "Take the Koran, or you must die. There is no other alternative!" You know from history how phenomenal was their success; for six hundred years nothing could resist them. And then there came a time when they had to cry halt. So will it be with other religions if they follow the same methods.

We are such babies! We always forget human nature. When we begin life we think that our fate will be something extraordinary, and nothing can make us disbelieve that. But when we grow old we think differently. So with religions. In their early stages, when they spread a little, they get the idea that they can change the minds of the whole human race in a few years, and go on killing and massacring to make converts by force. Then they fail and begin to understand better. These religions did not succeed in what they started out to do, which was a great blessing. Just think! If one of those fanatical sects had succeeded all over the world, where would man be today? The Lord be blessed that they did not succeed! Yet each one represents a great truth; each religion represents a particular excellence, something which is its soul. . . .

The fact that all these old religions are living today proves that they must have kept that mission intact. In spite of all their mistakes, in spite of all difficulties, in spite of all quarrels, in spite of all the incrustation of forms and rituals, the heart of every one of them is sound—it is a throbbing, beating, living heart. They have not lost, any of them, the great mission they came for. And it is splendid to study that mission. Take Mohammedanism, for instance. Christian people hate no religion in the world so much as Mohammedanism. They think it is the very worst form of religion that ever existed. But as soon as a man becomes a Mohammedan, the whole of Islām receives him as a brother with open arms, without making any distinction, which no other religion does. If one of your American Indians becomes a Mohammedan, the Sultan of Turkey would have no objection to dine with him. If he had brains, no position would be barred to him. In this country I have never yet seen a church where the white man and the Negro can kneel side by side to pray. Just think of that: Islām makes its followers all equal. So that, you see, is the peculiar excellence of Mohammedanism. In many places in the Koran you find very sensual ideas of life. Never mind. What Mohammedanism comes to preach to the world is this practical brotherhood of all belonging to their faith. That is the essential part of the Mohammedan religion; and all the other ideas, about heaven and of life and so forth, are not Mohammedanism. They are accretions.

With the Hindus you will find one great idea: spirituality. In no other religion, in no other sacred books in the world, will you find so much energy spent in defining the idea of God. They tried to describe God in such a way that no earthly touch might mar Him. The Spirit must be divine; and Spirit, as such, must not be identified with the physical world. The idea of unity, of the realization of God, the Omnipresent, is preached throughout. They think it is nonsense to say that God lives in heaven, and all that. That is a mere human, anthropomorphic idea. All the heaven that ever existed is now and here. One moment in infinite time is quite as good as any other moment. If you believe in a God, you can see Him even now. We Hindus think that religion begins when you have realized something. It is not believing in doctrines or giving intellectual assent or making declarations. If there is a God, have you seen Him? If you say no, then what right have you to believe in Him? If you are in doubt whether there is a God, why do you not struggle to see Him? Why do you not renounce the world and spend the whole of your life for this one object? Renunciation and spirituality are the two great ideals of India, and it is because India clings to these ideals that all her mistakes count for so little.

With the Christians, the central idea that has been preached by them is the same: "Watch and pray, for the kingdom of heaven is at hand"—which means: Purify your minds and be ready. You recollect that the Christians, even in the darkest days, even in the most superstitious Christian countries, have always tried to prepare themselves for the coming of the Lord by trying to help others, building hospitals, and so on. So long as the Christians keep to that ideal, their religion lives.

Now, an ideal presents itself to my mind. It may be only a dream. I do not know whether it will ever be realized in this world; but sometimes it is better to dream a dream than to die on hard facts. Great truths, even in a dream, are good—better than bad facts. So let us dream a dream.

You know that there are various grades of mind. You may be a matter-of-fact, common-sense rationalist. You do not care for forms and ceremonies; you want intellectual, hard, ringing facts, and they alone will satisfy you. Then there are the Puritans, the Mohammedans, who will not allow a picture or a statue in their place of worship. Very well. But there is another man who is more artistic. He wants a great deal of art—beauty of lines and curves, colours, flowers, forms; he wants candles, lights, and all the insignia and paraphernalia of ritual, that he may see God. His mind grasps God in those forms, as yours grasps Him through the intellect. Then there is the devotional man, whose soul is crying for God; he has no other idea but to worship God and praise Him. Then again, there is the philosopher, standing outside all these, mocking at them. He thinks: "What nonsense they are! What ideas about God!"

They may laugh at each other, but each one has a place in this world. All these various minds, all these various types, are necessary. If there is ever going to be an ideal religion, it must be broad and large enough to supply food for all these minds. It must supply the strength of philosophy to the philosopher, the devotee's heart to the worshipper; to the ritualist, it will give all that the most marvellous symbolism can convey; to the poet it must give as much of heart as he can absorb, and other things besides. To make such a broad religion, we shall have to go back to the very source and take them all in.

Our watchword, then, will be acceptance and not exclusion. Not only toleration; for so-called toleration is often blasphemy and I do not believe in it. I believe in acceptance. Why should I tolerate? Toleration means that I think that you are wrong and I am just allowing you to live. Is it not a blasphemy to think that you and I are allowing others to live? I accept all the religions that were in the past and worship with them all; I worship God with every one of them, in whatever form they worship Him. I shall go to the mosque of the Mohammedan; I shall enter the Christian's church and kneel before the Crucifix; I shall enter the Buddhist temple, where I shall take refuge in Buddha and his Law. I shall go into the forest and sit down in meditation with the Hindu, who is trying to see the Light which enlightens the heart of everyone.

Not only shall I do all this, but I shall keep my heart open for all the religions that may come in the future. Is God's Book finished? Or is revelation still going on? It is a marvellous Book—these spiritual revelations of the world. The Bible, the Vedas, the Koran, and all other sacred books are but so many pages, and an infinite number of pages remain yet to be unfolded. I shall leave my heart open for all of them. We stand in the present, but open ourselves to the infinite future. We take in all that has been in the past, enjoy the light of the present, and open every window of the heart for all that will come in the future. Salutation to all the prophets of the past, to all the great ones of the present, and to all that are to come in the future!

Part IX

Religion and the Meaning of Life

Three questions, it is said, concern humans above all others when they reflect seriously about their lives: Where did we come from? Why are we here? What will become of us in the end? Religion has often been regarded as the source of answers, if there are any answers, to these questions. Religion, however, is not the only source. Any comprehensive world view either explicitly or implicitly suggests answers. Theism tends to answer by reference to a God who created the world and us, who has a plan for each of us that constitutes the meaning of each individual human life, and who will determine ultimately what becomes of us after we die, perhaps based on our merits as determined by the kind of lives we have lived. Theism often teaches that worthy individuals live on in another idyllic realm after the death of their bodies; sometimes it also includes teachings about the destiny of unworthy or sinful individuals who may be depicted as suffering punishment for their misdeeds in this life.

Materialistic and naturalistic philosophies also imply answers to these three questions. According to evolutionary naturalism, for example, human life is a natural result of material forces that, through a long, slow process of natural selection, have made us what we are. The question of the purpose of our existence has no straightforward answer because the course of cosmic history was not planned or designed. We might say that our purpose, like that of all

585

other living beings, is to enjoy our lives and pass our genetic material—and, in the special case of humans, our cultural materials—down to future generations. What becomes of us ultimately is that individuals die like all other living things. Our immortality, if one wants to speak in this way, is only in our children and in anything we may have created that lasts after us. Our society lives on, but eventually it too will disappear when the earth is no longer able to sustain life.

For a great many people, these fundamental human questions come to focus most significantly on the puzzle of death. Once we reach a fairly sophisticated level of biological understanding, we discover that death seems to be a natural phenomenon. Nearly every living species appears to incorporate something like a built-in natural life span at the end of which each of its members dies. Viewed in this way, death needs no further explanation; it is just what naturally happens to every living thing. To ask, Why do we die? seems to be like asking a question like, Why is water wet? Being wet is a part of the nature of water; dying is a part of the nature of living things.

Humans find these answers satisfactory in the case of water—and of frogs, cows, trees, or chimpanzees. They have often found them utterly unacceptable in the case of their own death. When we demand to be told why humans have to die, our question implies a belief that humans ought not to die, that human death requires not just an explanation but a justification. There is an assumption, apparently, that each human is a being of such importance or value that he or she ought not to die but to continue to live and have that value preserved— perhaps forever. Thus many religious and philosophical traditions have developed the belief in the continued existence of human individuals after the death of their bodies. This belief has taken various forms in different religions. Such Eastern religions as Hinduism and Buddhism, for example, teach belief in reincarnation. According to the Hindu doctrine of reincarnation, the human soul occupies a series of bodies, some human and perhaps some animal. This form of the continued existence of the human self after the death of its body is not considered to be desirable, because earthly life involves suffering and every rebirth only leads to another death. Thus Hinduism includes the spiritual quest for *moksha*, or liberation from the process of rebirth and redeath. The ultimate destiny of the soul after it achieves *moksha* is said to be *nirvana*. *Nirvana* literally means extinction, but the term is often interpreted to mean not extinction of the self but only of its sufferings and its unsatisfied desires and cravings.

The West has fostered a wide range of beliefs about what happens to humans after death. The ancient Greeks, Romans, and Hebrews taught a rather vague doctrine that after death only a ghost or shade remains, which is consigned to a place called Sheol or Hades, a dark, dank, and quite unpleasant place. Plato (c. 428–347 B.C.E.), a leading ancient Greek philosopher, taught a doctrine of reincarnation remarkably similar to that of Hinduism, but he seems to have believed that the individual soul ultimately achieves immortality by escaping the prison house of the body, after which it apparently goes to live with the gods and other departed humans in a kind of paradise. In the Christian religious tradition, belief in the immortality of the soul was rejected in favor of a belief in resurrection. To form a complete person, it was thought, the soul needs to be connected to the body. Thus Christianity teaches that a time will come when all the dead will be resurrected to spend eternity in a paradise with God. To counter the objection that the body is a source of disease and suffering, a teaching developed about a "spiritual body" that would be a suitable eternal habitation for a resurrected soul. The evidence Christians offer to support this belief are two claims: that after Jesus was crucified God raised him from the dead and that God has promised also to resurrect those who follow Jesus. Philosophers, meanwhile, have rarely been satisfied simply to accept the assertions of the religious traditions about human destiny after death. They have attempted instead to analyze such concepts as immortality, resurrection, and individual identity and to supply arguments to support the doctrine thought to be most acceptable.

The suggestion that human life ends totally when the body dies has struck many people as implying that human life is without purpose or meaning. The spreading disbelief in the continuation of individual life after death among modern, scientific-minded Westerners has been one major contributor to a widespread sense in the twentieth century that human life is futile, absurd, perhaps not worth living. A more general explanation for the anomie characteristic of our times, expressed so poignantly in the literature of the philosophical movement called existentialism, is the fading out of a whole range of central doctrines and values that have integrated the belief system we call Western civilization.

The blending of systematic Greek philosophy with Christian theology during the Middle Ages produced an impressive system of beliefs that depicted the earth as the center of the universe, with the rest of the cosmos revolving around it; humans in turn were the center of the hierarchy of beings—the highest embodied beings, the lowest spiritual beings, the darlings of God created only a little lower than the angels. Christian theology also depicted space and time as strictly limited: Time began with creation some few thousand years ago and will end with the resurrection and judgment day, when God will punish all sinners but bring his righteous children home to live with him in heaven. Space consists of the perceived cosmos, with earth at the center; the sun, moon, planets, and stars revolving around it; hell a short distance down below and heaven immediately above. For faithful believers, it was a cozy and comforting world; they knew where they came from, what their life meant, and what destiny had in store for them.

Then came a series of episodes, the so-called humiliations of man, that pulled down the whole impressive structure and hurled humans into a vast, cold, apparently uncaring cosmos in which hope and meaning seemed entirely to disappear. The earliest was Copernican astronomy, which showed that the earth is not the center of the universe and which eventually led to the discovery of the vastness of the universe in which our sun is only a tiny star among billions of stars in one of millions of galaxies. That this whole vast universe, in which we occupy not the center but some tiny random place, should have been created exclusively for our benefit seems not only uncertain but even preposterous in light of this scientific discovery. This, however, was only the first humiliation. Darwin discovered the process of evolution, which demonstrated that humans developed through natural selection from primitive life forms, only the latest in a very long process that has also produced all of the other animals on earth. The beings who had proudly thought of themselves as created in the image of God, and only a little lower than the angels, were faced with the discovery that they were actually very little higher than the beasts. And soon the progress of literary scholarship applied to the holy scriptures began to discover that the Bible, that firm source of indubitable divine truth, was not at all what it had been thought to be: a coherent, divinely inspired account of reality, history, and morality given through revelation directly from the mouth of God. Rather, it turned out to be simply a collection of writings from the imaginations of many persons over many centuries, full of inconsistencies and incoherencies that make it impossible for us to regard it, as had been formerly claimed, as the full and inerrant truth correct in every detail literally understood.

Meanwhile, our hope for human progress, fueled by the successes of science and the growth of human knowledge, began to be dashed not only by a series of economic depressions, but also by a continuing series of ever more horrendous wars, characterized by acts of human brutality and barbarism that staggered and sickened the imagination. The suspicion that human existence might be no more than a tragic cosmic accident fraught with futility and meaninglessness is not new in the twentieth century; passages in the Bible and other ancient writings reflect this viewpoint clearly. Never before, however, have so many humans been so irresistibly lured by such forceful evidence to accept the truth of such a melancholy doctrine.

The existentialists gave voice to this sense of absurdity and futility in our century, raising in urgent tones the question of whether human existence had any meaning or any worth at all. Some of them intimated that no hopeful answer seemed forthcoming; others bravely affirmed, in the face of all of the suffering and the confusion, that meaning could be created and value could be enjoyed whether there is objective purpose to our existence or not.

At the close of the twentieth century, we seem to have entered an era when the terrifying threat of nuclear holocaust has receded in some measure. The shrill warnings of disaster and the heart-sickening images of human emptiness, futility, meaninglessness, absurdity ring a little less true and seem slightly less urgent in a time when superpowers seem to be holstering their guns and groping their way toward more humane relations with one another. And even if the threat of nuclear disaster has been replaced with perhaps equally dangerous threats of environmental devastation and the choking of the whole earth by the population explosion, we still seem to sense a slight breeze of optimism as we begin efforts to diminish these dangers.

It may be that the religious teachers are right, and time is destined soon to end with a judgment day and a transition to a completely different kind of existence. Or possibly the existentialists are right; perhaps such meaning as human existence can have is only the meaning we create by our own deliberate and thoughtful efforts. May it be that our efforts to deal with the population disaster and the environmental crisis is a path toward the creation of such meaning? Whatever the answer may be to the three fundamental questions, no position seems more reasonable and no course of action more sensible than to pitch in and make an effort to save our planet home and our human project—whether we do it in the name of our God or for the sake of our own souls and those of our human sisters and brothers, our animal cousins, and our plant relatives, all of whose destiny belong to a single path of history.

It is perhaps ironic that a thinker writing at the beginning of the twentieth century, before the worst of our existential horrors had occurred, should sound more contemporary and relevant to our end-of-the-century situation than the more recent existentialist writers. William James urges us to notice that the question of whether life is worth living depends on how we live it—and that if we live it well, it can have meaning whether God exists or not.

ANNOTATED GUIDE TO FURTHER READINGS

Camus, Albert. *The Myth of Sisyphus and Other Essays.* New York: Alfred A. Knopf, 1955.
The essays in this book address what Camus calls the only important philosophical question [suicide] by an analysis of the concept of absurd existence. Camus argues that meaning can be created even amidst an absurd world. He illustrates the claim through his retelling of the Myth of Sisyphus, included in this Part.

Flew, Antony. *The Logic of Mortality.* New York: Basil Blackwell, 1987.
A thorough and critical examination of the concept of immortality of the soul. Emphasizes the theories of Plato; the contributions of Descartes, Aristotle, and Aquinas are examined as well, along with a chapter devoted to parapsychology.

Frankl, Viktor E. *Man's Search for Meaning.* New York: Pocket Books, 1963.

The fascinating and powerful story of Frankl's experiences in a Nazi concentration camp and how this led him to the creation of a philosophy he calls logo-therapy. Each individual must decide on and affirm the thing that provides his or her life with meaning; in this action the meaning of life resides.

Hick, John. *Death and Eternal Life.* New York: Harper & Row, 1976.
The issue of what happens after death is approached from a number of perspectives: Eastern and Western religious thought; sociological, psychological, and humanist perspectives; the views of specific authors. Hick suggests the possibility of an all-inclusive eschatological reality that transcends worldly boundaries.

Klemke, E. D., ed. *The Meaning of Life.* New York: Oxford University Press, 1981.
An excellent collection of essays, divided into three sections: the theistic perspective, the nontheistic perspective, and the claim that the question "What is the meaning of life" does not make any sense.

Kramer, Kenneth. *The Sacred Art of Dying: How World Religions Understand Death* New York: Paulist Press, 1988.
A useful and easily understandable introductory text covering Hinduism, Buddhism, Taoism, Judaism, Christianity, and Islam as well as Native American, Egyptian, and ancient Greek thought.

Moody, Raymond A., Jr. *Life After Life.* New York: Bantam Books, 1975.
Examines case studies in which the subjects were clinically dead for a period of time and then resuscitated. Moody finds these near-death experiences suggestive evidence of an afterlife but stresses that they do not provide a definitive proof.

Pojman, Louis P., ed *Philosophy of Religion: An Anthology.* Belmont, Calif.: Wadsworth, 1987.
Contains a good selection of essays on death and immortality presenting both sides of the argument concerning immortality of the soul or resurrection of the body

Price, H.H. "The Problem of Life After Death." In *Philosophy of Religion: Selected Readings,* 2nd ed., edited by William L. Rowe and William J. Wainwright. New York: Harcourt Brace Jovanovich, 1989.
Price concentrates on such matters as ESP and mediums who claim to communicate with the dead. Other pieces on death and immortality in this anthology are by Anthony Quinton, Bertrand Russell, and J.M.E. McTaggart.

Sartre, Jean Paul. *No Exit and Three Other Plays.* New York: Vintage Books, 1956.
In these plays, especially "No Exit" and "The Flies," Sartre depicts the themes of bad faith, absurdity, and inauthenticity. "No Exit" seems to suggest that the task of choosing an authentic life is virtually impossible, but the outcome of "The Flies" seems more optimistic about creating a meaningful life.

Tillich, Paul. *The Courage to Be.* New Haven: Yale University Press, 1952.
Tillich states that the anxieties aroused by the threat of our nonexistence are best met with courage. Ideally, we need to accept our anxieties as a part of ourselves. This is the courage to be, and it is realized when the theistic God is transcended and the God that lies beyond is affirmed.

IX.A.   Death and Human Destiny

IX.A.1.   Regarding Immortality

ROY W. PERRETT

Roy W. Perrett, on the faculty of the University of Otago, New Zealand, addresses questions concerning the relationship of immortality to the meaning of life. He is convinced that immortality is not a necessary *condition for life to have a meaning; that is, he believes we can live meaningful lives even if death marks the final end of our existence. Most of his argument concerns whether or not immortality is a sufficient condition for life to have a meaning. We can imagine versions of immortality, he says, that would not be desirable; therefore immortality simply in the sense of continuing to exist forever is not sufficient. What can make life meaningful is rather the realization of certain desirable qualities of life. Those qualities, however, might be realized during this life; indeed, endless prolongation of life might even diminish them. But the realization of certain moral qualities does seem to Perrett sufficient to guarantee that life is meaningful— whether life ends or continues forever. And he also believes that a case can be made for the claim that this interpretation of immortality is compatible with the traditional religious view.*

I

Would personal immortality have any value for one so endowed? An affirmative answer would seem so obvious to some that they might be tempted to go so far as to claim that immortality is a condition of life's having any value at all. The claim that immortality is a *necessary* condition for the meaningfulness of life seems untenable.[1] What, however, of the claim that immortality is a *sufficient* condition for the meaningfulness of life? Though some might hold this to be the characteristic *religious* view, this is certainly disputable. Thus McTaggart reminds us, for instance, that 'Buddhism . . .

From *Religious Studies* 22, no. 2 (June 1986): 219–233.

[1] I have argued for this in my 'Tolstoy, death and the meaning of life', *Philosophy*/LX (1985), 231–45.

holds immortality to be the natural state of man, from which only the most perfect can escape.'[2] I want to argue that we can imagine variants of personal immortality which would not be valuable and hence immortality in itself cannot be a sufficient condition for value. What is required for the meaningfulness of life is that life exhibit certain valuable qualities. But then the endless exhibition of these qualities is not only unnecessary for the meaningfulness of life, but the endlessness of a life can even devalue those qualities that would make valuable a single, bounded life.

II

Before turning to this task, however, I want to consider a different sort of approach to the question of the relation between immortality and value. This consists in the claim that immortality is somehow a presupposition of our conceptions of value. This claim has been supported by various arguments. John Hick, for example, presents 'the basic religious argument for immortality' as follows.[3] True, a humanist view of death is compatible with an optimistic view of life insofar as some exceptional figures like Hume can successfully fuse the two together in their own lives. However such a possibility is realizable only for the fortunate few. Most humans are deprived of the opportunity of realizing their potential. Thus for most the realization of this potential would require some form of continued personal life after death. In denying the reality of an afterlife, humanism is committed to the view that for the vast majority existence is in the end irredeemably tragic. The stark fact of the enormity of human suffering through the ages presents the humanist with a problem: is this all sheer, meaningless, unredeemed and unredeemable suffering? Hick sees three ways to evade this possibility and justify this suffering. First, to say that this is all God's will. As Paul puts it (Romans 9:20–21): 'Will what is moulded say to its moulder, "Why have you made me thus?" Has the potter no right over the clay?' This is an attempt at a religious justification which does not require human immortality. Second, to try to justify this suffering in terms of a future state that will evolve out of this painful process. (For an example of such an attempt consider Teilhard de Chardin's picture of the evolution of man into a 'harmonized collectivity of consciousnesses equivalent to a sort of super-consciousness ')[4]

But Hick rejects both of these possibilities on moral grounds. They seem to treat persons as means rather than ends, to devalue the individual's moral status in favour of some future state in which the individual *himself* will not participate. Thus Hick opts for the third possibility and suggests we can justify this suffering in terms of a future state in which the individuals who suffered *themselves* participate. This is the Christian view of life: not a tragedy, but a divine comedy leading to a fulfilment which presupposes our continued existence after death. This is Hick's 'basic religious argument for immortality'.

---

[2] J. M. E. McTaggart, *Some Dogmas of Religion* (London: Edward Arnold, 1906), p. 278.

[3] John Hick, *Death and Eternal Life* (London: Collins, 1976), ch. 8.

[4] Pierre Teilhard de Chardin, *The Phenomenon of Man* (London: Collins, 1959), p. 251.

The argument is, of course, uncompelling. In the first place it doesn't show that *immortality* is a requisite for justifying suffering. All that is required by the argument is sufficient *post-mortem* existence to balance up the inequalities. Secondly, Hick offers no argument to block the possibility of human suffering being unjustifiable. It may be that a tragic view of life is the appropriate one given the facts.

Hick's allusion to the Kantian ethical doctrine that persons ought to be treated as ends and not means recalls to mind an ancestor of this sort of argument for immortality. In the *Critique of Practical Reason* (bk II, ch. II, sect. IV) Kant argues that immortality is a postulate of practical reason, a presupposition of morality. The argument goes as follows. In Kant's view the highest good (*summum bonum*) is the ideal union of moral perfection and complete happiness. This is the goal of practical reason and the possibility of this highest good is demanded by morality. Hence whatever must be presupposed to allow for this possibility is a practically reasonable postulate. Human immortality (together with human freedom and the existence of God) is such a postulate. In the case of immortality this is supposed to follow from the fact that the *summum bonum* is not actually achieved in the observable span of human life. Nevertheless the possibility of the highest good is practically necessary. Thus it is morally reasonable to suppose that human life extends beyond death in order to provide time for the required adjustment between virtue and happiness. Moreover, the argument continues, the finite agent's quest for moral perfection is inherently endless. Progress in virtue can continue *ad infinitum*. Thus it is necessary to postulate an endless duration within which this progress can take place. As Kant puts it, 'the highest good is practically possible only on the supposition of the immortality of the soul, and the latter, as inseparably bound to the moral law, is a postulate of pure practical reason.'[5] Kant concedes, of course, that immortality is 'not as such demonstrable', not a matter of knowledge. However, it is one of our most profoundly reasonable beliefs.

Kant's argument clearly rests upon his moral theory and as such is vulnerable to attack in this direction. However, there are also other ways in which the argument can be resisted. Firstly, we could deny that we are under any obligation to *attain* the highest good; we are only obliged to *strive towards* this unrealizable end. Secondly, the postulation of immortality cannot itself guarantee the attainment of the ultimate moral goal so long as the autonomy of the agent is retained. Finally, the postulate won't really satisfy the practical need for the highest good's achievement. Recall that Kant insists on the endlessness of the afterlife in order to accommodate the infinitely progressive character of virtue. That is, moral perfection remains an unachievable goal. But then immortality is merely the indefinite postponement of the state of affairs demanded by practical reason. What is gained by introducing the *eternal* frustration of the highest good? Why not admit the unachievability of the ideal and abandon any claims to its obligatory character? Since the afterlife will not

---

[5] Immanuel Kant, *Critique of Practical Reason*, trans. Lewis White-Beck (Indianapolis: Bobbs-Merrill, 1956), p. 127.

supply what morality supposedly demands, what warrant do we have for postulating immortality?

A different sort of argument from the conservation of value to immortality utilizes the 'degrees of perfection' principle.[6] Ordinary human life is characteristically imperfect and incomplete. Hence the perfection of humans would typically require an afterlife. But the possibility of perfection is not merely a presupposition of value, for the ability to recognize degrees of perfection implies that perfection exists. Thus immortality is in turn implied. This argument has some resemblance to Aquinas' Fourth Way (*Summa Theologiae* Ia, 2, 3) in that both utilize the 'degrees of perfection' principle.[7] Aquinas begins from the fact that we observe a gradation in things such that some things are more or less good, or true, or noble etc. But comparative terms describe varying degrees of approximation to a superlative, i.e. things are said to be more or less *F* insofar as they approach what is most *F*. Therefore there is something which is the truest and best and noblest of things and hence most fully in being. Moreover, whatever is most *F* is the cause of whatever else is *F*, just as fire is the cause of hot things. Hence there is something that is the cause of being and goodness and any perfection in all things. This, Aquinas concludes, we call 'God'.

Both arguments appeal, then, to the principle that the admission of comparative claims like 'Some things are better than others' commits us to the actual existence of a maximal exemplar of goodness. This Platonic assumption is entirely resistible. From the fact that superlative terms can be defined in terms of comparative terms, nothing significant can be inferred as to the existence of an exemplar of the superlative. Thus degrees of size do not imply that there exits a largest possible thing, except in the sense that there exists a *de facto* largest thing (i.e. if there exists anything, there exists a thing than which there is no larger).[8] Aquinas himself would concede this point with regard to the example of size since he believed that there can be nothing which is unlimited in size (*Summa Theologiae* Ia, 7, 3). He is only concerned that his principle about comparatives apply to perfections which involve absolutely no imperfections: 'transcendental perfections' like truth, goodness, beauty etc. But even so restricted the principle is dubious for it requires the further premise that existence is a perfection. That is, if transcendentally perfect truth did not exist it would not be the perfect truth that is implied by comparative judgments. But since existence is not a perfection, the argument is unsound.

To sum up so far, then, we have seen no reason to suppose that the

---

[6] Cf. J. A. Harvie, 'The immortality of the soul', *Religious Studies* v (1969), 219–20.

[7] Cf. also the proof from goodness in Anselm's *Monologian*, ch. 4. This passage might plausibly be seen as an argument for what Augustine merely asserts in *The City of God* (bk xii, ch. 1).

[8] My objection here assumes the universe to be a finite collection of objects, as Aquinas believed. Hence he rejects the suggestion that there can exist an unlimited number of things (except potentially): 'All created things must be subject therefore to definite enumeration. Thus even a number of things that happens to be unlimited cannot actually exist.' (*Summa Theologiae* Ia, 7, 4). If, however, the universe is unlimited there need not exist even a *de facto* largest thing

prospect of immortality is somehow a requisite of our conceptions of value. Let us now turn to the question of the value of personal immortality.

III

In discussing this question of whether personal immortality would have any value it is fairer not to load the dice by imagining, for example, an eternal future of hideous pain. Clearly this is a disvalue but that does not show immortality to be a disvalue. Rather let's take as our paradigm case the ordinary life with its share of pain and pleasure, joy and sorrow, satisfaction and frustration. Now most people consider their lives worth living: they do not contemplate suicide, but rather attempt to prolong their lives (provided, of course, that conditions do not degenerate too badly). Nor do they generally regret having been born. If their lives are valuable to them in this way, would not the endless extension of them also have value? Let's consider this question by examining some possible scenarios of immortality, stipulating that the quality of life in these imaginary cases can be comparable with the quality of life exhibited by an ordinary mortal life that is considered worthwhile by the person living it.

One possibility is the endless extension of this life. Here, however, we immediately see the importance of our stipulation about quality of life. Ordinary mortal life displays a typical pattern of gradual senility attending aging. That this pattern transposed onto an eternal scale would not be a blessing is well brought out in the tale of the Struldbruggs in Swift's *Gulliver's Travels*.[9] When Gulliver first hears of the immortal Struldbruggs he conceives of such a fate as an extraordinarily fortunate one. He imagines how if he himself had been born such a one he would have pursued the arts and sciences in the company of his fellow immortals, having 'by Thrift and Management' succeeded in the first two hundred years of his life in supplying the wealth necessary for these cultured pursuits. His Luggnuggian hosts are amused at his idealized picture and inform him that in fact the Struldbruggs pass their time quite differently. By the time they are eighty they have 'not only all the Follies and Infirmities of other old Men, but many more which arose from the dreadful Prospect of never dying' (p. 212). As their memories fail them they can no longer remember even the names of things, while the diseases to which they are subject still continue without increasing or diminishing. 'They were,' Gulliver recalls, 'the most mortifying Sight I ever beheld . . . Besides the usual Deformities in extreme Old Age, they acquired an additional Ghastliness in Proportion to their Number of Years' (p. 214). Gulliver's original naive expectations about the desirability of being an immortal were based, his Luggnuggian hosts point out, on an unfounded assumption:

> That the System of Living contrived by me was unreasonable and
> unjust, because it supposed a Perpetuity of Youth, Health, and Vigour,
> which no Man could be so foolish as to hope, however extravagant he

---

[9] Jonathan Swift, *Gulliver's Travels*, ed. Herbert Davis (Oxford: Blackwell, 1959), pp. 207–14.

might be in his Wishes. That, the Question therefore was not whether a man would chuse to be always in the Prime of Youth, attended with Prosperity and Health; but how he would pass a perpetual Life under all the usual Disadvantages which old Age brings along with it (p.211).

This difficulty can be eliminated by considering a different version of the endless extension of this life, a version that satisfies Gulliver's original assumption. Bernard Williams has offered an interesting discussion of such a possibility based upon Karel Čapek's play *The Makropulos Case*.[10] EM, the heroine of this scenario, is 342 years old. She swallowed an elixir of life and for 300 years has been 42. Her life has been frozen and with this unending life has come boredom. She refuses to take the elixir again and dies. Considering this case Williams plausibly locates two conditions that any worthwhile form of personal immortality must satisfy: (i) that it is *me* who survives forever; and (ii) that my eternal future life must be adequately related to the life I have led so far and the aims and values I presently hold.[11] (For brevity I shall refer to these two conditions as respectively 'the identity condition' and 'the adequacy condition'.) The first condition is required to eliminate forms of 'immortality' through one's children, one's deeds etc. that do not involve personal continuance. The second condition is vague, but inevitably so for it depends upon what sort of aims and possibilities I envisage for myself as of now.

Now in the case of EM her life fails to satisfy the adequacy condition. Her problem is boredom: everything has lost its freshness and her life has 'frozen up'. This problem seems inherent in her version of immortality. Her life is just too closely tied up to what has gone before for it to offer any new challenges and rewards. Williams sees this failure to satisfy the adequacy condition as inevitable with such a version of immortality, i.e. an eternal life that is an indefinite extension of the present one. Even if the present life has value for me, the infinite extension of it need not.

IV

Anyway, it does seem true that boredom requires memory of previous experiences. (Not, of course, total recall but at least some degree of recall.) Hence consider instead another scenario of immortality, viz. Nietzsche's 'eternal recurrence':

> This life as you now live it and have lived it, you will have to live once more and innumerable times more; and there will be nothing new in it, but every pain and every joy and every thought and sigh and every-

---

[10] Bernard Williams, *Problems of the Self* (Cambridge: Cambridge University Press, 1973), ch. 6. The EM scenario discussed here is the one presented by Williams. However it differs from that found in Karel Čapek, *The Macropulos Secret*, authorized English translation by Paul Selver (London: Robert Holden, 1927). There EM claims to be 337 years old (p. 170). She took the elixir at 16 (p. 179) but she is commonly taken to be about 30 (pp. 18, 169).

[11] Williams, p. 91.

thing unutterably small or great in your life will have to return to you,
all in the same succession and sequence. . . The eternal hourglass of
existence is turned upside down again and again, and you with it,
speck of dust![12]

How well does this possibility satisfy our identity and adequacy conditions? In the first place consider the identity condition. There are two possible
and contrasting objections that immediately arise here. The first is that the
series of identical lives envisaged means not the infinite repetition of one
person's life but an infinite series of numerically distinct and hence different
persons. The second objection concedes that the recurrence involves the same
person but insists that this 'sameness' entails that there is not an infinite series
of distinct lives but only one life.

Neither objection, however, is overwhelming. The first objection assumes
that a person (or at least his life) has a particular ontological status (like an
individual) such that recurrence will involve duplication. But if we hold (as
Nietzsche did) that a person is a pattern of actions and experiences, then the
repetition of this sequence is all that is required for recurrence to occur. A
person is repeatable just as is a melody (i.e. a sequence of tones). The second
objection appeals, of course, to Leibniz's Identity of Indiscernibles: if two lives
are identical in all respects there are not *two* lives but one. It is not (as with the
first objection) that the other lives are not *mine*. Rather the point is that, since
there is no addition to my present experience represented in the envisaged
recurrence, it makes no sense to talk of *this* occurrence as distinct from any
other exactly similar one. But this Leibnizian argument presupposes a Leibnizian account of time and space. On an absolutist account of space-time we
can conceive of the possibility of two identical and numerically distinct lives
occurring at different temporal points. True, the person involved in this recurrence cannot recognize that this repetition is taking place. But God (outside of
space-time) could.

Another difficulty arises, however, when we consider that on this scenario
the person involved can have no memory of his previous lives—necessarily,
since otherwise the memory of his last life would make him different from his
immediate predecessor who could not have any memory of a life he had not
yet lived. But with no memory of 'my' previous lives, will it be *me* who lives
them? Of course, personal identity can survive memory gaps in one life. Can it
also survive life to life memory gaps? Surely it can, particularly if we understand the notion of identity here not so much in the strongest metaphysical
sense but in a looser sense. That is, a sense such that personal identity is a
relative notion, a matter of degree. This is what Derek Parfit calls the 'complex
view' about personal identity.[13] On this view the identities of persons are

[12] Friedrich Nietzsche, *The Gay Science*, trans. by Walter Kaufmann (New York: Random
House, 1974), sect. 341.

[13] See 'Personal identity', *Philosophical Review* LXXX (1971), 3–27; 'On "The Importance of Self-
Identity"', *Journal of Philosophy* LXVIII (1971), 683, 90; 'Later Selves and Moral Principles' in

rather like the identities of nations. What is involved are certain continuities; psychological and bodily in the case of personal identity. Survival is a matter of degree. A life can be viewed as a succession of selves with no underlying, persisting person. The connections between past and future selves are connections of similarity, a relation that admits of degrees.

The importance of these weaker connections of similarity (perfect similarity in the case of eternal recurrence) can be highlighted by the consideration of the thought-experiment of choosing such a recurrence. Now on a practical level it seems reasonable to avoid future pain even if there is no memory connection between present and future selves. This is well brought out by Peirce:

> 'If the power to remember dies with the material body, has the question of any single person's future life after death any particular interest for him?', . . Now if we had a drug which would abolish memory for a while, and you were going to be cut for the stone, suppose the surgeon were to say, 'You will suffer damnably, but I will administer this drug so that you will during that suffering lose all memory of your previous life. Now you have of course no particular interest in your sufferings as long as you will not remember your present and past life, you know, have you?'[14]

Pragmatically speaking it appears that psychological continuities between present and future selves are sufficient to ground emotional empathy for, or a practical egoistic decision concerning the future self, even if metaphysically it is not identical with the present self but rather a duplicate.

So much for the identity condition then. What of the adequacy condition? There is, of course no memory of having lived this life before so no boredom of EM's type is possible. Nevertheless, even if I won't be bored in her manner, my life will still be frozen in that it will be endlessly repeated. Does this repetitiveness matter? Does it violate the adequacy condition? One possible difficulty that could seem to arise is that eternal recurrence seems incompatible with goal-oriented life planning. If a life is thought to have meaning insofar as it approaches a particular goal, then (given eternal recurrence) either that goal can never occur, or it has already occurred an infinite number of times. But to meet this objection we can relativize the notion of goal such that each iterated transformation has a goal which renders it meaningful.

Suppose, however, that we introduce the concept of our having *knowledge* of the eternal recurrence into our scenario. Such knowledge could, of course, effect no change in the recurrence. Nevertheless Nietzsche thought such

Alan Montefiore (ed.), *Philosophy and Personal Relations* (Montreal: McGill Queen's University Press, 1973). For the contrary claim that only the 'simple view' of personal identity can satisfy our hopes and fears about immortality see Richard Swinburne, 'Personal identity', *Proceedings of the Aristotelian Society* LXXIV (1973–4), 231–47; 'Persons and personal identity' in H. D. Lewis (ed.), *Contemporary British Philosophy, Fourth Series* (London: George Allen and Unwin, 1976).

[14] Charles Sanders Peirce, *Collected Papers*, ed. by Charles Hartshorne and Paul Weiss (Cambridge, Mass.: Harvard University Press, 1935), 6.521.

knowledge might be liberating. If this life is your eternal life then what matters is what you eternally do. The task is to give style to one's character and meaning to one's life to the extent that one can joyously affirm one's existence and welcome its eternal recurrence. This is, as it were, the optimistic perspective on eternal recurrence.

However the doctrine seems at least plausibly to allow of a pessimistic perspective. The knowledge that we will have to endlessly repeat all that we have done could just as easily be experienced as crushing. The tedium of the picture is depressing. Just as a gesture repeated endlessly ceases to have the significance it originally did, so too with every episode in our lives until the ceaseless recurrence is felt to make every gesture senseless. Besides, there is a moral difficulty involved. Most lives include many wrong actions. The prospect of an infinite repetition of such wrong doings is distressing morally. Indeed, given the option of choosing such a recurrence, it may be that one is morally obliged to refuse it.

V

Perhaps these difficulties only arise with the eternal recurrence because each recurrence is an exact duplicate of the last. Consider instead, then, a series of disjoint lives such as is posited by Indian doctrines of rebirth. This does, of course, present some difficulties for the identity condition. For example, if memory is invoked as a sufficient condition of identity then we're back with the EM scenario and not with an alternative prospect. However, let's suppose that these difficulties can be met. What, then, of the adequacy condition? Well at least EM's type of boredom can be avoided if we eliminate memory of past lives. Moreover, the possible variety of the disjoint lives presents an important disanalogy with the eternal recurrence scenario. Nevertheless the prospect of an infinite series of such lives ultimately may prove as nauseating as the prospect of eternal recurrence. Even allowing for considerable variety, human lives exhibit a number of characteristic general traits. And the prospect of this recurrence can just as easily be viewed pessimistically as the prospect of the eternal recurrence of this life.

Interestingly Bernard Williams seems to disagree here:

> . . . I must confess that out of the alternatives it is the only one that for me would, if it had sense, have any attraction—no doubt because it is the only one which has the feature that what one is living at any given point is actually *a life*. It is singular that those systems of belief that get closest to actually accepting recurrence of this sort seem, almost without exception, to look forward to the point when one will be released from it. Such systems seem less interested in continuing one's life than in earning one the right to a superior sort of death.[15]

Is it that this prospect (like that of eternal recurrence) seems also to admit of

---

[15] Williams, pp. 93–4.

both optimistic and pessimistic perspectives? What does the difference here consist in?

The difference between the optimist and the pessimist here is a difficult one to grasp. Is it a disagreement about the facts? Not necessarily, suggests a well-known aphorism: 'The optimist proclaims that we live in the best of all possible worlds; and the pessimist fears that this is so.' The point of this aphorism, of course, is that both agree on the facts. In the terminology of the emotivists, what we seem to have here is an agreement in belief but a difference in attitude. Is there any way to break this deadlock? One way would be to try to change the beliefs of those involved. But it seems possible that there could be agreement on these and yet disagreement on the attitudes taken to the prospect of immortality. Of course judgements like 'boring', 'painful' etc. are difficult to analyse here. Insofar as they are construed as hedonic judgements they seem incorrigible. Disputes over whether the pleasures of eternal existence would outweigh the disadvantages are disputes to which empirical beliefs are obviously relevant. However the assertion 'I find immortality enjoyable and hence it is' seems more a straightforwardly incorrigible report about the speaker's hedonic states. It cannot be overturned by a rectificatory judgement of the form: 'Immortality is not enjoyable, though you mistakenly feel it to be so'.

Now in the Indian context (to which, presumably, Williams is alluding) the beginningless cycle of birth, death and rebirth (saṃsāra) is held to be inevitably characterized by duḥkha (suffering, sorrow). But it is also recognized that the ordinary person, while not insensitive to the sorrows of life, generally feels that the transitory pleasures of life are sufficient in their intensity to compensate. This attitude of the worldling is considered by most Indian philosophers and religious thinkers to be one of the ordinary person's many ignorances. Indeed it is ignorance (avidyā) that keeps such a person caught in the vicious circle of saṃsāra. Clearly 'duḥkha' is not simply a descriptive hedonic term, for then there could be no disputing the claim 'I find saṃsāra enjoyable, hence it is so'. Rather it is an evaluative term to be construed as more objective than a mere subjective feeling. Moreover duḥkha is not to be identified with pain, for pleasure (sukha) is widely acknowledged to be included in duḥkha. This is because worldly pleasure is inextricably entangled with pain, though not *vice versa*. (This point leads in turn to a disagreement among Indian philosophers as to whether liberation from the bondage of saṃsāra would involve some kind of eternal, positive pleasure. Thus the Nyāya, for example, holds liberation merely to involve absence of pain, whereas Advaita Vedanta maintains that the liberated soul experiences a positive bliss.[16]

Empirical observations are, however, relevant to the claim 'Life is duḥkha'. Indeed close attention to the world is thought to bring this point home with particular force as we see how little our flickering joys alleviate the corresponding worries and dissatisfactions. But perhaps no entailment can be shown between such empirical observations and the judgement that all is duḥkha. However this in turn need not entail that duḥkha is merely a subjective

---

[16] For an interesting discussion of this debate, based primarily on Nyāya materials, see A. Chakrabarti, 'Is liberation (Mokṣa) pleasant?', *Philosophy East and West* xxxiii (1983), 167–82.

feeling, nor that the judgement 'Life is *duḥkha*' is not a more appropriate response to the prospect of *saṃsāra* than the view of the hedonistic Cārvāka who mocks that all this would be as foolish as to give up rice because rice comes enfolded in husks.

VI

Some further interesting aspects of Indian thought can be highlighted by considering yet another scenario of immortality. Thus consider the possibility of an eternal existence constantly improving in all ways. (This is rather like the possibility envisaged in the Kantian argument for the postulate of immortality we discussed earlier, but it also incorporates features from the other two arguments of that section.) This scenario may not represent a necessary condition for value, but it might be claimed to be a sufficient condition for value. However this claim too is unfounded. What makes such a life valuable is not its eternal extension but the valuable qualities it exhibits. Now the defender of this version of immortality will want to claim that the life's continuous improvement means that it would be a disvalue to end it at any point. However it cannot be a disvalue for the person who dies because that the person is in existence is a presupposition of any claim that something is a disvalue (or value) for them. But perhaps what is being suggested is that we accede to a Platonistic principle that it is better for a (valuable) thing to exist than for it not to exist.[17] This, however, is to commit the familiar error of treating existence as a perfection so that a thing is better for existing than for not existing. It may, of course, be better for us (as existing beings) that a good thing exist but the thing itself is no better for existing. Rather its existence is a precondition of its having any value at all. As Gassendi put it, criticizing Descartes:

> But, sooth to say, existence is a perfection neither in God nor in anything else; it is rather that in the absence of which there is no perfection. . . Hence neither is existence held to exist in a thing in that way that perfections do, nor if the thing lacks existence is it said to be imperfect (or deprived of a perfection), so much as to be nothing.[18]

Now the metaphysics of Platonism and Neo-Platonism assert the identity of being and goodness and this doctrine was in turn incorporated into Christianity. But Platonism aside, no argument seems to be offered for the view that it is greater to exist in reality than not to do so. Of course, it is true that we do

---

[17] I call this principle 'Platonistic' since it seems to have an ancestral link with Plato's view that Goodness itself is the source of both being and goodness in everything else (*Republic* 509). The identity of being and goodness is certainly evident in Neo-Platonism: witness Plotinus' claim that the One is both Being itself and Good itself. Augustine takes over this view when he says that 'every entity, even if it is a defective one, in so far as it is an entity, is good' (*Enchiridion*, ch. xiii). The principle that it is greater to exist in reality than not to do so is, of course, a presumption of Anselm's first ontological argument (*Proslogian*, ch. ii).

[18] *The Philosophical Works of Descartes*, trans. by E. S. Haldane and G. R. T. Ross (New York: Dover, 1955), vol. ii, p. 186.

tend unreflectively to believe that it is better for us to exist in reality than in thought only. Indeed it might seem that otherwise we would have no reason to remain voluntarily in existence. But is this assumption justified? In the first place it is unclear what it is to compare the value of a real object with a merely imaginary object of the same description. One of two real objects may be better than the other, but how are real objects better or worse than imaginary ones? The Platonic principle, however, requires such comparisons. But if we assume a Strawsonian account of referring here, then the truth-value of assertions of sentences of the form 'The *f* is *g*' presupposes the existence of the entity the subject noun phrase refers to. If the subject of the sentence is only an imaginary object then, though the sentence is meaningful, the statement made in asserting that sentence is neither true nor false because one of its presuppositions is false. (Of course some philosophers wish to deny that value judgements have truth-values anyway and thus neither, on this account, will comparative value judgements. But presumably this position will hardly appeal to the Platonist.) Secondly, it does seem true that my desires can create interests which would be frustrated by my ceasing to exist and in this sense I can have a reason for voluntarily remaining in existence. But then it is the fulfilment of my interests that is the intrinsic value, not my continued existence.

This point in turn brings out another important Platonistic assumption about ultimate value that underpins a good deal of Christian theology and indeed much of Western thought: viz. that perfection is an intrinsic value, a good valued not for what it leads to but for what it is.[19] Given the doctrine of the identity of being and goodness, this seemed plausible. Indian thought, however, considers the quest for perfection to be the pursuit of an instrumental value. Perfection is valuable because it leads to the elimination of suffering (*duḥkha*) and it is the elimination of suffering that is intrinsically valuable, indeed the ultimate value. This is clearly implied by the structure of the Four Noble Truths in Buddhism. It is also apparent in philosophical Hinduism. Thus the *Sāmkhyakārikā* begins: 'Because of the torment of the threefold suffering arises the desire to know the means of removing it.' And the *Nyāyasūtra* defines final release, the highest good (*niḥśreyasa*, literally 'having no better') in terms of the complete absence of *duḥkha*. (Compare the Buddhist concept of *nirvāṇa*.) Thus to the question, 'Why pursue the goal of perfection?' the Platonist has no answer other than, 'Because it is intrinsically valuable.' But Indian thinkers reply, 'Because it leads to the elimination of suffering.' This is a fundamental value difference between Western (Platonistic) thought and Indian thought. Moreover, the Indians also have a reply to the objection that if it is not better to exist in reality than merely in thought, then we can have no reason to remain voluntarily in existence. They hold that it is impossible to exit voluntarily from the circle of *saṃsāra* except by becoming a perfected being. The suicide is simply reborn in even more unfavourable circumstances.

With regard to the relative plausibility of claiming perfection or absence of

---

[19] On perfectionism in Western thought see A. Newton Flew, *The Idea of Perfection in Christian Theology* (London: Oxford University Press, 1934); John Passmore, *The Perfectibility of Man* (New York: Charles Scribner's Sons, 1970).

suffering to be ultimate intrinsic values, the situation is rather more difficult. Consider, however, these two questions: (i) Why do you want to be perfect?; and (ii) Why do you want to eliminate suffering? Now (ii) seems to be un-answerable in that anyone acting contrary to the general principle of eliminat-ing suffering would seem irrational. Of course there might appear to be some counterexamples. The masochist, for instance, seeks suffering; but that is because it provides a greater pleasure. The saint ignores his own suffering; but that is in favour of eliminating the suffering of others. Altruism is perfectly consistent with taking the elimination of suffering generally to be an intrinsic value. Consider (i), however. Fania Pascal recalls a conversation with Wittgenstein:

> At one stage I cried out: 'What is it? You want to be perfect?' And he pulled himself up proudly, saying: 'Of *course* I want to be perfect'.[20]

The anecdote has piquancy precisely because the 'Of *course*' is not trivial. What makes Wittgenstein's reply so revealing of his character is that this goal seemed so *obviously* the right one to him. Nevertheless it certainly does not seem irrational to set oneself a different goal in the way that denying the goal of eliminating suffering seems irrational. Now this feature does not show that perfection is not an intrinsic value—we could admit a plurality of intrinsic values. But it does lend plausibility to the suggestion that perfection is a less *basic* intrinsic value than elimination of suffering. Anyway, given that the elimination of suffering is a basic intrinsic value in this way and given also some not unreasonable empirical observations about the nature of the world, the Indians do not generally consider personal immortality to be of value. (Unless, of course, it is instrumentally valuable in eliminating the suffering of others: consider the *bodhisattva* ideal in Mahāyāna Buddhism.)

VII

One final scenario. It might be thought that my discussion so far is deficient in an important respect. I have taken 'immortality' to mean endless temporal duration, whereas it should be understood to mean *timelessness*. This inter-pretation chimes in with the Christian theological tradition that holds God to be a timeless being. Now the theological doctrine of God's timelessness was held by a number of influential figures including Augustine, Boethius and Aquinas—though whether the theist is wise to adopt such a view of God is dubious.[21] However it is clear that the notion of timeless *post-mortem* existence won't help make the doctrine of immortality any more attractive. Indeed immortality thus understood would fail to satisfy both the identity and the adequacy conditions.

---

[20] 'Wittgenstein: a personal memoir' in C. G. Luckhardt (ed.), *Wittgenstein: Sources and Perspec-tives* (Hassocks: Harvester Press, 1979), p. 48.

[21] A good discussion of this question is to be found in Nelson Pike, *God and Timelessness* (London: Routledge and Kegan Paul, 1970).

The identity condition will not be satisfied because a timeless being will not clearly be *me*. A timeless being could not deliberate and reflect since these mental acts take time, i.e. they require that the agent have temporal *extension*. Nor could a timeless being anticipate or intend, since these activities require that the agent have temporal *position* relative to what is anticipated or intended. Nor could a timeless being remember, since such a being cannot have a past. Thus there is a large class of actions that a timeless being must be incapable of. Indeed this class of actions is so large that it is unclear that such a being could even be counted as a *person* at all. But even if such a being were marginally to count as a person, just how much of a person would he be? This question impinges on both the identity and adequacy conditions. Firstly, even if the timeless being is a person, is he enough of a person to be *me*? Secondly, even if the timeless person is me, would such a circumscribed mode of existence be valuable? With regard to this latter question we have good reason for negative expectations. Not only would the timeless being be incapable of a huge range of actions, but such a being would be totally immutable. Indeed the logical connection between total immutability and timelessness seems to have been a major theological motive for the claim that God is timeless. Hence Aquinas held that 'something lacking change and never varying its mode of existence will not display a before and after' (*Summa Theologiae* Ia, 10, 1). Thus God's timelessness supposedly 'follows upon unchangeableness, and God alone . . . is altogether unchangeable' (Ia, 10, 3). Aquinas, however, mistook the entailment relation involved between the two doctrines and erroneously held that God's immutability entailed His timelessness, whereas it is God's alleged timelessness that would entail His immutability. But the important point for our purposes here is that the situation of the timeless and hence immutable 'person' is the EM scenario *par excellence*, a scenario that cannot satisfy the adequacy condition.

Finally, it is by no means obvious that the doctrine of timelessness can even be coherently expressed. This is trenchantly brought out in Wittgenstein's remark:

> Philosophers who say: 'after death a timeless state will begin', or: 'at death a timeless state begins', and do not notice that they have used the words 'after' and 'at' and 'begins' in a temporal sense, and that temporality is embedded in their grammar.[22]

VIII

To sum up then. Our first three scenarios each represent a version of immortality, but none of these versions is an attractive one. The fourth scenario is not so much unattractive as insufficient for value. The fifth (timeless) scenario satisfies neither the identity condition nor the adequacy condition. Hence even if a normal life has value for me, this does not entail that the infinite extension

---

[22] Ludwig Wittgenstein, *Culture and Value* (Oxford: Blackwell, 1980), p. 22e.

or repetition of it would. None of these versions of immortality is sufficient to guarantee the meaningfulness of a life. This has, of course, been recognized by some writers. Theists, for example, typically expect a transformed quality of life in the hereafter. But then there is no reason why a life cannot now instance this transformed quality and hence have eternal value. In this spirit Tolstoy insists in his *What I Believe* that 'eternal life' refers to a quality of life *now*. The fear of death is the response to the realization that one's life does not possess this quality and death will destroy its meaning. This line of argument is interestingly developed in D. Z. Phillips' *Death and Immortality*:

> Eternity is not an extension of this present life, but a mode of judging it. Eternity is not more life, but this life seen under certain moral and religious modes of thought.[23]

Immortality is the turning towards these moral attitudes, 'living and dying in a way which could not be rendered pointless by death' (p. 50).

With regard to the adequacy of this sort of account, two separate questions need to be distinguished: (i) Is this sense of 'eternal life' sufficient to guarantee the meaningfulness of a life; and (ii) Is this sort of account adequate to the traditional religious view of immortality? In answer to (i) it seems to me that it is. In answer to (ii) the matter is more complex. Accounts like Phillips' are frequently castigated as 'reductionist'.[24] About this charge I just want to make two points, First, the reductionist charge is always a delicate one to handle. After all (to take but one example), few modern Christian theologians believe all the dogmas that their predecessors did. What is central to a system of religious beliefs and what is not is very difficult to determine. It is prudent to be chary of labelling new interpretations of traditional concepts 'reductionist' if we mean by this 'inadequate'.[25] Secondly, even if Phillips' account is inadequate to traditional Christian understanding of immortality it is necessary to recall the context of his argument. Preliminary to the chapters in *Death and Immortality* that present this account is a critique of traditional views about disembodied existence and resurrection. If Phillips is correct in believing these views to be philosophically incoherent, then the only viable sense of 'eternal life' must be one like that he gives it. But to show this, of course, requires that traditional concepts like disembodied existence, resurrection and rebirth are indeed untenable. And this in turn requires detailed investigation and argument...

---

[23] D. Z. Phillips, *Death and Immortality* (London: Macmillan, 1970), p. 49. Phillips' account here has been influenced by similar suggestions presented in Stewart R. Sutherland, 'Immortality and resurrection', *Religious Studies* III (1968), 377–89; and '"What happens after death?"', *Scottish Journal of Theology* XXII (1969), 404–18. (Compare also to Wittgenstein's *Tractatus* 6.4312.)

[24] See, for example, Patrick Sherry, *Religion, Truth and Language-Games* (London: Macmillan, 1977).

[25] On this point compare J. C. Thornton, 'Religious belief and "Reductionism"', *Sophia* V, no. 3 (Oct. 1966), 3–16.

IX.B. Existentialism and the Creation of Meaning

IX.B.1. All Is Vanity

ECCLESIASTES

Existentialism is a twentieth-century philosophical movement that denies that there is an objective purpose for the existence of the world or human beings. It expresses the sense that life is absurd and meaningless unless individuals are able by their own free choices to create a meaning that will endow their lives with value. But the sense that life may be futile, "a walking shadow, a poor player that struts and frets his hour upon the stage and then is heard no more," as Shakespeare puts it, is by no means new in our century. It is expressed with a tone of cynical bitterness in the following selection from the Hebrew Bible. The author of the book of Ecclesiastes claims to have been a king in Jerusalem and a son of David. If we take this attribution literally, we would infer that it might have been written by King Solomon. In any case, the author depicts himself as wealthy and powerful yet unsatisfied, full of weariness, and anguished with the sense that human existence is futile and vain.

1

The words of the Preacher, the son of David, king in Jerusalem. Vanity of vanities, says the Preacher, vanity of vanities! All is vanity. What does man gain by all the toil at which he toils under the sun? A generation goes, and a generation comes, but the earth remains for ever. The sun rises and the sun goes down, and hastens to the place where it rises. The wind blows to the south, and goes round to the north; round and round goes the wind, and on its circuits the wind returns. All streams run to the sea, but the sea is not full; to the place where the streams flow, there they flow again. All things are full of weariness; a man cannot utter it; the eye is not satisfied with seeing, nor the ear filled with hearing. What has been is what will be, and what has been done is what will be done; and there is nothing new under the

---

Scripture quotations are from the Revised Standard Version Bible, copyright 1946, 1952, 1971 by the Division of Christian Education of the National Council of the Churches of Christ in the U.S.A. Used by permission. Ecclesiastes 1:1–3:14.

sun. Is there a thing of which it is said, "See, this is new"? It has been already, in the ages before us. There is no remembrance of former things, nor will there be any remembrance of later things yet to happen among those who come after.

I the Preacher have been king over Israel in Jerusalem. And I applied my mind to seek and to search out by wisdom all that is done under heaven; it is an unhappy business that God has given to the sons of men to be busy with. I have seen everything that is done under the sun; and behold, all is vanity and striving after wind. What is crooked cannot be made straight, and what is lacking cannot be numbered.

I said to myself, "I have acquired great wisdom, surpassing all who were over Jerusalem before me; and my mind has had great experience of wisdom and knowledge." And I applied my mind to know wisdom and to know madness and folly. I perceived that this also is but a striving after wind. For in much wisdom is much vexation, and he who increases knowledge increases sorrow.

2

I said to myself, "Come now, I will make a test of pleasure; enjoy yourself." But behold, this also was vanity. I said of laughter, "It is mad," and of pleasure, "What use is it?" I searched with my mind how to cheer my body with wine— my mind still guiding me with wisdom—and how to lay hold on folly, till I might see what was good for the sons of men to do under heaven during the few days of their life. I made great works; I built houses and planted vineyards for myself; I made myself gardens and parks, and planted in them all kinds of fruit trees. I bought male and female slaves and had slaves who were born in my house; I had also great possessions of herds and flocks, more than any who had been before me in Jerusalem. I also gathered for myself silver and gold and the treasure of kings and provinces; I got singers, both men and women, and many concubines, man's delight.

So I became great and surpassed all who were before me in Jerusalem; also my wisdom remained with me. And whatever my eyes desired I did not keep from them; I kept my heart from no pleasure, for my heart found pleasure in all my toil, and this was my reward for all my toil. Then I considered all that my hands had done and the toil I had spent in doing it, and behold, all was vanity and a striving after wind, and there was nothing to be gained under the sun.

So I turned to consider wisdom and madness and folly; for what can the man do who comes after the king? Only what he has already done. Then I saw that wisdom excels folly as light excels darkness. The Wise man has his eyes in his head, but the fool walks in darkness; and yet I perceived that one fate comes to all of them. Then I said to myself, "What befalls the fool will befall me also; why then have I been so very wise?" And I said to myself that this also is vanity. For of the wise man as of the fool there is no enduring remembrance, seeing that in the days to come all will have been long forgotten. How the wise man dies just like the fool! So I hated life, because what is done under the sun was grievous to me; for all is vanity and a striving after wind.

I hated all my toil in which I had toiled under the sun, seeing that I must leave it to the man who will come after me; and who knows whether he will be a wise man or a fool? Yet he will be master of all for which I toiled and used my wisdom under the sun. This also is vanity. So I turned about and gave my heart up to despair over all the toil of my labors under the sun, because sometimes a man who has toiled with wisdom and knowledge and skill must leave it all to be enjoyed by a man who did not toil for it. This also is vanity and a great evil. What has a man from all the toil and strain with which he toils beneath the sun? For all his days are full of pain, and his work is a vexation; even in the night his mind does not rest. This also is vanity.

There is nothing better for a man than that he should eat and drink, and find enjoyment in his toil. This also, I saw, is from the hand of God; for apart from him who can eat or who can have enjoyment? For to the man who pleases him God gives wisdom and knowledge and joy; but to the sinner he gives the work of gathering and heaping, only to give to one who pleases God. This also is vanity and a striving after wind.

3

For everything there is a season and a time for every matter under heaven: a time to be born, and a time to die; a time to plant, and a time to pluck up what is planted; a time to kill, and a time to heal; a time to break down, and a time to build up; a time to weep, and a time to laugh; a time to mourn, and a time to dance; a time to cast away stones, and a time to gather stones together; a time to embrace, and a time to refrain from embracing; a time to seek, and a time to lose; a time to keep and a time to cast away; a time to rend and a time to sew; a time to keep silence, and a time to speak; a time to love, and time to hate; a time for war, and a time for peace. What gain has the worker from his toil?

I have seen the business that God has given to the sons of men to be busy with. He has made everything beautiful in its time; also he has put eternity into man's mind, yet so that he cannot find out what God has done from the beginning to the end. I know that there is nothing better for them than to be happy and enjoy themselves as long as they live; also that it is God's gift to man that every one should eat and drink and take pleasure in all his toil. I know that whatever God does endures for ever; nothing can be added to it, nor anything taken from it; God has made it so, in order that men should fear before him.

IX.B.2.   The Myth of Sisyphus

ALBERT CAMUS

*Albert Camus (1913–1960), a journalist, novelist, essayist,
and director of a theatre, was active during World War II in
the French Resistance, editing an important underground
paper called* Combat. *He was awarded the Nobel Prize for
Literature in 1957. His essays and his works of fiction explored the themes of existentialism, particularly the question
whether life has meaning. In his book of essays,* The Myth
of Sisyphus, *from which the following selection is taken,
Camus asserts that there is only one significant philosophical
question, namely, suicide. Judging whether or not life is
worth living is the first and most essential human task. We
tend to think, he says, that the question depends on an
answer to the prior question of whether or not life has a
meaning. If we decide that life has no meaning, this seems to
imply that it is not worth living. Camus, however, insists that
this conclusion is mistaken. He is convinced that human
existence is absurd; there is no objective meaning waiting to be
discovered. There is, however, the possibility of creating meaning, and this is the point Camus illustrates in his resetting of
the myth of Sisyphus. One can hardly imagine a situation
more absurd, more futile, or more conducive to despair than
an eternity of pushing a stone up a hill over and over again.
And yet, to our surprise, Camus tells us we must imagine
Sisyphus as happy. If Sisyphus can create meaning and realize
happiness in his dismal situation, what excuse have we if we
do not do as much?*

The gods had condemned Sisyphus to ceaselessly
rolling a rock to the top of a mountain, whence the stone would fall back of its
own weight. They had thought with some reason that there is no more
dreadful punishment than futile and hopeless labor.

If one believes Homer, Sisyphus was the wisest and most prudent of
mortals. According to another tradition, however, he was disposed to practice
the profession of highwayman. I see no contradiction in this. Opinions differ
as to the reasons why he became the futile laborer of the underworld. To begin
with, he is accused of a certain levity in regard to the gods. He stole their
secrets. Aegina, the daughter of Aesopus, was carried off by Jupiter. The father
was shocked by the disappearance and complained to Sisyphus. He, who

From *The Myth of Sisyphus and Other Essays* by Albert Camus, translated by Justin O'Brien.
Copyright © 1955 by Alfred A. Knopf, Inc., pp. 3–8, 88–91. Reprinted by permission of the
publisher.

knew of the abduction, offered to tell about it on condition that Aesopus would give water to the citadel of Corinth. To the celestial thunderbolts he preferred the benediction of water. He was punished for this in the underworld. Homer tells us also that Sisyphus had put Death in chains. Pluto could not endure the sight of his deserted, silent empire. He dispatched the god of war, who liberated Death from the hands of her conqueror

It is said also that Sisyphus, being near to death, rashly wanted to test his wife's love. He ordered her to cast his unburied body into the middle of the public square. Sisyphus woke up in the underworld. And there, annoyed by an obedience so contrary to human love, he obtained from Pluto permission to return to earth in order to chastise his wife. But when he had seen again the face of this world, enjoyed water and sun, warm stones and the sea, he no longer wanted to go back to the infernal darkness. Recalls, signs of anger, warnings were of no avail. Many years more he lived facing the curve of the gulf, the sparkling sea, and the smiles of earth. A decree of the gods was necessary. Mercury came and seized the impudent man by the collar and, snatching him from his joys, led him forcibly back to the underworld, where his rock was ready for him.

You have already grasped that Sisyphus is the absurd hero. He is, as much through his passions as through his torture. His scorn of the gods, his hatred of death, and his passion for life won him that unspeakable penalty in which the whole being is exerted toward accomplishing nothing. This is the price that must be paid for the passions of this earth. Nothing is told us about Sisyphus in the underworld. Myths are made for the imagination to breathe life into them. As for this myth, one sees merely the whole effort of a body straining to raise the huge stone, to roll it and push it up a slope a hundred times over; one sees the face screwed up, the cheek tight against the stone, the shoulder bracing the clay-covered mass, the foot wedging it, the fresh start with arms outstretched, the wholly human security of two earth-clotted hands. At the very end of his long effort measured by skyless space and time without depth, the purpose is achieved. Then Sisyphus watches the stone rush down in a few moments toward that lower world whence he will have to push it up again toward the summit. He goes back down to the plain.

It is during that return, that pause, that Sisyphus interests me. A face that toils so close to stones is already stone itself? I see that man going back down with a heavy yet measured step toward the torment of which he will never know the end. That hour like a breathing space which returns as surely as his suffering, that is the hour of consciousness. At each of those moments when he leaves the heights and gradually sinks toward the lairs of the gods, he is superior to his fate. He is stronger than his rock.

If this myth is tragic, that is because its hero is conscious. Where would his torture be, indeed, if at every step the hope of succeeding upheld him? The workman of today works every day in his life at the same tasks, and this fate is no less absurd. But it is tragic only at the rare moments when it becomes conscious. Sisyphus, proletarian of the gods, powerless and rebellious, knows the whole extent of his wretched condition: it is what he thinks of during his descent. The lucidity that was to constitute his torture at the same time crowns his victory. There is no fate that cannot be surmounted by scorn.

If the descent is thus sometimes performed in sorrow, it can also take place in joy. This word is not too much. Again I fancy Sisyphus returning toward his rock, and the sorrow was in the beginning. When the images of earth cling too tightly to memory, when the call of happiness becomes too insistent, it happens that melancholy rises in man's heart: this is the rock's victory, this is the rock itself. The boundless grief is too heavy to bear. These are our nights of Gethsemane. But crushing truths perish from being acknowledged. Thus, Oedipus at the outset obeys fate without knowing it. But from the moment he knows, his tragedy begins. Yet at the same moment, blind and desperate, he realizes that the only bond linking him to the world is the cool hand of a girl. Then a tremendous remark rings out: "Despite so many ordeals, my advanced age and the nobility of my soul make me conclude that all is well." Sophocles' Oedipus, like Dostoevsky's Kirilov, thus gives the recipe for the absurd victory. Ancient wisdom confirms modern heroism.

One does not discover the absurd without being tempted to write a manual of happiness. "What! by such narrow ways—?" There is but one world, however. Happiness and the absurd are two sons of the same earth. They are inseparable. It would be a mistake to say that happiness necessarily springs from the absurd discovery. It happens as well that the feeling of the absurd springs from happiness. "I conclude that all is well," says Oedipus, and that remark is sacred. It echoes in the world and limited universe of man. It teaches that all is not, has not been, exhausted. It drives out of this world a god who had come into it with dissatisfaction and a preference for futile sufferings. It makes of fate a human matter, which must be settled among men.

All Sisyphus' silent joy is contained therein. His fate belongs to him. His rock is his thing. Likewise, the absurd man, when he contemplates his torment, silences all the idols. In the universe suddenly restored to its silence, the myriad wondering little voices of the earth rise up. Unconscious, secret calls, invitations from the faces, they are the necessary reverse and price of victory. There is no sun without shadow, and it is essential to know the night. The absurd man says yes and his effort will henceforth be unceasing. If there is a personal fate, there is no higher destiny, or at least there is but one which he concludes is inevitable and despicable. For the rest, he knows himself to be the master of his days. At that subtle moment when man glances backward over his life, Sisyphus returning toward his rock, in that slight pivoting he contemplates that series of unrelated actions which becomes his fate, created by him, combined under his memory's eye and soon sealed by his death. Thus, convinced of the wholly human origin of all that is human, a blind man eager to see who knows that the night has no end, he is still on the go. The rock is still rolling.

I leave Sisyphus at the foot of the mountain! One always finds one's burden again. But Sisyphus teaches the higher fidelity that negates the gods and raises rocks. He too concludes that all is well. This universe henceforth without a master seems to him neither sterile nor futile. Each atom of that stone, each mineral flake of that night-filled mountain, in itself forms a world. The struggle itself toward the heights is enough to fill a man's heart. One must imagine Sisyphus happy.

IX.B.3. The Humanism of Existentialism

JEAN-PAUL SARTRE

*The French philosopher, journalist, and political activist
Jean-Paul Sartre (1905–1980) is probably the most widely
read of the atheistic existentialists. He was captured by the
Nazi army during World War II, escaped, and thereafter
participated actively in the underground Resistance movement. Sartre's novels and plays not only laid out central
existentialist themes but also carried messages designed to stir
the French to action against the Nazi occupation. His thought
owed much to such earlier philosophers as Nietzsche,
Kierkegaard, and Heidegger—and his technical philosophical
writings are nearly as opaque as Heidegger's—but in his
popular works, especially his works of fiction, Sartre succeeded in translating complicated philosophical doctrines into
clear ideas that most people could understand and poignant
images with which everyone who has felt the anxiety of
existential groundlessness and absurdity can identify.*

*Offered the Nobel Prize for Literature, Sartre refused it,
fearing that it might have an effect he did not want on East-
West political relations. He hammered away relentlessly at
what he called "bad faith," the tendency of individuals to
refuse to acknowledge their freedom or take responsibility for
their deeds and their character. He asserted a radical doctrine
of freedom that maintains that an individual, by an act of
will, can literally transform his or her character. Instead of
making excuses by citing childhood hardships or by claiming
lack of opportunities, the individual has a moral responsibility to recognize that his or her personality and character are
the direct result of individual choices. If persons do not approve of who they are, they ought to decide to change and thus
become persons of whom they can approve. Sartre does not
pretend that such a radical transformation is easy. As he
portrays the struggle in his novels and play, his characters
nearly always act out of bad faith and rarely if ever succeed in
exemplifying the opposite and admirable trait that Sartre calls
authenticity. Yet authenticity is possible, and we ought always to strive for it.*

*Sartre's most concise definition of existentialism is em-
bodied in the saying, "Existence precedes essence." In the
following selection, he explains this saying, pointing out that
each person is responsible for what he or she is because what*

From *Existentialism* (New York: Philosophical Library, 1947), pp. 11–39.

we are is the result of what we do and the choices we make. To claim that one might have written the great novel, led a great revolution, or discovered the cure for a dread disease, if only one had had a better education or better opportunities, is bad faith. We do what we think is really important, and our opportunities, however great or small, limit us only to the extent that we allow ourselves to be limited. Because there is no God to determine our lives, and no human nature that we must embody, we are radically free. We exist first, and then we create our essences by our choices. Sartre calls us to avoid bad faith, to stop making excuses, to take on ourselves the responsibility of our freedom: In these ways we can create essences for ourselves that express the values we recognize as good.

I should like on this occasion to defend existentialism against some charges which have been brought against it.

First, it has been charged with inviting people to remain in a kind of desperate quietism because, since no solutions are possible, we should have to consider action in this world as quite impossible. We should then end up in a philosophy of contemplation; and since contemplation is a luxury, we come in the end to a bourgeois philosophy. The communists in particular have made these charges.

On the other hand, we have been charged with dwelling on human degradation, with pointing up everywhere the sordid, shady, and slimy, and neglecting the gracious and beautiful, the bright side of human nature; for example, according to Mlle. Mercier, a Catholic critic, with forgetting the smile of the child. Both sides charge us with having ignored human solidarity, with considering man as an isolated being. The communists say that the main reason for this is that we take pure subjectivity, the *Cartesian I think,* as our starting point; in other words, the moment in which man becomes fully aware of what it means to him to be an isolated being; as a result, we are unable to return to a state of solidarity with the men who are not ourselves, a state which we can never reach in the *cogito.*

From the Christian standpoint, we are charged with denying the reality and seriousness of human undertakings, since, if we reject God's commandments and the eternal verities, there no longer remains anything but pure caprice, with everyone permitted to do as he pleases and incapable, from his own point of view, of condemning the points of view and acts of others.

I shall try today to answer these different charges. Many people are going to be surprised at what is said here about humanism. We shall try to see in what sense it is to be understood. In any case, what can be said from the very beginning is that by existentialism we mean a doctrine which makes human life possible and, in addition, declares that every truth and every action implies a human setting a human subjectivity.

As is generally known, the basic charge against us is that we put the emphasis on the dark side of human life. Someone recently told me of a lady who, when she let slip a vulgar word in a moment of irritation, excused herself by saying, "I guess I'm becoming an existentialist." Consequently, existentialism is regarded as something ugly; that is why we are said to be naturalists; and if we are, it is rather surprising that in this day and age we cause so much more alarm and scandal than does naturalism, properly so called. The kind of person who can take in his stride such a novel as Zola's *The Earth* is disgusted as soon as he starts reading an existentialist novel; the kind of person who is resigned to the wisdom of the ages—which is pretty sad—find us even sadder. Yet, what can be more disillusioning than saying "true charity begins at home" or "a scoundrel will always return evil for good?"

We know the commonplace remarks made when this subject comes up, remarks which always add up to the same thing: we shouldn't struggle against the powers-that-be; we shouldn't resist authority; we shouldn't try to rise above our station; any action which doesn't conform to authority is romantic; any effort not based on past experience is doomed to failure; experience shows that man's bent is always toward trouble, that there must be a strong hand to hold him in check, if not, there will be anarchy. There are still people who go on mumbling these melancholy old saws, the people who say, "It's only human!" whenever a more or less repugnant act is pointed out to them, the people who glut themselves on *chansons réalistes*; these are the people who accuse existentialism of being too gloomy, and to such an extent that I wonder whether they are complaining about it, not for its pessimism, but much rather its optimism. Can it be that what really scares them in the doctrine that I shall try to present here is that it leaves to man a possibility of choice? To answer this question, we must re-examine it on a strictly philosophical plane. What is meant by the term *existentialism*?

Most people who use the word would be rather embarrassed if they had to explain it, since, now that the word is all the rage, even the work of a musician or painter is being called existentialist. A gossip columnist in *Clartés* signs himself *The Existentialist*, so that by this time the word has been so stretched and has taken on so broad a meaning, that it no longer means anything at all. It seems that for want of an advance-guard doctrine analogous to surrealism, the kind of people who are eager for scandal and flurry turn to this philosophy which in other respects does not at all serve their purposes in this sphere.

Actually, it is the least scandalous, the most austere of doctrines. It is intended strictly for specialists and philosophers. Yet it can be defined easily. What complicates matters is that there are two kinds of existentialist; first, those who are Christian, among whom I would include Jaspers and Gabriel Marcel, both Catholic; and on the other hand the atheistic existentialists, among whom I class Heidegger, and then the French existentialists and myself. What they have in common is that they think that existence precedes essence, or, if you prefer, that subjectivity must be the starting point.

Just what does that mean? Let us consider some object that is manufactured, for example, a book or a paper cutter: here is an object which has been made by an artisan whose inspiration came from a concept. He referred to the concept of what a paper-cutter is and likewise to a known method of production, which is part of the concept, something which is, by and large, a routine. Thus, the paper-cutter is at once an object produced in a certain way and, on the other hand, one having a specific use; and one can not postulate a man who produces a paper-cutter but does not know what it is used for. Therefore, let us say that, for the paper-cutter, essence—that is, the ensemble of both the production routines and the properties which enable it to be both produced and defined—precedes existence. Thus, the presence of the paper-cutter or book in front of me is determined. Therefore, we have here a technical view of the world whereby it can be said that production precedes existence.

When we conceive God as the Creator, he is generally thought of as a superior sort of artisan. Whatever doctrine we may be considering, whether one like that of Descartes or that of Leibnitz, we always grant that will more or less follows understanding or, at the very least, accompanies it, and that when God creates He knows exactly what He is creating. Thus, the concept of man in the mind of God is comparable to the concept of paper-cutter in the mind of the manufacturer, and, following certain techniques and a conception, God produces man, just as the artisan, following a definition and a technique, makes a paper-cutter. Thus, the individual man is the realisation of a certain concept in the divine intelligence.

In the eighteenth century, the atheism of the *philosophes* discarded the idea of God, but not so much for the notion that essence precedes existence. To a certain extent, this idea is found everywhere; we find it in Diderot, in Voltaire, and even in Kant. Man has a human nature; this human nature, which is the concept of the human, is found in all men, which means that each man is a particular example of a universal concept, man. In Kant, the result of this universality is that the wild-man, the natural man, as well as the bourgeois, are circumscribed by the same definition and have the same basic qualities. Thus, here too the essence of man precedes the historical existence that we find in nature.

Atheistic existentialism, which I represent, is more coherent. It states that if God does not exist, there is at least one being in whom existence precedes essence, a being who exists before he can be defined by any concept, and that this being is man, or, as Heidegger says, human reality. What is meant here by saying that existence precedes essence? It means that, first of all, man exists, turns up, appears on the scene, and, only afterwards, defines himself. If man, as the existentialist conceives him, is indefinable, it is because at first he is nothing. Only afterward will he be something, and he himself will have made what he will be. Thus, there is no human nature, since there is no God to conceive it. Not only is man what he conceives himself to be, but he is also only what he wills himself to be after this thrust toward existence.

Man is nothing else but what he makes of himself. Such is the first principle of existentialism. It is also what is called subjectivity, the name we are labeled with when charges are brought against us. But what do we mean by this, if not that man has a greater dignity than a stone or table? For we mean that man first exists, that is, that man first of all is the being who hurls himself toward a future and who is conscious of imagining himself as being in the future. Man is at the start a plan which is aware of itself, rather than a patch of moss, a piece of garbage, or a cauliflower; nothing exists prior to this plan; there is nothing in heaven; man will be what he will have planned to be. Not what he will want to be. Because by the word "will" we generally mean a conscious decision, which is subsequent to what we have already made of ourselves. I may want to belong to a political party, write a book, get married; but all that is only a manifestation of an earlier, more spontaneous choice that is called "will." But if existence really does precede essence, man is responsible for what he is. Thus, existentialism's first move is to make every man aware of what he is and to make the full responsibility of his existence rest on him. And when we say that a man is responsible for himself, we do not only mean that he is responsible for his own individuality, but that he is responsible for all men.

The word subjectivism has two meanings, and our opponents play on the two. Subjectivism means, on the one hand, that an individual chooses and makes himself; and, on the other, that it is impossible for a man to transcend human subjectivity. The second of these is the essential meaning of existentialism. When we say that man chooses his own self, we mean that every one of us does likewise; but we also mean by that that in making this choice he also chooses all men. In fact, in creating the man that we want to be, there is not a single one of our acts which does not at the same time create an image of man as we think he ought to be. To choose to be this or that is to affirm at the same time the value of what we choose, because we can never choose evil. We always choose the good, and nothing can be good for us without being good for all.

If, on the other hand, existence precedes essence, and if we grant that we exist and fashion our image at one and the same time, the image is valid for everybody and for our whole age. Thus, our responsibility is much greater than we might have supposed, because it involves all mankind. If I am a workingman and choose to join a Christian trade-union rather than be a communist, and if by being a member I want to show that the best thing for man is resignation, that the kingdom of man is not of this world, I am not only involving my own case—I want to be resigned for everyone. As a result, my action has involved all humanity. To take a more individual matter, if I want to marry, to have children; even if this marriage depends solely on my own circumstances or passion or wish, I am involving all humanity in monogamy and not merely myself. Therefore, I am responsible for myself and for everyone else. I am creating a certain image of man of my own choosing. In choosing myself, I choose man.

This helps us understand what the actual content is of such rather grandiloquent words as anguish, forlornness, despair. As you will see, it's all quite simple.

First, what is meant by anguish? The existentialists say at once that man is anguish. What that means is this: the man who involves himself and who realizes that he is not only the person he chooses to be, but also a law-maker who is, at the same time, choosing all mankind as well as himself, can not help escape the feeling of his total and deep responsibility. Of course, there are many people who are not anxious; but we claim that they are hiding their anxiety, that they are fleeing from it. Certainly, many people believe that when they do something, they themselves are the only ones involved, and when someone says to them, "What if everyone acted that way?" they shrug their shoulders and answer, "Everyone doesn't act that way." But really, one should always ask himself, "What would happen if everybody looked at things that way?" There is no escaping the disturbing thought except by a kind of double-dealing. A man who lies and makes excuses for himself by saying "not everybody does that," is someone with an uneasy conscience, because the act of lying implies that a universal value is conferred upon the lie.

Anguish is evident even when it conceals itself. This is the anguish that Kierkegaard called the anguish of Abraham. You know the story: an angel has ordered Abraham to sacrifice his son; if it really were an angel who has come and said, "You are Abraham, you shall sacrifice your son," everything would be all right. But everyone might first wonder, "Is it really an angel, and am I really Abraham? What proof do I have?"

There was a madwoman who had hallucinations; someone used to speak to her on the telephone and give her orders. Her doctor asked her, "Who is it who talks to you?" She answered, "He says it's God." What proof did she really have that it was God? If an angel comes to me, what proof is there that it's an angel? And if I hear voices, what proof is there that they come from heaven and not from hell, or from the subconscious, or a pathological condition? What proves that they are addressed to me? What proof is there that I have been appointed to impose my choice and my conception of man on humanity? I'll never find any proof or sign to convince me of that. If a voice addresses me, it is always for me to decide that this is the angel's voice; if I consider that such an act is a good one, it is I who will choose to say that it is good rather than bad.

Now, I'm not being singled out as an Abraham, and yet at every moment I'm obliged to perform exemplary acts. For every man, everything happens as if all mankind had its eyes fixed on him and were guiding itself by what he does. And every man ought to say to himself, "Am I really the kind of man who has the right to act in such a way that humanity might guide itself by my actions?" And if he does not say that to himself, he is masking his anguish.

There is no question here of the kind of anguish which would lead to quietism, to inaction. It is a matter of a simple sort of anguish that anybody who has had responsibilities is familiar with. For example, when a military officer takes the responsibility for an attack and sends a certain number of men to death, he chooses to do so, and in the main he alone makes the choice. Doubtless, orders come from above, but they are too broad; he interprets them, and on this interpretation depend the lives of ten or fourteen or twenty men. In making a decision he can not help having a certain anguish. All leaders know this anguish. That doesn't keep them from acting; on the contrary, it is the very condition of their action. For it implies that they envisage a number of possibilities, and when they choose one, they realize that it has value only because it is chosen. We shall see that this kind of anguish, which is the kind that existentialism describes, is explained, in addition, by a direct responsibility to the other men whom it involves. It is not a curtain separating us from action, but is part of action itself.

When we speak of forlornness, a term Heidegger was fond of, we mean only that God does not exist and that we have to face all the consequences of this. The existentialist is strongly opposed to a certain kind of secular ethics which would like to abolish God with the least possible expense. About 1880, some French teachers tried to set up a secular ethics which went something like this: God is a useless and costly hypothesis; we are discarding it; but, meanwhile, in order for there to be an ethics, a society, a civilization, it is essential that certain values be taken seriously and that they be considered as having an *a priori* existence. It must be obligatory, *a priori*, to be honest, not to lie, not to beat your wife, to have children, etc., etc. So we're going to try a little device which will make it possible to show that values exist all the same, inscribed in a heaven of ideas, though otherwise God does not exist. In other words—and this, I believe, is the tendency of everything called reformism in France—nothing will be changed if God does not exist. We shall find ourselves with the same norms of honesty, progress, and humanism, and we shall have made of God an outdated hypothesis which will peacefully die off by itself.

The existentialist, on the contrary, thinks it very distressing that God does not exist, because all possibility of finding values in a heaven of ideas disappears along with Him; there can no longer be an *a priori* Good, since there is no infinite and perfect consciousness to think it. Nowhere is it written that the Good exists, that we must be honest, that we must not lie; because the fact is we are on a plane where there are only men. Dostoievsky said, "If God didn't exist, everything would be possible." That is the very starting point of existentialism. Indeed, everything is permissible if God does not exist, and as a result man is forlorn, because neither within him nor without does he find anything to cling to. He can't start making excuses for himself.

If existence really does precede essence, there is no explaining things away by reference to a fixed and given human nature. In other words, there is no determinism, man is free, man is freedom. On the other hand, if God does not exist, we find no values or commands to turn to which legitimize our conduct. So, in the bright realm of values, we have no excuse behind us, nor justification before us. We are alone, with no excuses.

That is the idea I shall try to convey when I say that man is condemned to be free. Condemned, because he did not create himself, yet, in other respects is free; because, once thrown into the world, he is responsible for everything he does. The existentialist does not believe in the power of passion. He will never agree that a sweeping passion is a ravaging torrent which fatally leads a man to certain acts and is therefore an excuse. He thinks that man is responsible for his passion.

The existentialist does not think that man is going to help himself by finding in the world some omen by which to orient himself. Because he thinks that man will interpret the omen to suit himself. Therefore, he thinks that man, with no support and no aid, is condemned every moment to invent man. Ponge, in a very fine article, has said, "Man is the future of man." That's exactly it. But if it is taken to mean that this future is recorded in heaven, that God sees it, then it is false, because it would really no longer be a future. If it is taken to mean that, whatever a man may be, there is a future to be forged, a virgin future before him, then this remark is sound. But then we are forlorn.

To give you an example which will enable you to understand forlornness better, I shall cite the case of one of my students who came to see me under the following circumstances: his father was on bad terms with his mother, and, moreover, was inclined to be a collaborationist; his older brother had been killed in the German offensive of 1940, and the young man, with somewhat immature but generous feelings, wanted to avenge him. His mother lived alone with him, very much upset by the half-treason of her husband and the death of her older son; the boy was her only consolation.

The boy was faced with the choice of leaving for England and joining the Free French Forces—that is, leaving his mother behind—or remaining with his mother and helping her to carry on. He was fully aware that the woman lived only for him and that his going-off—and perhaps his death—would plunge her into despair. He was also aware that every act that he did for his mother's sake was a sure thing, in the sense that it was helping her to carry on, whereas every effort he made toward going off and fighting was an uncertain move which might run aground and prove completely useless; for example, on his way to England he might, while passing through Spain, be detained indefinitely in a Spanish camp; he might reach England or Algiers and be stuck in an office at a desk job. As a result, he was faced with two very different kinds of action: one, concrete, immediate, but concerning only one individual; the other concerned an incomparably vaster group, a national collectivity, but for that very reason was dubious, and might be interrupted en route. And, at the same time, he was wavering between two kinds of ethics. On the one hand, an ethics of sympathy, of personal devotion; on the other, a broader ethics, but one whose efficacy was more dubious. He had to choose between the two.

Who could help him choose? Christian doctrine? No. Christian doctrine says, "Be charitable, love your neighbor, take the more rugged path, etc., etc." But which is the more rugged path? Whom should he love as a brother? The fighting man or his mother? Which does the greater good, the vague act of fighting in a group, or the concrete one of helping a particular human being to go on living? Who can decide *a priori*? Nobody. No book of ethics can tell him. The Kantian ethics says, "Never treat any person as a means, but as an end." Very well, if I stay with my mother, I'll treat her as an end and not as a means; but by virtue of this very fact, I'm running the risk of treating the people around me who are fighting, as means; and, conversely, if I go to join those who are fighting, I'll be treating them as an end, and, by doing that, I run the risk of treating my mother as a means.

If values are vague, and if they are always too broad for the concrete and specific case that we are considering, the only thing left for us is to trust our instincts. That's what this young man tried to do; and when I saw him, he said, "In the end, feeling is what counts. I ought to choose whichever pushes me in one direction. If I feel that I love my mother enough to sacrifice everything else for her—my desire for vengeance, for action, for adventure—then I'll stay with her. If, on the contrary, I feel that my love for my mother isn't enough, I'll leave."

But how is the value of a feeling determined? What gives his feeling for his mother value? Precisely the fact that he remained with her. I may say that I like so-and-so well enough to sacrifice a certain amount of money for him, but I may say so only if I've done it. I may say "I love my mother well enough to remain with her" if I have remained with her. The only way to determine the value of this affection is, precisely, to perform an act which confirms and defines it. But, since I require this affection to justify my act, I find myself caught in a vicious circle.

On the other hand, Gide has well said that a mock feeling and a true feeling are almost indistinguishable; to decide that I love my mother and will remain with her, or to remain with her by putting on an act, amount somewhat to the same thing. In other words, the feeling is formed by the acts one performs; so, I can not refer to it in order to act upon it. Which means that I can neither seek within myself the true condition which will impel me to act, nor apply to a system of ethics for concepts which will permit me to act. You will say, "At least, he did go to a teacher for advice." But if you seek advice from a priest, for example, you have chosen this priest; you already knew, more or less, just about what advice he was going to give you. In other words, choosing your adviser is involving yourself. The proof of this is that if you are a Christian, you will say, "Consult a priest." But some priests are collaborating, some are just marking time, some are resisting. Which to choose? If the young man chooses a priest who is resisting or collaborating, he has already decided on the kind of advice he's going to get. Therefore, in coming to see me he knew the answer I was going to give him, and I had only one answer to give: "You're free, choose, that is, invent." No general ethics can show you what is to be done; there are no omens in the world. The Catholics will reply, "But there are." Granted—but, in any case, I myself choose the meaning they have.

When I was a prisoner, I knew a rather remarkable young man who was a Jesuit. He had entered the Jesuit order in the following way: he had had a number of very bad breaks; in childhood, his father had died, leaving him in poverty, and he was a scholarship student at a religious institution where he was constantly made to feel that he was being kept out of charity; then, he failed to get any of the honors and distinctions that children like; later on, at about eighteen, he bungled a love affair; finally, at twenty-two, he failed in military training, a childish enough matter, but it was the last straw.

This young fellow might well have felt that he had botched everything. It was a sign of something, but of what? He might have taken refuge in bitterness or despair. But he very wisely looked upon all this as a sign that he was not made for secular triumphs, and that only the triumphs of religion, holiness, and faith were open to him. He saw the hand of God in all this, and so he entered the order. Who can help seeing that he alone decided what the sign meant?

Some other interpretation might have been drawn from this series of setbacks; for example, that he might have done better to turn carpenter or revolutionist. Therefore, he is fully responsible for the interpretation. Forlornness implies that we ourselves choose our being. Forlornness and anguish go together.

As for despair, the term has a very simple meaning. It means that we shall confine ourselves to reckoning only with what depends upon our will, or on the ensemble of probabilities which make our action possible. When we want something, we always have to reckon with probabilities. I may be counting on the arrival of a friend. The friend is coming by rail or street-car; this supposes that the train will arrive on schedule, or that the street-car will not jump the track. I am left in the realm of possibility; but possibilities are to be reckoned with only to the point where my action comports with the ensemble of these possibilities, and no further. The moment the possibilities I am considering are not rigorously involved by my action, I ought to disengage myself from them, because no God, no scheme, can adapt the world and its possibilities to my will. When Descartes said, "Conquer yourself rather than the world," he meant essentially the same thing.

The Marxists to whom I have spoken reply, "You can rely on the support of others in your action, which obviously has certain limits because you're not going to live forever. That means: rely on both what others are doing elsewhere to help you, in China, in Russia, and what they will do later on, after your death, to carry on the action and lead it to its fulfillment, which will be the revolution. You even *have* to rely upon that, otherwise, you're immoral." I reply at once that I will always rely on fellowfighters insofar as these comrades are involved with me in a common struggle, in the unity of a party or group in which I can more or less make my weight felt; that is, one whose ranks I am in as a fighter and whose movements I am aware of at every moment. In such a situation, relying on the unity and will of the party is exactly like counting on the fact that the train will arrive on time or that the car won't jump the track. But, given that man is free and that there is no human nature for me to depend on, I can not count on men whom I do not know by relying on human goodness or man's concern for the good of society. I don't know what will become of the Russian revolution; I may make an example of it to the extent that at the present time it is apparent that the proletariat plays a part in Russia that it plays in no other nation. But I can't swear that this will inevitably lead to a triumph of the proletariat. I've got to limit myself to what I see.

Given that men are free and that tomorrow they will freely decide what man will be, I can not be sure that, after my death, fellow-fighters will carry on my work to bring it to its maximum perfection. Tomorrow, after my death, some men may decide to set up Fascism, and the others may be cowardly and muddled enough to let them do it. Fascism will then be the human reality, so much the worse for us.

Actually, things will be as man will have decided they are to be. Does that mean that I should abandon myself to quietism? No. First, I should involve myself; then, act on the old saw, "Nothing ventured, nothing gained." Nor does it mean that I shouldn't belong to a party, but rather that I shall have no illusions and shall do what I can. For example, suppose I ask myself, "Will socialization, as such, ever come about?" I know nothing about it. All I know is that I'm going to do everything in my power to bring it about. Beyond that, I can't count on anything. Quietism is the attitude of people who say, "Let others do what I can't do." The doctrine I am presenting is the very opposite of quietism, since it declares, "There is no reality except in action." Moreover, it goes further, since it adds, "Man is nothing else than his plan; he exists only to the extent that he fulfills himself; he is therefore nothing else than the ensemble of his acts, nothing else than his life."

According to this, we can understand why our doctrine horrifies certain people. Because often the only way they can bear their wretchedness is to think, "Circumstances have been against me. What I've been and done doesn't show my true worth. To be sure, I've had no great love, no great friendship, but that's because I haven't met a man or woman who was worthy. The books I've written haven't been very good because I haven't had the proper leisure. I haven't had children to devote myself to because I didn't find a man with whom I could have spent my life. So there remains within me, unused and quite viable, a host of propensities, inclinations, possibilities, that one wouldn't guess from, the mere series of things I've done."

Now, for the existentialist there is really no love other than one which manifests itself in a person's being in love. There is no genius other than one which is expressed in works of art; the genius of Proust is the sum of Proust's works; the genius of Racine is his series of tragedies. Outside of that, there is nothing. Why say that Racine could have written another tragedy, when he didn't write it? A man is involved in life, leaves his impress on it, and outside of that there is nothing. To be sure, this may seem a harsh thought to someone whose life hasn't been a success. But, on the other hand, it prompts people to understand that reality alone is what counts, that dreams, expectations, and hopes warrant no more than to define a man as a disappointed dream, as miscarried hopes, as vain expectations. In other words, to define him negatively and not positively. However, when we say, "You are nothing else than your life," that does not imply that the artist will be judged solely on the basis of his works of art: a thousand other things will contribute toward summing him up. What we mean is that a man is nothing else than a series of undertakings, that he is the sum, the organization, the ensemble of the relationships which make up these undertakings.

IX.C. Pragmatism and the Creation of Meaning

IX.C.1. Is Life Worth Living?

WILLIAM JAMES

William James (1842–1910) was an American pragmatist concerned to interpret philosophy in terms both intelligible and attractive to ordinary persons, who need what it has to offer but cannot take the time to pursue the subject in a technical way. He believed that the most important function of philosophy is to help ordinary persons understand the world and their place in it, and to offer guidance and encouragement as individuals attempt to live their lives. James did not live through the events of war and depression that positioned existentialism as a crisis philosophy, but he certainly was keenly aware of the personal sense of futility that was a central factor in existentialism. He went through a personal crisis when he was in his early twenties in which he had the sense of being like an automaton operated by forces beyond his control, and his studies of science and medicine also seemed to imply a determinism that deprived humans of all freedom and thus made their lives entirely meaningless. James, however, overcame his depression, along with the sense of futility that drove him to serious thoughts of suicide, by a sheer act of will not unlike that which Sartre would later call "authenticity." His first act of free will, James decided, would be to believe in free will to live in the faith that his choices made a difference. They did. Although keenly sensitive for the rest of his life to the possibility that human existence might be merely a cosmic accident and thus ultimately meaningless, James succeeded in living a life of faith in the power of individual choice, bolstered by a deliberately willed faith in the truth of religion.

In the following selection James addresses the question of whether life is worth living, and he answers that it depends on the "liver," the person who lives it. We may not be able to answer the questions of whether there is a God or whether

From *The Will to Believe and Other Essays* (New York: Dover, 1956), pp. 33–38, 51–62.

there is an objective purpose for human existence, but we can answer the question of whether life has a meaning by simply deciding that for us it will. The person who decides to live by the belief that life is futile and meaningless will find that this expectation is self fulfilling; living under such a shadow will indeed sap life of the joy and sense of significance it might have had. In the same way, the person who decides to live by the belief that life is worth living will also find that expectation fulfilled. It is possible, James insists, to exercise one's freedom of choice and decide to do those things that make life worth living. This affirmation is a ringing challenge to the reader to create meaning and make life good by living it well.

I

With many men the question of life's worth is answered by a temperamental optimism which makes them incapable of believing that anything seriously evil can exist. Our dear old Walt Whitman's works are the standing text-book of this kind of optimism. The mere joy of living is so immense in Walt Whitman's veins that it abolishes the possibility of any other kind of feeling.

"To breathe the air, how delicious!
To speak—to walk—to seize something by the hand! . . .
To be this incredible God I am! . . .
O amazement of things—even the least particle!
O spirituality of things! . . .
I too carol the sun, usher'd or at noon, or as now, setting,
I too throb to the brain and beauty of the earth and of all the growths
of the earth. . . .
I sing to the last the equalities modern or old,
I sing the endless finalés of things,
I say Nature continues, glory continues,
I praise with electric voice,
For I do not see one imperfection in the universe,
And I do not see one cause or result lamentable at last."

So Rousseau, writing of the nine years he spent at Annecy, with nothing but his happiness to tell:

"How tell what was neither said nor done nor even thought, but tasted only and felt, with no object of my felicity but the emotion of felicity itself! I rose with the sun, and I was happy; I went to walk, and I was happy; I saw 'Maman,' and I was happy; I left her, and I was happy. I rambled through the woods and over the vine-slopes, I wandered in the valleys, I read, I lounged, I worked in the garden, I gathered the fruits, I helped at the indoor work, and happiness followed me everywhere. It was in no one assignable thing; it was all within myself; it could not leave me for a single instant."

If moods like this could be made permanent, and constitutions like these universal, there would never be any occasion for such discourses as the present one. No philosopher would seek to prove articulately that life is worth living, for the fact that it absolutely is so would vouch for itself, and the problem disappear in the vanishing of the question rather than in the coming of anything like a reply. But we are not magicians to make the optimistic temperament universal; and alongside of the deliverances of temperamental optimism concerning life, those of temperamental pessimism always exist, and oppose to them a standing refutation. In what is called "circular insanity," phases of melancholy succeed phases of mania, with no outward cause that we can discover; and often enough to one and the same well person life will present incarnate radiance to-day and incarnate dreariness to-morrow, according to the fluctuations of what the older medical books used to call "the concoction of the humors." In the words of the newspaper joke, "it depends on the liver." Rousseau's ill-balanced constitution undergoes a change, and behold him in his latter evil days a prey to melancholy and black delusions of suspicion and fear. Some men seem launched upon the world even from their birth with souls as incapable of happiness as Walt Whitman's was of gloom, and they have left us their messages in even more lasting verse than his—the exquisite Leopardi, for example; or our own contemporary, James Thomson, in that pathetic book, *The City of Dreadful Night*, which I think is less well-known than it should be for its literary beauty, simply because men are afraid to quote its words—they are so gloomy, and at the same time so sincere. In one place the poet describes a congregation gathered to listen to a preacher in a great unillumined cathedral at night. The sermon is too long to quote, but it ends thus:

"O Brothers of sad lives! they are so brief;
A few short years must bring us all relief:
    Can we not bear these years of labouring breath?
But if you would not this poor life fulfil,
Lo, you are free to end it when you will,
    Without the fear of waking after death.—

In all eternity I had one chance,
    One few years' term of gracious human life:
The splendours of the intellect's advance,
    The sweetness of the home with babes and wife;

The social pleasures with their genial wit;
    The fascination of the worlds of art,
The glories of the worlds of nature, lit
    By large imagination's glowing heart;

And this sole chance was frustrate from my birth,
    A mockery, a delusion; and my breath
Of noble human life upon this earth
    So racks me that I sigh for senseless death.

My wine of life is poison mixed with gall,
    My noonday passes in a nightmare dream,
I worse than lose the years which are my all:
    What can console me for the loss supreme?

My Brother, my poor Brothers, it is thus;
This life itself holds nothing good for us,

But it ends soon and nevermore can be;
And we knew nothing of it ere our birth,
And shall know nothing when consigned to earth:
I ponder these thoughts and they comfort me."

"It ends soon and nevermore can be," "Lo, you are free to end it when you will"—these verses flow truthfully from the melancholy Thomson's pen, and are in truth a consolation for all to whom, as to him, the world is far more like a steady den of fear than a continual fountain of delight. That life is *not* worth living the whole army of suicides declare—an army whose roll-call, like the famous evening gun of the British army, follows the sun round the world and never terminates. We, too, as we sit here in our comfort, must "ponder these things" also, for we are of one substance with these suicides, and their life is the life we share. The plainest intellectual integrity—nay, more, the simplest manliness and honor forbid us to forget their case. . . .

IV

And now, in turning to what religion may have to say to the question, I come to what is the soul of my discourse. Religion has meant many things in human history; but when from now onward I use the word I mean to use it in the supernaturalist sense, as declaring that the so-called order of nature, which constitutes this world's experience, is only one portion of the total universe, and that there stretches beyond this visible world an unseen world of which we now know nothing positive, but in its relation to which the true significance of our present mundane life consists. A man's religious faith (whatever more special items of doctrine it may involve) means for me essentially his faith in the existence of an unseen order of some kind in which the riddles of natural order may be found explained. In the more developed religions the natural world has always been regarded as the mere scaffolding or vestibule of a truer, more eternal world, and affirmed to be a sphere of education, trial, or redemption. In these religions, one must in some fashion die to the natural life before one can enter into life eternal. The notion that this physical world of wind and water, where the sun rises and the moon sets, is absolutely and ultimately the divinely aimed-at and established thing, is one which we find only in very early religions, such as that of the most primitive Jews. It is this natural religion (primitive still, in spite of the fact that poets and men of science whose good-will exceeds their perspicacity keep publishing it in new editions tuned to our contemporary ears) that, as I said a while ago, has suffered definitive bankruptcy in the opinion of a circle of persons, amongst whom I must count myself, and who are growing more numerous every day. For such persons the physical order of nature, taken simply as science knows it, cannot be held to reveal any one harmonious spiritual intent. It is mere *weather*, as Chauncey Wright called it, doing and undoing without end.

Now I wish to make you feel, if I can in the short remainder of this hour, that we have a right to believe the physical order to be only a partial order; that we have a right to supplement it by an unseen spiritual order which we assume on trust, if only thereby life may seem to us better worth living again. But as such a trust will seem to some of you sadly mystical and execrably unscientific, I must first say a word or two to weaken the veto which you may consider that science opposes to our act.

There is included in human nature an ingrained naturalism and materialism of mind which can only admit facts that are actually tangible. Of this sort of mind the entity called "science" is the idol. Fondness for the word "scientist" is one of the notes by which you may know its votaries; and its short way of killing any opinion that it disbelieves in is to call it "unscientific." It must be granted that there is no slight excuse for this. Science had made such glorious leaps in the last three hundred years, and extended our knowledge of nature so enormously both in general and in detail; men of science, moreover, have as a class displayed such admirable virtues—that it is no wonder if the worshippers of science lose their head. In this very University, accordingly, I have heard more than one teacher say that all the fundamental conceptions of truth have already been found by science, and that the future has only the details of the picture to fill in. But the slightest reflection on the real conditions will suffice to show how barbaric such notions are. They show such lack of scientific imagination, that it is hard to see how one who is actively advancing any part of science can make a mistake so crude. Think how many absolutely new scientific conceptions have arisen in our own generation, how many new problems have been formulated that were never thought of before, and then cast an eye upon the brevity of science's career. It began with Galileo, not three hundred years ago. Four thinkers since Galileo, each informing his successor of what discoveries his own lifetime had seen achieved, might have passed the torch of science into our hands as we sit here in this room. Indeed, for the matter of that, an audience much smaller than the present one, an audience of some five or six score people, if each person in it could speak for his own generation, would carry us away to the black unknown of the human species, to days without a document or monument to tell their tale. Is it credible that such a mushroom knowledge, such a growth overnight as this, *can* represent more than the minutest glimpse of what the universe will really prove to be when adequately understood? No! our science is a drop, our ignorance a sea. Whatever else be certain, this at least is certain—that the world of our present natural knowledge is enveloped in a larger world of *some* sort of whose residual properties we at present can frame no positive idea.

Agnostic positivism, of course, admits this principle theoretically in the most cordial terms, but insists that we must not turn it to any practical use. We have no right, this doctrine tells us, to dream dreams, or suppose anything about the unseen part of the universe, merely because to do so may be for what we are pleased to call our highest interests. We must always wait for sensible evidence for our beliefs; and where such evidence is inaccessible we must frame no hypotheses whatever. Of course this is a safe enough position *in abstracto*. If a thinker had no stake in the unknown, no vital needs, to live or languish according to what the unseen world contained, a philosophic neutrality and refusal to believe either one way or the other would be his wisest cue. But, unfortunately, neutrality is not only inwardly difficult, it is also outwardly unrealizable, where our relations to an alternative are practical and vital. This is because, as the psychologists tell us, belief and doubt are living attitudes, and involve conduct on our part. Our only way, for example, of doubting, or refusing to believe, that a certain thing *is*, is continuing to act as if it were *not*. If, for instance, I refuse to believe that the room is getting cold, I leave the windows open and light no fire just as if it still were warm. If I doubt that you are worthy of my confidence, I keep you uninformed of all my secrets just as if you were *un*worthy of the same. If I doubt the need of insuring my house, I leave it uninsured as much as if I believed there were no need. And so if I must not believe that the world is divine, I can only express that refusal by declining ever to act distinctively as if it were so, which can only mean acting on certain critical occasions as if it were *not* so, or in an irreligious way. There are, you see, inevitable occasions in life when inaction is a kind of action, and must count as action, and when not to be for is to be practically against; and in all such cases strict and consistent neutrality is an unattainable thing.

And, after all, is not this duty of neutrality where only our inner interests would lead us to believe, the most ridiculous of commands? Is it not sheer dogmatic folly to say that our inner interests can have no real connection with the forces that the hidden world may contain? In other cases divinations based on inner interests have proved prophetic enough. Take science itself! Without an imperious inner demand on our part for ideal logical and mathematical harmonies, we should never have attained to proving that such harmonies lie hidden between all the chinks and interstices of the crude natural world. Hardly a law has been established in science, hardly a fact ascertained, which was not first sought after, often with sweat and blood, to gratify an inner need. Whence such needs come from we do not know: we find them in us, and biological psychology so far only classes them with Darwin's "accidental variations." But the inner need of believing that this world of nature is a sign of something more spiritual and eternal than itself is just as strong and authoritative in those who feel it, as the inner need of uniform laws of causation ever can be in a professionally scientific head. The toil of many generations has proved the latter need prophetic. Why *may* not the former one be prophetic, too? And if needs of ours outrun the visible universe, why *may* not that be a sign that an invisible universe is there? What, in short, has authority to debar us from trusting our religious demands? Science as such assuredly has no authority, for she can only say what is, not what is not; and the agnostic "thou shalt not believe without coercive sensible evidence" is simply an expression (free to anyone to make) of private personal appetite for evidence of a certain peculiar kind.

Now, when I speak of trusting our religious demands, just what do I mean by "trusting"? Is the word to carry with it license to define in detail an invisible world, and to anathematize and excommunicate those whose trust is different? Certainly not! Our faculties of belief were not primarily given us to make orthodoxies and heresies withal; they were given us to live by. And to trust our religious demands means first of all to live in the light of them, and to act as if the invisible world which they suggest were real. It is a fact of human nature, that men can live and die by the help of a sort of faith that goes without a single dogma or definition. The bare assurance that this natural order is not ultimate but a mere sign or vision, the external staging of a many-storied universe, in which spiritual forces have the last word and are eternal—this bare assurance is to such men enough to make life seem worth living in spite of every contrary presumption suggested by its circumstances on the natural plane. Destroy this inner assurance, however, vague as it is, and all the light and radiance of existence is extinguished for these persons at a stroke. Often enough the wild-eyed look at life—the suicidal mood—will then set in.

And now the application comes directly home to you and me. Probably to almost every one of us here the most adverse life would seem well worth living, if we only could be *certain* that our bravery and patience with it were terminating and eventuating and bearing fruit somewhere in an unseen spiritual world. But granting we are not certain, does it then follow that a bare trust in such a world is a fool's paradise and lubberland, or rather that it is a living attitude in which we are free to indulge? Well, we are free to trust at our own risks anything that is not impossible, and that can bring analogies to bear in its behalf. That the world of physics is probably not absolute, all the converging multitude of arguments that make in favor of idealism tend to prove; and that our whole physical life may lie soaking in a spiritual atmosphere, a dimension of being that we at present have no organ for apprehending, is vividly suggested to us by the analogy of the life of our domestic animals. Our dogs, for example, are in our human life but not of it. They witness hourly the outward body of events whose inner meaning cannot, by any possible operation, be revealed to their intelligence—events in which they themselves so often play the cardinal part. My terrier bites a teasing boy, for example, and the father demands damages. The dog may be present at every step of the negotiations, and see the money paid, without an inkling of what it all means, without a suspicion that it has anything to do with *him*; and he never *can* know in his natural dog's life. Or take another case which used greatly to impress me in my medical-student days. Consider a poor dog whom they are vivisecting in a laboratory. He lies strapped on a board and shrieking at his executioners, and to his own dark consciousness is literally in a sort of hell. He cannot see a single redeeming ray in the whole business; and yet all these diabolical-seeming events are often controlled by human intentions with which, if his poor benighted mind could only be made to catch a glimpse of them, all that is heroic in him would religiously acquiesce. Healing truth, relief to future sufferings of beast and man, are to be bought by them. It may be genuinely a process of redemption. Lying on his back on the board there he may be performing a function incalculably higher than any that prosperous canine life admits of; and yet, of the whole performance, this function is the one portion that must remain absolutely beyond his ken.

Now turn from this to the life of man. In the dog's life we see the world invisible to him because we live in both worlds. In human life, although we only see our world, and his within it, yet encompassing both these worlds a still wider world may be there, as unseen by us as our world is by him; and to believe in that world *may* be the most essential function that our lives in this world have to perform. But "*may* be! *may* be!" one now hears the positivist contemptuously exclaim: "what use can a scientific life have for maybes?" Well, I reply, the "scientific" life itself has much to do with maybes, and human life at large has everything to do with them. So far as man stands for anything, and is productive or originative at all, his entire vital function may be said to have to deal with maybes. Not a victory is gained, not a deed of faithfulness or courage is done, except upon a maybe; not a service, not a sally of generosity, not a scientific exploration or experiment or text-book, that may not be a mistake. It is only by risking our persons from one hour to another that we live at all. And often enough our faith beforehand in an uncertified result *is the only thing that makes the result come true*. Suppose, for instance, that you are climbing a mountain, and have worked yourself into a position from which the only escape is by a terrible leap. Have faith that you can successfully make it, and your feet are nerved to its accomplishment. But mistrust yourself, and think of the sweet things you have heard the scientists say of *maybes*, and you will hesitate so long that, at last, all unstrung and trembling, and launching yourself in a moment of despair, you roll in the abyss. In such a case (and it belongs to an enormous class), the part of wisdom as well as of courage is to *believe what is in the line of your needs*, for only by such belief is the need fulfilled. Refuse to believe, and you shall indeed be right, for you shall irretrievably perish. But believe, and again you shall be right, for you shall save yourself. You make one or the other of two possible universes true by your trust or mistrust—both universes having been only *maybes*, in this particular, before you contributed your act.

Now, it appears to me that the question whether life is worth living is subject to conditions logically much like these. It does, indeed, depend on you *the liver*. If you surrender to the nightmare view and crown the evil edifice by your own suicide, you have indeed made a picture totally black. Pessimism, completed by your act, is true beyond a doubt, so far as your world goes. Your mistrust of life has removed whatever worth your own enduring existence might have given to it; and now, throughout the whole sphere of possible influence of that existence, the mistrust has proved itself to have had divining power. But suppose, on the other hand, that instead of giving way to the nightmare view you cling to it that this world is not the *ultimatum*. Suppose you find yourself a very well-spring, as Wordsworth says, of

"Zeal, and the virtue to exist by faith
As soldiers live by courage; as, by strength
Of heart, the sailor fights with roaring seas."

Suppose, however thickly evils crowd upon you, that your unconquerable subjectivity proves to be their match, and that you find a more wonderful joy than any passive pleasure can bring in trusting ever in the larger whole. Have you not now made life worth living on these terms? What sort of a thing would life really be, with your qualities ready for a tussle with it, if it only brought fair weather and gave these higher faculties of yours no scope? Please remember that optimism and pessimism are definitions of the world, and that our reactions on the world, small as they are in bulk, are integral parts of the whole thing, and necessarily help to determine the definition. They may even be the decisive elements in determining the definition. A large mass can have its unstable equilibrium overturned by the addition of a feather's weight; a long phrase may have its sense reversed by the addition of the three letters *n-o-t*. This life is worth living, we can say, *since it is what we make it, from the moral point of view*; and we are determined to make it from that point of view, so far as we have anything to do with it, a success.

Now, in this description of faiths that verify themselves I have assumed that our faith in an invisible order is what inspires those efforts and that patience which make this visible order good for moral men. Our faith in the seen world's goodness (goodness now meaning fitness for successful moral and religious life) has verified itself by leaning on our faith in the unseen world. But will our faith in the unseen world similarly verify itself? Who knows?

Once more it is a case of *maybe*; and once more *maybes* are the essence of the situation. I confess that I do not see why the very existence of an invisible world may not in part depend on the personal response which any one of us may make to the religious appeal. God himself, in short, may draw vital strength and increase of very being from our fidelity. For my own part, I do not know what the sweat and blood and tragedy of this life mean, if they mean anything short of this. If this life be not a real fight, in which something is eternally gained for the universe by success, it is no better than a game of private theatricals from which one may withdraw at will. But it *feels* like a real fight—as if there were something really wild in the universe which we, with all our idealities and faithfulnesses, are needed to redeem; and first of all to redeem our own hearts from atheisms and fears. For such a half-wild, half-saved universe our nature is adapted. The deepest thing in our nature is this *Binnenleben* (as a German doctor lately has called it), this dumb region of the heart in which we dwell alone with our willingnesses and unwillingnesses, our faiths and fears. As through the cracks and crannies of caverns whose waters exude from the earth's bosom which then form the fountain-heads of springs, so in these crepuscular depths of personality the sources of all our outer deeds and decisions take their rise. Here is our deepest organ of communication with the nature of things; and compared with these concrete movements of our soul all abstract statements and scientific arguments—the veto, for example, which the strict positivist pronounces upon our faith—sound to us like mere chatterings of the teeth. For here possibilities, not finished facts, are the realities with which we have actively to deal; and to quote my friend William Salter, of the Philadelphia Ethical Society, "as the essence of courage is to stake one's life on a possibility, so the essence of faith is to believe that the possibility exists."

These, then, are my last words to you: Be not afraid of life. Believe that life *is* worth living, and your belief will help create the fact.

Author Index

Title Index